BRITAIN & IRELAND'S

BEST WILD PLACES

CHRISTOPHER SOMERVILLE

Please note

These are wild places, many of them in remote locations. Please be properly prepared before embarking on any of the walks. The publishers and author have done their best to ensure the accuracy of the information contained in this guide, however they cannot accept any responsibility for any loss, injury, or inconvenience sustained by any reader as a result of information or advice contained in this guide.

Photo credits

All photographs are by the author except those listed below.

Bamburgh © Dae Sasitorn/www.lastrefuge.co.uk
Bardsey © David Pearson/Alamy
Ben Bulben © Jason Hawkes/www.jasonhawkes.com
Boscawen-un © Dae Sasitorn/www.lastrefuge.co.uk
Brontë Moors © grough.co.uk/Alamy
Chesil Beach © Adrian Warren/www.lastrefuge.co.uk
Cheviots © Gail Johnson
Cwm Idwal © Mick Knapton
Eigg © Albaimages/Alamy
Fair Isle © Dave Wheeler/www.dave-wheeler.com
Flambourough © Steve Race/www.racebirding.blogspot.com
Gurnards Head © Andrew Wood/www.solochallenges.com
High Cup © Ann Bowker/www.madaboutmountains.com
Hoy © www.undiscoveredscotland.co.uk
Loch Coire © Dave Henniker/www.henniker.org.uk
Mendips © Hembo Pagi
Morcambe Bay © Simon Coning
Moseley Bog © Ted Spiller
Orford Ness © NTPL/Joe Cornish
Pendle © Wildscape/Alamy
Pilgrims Way © Pip Rolls/www.logicacmg.com
Redsands Fort – Historic Redsands Fort Stand In Thames Estuary © Bruno Vincent/Getty Images
Ring of Brodgar © David Lyons/Alamy
St. Mary's Church, Pilgrim rabbit, Beverley © Ros Drinkwater/Alamy
Skellig © Josh Roberts
Slieve Gullion © Chris Hill/www.secenicireland.com
South Uist © Martin Third
Spey © Garry McDonald at www.itraveluk.co.uk
Stiffkey, Norfolk © Tim Graham/Getty Images
Trenshish © Iain Morrison
Uffington Whitehorse © Dae Sasitorn/www.lastrefuge.co.uk
Unst © Doug Houghton/Alamy
Wast Water © Dae Sasitorn/www.lastrefuge.co.uk

ALLEN LANE

Published by the Penguin Group

Penguin Books Ltd, 80 Strand, London WC2R ORL, England
Penguin Group (USA) Inc., 375 Hudson Street, New York, New York 10014, USA
Penguin Group (Canada), 90 Eglinton Avenue East, Suite 700, Toronto, Ontario, Canada M4P 2Y3 (a division of Pearson Canada Inc.)
Penguin Ireland, 25 St Stephen's Green, Dublin 2, Ireland (a division of Penguin Books Ltd)
Penguin Group (Australia), 250 Camberwell Road, Camberwell, Victoria 3124, Australia (a division of Pearson Australia Group Pty Ltd)
Penguin Books India Pvt Ltd, 11 Community Centre, Panchsheel Park, New Dehli – 110 017, India
Penguin Group (NZ), 67 Apollo Drive, North Shore 0632, New Zealand (a division of Pearson New Zealand Ltd)
Penguin Books (South Africa) (Pty) Ltd, 24 Sturdee Avenue, Rosebank 2196, South Africa
Penguin Books Ltd, Registered Offices: 80 Strand, London WC2R ORL, England / www.penguin.com

First published 2008

1

Designed by Estuary English
Illustrations by Clifford Harper
Printed in Germany by Mohn Media
Colour reproduction by Altaimage Ltd
ISBN: 978–0–713–99967–9

BRITAIN & IRELAND'S

BEST WILD PLACES

500 WAYS TO DISCOVER THE WILD

CHRISTOPHER SOMERVILLE

ALLEN LANE

an imprint of

PENGUIN BOOKS

ACKNOWLEDGEMENTS

Richard Eales for showing me Exmoor red stags at the rut, Brian Roberts-Wray who first alerted me to the extraordinary dance of the starlings over Westhay Moor, Roz Bateman and Vince Simmonds who took me 'down under' into Mendip's GB cave, Andrew Syvret who brought me moonwalking through Jersey's tidal landscapes, Richard Adams for helping me to pinpoint all the sites in his masterpiece *Watership Down*, Betty Rasell for her fascinating accounts of Pagham Harbour, the Abbey family for showing me over the flowery meadows of Hunsdon Mead, Chris Fenwick for his companionship around Canvey Island, the members of BATTLE for their never-say-die defence of the Dengie peninsula, Grant Lohoar for his time and patience on Orford Ness, the members of Club Foot for accompanying me through Wentwood, Sian Musgrove and Digby for showing me the rockpools of the Worm's Head causeway, Richard and Anne Wilson for taking me up and over Cadair Idris and Plynlimon, Peter Rutherford on Snowdon, Peter Hewlett around Llyn and Bardsey, my godson Andrew Harrison who introduced me to the Wren's Nest in Dudley, the late Benny Rothman, Shane Bates and Belle for their companionship on Kinder Scout, Roly Smith for pointing me towards several wild places in and around the Peak District, Mark Reid for walking with me in Arkengarthdale, Phil Richards for an excellent hike over the Access Land of Grassington Moor, Vicky Seager the erstwhile Ranger of the Hilbre islands for her enthusiastic hospitality, Cedric Robinson for steering me safely across Morecambe Bay, Neil Dowie for braving a bloody awful day on Scafell Pike, the King of Piel for an audience, Andy Lyddiatt for exploring the Durham coast and moors with me, Dave Richardson for polymath enhancement of Scottish wild places from Galloway to Ben More Assynt, Steve Duncan and Irvine Butterfield across Rannoch Moor, Andrew Bateman up Ben Nevis and in his 'snowy abodes' on Cairngorm, Duncan Macdonald for a fascinating day tracking animals in the snow of the Monadhliath Mountains, Don Hind for steering me through the Corryvreckan whirlpool, Barry Meatyard for showing me some of the secrets of Ardmeanach, Duncan and Duncan Macdonald of Eilean nan Amadan for letting me camp in their bog ditch, the islanders of Shetland and Orkney (far too many to mention by name) for their roaring hospitality.

In Ireland: John Lahiffe and colleagues for unstinting hospitality, Michael Gibbons and Olcan Masterson for many magical explorations, Tim Robinson for his ever-reliable and inspirational Folding Landscapes, James McEvoy in the Mournes and Martin McGuigan in the Sperrins, Pat O'Hagan the Cookstown tale-teller for a hilarious and enthralling night on Lough Neagh, Oliver Geraghty for his brilliant guiding in the mist-wrapped Nephin Beg Mountains, Tom Joyce in the Slieve Blooms, Kevin and Ber O'Donnell in the Knockmealdowns, and Eleanor O'Driscoll and her late husband Concubhar of Cape Clear Island for their generosity.

Last, but not least, my dear lifelong friend Andrew Finlay, my first companion into Wild Places; my dear father John, for walking so many wild parts of England and Wales with me; and my beloved wife Jane, who came to many of these places with me and is looking forward to exploring all the rest and many more.

CONTENTS

Above: Worcestershire Beacon (pp. 224–5). Below left: Wark Forest (pp. 352–3). Right: Badbea village (pp. 421–2)

THE WILD PLACES

On a bright cold winter morning at the start of 2006 I set out before sunrise in search of the wild. It was a moment of tremendous excitement and uncertainty. In front of me was a challenge I had set myself: to travel the length and breadth of the British Isles and the island of Ireland, looking for wild places wherever I might find them. I would give myself a year to seek them out — long enough to see them in the light of all four seasons and a whole cycle of weathers, short enough to keep a hunger and momentum in the journey. That year on the road was to bring me delirious pleasure, bitter disillusionment and constant astonishment.

THAT FIRST MORNING, driving across the Severn Bridge from England into Wales with the rising sun throwing the shadow of the car along the road before me, I asked myself once more the question that had propelled me on this quest. What is wild? I have spent thirty years exploring and writing about the moors and mountains, the coasts, the wild birds and wild flowers of these unique islands, their tearing rainstorms and pounding waves. What exactly was that quality I found so magnetically attractive about these manifestations of everything that was not me, that was not human, which I so freely labelled 'wild' and yet could not define, which I could recognize instantly without at all being able to pin down?

What is wild? Is it a red stag bellowing in a misty dawn, or a mouse darting away from my footfalls in a meadow? Are the naked tors of Dartmoor wilder than the ploughlands of the Cotswolds, or newly planted willow saplings on the coal-mining wastelands of Leicestershire tamer than a grove of ancient oaks in County Londonderry? Would I have to travel to the rugged, unpopulated landscapes of the outermost north of Scotland, or the Atlantic outposts of the west of Ireland, to find truly wild places? Setting out on my journey, I would have said yes, absolutely. But I soon learned to see things differently. The very first wild place of my intended 500, the one I was heading for across the Severn at sunrise, was Russell's Inclosure in the Forest of Dean. No mountains here, no moorlands, no storm-battered coasts or inaccessible grandeurs of naked rock. I knew the Forest of Dean because I lived just across the bridge in Bristol and had often taken my children there when they were little to wander and play among the trees. The forest had tangled thickets, bog pools, winding ways. I thought of it as wild in essence, but I didn't know Russell's Inclosure at all. I had chosen this place more or less as an experiment, a selection made by a random jab of the thumb on the map. If the wild were to be found in lowland, southern Britain, it would be in a place such as the Forest of Dean. And that is what I did find, crunching over the frost-burned leaves into the heart of the old woodland enclosure: fallen trees sodden with mosses and ferns, speckled with lichens, rich with life even in the depth of winter. More than that: an early-day silence so profound that it rang in my city-deadened ears like a bell, sour smells of rotted leaves bubbling from an iridescent pond, and a sense of loneliness as I went on into the forest that had me looking over my shoulder, half entranced, half unsettled.

I was to rediscover these heightened senses, the sharpened eyes and ears and the prickling at the nape of the neck, in hundreds of locations over the year I spent in search of the wild. I learned to focus down and in, to enter a disused quarry near Birmingham on the lookout for orchids, or to search for ancient trees in a beechwood within sight and sound of London, with the same sense of expectation that I carried on to the Pennine moors and up into the Scottish mountains. A week of scrambling on glacier-scraped granite, watching mountain hares and golden eagles in the back-country highlands, would be followed by a few days hunting along canal banks in the Midlands for dripping brick tunnels full of bats, or following the 7,000-year-old trackways that seam the chalk hills of the south. All were wild places, I discovered.

I learned to think of the wild in different ways. In one sense it is simply an absence of man's control. But it also expresses something fundamental in the character and the appearance of a living creature or a landscape. Whatever seems neither to acknowledge nor to compromise with us is wild. It may need our solicitude when it is under threat, may even benefit from our care and maintenance. Yet fundamentally, and ultimately, it rejects us. It will get along just fine when we have blown or argued or poisoned ourselves out of existence. Once I embraced that way of looking at things, I found wild places waiting round almost every corner.

There is wild, and then there is wilderness. The vast boglands of central Ireland, the medieval coppice woods of the Chiltern Hills, the Yorkshire moors, the heathery glens of Scotland – all are wild, yet none are wilderness. All exist because of man's activities, his relentless clearing and exploitation of the land. If in these islands there still remains any true wilderness, in the sense of a natural place never controlled or altered by the hand of man, it resides in rare places such as the dwarf oak grove of Wistman's Wood, tucked down in a remote crevice of Dartmoor. In all of Britain and

Above: Black Bog (pp. 493–4). Above right: Cannock Chase (pp. 244–5). Right: the Gobbins cliff path (pp. 483–4)

Ireland there remain one or two such pockets of primeval woodland; there are the caves under the limestone hills, too, and the cliffs and shores washed bare by the sea. Other than these, we have sacrificed all our wilderness over the past 6,000 years to our need to eat and to increase, and to our unstoppable impulse to make and to build. But 'the wild', the seductive concept that we both fear and desire – that is another matter altogether.

I came to realize, as my wild year unfolded, that the wild is here and now, as much as it has ever been, though its focus has changed hugely in my own short time on earth. Those who grew up in post-war Britain, as I did, tend to look back through a romantic haze to a countryside that seems to have been bursting with wildlife. It was not as wonderful as all that. By the 1960s the use of organophosphates, agricultural pesticides and herbicides, hedge-ripping, drainage of wetlands and other intensive farming practices were well under way. Fields and coasts were being built on, road schemes pushed through, motorways built. Transistor radios and motorbike engines were loud across the commons and along country lanes. The otter was in seemingly terminal decline, the red kite clinging to survival in a few Welsh valleys, the peregrine population crashing as organochloride pesticides took their toll. In spite of that, what strikes me forcibly as I explore these islands at the outset of the third millennium AD is the quietness of everything now, compared with then, and the thinning out of what I grew up to think of as everyday manifestations of the wild – the reduced volume of birdsong in the fields and hedges, the decrease in soundings and sightings of hedgehogs and field mice, frogs and their spawn, water voles, brown hares, stoats and weasels, yellowhammers and greenfinches, wildflower lanes. In the past few years there has been a quantum shift in our awareness of such decline, however, thanks to the excellence of TV programmes on wildlife and wild places, and to the free exchange of information via the Internet. We wax indignant about wind farm developments in the Outer Hebrides, about house-building at the opposite end of the country, about road schemes across chalk downs we have never set eyes on and ancient woodlands we will never walk through.

The wild has an astonishing resilience. When I was a child growing up in Gloucestershire I ran free, day after day, through the curious lost-and-gone landscape of the River Severn's floodplain. Our tiny village possessed more farms than cars, and the meadows were managed on traditional principles. Inundated yearly by King Severn and unploughed since medieval farmers corrugated them with the furrows that I stumbled across in my gumboots, they were a riot of wild wetland flowers and birds. To a small boy, but also to discerning birdwatchers, amateur botanists and lovers of watery landscapes, they were the wild brought close to home. Returning to the village and the meadows in the 1980s with my own young

Below: Hardibutts Farm (pp. 297–8). Right: yellow flag growing on Wicken Fen (pp. 151–2)

children, I found a countryside devastated by drainage and by intensive chemical farming, a barren land of uniform green where no milkmaids or ragged robin grew in spring. The ditches were devoid of water voles, the hedges of yellowhammers, the skies of lapwing flocks, the headlands of hares. There were no headlands: they had all been ploughed away. Whatever was wild had fled in defeat, so it seemed, in the face of the modern world. Yet the wild was only in temporary retreat. The wheel turned once more; the meadows were recognized for what they had been, one of England's prime wetlands, and were bought for conservation as a nature reserve. The older and gentler agricultural regime was reintroduced, the margins of ditches and fields were allowed to grow bushy. Back came the wild birds and animals, the flowers and dragonflies. The springtime walk I took there during my travels in search of the wild was through drifts of cowslips and milkmaids, under skies clamorous once more with the mournful creaking and piping of lapwings. The wild had simply been biding its time.

In such apparently unemphatic and undramatic surroundings, up and down the country, I have heard the call of the wild just as urgently, if with different emphasis, as on the most rugged Hebridean mountain or wind-blasted northern moor. I have sensed it as a gentle whisper at the side of a pond among damselflies, as a subtle tug of the sleeve in a railway-siding jungle of buddleia at the heart of a city, and as a full-blown anarchic roar on western reefs in a terrifying Atlantic gale. This call drives out complacency and self-satisfaction. It makes me marvel, an unfashionable activity. It rushes through me, dragging terrors and wonders in its wake. A sense of the wild, a visceral response to rocks, skies and seas, a repulsion and an attraction felt deep in the gut, seem bound up inseparably with the human condition.

We are inextricably tangled up with the wild, like it or not. And more often than not the very survival of wild places depends on how we choose to exercise our current omnipotence on earth. This fine contradiction pervades the wild in today's Britain and Ireland. Think of the wild and you think of a place where nature holds sway, where the influence of man brushes lightly, if at all, across the landscape. Yet very many of our wild places qualify for that status only because they are preserved as nature reserves – probably the most controlled, managed and manipulated environments in these islands. The open water, reed-beds, marshy ground, wildflower meadows and wet carr woods of the wonderfully diverse Wicken Fen in Cambridgeshire, for example, would soon all revert to dense woodland if they were not artificially maintained by sluices and locks, by cutting and clearing. Parking in the National Trust car park, walking through the Visitor Centre, traipsing along the walkways behind a troupe of primary school children with pond-dipping nets and neat worksheets, I feared I would find the whole place too ordered and primped, too boxed and beribboned for there to be any vestige of wildness there. Yet after an hour or so spent strolling the grass paths among the dragonflies and damselflies, walking the meadows through early purple orchids and ragged robin, sitting in the hides with a privileged view of the private lives of kingfishers, marsh harriers and Cetti's warblers, I could only rejoice in the wild nature of such a place. The tiny dark hobby that dashed through my field of vision above the mere, snatching dragonflies on the wing and ducking its head to pick their nutritious bodies delicately from between its claws, existed, throve and did not care for me, for the chattering children or for the committee of experts that was sitting round a table at that moment to decide if funding would stretch to maintaining the mere and the reed-beds for another year.

We have been trying conscientiously to conserve our wildlife and wild places ever since Victorian times, when sportsmen and egg collectors, enclosers of commons, polluters of rivers and developers of heathland were seen to be on a fair way to wiping out nature altogether from these islands. Consider Lord Walsingham's bag for one day of shooting a century ago: on the last day of January 1899 he personally accounted for 65 coots, 39 pheasants, 23 mallard, 16 rabbits, 9 hares, 7 teal, 6 partridges, 6 gadwall, 4 pochard, 3 swans, 2 herons, 2 moorhens and 2 jack snipe, and one apiece of goldeneye, woodcock, snipe and pigeon. He also bagged an otter, a rat – and a pike, which he shot as it swam in the shallows. What with egg collectors, shooters and stuffers of songbirds and owls, amateur botanists who picked and took home everything they found, lepidopterists who killed butterflies with ether and pinned them to display boards, naturalists who had no modern cameras and killed wild creatures in order to study them at leisure, wildlife and the wild countryside had a tough time of it back then.

At the time of Lord Walsingham's successful day in the field the Society for the Protection of Birds (later the RSPB), the Commons Preservation Society and the National Trust for Places of Historic Interest and Natural Beauty were already in existence. Since then they have been joined by local Wildlife Trusts and by the Countryside Agency. Fourteen National Parks have been designated, and more are on the way. Thousands of local and national nature reserves across Britain and Ireland are staffed by trained wardens and maintained by volunteers who guard and man and clean up and plant. And that is not even to mention the raft of national and European designations, the Special Protection Areas and Environmentally Sensitive Areas, the Sites of Special Scientific Interest and Areas of Outstanding Natural Beauty.

We know full well how overcrowded are our islands. We are aware only too clearly of our inexorable need for elbow room, of our propensity to slap roads and houses on any scrap of green that shows its head above the parapet. Yet far from being confident of our power to preserve the wild in all its wildness, we seem to chew our nails and glance over our shoulders with ever-increasing uncertainty and anxiety. The shadow of power stations unbuilt, of pylons as yet unassembled and roads still unplanned looms over our little patch of saltmarsh,

Above: Twelve Bens (pp. 524–5)

of saltmarsh, our neighbourhood wood, our hundred yards of hedgerow. Money talks. At the time of writing, in the form of the American tycoon Donald Trump and his many billions, it is in the process of shouting down opposition to a gigantic housing and golf-course development on irreplaceable sand dunes on the Aberdeenshire coast near Forvie Dunes (see pp. 405–6). Here is proof that a Site of Special Scientific Interest, home to rare and declining bird and plant species, wild and unspoiled, can perhaps simply be bought, smothered and ruined if the proposer's financial clout and carrot are big enough.

Wild places such as these rely for their survival on the vigilance and persistence of their lay champions. What such places have to offer, what benefits or assets can be set against their commercial potential – what their worth is, in non-monetary terms - is almost impossible to quantify. We all need empty horizons, lonely shores, forgotten woods, huge skies with nothing but a tree or a church tower sticking up into them; places where nature just carries on doing what she does without caring if we are there or not; places where we don't make a mark or leave our stamp; places where we can feel truly and properly insignificant; places to feel a thrill of loneliness. Such a landscape is a piece of history, a haven, a refuge, a rich ground for fantasy and imagination, a landscape that tells us of what was and what might be, as well as what is.

Above: Llyn-y-Fan Fach (pp. 169–70). Right: Silent Valley (pp. 164–5)

In a way it never was to our forbears, the wild is available to us at several removes: we are offered the most extreme, the most jaw-dropping experiences of wild places and wildlife in an extraordinarily vivid but objectified way in books and magazines, on television and radio, through blogs and podcasts, websites and online advertisements. Reflecting on the wild and what its true nature might be, as I did to the point of obsession while travelling and researching for this book, I understood with a sense of shock and amazement how far I had myself unconsciously been sliding down the road of vicarious experience. Television and the internet in particular had been infiltrating their cosy kind of wild across my doorstep. Their images offer versions of the wild that seem supercharged and airbrushed – often the Greater Wild Abroad, whose cheetahs and water snakes and rainforest creepy-crawlies, filmed with an ever more breathtaking intimacy and wealth of detail, have come to seem more magical, more wonderful and somehow more valid than our own native wild places and their natural inhabitants, their often subtle and unspectacular appeal. Such experience is especially true of the newest generations of British and Irish urbanites, who since the Second World War have become decoupled as never before from an everyday experience of rural living and the rhythms and cycles of nature in the countryside. Filling the vacuum, and fuelled by reaction to the enormous destruction and misery of the two world wars, has been an attitude towards the countryside of nostalgia and romantic escapism.

This breaking of bonds with the wild is such a recent phenomenon. Only a few generations ago we welcomed the mummers and the morris across our thresholds, all dressed in greenery, to whip our egos with sharp jokes and exorcize our comfort and sloth. Gypsies used to come to my parents' door smelling of the wild: woodsmoke, earth, human waste, leaf-mould. We knew wild men who lived in the woods: charcoal-burners, tramps, dreadlocked eccentrics. In the 1970s and 1980s, wherever I walked, it seemed, I would stumble upon traveller convoys encamped in wild places, down a green lane, up a pebbly track. Were they turning the green lanes tame with their sump oil and plastic nappies, their discarded tin cans and blurred reggae? Or did they embody the spirit of the wild, tuning in to something I had forgotten how to receive on antennae blunted by consumerism?

Our current generation of city dwellers faces threats to the wild as acute as any of the past. There have been, and are planned, huge encroachments by house-builders and infrastructure developers on the Green Belt (that respectable, sanitized but precious buffer of semi-wild country that encircles our cities), on woods, farmland, coasts and other places our wiser or less arrogant forefathers never built on – the flood plains and estuary banks. Politicians aim to build a giant sprawl of towns along the disregarded marsh margins of the Thames Estuary on both sides of the river; low-lying, flood-prone country in the most drought-afflicted and overcrowded region of Britain. More city dwellers than ever before seek to escape all that and to touch the wild by walking in the countryside, by cycling out along the towpaths, by canoeing and windsurfing and rock climbing – albeit insulated and protected from that very wild by Goretex and neoprene, by mobile phone and GPS.

As for what I found for myself when I went in search of the wild in these islands – it came in a thousand forms. The wild ambushed me during that unforgettable year of searching. It took me by surprise day by day – its capacity to hide just inside the thicket, just beyond the skyline. I have continued to search for it, continued to recognize it like a sly old friend

Below: Spurn Head (pp. 272–3). Below right: Big Moor (p. 253)

Above: Barbury Castle (pp. 73–4). Right: Bog Meadows (pp. 486–7). Far right: Aran Islands (pp. 529–30)

behind a tree. Some days I go out on purpose to throw myself headlong at the wild, and I fail to find or feel it. Like treasure in a fairy tale, it has somehow kept itself in hiding. At other times, perhaps in the most unpromising of places, it reveals itself, as if a shaft of light has suddenly fallen on a dark place. Many of the places in this book owe their wildness to the signs they betray of the presence of man now vanished, or his ancient purposes no longer to be fathomed – freakish beasts carved by a Pictish sculptor on a blade-shaped stone glimpsed from the car window by the roadside in Aberlemno, an abandoned farm stumbled across along the boggy old mountain road from Killarney to Kenmare, or the ruins of Craswall Priory in the Black Mountains of the Welsh Borders, which I found clutched in the sinewy arms of ivy in a narrow cleft. Sometimes tough old tales of wild-mannered men have pressed the button, as when I heard tell of the eighteenth-century Essex smuggler Hard Apple, who would wrestle a bull and drink a keg of brandy while chewing broken glass to overawe the members of his gang. And sometimes the wild has more to do with intangible but powerful atmospheres. Walking the cracked and ploughed runways of the old USAF base at Greenham Common, now decommissioned and reverting to nature, I sensed a dark hum of menace exuded by the squat rank of disused cruise missile silos along the boundary fence, a low drone of discord under the pastoral melody of wild flowers and songbirds.

Weather conditions matter when you are seeking the essential wildness of a place. Seeing the Three Sisters in the Pass of Glencoe for the first time with the full light of a summer morning on their faces I thought them noble, even dazzling, but scarcely wild. Their dark and deadly aspect struck home only when I approached them on foot in winter, in a falling light on a dreadful evening of cloud and rain. Mood is important, too, and the set of the day, and the state of the season; Bardsey Island, so fair and lovely in summer sunshine off the Llyn peninsula of north Wales, is a wild beast of a place in a February gale and a thrashing sea. Storms bring wildness to a landscape, naturally, but so do mist and rain, blanketing snowfall or a baking drought. These are the times to be out among the wild places.

We need the wild as never before; and we are apprehensive about it, perhaps, as our more earthed and earthy forerunners never were. Our troubled waking dreams are of uncontrollable weather, of catastrophic floods and tsunami waves, of apocalyptic environmental punishments for our greed, laziness, consumerism, selfishness – and for our 200-year-long divorce, ever since the Industrial Revolution, from our truest and most constant love/hate 'partner', the wild. Part of what we fear is not the real wild of bog, moor or mountain, but a city dweller's troubled dream of the wild. Nothing is really going to jump out of the bushes of London or Glasgow or Belfast to rip us limb from limb, unless it's a tabloid beast: an 'evil' stranger, a 'feral animal' in a hoodie. Maybe it is within these blank young faces and deracinated urban lives in which no moor and no mountain ever figure that we find a truly haunting shadow of the wild. How do such boys grow up to be good men if they never pit themselves against wild nature as young men always used to - cutting, chopping, sparring, running, leaping, facing boars, dodging dangers? Of course they still do, but in negative contexts.

Man and the wild are far from mutually exclusive – in fact, they are two sides of the same coin, as much internally as externally. 'The Call of the Wild': that is one of the most seductive and stirring phrases ever coined. We visit our wild places of the mind along transcendent pathways: dreams, drugs, prayer, shamanic flights. We are visited by intimations of the wild, as was Alfred Watkins on a June day in 1921 when from a Herefordshire hilltop he saw, as if in a vision, a network of what he termed 'ley lines' – shining lines linking ancient sites, laid out in prehistoric times to guide travellers across a landscape they held sacred. And we go out to meet the wild in fields and copses, high on a rock face or deep under the ground. Those triumphant evangelists and engineers the Victorians might have thought they could conquer the wild, inside and out. Our angsty, more sophisticated, more guilty generation knows we can't. And even as we fear the wild, we never stop desiring it, and we never cease from seeking it out, even though we scarcely know what it is we are so keen to find up on the moors and out beyond the islands, over the hills and far away.

The wild waits for us everywhere – in the crack of a paving stone, in the crash of seas against cliffs, on a lonely moor, between the bricks of a sheepfold wall. I envy you the wonder and the delight of discovering these 500 Wild Places, or returning to them as lost familiars; of recognizing their fragility and their ever-increasing need for protection; of acknowledging with a deep thrill of fear and of awe the absolute insignificance of our species in the face of a raging storm on a mountainside, the uncurling of a maidenhair fern from a limestone gryke, or the drip of bearded lichen in the shadows of Wistman's Wood.

KEY TO THE SYMBOLS

A list of symbols used throughout the book to help identify sites of particular interest.

 Birds

 Sacred, pagan

 Industry

 Antiquity

 Fauna

 Coastal

 Urban setting

 Special habitat

 Flora

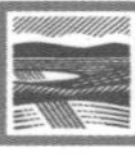 Dunes, beach, saltmarsh, mudflat, estuary

 Walking

 Inland wetland, bog, moor, heath

 Water feature

 Mountains, hills

 Historic site or event

 One of the best 50 wild places

 Myth, tale, literary, music

 Woodland

 Historic building or structure

UK DESIGNATIONS

- **Access Land** mountain, moor and upland in England and Wales that has been opened for public access on foot since the implementation of the Countryside and Rights of Way (CROW) Act 2000; shown in yellow-brown colour wash on Ordnance Survey Landranger maps.
- **ASP (Area of Special Protection)** public access restricted to protect vulnerable bird species
- **AONB (Area of Outstanding Natural Beauty)** landscape protected for its wildness and beauty
- **ESA (Environmentally Sensitive Area)** area where the landscape, wildlife or historic interest is of national importance
- **Heritage Coast** undeveloped coast for informal recreation
- **LNR (Local Nature Reserve)** nature conservation site owned and administered by the local authority
- **MNR (Marine Nature Reserve)** area where flora, fauna, geology or physical features are protected
- **NNR (National Nature Reserve)** nationally important nature conservation site
- **SSSI (Site of Special Scientific Interest)** of special interest for its flora, fauna, geology or physical features

EU DESIGNATIONS

- **SPA (Special Protection Area)** area of international importance for birds
- **SAC (Special Area of Conservation)** sites for the conservation of natural habitats and of wild fauna and flora of European importance.

INTERNATIONAL DESIGNATIONS

- **Ramsar** wetland site of international importance to birds
- **UNESCO World Heritage Site** natural or cultural area of outstanding universal value
- **UNESCO Biosphere Reserve** site forming part of a global network combining both conservation and sustainable use of natural resources

ORGANIZATIONS

- **The National Trust (www.nationaltrust.org.uk)** protects special places – historic houses, gardens, monuments and countryside – in England, Wales and Northern Ireland. National Trust for Scotland (www.nts.org.uk) does the same in Scotland; An Taisce (www.antaisce.org) in the Irish Republic.
- **Natural England (www.naturalengland.org.uk)** conserves and enhances the biodiversity, wildlife and landscapes of the natural environment of England, and promotes access and recreation. Sister organizations: Countryside Council for Wales (www.ccw.gov.uk), Scottish Natural Heritage (www.snh.org.uk), Environment & Heritage Service Northern Ireland (www.ehsni.gov.uk), National Parks & Wildlife Service (www.npws.ie) in the Irish Republic.
- **The Royal Society for the Protection of Birds (www.rspb.org.uk)** works for the conservation of wild birds in the UK; **Birdwatch Ireland (www.birdwatchireland.ie)** in the Irish Republic.
- **English Heritage (www.english-heritage.org.uk)** protects and promotes the historic environment – buildings and places – of England. Sister organisations: **CADW (www.cadw.wales.gov.uk), Historic Scotland (www.historic-scotland.gov.uk), Environment & Heritage Service Northern Ireland (www.ehsni.gov.uk), Office of Public Works (www.opw.ie)** in the Irish Republic.
- **The Woodland Trust (www.woodland-trust.org.uk)** works for the protection of the UK's native woodland heritage; Ireland's Native Woodland Trust (www.nativewoodtrust.ie) in the Irish Republic.
- **The Wildlife Trusts (www.wildlifetrusts.org)** comprises forty-seven local Wildlife Trusts across the UK, working to conserve the country's full range of wildlife species and habitats. The Irish Wildlife Trust (www.iwt.ie) has a similar function in the Irish Republic.
- **The Forestry Commission (www.forestry.gov.uk)** is a government agency responsible for protecting and expanding mainland Britain's forests and woodlands, and for promoting access and activities there. The Forest Service of Northern Ireland (www.forestserviceni.gov.uk) and the Irish Republic's Coillte (www.coillte.ie) do similar work.
- **The Ramblers' Association (www.ramblers.org.uk)** is the UK's most effective lobbying group for access on foot to the countryside. In the Republic of Ireland the situation is clouded by a lack of historic provision of access, by legal pitfalls over responsibility in case of accident, and by an aggressive and obstructive attitude among some landowners and farmers. Comhairle na Tuaithe, the Countryside Council, is a recently formed body that may make progress; www.discoverireland.ie/walking and www.walkingireland.ie are useful websites; Keep Ireland Open (www.keepirelandopen.org) lobbies for more and better access to the countryside.
- **The Wildfowl & Wetlands Trust (www.wwt.org.uk)** runs nine centres across the UK which conserve and protects wildfowl and the vulnerable wetlands they rely on, while allowing access to visitors.
- **The Ministry of Defence website: http://www.mod.uk/DefenceInternet/AboutDefence/WhatWeDo/DefenceEstateandEnvironment/AccessRecreation/** details walks and other access provision on MoD estates across the UK.

1

CORNWALL, DEVON, SOMERSET

THE WEST COUNTRY

The three West Country counties of Cornwall, Devon and Somerset form the south-western toe of mainland Britain. Between them they encompass two National Parks: Dartmoor and Exmoor. Any time spent here in rough weather reveals the harsh side of this sunny seaside region.

THE PALE LIMESTONE of Somerset and the red sandstone of the Devon coast darken, the silvery-grey granite of the Cornish cliffs turns to forbidding black as storm waves thunder in from the open Atlantic. The West Country is a wild place to walk then. Threatening weather summons ghosts here, too, in the coves that were once the stamping grounds of smugglers, and along cliffs that have been the scene of shipwrecks since men first started putting out to sea.

Many West Country places derive their wild nature from other influences. This region has been shaped by hard lives lived in difficult circumstances, and reminders of this rugged history lie all around the holiday coasts and hills. The moors of Penwith, Cornwall's westernmost tip, are open, empty country dotted with the stone circles, granite burial chambers and subterranean passages left by our ancestors. Nearer the coast stand the ruins of tin mine engine houses, their tottering chimneys raised against the sky like protesting fingers, and the man-made mountains of the Cornish Alps, whose slopes of china clay are already growing wild with gorse and old man's beard. You may hear wild Cornish legends of a horseman racing a tidal wave from the Isles of Scilly to Land's End, and of a city of gold buried deep beneath the dunes of Penhale. It is the same along the coasts of Devon, where huddled fishing villages have been wrecked by storms, and on the twin moors of the county: sandstone Exmoor of the lawless Doone tribe, and granite Dartmoor with its grim prison and litter of long-abandoned tin works and granite quarries.

Strange tales of strange people abound, wild men and women, spectral presences, eccentric characters such as Parson Hawker of Morwenstow with his seaweed wig and opium pipe. The West Country has always fired writers' imaginations. Here you walk in the footsteps of the dashing pirate of Frenchman's Creek, run in the pawprints of Tarka the otter, stride out across Dartmoor with Sherlock Holmes on the track of the Baskervilles' infernal hound.

The three counties are bonded by their traditional remoteness from the centres of power

Exmoor (pp. 48–9)

and government, their progression down the ever-narrowing tail of Britain to its vanishing point in the Atlantic Ocean. As for places that are still truly remote, there are plenty for adventurers to seek out: the caves deep under Mendip, for instance; the wild Western Rocks of the Scilly Isles; or the long granite bar of Lundy, out in the throat of the Bristol Channel, whose swirling tides hide a submarine world where only a handful of explorers ever venture.

LINKS

- South West Coast Path National Trail (www.southwestcoastpath.com; www.swcp.org.uk): Lynmouth, views of Lundy, Morte Stone, Baggy Point, Braunton Burrows, estuary of the Two Rivers, Morwenstow, Padstow Obby Oss, Penhale Sands, Pen-Enys Point, Gurnard's Head, Levant Mine, Land's End, St Levan's Well, Frenchman's Creek, Start Bay, Dawlish Warren, Lyme Regis Undercliff
- Two Moors Way (www.ramblers.org.uk/info/paths/twomoors.html): Huntingdon Warren, Grimspound, Pinkworthy Pond and the Chains, Hoaroak Water, Watersmeet

NATIONAL PARKS

- Exmoor: www.exmoor-nationalpark.gov.uk
- Dartmoor: www.dartmoor-npa.gov.uk

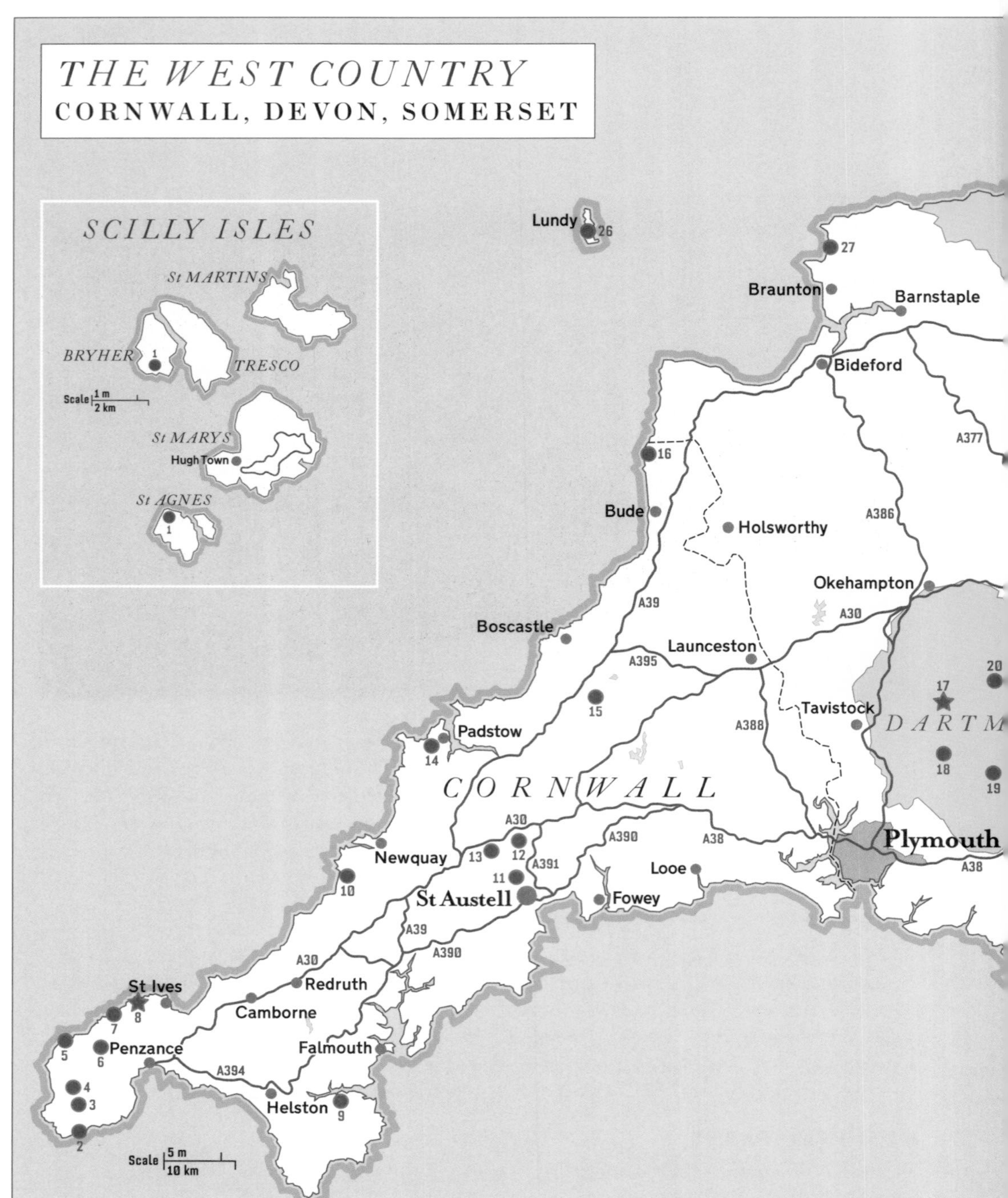
THE WEST COUNTRY
CORNWALL, DEVON, SOMERSET
SCILLY ISLES
St MARTINS
BRYHER
TRESCO
St MARYS
Hugh Town
St AGNES
Scale 1 m 2 km
Lundy
Braunton
Barnstaple
Bideford
A377
Bude
Holsworthy
A386
Okehampton
A30
A39
Boscastle
Launceston
A395
Tavistock
A388
DARTM
Padstow
CORNWALL
A30
Plymouth
A390
A38
Newquay
A391
Looe
St Austell
Fowey
A39
A390
A30
Redruth
St Ives
Camborne
Penzance
Falmouth
A394
Helston
Scale 5 m 10 km
1
2
3
4
5
6
7
8
9
10
11
12
13
14
15
16
17
18
19
20
26
27

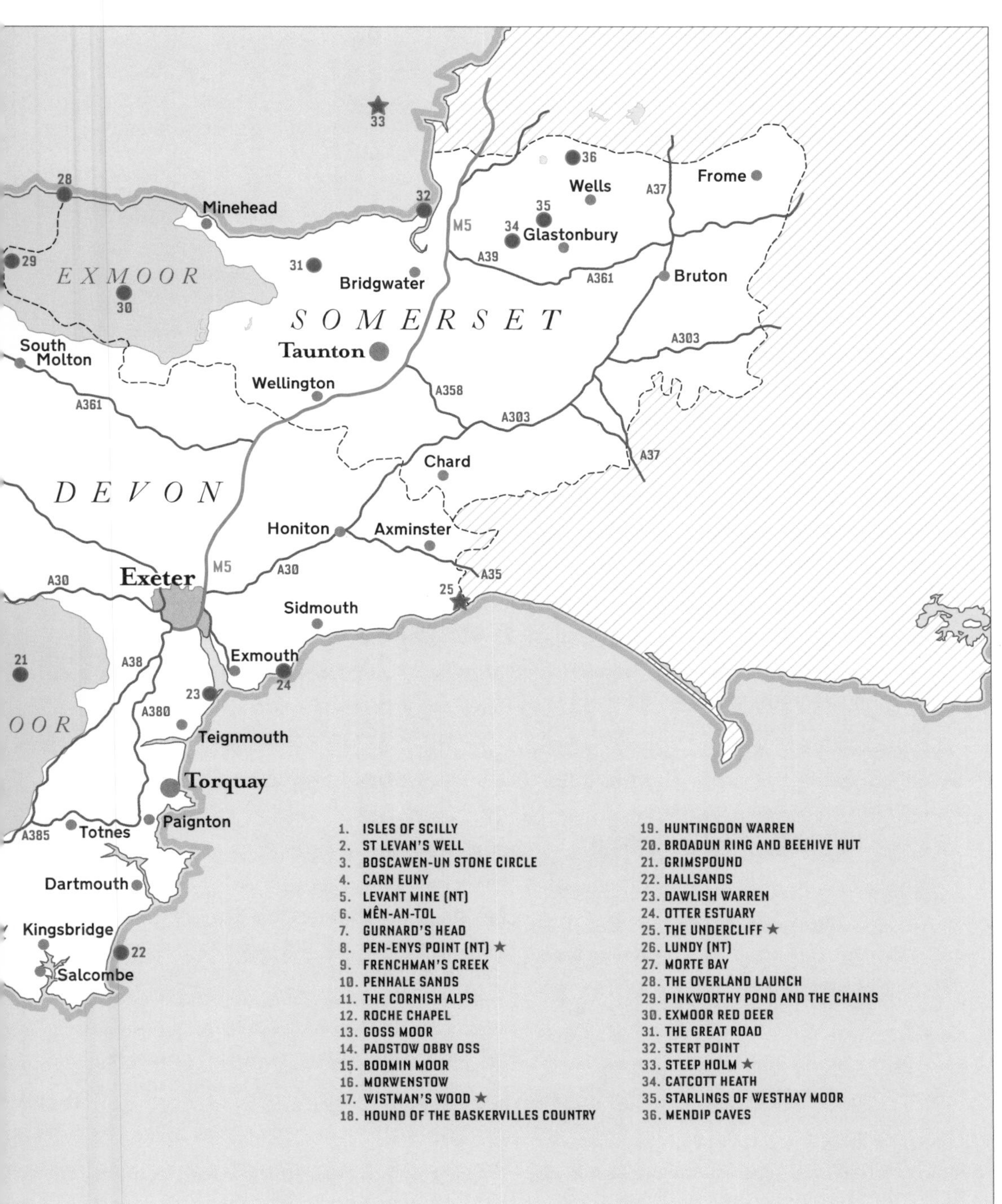
33
28
Minehead
32
29
EXMOOR
30
31
Bridgwater
36
Wells
35
34
Glastonbury
Frome
A37
M5
A39
A361
Bruton
SOMERSET
Taunton
South Molton
Wellington
A303
A361
A358
A303
A37
Chard
DEVON
Honiton
Axminster
A35
Exeter
M5
A30
A30
25
Sidmouth
Exmouth
24
21
A38
23
A380
OOR
Teignmouth
Torquay
Paignton
A385
Totnes
Dartmouth
Kingsbridge
22
Salcombe
1. ISLES OF SCILLY
2. ST LEVAN'S WELL
3. BOSCAWEN-UN STONE CIRCLE
4. CARN EUNY
5. LEVANT MINE (NT)
6. MÊN-AN-TOL
7. GURNARD'S HEAD
8. PEN-ENYS POINT (NT) ★
9. FRENCHMAN'S CREEK
10. PENHALE SANDS
11. THE CORNISH ALPS
12. ROCHE CHAPEL
13. GOSS MOOR
14. PADSTOW OBBY OSS
15. BODMIN MOOR
16. MORWENSTOW
17. WISTMAN'S WOOD ★
18. HOUND OF THE BASKERVILLES COUNTRY
19. HUNTINGDON WARREN
20. BROADUN RING AND BEEHIVE HUT
21. GRIMSPOUND
22. HALLSANDS
23. DAWLISH WARREN
24. OTTER ESTUARY
25. THE UNDERCLIFF ★
26. LUNDY (NT)
27. MORTE BAY
28. THE OVERLAND LAUNCH
29. PINKWORTHY POND AND THE CHAINS
30. EXMOOR RED DEER
31. THE GREAT ROAD
32. STERT POINT
33. STEEP HOLM ★
34. CATCOTT HEATH
35. STARLINGS OF WESTHAY MOOR
36. MENDIP CAVES

1. ISLES OF SCILLY, CORNWALL

Maps: OS Explorer 101; Landranger 203

Travel: From mainland: Isles of Scilly Skybus (www.ios-travel.co.uk), Air Southwest (www.airsouthwest.com), helicopter (www.islesofscillyhelicopter.com) or ferry (www.ios-travel.co.uk).

Inter-island travel: St Mary's Boatmen's Association (www.scillyboating.co.uk).

On a clear day the Isles of Scilly are just visible from the westernmost tip of Cornwall. Their geographical position alone, 28 miles south-west of Land's End, lends the five inhabited Scilly Isles and their hundreds of smaller satellite isles and rocks a romantic enchantment. Myths of the archipelago abound – that the islands are the mountain summit of sunken Atlantis; that the doomed knight and lover Tristan was born in a boat on the way to the mainland; that the islands were joined by dry land to the mainland until a catastrophic tidal wave overwhelmed them and drowned all but the famed horseman Tresilian, who raced the tsunami to Land's End and safety.

Of the five main islands St Mary's is the capital, Tresco is half filled with a wonderful subtropical garden, and St Martin's possesses superb beaches. But, for me, it is the two smallest, Bryher and St Agnes, that best reflect the wild spirit of the Atlantic. Bryher's east coast is sheltered by neighbouring Tresco, but once across the waist of the island you find a tremendously rugged west-facing coast indented with bays, particularly when winter gales hit Hell Bay, turning it into a maelstrom of white water. Down to the south-west stand the Norrard Rocks, black teeth against the white spray. Watching, the confrontation seems a matter of life and death.

St Agnes lies out by itself, unsheltered by any other isle. Its own off-island of Gugh is connected by the narrow isthmus of the Bar, and holds in its heathery flanks a couple of fine prehistoric monuments – the huge tumbled stones of a 4,000-year-old tomb called Obadiah's Grave, and a standing stone with a deeply grooved back, known as the Old Man of Gugh. The west coast of St Agnes, as of Bryher, is the place to be in dirty weather, looking out south-west to the Western Rocks fighting the waves, and beyond them to the Bishop Rock Lighthouse, 167 feet of grey granite rising from its rock 4 miles away, an admonitory finger in a lace cuff of foam.

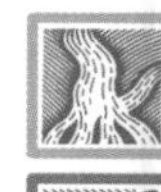

2. ST LEVAN'S WELL, CORNWALL

Maps: OS Explorer 102; Landranger 203

Travel: A30 from Penzance towards Land's End. At Catchall, left on B3283 through St Buryan to Sparnon; B3315 through Treen to Trethewy. Left here through Porthcurno to St Levan. Park near church. Returning down lane from church, right in 50 yards, then left on footpath to St Levan's Well (OS ref. 381219), just above the South West Coast Path National Trail.

St Levan's Well lies in a bend of the cliff path, somewhere to discover on a summer's day, walled in on three sides with great boulders of granite. There is a flat stone to kneel on, and the water (good for sore eyes and toothache) under its mat of pondweed wells gently from a stone lintel, seeping over a profusion of ferns and bright yellow ragweed.

The spring is named after the fifth-century Irish Christian pioneer Selevan, better known hereabouts as St Levan. He blessed the water, and made himself a hermitage just below the well. A flight of granite steps leads down to the oratory, which was built on the site of St Levan's cell three centuries after his death; but there is little these days to distinguish the stones of the two-roomed chapel from the lichen-bearded boulders all around.

The Irishman was a great fisherman, by all accounts. He was a bit of a wild man, too, with a rough edge to his tongue. There's a tale of how a local woman, Johanna, was gardening one Sunday when she saw the saint setting off on a fishing expedition and rebuked him for impiety. He retorted that fishing on the Sabbath was no more blasphemous than gardening, and that anyway she was a stupid woman, and furthermore if he had to baptize any children in his well with the name of Johanna from that day out, they'd grow up as stupid as her. The name instantly dropped out of existence in the parish.

Beyond the holy well and the obliterated hermitage, a rough scramble leads to St Levan's favourite fishing spot, the cove of Porthchapel, a tiny crescent of tan-coloured sand.

3. BOSCAWEN-UN STONE CIRCLE, CORNWALL

Maps: OS Explorer 102; Landranger 203

Travel: A30 from Penzance towards Land's End. A mile beyond Catchall and B3283 turning, bear left into entrance of Boscawenoon Farm (OS ref. 417280). Up track to lay-by parking place ('No cars past this point'). Continue on foot to farm; right up stony lane; in 300 yards, right at cattle grid up hedged path ('Boscawen-un Stone Circle') for 400 yards to stone circle (412274).

Holidaymakers in large numbers visit the ancient stones of the Merry Maidens a couple of miles down the valley; Boscawen-un Stone Circle, tucked away in the bracken at the end of its discouraging track, retains an air of aloofness and mystery. The approach is up a narrow, muddy and prickly path, one you are unlikely to share with any casual visitor. The circle lies concealed until the last moment, so that it comes as a shock when at the far end you are suddenly confronted by a great phallic stone 7 feet long, standing canted at a sharp angle in the centre of a wide ring of stones, set up perhaps 6,000 years ago. There are nineteen of these encircling stones, thick with lichen and standing shorter than an adult human, making the king stone in the middle seem all the more impressive. A gap on the west side might once have been filled by a twentieth stone.

One of the ring, on the south-west side, is not of sombre granite but of white quartz,

Boscawen-un stone circle

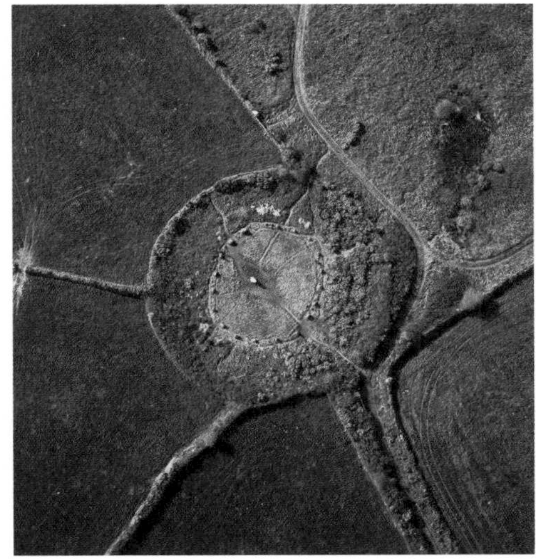

and it is on top of this stone that visitors occasionally leave offerings – a coin, a piece of rag or a bunch of flowers. In spite of that, there is a remote feeling to Boscawen-un.

4. CARN EUNY, CORNWALL

Maps: OS Explorer 102; Landranger 203

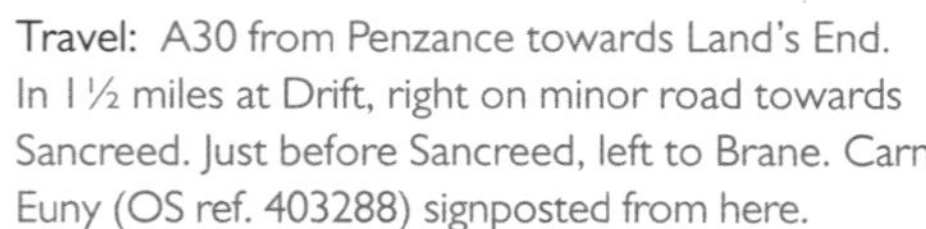

Travel: A30 from Penzance towards Land's End. In 1 ½ miles at Drift, right on minor road towards Sancreed. Just before Sancreed, left to Brane. Carn Euny (OS ref. 403288) signposted from here.

Coming up the lane from Brane, Carn Euny looks like an unremarkable hummocky green field. But stroll around the site, and it soon reveals its secrets. Here, sunken into the turf, lies what remains of one of the oldest villages in Britain. Walking at roof level around the small scatter of dwellings, you look down across fragments of stone-walling into grassy hollows which were once domestic rooms, animal pens and store chambers.

The huddled little settlement might have been of no more importance than a large Iron Age farmstead. It was certainly inhabited from around 200 BC, when wooden shelters were built here, and through the couple of centuries leading up to the Roman invasion, during which stone houses replaced the timber huts. The inhabitants of Carn Euny also developed a sophisticated artistic taste, decorating their pottery with wavy incisions and rope-like courses. After the Romans arrived, halfway through the first century AD, more houses were built, some of oval pattern, others around courtyards. Yet more sophisticated pottery of the smooth red Samian type found its way to Carn Euny from overseas, and there were glass beads for the women to wear. By about AD 300, however, the settlement was abandoned.

The most intriguing structure in the village pre-dates all the dwellings by several hundred years. It is a fogou, an underground passage that drives a straight course for nearly 70 feet, its ceiling of stone slabs running just below the surface. Experts argue as to whether it was a corn store, a place of concealment in times of danger, or a chamber designed for religious rituals. Descending from the ancient village in the wide moors into this dank, chilly tunnel is a trigger for anyone's imagination.

5. LEVANT MINE (NT), CORNWALL

Maps: OS Explorer 102; Landranger 203

Travel: B3306 coast road from St Ives towards St Just. At Pendeen or Trewellard, right (signs) on minor road to Levant Mine (OS ref. 368348).

All along the north coast of western Cornwall stand the ruined engine houses and tall chimneys that signal the sites of former tin mines. The price of tin collapsed many times over the centuries, but Cornwall's chief heavy industry continued through good times and bad for over 2,000 years until its complete shut-down at the end of the twentieth century. Such is the historical and cultural significance of the silent industrial landscape that it left along the cliffs, the area is now designated a UNESCO World Heritage Site.

The wild associations of these old mine workings are twofold: the gaunt, forlorn atmosphere of the ruins and their lonely, rugged setting; and the isolated and dangerous working lives of the miners.

Levant Mine (opened in 1820, closed in 1930) on the cliffs near Pendeen offers an excellent overview of the industry with its great green beam engine rhythmically pumping out water, its tunnels to the engine shaft, tin-dressing floors and engine pond. The nineteenth-century engine houses are sturdy buildings, plain but elegant in a late Georgian style. It is the setting that emphasizes the wildness of the scene – buildings, tall stone-banded chimneys and grassed-over spoil heaps all at the edge of the land, perched between a bleak, windswept moor and a fall of black cliffs nearly 300 feet to the sea. The mouths of shafts and tunnels open in the cliffs, and unseen levels run several hundred yards out under the seabed. As so often in Cornwall, fierce winter weather adds to the atmosphere as the wind whistles in the broken chimneys and the hidden sea thumps and booms at the feet of the cliffs.

6. MÊN-AN-TOL, CORNWALL

Maps: OS Explorer 102; Landranger 203

Travel: B3306 from St Ives towards St Just. At Trevowhan, 1 mile west of Rosemergy, left on minor road towards Madron. In 1 mile park near telephone box and walk up stony track to the Mên-an-Tol (signed) at OS ref. 426349.

The unique Mên-an-Tol stands in a wild and moody setting of bare pale moorland. The engine house and chimney of Ding Dong Mine loom in ruins on the skyline, and the ancient stone tomb of Lanyon Quoit is seen in the south as a huge slab hanging against the sky. Cornwall is littered with pre-Christian sites, but there is nothing like the enigmatic alignment of the Mên-an-Tol, in Cornwall or elsewhere in these islands.

The strange tripartite alignment of the 'stone with the hole' stands on its own, surrounded by bracken and gorse. A roughly rounded stone, pierced through its hub with a perfect circle, perches on its rim, flanked by two upright standing stones, all three stones in the group being about 3 feet high.

This ancient site seems always to have exerted power over people. Three centuries ago the locals were recorded as squeezing through the hole to cure their backaches. Anyone with rheumatism, it was believed, could ease the condition by crawling round the stones nine times 'from east to west' and then passing through the hole. In a ritual that twisted this cure back to front, tubercular children were posted through the central stone and then dragged in a circle 'on the grass three times against the sun' to make them strong. Today any visitor who waits patiently by the Mên-an-Tol can see modern-age pagans performing similar rituals and leaving floral offerings beside the holed stone.

7. GURNARD'S HEAD, CORNWALL

Maps: OS Explorer 102; Landranger 203

Travel: B3306 towards Land's End from St Ives. In 6 miles, park in Treen village. Walk up lane through village and follow field path to cross South West Coast Path National Trail. Continue seaward for 1/3 mile to reach the summit of Gurnard's Head (OS ref. 432387).

Gurnard's Head is, quite simply, one of the wildest places on the wildest coast in Cornwall. The dragon-head promontory pokes out northwards from the north coast

Gurnard's Head

of Penwith, Cornwall's most westerly region and the most exposed to the effects of wind and sea coming straight and hard off 3,000 miles of Atlantic. For such a formidable stronghold of a headland, Gurnard's Head is surprisingly easy to get to; you merely turn off the South West Coast Path National Trail and follow the path round the eastern flank of the promontory. There's an Iron Age fort, Trereen Dinas, at the outer edge of the Head. It's well worth climbing the stack of granite on the summit for the huge views, south-west to Pendeen Watch, north-east up the coast as far as St Agnes Head – 20 miles of rugged, dark coves, stacks, headlands and cliffs.

Many promontories along the coasts of Cornwall are lonely, dramatic places, but Gurnard's Head has something special: an exaggeratedly out-jutting form, sheer cliffs each side, and the rhythmic hollow thump and hiss of the sea in the invisible caves all round the skirt of the headland. The romantic young curate of Clyro, Francis Kilvert, recorded in his *Diary* a delightful expedition to Gurnard's Head on 29 July 1870. His omnibus party was so cheerful and jolly that he abandoned them and

wandered round the cliffs to the broken rocks at the furthest point of the Head, and sat alone among the wilderness of broken shattered tumbled cliffs, listening to the booming and breaking of the waves below and watching the flying skirts of the showers of spray. Perfect solitude. The rest of the party were climbing about in the rocks somewhere overhead, but not a voice or sound was to be heard.

High adventurers should try a walk here in a winter storm, when the waves thump into the shiny green-and-black cliffs with a force that sends a shiver through the promontory. Spray leaps high with each collision, to hang for an instance as a sheet, before being ripped apart and dashed away to nothing. At such times you have to hold on to the rocks, and fear and deep respect for the sea's power mix with the salt on your tongue.

8. PEN-ENYS POINT (NT), CORNWALL

Maps: OS Explorer 102; Landranger 203

Travel: Pen-Enys Point (OS ref. 490410) is 2 miles west of St Ives, along the South West Coast Path National Trail.

Nearest railway station: St Ives (2½ miles)

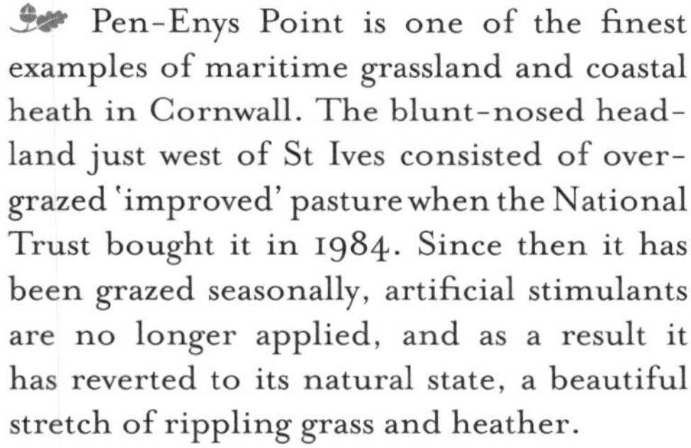

Pen-Enys Point is one of the finest examples of maritime grassland and coastal heath in Cornwall. The blunt-nosed headland just west of St Ives consisted of overgrazed 'improved' pasture when the National Trust bought it in 1984. Since then it has been grazed seasonally, artificial stimulants are no longer applied, and as a result it has reverted to its natural state, a beautiful stretch of rippling grass and heather.

The slopes tend to be wet with springs, and colonies of pink-purple southern marsh orchid can be seen here in summer, as can the trailing stems and crinkly-edged leaves of Cornish moneywort with its minuscule pink-and-yellow flowers. Pale butterwort is another uncommon flower, a bell of pale pink with a yellow throat that rises from the grass on a slender stem.

Moving to the less sheltered, more seaward side of Pen-Enys Point, you find a blaze of rich purple heather in sheets or in tussocks. In places the coastal heath is draped with tangles of madder, whose bright red stems flash in the sun. They are too weak to hold the plant upright, and have to spread for support across other species of plants with more solid structures. At the cliff edge you can find linnets skipping over the bracken, and may spot the dark shape of a peregrine on the hunt along the coast.

9. FRENCHMAN'S CREEK, CORNWALL

Maps: OS Explorer 103; Landranger 204

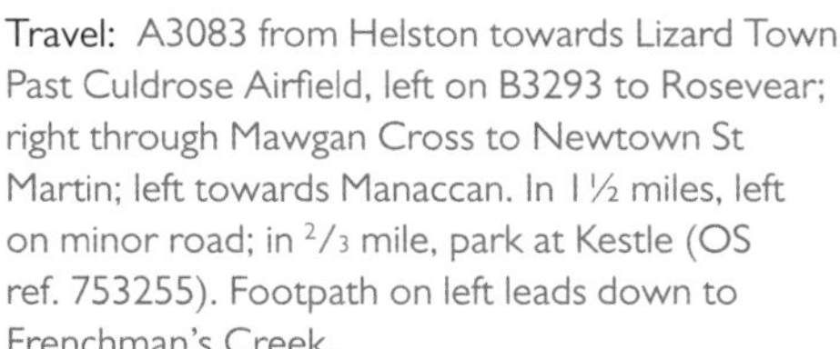

Travel: A3083 from Helston towards Lizard Town. Past Culdrose Airfield, left on B3293 to Rosevear; right through Mawgan Cross to Newtown St Martin; left towards Manaccan. In 1½ miles, left on minor road; in 2/3 mile, park at Kestle (OS ref. 753255). Footpath on left leads down to Frenchman's Creek.

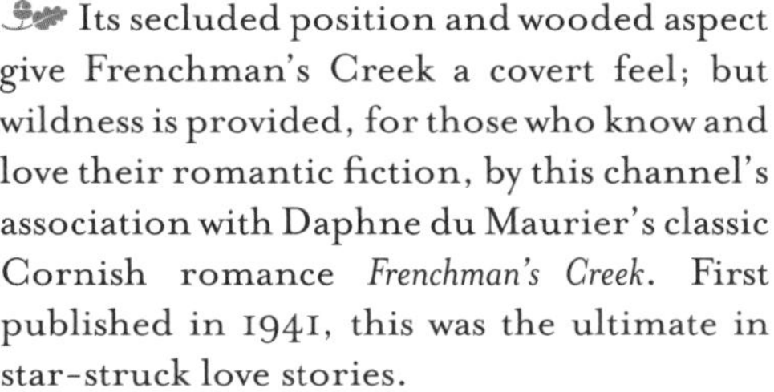

Its secluded position and wooded aspect give Frenchman's Creek a covert feel; but wildness is provided, for those who know and love their romantic fiction, by this channel's association with Daphne du Maurier's classic Cornish romance *Frenchman's Creek*. First published in 1941, this was the ultimate in star-struck love stories.

The creek itself snakes northwards into the estuary of Helford River – though 'sneaks' might be a better word, for there is something secretive about this tree-lined waterway. Muddy at ebb tide and dully gleaming with seawater at the flow, winding in and out of fallen tree trunks festooned with seaweed, Frenchman's Creek on a still, sunny afternoon seems more like an inlet in a mangrove swamp than a Cornish creek – particularly when a snow-white egret jumps up from its fishing stance and flaps away with trailing legs and a wheezy squawk. Yet here, among the mud-banks, the beautiful but bored Lady Dona St Columb throws caution (and her marriage) to the winds and finds excitement, passion and true love in the arms of the incredibly dashing yet superbly suave Jean Aubrey, French pirate and – naturally – philosopher.

With his white-sailed ship *La Mouette* moored safely in the creek, Jean and Dona spend a night of delight under a blanket. What a mad escape from everything rational, safe and sane! Read du Maurier's novel before you venture to Frenchman's Creek, and the murky little waterway will transmogrify before your eyes into a sweet and salty paradise.

10. PENHALE SANDS, CORNWALL

Maps: OS Explorer 104; Landranger 200

Travel: A3075 Newquay to Redruth; at Goonhavern, right on B3285 to Perranporth. Park near the seafront and walk north along Perran Beach. In 1/3 mile you pass Cotty's Point; in another 3/4 mile turn right to climb a steep pathway up the dunes to the top.

Nearest railway station: Newquay (5 miles)

In places Penhale Sands reach a height of 200 feet, a lumpy landscape shaggy with grasses and bright with wild flowers in spring and summer. Seen from the flat 3-mile strand of Perran Beach to the north of Perranporth, the enormous rise of sand hills that backs the beach looks more like a range of miniature mountains than a line of dunes. The holiday camp of Perran Sands Holiday Centre is a blot on the wild landscape, but turn your back and make for the tall cross that towers above the remains of St Piran's Oratory (OS ref. 768564).

Piran was a sixth-century Irish hermit who arrived on the Cornish coast aboard a millstone which God had miraculously caused to float. King Aonghus of Munster had ordered the stone to be tied round Piran's neck and the holy man himself to be hurled off a cliff after Piran had upset the king by rebuking him for taking a new wife while married to a former one. After stumbling ashore on Perran Beach, Piran lit a fire in one of the caves behind the beach. The heat melted the ore in the rocks, and hey presto! The saint had discovered how to make tin. Hermit and locals got roaring drunk to celebrate.

This agreeable and very human saint built an oratory high in the dunes where the great cross now stands. Perhaps it was a folk memory of this humble cell, linked to the old story of Piran's discovery of tin, that led to rumours of a great treasure lying buried beneath the dunes of Penhale Sands. These tales were elaborated into a full-blooded legend of a golden city, Langarrow, which stretched for 4 miles along the shore, filled with wonderful buildings, with feasting and the music of golden bells. However, the male inhabitants were unwilling to soil their hands and instead imported the lowest class of criminals and troublemakers from other cities to labour in the mines.

The inevitable came to pass. The slaves grew bolder as their masters became more decadent. The ladies of Langarrow came to prefer the lithe and muscular young slaves to their own blanched and flabby husbands. Such orgiastic scenes ensued that divine retribution was bound to descend. So it did, in the form of a terrible sandstorm that blew without ceasing for three days and nights. When the tempest abated, the golden city was nowhere to be seen. Langarrow lay far beneath the dunes heaped up by the storm, its golden bells never more to be heard by human ear.

Baal Pit, Cornish Alps

11. THE CORNISH ALPS, CORNWALL

Maps: OS Explorer 106, 107; Landranger 200

Travel: From St Austell, A391 Bugle and Bodmin road. At ½ mile north of St Austell, cross over roundabout beside 'St Austell' town nameplate. 100 yards up A391, park on right (OS ref. 021548). Blue 'Clay Trails' waymarks point away from both sides of road. Bear to the right for Baal and Carclaze pits (walking and cycling route).

Nearest railway station: St Austell (1 ½ miles)

For nearly 200 years travellers on the road between Launceston and Redruth have been exclaiming over the extraordinary sight that greets them on the southern skyline, behind St Austell and its bay. What appear to be snow-covered mountains, sharply peaked, stand in an impressive chain some 8 miles long where no mountain chain should be. A second glance at their stepped profiles and the abnormal flatness of their lower spurs confirms that these 'Cornish Alps' are man-made. They are the spoil heaps of the china clay industry, piled up well over 100 feet high in places. Deep extraction pits, flooded with brilliant turquoise water, lie alongside. Nowadays the Cornish china clay business is in decline, most of it residing in the hands of foreign companies who can obtain their china clay more cheaply from Brazil. The snowy whiteness of the Cornish Alps – so blinding on sunny days in the heyday of the industry that the inhabitants of the clay villages found it unpleasant to go out of doors – is becoming muted, as grasses and scrub bushes grow on their slopes. But they still form an infinitely strange, compelling landscape that is unique in Britain.

The National Cycle Network has developed a system of linking cycle routes known as the 'Clay Trails' – also open to walkers, and many to horse riders – which wind in and out of the Cornish Alps and their lakes. The trail from Wheal Martin to the Eden Project (whose famous geodomes are themselves built in an old clay pit) leads past one of the most impressive of the extraction holes, Baal Pit. Baal Pit and its parent mine of Carclaze were the largest in Cornwall in their day, producing hundreds of thousands of tons of white kaolinite, a product of decomposing granite used by industry for processes from coating paper to making weedkillers and cosmetics.

In 1971 the makers of the *Dr Who* TV series used Baal Pit as a setting for the planet Uxarieus in the year AD 2472. Looking at the strangeness of the scene today, the immense and devastated industrial site already back in nature's grip, you can appreciate the unsettling and unearthly atmosphere that brought the filmmakers here.

Baal Pit is immense, a 200-foot hole whose pale grey cliffs are streaked with crimson, their slopes deeply trenched by rainwater runnels. Huge boulders perch precariously on the steeply sloping screes. Roads snake downwards to vanish into the milky, poison-green water that fills the depths of the pit. A disused inclined railway slopes towards the pit bottom, its corrugated iron housings still in place, its tracks overgrown with weeds. Heather, rhododendron, birch and willow scrub are colonizing wherever the land is not too steep. Silence reigns.

12. ROCHE CHAPEL, CORNWALL

Maps: OS Explorer 106; Landranger 200

Travel: From A30 west of Victoria, B3274 to Roche. Park near church. Opposite church, walk along Bugle Road for 200 yards. Stile on right leads to path to chapel (OS ref. 991596).

NB: Unprotected climb up two ladders; ascend at your own risk.

Nearest railway station: Roche (2 miles)

Roche Chapel

The fifteenth-century 'Chapel in the Rock' outside the village of Roche is a very strange sight. It seems to have grown organically out of the purple-grey rock it clings to. Come here on a stormy day, or an evening of strong sunlight against heavy clouds, and the shell of the medieval hermitage wedged in its crack atop the 100-foot crag of Roche Rock seems truly sinister. The chapel was built in 1409 as a sanctuary dedicated to St Michael, and a more secluded situation for a prayerful hermit is hard to imagine. Yet Roche Chapel has also done duty as a leper's retreat – a local landowner of the Tregarnick family isolated himself here voluntarily, while his saintly daughter, Gundred, ministered to him.

Once you have ascended the first of the two rusty ladders and squeezed yourself into the roofless 'nave', there is a second ladder by which to climb the internal wall of the chapel, and then a set of worn stone steps up to the ramparts. From here there is a fine view over farmland to the stepped pyramids of the Cornish Alps (see p. 31).

A ruinous chapel in such a strange location could hardly escape being hedged round with legends. The most poignant concerns Tristan, nephew of the formidable King Mark of Cornwall, and beautiful Isolde, betrothed to the king but fated by the accidental intake of a love potion to fall hopelessly in love with Tristan. The chapel on the rock was one of the places they sought refuge from King Mark's men, and a version of the tale has Tristan leaping to safety from the chapel window. Perhaps it was this window, too, in which John Tregeagle got his head jammed in another wild Cornish fable. Tregeagle, a cheating steward who had returned to the earth in spirit form after his death, was condemned to an eternity of emptying Dozmary Pool on nearby Bodmin Moor with a leaking limpet shell. Like Tristan and Isolde, the unquiet spirit fled to Roche Chapel for sanctuary from his torment. But while the lovers were pursued by human enemies, it was a pack of howling, headless hellhounds that chased Tregeagle. Only frantic prayer enabled him to free his head at last and fall in through the window to safety; but the fiendish dogs, meanwhile, had bitten his bottom to ribbons.

13. GOSS MOOR, CORNWALL

Maps: OS Explorer 106; Landranger 200

Travel: From A30 west of Victoria, B3274 to Roche. Right in village along Harmony Road; in ½ mile, left ('Tregoss'). At T-junction, left ('St Dennis'). In 300 yards, park on left by gate (OS ref. 966601) and walk on to moor.

Nearest railway station: Roche (3 miles)

Anyone who has been stuck in a traffic jam crawling bumper-to-bumper between Victoria and Indian Queens on the A30 will have gazed out in mingled frustration and boredom over Goss Moor. It is the bleak-looking stretch of bushy ground that surrounds what used to be the single-track section of the busiest holiday road in Cornwall. Since the summer of 2007 the A30 has been upgraded, doubled and shifted further north, leaving Goss Moor free of the sight, sound and stink of slow-motion traffic.

Goss Moor is a hunting ground for hen harrier and hobby, a safe breeding site for the ground-nesting nightjar, and a place of refuge for walkers, naturalists, birdwatchers and lovers of quiet open spaces. It is also one of the UK's most important breeding sites for the beautiful orange-and-brown speckled marsh fritillary butterfly, and supports colonies of two other heathland butterflies in decline across England, the small pearl-bordered fritillary and the lovely silver-studded blue with white fringes round the borders of its blue wings.

Stepping out across the moor in summer you walk between patches of bell heather, willow scrub and gorse, with clumps of campion in the grassy margins. Boggy tracts of moor lie thick with rushes and marsh thistles. There are fleets of open water, too, miniature lakes formed in the hollows of former gravel pits and tin-mining scoops – this moor has been mined for its deposits of alluvial tin for perhaps 4,000 years. Every now and then the view opens, and looking south across the rushy moor between striding, skeletal pylons, you will see the volcanic-looking pyramids of the Cornish Alps (see p. 31).

14. PADSTOW OBBY OSS, CORNWALL

Maps: OS Explorer 106; Landranger 200

Travel: A39 south from Wadebridge; in 2 miles, right on A389 to Padstow.

NB: Padstow is extremely crowded on May Eve and May Day. Arrive early!

Eleven o'clock on a dark May Eve, and the narrow streets of Padstow are jam-packed with people. A group of women encircle the maypole on Broad Street, bending low to sweep their arms sideways, then leaping up to punch their hands at the sky. Drums thump, accordions blare, and thousands of voices are raised in the chorus of the May Song:

Unite and unite, and let us all unite,
For summer is a-come unto day;
And whither we are going we will all unite
In the merry morning of May!

It is a foretaste of what will engulf the little north Cornwall town tomorrow when Padstow's two Obby Osses, the Red Ribbon and the Blue, are let loose from their respective stables to celebrate the coming of spring with a wild and whirling dance through the streets. The ceremony of the Obby Osses may well pre-date the arrival of Christianity in Cornwall; it is certainly pagan, Celtic and unbridled in character.

On May Day morning itself Padstow wakes to the May Song as huge bass drums give out a big, bone-shaking beat. Drainpipes, lampposts and doorways are festooned with greenery. The streets are packed even more solid than the night before. When the Obby Osses do emerge – the Blue from Padstow Institute, the Red from the Golden Lion pub – everyone cheers thunderously. The Osses are revealed, not 'hobby horses' but demonic figures. The carrier of each Oss is strapped into a circular disk skirted with black drapes and topped by a sinister face, a painted mask in scarlet or blue, long-beaked like a bird, with clacking teeth that reach out to pinch the bystanders. The Oss twirls round and round, and in front of him prances the Teaser, high priest of this ceremony, waving a club and leaping as if both to goad and encourage. Now the Oss sinks to the ground in a simulation of death, and the lines of dancers who accompany him bend solicitously over his recumbent form as they croon an enigmatic lament:

Up flies the kite and down falls the lark O;
Aunt Ursula Birdhood she had an old ewe
And she died in her own Park O ...

'Oss! Oss!' yells a solitary voice. 'Wee Oss!' shout back the dancers. They raise the Oss from the deathly clutches of sterility and winter, and circle on with him in their midst in a celebration of fertility and spring, as the May Song sounds out once more.

Bodmin Moor

15. BODMIN MOOR, CORNWALL

Maps: OS Explorer 109; Landranger 200, 201

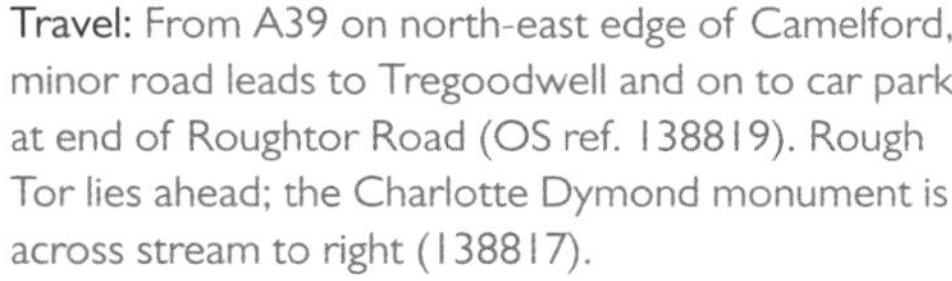

Travel: From A39 on north-east edge of Camelford, minor road leads to Tregoodwell and on to car park at end of Roughtor Road (OS ref. 138819). Rough Tor lies ahead; the Charlotte Dymond monument is across stream to right (138817).

Inland Cornwall boasts many wild places, but the 100 square miles of Bodmin Moor form by far the broadest wild expanse in the county. Like Dartmoor over the border in Devon, and the remote moors of Penwith in west Cornwall, Bodmin Moor is founded on granite, a rock that always seems to lend a sombre tone to an open landscape. Lapwings breed here in late spring and summer, their high-pitched cries adding a mournful note. There are wide patches of bog where the bright green or yellow sphagnum moss can quickly suck you in, and plenty of granite plates piled totem-like into tors on the hilltops.

A good introduction to the lonely and captivating atmosphere of Bodmin Moor is the climb up Rough Tor (pronounced 'Row-ter'), the second highest point on the moor at 1,311 feet, from whose summit you can see – and easily reach – Cornwall's highest peak, Brown Willy (1,375 feet). Setting off on foot from the car park at the end of Roughtor Road, a clear path leads you up the north-west flank of Rough Tor. On either side of the path lie stone circles, nearly 20 feet in diameter, the remaining foundations of the homes of the Bronze Age farmers who wrestled a living from this bare landscape some four millennia ago.

The summit of Rough Tor is piled with stacks of granite worn smooth and round-edged, undercut by wind and weather so that they appear to be resting one on another with very little to prevent them toppling over. In a couple of cases they are actually rocking stones, their site of contact with the stone below worn away to such a narrow point that you can rock a slab weighing many tons just by pushing down on its edge.

It's an easy descent down the east slope of

Rough Tor to cross the De Lank River, and from here twenty minutes uphill will put you on top of Brown Willy and reward you with a splendid view of brown moorland, shading in the distance into green farmlands, and bounded in the north-west by a line of cliffs and then the sea some 10 miles away.

Turn off to the left on your return journey, just before reaching the car park, to find the stone column of weathered, lichen-encrusted granite that forms the Charlotte Dymond monument. Charlotte was a young domestic maid murdered on a Sunday morning in April 1844 by her fellow servant Matthew Weeks as she walked over the moor. The lonely bleakness of the scene adds to the poignancy of this place.

16. MORWENSTOW, CORNWALL

Maps: OS Explorer 126; Landranger 190

Travel: A39 from Bideford towards Bude. At 7 miles after second 'Hartland' turn-off, right on minor road to Morwenstow. Park near church. Hawker's Hut (National Trust) signposted just off the South West Coast Path National Trail in the cliffs below.

This north Cornwall village, a clifftop settlement near the border with Devon, is gentle enough in atmosphere. In summer, with the gorse and campion in flower, the high-banked lanes and grey and white houses give out an air of contented permanence. In winter the tune changes as stiff gales blow in from the Atlantic and whip the smoke from the chimneys. It's then that you see why the trees all grow to lean so extravagantly inland. Hearing the sea crashing at the feet of the cliffs, you get a taste of Morwenstow as it was in the rough old days. Until the mid nineteenth century, to be shipwrecked here in a winter storm was as likely as not a ticket to an early grave. The Morwenstow villagers, like the inhabitants of many another remote seaside place in the West Country, were reputed to plunder wrecks without a thought of helping the victims to shore and safety.

The man who brought order into this wild place could claim to have been the wildest individual of them all. Robert Hawker, vicar of Morwenstow from 1834 until his death in 1875, instilled the fear of the Devil and of himself into his wayward flock, yet his parishioners came to respect and rely on him. But his behaviour and attitudes scandalized the church authorities of his day, and remain a byword for eccentricity around north Cornwall.

When Robert Hawker was nineteen he wed his forty-one-year-old godmother; when she died after forty years of happy marriage, the sixty-year-old clergyman took a twenty-year-old Polish girl as his bride, and fathered three daughters. He carried out his duties wearing tall sea boots, a pink coat, a yellow cloak and rows of holy medals on his fisherman's jersey. He would throw himself prone on the church floor during services, and pinch babies at the font to make them roar the Devil out. He designed each chimney of his vicarage to resemble one of the church towers of his previous incumbencies. He installed a ship's figurehead of a claymore-wielding woman among the churchyard graves. Once, he startled the stolid fishermen and farmers of Morwenstow by dressing as a mermaid with a wig of seaweed.

Like many wild men, Parson Hawker was a romantic through and through, a traditionalist in ecclesiastical matters who loved the symbols and mysteries of the Christian faith. He was also a practical benefactor, who left far more members of his flock able to read, write and count than could do so before his forty-one-year ministry. And he was a poet of great power, the composer of the defiant Cornish anthem 'The Song of the Western Men':

And have they found the where and why?
And shall Trelawny die?
Here's twenty thousand Cornish men
Will know the reason why!

Down on the cliff below the church stands a wooden hut that Hawker built as a retreat. Here you can rest and dream of the wild parson who would sit here, a pipe between his teeth, and write his verses in a fug of opium.

17. WISTMAN'S WOOD, DARTMOOR, DEVON

Maps: OS Explorer OL28; Landranger 191

Travel: B3357 Tavistock towards Dartmeet, or B3212 Moretonhampstead towards Princetown. At Two Bridges, park opposite Two Bridges Hotel in old quarry car park (OS ref. 609751). Follow 'Wistman's Wood' fingerpost along track past Crockern farmhouse and on for 1 mile to Wistman's Wood.

 The National Nature Reserve of Wistman's Wood, tucked down in a cleft of northern Dartmoor, is one of the strangest and wildest pieces of woodland in Britain. It is the nearest thing we have to true wilderness in an inland location, in the sense of somewhere unchanged by the hand of man. For that reason, visitors are asked to refrain from entering the wood, in order not to disturb the tiny, fragile ecosystem that is made up of ancient, stunted oak trees, their lichens and insects, and the ferns and mosses that sprout on the granite boulders in their shade.

Wistman's Wood lies in two neighbouring blocks on a clitter slope just above the West Dart River. 'Clitter' means a jumble of rocks in local dialect, and it is the sharp-edged boulders among which the trees grow that have repelled every attempt by man to farm the moorland slope, or by animals to graze inside the wood. The oaks have been left uncut to grow where their ancestors grew for 6,000 or 7,000 years.

Long streamers of pale green-grey usnea lichen – the 'old man's beard' that is an indicator of unpolluted air – trail from the branches of the trees. Stunted by the moor wind and the poor nutrients of the stony ground, the oaks grow no taller than about 16 feet, an eighth of the height of a full-grown specimen. They give the appearance of bent-up, bewhiskered old men, especially in a Dartmoor mist, and it is this aspect of Wistman's Wood ('Wise-man's Wood') that has lent it a reputation as a sacred grove where druidical ceremonies were carried out in pre-Christian days. That remains unproven. But visit the wood early on a misty morning when all is silent except for the drip of moisture from leaves and lichens, and you will taste the best of its mysterious and powerful atmosphere.

18. HOUND OF THE BASKERVILLES COUNTRY, DARTMOOR, DEVON

Maps: OS Explorer OL28; Landranger 191, 202

Travel: B3212 to Princetown. Opposite junction with B3357 Tavistock road, bear left by Fox Tor Café along minor road for 2 miles. Where road bends left to descend to Whiteworks, park car (OS ref. 604708). Follow moor track south for ½ mile to Nun's Cross Farm (606698).

Whenever a fan of Sherlock Holmes hears the name of Dartmoor, it is impressions from *The Hound of the Baskervilles* that come rushing like a savage mastiff out of the unconscious: a barren, mist-wreathed moor, a mysterious figure silhouetted on a tor against the rising moon, the face of an escaped convict 'all seamed and scored with vile passions', and the blood-freezing howl of the fiery, fiendish hound itself.

Something about Dartmoor, its dour dark granite and rolling heather so often swathed in mist, fascinated Arthur Conan Doyle from the moment he heard a yarn about a spectral hound that haunted the moor. Researching his tale in the field in 1901, Doyle drew inspiration from the gloomy baronial halls, sucking bogs, abandoned tin mines and lonely houses all round the moor, as well as from the greatest and grimmest Dartmoor monument of all – the huge, stark prison at Princetown.

There are several candidates for Doyle's inspiration for Merripit House, the remote moorland dwelling of the ominous naturalist Stapleton (in fact a disguised and murderous claimant to the Baskerville estates) and his exotically beautiful 'sister', Beryl, on the shores of the fearsome quagmire called the great Grimpen Mire. But only one really fits the bill geographically and in atmosphere – Nun's Cross Farm, near Fox Tor Mire in a remote corner of the moor south of Princetown.

Walking the puddled track to Nun's Cross Farm you come upon the building quite suddenly, hidden in a walled quarter-acre of rough garden, its grey walls battered by the weather. The farmhouse serves as an outdoor adventure centre these days, but nothing detracts from its remarkably isolated position on the moorland track near a rugged medieval way-cross. Along the track through a moor fog Arthur Conan Doyle set his likeable but rugged colonial character Sir Henry Baskerville, rightful heir to his family fortunes, to run screaming from the hellish, fire-breathing hound that Stapleton set on his trail. Here Holmes gunned the hound down in the nick of time. And just to the east, where the ruined walls of the old Whiteworks tin mine lie on the moor slopes above the vast flat brown waste of Fox Tor Mire, the desperate Stapleton ran from justice. In flight from the collapse of his evil schemes, he leaped across the tussocks of the mire until a false step sent him into the ooze, sucking him down to his awful end.

19. HUNTINGDON WARREN, DARTMOOR, DEVON

Maps: OS Explorer OL28; Landranger 202

Travel: A38 to Buckfastleigh; follow signs to Buckfast. From here follow 'Scorriton' signs. In 1 mile, at Hockmoorhead Cross (OS ref. 728673) left ('Bowden, Cross Furzes') for 2 miles to T-junction. Right; in 200 yards, at Cross Furzes, left ('Hayford'). In ½ mile, park on grass verge just short of Hayford Hall (692673).Continue on foot along lane for ½ mile, through Lud Gate (684673) on to moor. Follow

'Bridlepath Scorriton' fingerpost, half-right, for 200 yards to division of path. Take left fork, aiming for left flank of Puper's Hill. In 200 yards cross track and continue uphill. At top of rise cross Boundary Work track (676671); keep ahead on a distinct track for ½ mile to reach boundary wall of Huntingdon Warren (667670). Bear left for 600 yards to find ruin of Mattins Corner Chapel (666665).

Huntingdon Warren lies near the eastern edge of Dartmoor in a very lonely spot. Tracks made by tin miners, clay-pit workers and rabbit warreners approach the broad hill in its moorland waste, but all industry apart from sheep farming has been dead here for the past century. Following the track west from Lud Gate and climbing the slope of Puper's Hill to get your first sight of Huntingdon Warren on the skyline, it is remarkable to see the present-day emptiness and stillness of the moor. The same viewpoint in the nineteenth century would have disclosed tin workings and commercial rabbit farming all over the warren, other tinning operations to north and south, and beyond the hill the smoke and dust of Red Lake china clay works.

Turning left along the wall that forms the eastern boundary of Huntingdon Warren, sharp eyes will spot a little rounded stone shelter sunk in a hollow, a stone etched with a cross set up at its northern end. This is 'Mattins Corner', an open-air chapel established in 1909 by the three sons of the Reverend Martin of Dartington. The lads would come to camp in this lonely place and hold informal services. The oldest of the three, Keble, later became a clergyman himself. It is for his beautiful and scientifically accurate paintings and descriptions of wild flowers, gathered together and published as *The Concise British Flora*, that Keble is remembered and revered today.

Above: Mattins Corner. Below: Puper's Hill

Climbing to the top of Huntingdon Warren you pass the 'pillow mounds' or man-made burrows created on the hill from 1802 onwards. The warrener operated a farm as well as the warren, and was engaged in a long-standing confrontation with the tinners and china clay workers who would poach his preserves. Around the edge of the hill are the remains of stone shelters where the warrener would post lookouts to deter the rabbit-raiders.

The view from the summit of Huntingdon Warren is a splendid and dramatic one, especially to the north-west across 3 or 4 miles of sombre moor. Hidden from view beyond Crane Hill lies the bog of Fox Tor Mire, the best candidate to be the original of Sir Arthur Conan Doyle's 'great Grimpen Mire' in the classic Sherlock Holmes yarn *The Hound of the Baskervilles* (see p. 38). Was it across this stretch of moor that Doyle's imagination laid the 'narrow grassy path' connecting the villain Stapleton's dwelling, Merripit House, with Sir Henry Baskerville's residence of Baskerville Hall? It seems probable – the most likely model for the Hall in its 'cup-like depression, patched with stunted oaks and firs', is Hayford Hall, which lies just beyond Lud Gate at the start of this expedition.

20. BROADUN RING AND BEEHIVE HUT, DARTMOOR, DEVON

Maps: OS Explorer OL28; Landranger 191

Travel: B3212 to Postbridge. Park in the car park near the Clapper Bridge (OS ref. 647789). Follow bridleway signs north along The Drift, and up east bank of East Dart River for 1¾ miles to the beehive hut (639815), just north of where the river bends away to the left. If river is swollen after heavy rain, retrace steps to Postbridge from here; otherwise ford river and follow track south along west bank, to climb to Broadun Ring (637807) before continuing back to Postbridge.

Dartmoor is full of unfathomed mysteries, and among the most remarkable are the identifiable prehistoric sites – stone circles, round huts, enclosed settlements, stone alignments, cairns and dolmens – that litter the moor in extraordinary profusion. Probably most fertile areas of England could have shown as great a concentration of sites. But Dartmoor, having developed its empty moorland and bog landscape several thousand years ago, was only lightly touched by the ploughing that obliterated so many of these monuments.

Very little is known of the day-to-day lives and beliefs of the early dwellers on the moor. But you can get a very clear idea of the hard conditions of their existence by walking north from Postbridge into the heart of the moor, using the course of the East Dart River as a guide.

The river cuts a lonely channel in a deserted landscape. High shoulders of moorland rise all round. Nearly two miles into the moor a solitary stone hut stands just beyond the river, an Iron Age farmer's home from around 500 BC, shaped like a beehive, its walls of granite boulders sloping inward to give them the strength to support a stone roof. These walls stand in a horseshoe about 3 feet high, their doorway facing south-west away from the bitterest of the winter weather. At the widest point the house measures only 10 feet across.

This householder's family lived out on their own, but their distant ancestors up in Broadun Ring were dwellers in a close-knit community. The huts on the heights above the river were built perhaps 4,000 years ago at the start of the Bronze Age. Climbing up the flank of Broad Down you come to the walled enclosure where in 1893 the Reverend Sabine Baring-Gould excavated at least fifteen hut circles. You can see their ring-shaped foundations printed in the grass, some built into the stones of Broadun Ring's encircling wall. And just to the south, enclosed in the wall of Broadun Pound, are hundreds more circles on the slope of the hill. It is impossible now to count them all, but Baring-Gould reckoned there were more than 1,700 separate dwellings in and around Broadun Pound. He estimated that well over 2,000 people lived within a mile of Postbridge back then. The complete absence today of any human dwellings on these wide slopes and in the well-watered valleys of the moor only adds to the sense of vanished multitudes.

21. GRIMSPOUND, DARTMOOR, DEVON

Maps: OS Explorer OL28; Landranger 191

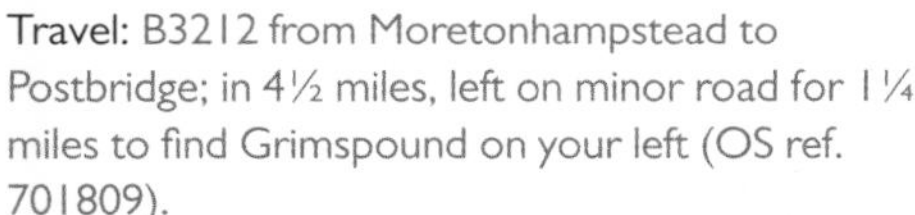

Travel: B3212 from Moretonhampstead to Postbridge; in 4½ miles, left on minor road for 1¼ miles to find Grimspound on your left (OS ref. 701809).

Winter is the time to visit the Bronze Age settlement of Grimspound. With a cold drizzle blowing and a hint of mist, you can fully appreciate the roughness of the everyday lives led by the hundred or so people who inhabited this circular walled settlement on the northern slopes of Hameldown Tor. They built the wall that enclosed their village 10 feet thick, strong enough to withstand any attack. The dead were buried in solitary magnificence up on the nape of the Tor; the living made do with a couple of dozen circular stone huts some 10 feet across, with a cooking pit and a hearth for a turf fire, a stone platform to sit or sleep on out of the mire, a conical roof of turf or bracken thatch, and a tunnel-like entrance sited to face east, away from the direction of the prevailing wind. The smoke, damp, mud and cold they endured would put paid to any modern Briton. Yet our ancestors toughed it out here, planting their thin cereal crops and hunting on the moor round about.

Grimspound has connections to the wildest of Dartmoor tales, *The Hound of the Baskervilles* (see also pp. 38 and 40). Arthur Conan Doyle and his friend Bertram Fletcher Robinson sat and smoked their pipes in Hut No. 3, at the centre of the enclosure, during Doyle's research trip to the moor in 1901. The hut was restored by local rector and archaeological savant Sabine Baring-Gould, and is still in good repair, with its stone lintels standing each side of a doorway 18 inches wide. The hearthstone and stone bench lie inside. Here the seeds were sown in Doyle's imagination for the stone hut where Sherlock Holmes camped out on the moor, and where he was discovered by the faithful Dr Watson towards the denouement of their most thrilling and Gothic adventure.

22. HALLSANDS, START BAY, DEVON

Maps: OS Explorer OL20; Landranger 202

Travel: A379 from Dartmouth to Kingsbridge; at Stokenham, left on minor roads through Kellaton to Start Point. Park in car park (OS ref. 821376) and walk down road to Start Point lighthouse (829371). Return to Hollowcombe Head and bear right for Hallsands (817385) where there's a viewpoint over the ruined village.

The cliffs at Start Point are the best place from which to view the enormous sweep of Start Bay. This 8-mile curve of coast cradles a bay that grows teeth in winter weather. The water of Start Bay is deceptively shallow; the Skerries Bank, a reef a long mile out from shore, shelves so steeply upwards that at certain states of tide (locals tell you) a tall man can stand with his feet on the Skerries and his head out of water.

The bank and the lee shore of the bay claimed thousands of ships in easterly gales during the days of sail. The disaster of Hallsands in January 1917, however, was not the work of a freak of nature, but of an act of folly by man. The fishing settlement of Hallsands was built hard under the cliffs and protected from the force of storm-driven waves by a high, stout shingle bank. More shingle below the water helped to limit the power of the sea. But when a new set of docks was being built at Devonport in 1897, the authorities decided to use shingle dredged from the section of Start Bay that faced the village. Within four years half a million tons had been removed, lowering the bank by 15 feet and exposing Hallsands to the full fury of the sea. It lasted another fifteen years, but when the January gales of 1917 set in, the whole village was smashed to pieces in one horrifying night. Those who could climb scaled the cliffs to safety; the old, young and infirm had to wait out the terrible night until rescuers could get to them.

Hallsands was abandoned, and the fishermen's cottages have been gradually disappearing into the sea ever since. Their broken walls and pathetically exposed interiors, viewed from the cliff today, stand witness to the tremendous power of the sea once its natural barriers have been removed.

23. DAWLISH WARREN, DEVON

Maps: OS Explorer 110; Landranger 192

Travel: A379 from Exeter towards Teignmouth. At ½ mile beyond Starcross, left on minor road to Dawlish Warren. Turn left off road towards railway station, bearing immediately right into car park. Cross railway by footbridge; left along seafront to end of concrete promenade, then along boardwalk to Visitor Centre (OS ref. 982790).

Dawlish Warren

The broad spit of Dawlish Warren reaches out from the turn of the south Devon coast on the west bank of the Exe Estuary. Tides have trapped the sand, gradually building the long arm of the spit over the past 7,000 years. Nowadays Dawlish Warren is 550 acres in extent, stretches the best part of 2 miles, and is well on the way to shutting off the mouth of the Exe. It's an extraordinary structure, heaped with dunes and hollows of reddish sand, a National Nature Reserve so ecologically rich that it supports over 600 different species of flowering plants, including many beautiful orchids and its own 'warren crocus' or sand crocus, a straggle of leaves like a starfish from which rises a pale lilac flower with six delicate petals.

The seaward-facing dunes of Dawlish Warren are exposed to rainstorms, drought, fierce sunlight, starvation, sandstorms, gales and showers of salt spray. Anything that lives in such a harsh and inconstant environment has to be tough to thrive. Marram grass is the hardy plant whose hair-like roots knit the dunes together, and where shelter can be found you'll see such resilient flowering plants as prickly blue sea holly, star-shaped sea aster, evening primrose with its big papery yellow petals, and the white-striped pink trumpets of sea bindweed.

Upwards of 25,000 birds spend the winter around the spit and in the estuary that it shelters; they include flocks of wigeon, dark-bellied brent geese and the black-and-white avocet with its stilt-like blue legs. In spring the scrub bushes come alive with nesting whitethroat and linnet, while summer sees plenty of waders busy along the shores – whimbrel (a smaller curlew cousin), black and bar-tailed godwit, greenshank and little tern. The warren is also a great place for sea-watching, with bottled-nosed dolphins often seen curving in and out of the water.

Choose your season and time of day carefully: on a sunny summer weekend Dawlish Warren can play host to 20,000 visitors in a single day. But come here for a walk in moody weather or when there is a stiff wind blowing, and you'll have the sands and shores pretty much to yourself.

24. OTTER ESTUARY, DEVON

Maps: OS Explorer 115; Landranger 192

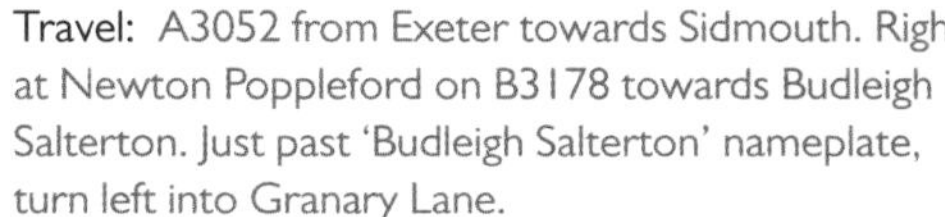

Travel: A3052 from Exeter towards Sidmouth. Right at Newton Poppleford on B3178 towards Budleigh Salterton. Just past 'Budleigh Salterton' nameplate, turn left into Granary Lane.

(a) To walk down River Otter to the sea, bear immediately left again along South Farm Road. In ½ mile cross River Otter, park beyond bridge in lay-by (OS ref. 075831) and follow footpath ('Coast Path') seaward along right (west) bank of River Otter.

(b) To explore estuary from seaward end, continue along Granary Lane to seafront car park (073820).

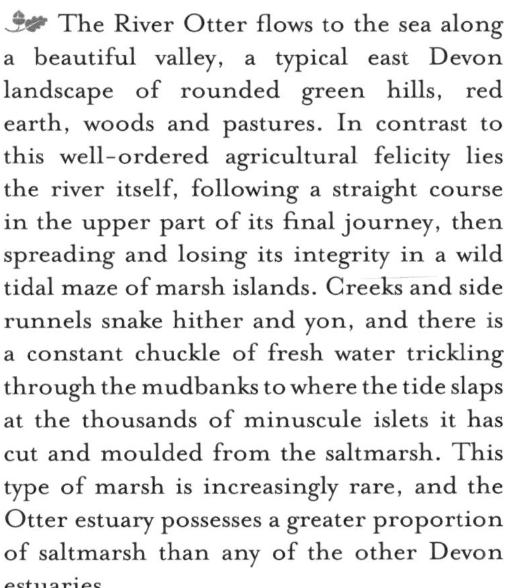

The River Otter flows to the sea along a beautiful valley, a typical east Devon landscape of rounded green hills, red earth, woods and pastures. In contrast to this well-ordered agricultural felicity lies the river itself, following a straight course in the upper part of its final journey, then spreading and losing its integrity in a wild tidal maze of marsh islands. Creeks and side runnels snake hither and yon, and there is a constant chuckle of fresh water trickling through the mudbanks to where the tide slaps at the thousands of minuscule islets it has cut and moulded from the saltmarsh. This type of marsh is increasingly rare, and the Otter estuary possesses a greater proportion of saltmarsh than any of the other Devon estuaries.

A long west–east shingle spit protects the mouth of the river and shelters the seablite and glasswort that grow in the estuary mud. These mudbanks attract large numbers of wintering birds. Waders include redshank and greenshank, ringed and grey plover, snipe and curlew. Wigeon, teal and shelduck spend the cold months here, too, as do brent geese and a number of red-breasted mergansers from the far north of Europe, with their double crests and white canonical collars.

Higher up the estuary is a zone of flowering plants that flush the marsh with colour in summer – white scurvy-grass with thick heart-shaped leaves, pale purple sea aster, and the much stronger pink-purple of sea lavender. Further inland the influence of the salt water lessens, and here grow reed-beds where reed and sedge warblers and reed buntings all make their nests, rarely disturbed except by walkers – and there are not many of those along these unfrequented paths.

25. THE UNDERCLIFF, LYME REGIS, DEVON / DORSET BORDERS

Maps: OS Explorer 116; Landranger 193

Travel: A35 from Bridport towards Axminster; in 9 miles, left on A3052 to Lyme Regis. Park in Pound Street car park (OS ref. 337921). From lower edge of car park, footpath descends to bear right along the South West Coast Path National Trail and reach the Undercliff entrance (327915).

Nearest railway station: Axminster (6 miles)

The Undercliff that lies west of Lyme Regis is a glorious tangle, the nearest thing to a jungle that the south of England can show. This 5-mile wilderness owes its pristine nature to the unstable character of the cliffs along which it runs. These cliffs of greensand and chalk are founded on a bed of dark slippery gault, a skid-mat after heavy rain, down which the feet of the cliffs slide from time to time. Spectacular cliff falls are the result, heaping the pebbly beaches with fans of rubble and exposing a fresh batch of the famous fossils of the region. The falls have another effect, too; they open fissures in the clifftops, toppling trees and swallowing footpaths, field walls and the remnants of the farm cottages and houses that once dotted the area. The last swineherds and woodmen quit the Undercliff in the early twentieth century, unable to cope with the instability of the ground beneath their house foundations. Now the jungle is a National Nature Reserve, threaded by a single narrow footpath that has to be re-routed further inland from time to time after more dramatic cliff falls.

Trees, plants, birds and butterflies thrive where man cannot. Blackcaps and nightingales sing in the scrub bushes, primroses line the mossy banks in spring, deer crash through the undergrowth. Yellow rockrose, hairy violet, horseshoe vetch, ploughman's spikenard; nuthatch, flycatcher, kingfisher, tree creeper, more than thirty species of butterfly, 200 kinds of moth ... the species lists go on and on, a roll-call of ecological riches. Signs of the vanished hand of man are there for sharp eyes to spot: sections of flint wall, paved pieces of carriageway, a corner of a cottage wall, borders of Victorian ilex, rhododendron and privet. They only point up the absence of any human inhabitants today.

Towards the west end of the Undercliff you pass a flat-topped, 15-acre table of rock – Goat Island – formed on Christmas Eve 1839 during the most monumental landslip recorded here, when 8 million tons of land dropped 200 feet and left a chasm half a mile wide with the 'island' standing in isolation.

From the road by which you return from Axmouth to Lyme Regis, neither island nor chasm nor any of the other geological wonders can be seen. The Undercliff to a casual passer-by seems just like any other stretch of woodland, its wild secrets hidden away beneath a green lid of leaves.

26. LUNDY (NT), DEVON

Maps: OS Explorer 139; Landranger 180

Travel: The Lundy ferry departs from either Bideford or Ilfracombe, depending on the tide. Helicopter services from Hartland Point. All information: www.lundyisland.co.uk.

Nearest railway station: Barnstaple (9 miles from Bideford)

Lundy lies off the coast of north Devon some 12 miles north-west of Hartland Point. The 3-mile-long bar of granite, edged by cliffs that rise over 400 feet in places, lies in the throat of the Bristol Channel. Lundy is a miniature world apart, a slip of land with a wild history which these days plays its role as a holiday haven, owned by the National Trust and administered by the Landmark Trust. But Lundy is far from tamed. Black-backed gulls, guillemots, cormorants and puffins haunt the cliffs; there are seals on the rocks, and so much subaqueous life fed and nurtured in the strong tides around the island that its underwater margins have been declared a Marine Nature Reserve.

The National Trust launched an appeal to buy Lundy in the 1960s, the latest in a long line of turning points in the island's bizarre roller-coaster ride of a story. Bronze Age settlers, early Christian hermits, Norman landowners, a Royalist garrison during the Civil War; then pirates, brigands, shipwrecked seafarers; owners who wagered Lundy at the card table, owners who loved the island to distraction, owners who loathed it with a passion – all came and went, leaving Lundy striped with stone walls, scattered with monuments and provided with a little granite-built village. The Heaven family reigned as supreme rulers in Victorian times – Lundy was then known, naturally, as the Kingdom of Heaven. They were followed by the Harmans, who held the island until 1968 when death duties forced them to sell it (they selected the National Trust, a purchaser they knew would be keen to preserve and improve Lundy, rather than richer buyers with less altruistic motives). Part of the fascination of a visit to Lundy is to find the houses and gravestones of these kings and queens in miniature, and to reflect on the magnetic attraction the island held for them.

Lundy's wild coasts are the setting for all kinds of sporty activities – sea kayaking, abseiling, rock climbing, caving, scuba-diving. Birdwatching is spectacular out here; Lundy offers migrating birds the only landfall for many miles. There is a herd of feral goats, and a colony of grey seals that live out on the rocks near the landing slip. In spite of its thousands of visitors each year, and those that stay on for a week or two in the island buildings restored as holiday homes by the Landmark Trust, Lundy retains a natural feel – even, in its cliffs and coves, a smack of wilderness that helps it remain a place apart.

27. MORTE BAY, DEVON

Maps: OS Explorer 139; Landranger 180

Travel: A361 from Barnstaple towards Ilfracombe.

(a) For Baggy Point, left in Braunton on B3231 to Croyde; follow 'Croyde Beach' sign to Baggy Point car park (OS ref. 433397) and follow the South West Coast Path National Trail.

(b) For Morte Point, continue on A361 to Mullacott Cross; left on B3343 to Woolacombe; right to Mortehoe. Park at Chichester Arms (please ask at the pub and give them your custom). Walk back down road for 200 yards to gate on right (456450); down path for 200 yards to follow the South West Coast Path National Trail.

Morte Bay boasts the superb 2-mile-long strand of Woolacombe Sand; but it is the two great headlands enclosing the bay, Baggy Point on the south and Morte Point to the north, that make this pincer-shaped stretch of coast a wild place. This is prime Henry Williamson country. In the years after the First World War the future author of *Tarka the Otter* lived as a young, unpublished writer in the village of Georgeham a mile inland. He roamed every inch of the two headlands, observing the lives of ravens, buzzards, peregrines, seals and otters, the movements of the sea and the always changing weather.

Morte Bay

Tamarisk, bramble and rhododendron flank the path along the green southern side of Baggy Point. The sandstone strata lie turned on end, presenting thousands of thin blades to the sky, the slit-like trough between each blade glinting with seawater. The path is best walked in winter with a good stiff westerly wind blowing. Better still, you can scramble down one of the side paths to the rocks where the waves crash. Out at the tip of Baggy Point lies the Long Rock, and here the narrow and slippery Wreckers' Path descends to the caves that Greymuzzle, the mate of Tarka, considered as a birthplace for their cub. In the end she gave birth behind the dunes of Braunton Burrows to a frostbitten runt of a cub in a savage winter, superbly described to the last icicle and frozen leaf by Williamson. Greymuzzle was beaten to death by a farmer's man, and her cub died, too.

Where Baggy Point forms a green-backed hump, Morte Point shows a rocky crest like a miniature Dolomite ridge. Morte is angular, bleak and harsh. At the far end the rock shows in slatey layers as thin as paper, jammed together and twisted. Out at sea the Morte Stone rises as a dark hump out of the fierce tide-rips that battle off the Point. Tarka came here after escaping the otterhounds further along the north Devon coast. He sighted a cormorant on the Morte Stone – its descendants still dry their wings and digest fish there today – and came ashore, sleeping at last on top of the hill under the tumbled stones of Morte Cromlech. You'll be lucky indeed to catch sight of an otter, though they still swim off both Baggy Point and Morte Point, and play on the rocks and in the caves, as they did when Henry Williamson walked here.

28. THE OVERLAND LAUNCH, LYNMOUTH (DEVON) TO PORLOCK (SOMERSET)

Maps: OS Explorer OL9; Landranger 180, 181

Travel: A39 to Lynmouth and Porlock.

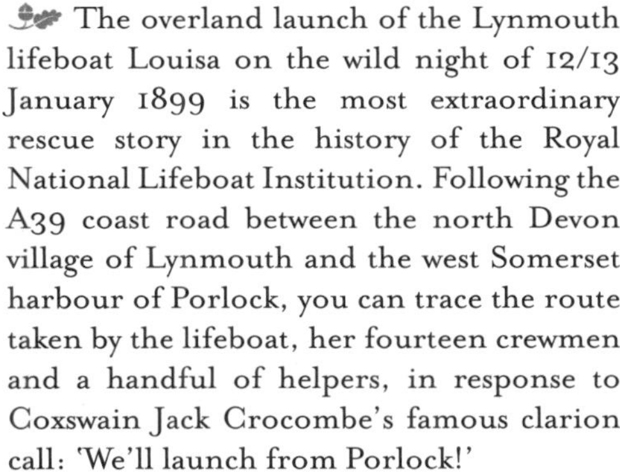

The overland launch of the Lynmouth lifeboat Louisa on the wild night of 12/13 January 1899 is the most extraordinary rescue story in the history of the Royal National Lifeboat Institution. Following the A39 coast road between the north Devon village of Lynmouth and the west Somerset harbour of Porlock, you can trace the route taken by the lifeboat, her fourteen crewmen and a handful of helpers, in response to Coxswain Jack Crocombe's famous clarion call: 'We'll launch from Porlock!'

The great storm of January 1899 caused chaos throughout the West Country. During the gale the 1,900-ton sailing ship *Forest Hall* anchored with a crippled rudder in the Bristol Channel, dangerously close to the Somerset shore and in desperate need of assistance. The lifeboat *Louisa* could not be launched from her home harbour of Lynmouth, because huge waves were sweeping the slipway. So Coxswain Crocombe decided to drag her to Porlock. Starting on the fearsome 1 in 4 slope of Countisbury Hill, the overland journey was carried out in pitch darkness and a howling gale, over a rough and stony track slippery with rain and mud. The men knocked down stone walls in their path, manhandled *Louisa* over the moor on a set of skids when her wheeled carriage proved too wide for the walled road, and demolished part of a cottage on Porlock Hill in order to squeeze her round a particularly tight corner. It took them over twelve hours to haul the boat from Lynmouth to Porlock, where they finally launched her into the storm shortly after dawn, rowing out to the stricken *Forest Hall* with the most difficult and dangerous part of their adventure still ahead of them.

Forest Hall was saved, and the exhausted Lynmouth crew landed at last in Barry Roads on the Welsh side of the Bristol Channel. A fortnight later the men were awarded a silver watch and £5 apiece, while the coxswains received gold watch-chains. For a brief moment the crew of *Louisa* became national heroes, albeit modest ones. Locally they are still well remembered, more than a hundred years after the overland launch, for their stolid, uncomplaining heroism on that wild January night.

29. PINKWORTHY POND AND THE CHAINS, EXMOOR, DEVON

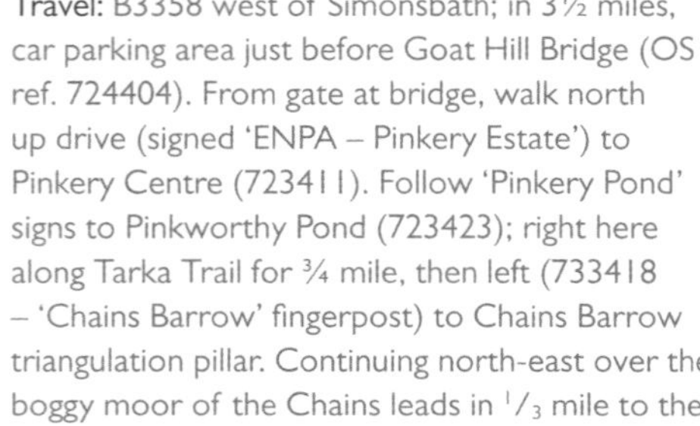

Maps: OS Explorer OL9; Landranger 180

Travel: B3358 west of Simonsbath; in 3½ miles, car parking area just before Goat Hill Bridge (OS ref. 724404). From gate at bridge, walk north up drive (signed 'ENPA – Pinkery Estate') to Pinkery Centre (723411). Follow 'Pinkery Pond' signs to Pinkworthy Pond (723423); right here along Tarka Trail for ¾ mile, then left (733418 – 'Chains Barrow' fingerpost) to Chains Barrow triangulation pillar. Continuing north-east over the boggy moor of the Chains leads in 1/3 mile to the head of Hoar Oak Water.

Within the moor is the Forest, a region high and treeless, where sedge grasses grow on the slopes to the sky. In early summer the wild spirit of the hills is heard in the voices of curlews. The birds fly up from solitary places, above their beloved and little ones, and float the wind in a sweet uprising music. Slowly on spread and hollow wings they sink, and their cries are trilling and cadent, until they touch earth and lift their wings above their heads, and poising, loose the last notes from their throats, like golden bubbles rising into sky again.

Henry Williamson caught the spirit of early summer over the heights of Exmoor in his 1927 masterpiece, *Tarka the Otter*. Williamson was writing of the Chains, still the wildest part of the moor, a great inverted bowl of peat, heather and tussocky golden grasses, sodden as a sponge after rain. Curlew still cry over these empty miles of moor, where you can find yourself thoroughly lost and bemired should mist creep down.

Pinkworthy Pond (pronounced, and often written, 'Pinkery') is the place to head for,

The Chains

a reservoir made in 1830 and abandoned to nature over 100 years ago. Frogs abound in spring – Tarka caught his share – and the banks are thick with sedges and rushes. Walking east along the Tarka Trail you follow an old boundary wall, squelching and slipping up to your knees in sloppy black peat. At last a fingerpost directs you away across the sedge of the open moor to the Bronze Age burial mound of Chains Barrow, topped by an Ordnance Survey triangulation pillar. A further slip and slide over the waterlogged ground leads to the shallow declivity, soon steepening as it drops to the east, of the Hoar Oak Water, one of the loneliest stream heads in the West Country. Henry Williamson has Tarka passing down the Hoar Oak Water towards the north Exmoor coast; but this is the place for walkers to stop and stare, filling their senses with the thrill of standing alone in the moor's wildest spot.

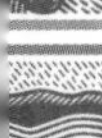

30. EXMOOR RED DEER, DEVON

Maps: OS Explorer OL9; Landranger 180, 181

Travel: Red deer are found in many places on Exmoor. For information on solo deer-watching and guided expeditions with a Ranger, contact Exmoor National Park Centre in Dulverton (www.exmoor-nationalpark.gov.uk).

It is impossible to be specific about where you will find the red deer of Exmoor. The 4,000-strong herd is widely dispersed across the moor and its combes or hidden valleys. You need some local advice, a sharp pair of eyes and a slice of luck.

Generally speaking, the red stags form a kind of loose gentleman's club for most of the year, staying on the high moor and keeping fairly clear of the hinds. The stags even tolerate each other's company, with only a little aggression coming to the fore if an individual's space is being encroached upon, or during the spring when their new antlers are feeling itchy. The hinds, too, maintain themselves and their young ones in small groups and stay away from the stags.

In the autumn it is a different matter. The stags approach the rutting or mating season in a mounting fever. They grow dark shaggy fur around their necks and throats, and spurn each other in favour of the hinds, for whose sake they come down from their high summer lodgings to lower ground around the farms and woods. This is the season when the famous roaring – known on Exmoor as 'belling' or 'belving' – is heard at dawn and dusk as the testosterone-charged stags warn each other off. Their only aim during the month-long rut is to gather, retain and impregnate as many hinds as possible. It is a frantic time for the stags, constantly on guard, seeing off one challenge after another (sometimes in more or less bloody combat), snatching a small amount of food from time to time. Their appetites are tiny, their tempers foul and their excitement immense. To see a full-grown stag, the size of a large horse, cantering menacingly towards an opponent, or stalking contemptuously away with a defeated rival's group of hinds, and to hear that extraordinarily powerful, throaty bellow, is to be a spectator of wild nature in free flow.

31. THE GREAT ROAD, QUANTOCK HILLS, SOMERSET

Maps: OS Explorer 22; Landranger 181

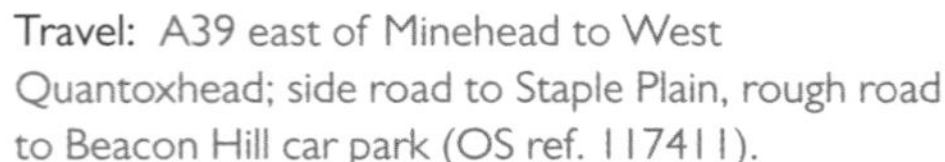

Travel: A39 east of Minehead to West Quantoxhead; side road to Staple Plain, rough road to Beacon Hill car park (OS ref. 117411).

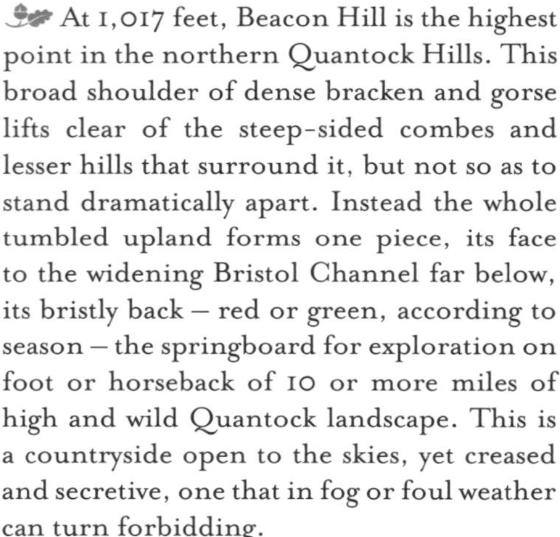

At 1,017 feet, Beacon Hill is the highest point in the northern Quantock Hills. This broad shoulder of dense bracken and gorse lifts clear of the steep-sided combes and lesser hills that surround it, but not so as to stand dramatically apart. Instead the whole tumbled upland forms one piece, its face to the widening Bristol Channel far below, its bristly back – red or green, according to season – the springboard for exploration on foot or horseback of 10 or more miles of high and wild Quantock landscape. This is a countryside open to the skies, yet creased and secretive, one that in fog or foul weather can turn forbidding.

Nowadays, gorse bushes, birch scrub and bracken are encroaching so vigorously that the Quantock wardens have their work cut out to keep them at bay. Wheatears, stonechats and pipits thrive in the thick cover, as do red deer. The northern Quantocks are a wilder place than for many years. But in times gone by these hills were intensively grazed. When the Great Road was in its heyday they were busy with traffic making its way between the ports of the Somerset coast and the trading towns inland.

Could there be a more evocative name for an ancient trackway than the Great Road? The rutted old highway that climbs the flank of Beacon Hill, winding in and out of the shadow of a clearer and much more junior track, could well date back to the Bronze Age,

Quantock Hills

when tomb-builders erected the memorial cairns that still crown the hill. Stand chest-high in the bracken at the apex of the Great Road and watch the sun go down behind the long Exmoor skyline to savour properly this high, lonely place.

32. STERT POINT, SOMERSET

Maps: OS Explorer 22; Landranger 182

Travel: A39 west from Bridgwater; Cannington, Combwich, Stockland and Steart signposted by minor roads. Car park near Dowells Farm (OS ref. 275459).

This is a low-tide place, best visited on a day of sun and high breeze when the reed-beds glint as they thrash in the wind. The approach to the Point is by way of Stert Drove, at first over a shaggy grass plain, then beside grazing meadows. This is the last piece of land shaped by the River Parrett before it curves into the Severn Estuary. The slow-flowing Parrett drags fertile silts down to the coast from the peaty Somerset Levels where it rises, forming the mudflats out in Bridgwater Bay and building up soil that grows lush grass for the cattle of a small cluster of dairy farms at the seaward end of the Point.

Out on the sea wall the scene is of estuarine flatness. Colours are mostly grey and blue. Creeks snake away from the land, carving shallow paths through a ledge of coarse grass and reed-beds to reach the outer shore. Here ridges of mud coated with bright green weed lead out to sand and mudflats that disappear under each advancing tide. In the distance rise the Mendip Hills, and further off a suggestion of the Welsh mountains.

A pebble path along the sea bank leads in a mile to a wood-slatted hide from whose tower there are far views across mud, marsh and sea. Stert Flats are a part of Bridgwater Bay National Nature Reserve, several square miles of saltmarsh and mudflats packed with invertebrates that form one enormous larder for wading birds. Summer is a very good time for spotting greenshank and redshank. Shelduck gather on the mud in their tens of thousands to moult in late summer, seeking safety in numbers during these weeks when they cannot fly. Black-tailed and bar-tailed godwit rest here and feed during their spring and autumn migration flights. You are more likely to hear the babbling burst of song from a Cetti's warbler in the bramble bushes than to see the shy, dark-backed little bird. As for birds of prey, short-eared owls quarter the marshes and grasslands, and a peregrine sometimes flashes through.

Stert Point

Stert Point

Four miles west of Stert Point the stark shape of Hinkley Point nuclear power station stands at the feet of the Quantock Hills. The station was opened in 1976, but its advanced gas-cooled reactors no longer operate, and the plant is due to be decommissioned in 2011. In spite of constant monitoring, concern continues about the contamination of the estuary's intertidal mud with radioactive isotopes, about cancer incidence and risks of accident or sabotage. Now the possibility of building a new nuclear power station on the site is being mooted. Plans for a huge wind farm here have come and gone and come again. These flat, lonely, windy coastal places are always prime sites for such big, intrusive and unsettling installations.

33. STEEP HOLM, SOMERSET

Maps: OS Explorer 153; Landranger 182

Travel: Boat trips to Steep Holm run from Knightstone Harbour, Weston-super-Mare. Timetable and information: www.steepholm.freeserve.co.uk.

Nearest railway station: Weston-super-Mare

The oval island of Steep Holm rises from the brown waters of the Bristol Channel about 5 miles out from Weston-super-Mare. Two miles away and 5 miles from the Welsh shore lies its round sister island of Flat Holm. Apart from their small size – neither measures much more than half a mile across – the two islands are as chalk and cheese. On the wedge of Flat Holm a polite warden greets visitors with a cup of tea and shepherds them in a group from one feature to the next. Arrive on the hunched green dome of Steep Holm and you crunch up a steep and rubbly path alone, to pilot yourself round the summit through an exuberant jungle of plant growth. A trip to Steep Holm is a wilderness expedition in miniature.

Steep Holm is administered and maintained by a paid warden and by the hard-working volunteers of the Kenneth Allsop Memorial Trust, which bought the island in 1976 in memory of the broadcaster, writer and conservation activist. Dotted with relics of a long and varied history, Steep Holm has been a Roman observation post, the site of a medieval priory, a base for smugglers and a fortress against the French. Rusted cannon lie among the brambles and alexanders, relics of the 1860s when Steep Holm became one of 'Palmerston's Follies' – a string of sites around the coasts of southern England that were fortified at the order of the Prime Minister, Lord Palmerston, against an invasion by the French that never materialized.

Wildlife flourishes here. Wild peonies with huge pink petals – great rarities – grow alongside wild leeks, introduced many hundreds of years ago by the monks of Steep Holm. Black-backed gulls use the island as a hatchery, and one of the thrills of a visit in

May is to watch the fluffy chicks emerging from eggs laid by the paths, in the old cannon mouths and on every available flat surface. The parent gulls stand sentry on the Second World War pillboxes, the tumbled medieval walls of St Michael's Priory and the tall chimneys of the old barracks, now the Visitor Centre. They are extremely active in defending their chicks, dive-bombing visitors with claws and beaks to the fore – another of the excitements of this wild place.

34. CATCOTT HEATH, SOMERSET

Maps: OS Explorer 140, 141; Landranger 182

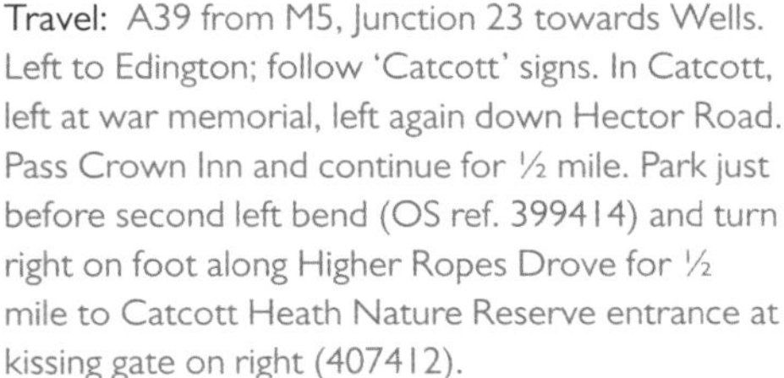

Travel: A39 from M5, Junction 23 towards Wells. Left to Edington; follow 'Catcott' signs. In Catcott, left at war memorial, left again down Hector Road. Pass Crown Inn and continue for ½ mile. Park just before second left bend (OS ref. 399414) and turn right on foot along Higher Ropes Drove for ½ mile to Catcott Heath Nature Reserve entrance at kissing gate on right (407412).

The peat moors of the Somerset Levels lie largely unvisited by tourists and holidaymakers. Yet they form a unique landscape, a dead-flat wetland at the southern feet of the Mendip Hills, which has somehow resisted centuries of effort to drain and improve it for arable agriculture. There are cornfields and vegetable fields here, but they are few and far between. Even the widespread grazing meadows are interspersed by tracts of fen and of wet carr woodland. The watery ditches known as 'rhynes', which form liquid fences between the fields, grow a rich aqueous flora. Catcott Heath, in the flatlands north of the low Polden Hills, is a classic example of a preserved Levels wetland, juicy and oozing

Catcott Heath

with water, a sodden peaty area full of wild flowers, dragonflies, butterflies and bird life.

Bushy, pale pink hemp agrimony and the large deep pink flowers of marsh willowherb line the approach drove, and once into the reserve itself you walk through dense cover of bog myrtle and purple moor grass. Marsh orchids, marsh and meadow thistles, meadowsweet and ragged robin all thrive. The southern edge is all carr, a waterlogged woodland where silver birch and willow shoot up tall, fungi sprout on decaying boughs, and alders suck up moisture from ground that is partly wet black peat, partly a rich midden of rotting boughs and logs. This is a lush, green-tinted world, a haven for tree creepers, willow tits and great spotted woodpeckers. Every step squelches as you walk the woodland paths. There are 'exclosure' pens from which rabbits and grazing animals are excluded, giving an exuberant flora that features the orange stars of bog asphodel, frothy pale pink bogbean and the fat blue-cheeked flowers of marsh pea; also saw sedge, with spiky leaves whose toothed edges will cut an exploring finger.

Looking out between the trees and over the rushy rhynes around the reserve to the uniform greenness of the chemically enriched grass fields near by, the contrast is startling. It's as if nature, hemmed in on all sides, has responded with a bright explosion of colour and defiance.

35. STARLINGS OF WESTHAY MOOR, SOMERSET

Maps: OS Explorer 141; Landranger 182

Travel: A39 or A361 to Glastonbury; B3151 through Meare and Westhay towards Wedmore. At ½ mile north of Westhay, right on minor road ('Godney'). In 1 mile, road takes sharp left bend; on following sharp right bend, park in car park (OS ref. 457437). Walk north up Dagg's Lane Drove for 400 yards to bird hide on right; grass paths lead to London Drove and adjacent reed-beds.

The evening dance of the starlings over Westhay Moor is a wild phenomenon well known to dwellers on the Somerset Levels. The first time that you encounter this winter congregation of starlings in full flood is a truly overwhelming experience. The exact location can vary from year to year, but the reed-beds of Westhay Moor nature reserve just west of Glastonbury are a good bet in most winters. A secure perch on a slender reed stem, surrounded by water, makes as safe a place as any for a starling to sleep out the night.

The reason why the starlings mass above the moors is much debated. Most likely they are seeking safety in numbers as they congregate over their chosen roosting place. 'Numbers' is a term quite inadequate. Upwards of 4 million birds can be present, one gigantic aerial army. They arrive in groups, in dribs and drabs, from all quarters of the compass. The flying mass of birds thickens and darkens, now coalescing into a ball, now elongating and twisting, a silk scarf trailed here and there across the sky. Wave after wave skims the reed-beds and wet woodlands of the moor until half the sky is full. The aerial currents ebb and flow.

After half an hour or so of communal roller-coasting, the immense mass of birds makes a final pass across the sky and drops to the reed-bed, where it shifts, rises and falls with a deep bass thunder of wings and a piercing shrilling of voices. Gradually the roost settles, the movements subside and the shrieking mutes to a sound like a shallow river over stones. Three or four million starlings have settled for the night, and the dance over Westhay Moor is finished until the following evening.

36. MENDIP CAVES, SOMERSET

Maps: OS Explorer 141, 142; Landranger 182, 183

Travel: The Mendip Hills lie east of the M5, between Junctions 22 and 21. A368 and A362 follow the northern edge, A371 and A361 the southern. Hunter's Lodge Inn, 'headquarters' of Mendip caving, is 1½ miles east of Priddy at a crossroads on the old Wells–Bristol road (OS ref. 549502). Enquire here about caving locally. General information from the British Caving Association: www.british-caving.org.uk.

You walk down into the hollow in the middle of the field and enter a tiny concrete hut with a square hatch in the floor. The lamp on your helmet picks out

Mendip caves

a metal ladder and a narrowing tunnel of rock sloping downwards and out of sight. It leads to an A-shaped passage, coated a monochrome khaki by mud. You shuffle ahead, now bending low as the cave roof drops to 3 feet high, now straightening as you pass through a chamber. At a certain spot the passage roof lowers sharply and the sides narrow to form a tunnel the length of your body, perhaps 2 feet square. It's called a squeeze, the first of many, says the caver who has brought you here. You get down on your belly, shove your right arm out in front of you, and worm your way forward. It feels impossible; no muscle you possess seems adequate to the motion required to get you through the squeeze. 'Turn on your side,' advises your companion calmly, 'and just pull yourself forward.' You do as told, and find yourself slithering out in a squelch of mud and water, as wet and greasy as a newborn baby. It's a cathartic moment. You feel a wonderful dragon-slaying sensation.

Next comes a descent down a slippery 15-foot rock wall. It looks formidable, but now you have the confidence to tackle it by finger-end and boot-tip. 'Prepare to be gobsmacked,' warns the caver ahead. You inch round a corner. 'Welcome to GB ...'

Two hundred feet below the grazing fields of the Mendip Hills, GB cave is breathtaking. A vast cavern opens in front of you, nearly 100 feet from floor to roof, as tall and impressive as a cathedral. A rock bridge springs outwards across a ravine. Long stalactites hang in the glow of your lamp among wavy white calcite and haphazard lines of helectite, which bunches like coral and forms delicately frosted cauliflower heads. Smooth knobs of stalagmites bobble the chamber floor. An unseen waterfall crashes near by.

Such are the pleasures and excitements of caving under Mendip. Burrowing in the bowels of the earth like this, your eyes are opened to treasures that remain unseen by all but a tiny, select group – pioneers in the last unexplored wilderness.

2

CHANNEL ISLANDS, DORSET, HAMPSHIRE, WILTSHIRE, WEST SUSSEX, EAST SUSSEX, KENT

THE SOUTH COUNTRY

Chalk defines the South Country. High chalk downs and outcropping sea cliffs undulate for 200 miles, all the way from Dorset to Kent. The elasticity of chalk, its capacity to weather into smoothly billowing downs where beechwoods thrive, its tendency to shear off sharp into huge cliffs when pounded by the sea, have given distinctive shape to these hills and coasts.

THE WILD PLACES of the South Country owe most of their character to this mighty barrier of close-packed marine animal skeletons and shells, laid down over the course of many millions of years. Woods rooted easily in such lime-rich foundations once the Ice Age glaciers had melted. Flints lay ready to hand, to be shaped into the most effective tools of the Stone Age. When humans came to clear the wildwood of the South Country they found the chalk ideal for farming; they settled, built, carved graceful white horses and giants and built earthen strongholds in the high places of the downs, and left behind great numbers of splendid tombs and other, more mysterious structures.

The South Country is rich in such landscapes. Each of the region's counties is littered with burial mounds and standing stones, to be traced along the ancient rutted trackways of the Ox Drove, Pilgrim's Way and Ridgeway. The oldest and least-known of all these primitive highways, the Harroway, has been scored into the landscape by the feet, hooves and cartwheels of 7,000 years. Wiltshire is the supreme county for these signs and symbols of the 'old folk', their climax the unique calendar of star and moon activity that is Stonehenge in its splendour. The county has retained uncultivated landscapes, too. Salisbury Plain owes the remarkably untamed character of its interior to its long-term use as a military training ground – apparently a contradiction in terms. The presence of phenomenal amounts of unexploded ordnance, the frequency of fires and explosions, has prevented any modern agriculture over big swathes of the plain, leaving a region of chalk grassland flowers and

Left: Malling Down (p. 80). Above: Bedlam's Bottom (p. 88). Right: Pevensey Levels (p. 82)

creatures unique in Britain. Ancient woods and patches of heath clothe the flanks of the Sussex downs; and the wide heaths of the New Forest and of Dorset, sombre blankets of heather and bogs full of lizards, songbirds and butterflies, have not changed in essential character since Thomas Hardy immortalized them as 'Egdon Heath'.

Sea journeys begin and end our tour through the wilds of the South Country, among the salt-rusted modern-day hulks of forgotten Thames forts, and out to the lonely Channel Island reefs, haunts of intrepid sea kayakers and connoisseurs of the bizarre.

LINKS

- Harroway: Five Lanes End, 'Efrafa', Stonehenge, Salisbury Plain, Groveley Wood
- Pilgrim's Way/North Downs Way National Trail (www.nationaltrail.co.uk/northdowns): Oldbury Fort, Coldrum Stones, North Downs Way near Hollingbourne
- Saxon Shore Way (www.ramblers.org.uk/info/paths/saxonshore.html): Dickens's marshes, Bedlam's Bottom, Isle of Sheppey (view from Swale), Romney Marsh (overview from inland cliffs)
- South Downs Way National Trail (www.nationaltrail.co.uk/southdowns): (short detour to West Dean Woods), Lullington Nature Reserve, Seven Sisters
- Ridgeway National Trail (www.nationaltrail.co.uk/ridgeway; www.ridgewayfriends.org.uk): Silbury Hill and West Kennet Long Barrow, Avebury, Barbury Castle (link to South Midlands: Wayland's Smithy, Oxfordshire)
- South West Coast Path National Trail (www.southwestcoastpath.com; www.swcp.org.uk): Dancing Ledge, Winspit, Isle of Portland, Chesil Beach (link to West Country: Lyme Regis Undercliff, Devon)

NATIONAL PARKS

- New Forest: www.newforestnpa.gov.uk
- South Downs (designated, not confirmed): www.southdowns.gov.uk

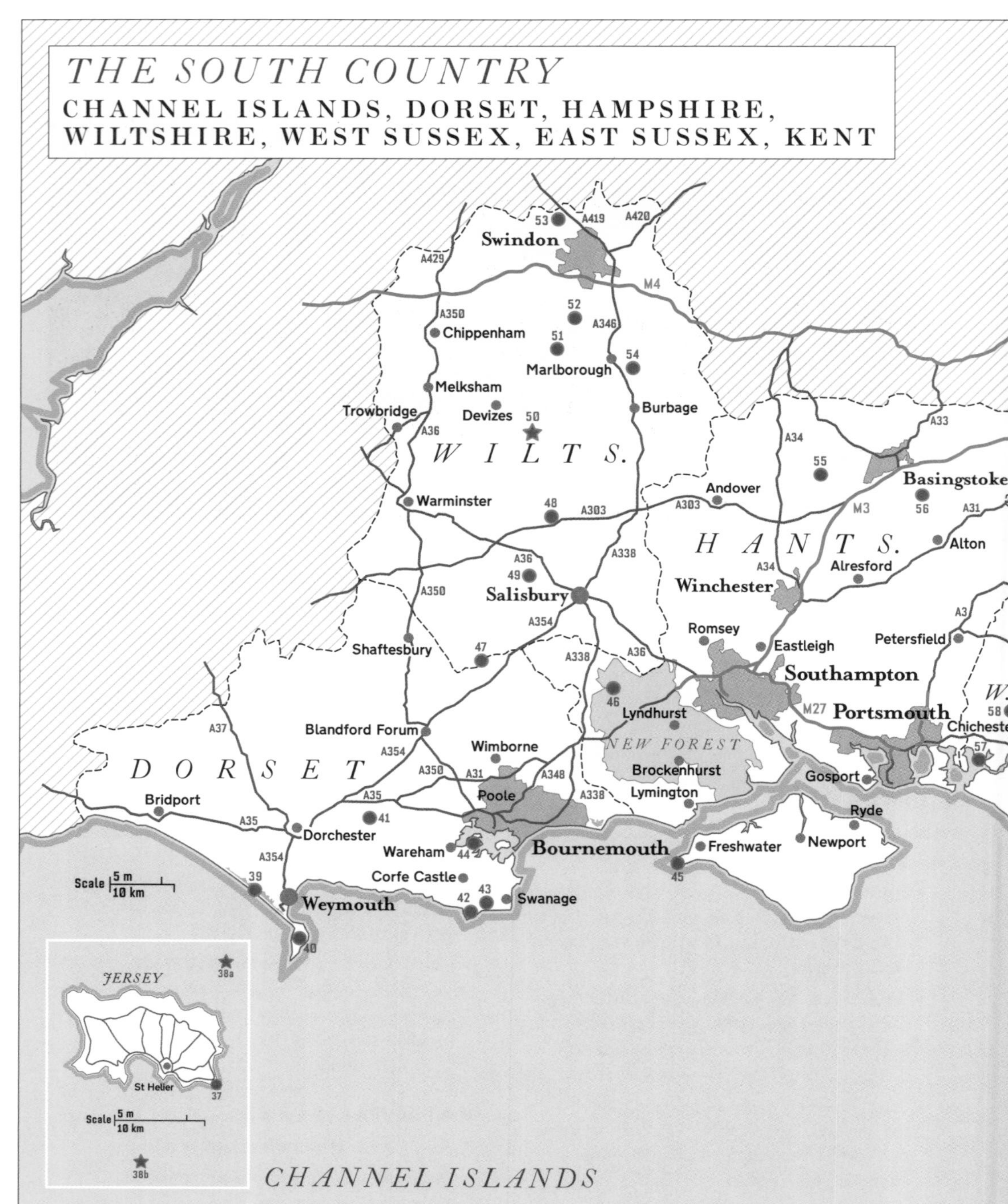
THE SOUTH COUNTRY
CHANNEL ISLANDS, DORSET, HAMPSHIRE, WILTSHIRE, WEST SUSSEX, EAST SUSSEX, KENT
Swindon
A419
A420
A429
M4
A350
Chippenham
A346
Marlborough
Melksham
Trowbridge
Devizes
Burbage
A36
W I L T S.
Warminster
A303
Andover
Basingstoke
M3
A31
H A N T S.
Alton
A338
A34
Alresford
A33
Salisbury
Winchester
A354
Romsey
Eastleigh
Petersfield
A3
Shaftesbury
Southampton
Lyndhurst
M27
Portsmouth
Chichester
Blandford Forum
NEW FOREST
Wimborne
Brockenhurst
D O R S E T
A37
A35
A348
Poole
Lymington
Gosport
Bridport
Ryde
Dorchester
Wareham
Bournemouth
Freshwater
Newport
Corfe Castle
Swanage
Weymouth
Scale 5 m 10 km
JERSEY
St Helier
CHANNEL ISLANDS

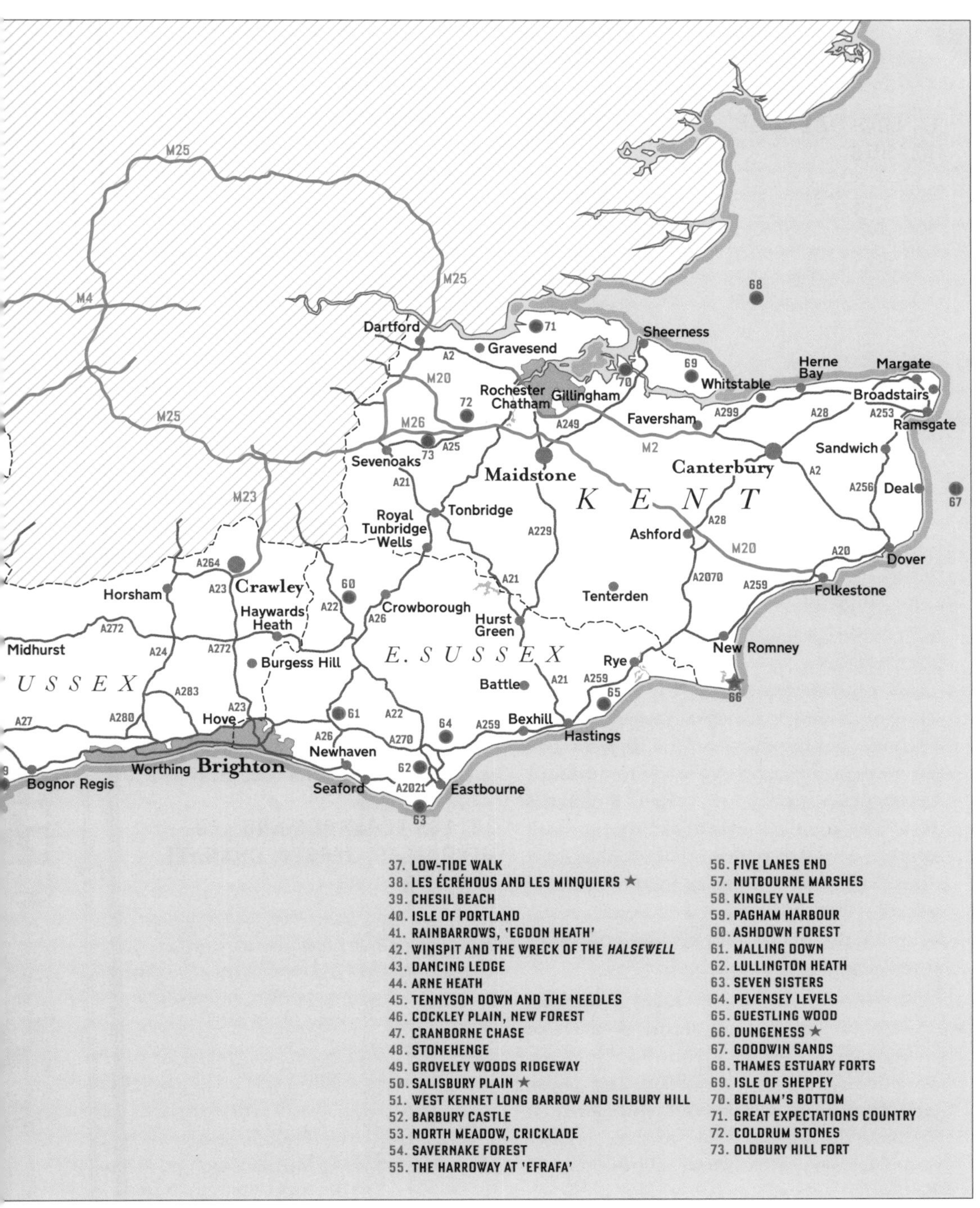
M25
M4
M23
M26
M20
M2
Dartford
Gravesend
Sheerness
Rochester
Chatham
Gillingham
Whitstable
Herne Bay
Margate
Broadstairs
Ramsgate
Faversham
Sandwich
Canterbury
Deal
Sevenoaks
Maidstone
KENT
Tonbridge
Royal Tunbridge Wells
Ashford
Dover
Folkestone
Tenterden
Crawley
Horsham
Haywards Heath
Crowborough
Hurst Green
Midhurst
Burgess Hill
E. SUSSEX
USSEX
Rye
New Romney
Battle
Hove
Bexhill
Hastings
Newhaven
Worthing
Brighton
Bognor Regis
Seaford
Eastbourne
A2
A249
A299
A28
A253
A256
A25
A21
A229
A20
A2070
A259
A264
A23
A22
A26
A272
A24
A283
A280
A27
A270
A2021
37. LOW-TIDE WALK
38. LES ÉCRÉHOUS AND LES MINQUIERS ★
39. CHESIL BEACH
40. ISLE OF PORTLAND
41. RAINBARROWS, 'EGDON HEATH'
42. WINSPIT AND THE WRECK OF THE *HALSEWELL*
43. DANCING LEDGE
44. ARNE HEATH
45. TENNYSON DOWN AND THE NEEDLES
46. COCKLEY PLAIN, NEW FOREST
47. CRANBORNE CHASE
48. STONEHENGE
49. GROVELEY WOODS RIDGEWAY
50. SALISBURY PLAIN ★
51. WEST KENNET LONG BARROW AND SILBURY HILL
52. BARBURY CASTLE
53. NORTH MEADOW, CRICKLADE
54. SAVERNAKE FOREST
55. THE HARROWAY AT 'EFRAFA'
56. FIVE LANES END
57. NUTBOURNE MARSHES
58. KINGLEY VALE
59. PAGHAM HARBOUR
60. ASHDOWN FOREST
61. MALLING DOWN
62. LULLINGTON HEATH
63. SEVEN SISTERS
64. PEVENSEY LEVELS
65. GUESTLING WOOD
66. DUNGENESS ★
67. GOODWIN SANDS
68. THAMES ESTUARY FORTS
69. ISLE OF SHEPPEY
70. BEDLAM'S BOTTOM
71. GREAT EXPECTATIONS COUNTRY
72. COLDRUM STONES
73. OLDBURY HILL FORT

37. LOW-TIDE WALK, JERSEY, CHANNEL ISLANDS

Map: OS 1:25,000 Official Leisure Map of Jersey

Travel: Flybe (www.flybe.com) flies to Jersey from many British regional airports. A12, A2, A1, A5 through St Helier to La Rocque. Park here and walk out across the foreshore at low tide, to reach Seymour Tower. Beware! Allow 3 hours at least for the round trip, and start off while the tide is still falling.

On the map, the Channel Island of Jersey measures about 9 miles by 5, an area of around 45 square miles. But the tide rises and falls 40 feet hereabouts. At low water, thanks to the large area exposed by the retreating sea, the dry land of Jersey doubles in size. What is exposed is a true wilderness, a vast collar of rock and sand that in parts stretches some 2 miles between the land and water's edge.

The south-east corner of the island possesses the largest expanse of this amphibian territory. Setting out from La Rocque, you can make an adventurous sortie to Seymour Tower, provided you keep a strict eye on the tides. The solid stone-block tower was built in 1782, a case of slamming the stable door after the horse had bolted: the previous year the French had tried without success to invade the island, and building Seymour Tower was a knee-jerk reaction.

On the way out to the tower you cross a desert of wet sand cut across by fleets of seawater and flowing channels. Here are the burrow holes of razorfish and green hanks of *vraic*, or wrack weed, still spread as fertilizer on the fields by some of Jersey's potato farmers. If you have the eye to spot the ragged leaf shape of pepper dulse on the rocks, it makes a tongue-tingling snack. Children love these sands, wide enough to scamper on, and the rock outcrops which rise on all sides, jagged miniature mountain ranges with hidden rock pools where you can search for blennies, sea anemones, crabs, starfish and, if you are lucky, the ear-shaped silvery shell of the ormer, a succulent delicacy.

Oystercatcher, curlew and turnstone are seen and heard on the tideline as you approach Seymour Tower. You can climb on to the terrace to admire the long views over the rocks and up the sandy beach of the Royal Bay of Grouville to Mont Orgeuil Castle looming massively on its headland. But don't linger too long, or you may emulate the riders who became marooned at the tower along with their three horses. They triggered a rescue operation that necessitated the use of two JCBs and a ramp of sand, hastily built between one tide and the next for the horses to descend. It's still talked about in the La Rocque pubs.

38. LES ÉCRÉHOUS AND LES MINQUIERS, JERSEY, CHANNEL ISLANDS

Travel: Sea kayak from Jersey (www.seapaddler.co.uk) is the adventurous way to reach Les Écréhous and Les Minquiers. Yachts with modern navigation aids may moor there; or ask a Jersey fisherman to take (and collect!) you.

Off the coast of Jersey rise two extraordinary rock reefs. Les Écréhous, the larger group, lie 6 miles offland, some 8 miles from the French coast; while Les Minquiers ('The Minkies' to Jerseymen) lie 12 miles south of the island. Ownership of both reefs was disputed for centuries between England and France; a decision at the International Court of Justice in 1973 awarded them to Jersey.

Intrepid sea kayakers paddle out to both reefs, a more adventurous means of access than buzzing out there in a yacht. However you approach, the reefs present entirely different aspects depending on the state of the tide. The sea's twice-daily local rise and fall of up to 40 feet exposes enormous stretches of rock, sand and lagoon at low tide. In the case of Les Minquiers, a reef which extends only a few hundred yards at high tide expands to some 25 square miles at the ebb. This is the best time for dry land and rock-pool exploration. At high tide the reefs look much odder; for each is topped by a cluster of houses, those on Les Écréhous former fishermen's cottages, those on Les Minquiers mostly built by the quarrymen who inhabited the reef early in the nineteenth century while quarrying it for stone used in fort-building on Jersey. The houses – some derelict, others now holiday homes – appear to float on the surface of the sea, so that one wonders how they do not sink beneath it, Atlantis-like.

The Écréhous group has three main islets – Maîtr'île (Mistress or Mother Island), La Marmotchiéthe (Little Boy) and Lé Bliantch'île (White Island). The ruin of a Cistercian cell lies on Maîtr'île. Lé Bliantch'île was a refuge for two contrasting figures: Philippe Pinel the 'King of the Écréhous', who lived here for fifty years in the nineteenth century, and the wretched Alphonse Le Gastelois, who fled to this outpost after being falsely named as the paedophile 'Beast of Jersey'. Les Minquiers were briefly captured in 1998 by a group of French invaders operating in the name of the King of Patagonia, as a retaliation for British actions in the South Atlantic during the Falklands War. As with the Thames Estuary forts (see pp. 86-7), wild deeds seem endemic to such remote sea outposts.

39. CHESIL BEACH, DORSET

Maps: OS Explorer OL15; Landranger 194

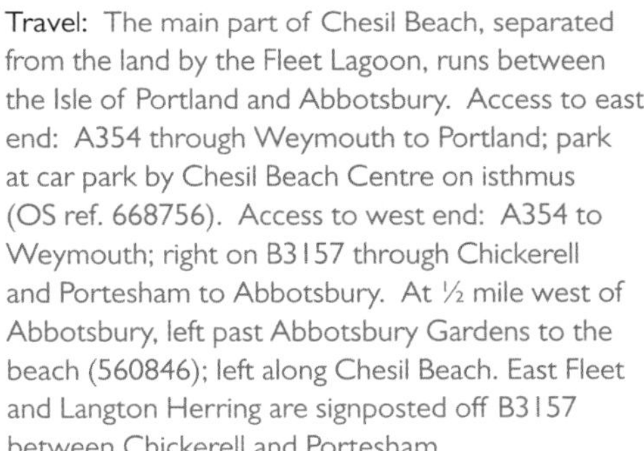
Travel: The main part of Chesil Beach, separated from the land by the Fleet Lagoon, runs between the Isle of Portland and Abbotsbury. Access to east end: A354 through Weymouth to Portland; park at car park by Chesil Beach Centre on isthmus (OS ref. 668756). Access to west end: A354 to Weymouth; right on B3157 through Chickerell and Portesham to Abbotsbury. At ½ mile west of Abbotsbury, left past Abbotsbury Gardens to the beach (560846); left along Chesil Beach. East Fleet and Langton Herring are signposted off B3157 between Chickerell and Portesham.

Nearest railway station: Weymouth (1½ miles from Chesil Beach Centre)

Chesil Beach is the longest shingle bar in Europe, a mighty ridge of pebbles that runs for 18 miles west from the Isle of Portland to the village of Burton Bradstock. For eleven of these miles, between the Portland isthmus and the shore at Abbotsbury, it is separated from the mainland by the narrow, brackish lagoon called the Fleet, which makes Chesil Beach not quite of the land nor yet of the sea. The process by which the bank built up, longshore drift from west to east, is well understood, yet no expert has been able to explain for sure how the flinty shingle of Chesil Beach is so perfectly graded from pebbles the size of large peas around Burton

Chesil Beach

Bradstock to cobbles the size of potatoes at Portland.

To experience Chesil Beach properly as a wild place, choose a day of stormy weather when waves roll in as high as houses to thunder down on the pebble bank. Chesil Beach has always been a deadly coast to sailors. So many wreck victims were pounded and drowned on Chesil in the eighteenth and nineteenth centuries that they fill two large graveyards around Wyke Regis church near Portland. One who lies in an unmarked grave is William Wordsworth's sea-captain brother, John, who drowned along with 300 passengers when his ship *Abergavenny* was wrecked in 1805. Walking the crunchy, slippery pebble ridge on a stormy day you can see only too clearly why a shipwrecked sailor had so little hope of rescue. Each wave rushes up the beach, then drags back with a vicious hiss of undertow. Ships and men would be revolved in the breakers, cast up and dragged back time and again until there were only shattered remains left of either.

All the villages behind the Fleet were up to their elbows in smuggling during the eighteenth century, when the 'preventive officers' were few and far between. Many cargoes were taken on moonless nights to hides in the Fleet marshes, or further inland up the flint tracks to lonely farms on the downs. John Meade Falkner set his breathless old smuggling yarn *Moonfleet* here in 1898, and in the chancel of the old church at Fleet you can stamp on the flagstones to hear the hollow echo of the vault where Falkner's young hero, John Trenchard, was trapped by the smugglers – wild men in wild times.

40. ISLE OF PORTLAND, DORSET

Maps: OS Explorer OL15; Landranger 194

Travel: A354 through Weymouth to Portland.

Nearest railway station: Weymouth (5 miles)

The Isle of Portland lies out in the English Channel, a crouching white lion on a blue stretch of savannah, its great breakwaters enfolding Portland Harbour like paws. Seen from the shore in profile, Portland seems all straight lines and sharp steps, a legacy of 600 years of intensive quarrying. Thomas Hardy, who set his last novel, *The Well-Beloved*, here, called the isle 'the Gibraltar of Wessex', and that nicely catches both its lumpy stance in the sea and its air of defiance, even of menace, as it pushes its bald flank and forehead into wind and waves.

Walking the maze of Portland's footpaths is the best way to appreciate its stark appeal, taking a long day to make a circuit of the island's rough-hewn perimeter. It was Sir Christopher Wren who ensured the success and fame of Portland stone when he chose this easy-to-work yet durable Upper Jurassic limestone or 'freestone' for the rebuilding of London after the Great Fire of 1666. But Portland had been quarried since at least Roman times, and as you walk you will see great downfalls of broken rock everywhere – the spoil rock that was shovelled over the quarry cliffs to litter the beaches and ledges below. Now the cliffs are no longer quarried, and nature has clothed the abandoned stone blocks with deep pink drifts of valerian, yellow ragwort and strong-scented mugwort. Whinchats send their clicking calls out from scrub bushes, for all the world like tiny quarrymen breaking minuscule stones.

Stone-breaking was the chief employment of the inmates of Portland's notoriously cruel prison in the nineteenth century. On the plateau that forms the crest of the island looms the huge building (now a Young Offender's Institution) with its great chimneys and grim rows of tiny windows. Its intransigent bulk in the harsh landscape of bare stone and scattered scrub seems as alien to Dorset's cosy cream-tea image as one can possibly imagine.

The Rainbarrows

41. RAINBARROWS, 'EGDON HEATH', DORSET

Maps: OS Explorer OL15; Landranger 194

Travel: A35 from Dorchester towards Puddletown; in 2½ miles, Higher Bockhampton signed off main road. Follow signs for Hardy's Cottage; park in car park and follow footpath signs to pass cottage (OS ref. 728925) and American monument. Continue past Forestry Commission barrier up gravel track, through trees and over heath. In 300 yards keep ahead over crossing of tracks; in 100 yards ignore grassy track off to right. In another 40 yards, four tracks meet (732928); take track that is first on the right (it hairpins back with a fence on the right and yellow waymark arrow). In ¼ mile pass path on left, and in 200 yards another where Roman road crosses track (734923). In another 300 yards, stile on right just before a steep downward slope leads to Rainbarrows, 50 yards beyond fence (735920) and ¾ mile from Hardy's Cottage.

Nearest railway station: Dorchester (3½ miles from Hardy's Cottage)

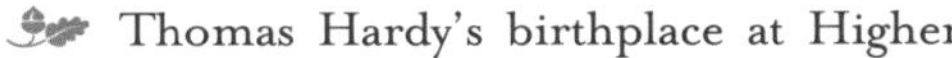

Thomas Hardy's birthplace at Higher

Bockhampton, now called Hardy's Cottage (NT), lies on the edge of Puddletown Forest, an area which was mostly wild heath in the mid nineteenth century when Hardy was growing up. The 'Egdon Heath' of *The Return of the Native* and several other of his Wessex novels was inspired by this rolling, open landscape, nowadays planted with coniferous forests to the extent that the writer would scarcely recognize it. But Duddle Heath on the south-west corner of Puddletown Forest still looks much as Hardy knew it.

It is less than a mile on foot from Hardy's Cottage to Rainbarrows, a cluster of ancient burial mounds on the edge of the steep escarpment fringing Duddle Heath that drops away to the valley of the River Frome – the 'Vale of the Great Dairies' in *Tess of the D'Urbervilles*. Here Hardy played as a child, and heard of the death of a shepherd boy from starvation in the area of the heath – a small, local tragedy he never forgot.

Birch, pine, gorse and heather all thrive in the sandy soil, and honeysuckle twines over the bushes. Bracken-filled hollows show where deep old sandpits lie. The three Rainbarrows stand out clearly on the edge of the slope; the most prominent of them is carpeted with mosses and lichens, ling and bell heather, with a knotty and vigorous old holly tree growing out of the top. Here Hardy came as a boy; and after he gave up novel-writing at the turn of the twentieth century and turned to writing poetry, the location stayed in his mind. One of his most mysterious poems, 'The Sheep Boy', describes a fog creeping up on a shepherd boy on Rainbarrows as he looks out over the Frome vale:

A yawning, sunned concave
Of purple, spread as an ocean wave
Entroughed on a morning of swell and sway
After a night when wind-fiends have been heard to
rave
Thus was the Heath called 'Draäts' on an August day.

42. WINSPIT AND THE WRECK OF THE *HALSEWELL*, DORSET

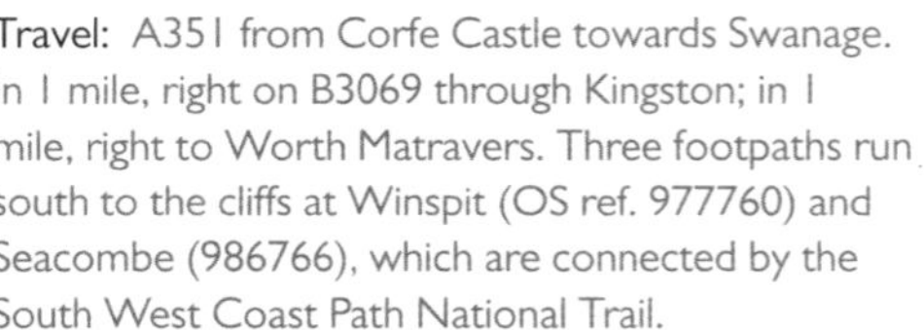
Maps: OS Explorer OL15; Landranger 195

Travel: A351 from Corfe Castle towards Swanage. In 1 mile, right on B3069 through Kingston; in 1 mile, right to Worth Matravers. Three footpaths run south to the cliffs at Winspit (OS ref. 977760) and Seacombe (986766), which are connected by the South West Coast Path National Trail.

Around 2 a.m. on 6 January 1786, in a full gale and a wild snowstorm, the 758-ton passenger ship *Halsewell* drove into the Purbeck cliffs between Seacombe and Winspit. Of all the terrible shipwrecks along this dangerous Dorset coast, the *Halsewell* has lingered longest in local imagination – perhaps because of the wild location of the wreck, far from help, or maybe because of the desperation of the survivors as they tried to climb the sheer cliffs in the snow and wind.

Halsewell was on passage to Bengal with a complement of 250 souls. Two days before the wreck, Captain Richard Pierce found that the ship would not steer and was taking on water. He ordered the mizzenmast and then the mainmast to be cut away, and put out bower and sheet anchors; but *Halsewell* could not be prevented from drifting towards the cliffs. The crew and passengers had to wait two days and nights for the disaster they could all see was inevitable. When she did eventually strike, she was thrown broadside into the mouth of a cave. Newspaper reports of the day described with full tabloid-style relish how 'the ship struck with such violence as to dash the heads of those who were standing on the cuddy against the deck above them, and the fatal blow was accompanied by a shriek of horror, which burst at one instant from every quarter of the ship'.

The *Halsewell* seamen were roundly condemned for 'skulking in their hammocks' and leaving the officers to do all the rescue work. Those that did clamber on to the rocks had to inch along a hand's-breadth ledge and then scale a 200-foot cliff, many of them falling to their deaths in the attempt. The first men to reach the top were the cook and the quartermaster, who struggled a mile inland to Eastington Farm where they raised the alarm. The Reverend Jones, vicar of Worth Matravers, the nearest village, described how a bunch of quarrymen gathered on the cliffs, though they 'were more eager to get their share of the two casks of spirits which had just been sent them, than to attend to the cries of the sufferers below'.

In a letter to the *Hampshire Chronicle*, Mr Jones later described the aftermath of the wreck as he viewed it from the cliffs at daylight:

Such a horrid, tremendous scene never did my eyes behold, and God of His mercy grant that they may never again. The sea ran mountains high, and lashed the rocks with all the appearance of insolence and anger. The ship's rigging on the water was wound up like garbage of an animal and rolling to and fro in sullen submission to the imperious waves. In the different recesses of the rocks, a confused heap of boards, broken masts, chests, trunks, and dead bodies, were huddled together, and the face of the water as far as the eye could extend was disfigured with floating carcasses, tables, chairs, casks, and part of every other article of the vessel. I do not think that any two boards remained together.

Of the 250 on board *Halsewell*, 168 were lost, including seven young women on their way out east to find husbands. Most of the victims lie buried in a mass grave on the slopes of East and West Man just to the west of the wreck site. Glass bottles, coins and other relics of *Halsewell* are still thrown up by the sea from time to time, to ignite yet another retelling of the story.

43. DANCING LEDGE, DORSET

Maps: OS Explorer OL15; Landranger 195

Travel: A351 to Swanage. South West Coast Path National Trail runs west to Dancing Ledge (OS ref. 998769) in 3½ miles. Alternatively, bear right on B3069 just outside Swanage into Langton Matravers. Park here and take footpath due south for 1¼ miles to Dancing Ledge.

The south coast of the Isle of Purbeck is one of the wildest coasts in the South Country. The tall cliffs were quarried for the pale, durable yet workable freestone over many hundreds of years; their moment of glory arrived with the rebuilding of London after the Great Fire of 1666, and then again in another vast development surge in the city during Imperial Britain's apex of nineteenth-century prosperity.

Dancing Ledge, easily reached from the South West Coast Path, is a good place to view the interaction of natural and industrial effects. There are actually two ledges here – an upper, artificial one cut by the quarrymen, and a lower one beside the sea floored by the

Prickly Bed, a formation of lumpy limestone full of fossils and washed regularly by the tide. Deep grooves in the lower ledge were made by the runners of the quarrymen's sledges as they dragged the stone to the water's edge to be loaded into boats for onward transportation – most of it destined to end up in the harbour wall at Ramsgate.

To this lonely ledge in the cliffs came the young boys of Durnford Prep School in Langton Matravers, a mile or so to the north, for a naked swim in the sea each morning. The ritual was instigated by the school's headmaster, Thomas Pellatt, around the turn of the twentieth century. In the lower ledge at the edge of the sea is the tidal swimming pool that Pellatt had excavated for his boys. A swim there in fresh swirling seawater among small fish and shrimps, with limpets and brightly coloured seaweed decorating the rough pool walls, is a plunge you will never forget.

44. ARNE HEATH, DORSET

Maps: OS Explorer OL15; Landranger 195

Travel: A351 from Wareham towards Corfe Castle. Cross bridge over River Frome; in ¼ mile, left ('Stoborough'). In 300 yards, left into Stoborough. In 200 yards, right along Nutcrack Lane and follow 'Arne' for 3½ miles to park in RSPB car park (OS ref. 972878). Long and short trails lead over Arne Heath (leaflet guide available in car park).

Arne Heath is one of the best preserved of Dorset's heaths, which once covered much of the coastal area of the county but have now mostly disappeared under agricultural 'improvements' or house building. Arne occupies a hook-shaped peninsula poking out north into Wareham Channel on the north-west side of Poole Harbour, itself a rare phenomenon of a place where the tide ebbs and flows twice as often as it should. The most expensive and exclusive dwellings in the region (the houses on the Sandbanks peninsula at the mouth of the harbour) look across at some of the most deserted and natural land in the South Country. Developers would love to get their hands on Arne, but the Royal Society for the Protection of Birds, who maintain the heath, and the local residents, who watch and ward it jealously, won't allow them anywhere near it.

Well over 1,000 acres of heath and woodland, muddy foreshore and saltmarsh are yours to enjoy via a network of footpaths and a cycleway. From the beechwoods you reach a heathland plateau purple with

Arne Heath

heather, from which there are far views between pine clumps over the green marshes and tideways of Poole Harbour. Rowan trees show white blossom in spring and intensely scarlet berries in autumn. In among the heather and birch scrub you may spot goldfinch and greenfinch, spotted flycatcher and stonechat, and if you are lucky a glimpse of the heath's most celebrated resident, the Dartford warbler, with dark red waist-coat and grey cap. The British population of these shy and scarce little birds, very characteristic of heathland, declined hugely during the twentieth century, but the RSPB's conservation efforts have seen numbers on Arne Heath rise towards 100 pairs.

In the past two centuries Europe as a whole has lost nearly 90 per cent of its heaths, which have existed since just after the last Ice Age. Thanks to the handsome efforts of man, Arne Heath, with its spotted roe deer, its hornets and raft spiders, its dragonflies and lizards and nightjars, survives as a wild place against the odds.

45. TENNYSON DOWN AND THE NEEDLES, ISLE OF WIGHT, HAMPSHIRE

Maps: OS Explorer OL29; Landranger 196

Travel: Ferries run from Southampton to Cowes, or Lymington to Yarmouth (www.redfunnel.co.uk; www.wightlink.co.uk).

(a) For the Needles: A3054 to Freshwater; B3322 to Alum Bay car park; signposted footpath up to Old Battery overlooking the Needles (OS ref. 295849).

(b) For Tennyson Down: A3055 to Freshwater Bay. Park on seafront; 'Tennyson Trail' footpath signed from here, along Tennyson Down to Old Battery (7-mile walk, there and back).

Tennyson Down is a masterpiece of a cliff walk, a great windy blow-through atop 500 feet of solid chalk cliff. In the 1850s and 1860s Alfred, Lord Tennyson lived at Farringford just outside Freshwater. He often came walking here, striding as a Poet Laureate should with wildly flapping hair and cloak, and the granite cross that stands on the summit of the down is his memorial.

Standing here in a proper old Isle of Wight wind you look out on a sea whitened and misty with spray. It is another couple of miles to the western end of the down, a promontory that gradually narrows until the sea on either side seems to be squeezing you out like toothpaste along the back of West High Down. You pass a row of wind-blasted coastguard cottages, and then the Needles Battery, which was sited up here in Tennyson's day to defend Portsmouth from the French invaders that never came. Here, too, British scientists a century later tried unavailingly to launch the UK into the Space Race on the back of the Black Arrow and Black Knight rocket experiments.

Beyond comes the final thrill of the walk, as you reach a well-guarded viewing platform from which to look down on the Needles. If it is a blowy day these three slender blades of chalk, rising from the sea just off the tip of the down, will be half smothered in a welter of foam and spray. Their bases show slimy green with algae and sea-staining, their upper halves look salt-grey until bright sun points up the whiteness of their chalk. The most seaward of the Needles is capped by a red-and-white striped lighthouse, automated these days but furnished with a helipad for a roof. The three sea stacks, slowly crumbling under the attack of wind and waves, make a curiously defiant and moving spectacle off Hampshire's coast.

46. COCKLEY PLAIN, NEW FOREST, HAMPSHIRE

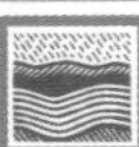

Maps: OS Explorer OL22; Landranger 195, 196, 184

Travel: The New Forest National Park lies west of Southampton and east of Ringwood. A338 Bournemouth to Fordingbridge runs up its west flank, A31 Ringwood to M27 bisects it, and A36 gives access to the northern section, north-west of Southampton. For Cockley Hill and Plain: A338 from Ringwood to Fordingbridge; right on B3078 through Godshill; ¾ mile beyond Godshill, park on right in Ashley Walk car park (OS ref. 186157). Follow gravel track east across Ditchend Brook, up Cockley Hill on to Cockley Plain (195155).

Notwithstanding its name, the New Forest is in fact the oldest of Britain's royal hunting forests. These 150 square miles of trees, fields, heaths and common lands were hunted by Saxon nobles and royalty long before the Normans muscled in. Yet it is the Normans that people associate with the New Forest, partly because of their penalties for poaching, fantastically harsh for today's sensibilities – mutilation, blinding or death – and partly because it was here that King William Rufus, son of William the Conqueror, was killed by an arrow while out hunting on 2 August 1100. The Commoners of the New Forest still exercise ancient rights of grazing and gathering wood, and the agisters or officers of the centuries-old Verderers Court of Forest Law can be seen patrolling on horseback in their forest-green jackets.

Among all this tradition and these checks and balances, the New Forest – designated a National Park in 2005 – maintains the delicate equilibrium of its mosaic of water, woodland, wetland and heath. From the lizards and adders on its sandy commons to the frogs and newts in its ponds, the nightjars and hobbies on the heaths and the fritillary and silver-studded blue butterflies at their margins, there are many wildlife delights for quiet, observant walkers.

A really fine walk is along the gravel tracks of Cockley Plain in the north-west sector of the forest, an area far less frequented than further east near Southampton. Within a few minutes you get into a broad, shallow valley of heather, empty and rolling, where ridges and hollows are concealed until you are right on top of them. Silver birch scrub and stands of pine provide shelter for the New Forest ponies with their long coarse manes and tails. Groups of cattle wander at will over the heath. From the heights of Cockley Plain, walk on east into Ashley Hole, a gully descending nearly 100 feet to a boggy bottom where you can picnic beyond sight and sound of the outside world.

47. CRANBORNE CHASE, DORSET/ WILTSHIRE BORDERS

Maps: OS Explorer 118; Landranger 184 (also 183, 194, 195)

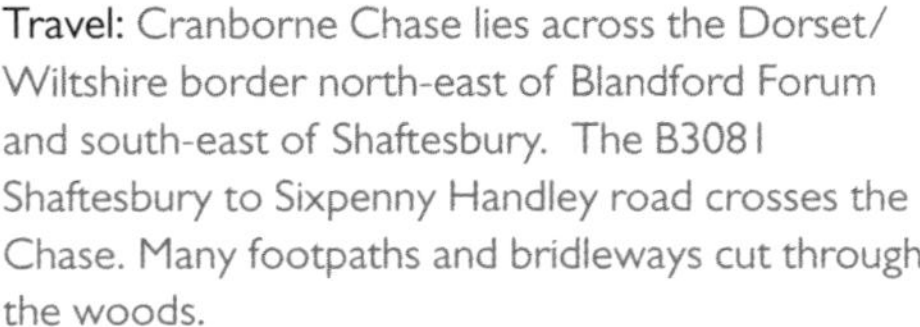

Travel: Cranborne Chase lies across the Dorset/ Wiltshire border north-east of Blandford Forum and south-east of Shaftesbury. The B3081 Shaftesbury to Sixpenny Handley road crosses the Chase. Many footpaths and bridleways cut through the woods.

'A truly venerable forest,' wrote Thomas Hardy in *Tess of the D'Urbervilles*, 'one of the few remaining woodlands in England of undoubted primeval date, wherein Druidical mistletoe is still found on aged oaks, and where enormous yew trees, not planted by the hand of man, grow as they had grown when they were pollarded for bows.'

It is probably Hardy's novel, more than any other single influence, that draws visitors to Cranborne Chase. The seduction of innocent Tess by her caddish kinsman Alec D'Urberville in the wild wood is the stuff of every self-respecting scary fairy tale from Little Red Riding Hood to Snow White. And Cranborne Chase fulfils the fantasy to perfection, with its great acreage, dark depths and abundance of tremendously twisted ancient oaks and yews.

Walking the rides and their flint-strewn side paths, once the deer have plunged away through the bracken and ragwort, a solemn silence closes in, shadowed by the hum of countless insects at work.

Woods are wild places where dark deeds may be hatching, as poor Tess discovered when she and Alec D'Urberville approached Cranborne Chase:

'Why, where be we?' she exclaimed.

'Passing by a wood.'

'A wood – what wood? Surely we are quite out of the road?'

'A bit of the Chase – the oldest wood in England. It is a lovely sight, and why should we not prolong our ride a little?'

Why, indeed? Beware of the woods, Tess, and wolves in human clothing ...

48. STONEHENGE, WILTSHIRE

Maps: OS Explorer 130; Landranger 184

Travel: A303 from Winterbourne Stoke or A344 from Shrewton towards Amesbury; Stonehenge (OS ref. 122422) signposted from roads. Park in Stonehenge car park.

NB: The visitor path encircles the stones at a distance of about 40 yards. English Heritage organize a number of Stone Circle Access Visits (www.english-heritage.org.uk), during which visitors can walk among and touch the stones.

Nearest railway station: Salisbury (11 miles)

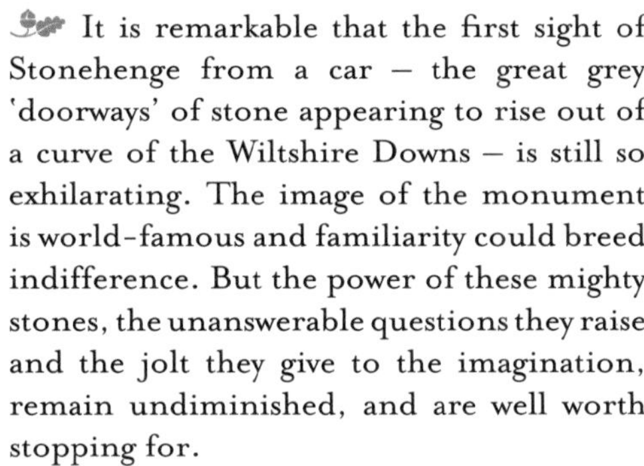

It is remarkable that the first sight of Stonehenge from a car – the great grey 'doorways' of stone appearing to rise out of a curve of the Wiltshire Downs – is still so exhilarating. The image of the monument is world-famous and familiarity could breed indifference. But the power of these mighty stones, the unanswerable questions they raise and the jolt they give to the imagination, remain undiminished, and are well worth stopping for.

Stonehenge was built in several phases, the earliest around 3100 BC when the circular bank around the site was constructed. Inside this bank almost 1,000 years later, Stone Age architects erected a double circle of bluestones 4 or 5 tons in weight, quarried from the dolerite of the Preseli Hills in south-west Wales and transported over 200 miles to Salisbury Plain, probably by sea and then on rollers. In about 2000 BC these were rearranged and partly replaced by stones from the Marlborough Downs 25 miles away, the heaviest of which weighed as much as 50 tons. These 'sarsens' or saracen ('stranger') stones were erected much as they still stand, pairs of uprights with a lintel laid across the top to form an outer ring of 25 trilithons, rectangular doorways about 14 feet tall. The lintels were carefully secured with mortice and tenon joints. Inside this new ring a horseshoe arrangement of five more trilithons was put up. Five hundred years after this, some of the bluestones that had been abandoned were put on end again in the space between the inner and outer rings; and the whole monument was furnished with a central stone, another of the bluestones (now known as the Altar Stone), which was erected in the centre of the horseshoe. And there the builders of Stonehenge finally ceased, some 1,400 years after the monument was begun.

The selection and transport of such huge blocks of material from specific but faraway sites, and the planning and execution of the work, interrupted perhaps for tens of generations and then resumed or reordered according to some new refinement – these facts are astonishing in themselves, considering the technology available to the Stone Age and then the Bronze Age builders: wooden rollers and lifting tackle, cutting and digging tools of flint or bronze. The why and wherefore of the giant trilithons, the feasibility of their function as a temple, observatory or celestial recording device, remain obscure to us. All that can be said for sure is that the sun, when viewed from the Altar Stone, rises directly over the Heel Stone, 256 feet away, at dawn on the summer solstice, 21 June.

Some people feel a strong but unquantifiable connection to the stones; some use them as the focus for druidical or other solstice worship; others remain sceptical of any power emanating from the monument. Whatever the call that our ancestors responded to in this place, only the most overwhelming imperative could have commanded such an outlay of time, effort and calculation from people for whom every day was a struggle for mere existence.

49. GROVELEY WOOD RIDGEWAY, WILTSHIRE

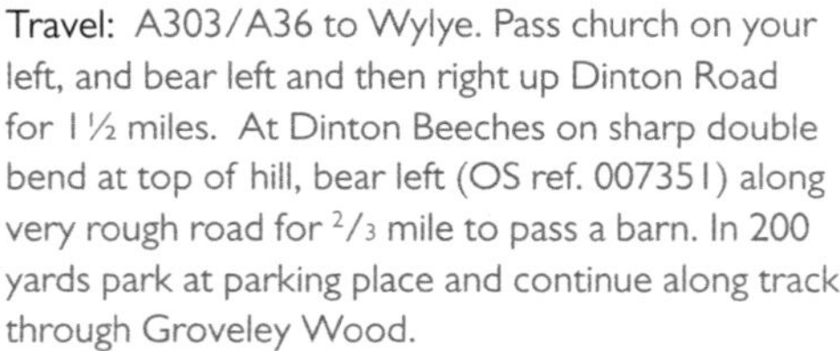

Maps: OS Explorer 130; Landranger 184

Travel: A303/A36 to Wylye. Pass church on your left, and bear left and then right up Dinton Road for 1½ miles. At Dinton Beeches on sharp double bend at top of hill, bear left (OS ref. 007351) along very rough road for ⅔ mile to pass a barn. In 200 yards park at parking place and continue along track through Groveley Wood.

Groveley Wood is an ancient wood, and the Groveley Wood Ridgeway track that threads it from west to east has been in use as a thoroughfare for perhaps 7,000 years. The wood lies along a ridge between the Nadder and Wylye valleys, with a fording place just to the east at Ditchampton. This is exactly the topography that travellers in prehistoric times preferred. To stay high with a good viewpoint all round, and to be able to descend to cross a river at a reliable ford, was to give oneself the best chance of travelling safely through what was then extremely wild country.

Dinton Beeches, the grove at the summit where you enter the wood, is the point where the Ridgeway is crossed by a trackway equally old, if not older – the Harroway (see p. 75), an ancient route that arcs 200 miles across the chalk downs of southern England from Devon to the Kentish coast. Soon the Harroway is left behind, as you follow the

Ridgeway through Groveley Wood. The way is partly under tarmac, evidence of its former use as a motor road, though nowadays walkers and cyclists follow its course. Tall beech and oak make up much of the woodland; there is a pungent smell of wild marjoram, and an abundance of wild strawberries.

The OS map names the Ridgeway 'Roman Road', and the Romans certainly used it as a through route from the Bristol Channel and their lead mines on the Mendip Hills to their forts and towns across the south of Britain. Mendip coal has been found at the ancient settlement site of Stockton Earthworks just to the west of Dinton Beeches, demonstrating the longevity of the Groveley Wood Ridgeway as a trading route; and its name in that section of the trackway, the Ox Drove, recalls how drovers and packmen once crossed the country on such highways.

50. SALISBURY PLAIN, WILTSHIRE

Maps: OS Explorer 130; Landranger 173, 184

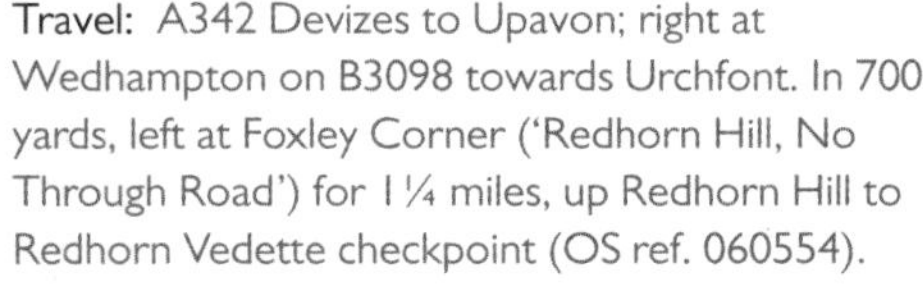

Travel: A342 Devizes to Upavon; right at Wedhampton on B3098 towards Urchfont. In 700 yards, left at Foxley Corner ('Redhorn Hill, No Through Road') for 1¼ miles, up Redhorn Hill to Redhorn Vedette checkpoint (OS ref. 060554).

NB: Access to the Imber Range Perimeter Path (IRPP) is available at all times. Access to the Byway Open to All Traffic southwards across Westdown Artillery Range depends on Ministry of Defence activities. Red flags at Redhorn Vedette signify 'No Access'. Firing times are posted at Redhorn Vedette. Information: www.mod.uk; tel: 01980 674763.

On the OS maps, Salisbury Plain resembles a great spider's web. Thinly dotted lines of tank tracks and red blobs of footpaths cross enormous tracts of empty ground – 94,000 acres in all, an area roughly the size and shape of the Isle of Wight. Yet access is severely restricted, and in many places would be extremely bad for your health. The reason is that the Ministry of Defence has owned this ground and used it as a training area since before the First World War. So much high explosive and so many combustibles have landed here, so much unexploded ordnance lies around, that the public cannot wander and farmers cannot farm the vast majority. As a result, the 1,700 ancient monuments on the plain – Romano-British villages, enigmatic earthworks, Bronze Age burial mounds and Dark Age field systems – have been saved from the deep ploughing that has grubbed similar sites apart all over Wiltshire, and from the road-building and housing development that has gobbled up land like a hungry ogre.

Ancient monuments are not the only beneficiaries of the Army's presence on Salisbury Plain. The MoD land here comprises 60 per cent of all Europe's chalk downland left unspoiled by modern farming. The plain is an SSSI (Site of Special Scientific Interest), and also an SPA (Special Protection Area) for birds: hen harrier and hobby hunt here, skylark and whinchat nest, the rare stone curlew breeds in shallow scrapes. The great bustard, a giant turkey-like bird in handsome chestnut-and-white plumage, has been reintroduced after an absence of nearly 200 years. As for the rare marsh fritillary (the largest population in the UK) and the uncommon chalkhill blue butterflies, the brown hares that breed and feed in the long grass, the beautiful Deptford pinks and yellow

horseshoe vetch and reddish-purple betony and other plants of dry chalky grasslands – they flourish here among the crumps and bangs of military training.

One of the best ways to enjoy an overview of the plain is to follow the Imber Range Perimeter Path, a 30-mile footpath around the rim. Huge bowls of open chalk grassland lie beyond the safety strip inside the path, a snapshot of the southern downs of England as they were in the days before modern agriculture. No trees have been planted because of the necessity of keeping lines of artillery fire clear. The fires caused by shells and other explosions have the effect of clearing scrub and cleaning up any disease in the soil, as well as turning over the earth. Scrub trees make green patches in the seas of pale grass, and you can watch the hawks and harriers planing over the wide expanses of the Westdown Impact Area. There is so much colour from the wild flowers, so much birdsong and insect humming, that the experience of walking the plain becomes almost hallucinatory – and poignant, too; a savouring of the natural treasures of a now vanished countryside.

51. WEST KENNET LONG BARROW AND SILBURY HILL, WILTSHIRE

Maps: OS Explorer 157; Landranger 173

Travel: A4 from Marlborough towards Calne. Pass B4003 turning for Avebury. Silbury Hill (OS ref. 100685) is another ¾ mile on the right off A4. Park here on left, near entrance to footpath to West Kennet Long Barrow (105677).

Though 1,000 years separates the building of West Kennet Long Barrow from that of Silbury Hill, the two ancient monuments make such a striking pair in the billowing chalk downland of north Wiltshire that they seem to belong together. Nearby Avebury, the village that lies caught inside a giant stone circle, is a good base from which to explore a landscape extraordinarily full of stone and earth monuments – standing stones, circles, avenues, alignments and tombs.

Of the tombs, West Kennet Long Barrow is the most remarkable, lying at the crest of a rise in full view of Silbury Hill. This is the largest communal chambered tomb in Britain, its entrance guarded by massive stones like a giant's broken teeth, each many tons in weight, which look as impressive today as they must have done to those who built the structure around 3250 BC. Its long green back is bright with cornfield flowers: field scabious, knapweed, corn cockle. Crouching to shuffle inside, you find at the eastern end of the stone-lined passage a chamber, lit by a roof opening, with five burial compartments opening off it. Here the remains of forty-six people have been excavated – men and women, old and young. Bone analysis shows that arthritis and tooth trouble were two of their afflictions, and this homely detail seems to bring these distant ancestors close and into focus.

The long barrow was in use for around 1,000 years, and was then sealed up. This happened at about 2500 BC – the era when descendants of the original tomb-builders were constructing Silbury Hill in the shallow valley half a mile to the north. What was it that drove people already fully stretched by the rigours of subsistence living to create a flat-topped artificial hill 130 feet high?

They planned their creation very carefully, mounding it up around a core of chalk-block walls radiating out like spokes from a wheel hub. They shifted over a million cubic feet of chalk to build the mound.

Silbury Hill must have shone like a beacon in the landscape when completed, a gleaming, snow-white magnet for all eyes. Was it a focus for ceremonies, a royal place of enthronement, a grandstand for priestly ritual or pronouncement? The core has been probed, the top bored into, the sides trenched and examined over the centuries; but we are no nearer discovering the whys or the wherefores of Silbury Hill.

52. BARBURY CASTLE, WILTSHIRE

Maps: OS Explorer 157; Landranger 173

Travel: From M4 Junction 16, follow 'Wroughton' signs. In Wroughton, left on A361 for 200 yards to roundabout; right up Priors Hill. In 2½ miles park at top of hill (OS ref. 145764) and follow Ridgeway National Trail up to Barbury Castle.

The Marlborough Downs are rich in ancient sites, and the Iron Age hill fort of Barbury Castle is one of the most impressive. Its double ramparts on the crest of Barbury Down are seen from miles away. Close to, you can appreciate how formidable such a chalk and soil earthworks, the outer ring solidified with stone and the inner topped with a wooden palisade, would have seemed to any potential attackers. Even so, in AD 556 a Saxon army beat a force of British defenders here, and named the hill fort Beranburgh in honour of their king, Bera. Walking the ramparts in fine summer weather among blue drifts of harebells and scabious, you can see 30 miles across the downs, with the hill forts of Liddington and Uffington clearly in view away to the north-east. Supply was no problem for inhabitants of Barbury Castle: the ancient track known as Smeathe's Ridge (nowadays the Ridgeway National Trail) runs right through the fort, while the original course of the Ridgeway passes immediately to the north.

Barbury was superbly sited for defence. This was a valuable place to have and hold for at least 1,000 years of turbulent history in the South Country. Those who commanded the stronghold left their possessions in the earth to be excavated 2,000 years later: the nave-ring or hub-cap of a chariot wheel, Iron Age blacksmith's tools and Roman coins and jewellery. Barbury was a place of burial, too. A woman of royal descent was interred in the Bronze Age disc barrow on the hill, and skeletons have been found elsewhere in the hill fort, which confirm the status of the summit as a favoured cemetery.

In among the grassland flowers in summer

Barbury Castle

you'll find brimstones, the butter-yellow butterflies with the single orange dot on each wing. They are essentially creatures of woodland, but here on the chalky down they find their food plant, buckthorn, and so breed and thrive. Fritillaries are here – another species you would generally associate with woods, but they have their food plant, violets, available on Barbury. The grasses are alive with bees and grasshoppers, too, making soft creaky summer music.

53. NORTH MEADOW, CRICKLADE, WILTSHIRE

Maps: OS Explorer 169; Landranger 163, 173

Travel: A419 to Cricklade, Thames Path National Trail through reserve is signed from north-west edge of town (OS ref. 095942).

North Meadow National Nature Reserve is a rare survival, a traditionally managed wildflower meadow in the valley of the River Thames where most such hayfields have been 'improved' out of existence or destroyed by gravel quarrying. The meadow is managed by Natural England in partnership with its long-time owners and farmers, the burgesses of Cricklade. Keeping to the old ways of management has preserved a hay-meadow flora of a type which has all but disappeared from Britain since intensive farming and the widespread use of chemicals were introduced in the later half of the twentieth century.

The grass and its flowers are left uncut until after the beginning of July, by which time they have set their seeds. Grass cutting for hay is finished by mid-August, and then cattle are put on to graze and dung the meadow until winter, when the adjacent Thames and Churn rivers spill over and spread nutritious silt with their floodwater. From early spring onwards the floods recede and the cycle begins again with the growth of new grass. This natural process produces a wonderful spring and summer flora which spatters the meadow with yellow of cowslips and yellow rattle, pale pink and mauve of marsh orchids and milkmaids, and creamy white of ox-eye daisies and frothy champagne-scented meadowsweet.

The flower that people flock here to see each April and May, however, is the snake's-head fritillary, a showy member of the lily family with a large drooping head, purple with pale spots, shaped like a bell and nodding with every breath of wind. The colony of many thousands in North Meadow is Britain's largest, and may account for up to 80 per cent of the total UK population – for the snake's-head fritillary is a flower of damp, unploughed meadows, and those are no longer part of a modern farmer's agenda.

54. SAVERNAKE FOREST, WILTSHIRE

Maps: OS Explorer 157; Landranger 174, 173

Travel: A346 from Marlborough towards Salisbury. In ½ mile, turn left into Savernake Forest to find Postern Hill Forestry Commission Office (OS ref. 198679; leaflets and information).

Savernake Forest occupies a neat triangle just south of Marlborough and the valley of the River Kennet. These 5,000 acres of beech and oak woods are at least 1,000 years old, a royal hunting forest of Norman kings that carefully preserves its deer, rare plants and fungi. The current Earl of Cardigan is the 31st Hereditary Warden of Savernake, a line that stretches back to the Norman Conquest. This is an ancient place.

A good way to explore the forest is to follow the paths as laid out in Savernake Parish Council's handy map-and-information pamphlet. Walkers can wander where they like here, and soon come to appreciate the great network of radial rides that all meet at the central point known as Eight Walks. These rides were laid out in the eighteenth century by Warden Thomas Brudenell Bruce, and still form the basis of paths and bridleways in the forest.

Dotted through the forest are some huge old veteran trees. The Great Beech stands a little back from Grey Ride, off White Road, its stout branches stretching 100 feet upwards from where they sprout at the top of a massive stub of a trunk. How its slender 'wrist' supports such an enormous canopy is a mystery. Further along Grey Ride the giant Great Sweet Chestnut displays deeply fissured bark like the skin of a very old man, its limbs splintered and partly shed. Off Church Walk, the oak known as Old Paunchy projects a belly more ponderous than John Bull's; while just to the north, by the boundary fence, the Cathedral Oak, more of a monolith than a tree, measures 37 feet round the waist and hoists a widespread and shattered crown murmurous with bees and flies. The oldest tree of all is probably the Big Belly Tree, which stands at the edge of Savernake, beside the A346. Its waist measures a mighty 36 feet, and round the base it is almost 50 feet. This king of oaks, gnarled and contorted, with goblin faces to be imagined in the lumps and bumps of its battered trunk, could well date back to Saxon times, long before the Normans ever hunted through the forest.

55. THE HARROWAY AT 'EFRAFA', NEAR OVERTON, HAMPSHIRE

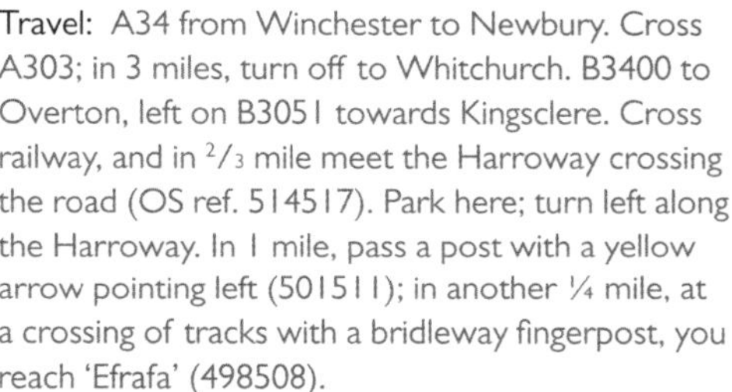

Maps: OS Explorer 144; Landranger 185

Travel: A34 from Winchester to Newbury. Cross A303; in 3 miles, turn off to Whitchurch. B3400 to Overton, left on B3051 towards Kingsclere. Cross railway, and in 2/3 mile meet the Harroway crossing the road (OS ref. 514517). Park here; turn left along the Harroway. In 1 mile, pass a post with a yellow arrow pointing left (501511); in another ¼ mile, at a crossing of tracks with a bridleway fingerpost, you reach 'Efrafa' (498508).

Nearest railway station: Overton (1 mile)

'Harrow Way' says the OS map legend beside the old track, in the Gothic font that signifies an antiquity. And there is no more antique road in Britain than the old Harroway track. It runs some 200 miles across the south of England, in some parts a modern motor road, in others a sunken lane. That is its condition up here on the Hampshire Downs, a rutted, deeply scored highway between vast old hedges, used nowadays by no one except walkers, riders and occasional off-road drivers. The Harroway may have been in use for as long as 7,000 years, but it runs all but forgotten these days, a magnificent ancient trackway gone back to the wild with a covering of beech and ash, oak and venerable yews, with spindle berries and bryony in its margins and birds thronging its hedges.

A mile or so along the Harroway west of its crossing with the Overton road is another crossing, this one of woodland tracks. This is the location that Richard Adams chose in his classic animal tale *Watership Down* for Efrafa, the rabbit warren run like a fascist dictatorship by the enormous and fearsome

General Woundwort. This is the spot to which our heroes Bigwig and Hazel come to steal does for their warren on Watership Down, a couple of miles to the north. Their seduction of the does, the chase down the hill with General Woundwort on their heels, and their audacious escape downriver are the stuff of dreams – or nightmares. There are still rabbits burrowing in the banks of the Harroway around the old crossroads, and children with very sharp eyes and even sharper imaginations may possibly spot some familiar faces …

56. FIVE LANES END, HAMPSHIRE

Maps: OS Explorer 144; Landranger 186

Travel: From M3 Junction 5, A287 towards Farnham. Turn immediately right to reach Greywell in 1 mile. Park at Fox & Goose pub (please ask permission first, and give the pub your custom). Walk forward along village street and out along Nately Road. At ¼ mile out of Greywell on a right bend, keep ahead (OS ref. 712509) along White Lane farm track. Follow it for 1 mile to Five Lanes End (696502).

Nearest railway station: Hook (3½ miles)

Five Lanes End is a mysterious place, full of resonance for anyone with a feeling for ancient landscapes and their trackways. You can approach it from five directions, as the name suggests. The first, recommended above, comes up south-west from Greywell village along an old track called White Lane, probably named because of the colour of its surface – chalk white in the dust of summer, pale batter colour in the sludge of winter. From the opposite direction White Lane climbs gently north-east all the way from Alton, an ancient fording place across the River Wey. A third approach is from the direction of Old Basing in the north-west by way of Down Lane, which joins up below Five Lanes End with a very old droving route known as Andwell Drove.

The fourth and fifth old roads to meet at Five Lanes End are the east and west continuations of the Harroway (see p. 75), a trackway so old that it has probably been in use for 7,000 years and pre-dates all other roads in Britain. Any of these ancient ways is worth exploring. Their deeply rutted courses, overhung with bushes, and the glimpses of rolling downland country they permit every now and then through their thick hedges, mean they are hidden away in the landscape, so that only those who set out on foot can find them. The presence of the occasional mountain biker or 4-wheel driver does not dispel their sense of secrecy. Even when they converge at the gentle summit of Five Lanes End, a place of rest and rendezvous for travellers, drovers and packmen in past centuries, the big old beeches that grow widely spaced there do not allow more than a partial, green-tinted view of the outer world.

57. NUTBOURNE MARSHES, WEST SUSSEX

Maps: OS Explorer 120; Landranger 197

Travel: A259 Chichester towards Havant; turn left in Nutbourne beside church; in 300 yards, footpath on left (OS ref. 777053) leads to Nutbourne Marshes and sea-wall path.

Nearest railway station: Southbourne (1 mile)

The 940 acres of Nutbourne Marshes form a wide stretch of intertidal saltmarsh and mudflats between the chunky peninsulas of Thorney Island and Chidham. The mudflats are accessible to humans only by shallow boat or canoe, inaccessible at low tide except along the narrow Thorney Channel. There was a quarry, a busy mill and plenty of toing and froing of coastal boats in former times. In the late nineteenth century attempts were made to reclaim two areas of marsh for agriculture, North and South Stakes. The sea soon broke through. Nowadays the wooden stakes that shored up the sea banks of the two artificial islets are the only reminders of the venture. The flat muds are left to the shelduck, oystercatchers and egrets, and the countless trillions of tiny invertebrates that inhabit the banks of the rithes or creeks.

The marshes offer winter refuge to more than 50,000 waders and wildfowl, and the birdwatching is tremendous at this time of the year, with brent geese, wigeon, godwit, dunlin and other species gathered in large flocks. In late summer the muds are green with the fleshy branched sprouts of glasswort, while down at the tip of the peninsula pink catkin-like flowers haze the tamarisk bushes and striped acorns swell in the twisted branches of a line of bent old oaks clinging precariously to the crumbling yellow clay cliffs.

Erosion is also a problem for humans here, as the rising sea eats away at the margins of the peninsula. Smashed and smoothed chunks of concrete along the shore show where old defences have been broken by the tides, and a new sea bank has been built well inland, part of the process of yielding farmland to the encroaching sea that is diplomatically styled 'managed realignment'. This wild place, like many along our southern shores, looks set to become wilder still.

58. KINGLEY VALE, WEST SUSSEX

Maps: OS Explorer 120; Landranger 197

Travel: From Chichester, B2178 to East Ashling; at left bend, right on minor road ('West Stoke, Lavant'). In $^{2}/_{3}$ mile, left (brown 'National Nature Reserve' sign) to West Stoke car park on right (OS ref. 825088). Through kissing gate; follow track north to kissing gate into NNR. Bear left on footpath just inside fence; follow uphill for $^{1}/_{3}$ mile to yew grove on right (819105). Continue along waymarked path to make clockwise circuit of reserve.

Nearest railway station: Bosham (3 miles from West Stoke car park)

At one time motorists could drive from West Stoke to the foot of Kingley Vale. Pedestrianizing the approach road seems to have deterred a great proportion of car-borne visitors, much to the benefit of the downland nature reserve, with its air of being not quite part of this world. Hurtling cyclists on the flint and chalk trackways add their own brand of hazard to the expedition, though.

Essentially there are two parts to Kingley Vale National Nature Reserve – the cool, dark and secretive woodlands blanketing its slopes, and the warm, dry and open chalk grassland that lies on the south-facing brow of the downs above the trees. These grazed grasslands are composed more of flowering plants than of grasses, a tight-packed sward rich in thyme and marjoram, with scabious, harebells, pink centaury, bird's-foot trefoil and dozens more species attracting clouds of blues, coppers, browns and other butterflies. By contrast, the sombre yew grove that colonizes the steep east-facing slope on the west edge of the reserve seems barren of all life except that of its ancient occupants.

Unlike the overall sprouting growth of the solitary Crowhurst Yew (see p. 96), the yews of Kingley Vale are green only in their upper canopy. They have shaded out the sun from their whole company. Their limbs, contorted with age and effort to reach a glint of sunlight, are iron-hard close to the trunks, but so brittle towards the extremities that they snap off at any pressure. The trunks of the oldest yews in the grove – at least 500 years old, but some of them harking back 2,000 years or more – resemble skinless torsos rather than living wood, knotted and seamed with raised ridges like a strongman's muscles. The yews grow in a wide variety of forms; some give the appearance of having been coppiced, with multiple limbs swirling this way and that from a central stool. Perhaps they were indeed used in this way; yew wood, hard and springy as steel, was the choice of bow-makers in medieval times.

Nothing grows in the shadow of the yews. They preside over empty, shady slopes of flint, chalk and their own tindery flakings and droppings. Druids worshipped them and armourers harvested them, but nothing can live with them.

59. PAGHAM HARBOUR, WEST SUSSEX

Maps: OS Explorer 120; Landranger 197

Travel: A27 to Chichester; B2145 towards Selsey. Pagham Harbour Local Nature Reserve Visitor Centre is signposted on left 1 mile south of Sidlesham. Park here (OS ref. 865976). Footpaths encircle Pagham Harbour.

Nearest railway station: Chichester (6 miles)

Pagham Harbour's 1,600 acres of reed-beds and mudflats, meadows and woodlands, shingle and seashore resemble a big salty bite taken out of the southern flank of the West Sussex shoreline. They are a birdwatcher's delight. Dedicated twitchers who visit this reserve can tick nearly 300 species off their lists. In winter it is packed with wildfowl on retreat from the big freeze further north, while in summer the waders take over.

But you don't need to be an ornithologist to appreciate this wonderful place. People come to stroll the seawalls of Pagham Harbour to get away from the crowded holiday beaches and tourist traps of the Sussex coast, to wind down and be easy where everything is green and slow-going. Into a coastline of almost unbroken ribbon development Pagham Harbour pushes its meandering creeks, silty lagoons and channels, a gleaming world of low-tide mudflats and weed-green islets. At high tides the sea moves in through a narrow gap in the shingle bank, spreading out to fill the shallow basin of the harbour and lap up against flood walls more than a mile inland.

The heart of Pagham Harbour, washed twice a day by tides, picked over by seabirds, is free of human influence. That wasn't always the case. The harbour began to silt up from the eighteenth century onwards, and by the turn of the twentieth century the narrowing sea entrance had become blocked. The whole area was reclaimed for corn growing. Contemporary photographs show a solid prairie of barley stretching from one side of Pagham Harbour to the other. But at Christmas 1910 a ferocious gale drove a high tide onshore to punch a new hole in the shingle bank and recapture the basin for the sea. This present century will see high tides reclaim far more of the flat Selsey Peninsula than merely Pagham Harbour as sea levels continue to rise. But for now the wide inlet continues to thrive half in and half out of the sea.

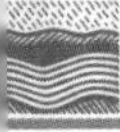

60. ASHDOWN FOREST, EAST SUSSEX

Maps: OS Explorer 135, Landranger 187, 188

Travel: From M25 Junction 6, A22 through East Grinstead. At Wych Cross, 2 miles south of Forest Row, left at traffic lights. Ashdown Forest Centre is 1 mile on left, opposite Ashdown Park Hotel. Park in car park (OS ref. 433323).

Nearest railway station: East Grinstead (5 miles)

Along the High Weald of Sussex lies Ashdown Forest, a delicate, irreplaceable mosaic of heath and scrub, woodland and wetland – not quite the dark, impenetrable blocks of trees that most people associate with the word 'forest', nor the dull and uniform conifer armies of the old-fashioned Forestry Commission kind. Ashdown is a real forest, wild in its diversity and in the way that nature operates so many systems with such brilliant counterbalance, requiring only as much human influence as will keep road-building, housing development, litter and fag-end fires at bay.

That is the job of the Conservators of Ashdown Forest, and their Forest Centre is a good place to get an overview before setting out on foot to explore. This was a Norman royal hunting forest, an exclusion zone where only local commoners were allowed to enter for the purpose of gathering firewood and animal bedding, and grazing their cattle and pigs. By the end of the seventeenth century the forest was beginning to be broken up for private ownership; it took another 200 years for the Board of Conservators to be set up, but once they were in control they made sure that what remained was properly protected.

By the middle of the twentieth century Ashdown was bald, a place of bare slopes whose tree cover had almost all been felled for iron-working charcoal or for timber or fuel. Since the Second World War trees have been growing at a great rate – so much so that grazing has been reintroduced to control the scrub. As a direct result songbirds, fallow deer, dragonflies, rare plants and a whole cornucopia of insects flourish here in a way they do not in the surrounding intensively farmed or built-up areas. Boggy stream valleys rich in mosses and ferns lead to heathery hillsides and wooded ridges.

Here and there clumps of conifers stand out; they were introduced by former landowners to vary the monotony of the bald hillsides. The clump at Gill's Lap (OS ref. 469319), 2 miles east of the Forest Centre, was inspiration for A. A. Milne's enchanted wood, Galleon's Lap, where Christopher Robin and Pooh bid a poignant farewell to childhood and to innocence in the last Pooh Bear story.

61. MALLING DOWN, EAST SUSSEX

Maps: OS Explorer 122; Landranger 198

Travel: Either on foot from Wheatsheaf Gardens or Mill Road in Lewes, or follow footpath from lay-by with parking spaces on B2192, ½ mile west of Ringmer (OS ref. 434115), off A26 on northern outskirts of Lewes.

Nearest railway station: Lewes (1 mile)

Viewed from southern Lewes during the spring, the slopes of Malling Down immediately to the east seem to have been washed pale yellow. The same effect is seen on the cushion of ground that swells at the far end of the Coombe, the tremendously steep east–west valley that cleaves the down in two. The yellow drifts are cowslips, to be replaced later in the year by the stronger, more sulphurous yellow of horseshoe vetch. These are just two of the dozens of flower species flourishing here that are characteristic of ancient, unploughed chalk grassland, a rare habitat that is becoming rarer by the decade.

A casual glance into the Coombe with its precipitous slopes tells you why it has escaped the plough, and a struggle up its flanks reinforces the lesson. Here on the north-facing slope common spotted orchids spread a mauve sheet in summer, while the south-facing flanks are full of the orange-yellow conquistadors' helmets of bird's-foot trefoil,

Malling Down

the yellow tresses of lady's bedstraw and the round sky-blue buttons of scabious. Intensely blue adonis blue butterflies and their more silver-blue and gregarious chalkhill blue cousins flit around the horseshoe vetch, which is their source of nectar and the food plant of their green-and-yellow caterpillars. A careful search will reveal the tiny white flowers of eyebright (bathe your eyes in their dew to gain a pair of irresistibly lustrous orbs, says the old wives' tale) and the pink stars of common centaury.

These treasures of flowers and blue butterflies are the chief glory of the Coombe. Footpaths lead through the old abandoned chalk quarries in the north face of Malling Hill, up round the inner end of the Coombe and through scrubland and trees on to the back of Malling Down itself, the more southerly of the two halves of the down. Here, high above the town, you can stand among horseshoe vetch and pinky-purple wild thyme, looking south over a magnificent prospect of the South Downs and the gap carved in their chalk rampart by the snaking River Ouse.

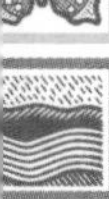

62. LULLINGTON HEATH, EAST SUSSEX

Maps: OS Explorer 123; Landranger 199

Travel: From A259 between Eastbourne and Seaford, turn north on minor roads either to Litlington or Jevington. The east–west downland footpath that connects these two villages runs through Lullington Heath (OS grid square 5401), which is about 1 mile from either village.

Nearest railway station: Eastbourne (4½ miles via South Downs Way, 6 miles by road from Jevington)

Lowland heath is a tremendously diminished habitat in the south-east of England, thanks mostly to twentieth-century ploughing, road-building and housing development. Lullington Heath Nature Reserve, carefully maintained by Natural England, lies in a superb location high on the South Downs north of the white chalk cliffs of the Seven Sisters (see below). The heath straddles a ridge and slopes quite steeply to the south and west. Plenty of sun reaches Lullington Heath, warming the bell heather and ling and causing the bilberries to swell purple and plump by autumn.

Lullington Heath

Heathers and bilberries are plants of acid soils; the remarkable thing about Lullington Heath is that it is based on soil that is slightly acid but also retains the alkaline properties of chalk. So here are fragrant wild thyme and the brushy, red-bristled heads of salad burnet, which both appreciate the lime in the grassland that mixes with the lowland heath. Insect species abound; there are sixty or more kinds of spider, for example. Bird life is abundant. All this wildlife thrives here in a habitat which has been vanishing rapidly from this part of the world. East Sussex probably retains only half the lowland heath it possessed two centuries ago, and most of that is in Ashdown Forest (see p. 79); West Sussex has lost over 90 per cent of what it had around the turn of the nineteenth century. These 140 acres are a rare and precious survival of this highly specialized and fragile wild environment.

63. SEVEN SISTERS, EAST SUSSEX

Maps: OS Explorer 123; Landranger 199

Travel: From A259 Eastbourne towards Seaford, take minor road south from East Dean to Birling Gap and park car here (OS ref. 555960), or take footpath south from Exceat (car park at 518995) for 1½ miles to Cuckmere Haven (516977). The Seven Sisters lie between Birling Gap and Cuckmere Haven.

Nearest railway station: Eastbourne (5 miles on foot from Birling Gap via Beachy Head and South Downs Way)

The Seven Sisters and their neighbouring cliffs of Belle Tout and Beachy Head

Seven Sisters

form the most impressive run of chalk cliffs in Britain. The Seven Sisters present a magnificent 2 miles of white sea rampart that stretches west from Birling Gap to the mouth of the Cuckmere River at Cuckmere Haven. They are topped by a sward of chalk downland grasses and flowers, and have at their feet a jumbled beach of fallen boulders and round flint pebbles. The seven peaks are not too easy to distinguish, but reading westward they are Went Hill, Bailey's Hill, Flat Hill (it truly is flat), Brass Point, Rough Brow, Short Brow and Haven Brow. Between the hills, points and brows lie the Bottoms, dry valleys that decline to the edges of the cliffs. The Seven Sisters do not even reach 300 feet in height. In comparison to the 530-foot monster of Beachy Head they are small fry. But something in their solid togetherness, the extent of the high wall and the battered beach, lend them a special force and impressiveness.

The Seven Sisters are eroding on average about 16 inches a year, and at a rate that is increasing as sea levels rise and storms – probably owing to the effects of climate change – become fiercer. The sea eats into and undercuts the base of the cliffs, causing them to become unstable; rainwater seeps through crevices in the chalk and cracks them apart from on high. Occasionally there are spectacular cliff falls, but mostly it is a steady and gradual rate of attrition, sending more chalk and flint on to the beach, staining the water a milky grey after a storm and exposing fossils of sea urchins, crinoids and bivalve shellfish for hunters to collect. Seen at such times in a mist of sea spray, shuddering to the thump of big waves, it is hard to reconcile these wild Seven Sisters with the calm and reassuringly solid white face they show on gentle sunny days.

64. PEVENSEY LEVELS, EAST SUSSEX

Maps: OS Landranger 199; Explorer 123, 124

Travel: From A27/A259 roundabout at Pevensey on north-east outskirts of Eastbourne, take the Wartling road. In 300 yards, turn left ('Rickney') on minor road across Pevensey Levels.

At first glance the Pevensey Levels, like their larger eastern neighbour Romney Marsh, seem thoroughly tamed by agriculture. The former tidal flats, drained and brought under cultivation from medieval times onward, lie in hedged and ditched oblongs of green pasture grazed by sheep and cattle, with isolated clusters of farmhouses and buildings standing out along the minor road that snakes from Pevensey to Horse Eye. A lonely, cut-off place, bleak enough in foul weather – but not really wild.

For me, the key to the wildness of the levels lies in the very thing that has served to tame them – the system of man-made watercourses and ditches that drain the fields while giving them shape. In the lush overgrowth of summer these fleets, sewers, streams, havens, dykes and guts (what a pungent treasure of names for muddy ditches) burst out in a smother of green weed, crowfoot and marsh marigold, which swells from the watercourses to invade the margins of roads and fields. Feathery reeds and busby-flowered bulrushes reach skywards, and colour comes from the shocking pink of great willowherb, the flat orange-yellow flowers of common fleabane, and the powder-puff blue flower heads of water mint, whose leaves, when you squeeze them, release a beautiful minty fragrance.

Pevensey Levels

Apart from the distant growl of a tractor all is quiet out among the ditches; but a background murmur is always present on hot summer days, the drowsy hum of bees and iridescent flies on the flowering plants. The large dragonflies that hover over the weed-choked ditches before flicking abruptly away seem, by contrast, completely silent, until you catch the almost imperceptible whirr of their glassy wings. As with many wild places throughout Britain, the wildness of the Pevensey Levels is of narrow and very localized focus.

65. GUESTLING WOOD, EAST SUSSEX

Maps: OS Landranger 199; Explorer 124

Travel: On A259 from Hastings towards Rye, turn right at Robin Hood pub in Icklesham down Water Mill Lane. Guestling Wood car park is 1½ miles on right (OS ref. 863145).

Nearest railway station: Three Oaks (2 miles by roads and paths)

Clinging to the flanks of a knoll deep in the countryside, Guestling Wood is full of surprises. Though apparently a dense mass of trees, it is seamed with old holloways cutting down through the Wealden clay banks to clearings in the woodland floor. The banks of the stream here at the bottom of the slope are dense with the strong-scented leaves and tiny green flowers of dog's mercury, a plant characteristic of shady old woods. The humps and hollows of former clay-pits lie under the trees, and you can follow the course of the ancient banks and ditches, now flattening out, which once delineated different segments of the wood.

There are stands of oak coppice and a little hornbeam, but the chief glory is the sweet chestnut coppice, which accounts for at least three-quarters of the tree cover. Sheltered by tall oak standards, the sweet chestnut coppice varies from the most recent harvesting by the Woodland Trust who care for Guestling Wood, with tender shoots just beginning to emerge, to huge overshot stands where the stools (base tree stubs) are up to 5 and 6 feet across and the poles can be as thick as a man's leg and stretch up 60 feet high.

In the clearings grows a wonderful spring flora – carpets of bluebells and wood anemones, and later the tall nettle-like flowers of yellow archangel and mats of blue bugle. With their columnar rods reaching as high as a church nave and their leathery sawtoothed leaves thatching in the sky, the tall old sweet chestnuts cast a dappled shade over the holloways and bring an air of solemn dignity.

66. DUNGENESS, KENT

Maps: OS Explorer 125; Landranger 189

Travel: From M20 Junction 9, A2070 through Ashford to Brenzett; A259 to Old Romney; left to Lydd. Left past church, right down Ness Road, over roundabout and on along Dungeness Road to the shore (OS ref. 090185)

Nearest railway station: Dungeness (Romney, Hythe & Dymchurch Railway – www.rhdr.org.uk)

There is no place in Britain like Dungeness – nowhere with such a bizarre combination of empty space and man-made eccentricity. Here on the south-east tip of Kent, poking into the English Channel, is a vast arrowhead of shingle that plays host to hundreds of rare bird and animal species, lonely, unspoiled and beautiful. Here, too, are the giant grey blocks of twin nuclear power stations, rows of marching pylons and a spatter of shack-like dwellings shaped and decorated exactly as their owners please. Dungeness challenges us to reflect on what we mean by 'wild'. Unsullied, untouched by human influence? Certainly not. Remote, huge, moody? Absolutely.

With its RSPB reserve and observatory Dungeness is one of Britain's prime bird-watching and recording sites. Here in winter you can expect to see pintail and wigeon, teal and greylag geese, with seabirds cutting over the sea: eider drakes, Arctic skua with scarlet bills, scoter, kittiwakes with dark-tipped wings. Salt-tolerant shore plants sprout in the spring and summer – blue sea holly, crinkle-leaved sea kale, delicate yellow-horned poppy, sky-blue viper's bugloss. In among the birds and flowers trudge the Dungeness fishermen, members of tight-knit families who have fished from the shingle bank for generations. Home-made tram tracks across the pebbles carry their gear between the boats and their black-tarred huts. Tangles of fishing net, bulbous pink floats, fish boxes and rusty winches lie scattered around.

In spite of all this human clutter it is the birds and the shore plants, the enormous inverted bowl of the sky and the long reach of shingle that hold your attention. Boats, huts, shingle ridges and sea make a composition for an Impressionist. The giant grey cubes and pylon ranks of the power station seem insubstantial by comparison, in a place where you can walk away and soon see no one at all.

67. GOODWIN SANDS, KENT

Maps: The Goodwins do not appear on any OS map, so you will only be able to reach them if you're very lucky or resourceful!

The Goodwin Sands lie 3 miles off Deal on the east Kent coast, a ragged-edged block of sand 10 miles from tip to toe and about 5 across the waist. Twice a day they break the sea surface. Seen from the Saxon Shore Way on the cliffs, they roll clear of the falling tide like the gleaming shoulder of the Leviathan.

> *Antonio hath a ship of rich lading wracked on the narrow seas; the Goodwins, I think they call the place; a very dangerous flat, and fatal, where the carcasses of many a tall ship lie buried …*

So Shakespeare framed the bad news of Antonio's lost cargo in *The Merchant of Venice*. Mention of the Goodwins would have sent a prickle of fear up the necks of his audience. Back in the days of sail, negotiating the Goodwin Sands in a Dover Straits fog or a south-west gale was a sailor's nightmare. Situated where they are, right in the path of vessels plying between London, the Channel ports and the Continental coast, the sands form a deadly obstacle. Running aground here usually meant a violent and terrifying death. Survivors spoke of ships striking the sands with a thunderous crash, masts and rigging tumbling. Most of those who survived the impact would be crushed to death between waves and sand, or drowned as the tide swept them away. The glutinous sand of the reef, liquefying as the rising tide separated its particles, would hold and suck down the remains of the wreck. Come daylight, investigating boatmen from Deal might find a complete ship stuck in the sands, or perhaps only a funnel or a set of disembodied masts. Sometimes the suction was so powerful that a vessel wrecked at night would entirely vanish before morning.

Famous wrecks are legion. A Dover-to-Ostend steamer rammed the Goodwins in a snowstorm in 1857; all that was found of her was a single lifebelt marked with her name, *Violet*. There was the wreck of the schooner *Lady Lovibond* in February 1748, in which her captain and his newly wed bride were drowned; the wreck was engineered by the mate, who was hopelessly in love with the skipper's wife. Then there was the extraordinary reappearance of *Sterling Castle*, a battleship wrecked on 27 November 1703 with the loss of 279 lives. She was found by divers in 1979, and in 1998 she became exposed again when the sands shifted, far down in the sides of a giant sand hole, her all but complete hull piled with swords, musketoons, navigation instruments, the leather hats of the sailors, and also their skulls and bones.

The Goodwins are not always so savage. In calm weather on a low tide, cricket matches have been played here. People have bicycled here and played golf, bowls and football. In 1705 the diarist John Evelyn's brother-in-law, Granville, was buried in the Sands wrapped in lead. There is even a Goodwin Sands Potholing Club, a charitable organization that arranges ad hoc visits to the sands on low tides. The vast sandbank, accessible only at haphazard times, makes the perfect display ground for the multiform branches of British eccentricity. But this 'most dreadful gulfe and shippe swallower' allows no liberties. One hour on sufferance, and then trespassers must be gone before the solid ground turns to a sucking morass and the brief welcome of the Goodwin Sands becomes a deadly embrace.

68. THAMES ESTUARY FORTS

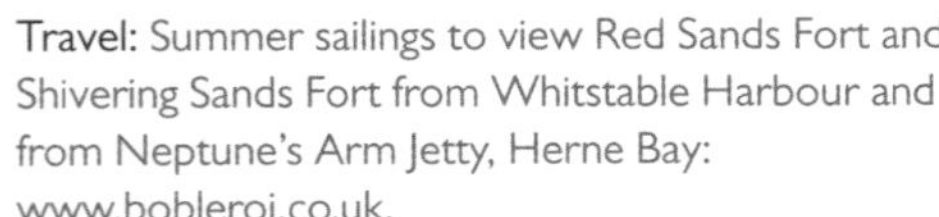

Travel: Summer sailings to view Red Sands Fort and Shivering Sands Fort from Whitstable Harbour and from Neptune's Arm Jetty, Herne Bay: www.bobleroi.co.uk.

Nearest railway stations: Whitstable, Herne Bay

Of all the wild places in the south of England, the Thames Estuary Army and Navy forts are the most strange and remote. As you sail out from Whitstable across the mouth of the Thames, a cluster of dots on the northern horizon gradually resolve themselves into a group of six structures that resemble robots from *Star Wars* more than they do any conventional fortification. Battered by storms, salt-bitten, rusty and decrepit, standing in the sea on four splayed legs, they are the component parts of Red Sands Fort, built to guard the Thames Estuary during the Second World War and the subject of controversy ever since. They are too dangerous to enter, too much of a hazard to be left where they are – and yet too historic to be demolished out of hand.

Altogether seven forts were built to the plans of designer Guy Maunsell, heavily armed and towed out to be grounded on sandbanks off the Kent and Essex coasts. Of the originals, three have been destroyed. Four remain in situ, a headache to maritime authorities, a delight to lovers of outlandish wild places. Red Sands Fort's sister fort at Shivering Sands, another cluster of four-legged towers, was used to house Radio City and Radio Sutch, two of the short-lived pirate radio stations that broadcast from the abandoned forts in the 1960s.

The two other forts are of different construction: Knock John and Rough Tower are both composed of a pair of mighty cylindrical legs joined by a rectangular platform. Knock John, 8 miles out from Foulness Island, was the home of pirate

Red Sands Fort, Thames Estuary

station Radio Essex in the 1960s, and still stands on its sandbank today. As for Rough Tower, it has had a marvellously exciting and chequered history. It saw more action in the peacetime 1960s and 1970s than ever it did in the wartime 1940s, as rival groups of would-be pirate radio operators battled for control of the fort with petrol bombs, gunshots, helicopter raids and fisticuffs. The eventual victor, Roy Bates, proclaimed Rough Tower the 'Independent Principality of Sealand' in 1976, and as Prince Roy of Sealand he and his wife, Princess Joan, together with their daughter, Princess Penelope, and son, Crown Prince Michael, have ruled this tiny realm ever since. Within the hollow legs of Sealand are luxury apartments fit for a prince and his princess. Sealand has its own flag (a white diagonal on a red-and-black background) and a wordless national anthem entitled 'E Mare Libertas'. The royal family have issued their own stamps, passports and currency (the Sealand dollar). Their website, www.sealandgov.org, is a model of informative solemnity. The entire principality measures not more than 450 feet long and 130 feet wide.

69. ISLE OF SHEPPEY, KENT

Maps: OS Explorer 149; Landranger 178

Travel: From M25 Junction 2, A2 and M2 to Junction 5, A249 towards Sheerness. Right on B2231 through Eastchurch; in 1 mile, right on minor road for 4 miles via Elliotts Farm and Mocketts to St Thomas's Church (OS ref. 022662) and Ferry House Inn.

Nearest railway station: Queenborough at north-west end of Sheppey

Sheppey is an island of two halves. To the north rolls the clay ridge, lined with settlements of holiday chalets and caravan parks which peter out at the eastern end near Warden Point. Here the road comes to an end on the cliff edge, among the shells of abandoned houses and gardens that are falling one by one into the estuary.

To the south the ridge dips, levelling out in a great broad apron of dead-flat grazing marshes and damp green fields skirted by saltmarshes and broad hems of gleaming silver mud. Here the sounds are of wind in bent grasses, sheep bleating, and the cries of hundreds of thousands of seabirds. Gaunt, wind-bitten farms with bleak names – Mocketts, Great Bells, Old Hook – stand four-square among their big lonely marsh fields. This southern half of Sheppey is also divided in two. Elmley Island lies in the west, an RSPB reserve where redshank and dunlin probe the mud of the Swale channel and shaggy long-horned cattle graze the marshes. The south-eastern corner of Sheppey is known as the Isle of Harty, where a sea-wall path leads out to the isolated community of Shell Ness on a cockleshell strand. Saltmarsh and mudflats stretch out east, the winter larder of tens of thousands of wading birds: knot, dunlin, bar-tailed godwit, oystercatcher. Dark-bellied brent geese winter here, too, feeding on eel-grass.

On the southernmost point of Sheppey stands the tiny Norman church of St Thomas, the remotest church in Kent, just inland of the Ferry House Inn, the loneliest pub. Parts of the inn date back 500 years. It catered for travellers reaching Sheppey by the only means before Kingsferry Bridge was built – a small ferryboat across the Swale.

You can take your beer a few yards along the marsh path and feel as if you have the whole muddy, bird-haunted world to yourself. It seems quite impossible that central London is only an hour away.

70. BEDLAM'S BOTTOM, MEDWAY ESTUARY, KENT

Maps: OS Explorer 149, 163; Landranger 178

Travel: From M2 Junction 5, A749 towards Sheerness. Immediately before Kingsferry Bridge on to Isle of Sheppey, turn left ('Iwade'). Ignore Iwade turning immediately on left; continue along unsigned road. In 1 mile turn right up Raspberry Hill Lane; in 700 yards, park in little lay-by near stile on your right (OS ref. 894687). Go over stile ('Saxon Shore Way' fingerpost and waymark); follow path around shoreline of Bedlam's Bottom.

Nearest railway station: Swale Halt (1½ miles)

The estuary of the River Medway is wide, moody and muddy. Here, downriver of London, is a no man's land, a broad swathe of rivermouth country where the Medway winds lazily out between marsh islands to merge with the greater tideway of the River Thames. There are forts on some of these islands, redolent of mid nineteenth-century fears of a French invasion. The French grew to know the Medway well – not the dreaded invasion army (that never arrived), but Frenchmen of an earlier generation, prisoners of war from Napoleonic times. They were marooned in the estuary, many to sicken and die, on board rotting old prison ships, the famous 'hulks' of Charles Dickens's Kent marshes (see opposite). Their bodies were dug into the mud of Deadman's Island and Prisoner's Bank, where the earth is still blackened by the chemicals of their bones.

Bedlam's Bottom

This history lends melancholy to the muddy inlets here, and Bedlam Bottom is a fine example of such a place. A huge field of pale, ungrazed grass slopes to the sloppy brown shore. Golden eel-grasses and bright green weed fringe the mud where ancient wooden boats slowly rot, their strakes all split apart to show their barnacled and lichened ribs. In the distance the giant bow of Kingsferry Bridge and the power-station chimneys and pylons on the northern horizon are reminders of the modern world. But walking the sea wall of Bedlam's Bottom into a remote marsh peninsula with no roads or houses, hearing the piping of plovers and curlew, you feel you've travelled back a century in time.

71. GREAT EXPECTATIONS COUNTRY (CLIFFE, COOLING AND HALSTOW MARSHES), KENT

Maps: OS Explorer 163; Landranger 178

Travel: From M25 Junction 2, A2 east to Junction 1; A289, B2000 to Cliffe.

(a) Park here and walk west between lagoons for 2 miles to reach Cliffe Fort overlooking River Thames (OS ref. 707767).

(b) Turn right beyond Cliffe Church for 2 miles past Cooling Castle to reach Cooling Church (756760).

(c) Continue through Cooling and on for another 2 miles through High Halstow. At ¼ mile beyond village, left up minor road for 1½ miles to Swigshole (788775). Park (neatly, please) here and continue on foot, north for 1½ miles to reach Egypt Bay.

The great nose of marshes that sticks out north of Rochester along the southern shore of the Thames is forever associated with Charles Dickens – especially with the wildest of his tales, *Great Expectations*. As a boy growing up in early nineteenth-century Chatham, Dickens knew the marshes as a desolate place of fog, clanking gibbets and the deadly malarial fevers that were known as marsh agues. The opening scenes of *Great Expectations* carry that grim and forbidding atmosphere superbly, as young Pip is accosted by the dreadful Magwitch and scared into stealing for him. Despite the pylons and the flares and pipework of the giant Coryton oil refinery on the Essex shore, these 10 square miles of flat green country are still remarkably wild in aspect and mood.

The settings of four of the most atmospheric scenes from *Great Expectations* are easy to find. At Church Street just north of Higham stands St Mary's (OS ref. 716742), the lonely marsh church where Pip was terrified by Magwitch starting up from among the graves and tipping him upside down so that the steeple flew under his feet. Out on the bank of the Thames beyond some flooded pits is Cliffe Fort (707767), a fortification constructed in the 1870s to deter a possible invasion by the French. It stands on the site of the Tudor fort, also built against the French, where Pip ran through a Christmas morning fog to bring Magwitch a file and some 'wittles' that he had stolen from home. A gibbet on which were hung the corpses of executed pirates used to stand near by, and Dickens used his memories of it to put the frighteners yet further on poor Pip. Cliffe Fort, with its yawning tunnel mouths sprouting bushes, wildly overgrown, is a strange and creepy sight.

Across in Cooling, the village churchyard contains thirteen little lozenge-shaped stone tombs of infants from the local families of Comport and Baker, who died of marsh ague between 1771 and 1800. These were Dickens's inspiration for the tombs of Pip's brothers; Pip's childish belief from the shape of the monuments was that 'they had all been born on their backs with their hands in their trouser pockets'.

Out to the north of High Halstow a lonely marsh path brings you to Egypt Bay on the Kentish shore. Here Dickens saw the coastguard vessel *Swallow* at anchor, and remembering the convict prison ships that once moored in the Medway Estuary (see opposite) he transformed her into the terrible 'hulks' from which Magwitch had escaped – sinister presences among the fogs, from which cannon would boom out a warning to the villages of wild men on the run.

72. COLDRUM STONES, KENT

Maps: OS Explorer 148; Landranger 188

Travel: From M25 Junction 3, M20 to Junction 2; A227 towards Gravesend. In just over a mile, right on minor road signed 'Trottiscliffe'. Left along Church Lane in village, to pass church. In 300 yards, follow brown signs to parking place, then footpath fingerposts to the monument (OS ref. 654607).

Nearest railway stations: Borough Green and West Malling (5 miles)

The Neolithic long barrow of Coldrum Stones was raised on its steep little chalk knoll at the foot of the North Downs some time between 3000 BC and 2000 BC. The ancient trackways, now partly mingled together and known as the Pilgrim's Way and the North Downs Way, pass a few hundred yards to the north; they may have been in use for 1,000 years and more when the Coldrum Stones were erected.

The builders selected four enormous sarsens ('saracen' or 'stranger' stones from elsewhere) of grey-blue sandstone, which they squared and positioned as a tomb in the shape of a box, its mouth open towards the east. A fifth, smaller stone chocks in a gap. If there was a capstone, it has somehow vanished along with the earthen mound that originally enclosed the stone chamber. The tomb stands at the opening of a horseshoe of standing stones, fallen from the upright position in which they were first set. They frame the chamber stones like a necklace, lying in the shadow of ash, beech and field maple trees.

When the chamber was excavated in 1912 the remains of twenty-two people – men, women and children – were unearthed. Their status in life can only be guessed at, but they were probably of the Neolithic aristocracy. Communal burials of this sort are known in Denmark, and date from the most ancient late Stone Age culture of northern Europe.

Coldrum Stones

Pagan ceremonies at the site are not uncommon. When I visited the stones on a cold winter's night, I found a fire left smouldering in a neat little hearth dug into the turf. The branches of one of the guardian beech trees were hung with charms and tokens, ranging from a necklace of twisted silver strands to flints tied up in cloth strips and bows of gauze. Apart from the massive solidity of its chamber stones and their eye-catching positioning, what distinguishes the Coldrum monument is the continuing veneration in which some still hold it.

73. OLDBURY HILL FORT, KENT

Maps: OS Explorer 148; Landranger 188

Travel: M25 to Junction 3 (M20) or Junction 5 (M26).

(a) M20 to Junction 2, then A20, A227 to Borough Green; or M26 to Junction 2, then A20 to Wrotham Heath, A25 to Borough Green.

(b) From Borough Green, A25 towards Sevenoaks. Oldbury Hill lies ½ mile west of the Cob Tree Inn (OS ref. 592565) on A25.

Concealed perfectly among the woods on Oldbury Hill, so that you could very easily pass by on the A25 and never suspect the presence of one of the largest Iron Age fortified sites in Britain, Oldbury Fort is enormous. It occupies some 124 acres, a teardrop-shaped enclosure outlined by steep ramparts, built some time between 100 BC and 50 BC by a Wealden tribe of people native to north Kent. What they actually constructed it for is still, as with all these painstakingly fortified hilltop enclosures of the Iron Age, a mystery. Probably it was not continuously occupied. The most likely guess is that it was a place of temporary refuge for people and their animals in times of strife; though it's hard to see why they took such time and trouble to mound up earthen banks of such magnitude.

During its periods of occupation, Oldbury Hill Fort was a refuge for large numbers of people. Excavations have found traces of many hut circles and of pits that were used to hoard grain. There were gateways on the north and south angles of the enclosure to accommodate an ancient trackway running north from a port at Pevensey, on the south Kent coast, to settlements far inland. You can follow the course of this trackway through the interior of the fort to its junction with a deeply sunken east–west track, a main route for coach traffic in the eighteenth century. The track lies carved deep into the greensand by coach wheels, boots and the hooves of driven flocks and herds.

Woods of oak and chestnut blanket this place. Coppicing has been going on here since Saxon times and maybe much earlier. Perhaps this forest harvest was practised by the Wealden builders of Oldbury, or the Belgae people who captured it from them. The Romans overran the fort in AD 43 on the initial thrust of their second and triumphant invasion of these islands.

The Iron Age hill forts of Dorset and Wiltshire stand out proudly on their treeless hilltops, bald grassy crowns rising boldly above multiple collars of ramparts. Oldbury, by contrast, hides itself away. Discerning the fort's shape under its smother of trees feels like stumbling upon a secret.

3

SURREY, BERKSHIRE, BUCKINGHAMSHIRE, BEDFORDSHIRE, HERTFORDSHIRE

THE HOME COUNTIES

The very name of the Home Counties — solid, reassuring and indoorsy — and the presence of London at their centre make it seem unlikely that the Home Counties could be anything other than tame country. After all, there are no moors, mountains or stormy coasts. But the wild clings on, and indeed flourishes, in the most unexpected places.

LONDON IS RINGED with ancient heaths and commons. The wide swathes of scrubby, bushy heathland developed once wildwood forests – bedded on thick belts of sand and clay, a foundation perfect for the establishment of heaths – had been cut down for primitive agriculture. Many heaths became common land, a bare and open no man's land where people with no land or forests of their own had the right to gather wood for the fire, collect bracken for bedding, and graze their pigs, cows and geese. The Enclosures of the eighteenth and nineteenth centuries saw much of this common land bought and fenced off by rich men. Large areas reverted to scrub and then to woodland, too, as the domestic pig and cow followed the poor woodcutter into history. But in a remarkable display of forward-thinking, many commons and heaths were bought up for preservation in the second half of the nineteenth century, some by the City of London Corporation, others by philanthropic individuals. These form the wild places of today, rigorously preserved from destruction, yet always under potential threat from housing development and road-building, as well as fly-tipping and similar private acts of selfishness.

Woodlands are the other chief stronghold of nature in the Home Counties. The clay of the London basin and the chalk of the North Downs and Chiltern Hills make fine nurseries for trees. The Chilterns in particular, those easy and domesticated chalk downs that form an arc to the north-west of London, are famous for their beechwoods, and these harbour some really remarkable old pollard trees that have run completely wild. You'll find an especially fine group of these distorted ancients, crouching in the shadows like untamed old men of the woods, at Frithsden Beeches on the edge of Berkhamsted Common in Hertfordshire – a county with its fair share of eccentric figures, both arboreal and human. Here you'll discover the setting for the licentious activities of the gentlemen of the Hellfire Club and their goings-on in the caves of West Wycombe, and also the unbridled behaviour during the remarkable 'games' between men and women at Hocktide Revels on Waytyng Hill. The hill is skirted by the prehistoric track of the Icknield Way with its cargo of 7,000 years of travelling ghosts; and south of London the tree-smothered escarpment of the North Downs is likewise threaded by a pair of ancient trackways, the Pilgrim's Way running through the valleys in parallel with the old road we now style the North Downs Way, high above along the crest of the downs.

London is in a category of its own, one of the world's great cities that nevertheless nourishes its own wild places in urban surroundings – old flowery commons, bird-haunted marshes, bits and pieces of ancient woodland, and other more Gothic treasures such as the stone urns and shrouded pillars of Abney Park Cemetery, standing forgotten in the gloom of trees that are steadily absorbing them as if they had never been.

LINKS

- London Outer Orbital Path (LOOP) (www.ramblers.org.uk/info/paths/londonloop.html): Riddlesdown, Kenley Common, Coulsdon Common, Happy Valley and Farthing Downs; Monken Hadley Common, Epping Forest (via Forest Way and Three Forests Way – www.ramblers.org.uk/info/paths/threeforests.html), Rainham Marshes
- Capital Ring (www.ramblers.org.uk/info/paths/capitalring.html): Horsenden Hill, Abney Park Cemetery, Oxleas Wood (via Green Chain Walk – www.greenchain.com)
- Thames Path National Trail (www.nationaltrail.co.uk/thamespath): Wildfowl and Wetlands Trust at Barnes; 'Wild Wood', Cookham
- Icknield Way (www.ramblers.org.uk/info/paths/icknield.html): Ivinghoe Beacon (link to Ridgeway), Pegsdon Hills, Sharpenhoe Clappers
- John Bunyan Trail: Waytyng Hill and Hocktide Revels, John Bunyan's Oak, Sharpenhoe Clappers
- Beeches Way (http://www.ramblers.org.uk/info/paths/londonwest.html#beeches): Stoke Common, Burnham Beeches

Top: grotesques from Benington Church (p. 114).
Right: Burnham Beeches (p. 103)

THE HOME COUNTIES

SURREY, BERKSHIRE, BUCKINGHAMSHIRE BEDFORDSHIRE, HERTFORDSHIRE

74. THE CROWHURST YEW
75. ASHTEAD COMMON
76. NORTH DOWNS WAY AND PILGRIM'S WAY
77. PIRBRIGHT COMMON
78. CHOBHAM COMMON
79. GREENHAM COMMON ★
80. BOWDOWN WOODS
81. WILDMOOR HEATH
82. 'THE WILD WOOD', COOKHAM DEAN
83. BURNHAM BEECHES
84. STOKE COMMON
85. DASHWOOD MAUSOLEUM AND THE HELLFIRE CLUB
86. HEARNTON WOOD AND BUTTLERS HANGING
87. IVINGHOE BEACON
88. BUNYAN'S OAK, HARLINGTON
89. PEGSDON HILLS
90. ICKNIELD WAY
91. BARTON HILLS NNR, RAVENSBURGH CASTLE AND WAYTYNG HILL
92. MINSDEN CHAPEL
93. BERKHAMSTED COMMON
94. FRITHSDEN BEECHES (NT)
95. ST PETER'S CHURCH, BENINGTON
96. HUNSDON MEAD
97. BAYFORD WOOD
98. MONKEN HADLEY COMMON, BARNET
99. ABNEY PARK CEMETERY, STOKE NEWINGTON ★
100. RUISLIP WOODS
101. HORSENDEN HILL, PERIVALE
102. THE LONDON WETLAND CENTRE, BARNES
103. COMMONS AND DOWNS OF SOUTH CROYDON
104. OXLEAS WOOD, FALCONWOOD
105. RAINHAM MARSHES

BEDS.
BUCKS.
HERTS.
LONDON
SURREY
Bedford
Newport Pagnell
Biggleswade
Bletchley
Baldock
Letchworth
Hitchin
Luton
Leighton Buzzard
Stevenage
Bishop's Stortford
Aylesbury
Harpenden
Welwyn Garden City
Hertford
Berkhamsted
Hoddesdon
Hemel Hempstead
Princes Risborough
Chesham
Amersham
Potter's Bar
High Wycombe
Watford
Gerrards Cross
Maidenhead
Slough
Reading
Windsor
Bracknell
Wokingham
Camberley
Weybridge
Esher
Woking
Leatherhead
Reigate
Dorking
Guildford
Farnham
Godalming
Haslemere
Scale 5 m 10 km

74. THE CROWHURST YEW, SURREY

Maps: OS Landranger 187; Explorer 146

Travel: M25 to Junction 6; A22 towards East Grinstead. In 3 miles, left on minor road, following 'Tandridge' and then 'Crowhurst' signs.

NB: Crowhurst Church (OS ref. 390475) stands on a blind summit. Please park well away from this, and walk to the church.

Nearest railway station: Godstone (3 miles)

Above all else, yews are survivors, and the tree that stands propped at the east end of St George's Church in Crowhurst has survived much. Struck by lightning, fissured and hollowed, it raises its pink-green crown defiantly above the shattered remnants of its body.

How old is the Crowhurst Yew? Some say 1,500 years. That would put its genesis back in the very earliest days of Christianity in these islands, long before any church stood on this ridge, back in the era of the great unbroken Wealden Forest. Rather than this yew having been planted as a churchyard ornament, each successive church must have been built alongside the tree. The Crowhurst Yew might already have been seven centuries in existence when the oldest parts of the present church were raised some 800 years ago; a venerable presence, even then.

The trunk of the yew measures 33 feet around. It stands shredded into several strakes, like the staves of a burst barrel. Some of these vegetable pillars still retain their hairy pink bark; others have been stripped by weather and decay to their inner structure, a stringy musculature. What branches still belong to the yew are contorted like arthritic limbs; some are propped on staves.

A wooden door is hinged to one of the apertures in the trunk; a publican in 1820 inserted a door and a circular bench inside the hollow trunk to accommodate up to fourteen drinkers. For a while a fair was held in the shade of the canopy on Palm Sundays. But by 1850 this occasion had degenerated into a drunken orgy, and the Church authorities put a stop to it.

Yews have always been totems of worship: yew groves were gathering points and objects of veneration in the druidical religion. The careful preservation of the Crowhurst Yew, its association with drinking, jollity and unbridled behaviour, carry echoes of those wildwood traditions.

75. ASHTEAD COMMON, SURREY

Maps: OS Explorer 146, 161; Landranger 187

Travel: From M25 Junction 9, A243 north towards Kingston-upon-Thames. In 1 mile, Ashtead Common lies on your right.

Nearest railway station: Ashtead (½ mile)

It is a never-ending source of surprise to find wild commons and heaths close to London. Ashtead Common is a very fine example; it lies inside the M25, yet offers

500 acres of woodland and open spaces. A maze of footpaths crosses the common, so that you can easily track within a couple of hundred yards from one to the next, making it hard to get lost – even when temporarily bewitched by nightingale song.

The common is dotted with a large number of ancient oaks. They hold up enormous branches, or stand over the ruins of their own boughs, which form long baulks of timber on the ground, made powdery by the insects that thrive on the damp wood. Ashtead Common is a haven for woodland butterflies, especially the startlingly coloured purple emperor, a rare butterfly that lives in ancient oak woods with a supply of broad-leaved sallow, its food plant. The big male butterflies with their bright purple, white-spotted wings spend most of their time in the tops of the oak trees; you may have a better chance of seeing the females, brown-winged with the same pattern of spots, as they descend in July to lay their eggs on the sallow leaves. Purple hairstreak, with an iridescent sheen to the wings, is another oak woodland butterfly sometimes seen here. Because of the presence of these butterflies, the number of ancient trees and a rich woodland flora, about half of Ashtead Common is designated a Site of Special Scientific Interest (SSSI). This is a quiet, secluded wild place to escape from the press of suburbia all round.

76. NORTH DOWNS WAY AND PILGRIM'S WAY (ST MARTHA'S HILL TO RANMORE COMMON), SURREY

Maps: OS Explorer 145, 146; Landranger 186, 187

Travel: From M25 Junction 9, A24 south to Dorking; right on A25 through Shere; in 1 mile, left on A248 through Albury to Chilworth. At 600 yards past station, right up minor road for 1 mile to intersect North Downs Way/Pilgrim's Way National Trail (OS ref. 021484). Park neatly near by and turn right (east) along North Downs Way.

Nearest railway station: Chilworth. Return from Dorking West station after a walk of 10 miles

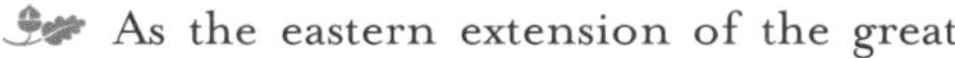

As the eastern extension of the great

Pilgrim's Way

old trackway called the Harroway (see pp. 75–6), the ancient highway now known as the North Downs Way can lay claim to being part of the oldest road in Britain. Travel along the high road of the chalk downs of southern England dates back perhaps 7,000 years. Everyone from market-goers to warriors used the old road. Their aim was to stay high and dry, out of the overgrown and potentially dangerous valleys, concealed from view and shielded from bad weather, but with a good view themselves.

In medieval times the shrine of St Thomas à Becket at Canterbury Cathedral drew millions of penitents east into Kent. By then villages, with their comforts, their bed and board, had become established along the river valleys below the hills, and this was where those journeying to Canterbury beat out a 'Pilgrim's Way' east. Nowadays the two tracks run parallel courses along the valley of the Tilling Bourne stream, the Pilgrim's Way below, the North Downs Way high above.

The 10-mile walk, east from the dark ironstone church of St Martha-on-the-Hill to the tangled woodlands of Ranworth Common, gives you a wonderful sense of what it must have been like getting from one place to another through a much wilder Britain. The Pilgrim's Way in the valley is the harder track to follow, snaking in and out of woods, dodging through the villages of Shere and Gomshall in the guise of modern roads, lanes and footpaths. The older trackway on the ridge seems both wilder and easier to follow, running boldly through dark groves of yew and holly, then out under lighter oak and beech. Sometimes the OS map labels it 'Drove Road'; in other parts it runs unnamed. Towards the end of the walk it skirts Ranmore Common, a wood maintained by the National Trust that has grown to smother the old grazing common. Spring is the time to explore here, walking past drifts of bluebells before descending to the civilization of the valley once more.

77. PIRBRIGHT COMMON, SURREY

Maps: OS Explorer 145; Landranger 186

Travel: From M25 Junction 11, A320 to Woking, A324 through Pirbright towards Ash. In 1½ miles park near Standinghill Wood with Pirbright Common on your right (OS ref. 939543) and follow bridleway to right on to the common and Ash Range.

NB: Ash Range is MoD property. Public access is permitted when red flags or lamps are not showing. When access is denied, use network of footpaths around the edge of the range.

Nearest railway station: Brookwood (3 miles)

Pirbright Common is an area of lowland heathland near London that has survived undeveloped because of its usefulness as a training ground for the Ministry of Defence. The common is part of the Thames Basin Heaths Special Protection Area, a scatter of lowland heaths to the south and west of London that amount to about 20,000 acres.

Pirbright Common lies over the Folkestone Sands, deep sand beds that underpin sterile soils and an arid environment. They support heath of bracken, bilberry and heather. The heath is dry on the summits and steeper slopes, wetter where the slopes are more shallow and retain more rainwater, boggy and squelchy down in the hollows. Larch and spruce rise in tall stands among silver birch scrub. It is a peaceful place, so much so that the pop and rattle of small-arms fire from Ash Range soon fade into the background of birdsong and wind in treetops.

Army movements and firing on the common are nothing new. In Victorian times military training and exercises were all the rage, and Pirbright was chosen for the establishment of military depots and training camps because it was conveniently close to London and possessed a big stretch of suitable open, heathy country. The Army is still here, which is lucky for the Dartford warblers and nightjars who need the mixture of dry sandy heath, fallen trees and open ground that this common affords.

If Ash Range is open you can walk past the firing butts and on along the wide track over the central common. It is an eerie sensation being surrounded by so much open, empty country so close to London. North across the railway and Basingstoke Canal is Pirbright Range, littered with unexploded ordnance and permanently closed to the public. That is a wilder place still, but a trespasser is unlikely to return to tell the tale.

78. CHOBHAM COMMON, SURREY

Maps: OS Explorer 160, Landranger 175

Travel: From M25 Junction 11, A317 west for ¾ mile to roundabout; right on A320 towards Chertsey; in ½ mile, left on B386 for 3½ miles to Longcross. Park in car park (OS ref. 979651). Follow bridleway across Chobham Common.

Nearest railway station: Longcross

The broad heathland of Chobham Common is a stunning place to walk in late summer when the heather flushes purple. At other times, even in sunshine, the common can seem a dour and moody place. The M3 motorway rushes past its northern perimeter and the jets of Heathrow whistle overhead, but Chobham Common retains the heavy, dark atmosphere that caused dismay and apprehension to the travellers of the pre-motor-car world.

The common was notorious in the coaching era for highwaymen who would wait among the trees for London-bound travellers. 'A vast tract of land given up to barrenness,' was Daniel Defoe's opinion of it when he passed this way in 1724, 'horrid and frightful to look upon, not only good for little, but good for nothing.' The gentry avoided Chobham Common, and the commoners exploited it for grazing and for collecting bracken for animal bedding. It wasn't until the Romantic Movement of the late eighteenth century that such empty landscapes were imbued with nobility and grandeur.

The wildlife of the common is spectacular, for those with the patience and eyesight to appreciate it: foxes and rabbits, roe deer, small dark-winged hobbies floating over the heather to clutch at grasshoppers or dragonflies, nightjars keeping still and perfectly camouflaged in their scrape nests on the ash-grey, speckled sandy soil. Today's wanderer on Chobham Common glimpses the wildlife, sees the sombre colours, senses the loneliness of the heath. Rather than turn away in fear, he revels in all of it.

79. GREENHAM COMMON, BERKSHIRE

Maps: OS Explorer 158; Landranger 174

Travel: From M4 Junction 13, A34 past Newbury; left on A343 ('Newbury'); in 1½ miles, right on minor road ('Greenham, Thatcham'). In ¾ mile go over A339 roundabout. In another ⅔ mile, where Greenham Road meets Pinchington Lane, park on right by entrance to Greenham Common Nature Reserve (OS ref. 484653).

Nearest railway station: Newbury (1¼ miles)

The countryside west of London is well supplied with commons, and many of them are wild places. But for a common that has witnessed wild and improbable scenes, and exists now in a state many thought beyond their wildest dreams, Greenham Common takes the biscuit. Wandering here on the ridge just south of Newbury, a stranger to the area's history might accept the stubby superannuated buildings, the flatness and regularity of the 3-mile-long site, as in the natural order of things. Quite how a rusty, full-size model of a military aeroplane in a purpose-built pool of water comes to be here, or what the significance of the big, black-mouthed grass hummocks in the south-west might be, demands more explanation.

For fifty-six years, until 1997, Greenham Common was an airbase. Between 1951 and 1992 it was run by the United States Air Force, and for eight of those years, 1983–91, it housed cruise missiles with a nuclear capability. No British citizen who watched television news in the 1980s could forget the Women's Peace Camp that established itself outside the perimeter fence, nor the fence-scalings, incursions, sit-down protests and other ways that the women found to publicize

Greenham Common

their cause and keep it in the headlines. In 1997, five years after the USAF left the base, the Ministry of Defence handed Greenham Common over to Newbury District Council and the Greenham Trust, and since then the 1,200 acres have been managed as one enormous nature reserve.

Two things vie for your attention as you walk the common: the natural world that is re-establishing itself with astonishing speed, and the ominous remains of the airbase that still lie in situ. Here are mires and sphagnum bogs, ponds and streams, mown meadows where orchids thrive – bee orchids with their bumble-bee patterns, green-winged orchids, autumn lady's tresses with tiny white flowers. Hares, rabbits, weasels and foxes find refuge here. Dartford warblers nest, as do skylarks and woodlarks. You find great blue drifts of viper's bugloss, yellow of ragwort and purple-pink of rosebay willowherb, and the pink five-petalled stars of lime-loving common centaury. These thrive next to acid-soil plants such as bell heather, in patches where lime leaching out of the broken old runways has enriched the surrounding heathland.

In the midst of this, old airbase buildings quietly crumble. The cruise missile silos, green flat-topped pyramids with dark entrances, squat on the edge of the demolished runways behind a triple layer of fencing, the burial mounds of long-superseded warriors. And the fire-plane lies on in its protective pool, no longer blasted with flame in simulated emergency, silently rusting away.

80. BOWDOWN WOODS, BERKSHIRE

Maps: OS Explorer 158; Landranger 174

Travel: From M4 Junction 13, A34 past Newbury; left on A343 ('Newbury'); in 1½ miles, right on minor road ('Greenham, Thatcham'). In ¾ mile go over A339 roundabout. In another 2/3 mile pass entrance to Greenham Common Nature Reserve on right (see opposite). Continue along Bury's Bank Road, and in 1½ miles, beyond Bury's Bank and the following long right-hand bend, bear left past 'Greenham Common' notice on a rough concrete track and on for 300 yards to car park (OS ref. 506653). Follow paths through the woods.

Bowdown Woods lie opposite Greenham Common, but the two places could not be more different in character. Where Greenham Common lies flat and open, its military relics exposed to the sky, Bowdown Woods is secretive and enclosed. The woods were once fringed by wartime munitions dumps and as you walk you will notice crumbling tarmac under your feet and a scatter of remnants of brick structures now being reabsorbed by the trees.

The slopes of Bowdown Woods have been furrowed by springs, making wet holloways thick with mosses and ferns. In parts there are open patches of heath and acid grassland, where lizards and grass snakes bask. Tall mulleins, mats of scarlet pimpernel and bright blue viper's bugloss catch the sun out here, before the path plunges back among bulbous oaks and silver birch. Come in spring and you will find these quiet woods cloaked in bluebells. But there are many other beautiful and unusual woodland flowers to enjoy too – carpets of green-flowered moschatel, white wood-sorrel with delicate pink veins, and the hanging white bells of Solomon's seal, of whose root the old herbalist John Gerard wrote in 1597: 'It taketh away in one night or two at the most, any bruse, blacke or blew spots gotten by fals, or womens wilfulnes, in stumbling upon their hastie husbands fists, or such like.'

81. WILDMOOR HEATH, BERKSHIRE

Maps: OS Explorer 160; Landranger 175

Travel: From M4 Junction 10, A329(M) to Bracknell; A3095 towards Sandhurst. In 2½ miles, right on B3348 to Crowthorne. Left at the Prince pub ('Sandhurst') down Crowthorne High Street. In ¾ mile, just after left bend, turn left into Wildmoor Heath car park (OS ref. 838631).

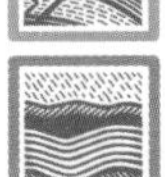

Nearest railway station: Sandhurst (1 mile)

Wildmoor Heath is a snippet of lowland heath, an increasingly rare and fragile habitat, that has survived in the Home

Wildmoor Heath

Counties against all the odds. The pressure from developers and road-builders on these 200 acres, unspoiled in the middle of prime commuter-belt country, has been enormous, but vigilance by local residents and the conservation efforts of the Berks, Bucks and Oxon Wildlife Trust have safeguarded them so far.

From the car park you step suddenly into a wild place, walking among broadleaved trees before emerging into open heathland. Higher up the slopes it is a dry scene of silver sandy soil, good basking ground for lizards and slow-worms; further down in the shallow valleys the heath turns wet, declining in the bottoms to oily bog pools where dragonflies and damselflies hover. Paths over Wildmoor Heath run under hollies, sweet chestnut and rowan before winding off across the open heath. Although the heath is well used by locals, the built-up world is still held at bay.

A summertime stroll at nightfall yields two big thrills. Nightjars nest on the open heath, and can be heard making their throaty 'churring' call around dusk. And if you are lucky and observant you may spot points of yellow luminescence among the grasses, emanating from the hindquarters of female glow-worms as they turn on their love lights.

82. 'THE WILD WOOD' (QUARRY WOOD AND WINTER HILL), COOKHAM DEAN, BERKSHIRE

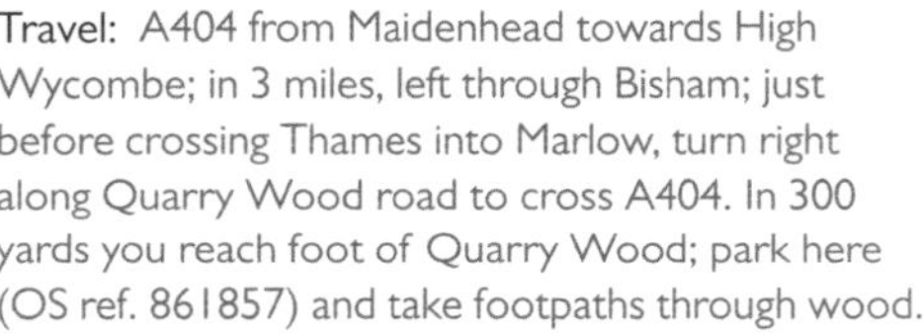

Maps: OS Explorer 172; Landranger 175

Travel: A404 from Maidenhead towards High Wycombe; in 3 miles, left through Bisham; just before crossing Thames into Marlow, turn right along Quarry Wood road to cross A404. In 300 yards you reach foot of Quarry Wood; park here (OS ref. 861857) and take footpaths through wood.

Nearest railway station: Marlow (1 mile)

'What lies over there*?' asked the Mole, waving a paw towards a background of woodland that darkly framed the water-meadows on one side of the river.*

'That? O, that's just the Wild Wood,' said the Rat shortly. 'We don't go there very much, we river-bankers.'

In this elliptical way Kenneth Grahame first slides the sinister Wild Wood into his great 1908 children's classic, *The Wind in the Willows*. The Wild Wood, with its wicked weasels and stoats, its illimitable depths and pathways that seem to disappear, does duty for all that is dark and unfathomable in the human psyche – as it did for Grahame, motherless son of an alcoholic Edinburgh lawyer, when he was sent to live with his grandmother at Cookham Dean, on the edge of Quarry Wood. It was almost certainly this tangled and overgrown place that Grahame had in mind when he wrote his fable based on familiar Thames-side scenes, partly to please his son, Alistair (known as 'Mouse'), partly as an escape from his own miserable marriage.

Of course inquisitive Mole does eventually go into the Wild Wood, against the advice of the sensible Water Rat. Soon the faces begin 'coming and going rapidly, all fixing on him glances of malice and hatred: all hard-eyed and evil and sharp'. They are quickly followed by the whistling and the pattering. 'The whole wood seemed running now, running hard, hunting, chasing, closing round something or – somebody?'

Quarry Wood is a particularly deep piece of woodland, overhanging the Thames on a steep bank, so thickly grown that little sunlight penetrates. Kenneth Grahame's association with this queer, shadowy place was tinged with tragedy. Alistair, for whom the tale was conceived, died by suicide while an undergraduate at Oxford University, two days short of his twentieth birthday.

Walking the paths of Quarry Wood today, it is easy to recall the thrill and fear of the Wild Wood as Mole ran hither and thither, darting under things and dodging round things, until he took refuge in the hollow of an old beech tree:

> *And as he lay there panting and trembling, and listened to the whistlings and the patterings outside, he knew it at last, in all its fullness, that dread thing which other little dwellers in field and hedgerow had encountered here, and known as their darkest moment – that thing which the Rat had vainly tried to shield him from – the Terror of the Wild Wood!*

83. BURNHAM BEECHES, BUCKS.

Maps: OS Explorer 172; Landranger 175

Travel: From M40 Junction 2, A355 south towards Slough. In Farnham Common village, pass turning on left to Stoke Common and Fulmer; in 150 yards, right down Beeches Road. In 300 yards cross road and enter car park on Lord Mayor's Drive. Forward along drive to Victory Cross (Corporation of London noticeboard); right here to park in car-parking bay (OS ref. 950851). Walk through gate and on along Halse Drive.

Nearest railway station: Burnham (3½ miles)

As so often in the countryside around London, it took a dedicated individual to ensure the preservation of Burnham Beeches. It was a naturalist, Mr Heath, who persuaded the City of London in 1880 to buy the 600-acre wood on the south-east edge of the Chiltern Hills. The famous beechwoods, remnant of a great Saxon forest, were beginning to fall to developers at an alarming rate. Burnham Beeches was one of the best-known woods: an inspiration to countless artists, among them composer Felix Mendelssohn and poet Thomas Gray. In 1737, while staying with his aunt, Anne Rogers, at nearby Stoke Poges, Gray had written to his friend Horace Walpole:

> *I have at the distance of half a mile through a green lane a forest all my own, for I spy no human thing in it but myself... Both vale and hill are covered with most venerable beeches, and other very reverend vegetables, that, like most other ancient people, are always dreaming out their old stories to the winds.*

Today these 'very reverend vegetables' are monsters. For a century or more before the Corporation of London bought the wood the trees had stood neglected, denied the regular pollarding that kept their crowns in check, so that the smooth trunks grew knotted and deformed, the branches hugely overshot and bulbous. The intervening decades have only increased the effect. Wander off the rides and into the darker depths of the wood for a few hundred yards, and the old trees look even more impressive in the subdued light. These are the trees of Arthur Rackham illustrations, mouths agape, knobbly fingers reaching for a victim.

84. STOKE COMMON, BUCKS.

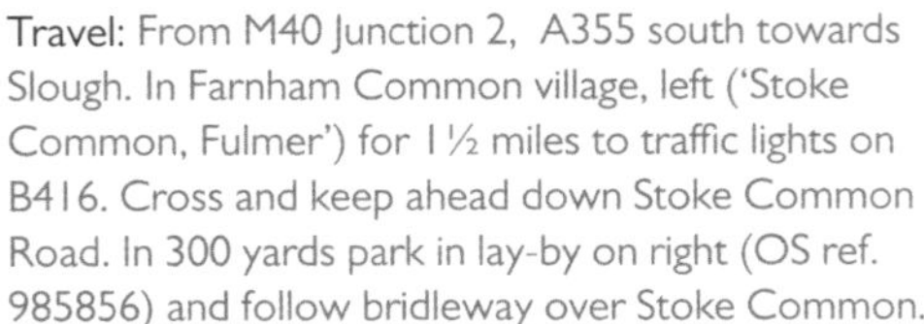

Maps: OS Explorer 172; Landranger 176

Travel: From M40 Junction 2, A355 south towards Slough. In Farnham Common village, left ('Stoke Common, Fulmer') for 1½ miles to traffic lights on B416. Cross and keep ahead down Stoke Common Road. In 300 yards park in lay-by on right (OS ref. 985856) and follow bridleway over Stoke Common.

Silver birch scrub and buttery clumps of gorse; bracken swathes and sedgy hollows; birdsong from all quarters and the brilliant orange flash of small copper butterflies; these are the keynotes of Stoke Common. Autumn is a good time to visit, when the heather flowers, the birch leaves turn a translucent lemon yellow and the hazel bushes grow fat with milky nuts. Forget-me-nots can last this late in the year, too, their

Stoke Common

sky-blue petals jewelling the grasses where black and brown cattle graze.

Dwarf oak thrives here, and so does goat willow or sallow, with its soft white-furred 'pussy willow' catkins – they show as one of the first signs of spring. And there are great carpets of star mosses; get down on your knees, and their subtle range of colour comes alive, an earthy palette of orange, ochre, emerald and many more. Spiders with round toffee-coloured bodies and immensely long hair-thin legs labour over this awkward terrain like oddly shaped experimental craft on a choppy sea, occasionally slipping sideways into a crevasse a quarter of an inch deep where they thrash around, apparently at random, until they have got themselves upright and can row on stolidly once more.

85. DASHWOOD MAUSOLEUM AND THE HELLFIRE CLUB, BUCKINGHAMSHIRE

Maps: OS Explorer 172; Landranger 165, 175

Travel: A40 from High Wycombe towards Stokenchurch. In 2 miles, pass A4010 turning to Princes Risborough; in another 1/3 mile, reach crossroads in West Wycombe. Right up Church Lane; park at Hellfire Caves (www.hellfirecaves.co.uk – OS ref. 829948). Leaving caves turn left outside gates up steep stepped path to mausoleum and St Lawrence's Church.

Nearest railway station: High Wycombe (3 miles)

Exactly how much wild behaviour actually went on in Sir Francis Dashwood's notorious Hellfire Club is open to debate. Back in the 1750s anything a gentleman and his aristocratic friends got up to was the subject of tremendous local tittle-tattle – just like today, in fact. The difference back

Dashwood Mausoleum

then, though, was that a gentleman could keep the details hidden if he wished. No one papped the members of the Hellfire Club, or infiltrated a kiss-and-tell babe into the orgies they held in their club premises, deep within the caves that had been hollowed out by Sir Francis under West Wycombe Hill. In fact, in excavating the caves the baronet was simply providing paid work for his impoverished farm tenants after a series of bad harvests, getting them to dig out chalk and flint to surface the local roads. But when did facts ever get in the way of a good scandal?

A visit to Hellfire Caves today involves a likeable over-the-top tourist romp through the facts and fancies of the old story. Here Dashwood would entertain such luminaries and statesmen as Lord Sandwich, Benjamin Franklin and the future radical politician and champion of liberty John Wilkes. Young and not-so-young ladies of varying blueness of blood were entertained, too – to what extent, and how willingly, local rumour could only speculate.

On top of the hill stands St Lawrence's Church, rebuilt in flint by Dashwood. The huge, hollow golden globe that still stands moored to the top of the tower was provided by the baronet to serve as a club room for the Hellfire Club members. Up to ten of 'Dashwood's Apostles' at a time could squeeze in to gamble and drink together. 'The best Globe Tavern I ever drank in,' asserted John Wilkes. Tales circulated of Black Masses celebrated there, of rites of the 'old religion' carried out.

There is little sinister about either the caves or the church these days; that is reserved for the great dark stone mausoleum that stands on the hilltop next to the church. Built of solid flint, three sides of the hollow hexagon are pierced with arches. Statuary urns with gurning faces stand along the balustrade, and there are more in the inside walls, facing into the central court. Here one large urn stands in a railed area under a central canopy. These vessels were intended to hold the hearts of 'Dashwood's Apostles'. That never happened; but one heart did end up in an urn here, that of the Hellfire Club's steward, Paul Whitehead, who died in 1774 and bequeathed his organ to Sir Francis Dashwood 'as a token of his warm attachment to the noble founder'. Later the heart was stolen from the mausoleum. Steward Whitehead now haunts the caves, searching in vain for his lost heart.

86. HEARNTON WOOD AND BUTTLERS HANGING, BUCKINGHAMSHIRE

Maps: OS Explorer 172; Landranger 165

Travel: From M40 Junction 4, A4010 north from High Wycombe towards Princes Risborough. In 2 miles park at Saunderton railway station (OS ref. 813981). From the station turn right up lane, round hairpin bend, and in 150 yards left (fingerpost) up the old track through Hearnton Wood to Nobles Farm. At 700 yards past Nobles Farm, bear right to leave Hearnton Wood (819960) and enter Buttlers Hanging Nature Reserve.

Nearest railway station: Saunderton

Hearnton Wood hangs along its ridge, a long dark bar of ash and beech trees with an ancient ridgeway at its heart. Holly and yew flank the flinty track, whose banks grow a profusion of large purple bellflowers. This is a beautiful place to walk, but leaving it for Buttlers Hanging, after half an hour or so, means you enter a completely different - but equally rewarding - landscape.

Buttlers Hanging slopes to the south-west, a hillside of rare chalk grassland preserved and managed as a nature reserve, nibbled close by sheep to maintain a flowering sward. Early purple orchids in spring give way to summer's common spotted and pyramidal orchids, the latter's tight little cone giving off a strong animal scent to compete with the wild thyme and marjoram. The purple trumpets of Chiltern gentian with their wide-open mouths and pale throats are a great rarity that you may spot here. Finches and warblers sing from the dogwood and sweet briar scrub, and big green bush crickets creak in the long grasses. Buttlers Hanging is full of wildlife, in stark contrast to its intensively farmed surroundings. It is grazed, fenced, cut and cleared with meticulous care by the local wildlife trust. This is a fine example of that widespread paradox of the British landscape, a wild place that can remain wild only with our help.

87. IVINGHOE BEACON, BUCKS.

Maps: OS Explorer 181; Landranger 165

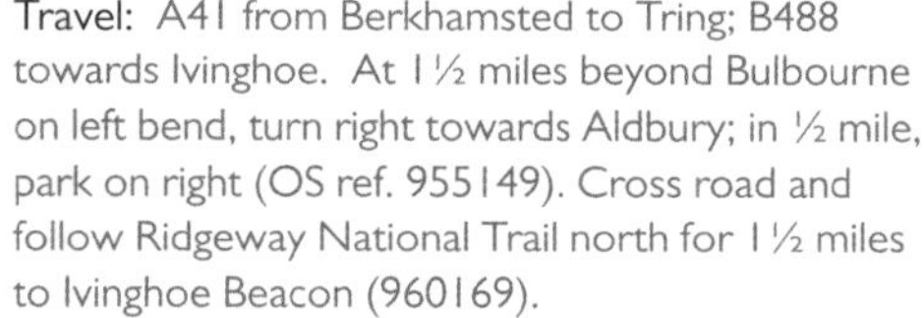

Travel: A41 from Berkhamsted to Tring; B488 towards Ivinghoe. At 1½ miles beyond Bulbourne on left bend, turn right towards Aldbury; in ½ mile, park on right (OS ref. 955149). Cross road and follow Ridgeway National Trail north for 1½ miles to Ivinghoe Beacon (960169).

Nearest railway station: Cheddington (3½ miles by road to car park)

The best way by far to approach the summit of Ivinghoe Beacon is to mount it along the steadily rising track of the Ridgeway National Trail. And the best time without a doubt is very early in the morning, preferably at sunrise on a misty summer's day before anyone else is about, for the enormous views and clear air, 755 feet up, make Ivinghoe Beacon a very popular place.

This is the highest point of the ancient Ridgeway, the summit and end of its 90-mile course from the great stone circle at Avebury in Wiltshire. Here on the heights the Ridgeway hands over to the Icknield Way (a continuation of itself under another name, in fact) to forge on along the chalk and clay ridges for another 100 miles into East Anglia. This ancient meeting place has attracted men for thousands of years – witness the burial mounds and the remnants of an Iron Age hill fort.

On a clear morning you have dozens of miles of Buckinghamshire, Hertfordshire and Bedfordshire spread at your feet. But if you come here when the mist is still thick in the plain below, you have the thrill of being marooned on the brow of the downs, a green island in a white sea. This was the view that the supreme South Country writer Edward Thomas found in 1911 when he was researching his book *The Icknield Way*. Thomas arrived on Ivinghoe Beacon on a murky summer's morning, 'stumping along on a shoeful of blisters', having walked 80 miles in three days. The view from the summit revealed itself to him on 'a hot day slowly and certainly preparing in mist and silence. I saw Ivinghoe Church tower and the silly spire, short and sharp, on top of it, the misty woods behind, the Pitstone Church tower and an elm throned on a rise together, and the broad wooded valley beyond. Larks sang ...'

88. BUNYAN'S OAK, HARLINGTON, BEDFORDSHIRE

Maps: OS Explorer 193; Landranger 166

Travel: From M1 Junction 12, A5120 for ½ mile, towards Ampthill; right on minor road to Harlington. Over crossroads in village, past church; park where 'Westoning, Toddington' is signed to right (OS ref. 044308). Continue on foot along Sharpenhoe Road for 70 yards (take care!); left over stiles into field. Aiming for water tower on skyline, follow 'Pulloxhill' fingerpost into dip, to pass spinney. Bunyan's Oak is up slope to the left (046313).

Nearest railway station: Harlington (1 mile)

In November 1660, when John Bunyan came to preach in the Bedfordshire parish of Lower Sampshill, the thirty-two-year-old tinker's son was a marked man. It was a nervous time in England, with King Charles II only just restored to his throne after a

Bunyan's Oak

decade of exile. The bloody misery of the Civil War and the dour fanaticisms of Oliver Cromwell's Commonwealth were still fresh in everyone's mind; religious nonconformists were the new folk devils. Local magistrate Sir Francis Wingate of Harlington Manor had his eye on the fiery young preacher from Elstow village; and when large crowds began to gather round a great oak tree in the fields beyond Harlington, where Bunyan had taken up his stance and begun to let fly with his independent religious views, Sir Francis ordered his men to detain the miscreant as soon as he'd finished his rant. Bunyan was hauled off and committed to Bedford Jail. The open-air missionary was destined to spend the next twelve years incarcerated there.

Bunyan's Oak still stands, though it is long dead. Seven limbs, like the spikes of a crown, are held aloft by a massive trunk, warty and bulbous, the silvery-grey wood still retaining a few scabs of saurian bark. Patterns of splits and cracks in the old timber run down the body of the tree in runnels like raindrops on a window.

When John Bunyan stood in the oak's shelter to speak what was in his heart, he looked out over the heads of the crowd, across the valley to the long ridge of the Sundon Hills ending in the steep chalk promontory of Sharpenhoe Clappers. The Sundon Hills were in Bunyan's view for much of his life as he roamed around this part of Bedfordshire, preaching wherever the spirit moved him. When he wrote the first part of *The Pilgrim's Progress* in 1676, during a second spell in Bedford Jail for preaching 'Independency', it was partly these hills that formed the inspiration for the 'Delectable Mountains' of his fable.

Bunyan had been a bit of a lad in his youth, very fond of singing, dancing and playing the fiddle. But the preaching spirit, when it struck him in his twenties, propelled him forth from then on to defy wind, weather and the fear and loathing of the orthodox majority. *The Pilgrim's Progress* was published in 1678. Its author had ten more years of life, and spent them wandering, preaching and praying, until he caught a chill in a rainstorm in August 1688 which soon sent the tireless traveller for the Lord to his reward in the Celestial City.

Bunyan's Oak, though dead, is far from lifeless. A young oak planted in front of the old tree in 1988, the tercentenary of Bunyan's death, is flourishing. In the shelter of the ancient hulk itself an elder tree thrives, while from the split and hollow heart of Bunyan's Oak springs – most appropriately – a vigorous sapling of the wayfaring tree.

89. PEGSDON HILLS, BEDFORDSHIRE/HERTFORDSHIRE BORDER

Maps: OS Explorer 193; Landranger 166

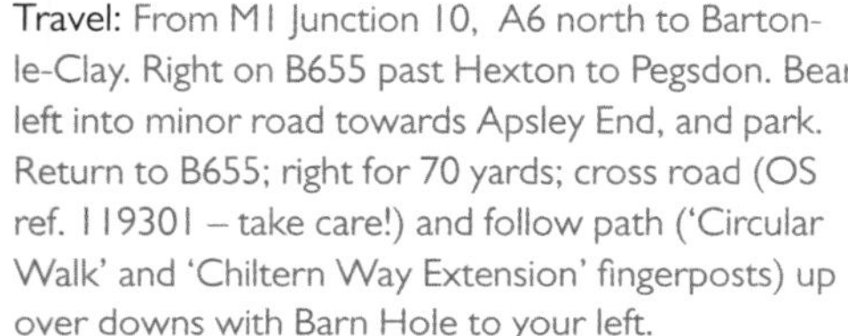

Travel: From M1 Junction 10, A6 north to Barton-le-Clay. Right on B655 past Hexton to Pegsdon. Bear left into minor road towards Apsley End, and park. Return to B655; right for 70 yards; cross road (OS ref. 119301 – take care!) and follow path ('Circular Walk' and 'Chiltern Way Extension' fingerposts) up over downs with Barn Hole to your left.

Nearest railway stations: Hitchin or Harlington (5 miles)

Among the chalk ramparts of John Bunyan's 'Delectable Mountains' (see opposite) at the north-east extremity of the Chiltern escarpment you will find the Pegsdon Hills. They rise only 300 feet at most, but stand out as especially steep and deeply indented. Dry valleys cut into their flanks and their sides are too steep to be ploughed by modern machinery. They escaped twentieth-century intensive farming, and preserve an increasingly rare chalk grassland landscape – now added to by Bedfordshire Wildlife Trust, who have recreated chalk grassland on 100 acres of former farmland in and around Barn Hole.

As you climb the slope of the down from Pegsdon village, Barn Hole lies on your right, a deep hollow in the hills. From a seat placed half-way up you can look down the length of the cleft, and a gate towards the top leads into it. Spring and summer are the seasons to come. Wild thyme, marjoram and basil turn your pinching fingers green and fragrant. Pale blue harebells nod in the wind, and other flowers of lime-rich grasslands thrive – cowslip, yellow rattle, milkwort with its tiny bright blue bells, the yellow five-petalled flowers of rock-rose, big blue heads of field scabious. Butterflies include the gleaming chalkhill blue, whose food plant of horseshoe vetch grows on the slopes, and the big brown-and-white dotted marbled white.

These hills were farmed in Bronze Age times, as the strip lynchets along their sides show, but they were grazed by sheep for hundreds of years during the Middle Ages and on up to the nineteenth century. The teeth of sheep and rabbits nibble plants down to ground level but leave the roots intact, creating a tight-knit sward of herbs, flowering plants and grasses. This is the sward that today clothes Barn Hole and the other reserves along the Pegsdon Hills.

90. ICKNIELD WAY ON TELEGRAPH HILL, BEDFORDSHIRE

Maps: OS Explorer 193; Landranger 166

Travel: From M1 Junction 10, A6 north to Barton-le-Clay; right on B655 through Pegsdon. Pass Live & Let Live pub; in ½ mile, park on right of road in lay-by car park (OS ref. 132300). Turn back to your right along Icknield Way, climbing gently for 1/3 mile till it levels off. In another 1/3 mile, kissing gate with Access Land on right (120290) leads to Pegsdon Hills and Barn Hole Nature Reserve (see above). Another ¼ mile along Icknield Way will give you a sight on the left of the grassland summit of Telegraph Hill (118288).

Nearest railway stations: Hitchin or Harlington (5 miles)

At first sight the Icknield Way may seem like any other broad footpath as it climbs south-west up the gentle slope of Telegraph Hill. Soon your eyes and senses become adjusted, and the breadth of its hedges – in some places 50 yards across – and the

Icknield Way

straightness and depth of its rutted course tell you that here is a high road that has run this outermost ridge of the Chiltern Hills for a very long time. In fact the Icknield Way is one of the oldest roads in Britain, a trackway that has been in use since Neolithic times.

Before the trees grew so thickly along its course, the Icknield Way on Telegraph Hill must have commanded an enormous view north and west over the Bedfordshire Plain. Today it runs cloaked in field maple, oak, hazel, beech and the suckers of elms, with the white flowers and red and blue fruits of hawthorn and blackthorn splashing colour over the springtime and autumn verges. Wild garlic sends out its pungent stink, and every now and then a scribble of blackcap or blackbird song bursts out of the hedges.

There is a peaceful green light in this tunnel of a thoroughfare, between the hedges as it nears the summit of Telegraph Hill. At 602 feet the hill is the highest for many miles. On its top a wooden telegraph station was built in 1808, one of a chain whose jerky semaphore arms could pass messages between the Admiralty in London and the shore-station at Great Yarmouth in a fraction of the time a horse would take. The Icknield bypasses Telegraph Hill and runs on south-west through avenues of largely smooth-trunked old beeches, dignified as guardsmen. If you were to follow the track another dozen miles you would come to Ivinghoe Beacon (see p. 107), from where Icknield Way continues under the name of the Ridgeway – a new name for the same old and beautiful road.

91. BARTON HILLS NNR, RAVENSBURGH CASTLE AND WAYTYNG HILL, HERTFORDSHIRE/BEDFORDSHIRE BORDER

Maps: OS Explorer 193; Landranger 166

Travel: From M1 Junction 10, A6 north to Barton-le-Clay. Right on B655 to pass through village, right in 200 yards to church. Park here (OS ref. 085304). Just beyond church, left along a track (fingerpost) that climbs slope of Barton Hills to reach kissing gate on right and noticeboard of Barton Hills National Nature Reserve (092296). To your left a path approaches a viewpoint to Ravensburgh Castle hill fort (under trees), with Waytyng Hill beyond (102299).

Nearest railway station: Harlington (3½ miles)

Three wild places abut each other among the abrupt valleys and rounded ridges of the Barton Hills. The most easily accessible is the National Nature Reserve of Barton Hills, the steep dry slopes whose appearance on the skyline caught the eye of John Bunyan in the 1660s (see p. 108). Barton Hills are one of the strong candidates to have been the inspiration for the 'Delectable Mountains' in Bunyan's epic Christian allegory *The*

Pilgrim's Progress. These days the hills sustain some of the largest remnants of chalk grassland north of London, a specialized and increasingly rare habitat where cowslips and the beautiful purple bells of pasque flowers in spring give way to a summer show of pale purple fragrant orchids with a subtle scent of sweet cloves.

Just east of the reserve lie two neighbouring hills where wild battles were enacted. The struggle that took place on the Iron Age hill fort of Ravensburgh in 54 BC pitted the legions of Imperial Rome under Julius Caesar against the British leader Cassivellanus and his warriors. Caesar stormed the hill from two sides at once and achieved a crushing victory, capturing a British lord for whose safety Cassivellanus had to agree peace terms.

The old hill fort, the largest in the south-east of England at 22 acres, lies half hidden under trees. Just north is Waytyng Hill, otherwise known as Bonfirehill Knoll, probably the scene of the Celtic summer fire rituals of Beltane. Legends tell of a warrior who lies sleeping under the hill, waiting to be awoken and ride to a great victory. It's amazing that he managed to sleep through the shouting and shrieking of Hocktide Revels, a rustic celebration that used to take place on the hill in the second week after Easter. The men of Hexton, the village below the knoll, would set up an ash pole on Waytyng Hill and try to maintain it in an erect position, while the women would endeavour to topple it and pull it down the hill. The women invariably succeeded. Now what could possibly have been the symbolic significance of that?

92. MINSDEN CHAPEL, HERTS.

Maps: OS Explorer 113; Landranger 166

Travel: From A1(M) Junction 8, A602 into Hitchin, left on B656 towards Langley. In 2 miles, park at Royal Oak pub (OS ref. 199253 – please ask permission, and give the pub your custom). Follow sunken lane, then field path south for 400 yards to Minsden Chapel Plantation. Continue along wood edge; in a few yards turn right into wood to find ruin of Minsden Chapel (198246).

Nearest railway station: Stevenage (4 miles)

Some wild places rely on atmosphere and the stories that surround them for their sense of wildness; some plunge you straight into the wild by virtue of their setting in uncontrolled surroundings. The ruin of Minsden Chapel displays both these characteristics. In the skirts of a Hertfordshire wood, overgrown and half tumbled under the onslaught of nettles and elders, the chapel that refreshed and revived medieval pilgrims en route for St Albans Abbey stands with its tall flint walls and window arches crumbling into the mossy green earth. It is a strange, melancholic sight, the slowly falling church screened by trees from any casual passer-by.

Stranger still are the tales that have gathered round the old ruin in the wood. A psychic brought to the site in 1993 saw visions of the bricked-up entrance to a vault, and of barrels being unloaded from a farm cart in which a group of fugitives was hiding in terrible fear. Minsden Chapel is said to be haunted by the ghost of a monk who appears at midnight on All-Hallows Eve and climbs a set of invisible steps. Sweet organ music is heard as the monk goes through his paces. It is the only frivolity to touch this relic, with its sad aspect and forlorn setting.

93. BERKHAMSTED COMMON, HERTFORDSHIRE

Maps: OS Explorer 181; Landranger 165

Travel: A41, A416 to Berkhamsted. Left on A4251 towards Tring; right on B4506 towards Dagnall. In 2 miles you reach Berkhamsted Common; park here (OS ref. 977117) and follow paths to right.

Nearest railway station: Berkhamsted (2½ miles by footpaths, 4 miles by road)

Berkhamsted Common today is overgrown with trees and presents a wilder aspect than in the past. The wood north of Berkhamsted is a remnant of an ancient common wood, the Frith, a hive of ordered activity in medieval times when the commoners gathered bracken and grazed their pigs and cattle there. When Carl Linnaeus, the Swedish botanist and zoologist, visited England in the summer of 1736 and saw the gorse in bloom on Berkhamsted Common, he knelt down and thanked God for showing him such a glorious sight. Nowadays the big wood is a favourite with walkers and birdwatchers, a setting whose secluded quiet might never have been disturbed. Yet back in 1866 a confrontation that became known as the 'Battle of Berkhamsted Common' brought down an army of toughs from London and signalled a convulsion in the old social order.

It was Lord Brownlow of the adjacent Ashridge Estate who sparked the trouble by enclosing one third of the common inside iron fences with no means of access. Another local grandee, Augustus Smith, decided to stand up for the rights of the dispossessed commoners, and paid for a gang of labourers to be brought down from London on a night train to dismantle the railings. The enterprise nearly met with disaster; the two men Smith had hired to oversee proceedings got incapably drunk before the train left Euston, and the navvies disembarked leaderless at Tring station in the early hours. But a lawyer's clerk summoned enough authority to get the men in order, and they marched to Berkhamsted Common where by sunrise they had dismantled and neatly rolled up 3 miles of fencing. The folk of Berkhamsted, gathering on the common that morning to lament their loss, found that all was open once more, and 'took away morsels of gorse to prove, they said, the place was their own again'.

Lord Brownlow conceded defeat. His enclosure attempt was one of several around the same time, and this spate of land grabs provoked the formation of the Commons, Open Spaces and Footpaths Preservation Society, which continues to safeguard access rights to wild places today.

The versifiers at *Punch* went to town on the subject of the Battle of Berkhamsted Common:

Spoke out their nameless leader,
'That railing must go down.'
Then firmer grasped the crowbar
Those hands so strong and brown.
They march against the railing,
They lay the crowbars low,
And down and down for many a yard
The costly railings go ...

At the conclusion of a lengthy, mock-heroic celebration of deeds of arms and the rights of the common man, *Punch* summed up the zeitgeist with a plea for justice:

Bold was the deed and English
The Commoners have done,
Let's hope the law of England
Will smile upon their fun.
For our few remaining Commons
Must not be seized or sold,
Nor Lords forget they do not live
In the bad days of old.

94. FRITHSDEN BEECHES (NT), HERTFORDSHIRE

Maps: OS Explorer 181; Landranger 165, 166

Travel: A41, A416, A4251 to pass Berkhamsted railway station. Bear left under railway bridge, right past Berkhamsted Castle, and follow road to left around castle for 1 mile to T-junction by war memorial. Turn left and follow Ashridge road until you pass 'Toll Road' notice. In 400 yards park on left by 'Ashridge' National Trust sign (OS ref. 998111). Turn sharp left up track ('Brick Kiln Cottage only'), and bear left at top into Frithsden Beeches (NT sign).

Nearest railway station: Berkhamsted (2½ miles by road, 1½ miles by path via Well Farm)

The old trees known as Frithsden Beeches have a rare presence, standing like gods on their ridge above Berkhamsted with arms raised 100 feet high or more. The medieval wood pasture of which they are the remains was last pollarded well over a century ago. The boles of some of the huge coppice trees that stand protected at the heart of the wood might date back 400 years – a Methuselah-like age for a tree as shallow-rooted and inherently unstable as the beech. Spider webs fill the holes that have been torn by the dropping of limbs; the boughs lie in the twig and leaf litter on the forest floor, some weighing many tons, all slowly reduced by burrowing insects to powder that will blow away in the wind.

Frithsden Beeches, a rare survival of the medieval landscape of the Chilterns, was acquired by the National Trust in 1925 after the owner planned to fell the trees. A little further east along the ridge are two more pieces of woodland owned by the National Trust, Great and Little Frithsden Copse. These embanked woods, coppiced for hundreds of years, were appropriated from the Commoners in the 1640s by the Earl of Bridgewater – he simply enclosed the common land and then 'persuaded' a magistrate to back up his claim. The authenticity of Great Frithsden Copse was compromised in 1953 when it was replanted to commemorate the coronation of Queen Elizabeth II. But Little Frithsden Copse remains largely as it was in medieval times: a lovely wood of oak, hornbeam and cherry with some fine old beeches clinging to the ancient hedge banks, somehow defying every winter gale.

95. ST PETER'S CHURCH, BENINGTON, HERTFORDSHIRE

Maps: OS Explorer 193; Landranger 166

Travel: From Stevenage, A602 towards Ware; at Bragbury End on outskirts of Stevenage, left on minor road through Aston to Benington. Park near St Peter's Church (OS ref. 297236).

Nearest railway station: Watton-at-Stone (4 miles)

Standing next to the twelfth-century castle of Benington Lordship – an 'adulterine' castle, built without the permission of the crown – a snook-cocking, devil-may-care air hangs around St Peter's. The external and internal carvings are extravagant and fanciful, products of nonconformist medieval minds.

The church is beautifully built of knapped flint, with headstops to most of the windows. These tiny kings, queens and nuns look more or less conventional (though you notice a swollen cheek here, a poked-out tongue there); not so the grimacing gargoyles along the gutters. But even these are nothing compared to the strangeness of the carvings inside St Peter's. Supporting the chancel arch are two Green Men of contrasting types: one sprouts branches from his wide-stretched mouth, the other thrusts forward from a collar of acorns and oak leaves with an expression of concentrated strain. Near by a wonderfully ugly goblin who can scarcely be a Christian symbol yanks the corners of his mouth apart, and his two chums on the north side of the sanctuary arcade sport faces contorted in pain or fear. On the reverse side a little crowned figure of King Edward II struggles to remove a sword that has been plunged clean through him.

Weirdest and wildest of all is the tiny imp that props up a lone corbel stone. With clumsy fingers propped on his faun-like knees he leers forward with goatish eyes, frowning under a mat-like fringe – hair, ears or horns, it is difficult to say which. From which vault of a medieval mind did such a little demon spring?

96. HUNSDON MEAD, ESSEX/HERTFORDSHIRE BORDERS

Maps: OS Explorer 194; Landranger 167

Travel: From M25 Junction 25, A10 towards Hertford; in 7 miles, A414 to Stanstead Abbotts, B181 to Roydon. Park in village and walk back to railway level crossing by Roydon station (OS ref. 406105). Turn right along north bank of River Stort Navigation; in 300 yards go under railway line to reach Roydon Lock. Turn right across it and continue along same bank of Stort Navigation for ¼ mile to reach gate on left, beside noticeboard, into Hunsdon Mead (415106). Please keep to footpaths as shown on noticeboard.

Nearest railway station: Roydon

As a superb wildflower meadow, Hunsdon Mead owes its existence to the willingness of local farming family the Abbeys to take less than half the annual yield of hay that they could get if they farmed the big meadow intensively. Their persistence in using traditional 'lammas meadow' methods of husbandry, allied to the ancient rights of grazing that locals enjoy, means that sheets of wild flowers – and the insects they attract, and the birds that are drawn by the insects – inhabit Hunsdon Mead to the delight of those who venture far enough away from the road to discover this natural yet man-dependent treasure.

Sheep and cattle are run on the meadow from each autumn through until March, fertilizing the grass and flower seed with their dung and nibbling the sward short. Winter floods from the nearby River Stort usually turn the meadow into a lake, and when they retreat they leave behind a layer of rich silt where golden plover and lapwings feed. Wild flowers grow in the fertile ground, along with the grass, until after they have set seed; generally by late July or August, when the year's one cut of hay is taken. Then the meadow is left to recover, and the grazing animals are reintroduced for autumn.

Hunsdon Mead

Spring here sees primroses in the hedges, cowslips out in the meadow and marsh marigolds in the wet parts. A bright sea of buttercups, patched with the paler gold 'parrot beak' flowers of yellow rattle, spreads across the meadow in summer. Sulphurous bird's-foot trefoil completes the yellow palette. Feathery pink heads of ragged robin show in the damp patches where damselflies and dragonflies flit, pausing in mid-air before suddenly disappearing, only to re-materialize 5 feet off. Leave plenty of time for a visit to Hunsdon Mead; it's a hard task to drag yourself away from so much beauty, especially when the path back to the road traverses the plain green, flowerless grass fields of modern agriculture's making.

97. BAYFORD WOOD, HERTFORDSHIRE

Maps: OS Explorer 174, 182; Landranger 166

Travel: From M25 Junction 25, A10 and A414 into Hertford. Left on B158 towards Essendon; in 2 miles, left on minor road to Bayford. Right past Baker Arms pub towards Epping Green. In ½ mile you reach Bayford House on right; park near by (OS ref. 306079) and take Hertfordshire Way path on right, down hedge and into Bayford Wood (303080).

Nearest railway station: Bayford (1 mile)

You approach Bayford Wood by way of

Bayford Wood

a wonderful wildflower meadow. In early summer this is a sheet of rich buttercups, hazed with forget-me-nots and speedwell. It makes a beautiful introduction to the old overshot coppice of Bayford Wood. The meadow is not the only bright note of colour; garden-escaped rhododendrons flourish in the shade of the trees, splashing the gloom with showy purple blooms. Along the woodland paths you may spot orange-tip butterflies, the pure white of their wings contrasting startlingly with their intensely orange wing-tips; also speckled woods (white dots on brown wings) and, if you are lucky, a glimpse of the gorgeous white admiral whose dark wings carry a striking band of white.

Silver birch and sycamore are dotted throughout Bayford Wood, but of the trees it is the ancient hornbeam pollards and coppice stumps that give the wood its great character. Hornbeam timber is the hardest among our native trees, and was harvested for making items that needed to resist a lot of rough treatment: the soles of clogs, for example, the butts of rifles, the centres of butcher's blocks. It was resistant to the nibbling of deer and squirrels, too, and was used to make boundary posts and fences. Coppiced as they were in Bayford Wood, the slim poles, cut every few years, could also be turned into charcoal – hornbeam charcoal burned hotter than any other kind. Nowadays we have left such country practices for dead, and the hornbeams of Bayford Wood are left unmolested to grow as crooked as nature pleases.

98. MONKEN HADLEY COMMON, BARNET, NORTH LONDON

Maps: OS Explorer 173; Landranger 166; London A–Z, pp. 4 (E2), 5 (G1, H1, F2, G2, H2)

Travel: Tube (Piccadilly Line) to Cockfosters; cross A111, follow Chalk Lane for ¼ mile to T-junction with Games Road. Left past Cock & Dragon Inn to east end of Monken Hadley Common (OS ref. 278967), and follow path along common.

By road: From M25 Junction 24, A111 south towards London; in 2¼ miles, right (279967) into Chalk Lane and follow Games Road as above.

There is no prescribed route on Monken Hadley Common. You can wander as you will through this narrow strip of

Monken Hadley Common

wilderness where north London meets rural Hertfordshire, a remnant of the royal hunting forest of Enfield Chase; King James I was the last monarch to exercise his right to hunt here. After such hunting ceased, Enfield Chase was encroached upon by casual felling and piecemeal reclamation for agriculture until the rest of the forest was enclosed and sold off in small parcels. Luckily for posterity, the 'stint holders' or commoners of Monken Hadley village could not agree on who should get which allotment of Chase land, and so their entire portion ended up in trust, in which legal state it remains. No one can sell it, so no one can buy it and build on it.

Monken Hadley Common is studded with big old oaks; also with beeches, and a large number of fine old holly trees. Ponds and marshy hollows indent the long triangle of land. Three of these ponds, in a line near the eastern boundary, are connected by a stream called Monkey Mead, a reminder of the monks of the ancient hermitage that stood here long before the Norman kings appropriated the land. The whole common is wonderfully tangled, and so are the many footpaths that cross it – they have arisen in haphazard fashion over the centuries because of the common's ancient wayfaring rights, which allowed anyone to cross it any way he chose. Monken Hadley Common, in fact, was Access Land many centuries before the Countryside and Rights of Way Act 2000 enshrined in law everyman's right of access to all such open land.

99. ABNEY PARK CEMETERY, STOKE NEWINGTON CHURCH STREET, STOKE NEWINGTON, LONDON N16

Maps: OS Explorer 173; Landranger 176; London A–Z, p. 50 (2E)

Travel: From Stoke Newington station, left along Stamford Hill and Stoke Newington Hill Street; right along Stoke Newington Church Street. Abney Park Cemetery lies on the right.

Of the jungly, overgrown cemeteries for which London is famous, Abney Park is one that often escapes attention. This is a truly wild place in the heart of the city, tremendously overgrown, in a state of benign disorder carefully maintained by the Abney Park Trust that was established in 1991 to look after the neglected old burial ground. It was opened in the 1830s in the grounds of two grand residences, Abney House and Fleetwood House, as a non-denominational 'garden' graveyard, the first of its kind in Europe. After 100 years of use it began to be overcrowded and poorly looked after, and was finally closed in 1979. The Abney Park Trust does an excellent job in a sensitive way, looking after the

Abney Park Cemetary

cemetery's thousands of monuments while managing and maintaining the trees and shrubs that half swallow them.

To walk into Abney Park Cemetery is to step into a parallel universe where sorrowing women and trumpeting angels glimmer whitely inside the clasp of elder bushes and yew tree limbs. In among the silver birch and sycamore thickets stands a white lion, guarding the tomb of Victorian menagerie owners. A loop of pathways and interconnecting tracks leads round the 32-acre site, which seems infinitely larger once you are inside it.

Famous folk are buried here, and some of their tombs are kept respectfully clear of growth: notably William Booth ('Born 1829. Born again of the Spirit 1845. Founded the Salvation Army 1865. Went to Heaven 20 August 1912', his inscription sums up with crisp certainty) and his wife, Catherine. All round the Booths' graves are those of other Salvationists 'promoted to Glory' or 'left for Higher Service'. At the centre of the cemetery stands Isaac Watts. The 'Father of Hymnody' (1674–1748) stares over the surrounding jungle from a tall plinth. Watts, an ecumenical dissenting Christian, lived at Abney Park House for many years as a guest of his patron Lady Mary Abney. He wrote some splendid and resounding hymns, among them 'Jesus Shall Reign Where'er the Sun' and 'When I Survey the Wondrous Cross' – also some more obscure numbers, including 'Lord, I would Spread my Sore Distress', and 'Blest is the Man whose Bowels Move'.

100. RUISLIP WOODS, RUISLIP, NORTH-WEST LONDON

Maps: OS Explorer 172; Landranger 176; London A–Z, pp. 22–3 (D2–H5)

Travel: Tube (Metropolitan Line) to Northwood Hills; left down Joel Street. In 1/3 mile, right along Norwich Road, then Wiltshire Lane, passing hospital to enter Park Wood (OS ref. 095897).

By road: From M25 Junction 18, A404 towards London. In 4 miles, right on A4180 ('Ruislip'); in 1½ miles, Mad Bess Wood car park on right (080896), and Copse Wood on left.

Out on the north-west rim of London, turning their backs on suburbia, lie four ancient blocks of woodland that together form Ruislip Woods. This whole site is a

National Nature Reserve, and no wonder – although not directly threatened by development as Oxleas Wood in south-east London has been (see p. 122), Ruislip Woods have always been in danger of encroachment. These 650 acres of oak, hornbeam, scrub and heathland need all the protective designation they can get to safeguard their status as a vital patch in London's Green Belt.

Park Wood is the most easterly of the three, where silver birch and aspen shiver in every breath of wind. To the north is Copse Wood, with plenty of indicators of ancient woodland – wild cherry with its bright fruit that bites like acid on the tongue, guelder rose with white flowers and scarlet berries, wild service trees with toothed leaves shaped like hands. These beautiful trees are also in evidence as you walk across Duck Hill Road, through Mad Bess Wood and on into Bayhurst Wood on the western edge of the reserve. Old hornbeam coppices shoot unharvested limbs up to the woodland canopy, and squirrels bounce and scutter among them.

How Mad Bess Wood got its name is open to question. Some tales say Bess was a gamekeeper's wife, a harridan whom even hardened poachers would avoid when she patrolled the wood by night. Others speak more gently of a woman betrayed by her lover who found shelter and solace among these quiet old trees.

101. HORSENDEN HILL, PERIVALE, MIDDLESEX

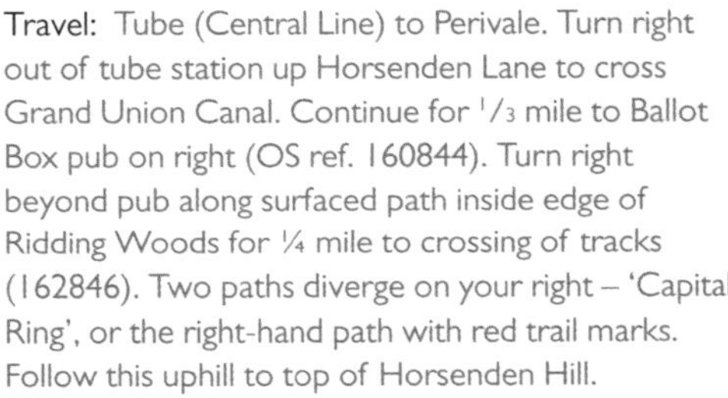

Maps: OS Explorer 173; Landranger 176; London A–Z, pp. 44, 62

Travel: Tube (Central Line) to Perivale. Turn right out of tube station up Horsenden Lane to cross Grand Union Canal. Continue for 1/3 mile to Ballot Box pub on right (OS ref. 160844). Turn right beyond pub along surfaced path inside edge of Ridding Woods for ¼ mile to crossing of tracks (162846). Two paths diverge on your right – 'Capital Ring', or the right-hand path with red trail marks. Follow this uphill to top of Horsenden Hill.

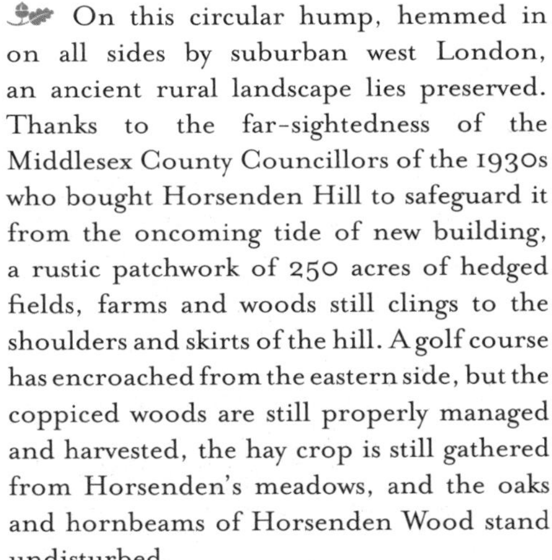

On this circular hump, hemmed in on all sides by suburban west London, an ancient rural landscape lies preserved. Thanks to the far-sightedness of the Middlesex County Councillors of the 1930s who bought Horsenden Hill to safeguard it from the oncoming tide of new building, a rustic patchwork of 250 acres of hedged fields, farms and woods still clings to the shoulders and skirts of the hill. A golf course has encroached from the eastern side, but the coppiced woods are still properly managed and harvested, the hay crop is still gathered from Horsenden's meadows, and the oaks and hornbeams of Horsenden Wood stand undisturbed.

Paths lead up and round through the wood, meandering to the top of the hill. In the early 1800s this was an 80-acre wood. Now it covers an eighth of that area. It's a small miracle that any survives at all. A grassy woodland floor lies between widely spaced old standard trees. Wild service trees, infallible signs of ancient woodland, are dotted through Horsenden Wood. An especially fine one stands by the path near the summit.

Once out in the open air, you can stroll a circuit of the hilltop and picture beautiful Ealine, Saxon wife of a boorish drunk and lecher named Bren. When Ealine's father Horsa heard from a talking starling how badly Bren was treating his lovely daughter, he sallied forth against him. Both men died in the ensuing battle, and in sorrow and pride – so legends say – Horsenden Hill was built as a vast burial mound over the tomb of bold Horsa. On misty moonlit nights he walks abroad, and those with keen ears can hear his restless charger clopping around inside the hill.

102. THE LONDON WETLAND CENTRE, QUEEN ELIZABETH WALK, BARNES, LONDON SW13

Maps: OS Explorer 161; Landranger 176; London A–Z, pp. 100 (1D) and 82 (7D)

Travel: Walk from Barnes station (north on Rocks Lane for ¾ mile, right into Queen Elizabeth Walk) or Barnes Bridge station (The Terrace, Barnes Hill St, Church Road, Queen Elizabeth Walk – ¾ mile); or tube (District, Piccadilly or Hammersmith & City lines) to Hammersmith, and bus 283 to Wetland Centre entrance in Queen Elizabeth Walk.

Wildfowl and Wetland Trust: www.wwt.org.uk

The London Wetlands centre

The gabble of geese, honking of ducks and screech of black-headed gulls greet you here. Bridges span channels between open fleets of water where wildfowl land with skidding splashes, delighting the children who throng the Wetland Centre. These former reservoirs on the south bank of the Thames, in a densely built-up area, have been transformed by the Wildfowl and Wetlands Trust into a network of complementary wetlands.

The Visitors Centre tells you much about the world's wetlands – Arctic tundra with its bogs and permafrost areas where barnacle geese breed, coniferous northern forests whose lakes hold goldeneye and smew, wetland islands of the tropics. These habitats, fourteen in all, are reproduced in miniature outside, and strolling through them you can admire their native wildfowl installed in these artificial homes-from-home in west London.

Stout gates lead you into the Wildside, a lightly managed area of ponds, reed-beds, willow and poplar groves, with patches of wet woodland where coot bob and moorhens run panicking on long green toes. There is a faint hum of traffic, but it is overlaid by birdsong, the screech of gulls and the throaty grunting of amorous toads in springtime. Wandering here, it is astonishing to look up across the feathery heads of the reeds and discover the tower blocks of Hammersmith peeping over the treetops like uninvited guests outside the gates.

103. COMMONS AND DOWNS OF SOUTH CROYDON

Maps: OS Explorer 146; Landranger 187

Travel: Coulsdon South, Riddlesdown, Whyteleaf or Whyteleaf South railway stations, or bus from West Croydon bus station to Hamsey Green Pond.

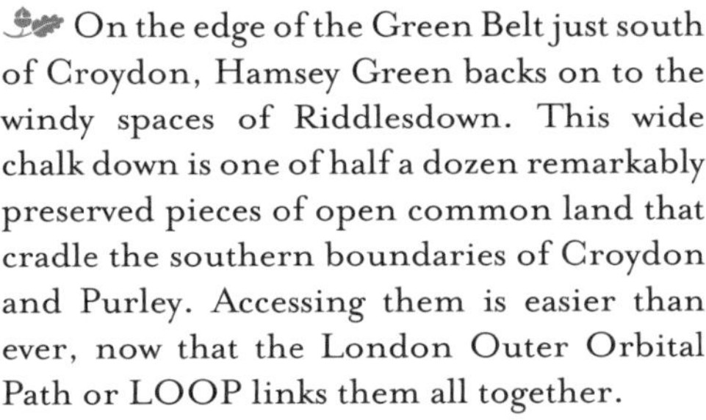

On the edge of the Green Belt just south of Croydon, Hamsey Green backs on to the windy spaces of Riddlesdown. This wide chalk down is one of half a dozen remarkably preserved pieces of open common land that cradle the southern boundaries of Croydon and Purley. Accessing them is easier than ever, now that the London Outer Orbital Path or LOOP links them all together.

These commons – Riddlesdown, Kenley Common, Coulsdon Common, Happy Valley and Farthing Downs – billow up from their deep dividing valleys. These hundreds of acres of wild ground would have been lost to the public, first enclosed for agriculture and then in all likelihood built over, if the Corporation of London had not stepped in with £7,000 and bought them all in 1883. Now carefully maintained by the Downlands Countryside Management Project, the unimproved chalk grassland of the common is traditionally managed, grazed by sheep and cattle, and mown for hay. It supports a wonderful display of lime-loving plants including marjoram and thyme, wild parsnip and yellow rattle, harebells, cowslips and orchids.

Junipers and wayfaring trees grow on the downs; small blue and chalkhill blue butterflies have thriving colonies; long hangers of beech and yew, oak and white-beam clothe the ridges. Only the far-off rush and swish of the M25 carries any reminder of the world that dashes by far below.

Follow the London LOOP path across the downs and marvel at their wildlife riches. On Farthing Downs, descending across Iron Age field banks with a tremendous view to the towers of the capital on the northern skyline, you may well give thanks for the far-sightedness of those now anonymous Victorian aldermen who realized the priceless importance of these high wild places and saved them for us in the nick of time.

104. OXLEAS WOOD, FALCONWOOD, SOUTH-EAST LONDON

Maps: OS Explorer 162; Landranger 177; London A–Z, p. 109 (G2, H2, G3, H3)

Travel: Rail to Falconwood station; right out of station, right across railway bridge ('Welling, Eltham') and continue along Rochester Way. Keep on right-hand pavement. In 300 yards cross over Welling Way at traffic lights, bear right and in 10 yards left ('Capital Ring' waymark, yellow arrow) into Oxleas Wood (OS ref. 443757).

The moment you step from the surrounding roads into the green haven of Oxleas Wood, the modern world seems irrelevant. Here in the heart of south-east London a strip of ancient woodlands is preserved, an enclave that includes Jack Wood to the west, Shepherdleas Wood to the south, and Oxleas Woods on the north and east. These three woods and the common land that links them could have disappeared under bricks and mortar at any time in the past 150 years. They certainly would have been torn apart by the East London River Crossing scheme of the 1990s, which would have sent a major highway slap through Oxleas Wood. Locally generated, nationally orchestrated protest put a stop to that. Somehow these woods – established here for many millennia, perhaps as much as 8,000 years in the case of Oxleas – have clung on.

'Oxleas' derives from the Saxon for 'ox pasture', and the wood itself was used to graze cattle as far back as the Dark Ages. Swollen oaks and hornbeams, their lower limbs pollarded until relatively recent times to allow the beasts free passage, stand deep in the wood. The hornbeams have flourished on the lower slopes to which the heavier and richer soils have been washed over the centuries. Chalk-loving trees are here, too, wayfaring trees, and London's biggest and healthiest population of wild service trees with their serrated, hand-shaped leaves – benchmarks of ancient woodland, as are the bluebells, wood anemones and yellow pimpernel that show themselves in spring. You'll find spider threads winking between the hornbeam shoots, and strange moths with wonderful names – festoon, with furry brown wings, ash-grey seraphim and oak lutestring. Tree creepers, chiffchaffs and nuthatches breed in Oxleas Wood, along with the wood warbler with its yellow cravat and white shirtfront – a bird you'll struggle to spot anywhere else in London.

105. RAINHAM MARSHES, EAST LONDON

Maps: OS Explorer 162; Landranger 177

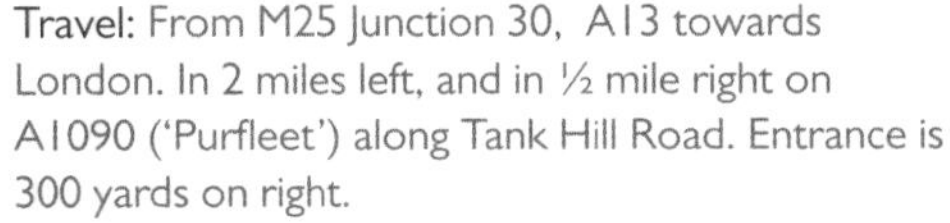

Travel: From M25 Junction 30, A13 towards London. In 2 miles left, and in ½ mile right on A1090 ('Purfleet') along Tank Hill Road. Entrance is 300 yards on right.

Nearest railway station: Purfleet (1 mile)

From the big picture windows of the large modern RSPB Visitor Centre at Rainham Marshes you get a fine overview of this remarkable place on the north shore of the Thames. Green grazing fields populated with stolid cattle stretch away among wide lagoons and long straight channels of water. Extensive reed-beds form pale blocks against the green.

A functional-looking concrete building squats in the middle distance. Towards the end of the twentieth century these empty flatlands were regarded as waste ground, fit only for military ranges (hence the bunker-like ammunition store) and as dumping grounds for rubbish. When the MoD ceased to use them in the 1990s, developers were ready to move in, but instead the 1,200 acres of Rainham, Wennington and Aveley marshes (collectively known as the Inner Thames Marshes) were bought by the RSPB, designated a Site of Special Scientific Interest, and saved – for the present – from the threat of development.

The part of the RSPB's Rainham Marshes nature reserve that is currently open to the public is actually Aveley Marshes, formerly Purfleet Rifle Range, where the grass tussocks and threading creeks have been augmented by purpose-built scrapes, lagoons and flashes of water. Bearded tits nest in the reed-beds, lapwings and skylarks in the grasses. Water voles, now an endangered species, plop into the weedy ditches at your approach along the boardwalk paths. Rare docks and sedges thrive. Water rail skulk along the water channels, and barn owls are seen floating like ghosts across the marshes at night.

At present the marshes, particularly at the western end, are rather forlorn, but one day the entire site will be open to birdwatchers, walkers, cyclists and other users of green open spaces. There are plans to develop the whole of the southern half as a public park under the name of 'Wildspace'. Whether that will destroy the current atmosphere of wildness remains to be seen.

4

ESSEX, SUFFOLK, NORFOLK, CAMBRIDGESHIRE, LINCOLNSHIRE

EAST ANGLIA

It's often said that no one goes to East Anglia without meaning to. No motorway penetrates the rural core, and low-lying Cambridgeshire, in spite of the M11 that crosses its heart, is nobody's idea of a suburban county. It is an old-fashioned, slow-moving region, and it is to its marshy, secretive shores that we go for wild birds, empty horizons (though threatened now with the visual intrusion of wind turbines) and windy vistas.

FENS, BROADS AND MARSHES form a trio of characteristic East Anglian landscapes. Though the broads, remnants of the peat diggings of medieval peasants, are man-made, they share with the other two the properties of great flatness, wateriness and loneliness. Under the vast skies of Norfolk and Cambridgeshire these flatlands, reflecting the blue or grey whirling overhead in their creeks and fleets of water, have a moody and seductive beauty. I walk them to be in isolation, to let mind and spirit roam beyond the point where land meets water and sky.

East Anglians have always been individualists. Rough men of the coast of former days have their contemporary counterparts here, living on the fringes of the law in creek-bound houseboats or home-made chalets. The wonderful parish churches of the Middle Ages, in which the region is richer than any other of comparable size in Britain, form an incomparable fleet of elaborate 'ships of God' – a curious fact in an area almost completely devoid of good building stone. Flint cobbles, ragstone and brick were all pressed into service. And into these ordered places their builders smuggled a heterodox treasure of painted and carved embellishments that speak more of the wild than they do of calm and contemplation – Green Men, red dragons and, in the chancel arch of St Peter's Church at Wenhaston in Suffolk, a depiction of the torments of the medieval damned lively and savage enough to stop any sinner in his tracks.

Nature is busy absorbing the works of man at South Elmham on the Suffolk/Norfolk border, where a Saxon minster church stands forgotten in a wood, and up on the Norfolk Broads, where the old flooded peat pits are now the weedy breeding grounds of dragonflies,

Above: Dunwich Heath (pp. 138–9). Below: Benfleet and Hadleigh Marshes (p. 129)

frogs and rare water plants. Man is giving this process a helping hand in such diverse reserves as Wicken Fen in the heart of Cambridgeshire, Scolt Head Island of the seals and shore plants on the North Norfolk coast, and Wallasea Island in the remote marsh creeks east of everywhere. Here on the low-lying Essex shore the rising level of the sea is expected to overwhelm much of the coast. The sea walls are being bent far inland to create new saltmarshes at the expense of good farmland – land which was itself initially created by walling off and draining the tidal grounds of the coast. And so the wheel turns, from wild to tamed, and back again to wild.

LINKS

- Peddars Way and Norfolk Coast Path National Trail (www.nationaltrail.co.uk/peddarsway): (link to the Wash), Scolt Head Island, Stiffkey, Blakeney Point, Poppyland cliffs
- Suffolk Coast and Heaths Path (www.suffolkcoastandheaths.org): Walberswick marshes, Dunwich Heath, Shingle Street

NATIONAL PARK

- The Broads: www.broads-authority.gov.uk

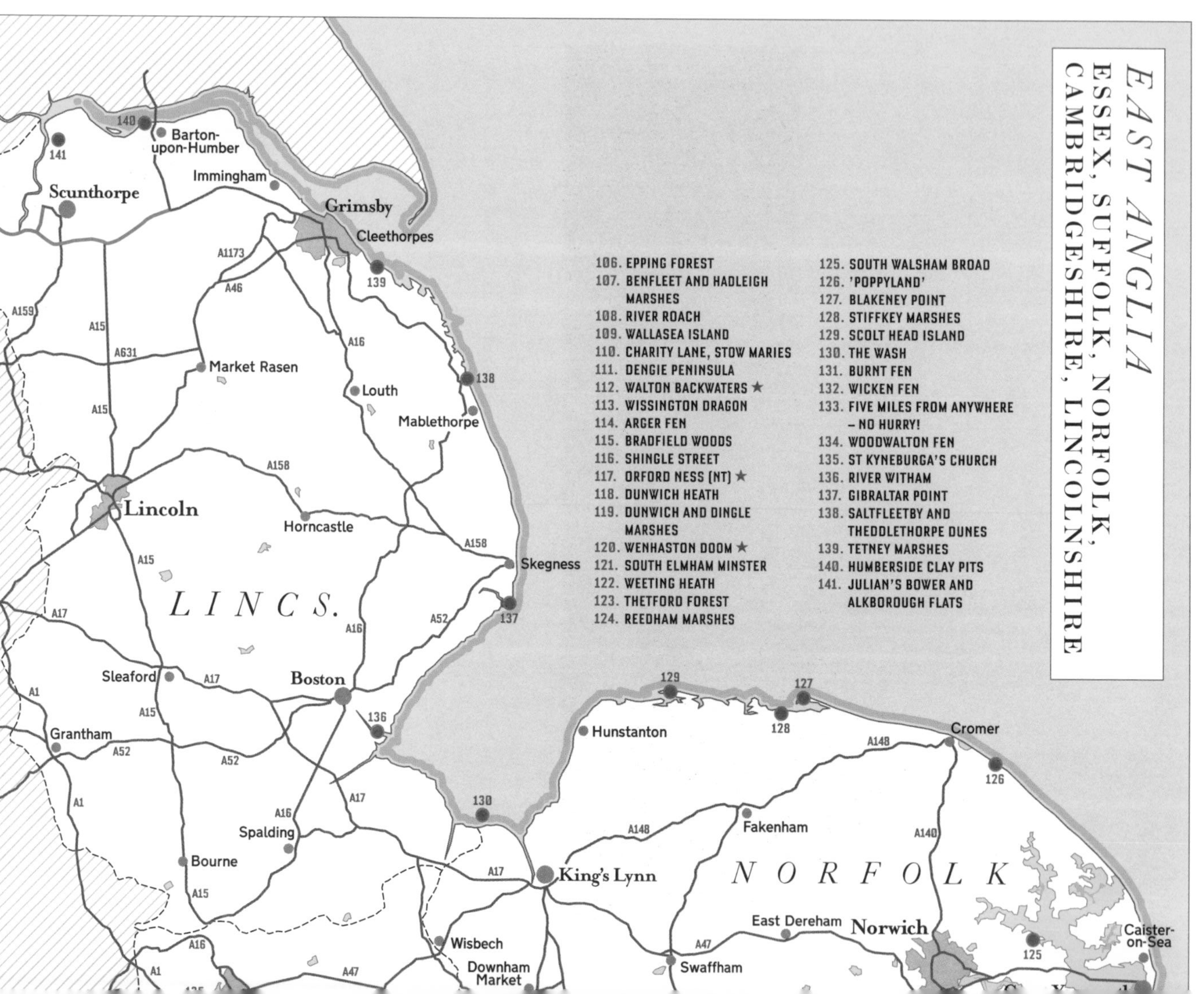

EAST ANGLIA
ESSEX, SUFFOLK, NORFOLK, CAMBRIDGESHIRE, LINCOLNSHIRE
106. EPPING FOREST
107. BENFLEET AND HADLEIGH MARSHES
108. RIVER ROACH
109. WALLASEA ISLAND
110. CHARITY LANE, STOW MARIES
111. DENGIE PENINSULA
112. WALTON BACKWATERS ★
113. WISSINGTON DRAGON
114. ARGER FEN
115. BRADFIELD WOODS
116. SHINGLE STREET
117. ORFORD NESS (NT) ★
118. DUNWICH HEATH
119. DUNWICH AND DINGLE MARSHES
120. WENHASTON DOOM ★
121. SOUTH ELMHAM MINSTER
122. WEETING HEATH
123. THETFORD FOREST
124. REEDHAM MARSHES
125. SOUTH WALSHAM BROAD
126. 'POPPYLAND'
127. BLAKENEY POINT
128. STIFFKEY MARSHES
129. SCOLT HEAD ISLAND
130. THE WASH
131. BURNT FEN
132. WICKEN FEN
133. FIVE MILES FROM ANYWHERE – NO HURRY!
134. WOODWALTON FEN
135. ST KYNEBURGA'S CHURCH
136. RIVER WITHAM
137. GIBRALTAR POINT
138. SALTFLEETBY AND THEDDLETHORPE DUNES
139. TETNEY MARSHES
140. HUMBERSIDE CLAY PITS
141. JULIAN'S BOWER AND ALKBOROUGH FLATS
LINCS.
NORFOLK
Barton-upon-Humber
Scunthorpe
Immingham
Grimsby
Cleethorpes
Market Rasen
Louth
Mablethorpe
Lincoln
Horncastle
Skegness
Sleaford
Boston
Grantham
Spalding
Bourne
Hunstanton
Cromer
Fakenham
King's Lynn
East Dereham
Norwich
Caister-on-Sea
Wisbech
Downham Market
Swaffham

Peterborough
THE BROADS
Lowestoft
Attleborough
Thetford
Bungay
Diss
Southwold
CAMBS.
Ely
Huntingdon
Newmarket
SUFFOLK
Bury St Edmunds
Saxmundham
Cambridge
Stowmarket
Aldeburgh
Woodbridge
Duxford
Ipswich
Sudbury
Saffron Walden
Felixstowe
ESSEX
Manningtree
Harwich
Colchester
Braintree
Wivenhoe
Kelvedon
Frinton-on-Sea
Clacton-on-Sea
Chelmsford
Maldon
Brentwood
Basildon
Benfleet
Southend-on-Sea
Canvey Island
Tilbury
Scale 5 m 10 km
A141
A1(M)
A1
A14
A10
A142
A428
A1033
A11
A1066
A143
A140
A12
A134
A131
A154
A120
A133
A130
A414
A127
A13
M11
M25
106
107
108
109
110
111
112
113
114
115
116
117
118
119
120
121
122
123
131
132
133
134

106. EPPING FOREST, ESSEX

Maps: OS Explorer 174; Landranger 167

Travel: From M25 Junction 26, A121, A104 to Ranger's Road car park near Chingford (OS ref. 405951 – south end of Epping Forest) or A121, B172 to Jack's Hill car park (435995 – north end). The Three Forests Way/Green Ride runs through Epping Forest, with numerous side turnings for pedestrians and riders.

Nearest railway stations: Loughton or Epping tube stations (Central Line)

It seems remarkable that Epping Forest's 6,000 acres of tangled old woodland have survived right on London's doorstep. But this 'green lung' of the capital, wide and wild though it is, represents only a fragment of the vast Royal Forest of Waltham where the monarchs of England once went to hunt. Even in the mid eighteenth century Epping Forest covered nearly ten times its present area. By then the forest was notorious as a hang-out for rogues and vagabonds. Epping had become as much a place of fear and apprehension for ordinary citizens as it was of resource for the commoners who grazed their animals in the woods and pollarded the trees for the thinnings that went to make tool handles and the raw materials of houses and cattle sheds.

Walking the Three Forests Way today, one sees straight away that the largest specimens of Epping's magnificent old beeches and hornbeams have not been pollarded for a very long time. The branches that were once snipped off short every few years now reach up to the forest canopy 70 or 80 feet overhead. These wildly overshot trees were last trimmed back in the years before 1878, when the City of London Corporation took over Epping Forest to safeguard what was left of it. The forest had been decimated by centuries of neglect, of encroachment and of tree-felling for house-building and agricultural development. The takeover was bitterly resented by the commoners, now forbidden to exercise their ancient rights, and Epping Forest soon faced problems of pollution, noise and vandalism in its new role as a green place of resort for day-tripping Londoners. Drunken parties, fairground stalls and rowdy behaviour threatened to destroy what was left of the forest's peace, until stringent by-laws were enforced and a new culture of quiet enjoyment took hold.

Under the trees are hidden the earthworks of two Iron Age camps with strange histories. Ambresbury Banks, towards the northern end of the forest (OS ref. 438003), was probably the site of Queen Boudicca's last stand against the invading Romans in the first century AD. Further south, near the Epping Forest Centre, lie the ramparts of Loughton Camp (418975). In one of the hut circles inside the earthworks, the Whitechapel butcher's-apprentice-turned-highwayman Dick Turpin had a hideout in the 1730s during the early part of his short and riotous career of crime.

Back then you wouldn't have wanted to stray anywhere near Loughton Camp. These days the old earthen stronghold lies under a smother of great beech trees, silent and forgotten at the heart of the forest.

107. BENFLEET AND HADLEIGH MARSHES, CANVEY ISLAND, ESSEX

Maps: OS Explorer 176; Landranger 178

Travel: From M25 Junction 30, A13 towards Southend-on-Sea; right on A130 at South Benfleet on to Canvey Island. At roundabout, left on B1014. Park near sea wall (OS ref. 780853) and walk east above the marshes.

Nearest railway station: Benfleet (½ mile)

For many people Canvey Island is the antithesis of a wild place. The big flat island off the Essex shore of the Thames Estuary is completely built up for the eastern two-thirds of its area. There are gas and oil storage silos along its Thames-facing shore. Only at the western end do green acres lie, and they are all sunken grazing marsh below the level of high tide. Yet along the north side of Canvey Island, and off its eastern tip, stretches a world of saltmarshes and mudflats untrodden by anyone, apart from the occasionally adventurous island youngster. Walk here, along the low old sea wall, amongst the piping of oystercatchers and the scolding of black-headed gulls, and workaday Canvey fades away.

Before 1620, when Dutchman Joos van Croppenburgh built the first sea wall here, Canvey was six islands, good sheep-grazing ground that was covered by the sea at high spring tides. At low tides the flocks were driven on to the islands, and milked in the pastures by shepherds with three-legged stools strapped to their buttocks for ease of squatting. The sea wall created one island out of six – but Canvey Island still lies wholly below high spring-tide level.

The island is separated from the Essex shore by 12 miles of narrow, winding creek – Holehaven Creek on the west, Benfleet Creek and Hadleigh Creek close to the north coast of the island, and then Hadleigh Ray and Ray Gut where the gap widens between Leigh and Chapman Sands to the east. Here lie long mud and marsh islets in a maze of creeks, thronged with oystercatchers, plover and black-headed gulls at low water when the food-laden mudbanks are exposed. At high tide it is a different story, as the islands disappear and the gut, the ray and the creeks fill with the tide.

Nowadays a high concrete sea wall runs 15 feet above normal high-tide level. It scarcely looks as if it needs to be so tall. But in January 1953, an era when the wall was lower and weaker, an exceptionally high tide broke through at Newlands. It flooded Canvey Island and drowned fifty-eight people – a tragedy no one here has forgotten.

108. RIVER ROACH, ESSEX

Maps: OS Explorer 176; Landranger 178

Travel: From M25 Junction 29, A127 to Southend-on-Sea; left on B1013 to Rochford. Broomhills (OS ref. 889903) lies a mile east of Rochford on north bank of River Roach.

NB: Broomhills is private property and not open to the public, but you can glimpse it from the Roach Valley Way footpath.

For Paglesham Churchend (925931) take minor road east from Rochford through Great Stambridge and Ballards Gore.

Nearest railway station: Rochford

The Roach Valley Way's symbol shows a goose flying over the reed-beds of a wide river. That perfectly sums up the River Roach landscape, a flat and lonely one through which the tidal river creeps between high-piled mudbanks. This moody corner of coastal Essex has produced strong, not to say idiosyncratic, characters – in particular, two notably wild men from this area.

The riverbank house of Broomhills, a mile east of Rochford, was where the great eighteenth-century adventurer John Harriott came to end his days. Born in the parish in 1745, Harriott was inspired by reading *Robinson Crusoe* to go out and see the world. First he sailed as a midshipman in a Royal Navy vessel-of-war to New York, where he rescued an Irishwoman from a compromising situation and restored her to her friends. A cruise in the Mediterranean and a shipwreck followed. Rescued and put on dry land, Harriott shipped again and took part in the Royal Navy capture of Havana in July 1762. Next he voyaged to St Petersburg, sailed to Jamaica and fought a duel there; then he went to America and joined an Indian tribe.

By now Harriott was twenty-one, and extremely lucky to be still alive. Undaunted, he sailed to Madras and joined the East India Company's campaign of 1767–9 against the usurping ruler Hyder Ali. The wound he received in this fighting seems to have cooled him off, for he returned home to become a farmer and insurance broker. He lost all his East India money investing unwisely in the spirit trade, and subsided into the comparative peace of his riverside abode. *Robinson Crusoe* had a lot to answer for.

The second River Roach wild man never travelled far from home, but he made his mark all the same. William Blyth, born in 1756 in Paglesham Churchend and known far and wide as 'Hard Apple', was a fantastically successful smuggler, operating at roughly the same time as John Harriott was living up the river at Broomhills. Hard Apple's cutter *Big Jane* was well known to the Excise men. Once they actually had the smuggler and his gang imprisoned on board the Excise boat, having caught them red-handed with a hold full of brandy kegs. But the Revenue captain made the mistake of inviting Hard Apple to his cabin for a drink. While the two were toasting each other, the smuggler crew were down below carousing with the Revenue men and 'helping' them transfer the kegs from *Big Jane*. The king's men became so drunk they fell asleep, whereupon the smugglers reversed the direction of the kegs. *Big Jane*'s hold refilled, they sailed away to scoff another day.

Hard Apple was a grocer by trade. He was also the Paglesham churchwarden, and would tear out pages from the parish register to use as wrapping for his customers' goods. The church tower made a handy hiding place for contraband. He was a showman who kept his hold over the ruffians of his gang by amazing them with his extravagant deeds. These included wrestling a bull to the ground, munching wine glasses and drinking a whole keg of brandy at a sitting.

Hard Apple died in 1840, at the age of eighty-four. On his deathbed he had a chapter of the Bible read to him, then turned his face to the wall and uttered his final words: 'Thank you – now I'm ready for the launch.'

109. WALLASEA ISLAND, ESSEX

Maps: OS Explorer 176; Landranger 178

Travel: From M25 Junction 29, A127 to Southend-on-Sea; left on A1159; in ¾ mile, right at roundabout for 1 mile to Rochford. Right on minor road for 5 miles, through Great Stambridge and Ballards Gore to Wallasea Island. Park at Grapnells Farm (OS ref. 943947) – neatly, please! Follow 'Wetlands' signs along concrete farm road (a permissive path). In ¾ mile, left over ditch and up to noticeboard on sea wall (955946).

NB: Owing to future coastal realignment schemes, walking routes on Wallasea may change.

Out at the eastern tip of south Essex lies Wallasea Island, as green and flat as the landscape around it, a great 1,800-acre slab of intensively farmed land shaped like a back-to-front Cyprus. Wallasea was composed of several islands before Dutch engineers began to build sea walls and drain the marsh back in Tudor times. Over the years a single piece of land emerged, to be worked as first-class farmland. The island lies in a remote corner between the muddy rivers Crouch and Roach, one of a number of islands that form a complicated jigsaw of fractured land. Few outsiders venture here. But that is all due to change, for Wallasea Island is the setting of a bold experiment by the RSPB, which will give back to the sea what has been painstakingly retrieved from it over the centuries.

No one would call Wallasea Island wild just at present. With its ruler-straight, sterile water channels and blank prairies of corn it seems a perfect exemplar of modern agriculture. Yet it is set to be returned to the wild. The flood walls will be breached and the sea allowed to flood the island. That would happen in the natural order of things in any case, as sea levels rise in the twenty-first century. But on Wallasea Island it will be carefully controlled with sluices, shallow pools, internal banks, spillways and other devices to create a new network of saltmarsh and lagoons, mudflats and islets.

In 2006 the first breaches were made in the north coast sea wall. Low-tide lagoons and

Wallasea Island

acres of new mud formed almost at once. A green flush of algae and haze of marsh plants spread within months. A 300-acre wetland had come into being, and sightings of avocet and godwit, wigeon and dark-bellied brent geese, peregrines and marsh harriers rose significantly. When the 'Big Flood' is established, there are strong hopes of seeing the return of species that have been driven away from these coasts by loss of habitat or persecution in former times – spoonbills, which last nested here before Wallasea became one island, and perhaps the little wading Kentish plover, which vanished from its English coastal breeding grounds shortly after the Second World War.

110. CHARITY LANE, STOW MARIES, ESSEX

Maps: OS Explorer 183; Landranger 168

Travel: From M25 Junction 29, A127 towards Southend-on-Sea; A130 north towards Chelmsford. In 3 miles, right on A132 to South Woodham Ferrers; left on B1418 towards Bicknacre. At ½ mile beyond Woodham Ferrers, right ('Stow Maries'); follow zigzag lane for 1¼ miles to turn left at grassy triangle (OS ref. 810001). In 300 yards pass Charity Farm; in another 400 yards, round sharp left bend. Park here (816004). Where the road bends right walk ahead, north along Charity Lane.

Nearest railway station: South Woodham Ferrers (4 miles)

In the ordered, intensively farmed landscape of rural south Essex, ancient lanes are one of the few manifestations of the wild. Some old green lanes have been ploughed out, or are so little used that they have declined to become thick hedgerows. But many others are still there, smuggling in their loads of birdsong, wild flowers and tree species among the cornfields and ploughlands. In the hinterland near Woodham Ferrers, inland of the Dengie Peninsula (see below), Charity Lane performs that function in its mile-long northward course through a landscape of new farming methods and old farmsteads. England's green lanes have been around a long time. Charity Lane itself dates back to the Middle Ages; others are the remnants of Saxon warpaths, Roman thoroughfares, or ancient trackways. They mesh the countryside together, though the motor car has made them redundant.

The old green lane runs straight and true in a wild tunnel of trees, a purposeful thoroughfare between farms, now superseded by tarmac roads. Dating old lanes by the woody species in their hedges – a hundred years for every species in a randomly chosen 100-yard stretch – may be scientifically inaccurate, but it's a fair rule of thumb. Judging by the oak, ash, holly, elm, hawthorn, blackthorn and hornbeam in the hedges of Charity Lane, the green lane might be as old as the medieval farmsteads all round: Hobclerk's, Flambird's, Jacklett's, Wickham's.

111. DENGIE PENINSULA, ESSEX

Maps: OS Explorer 176; Landranger 168

Travel: A12 to Chelmsford bypass, A414 towards Maldon; B1010 and B1018 to Latchingdon. Keep ahead by Latchingdon Church on minor road through Mayland and Steeple for 8 miles; left on B1021 to Bradwell Waterside. Park here (OS ref. 995079) and walk east on sea-wall path.

Nearest railway stations: Burnham-on-Crouch or Southminster

The blunt-nosed peninsula of Dengie,

pushing out east between the estuaries of Crouch and Blackwater, is less than an hour's journey from central London. This is a moody, haunting retreat on the capital's doorstep, overlooked and ignored by outsiders. Here are saltings and mudflats, decoy pools, marshes and curious weather-boarded villages. Anything less 'London' would be hard to imagine.

Dengie dwellers reclaimed the marshes from early medieval times; you can trace the original shoreline along the course of the B1021 from Burnham-on-Crouch to Bradwell on the River Blackwater. These wildfowlers, duck-netters, fishermen and reed-cutters lived a precarious existence that often proved terminally unhealthy for outsiders. In 1720 Daniel Defoe recorded how local men would take a young wife from the uplands, 'healthy, fresh and clear, and well; but when they came out of their native air into the marshes among the fogs and damps, there they presently changed their complexion, got an ague or two, and seldom held it above a half a year'. When Defoe asked his Dengie-born interlocutor what local men did when their wives died, he replied, 'We go to the uplands and get another.'

It is on the sea wall that you properly appreciate the wildness of Dengie. From Bradwell to Burnham around the coast is 16 long miles, and you rarely see a soul. Once past the grim cubes of Bradwell's redundant nuclear power station, you quickly approach one of the oldest and loneliest churches in Britain, the Saxon chapel of St Peter's-on-the-Wall, out at the north-east tip of the peninsula. At the time of writing there are plans to destroy the sublime flatness of its prospect, out across saltmarsh and cockleshells, by erecting a clutch of 400-foot-tall wind turbines. The question is: where will people turn for an empty horizon and sense of their own insignificance, when every skyline is busy with man-made shapes?

112. WALTON BACKWATERS, ESSEX

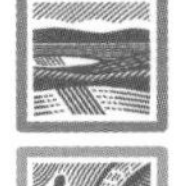

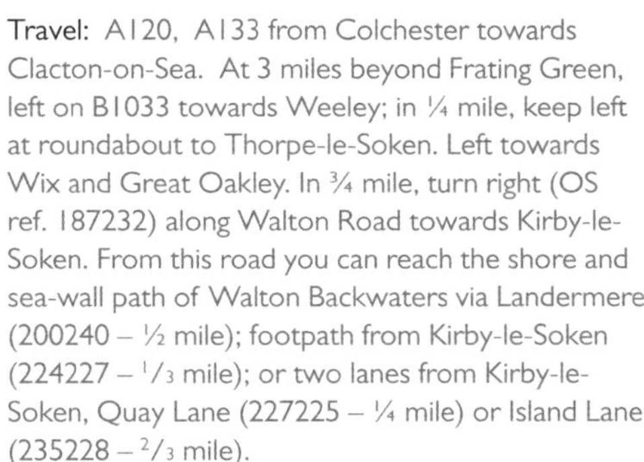
Maps: OS Explorer 184; Landranger 169

Travel: A120, A133 from Colchester towards Clacton-on-Sea. At 3 miles beyond Frating Green, left on B1033 towards Weeley; in ¼ mile, keep left at roundabout to Thorpe-le-Soken. Left towards Wix and Great Oakley. In ¾ mile, turn right (OS ref. 187232) along Walton Road towards Kirby-le-Soken. From this road you can reach the shore and sea-wall path of Walton Backwaters via Landermere (200240 – ½ mile); footpath from Kirby-le-Soken (224227 – 1/3 mile); or two lanes from Kirby-le-Soken, Quay Lane (227225 – ¼ mile) or Island Lane (235228 – 2/3 mile).

Nearest railway stations: Kirby Cross (1½ miles from sea wall by footpath) or Frinton-on-Sea (1¾ miles by Turpins Lane and Island Lane)

This vast waste of mud and marsh, 12 square miles in area, has a wildly indented shoreline that measures some 20 miles or more, and lies like an inland sea behind Walton-on-the-Naze. Twice every twenty-four hours it is filled by the sea. Then the flat marsh islands, indistinguishable at low tide from the marsh and mud around them, separate and take on individual characters – Hedge-end Island, New Island and Pewit Island with their dozens of tiny, wriggling creeks, the green and bushy nature reserve of Skipper's Island, and Horsey Island, five times the size of the others, the only one with a properly negotiable causeway and inhabited farmhouse.

A keen amateur sailor of the Essex creeks, Arthur Ransome felt the seductive wildness of the Walton Backwaters. Here he set his seventh Swallows and Amazons yarn, *Secret Water*. The children camp out on Horsey Island, almost drowning on the causeway. Today, seals lie out on the mudbanks, fieldfares and brent geese overwinter, brown hares run through the grasses. Seen from the sea-wall path the Backwaters gleam olive and purple in bunched horizontal lines as far as the horizon. Seen from the air they are a jigsaw of brown and green. Either way they never cease to fascinate.

113. WISSINGTON DRAGON, SUFFOLK

Maps: OS Explorer 196; Landranger 168

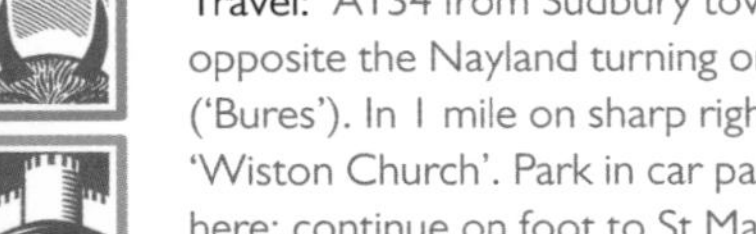

Travel: A134 from Sudbury towards Colchester; opposite the Nayland turning on left, bear right ('Bures'). In 1 mile on sharp right bend, follow 'Wiston Church'. Park in car parking space along here; continue on foot to St Mary's Church (OS ref. 955333).

Nearest railway station: Bures (4 miles)

The church of St Mary the Virgin at Wissington (pronounced and sometimes spelled 'Wiston') stands beside Wiston Hall on the north bank of the River Stour where Suffolk looks across the river into Essex. This is peaceful, quintessentially English countryside, perfectly caught in the paintings of local boy John Constable. The damp little Norman church holds some fine red ochre frescoes of a very early date – probably around 1280. Here are St Nicholas in a tub-like sailing boat, St Francis feeding the birds, and the angel stirring the Three Wise Men from their communal slumber.

Over the north doorway stretches a figure far stranger than any of these – a great red dragon, his mouth open, bat-like wings raised and tail splendidly curled. He brings a bracing smack of exotic oddness to the conventional Christian depictions.

A local legend tells of a dragon suddenly appearing in the nearby town of Bures in the spring of 1405. The monster was described by the monk who chronicled the episode as 'vast in body with a crested head, saw-like teeth and a tail of enormous length'. Its armour was so strong that arrows bounced off it. The beast turned savage, devoured the villagers, and then dived into the river and swam away to hide itself in Wormingford Mere – the 'pool of the dragon's ford'. An old tradition says that either the Devil or his horrible creature still disturbs the waters there.

Perhaps the dragon was really a crocodile; one was reported as having escaped from the royal menagerie in the Tower of London around that time. None of the superstitious Suffolk peasants who gathered to repel the beast would have seen a crocodile before, but most would have seen the painting of the monster over the door of Wissington Church – and, however ill-educated, were quite as capable as we are today of putting two and two together to make five. The beast they saw looked like the dragon on the church wall – *ergo* it, too, must have been a dragon.

Or maybe there is a further twist to the tale. The dragon fresco may not be of early medieval date at all. Some experts say it was painted half a century or so after the dragon/crocodile episode. Such a tale would have been currency in the local countryside for decades. Maybe the painting actually *represents* the crocodile – and its long, snarling jaws are the artist's depiction of those that caused such wonder and terror in his grandfather's day.

114. ARGER FEN, SUFFOLK

Maps: OS Explorer 196; Landranger 155

Travel: A134 Sudbury towards Colchester. In 4 miles, right through Assington. At ½ mile beyond Assington, left ('Arger Fen'). In 1 mile, pass through a watersplash; car park is 300 yards up hill on left (OS ref. 930353) beside entrance to Arger Fen.

Nearest railway station: Bures (2 miles on foot)

Arger Fen is a work in progress, a former Forestry Commission wood which was planted in 1962 with heavy conifers, fast-growing grand fir and Corsican pine, and which for the last twenty years has been undergoing regeneration as a local nature reserve. The big conifers are being felled and taken out, light is being allowed in to the understorey again, and the whole wood is coming back to life.

Arger Fen's few decades with the Forestry Commission represent only a tiny blip in an extremely long existence. This is a remnant of England's ancient wildwood, and has been in use (more sustainably than under the FC of the 1960s) since the early Middle Ages as a commoners' wood where locals had the right to collect firewood. Medieval parish boundary banks cross the centre of the wood, and as you walk the paths you'll spot the hollows where clay was dug several hundred years ago to daub the walls of houses.

Bluebells and wild garlic carpet Arger Fen in spring. Greater spotted woodpeckers breed here, as do goldcrests. A splendid feature of the wood is the huge, gnarled old cherry trees,

Arger Fen

their bark cracked laterally, shining a dull red where the light strikes through. Some stand 80 feet tall, leafless except for the uppermost canopy – they have had to fight for light against the swiftly growing conifers. Now they look strangely naked, standing solitary in the centre of patches crammed with firs and pines not so long ago.

At present there are jungly parts and bald parts in Arger Fen; lush undergrowth full of flowers, and bare slopes not yet recovered from their long lack of light. But this is a wood getting back on its feet, and it is endlessly fascinating to watch it slowly assume a wilder, less regimented atmosphere.

115. BRADFIELD WOODS, SUFFOLK

Maps: OS Explorer 211; Landranger 155

Travel: A14 Bury St Edmunds towards Stowmarket; in 3 miles right to Beyton. Follow 'Hessett' and 'Felsham'. In 4 miles, right at T-junction ('Bradfield St George' and brown 'Bradfield Woods' sign). Car park ½ mile on left (OS ref. 935580).

Nearest railway station: Thurston (6 miles)

This is one of the finest and oldest coppiced woods in Britain. Felsham Hill and Monks Park Wood – together known as Bradfield Woods – were owned by Bury St Edmunds Abbey in medieval times, and have been coppiced since at least that era. Some of the ash and alder stools date back to the Middle Ages, measure 10 feet across, and are still productive. The whole 151-acre site is a wildlife treasure, though Monks Park, 58 acres at present, was more than three times that size until the late 1960s. The great age, productivity and ecological value of the woods did not prevent 130 acres of it being felled and cleared for intensive agriculture. Eventually the Royal Society for Nature Conservation stepped in and bought what was left in the 1970s, and Suffolk Wildlife Trust has managed it ever since.

Paths wind around the woods, weaving between alder coppice and mighty oak and ash pollards, trees that had their lower limbs docked to allow animals to graze underneath. Deer crash away among the trees – tiny muntjac shelter here, along with fallow and roe deer from time to time. The wood is full of butterflies; red admiral and painted lady are two of the most spectacular, but you can also spot the beautiful speckled wood, large cream-encircled dark dots along the scalloped edges of its trailing wings.

The woods stand on soil that varies from wet to dry, exposed to sheltered, alkaline clay to acid sand. So much variety in such a small area means wonderful flora, with nearly 400 species recorded – wood anemones and bluebells on the sand, spindle and early purple orchids on the clay. And it is the alkaline soil that sustains one of the rarities of Bradfield Woods, the beautiful pale yellow oxlip, like a cross between a primrose and a cowslip, which grows by the dozen in newly coppiced areas in spring.

What with the nightingales and the dormice, the frogs in the ponds and the stoats in the old logs, Bradfield Woods seems a Tardis in an alien world of hedgeless, charmless East Anglian agriculture.

116. SHINGLE STREET, SUFFOLK

Maps: OS Explorer 197; Landranger 169

Travel: A12 from Ipswich to Woodbridge; A1152 ('Orford, Rendlesham, Melton'). At ½ mile beyond Melton level crossing, right at roundabout on B1083 ('Hollesley, Bawdsey'). In 1 mile, left ('Hollesley'). In Hollesley, follow 'Shingle Street'; park at end of road (OS ref. 366426).

Nearest railway station: Melton (8 miles)

Shingle Street is only a strip of houses on a barren shore at the end of a lonely road. Yet I have always been drawn here. The old coastguard barracks and weather-boarded cottages flank a pebbly shore whose high-piled shingle bank grows leather-leafed sea kale with tiny white flowers, and great bushes of yellow-horned poppy whose large papery petals fall at a touch. The shore sweeps to the south in a gentle curve, and walking here away from the hamlet you can hardly imagine hearing another voice, there is so much time and space. It was in places such as this that England waited grimly to be invaded by the forces of Napoleon Bonaparte at the turn of the nineteenth century.

On the shore at Shingle Street, four Martello towers bear witness to that era of tension and defiance. Three of the four stubby structures have been converted into

Shingle Street

houses; the fourth stands in a cornfield behind the sea wall. Where a nineteenth-century cannon once stood on the roof, a pillbox now squats, placed there during the Second World War to gain a view over the bank. The grey cladding on the old tower's brick walls is crumbling, and its semi-elliptical windows look out blankly towards the sea wall. Owls and mice are the only creatures that use the tower nowadays.

Standing on guard in the corn, bounded by a brackish marsh where kestrels hang in the wind, the abandoned Martello tower wears an air both forlorn and poignant. Had Napoleon's men ever come ashore, they would simply have walked round the towers and gone on inland, to London and victory.

117. ORFORD NESS (NT), SUFFOLK

Maps: OS Explorer 212; Landranger 156

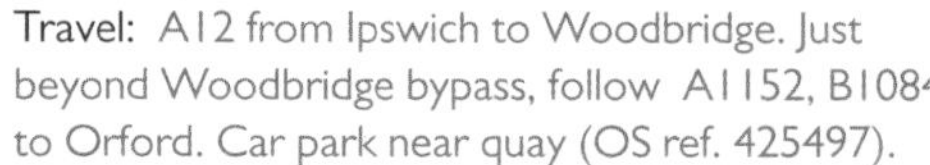

Travel: A12 from Ipswich to Woodbridge. Just beyond Woodbridge bypass, follow A1152, B1084 to Orford. Car park near quay (OS ref. 425497).

Ferry to Orford Ness: Check on dates and times: tel: 01394 450047 / 450900; www.nationaltrust.org.uk

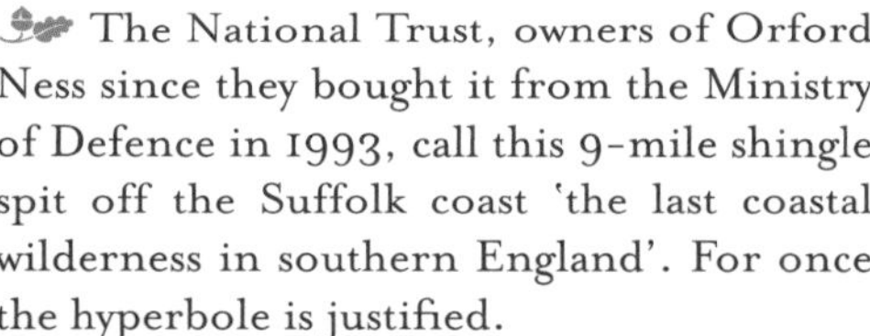

The National Trust, owners of Orford Ness since they bought it from the Ministry of Defence in 1993, call this 9-mile shingle spit off the Suffolk coast 'the last coastal wilderness in southern England'. For once the hyperbole is justified.

Crossing the River Alde to walk on Orford Ness is the nearest thing in Britain to entering the desert. And the shapes that pierce the level horizons seem as outlandish as any mirage: a bleak tower straight out of Mordor, a grim metallic building as big as a city block, a scatter of enigmatic structures like Chinese pagodas, half buried in the shingle. Orford Ness is one of those places where resurgent nature engages with and undermines man's abandoned structures. The pagodas housed Cold War experiments on atomic bombs (without their fissile material, we are told), which were baked, frozen, spun and dropped to test their reactions. The gaunt tower was the Black Beacon, a marine radio beacon that doubled as a top-secret transmitter. And the huge grey tin box, which nowadays broadcasts the BBC World Service, was the nerve centre of Cobra Mist, an over-ambitious radar system forever plagued by a mysterious hum, which was supposed to be able to monitor Soviet rocket and bomber flights far behind the Iron Curtain and beyond the curve of the

Orford Ness

Earth. The outline of its enormous, fan-shaped aerial reflector can still be traced on the ground like the ghost of a monstrous spider's web.

There are colour-coded trails that take you around Orford Ness and show you these sites; they also put you in among a stunning variety of seabirds and plants of marsh and shingle. To walk on the Ness is to witness a minor miracle: the survival of a fragile, highly specialized environment that would probably have been driven over, dug and drained out of existence if the MoD had not settled here during the First World War and excluded all outsiders for the next eighty years. The destructive effects of twentieth-century agriculture and development did not register on this side of the River Alde.

In the hollows of the shingle you lose sight of both sea and land, and walk in a world of dry stones and their tough, colourful plants. The only sound apart from gull cries is the hiss and drag of the North Sea at the edge of the spit, the essential backdrop of the Suffolk coast that Benjamin Britten wove into the fabric of *Curlew River* and *Peter Grimes*. This is a place to savour, strange and unique.

118. DUNWICH HEATH, SUFFOLK

Maps: OS Explorer 231; Landranger 156

Travel: A12 from Saxmundham towards Lowestoft; just past Yoxford, right to Westleton. Continue on Dunwich road for 1½ miles; just before Dunwich, right along Minsmere road for 1 mile to Dunwich Heath car park (OS ref. 476685).

The Sandlings of the Suffolk coast are lonely country. These heaths once spread all the way from Ipswich to Lowestoft, a low-lying, rolling landscape of heather, silver birch, gorse and shingly sand. Chalk and clay underlie them, but these benign elements were covered 10 million years ago by huge deposits of sand and gravel. A retreat by the sea 1 million years ago dumped more vast beds of shingle, and these were piled still higher – in places up to 50 feet – by a receding glacier at the end of the last Ice Age. Forests grew here and were cleared for agriculture and grazing; their shoots were kept under control by sheep and rabbits, and heather grew in their place, producing a wide belt of heath open to coast winds, salt spray and occasional inundations.

Since the Second World War conifer planting, intensive farming and building development have all decimated the Sandlings heaths. Dunwich Heath remains, a sombre tract of isolated scrub and heather inland of a pebbly coast. Birds of stony open places nest here – visiting whinchats with their bold eyeliner and rattling little calls, and their residential cousins the stonechats with black caps and pinky-red waistcoats, whose call sounds like two flints being clicked together. Long-eared owls swoop from the pine trees fringing the heath and hunt the open ground at nightfall. Walk here in the dusk and you'll hear their deep, abrupt hoots, and also, if you're lucky, the *churrrr* of a nightjar, sitting tight on its ground scrape, camouflaged to resemble a dead pine log, before it flies off to hunt moths through the half-light.

Dunwich Heath

119. DUNWICH AND DINGLE MARSHES, SUFFOLK

Maps: OS Explorer 231; Landranger 156

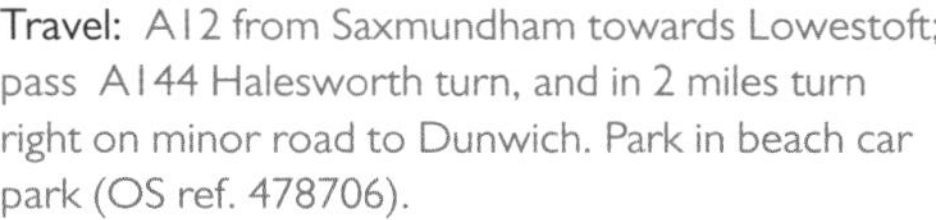
Travel: A12 from Saxmundham towards Lowestoft; pass A144 Halesworth turn, and in 2 miles turn right on minor road to Dunwich. Park in beach car park (OS ref. 478706).

Nearest railway station: Darsham (5 miles)

As you walk down the single modest street at Dunwich with its church, pub and handful of houses, you might imagine that it had never been anything more than a little fishing village on the Suffolk shore. Only the fragment of a monastery wall on the cliff to the south and the corner of a leper hospital beside the church hint at the glorious past of Dunwich, ancient capital of East Anglia and seat of the region's first bishop.

The Romans called Dunwich the Great Town, the Anglo-Saxons the 'town with the deep water harbour'. In medieval times a prosperous city stood on the shore, a heavily populated place of nine churches, two monasteries and a hospital. Dunwich owned large fishing and trading fleets and its own mint. But the sea, which for centuries had been nibbling at the eastern fringes of the town, took it all in the course of 300 years. The 'City surrounded with a Stone-wall and brazen Gates' disappeared beneath the waves; the clifftop churches and monastery fell into the sea.

Dunwich stands diminished, a parable of man's pretensions and their fate at nature's hand. North of the village lie Dingle Marshes; and now the sea seems intent on devouring this 3-mile stretch as well. Dingle Marshes are maintained as a nature reserve, with special attention to creating the kind of reed-beds in shallow fresh water which attract the rare bittern to breed. Footpaths cross the marshes, giving some of the loneliest and best coastal walking in Suffolk. The shingle bank that lies seaward of them has been breached by the tide and repaired by man many times. It is a barrier more fragile than it looks. With rising sea levels predicted to drive higher tides on to this low-lying coast, Dingle Marshes, like Dunwich, seem set to be victims of the sea and of its insatiable hunger to mould new shorelines ever further inland. Go now, before they disappear for ever.

120. WENHASTON DOOM, SUFFOLK

Maps: OS Explorer 231; Landranger 156

Travel: A12 north of Saxmundham to Blythburgh; B1123 to Blyford; minor road to Wenhaston. Park near church (OS ref. 425755).

Nearest railway station: Halesworth (3½ miles)

The sexton of St Peter's Church at Wenhaston was crossing the churchyard on a rainy day in 1892, when he suddenly got the uncomfortable feeling that someone was watching him – someone most unpleasant.

Wenhaston Doom

To his growing astonishment and horror he became aware that evil, glaring eyes were manifesting themselves, pair by pair, all over the old chancel-arch boarding that had been thrown out of St Peter's and left to rot. It was quite some time before the unfortunate man realized the truth – the rain was sluicing off the whitewash of centuries, to reveal in all its terror and power a medieval Doom painting.

Now restored to the interior of St Peter's, the early sixteenth-century Wenhaston Doom is a vivid reminder of just how real the concepts of Heaven and Hell were to the pre-Reformation mind. Christ sits in glory on a rainbow above a scene of Judgement in which the souls of the departed are being weighed in a large balance. The Saved troop off with meek smiles of relief to the gates of Heaven, where St Peter waits to welcome them into the celestial city. The Damned, however, have nothing but ghastly torments as their portion. The Devil himself, with outsize warty nose and fiendish grin, stands beside the balance, taking a keen interest in the outcome of the weighing. At the bottom right-hand corner of the painting Hell is depicted as a gigantic beast, perhaps a man-eating fish, into whose yawning jaws a cast of triumphant red-skinned devils are loading their catch of naked sinners. Serpents are blown into the ears of the Damned; harlots are slung upside down across the shoulders of capering demons; all is vigorous, lusty and out of control. The message was crystal clear: be good, you fools, or else.

121. SOUTH ELMHAM MINSTER, SUFFOLK

Maps: OS Explorer 231; Landranger 156

Travel: A143 from Harleston towards Bungay; in 2 miles, right on B1062 ('Flixton, Bungay'). In 700 yards, right on minor road through Homersfield to St Cross South Elmham. Right on minor road towards St James South Elmham; in 1 mile, park on road where footpath crosses it (OS ref. 303823) just before Top Farm. Turn left along footpath across two fields, to bear left into wood and find the minster (308827).

In a dense wood of oak and hornbeam, hidden away until you are right upon it, a great Saxon building quietly crumbles away. The facts cannot prepare you for the extraordinary spectacle of shattered walls of flint and rough mortar standing as high as a cathedral's upper storey, windows whose arches are now remembered only by gaps, all dappled by sunlight through the surrounding trees so that in certain phases of the light it is hard to see if anything is there at all.

The minster has been dated to both the seventh and the tenth centuries AD; it is probably nearer the latter. It stands inside a bank that might pre-date it by 1,000 years. At the west end a square shape represents the porch; at the east the ground plan of an apse stretches nearly as wide as the nave. The whole building is 100 feet long, far bigger than the average parish church, even in East Anglia, the land of splendid churches. But perhaps it was never a church at all. 'Minster' is generally taken to be a courtesy title. No one knows the origin or purpose of the building – except that it almost certainly was not a minster, or large church directing the work of many small ones. It could have been a house, or some kind of fortification. But an ecclesiastical function seems most likely, especially as South Elmham was a privileged place, the seat of summer retreat of the bishops of Norwich from Saxon times until well into the Middle Ages.

Whether the minster was church or fort, highly important or merely functional, public or private, remains unknown. Its presence in the wood is peaceful. There is more than a touch of greenwood strangeness about it, nonetheless.

South Elmham Minster

122. WEETING HEATH, BRECKLAND, NORFOLK

Maps: OS Explorer 229; Landranger 143

Travel: M11, A11 to Mildenhall; A1065 through Brandon. At Weeting, left on minor road towards Hockwold-cum-Wilton. In 1½ miles, Weeting Heath National Nature Reserve car park and Visitor Centre on left (OS ref. 741880).

Nearest railway station: Brandon (3 miles)

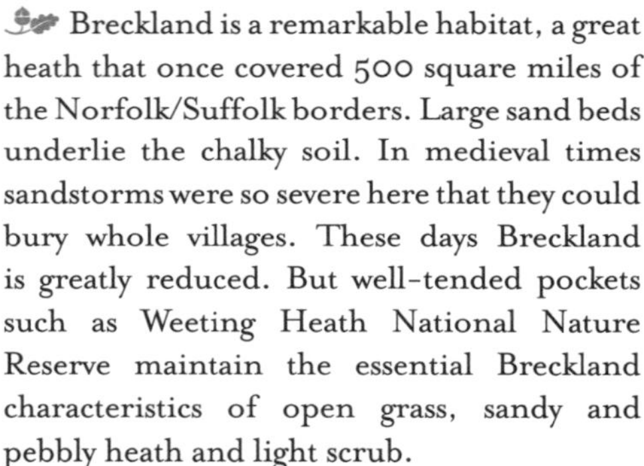

Breckland is a remarkable habitat, a great heath that once covered 500 square miles of the Norfolk/Suffolk borders. Large sand beds underlie the chalky soil. In medieval times sandstorms were so severe here that they could bury whole villages. These days Breckland is greatly reduced. But well-tended pockets such as Weeting Heath National Nature Reserve maintain the essential Breckland characteristics of open grass, sandy and pebbly heath and light scrub.

Breckland is not to everyone's taste. Some find it too arid and open, too dry, too monotonous. But better acquaintance can produce a fascination with this uncompromising landscape. Weeting Heath preserves many bird species in retreat from the intensively farmed and forested country all round: spotted flycatchers and speckle-breasted woodlarks in the pines, lapwings and pied wagtails further out on open ground. The pride and glory of the reserve, though, is the stone curlew, a long-legged bird that scutters in pattering runs over the bare ground and utters a haunting, mournful pipe of a cry. Stone curlews cannot cope with disturbance; they must have stony, open, empty ground to nest on, a commodity in short supply in modern Britain.

The rabbits of Weeting Heath are also a privileged lot; instead of being fenced out and persecuted, they are fenced in and welcomed for their unrivalled expertise in producing the flat, tight grass sward and pebbly ground the stone curlews need. From hides on the reserve you can watch the springtime interactions of the two species as the rabbits nibble, pause and nibble, and the newly arrived stone curlews patter, pause and patter again before settling on a nesting site. Soon the bumble-bee-striped chicks are staggering about the heath after their parents, continuing an age-old cycle that Breckland has been witnessing for several thousand years.

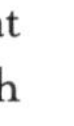

123. THETFORD FOREST, NORFOLK/SUFFOLK BORDERS

Maps: OS Explorer 229; Landranger 144, 143

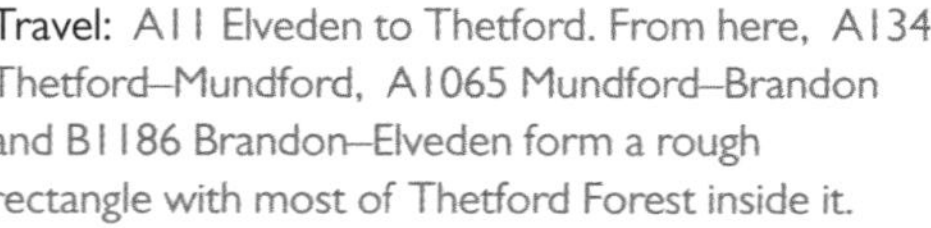

Travel: A11 Elveden to Thetford. From here, A134 Thetford–Mundford, A1065 Mundford–Brandon and B1186 Brandon–Elveden form a rough rectangle with most of Thetford Forest inside it.

Nearest railway stations: Thetford and Brandon

The enormous coniferous woodlands planted by the Forestry Commission are rarely seen as wild places – rather, they tend to be thought of as replacing all that is wild and natural with something regimented, artificial and baleful. Thetford Forest is one such place, planted from 1922 to ensure that Britain, stripped of huge acreages of broadleaved woodland during the Great War to satisfy military needs for trench props and boards, would never again have to squander such precious resources. Quick-growing, close-packed Corsican pines were the preferred crop, and the sandy heaths of

Breckland (see opposite) soon went under the giant forest – 80 square miles of trees in all.

Since those days a lot of amenity planting has taken place, a lot of the original planting has been harvested, and Thetford Forest has softened in appearance and atmosphere. There is open access to the forest now, and it has become a popular place for a day out – so much so that around the High Lodge Visitor Centre and the forest centre village of Santon Downham you could struggle to find peace and quiet. Step down any ride, though, and within five minutes you can be away from everyone.

On a dull day the heart of the forest can be a gloomy, even a threatening place. The sunken meres give out a chilly gleam, and the air seems still and heavy among the tight-packed conifers. Sunlight has a more profound effect here than in a broad-leaved wood, especially after heavy rain. It strikes in dusty but dazzling beams between the tall bare trunks of the pines. The meres sparkle. Heavy fruity smells of pine resin arise. Tree trunks that in shadow seem featureless grey sawmill fodder resolve into flaky tissues alive with boring beetles, spiders and tiny flies, centipedes and wood wasps. An hour in close communion with one of these generous hosts, and you come to see that you yourself are the tamest thing in the forest.

124. REEDHAM MARSHES, NORFOLK

Maps: OS Explorer OL40; Landranger 134

Travel: Train to Berney Arms station (request halt) (OS ref. 460053).

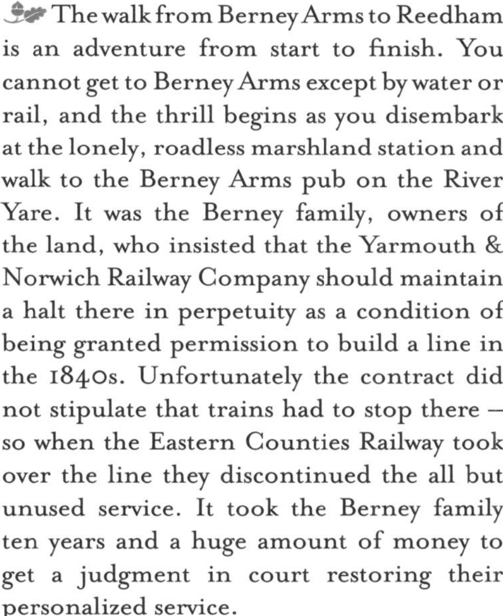

The walk from Berney Arms to Reedham is an adventure from start to finish. You cannot get to Berney Arms except by water or rail, and the thrill begins as you disembark at the lonely, roadless marshland station and walk to the Berney Arms pub on the River Yare. It was the Berney family, owners of the land, who insisted that the Yarmouth & Norwich Railway Company should maintain a halt there in perpetuity as a condition of being granted permission to build a line in the 1840s. Unfortunately the contract did not stipulate that trains had to stop there – so when the Eastern Counties Railway took over the line they discontinued the all but unused service. It took the Berney family ten years and a huge amount of money to get a judgment in court restoring their personalized service.

The Berney Arms stands in the shadow of a huge old windmill – in fact a wind-pump which once drained the marshes into the River Yare. From here south-west

Reedham Marshes

to Reedham is a 5-mile walk, a supremely lonely trek through a landscape utterly alien to anyone not accustomed to it. The map shows only one contour to left or right for many miles, and the legend on that reads '0 metres'.

Much of this peaty land has been pumped and drained until it lies below sea level. Cattle graze in fields split up by thousands of capillary ditches. The skeletons of disused wind-pumps stand black along the ditches. From far and near comes the gentle whispering of reed heads, feathering together in the breeze.

The Yare is lined with reed-beds, a hidden world where coot and moorhen skulk and reed buntings drop little sharp strings of song. The reeds gave their name to Reedham village, and they provided a living for local thatchers until modern materials put most of them out of business. Nowadays the reed-beds are prized as wildlife habitat. In their sibilant company you could walk on up the Yare for 15 miles by way of Reedham and Cantley, a stretch of marshy river country that winds its way to the heart of the Norfolk Broads, and hear nothing but bunting chatter and moorhen squeak.

125. SOUTH WALSHAM BROAD, NORFOLK

Maps: OS Explorer OL40; Landranger 134

Travel: B1140 north-east from Norwich's ring road to South Walsham; left on minor road towards Ranworth; in ½ mile, cross west end of South Walsham Broad. Round next bend, bridleway leads beside the broad. In Ranworth (¾ mile along the road), the view from church tower (91 steps, 2 ladders) over the Broadland landscape is superb.

The Fairhaven Garden Trust in School Road, South Walsham (tel: 01603 270449/270683; www.fairhavengarden.co.uk) has paths leading down to South Walsham Broad.

Nearest railway station: Acle (4 miles)

Unless you have a boat, or even better a canoe, it's hard to get at the heart of a Norfolk broad. From the lanes and roads it seems always on the sly, its soupy waters peeking at you from behind thickets of alder or sliding off under a bridge like a snake to where they widen, invariably just out of sight, past the willows and round the bend. This modesty, or reluctance to be in plain view to land-bound observers, is frustrating, but seductive.

Many of Norfolk's fifty or so broads are unregenerate, left to their own devices in a reedy and weedy tangle of slimy tree roots, rushy bog and fen plants. Some, however, are

South Walsham Broad

maintained and managed for the benefit of visitors. Such broads as Ranworth, Hickling and Cockshoot have been painstakingly restored to health from a state of diesel-polluted, mud-choked, nitrate-enriched degradation into which all the broads had fallen by the 1950s. With their well-appointed Visitor Centres, duckboard trails through the reed-beds and programmes of guided walks and talks, these carefully maintained nature reserves are the best places to learn the history of Norfolk's once mysterious broads – thought to be arms of the sea marooned inland, until towards the middle of the twentieth century research showed them to be pits, subsequently flooded, where medieval workers had dug peat to satisfy the demands of the city of Norwich for fuel. If the National Trust, English Nature, the local Wildlife Trusts and the Broadland Authority had not invested such enormous amounts of time and money in restoring these showpiece broads, in reed-cutting and mud-pumping, in encouraging conditions where rarities such as the swallowtail butterflies and bitterns and water soldier plants could thrive alongside more common if no less valuable birds and plants – all of this would have been lost as the broads reverted to fen and then to woodland, melting back into the landscape as if such man-made lakes had never existed at all.

South Walsham Broad is no better or worse than other unregenerate Norfolk broads – it is just a very typical example of the understated charm of these secret waters. Duckweed coats its surface, cut into black channels by cruising mallard and coot. Rushes line its banks, hissing softly in the rare winds that manage to penetrate the sheltering circle of willow and alder. Occasionally the sharp grating cry of a moorhen rings out with a curious echo, clinging to the lagoons. If you want to get close to the water, you'll have to be prepared for a shoe full of mud. This is the nearest to swamp that England comes, and the same sense of quiet is all around.

126. 'POPPYLAND' (CROMER TO SIDESTRAND), NORFOLK

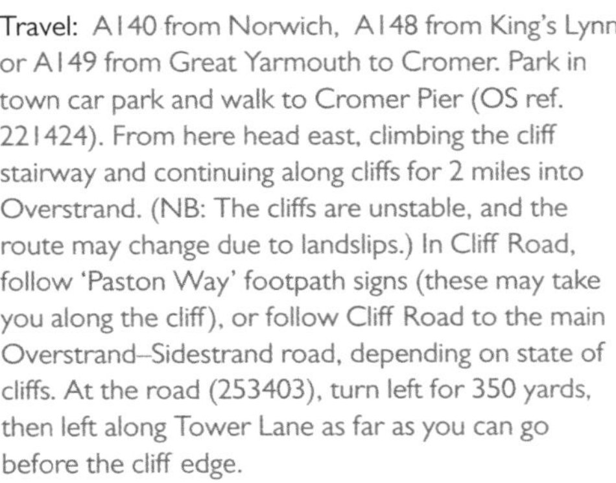

Maps: OS Explorer 252; Landranger 133

Travel: A140 from Norwich, A148 from King's Lynn or A149 from Great Yarmouth to Cromer. Park in town car park and walk to Cromer Pier (OS ref. 221424). From here head east, climbing the cliff stairway and continuing along cliffs for 2 miles into Overstrand. (NB: The cliffs are unstable, and the route may change due to landslips.) In Cliff Road, follow 'Paston Way' footpath signs (these may take you along the cliff), or follow Cliff Road to the main Overstrand–Sidestrand road, depending on state of cliffs. At the road (253403), turn left for 350 yards, then left along Tower Lane as far as you can go before the cliff edge.

Nearest railway station: Cromer

If 'wild' is in the eye and heart of the beholder, then Clement Scott found a wild place in Poppyland. That was the name the London-based *Daily Telegraph* journalist coined for the coastal landscape east of Cromer which he 'discovered' in the summer of 1883. Scott came to write a few light-hearted pieces on the summer season; he stayed to fall hopelessly in love with Poppyland, its apple-cheeked girls, quiet clifftop farms, and the poppies that flooded the cornfields with scarlet.

There was no wilderness about the north Norfolk coast back then, apart from the propensity of its yellow clay cliffs to fall without warning – as they are still doing today. But Clement Scott was marching to his own drum. He turned his back on the crowded, pseudo-sophisticated (as he saw it) resort of Cromer, and struck out on foot along the cliffs to fulfil a romantic ideal, to discover an Eden of natural, uncomplicated simplicity.

A blue sky without a cloud across it, a sea sparkling under a haze of heat, wild flowers in profusion around me, poppies predominantly everywhere, the hedgerows full of blackberry-blossom and fringed with meadow-sweet; the bees busy at their work, the air filled with insect life, the songbirds startled from the standing corn as I pursued my solitary way.

Clement Scott turned out to be the serpent in his own enchanted garden. He published his articles as *Poppyland Papers* in 1886, and found that the public couldn't get enough of Miller Jermy of Sidestrand and his wholesome daughter, Louie, the hearty fare, the clean crisp sheets, the nodding poppies, the flowery lanes and even more flowery prose. The idea of the wild as a retreat from civilization proved so seductive that the world and its architect came to Poppyland. Building proliferated, hotels sprang up, louche celebrities arrived to rediscover the fountain of youth and innocence. In short, Poppyland was ruined. Scott began calling it 'Bungalowland', and set his face vehemently against the whole sorry mess.

The Mill House where Scott lodged with the Jermys still stands near Tower Lane. But the old abandoned tower and graveyard of St Michael's Church, apostrophized by Scott in his poem 'The Garden of Sleep', slipped over the cliff edge long ago. The wildest part of Poppyland, now as then, is the crumbling cliff edge, and the image of Clement Scott standing with an ache in his romantic heart on the edge of the Eden he created and then destroyed:

O! heart of my heart! where the poppies are born,
I am waiting for thee, in the hush of the corn.
Sleep! Sleep!
From the Cliff to the Deep!
Sleep, my Poppy-land,
Sleep!

127. BLAKENEY POINT, NORFOLK

Maps: OS Explorer 251; Landranger 133, 132

Travel: A149 from Hunstanton or Cromer to Blakeney. Access to Blakeney Point by boat from Blakeney Quay or Morston Quay (www.exploring.co.uk/boatmen_blakeney). Access on foot via Cley-next-the-Sea beach (OS ref. 048452), a 7-mile walk, there and back.

It has taken the sand and shingle spit of Blakeney Point something over a thousand years to reach its current length of 3½ miles. And if the process of longshore drift by which the spit is inching westwards continues at the same rate, in another 1,000 years the fingertip of this skinny coastal arm will be stopping the mouth of Wells-next-the-Sea harbour, 4 miles along the coast.

The whole north Norfolk coast is dynamic, the shingle banks and mudflats changing with the tides. Five hundred years ago Blakeney village was open to the sea, but now at low tide a sailor has to embark on a 5-mile meander along a narrow channel through a vast muddy plain that has built up within the crook of Blakeney Point's sheltering arm. The spit is a National Nature Reserve managed by the National Trust, a haven for wildlife at the bulbous westward end, well out of the way of humans. This is a real wilderness, a breeding ground in summer for little, common, Arctic and roseate tern, and a place where grey seals sometimes haul out to bask alongside the spit's resident colony of common seals. In winter the Arctic geese arrive and bad weather howls in from the North Sea.

There are three ways to enjoy this lonely peninsula. You can boat in summer to the west end and be quickly among the seals and terns. You can crunch out there from Cley Beach, a 7-mile there-and-back walk along shingle and sand dunes with the smooth sea on your right and the long gleaming expanses of the mudflats on your left. Or you can climb Blakeney church tower and gaze out across the whole picture, the great claw of the spit, imperceptibly creeping westward.

128. STIFFKEY MARSHES, NORFOLK

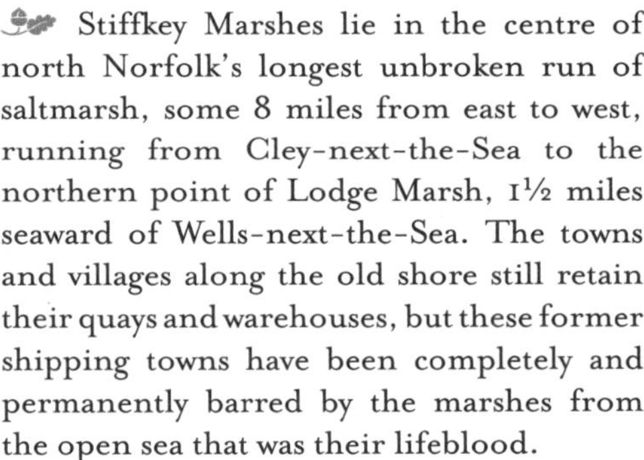

Maps: OS Explorer 251; Landranger 132

Travel: A149 from Cromer or Hunstanton to Stiffkey. Park in the coastal car park (OS ref. 964439) and walk on to Stiffkey Marshes.

Stiffkey Marshes lie in the centre of north Norfolk's longest unbroken run of saltmarsh, some 8 miles from east to west, running from Cley-next-the-Sea to the northern point of Lodge Marsh, 1½ miles seaward of Wells-next-the-Sea. The towns and villages along the old shore still retain their quays and warehouses, but these former shipping towns have been completely and permanently barred by the marshes from the open sea that was their lifeblood.

Looking back to shore from out on Stiffkey Marshes, then on north-east towards the distant hump of Blakeney Point (see opposite),

Stiffkey Marshes

you can see how the land lies now this shift has happened. Longshore drift has caused a gradual building-up of offshore shingle banks, a consequence of the prevailing west-flowing tide. The silt that washes seaward down the River Stiffkey piles up behind the pebble spits with nowhere to go and forms a fertile bed for the growth of long-rooted plants like spartina grass and sea purslane that consolidate the ever-growing marshes.

Only wildfowlers, walkers and bird-watchers venture on to the marshes. It's possible to get trapped by the incoming tide if you go out far enough and don't watch your step as you wander this strip of mud that is neither of the land nor the sea. In summer the sickly green face of the marsh develops a purple flush like that of a heavy drinker, as carpets of sea lavender open their flowers. But it is the winter that exposes the moody soul of this place. Bring your binoculars then, because these marshes are a wildfowl-watching site supreme. Up to 150,000 pink-footed geese arrive from Iceland to spend the winter in Britain, around a third of them hereabouts. At dusk and dawn the power and spectacle of their roosting and feeding flights over the north Norfolk marshes is something to behold. Dark-bellied brent geese and white-fronted geese are here in large numbers from Russia at that season, too. But it is the sheer weight of numbers and the deafening roar of wings and cries that is so stunning, as wave after wave of pinkfeet sweep overhead in long lines. One can only stand and marvel at the imperative that brings these birds 1,000 miles from their breeding grounds to the exact spot to which their ancestors also came, 10,000 years ago.

129. SCOLT HEAD ISLAND, NORFOLK

Maps: OS Explorer 251, 250; Landranger 132

Travel: A149 from Hunstanton to Burnham Overy Staithe. Access to Scolt Head Island by boat from the quay (OS ref. 845493), April–September: www.english-nature.org.uk.

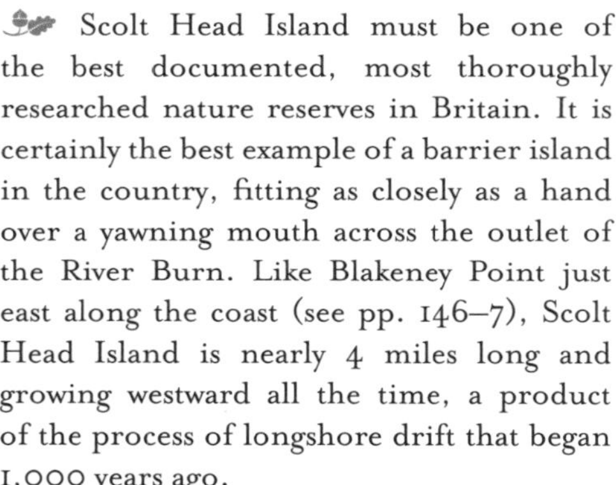

Scolt Head Island must be one of the best documented, most thoroughly researched nature reserves in Britain. It is certainly the best example of a barrier island in the country, fitting as closely as a hand over a yawning mouth across the outlet of the River Burn. Like Blakeney Point just east along the coast (see pp. 146–7), Scolt Head Island is nearly 4 miles long and growing westward all the time, a product of the process of longshore drift that began 1,000 years ago.

Scolt Head's northern edge is mainly smooth, firm sand dunes cut knife-straight by the sea. The south is utterly different, a wriggling mass of creeks that invade a solid wedge of saltmarsh a mile broad. Every tide changes its aspect in some almost imperceptible way; every 100 years of tides swings the hooked tip of the spit another half-mile to the west.

Although botanists, ecologists and marine scientists come to study the forms and movements of Scolt Head, the island stays wild by virtue of its isolation. Only a few visitors can be catered for at one time, and they have to come by boat from Burnham Overy Staithe. So the jittery terns that are so sensitive to human presence around their summer nesting sites feel secure here – even the delicately pink-bellied roseate terns, so rare their British breeding numbers are

under 100 pairs, and the sandwich terns with their punky little crests who breed in several thousands, up to a quarter of the total UK population. The marshes grow a fine display of flowering plants in summer: white sea campion, beautiful sprigs of pink sea heather, and the muted purple of matted sea lavender with a net of coarse little branchlets – a very rare coastal plant.

Winter brings snow buntings down from the cold hills to the warmer shore of the island and the skies all around are full of wild geese and ducks. The boats don't run then, and so this wild island is accessible only through the end of a telescope.

130. THE WASH, LINCOLNSHIRE/ NORFOLK BORDERS

Maps: OS Explorer 249; Landranger 131

Travel: A17 west of King's Lynn to Sutton Bridge; right just before bridge on minor road to East Light lighthouse (OS ref. 493258). Peter Scott Walk runs for 11 miles from here, east round sea walls of the Wash to King's Lynn.

When Peter Scott came to live in the East Light lighthouse at the mouth of the River Nene, he was a young man with a deeply ingrained love of wildfowling. By the time he left to go to war in 1939, Scott had put away his shotguns and his punt gun. He had become that rare phenomenon back then, a pioneer conservationist, a painter and photographer rather than a slaughterer of pinkfooted geese, wigeon, curlew and teal. No wonder – for this dead-flat region lying under vast swirling skies, at the point where Lincolnshire and Norfolk meet, is crammed and thronged with birds and all kinds of wildlife, an inspiring landscape.

The Wash is the largest estuary in Britain. It shelters and sustains many thousands of common seals, nearly half a million wildfowl each winter, millions of migrating birds on passage every spring. It contains 10,000 acres of saltmarsh (a tenth of the UK total), and 65,000 acres of tidal sand and mudflats that support uncountable trillions of invertebrates, food for the birds. The Wash, in other words, is one of Britain's most important, most vibrant and most precious wild areas. The reason is plain: almost all its territory lies beyond the sea walls, out of reach of humans.

The Peter Scott walk starts at Scott's lighthouse and makes a great clockwise arc around the margins of the Wash. A belt of prime arable silt 4 miles broad inside the walls has been reclaimed from the sea since Roman times; within the next 100 years the greedy sea will perhaps have risen high enough to retake it all. The Wash with its giant empty skies and broad empty horizons is a place for contemplation. It is simply beautiful, a plate of land and sky where weather systems collide to technicolour effect, where you follow a creek out through the saltmarsh at low tide to the edge of the sandbanks. Gazing at their purple and ochre backs, you become aware that the sea is 5 miles away on the northern horizon, that there are more wild birds than you can imagine between you and it, and that no other human being is drawing breath within eye or earshot.

131. BURNT FEN, CAMBRIDGESHIRE

Maps: OS Explorer 228; Landranger 143

Travel: A10 from Ely towards Downham Market; in 6 miles, take A1101 ('Mildenhall'). In 1½ miles, left along Little Ouse road (OS ref. 600863) into Burnt Fen.

Nearest railway station: Littleport (2 miles)

Back before the 4th Earl of Bedford hired Dutch water engineer Cornelius Vermuyden to drain the Fens in the mid seventeenth century, there were half a million acres of wetland sprawling through the heart of East Anglia. In *Poly-Olbion*, Michael Drayton's huge topographical survey of England, the poet describes the Fens as he saw them in the 1620s – a lush Eden-like wilderness:

The horse, or other beast, o'erweigh'd with his own mass,
Lies wallowing in my fens, hid over head in grass;
And in the place where grows rank fodder for my neat,
The turf which bears the hay is wondrous needful peat;
My full and batt'ning earth needs not the ploughman's pains,
The rills which run in me are like the branchéd veins
In human bodies seen; those ditches cut by hand,
From the surrounding meres to win the measur'd land,
To those choice waters I most fitly may compare,
Wherewith nice women use to blanch their beauties rare.

You wouldn't want to blanch your beauties rare in a nitrate-fouled Fenland river these days. Even in Drayton's day the ditches were being cut by hand 'to win the measur'd land'; and soon the greatest feat of drainage ever accomplished in Britain would be getting under way. The legacy of Bedford and Vermuyden is a land regulated, dried and ploughed into the most productive farmland in Britain. The rivers run wildly polluted, the rich black peat has sunk by as much as 20 feet, and the twenty-first-century ploughman's pains and those of his suppliers of fertilizer and pesticide and insecticide are exerted every day in every way.

Burnt Fen is a typical Cambridgeshire fen of the modern age. Walking its straight drove roads, rows of lettuces, gaily caparisoned with bird-scaring streamers of yellow and white, run to the horizon like a lesson in perspective painting. Giant sprayers crawl like insects through the knee-high corn. Lines of telegraph poles diminish to vanishing point, and farmhouses lie low in protective collars of dark conifers. This is country where strangers stick out like sore thumbs, are stared at, and are sometimes challenged as to their intentions.

This is, then, a landscape thoroughly tamed, but it is capable of wearing a very wild aspect when inland gales pick up after a long, dry spell. The powdery topsoil is whipped from the land and blows in sky-darkening clouds across the Fens. The dust cloaks the trees, blackens the roads and clogs the eyes and nose of anyone caught outside. A Fen Blow plunges the flat world into fog. It is a terrifying phenomenon, a product of the processes that have abolished the old green Eden of Michael Drayton.

132. WICKEN FEN, CAMBRIDGESHIRE

Maps: OS Explorer 226; Landranger 154

Travel: From A14 Newmarket bypass, A142 towards Ely; in 4 miles, left on A1123; in 3 miles, left in Wicken village (brown 'Wicken Fen' sign). Park at Wicken Fen car park (OS ref. 564705).

Approaching this 800-acre National Nature Reserve through intensively cultivated arable farmland, your first impression is of a shaggy sprawl of trees and bushes, dark olive and dun brown, rising like an unkempt little island in an ocean of neat, uniform green corn. This place is a paradox, a subtle mosaic of water and woodland, fen, sedge and reed-bed, where rarities are commonplace and wildlife lives truly wild in an artificially maintained oasis of just 1 square mile.

In May 1899 the infant National Trust paid out £10 for 2 acres of undrained, uncultivated fenland near the village of Wicken, 10 miles north-east of Cambridge. The reserve has been managed by the Trust ever since. Management is the keynote. If a piece of fen country is abandoned to nature, its open water quickly becomes reed swamp, then fen. It reverts to wet carr, which dries up and grows on into mature woodland. At Wicken Fen all these stages, and the wildlife associated with each, are maintained carefully. Water levels are adjusted, scrub cut back here, reed-beds planted there, and the result is a highly impressive list of rarities. More than 200 bird species have been recorded on the reserve, including very localized or rare inhabitants such as the marsh harrier, water rail with its red beak and pink legs, and the long-tailed bearded tit. Plants of the reserve include fen violet and fen ragwort, and the marsh pea with flowers of a delicate musky blue. As for the insects of this damp green world, apart from the dragonflies and water-skaters, there are 1,300 species of fly alone, and 1,400 kinds of beetle.

If lists and records daunt you, just take a stroll along the mown paths and stop in one of the bird hides or beside a fleet of water. Swifts and swallows dart after midges. Tall stems of water violet push up from ponds. In the carr woods, mosses and ferns sprout from wet timber and the air is thick with insect hum. Water voles cut ripples in the dark water of the channels. The wildlife cycle wheels on, regardless of the human management on which it so completely depends.

133. FIVE MILES FROM ANYWHERE – NO HURRY!, UPWARE, CAMBRIDGESHIRE

Maps: OS Explorer 226; Landranger 154

Travel: From A14 at Newmarket, north on A142 towards Ely. Approaching Soham, left on A1123 through Wicken; next left to Upware.

Out in the flatlands north of Cambridge a bumpy fen road leads eventually to Upware. The hamlet with its modern pub sits on the east bank of the River Cam at the point where the lodes or cut channels from Burwell and Reach join the river. It would be hard to light on anywhere quieter or more sedate; it's harder still to imagine the riotous days of the mid nineteenth century when this hamlet was proclaimed the 'Republic of Upware' and had its own eccentric and quarrelsome king.

Upware lies in Adventurers Fen, which in the 1850s was still a wild, undrained place, a remote fenland fastness noted for ague and lawlessness. Cambridge University characters were drawn to the area – botanists and lepidopterists by the wildlife, others because it was a great place to have a wild and drunken time. There were three pubs at Upware to cater for the bargees and lightermen who passed on the waterways, and one, the Lord Nelson, became the centre of revels for two undergraduate drinking clubs, the Idiots and the Beersoakers.

The Lord of Misrule at Upware was Richard Ramsay Fielder, a graduate of Jesus College, black sheep of a good family, who was well paid to keep away and live his anarchic life elsewhere. He fixed on the Lord Nelson in 1850, renamed it the Five Miles from Anywhere – No Hurry!, and settled down as the self-proclaimed 'King of the Republic of Upware' – not the only contradiction in his life. Fielder was a firework of a man, a bit of a genius, a bit of a bully. He needed an audience for his doggerel and monologues, and found it in the unlettered fenmen of Upware. They looked up to him for the scholarship he loved to display, while better-educated locals held him in contempt.

The King of Upware sported long hair and talon-like nails. He gave forth 'a far from aromatic odour'. Dispensing punch from his private 7-gallon gotch as largesse to his subjects, he would keep strangers up all night while he smoked coarse tobacco, drank, opined and challenged the lightermen to fist fights. Around him other ne'er-do-wells did likewise.

The annual Bustle Fair at Upware had its own notoriety. At the fair of 1862 undergraduates, locals and strangers conducted a day-long drunken battle that culminated with the police being thrown into the river.

Eventually Richard Ramsay Fielder left his fenland realm under mysterious circumstances. The self-mythologizer who signed himself 'Rex Primus Upware' and adopted the motto 'Celer et Acer' – 'Quick and Smart' – died in Folkestone in 1886, aged sixty-four, his riotous reign forgotten. Upware's riverside pub is still called Five Miles from Anywhere, but no one working there today has heard of the man who named it.

134. WOODWALTON FEN, CAMBRIDGESHIRE

Maps: OS Explorer 227; Landranger 142

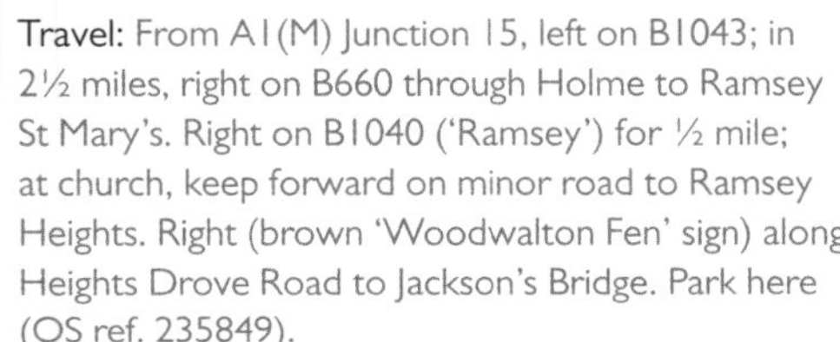

Travel: From A1(M) Junction 15, left on B1043; in 2½ miles, right on B660 through Holme to Ramsey St Mary's. Right on B1040 ('Ramsey') for ½ mile; at church, keep forward on minor road to Ramsey Heights. Right (brown 'Woodwalton Fen' sign) along Heights Drove Road to Jackson's Bridge. Park here (OS ref. 235849).

In this 1½-mile block of undrained fenland the grass and fen vegetation grows chin high, so that grazing cattle emerge like whales from a green sea. This priceless refuge for wildlife, leased to Natural England by its owner the Royal Society of Wildlife Trusts, is an oasis of insect hum and birdsong in a desert of intensively farmed, drained and shrunken peatland prairie. The ditches are full of pondweed as thick and green as pea soup. The peaty ground is so soft and sodden with water it bounces gently underfoot as if a trampoline were hidden under the turf.

In times of rain, water enters the fen by gravity, but in dry weather it has to be pumped in, because the level of the surrounding land has dropped some 20 feet since it was drained for agriculture. Waterproof banks have been built all round the site to keep the precious water in. The old fen engineers of the seventeenth and eighteenth centuries, and the 'adventurers' or speculators who funded them to dry out the land, would stare in amazement to see the water being pumped back in again. But it is Woodwalton Fen's amazing wetness that maintains it in its wild state for the woodcock, the red damselflies and the grasshopper warblers of spring, the reed and sedge warblers who nest here in summer, and the bitterns that winter in the reed-beds over which ghost-like hen harriers float in search of frogs and mice.

Woodwalton Fen has gone through some big changes. It was bought in 1910 by the Hon. Charles Rothschild, a pioneer ecologist and founder of the Society for the Promotion of Nature Reserves, as a tract of open sedge, reed-bed and raised bog. It quickly reverted to scrub, before a painstaking programme of clearance, of ditching and flooding, bank-building and planting saw its current richness of variety emerge. Now Natural England is planning the next phase, the seasonal flooding and traditional management of the adjacent Darlow's Farm. One day, if long-term plans come to fruition, almost 10,000 acres of what is now intensively farmed land between Huntingdon and Peterborough will be one vast wetland.

135. ST KYNEBURGA'S CHURCH, CASTOR, CAMBRIDGESHIRE

Maps: OS Explorer 227; Landranger 142

Travel: A47 from Peterborough towards Wansford; in 2 miles, left into Castor. Right at Royal Oak pub, up Stock's Hill; park outside St Kyneburga's Church (OS ref. 125995).

Nearest railway stations: Wansford or Ferry Meadows stations on Nene Valley Railway (5 miles): www.nvr.org.uk

Hidden away in St Kyneburga's are some notably wild carvings. These are bas-relief sculptures on the capitals of the columns, executed with great vigour some time in the twelfth century. Several are of Green Men – two of these flank the Romanesque south door. A Green Man with tremendous wolf's

St Kyneburga's Church

ears, on the north capital of the tower arch, seems to be clawing a tangle of foliage out of his mouth in a panic. Another carving shows a hunting scene of real savagery in which a snarling wild boar, having sliced a dog in two, tosses its victim's hind quarters high in the air. Meanwhile the dog's master levels a spear with a double barb and prepares to thrust it down the boar's throat. Near by a hero, perhaps Samson, forces open the jaws of a madly struggling lion.

The battle scene on the south capital opposite may have a bearing on the story of the church and its rare dedication. It shows two helmeted warriors with pointed Saxon shields locked in combat, one wielding a mace and the other a whip. A horrified woman looks on, her knee-length sleeves billowing, her hands raised to cover her face in the universal symbol of terror. She may be St Kyneburga herself, otherwise called Cyneburh, daughter of the ferocious and confirmedly heathen King Penda of Mercia in the seventh century AD. Cyneburh was married to Alhfrith, son of the Christian King Oswin of Northumbria, and it was Alhfrith who took part in the killing of Penda at the Battle of Winwaed in AD 654. Perhaps the carving shows the grief and horror of Cyneburh as her father dies at the hands of her husband. Ten years later she founded a monastery here on the site of a Roman praetorium; and it was on the same site that the Normans built the church that still carries her name today.

136. RIVER WITHAM, BOSTON, LINCOLNSHIRE

Maps: OS Explorer 261; Landranger 131

Travel: A16 Spalding to Boston. Park in Skirbeck Quarter near bridge over South Forty Foot Drain (OS ref. 326428), and walk east along the bank of River Witham ('The Haven') as far as the Wash (5 miles).

Nearest railway station: Boston

The Wash has always been a wild and treacherous place. High tides come creeping or racing in across the mudflats and marshes, and woe betide anyone caught out in the middle. It was a flood tide that trapped King John's retinue in 1216 as they crossed the mouth of the River Nene; perhaps one of the dreaded aegres or tidal bores that would rush in like a tsunami. 'The ground was opened up in the middle of the waves,' reported Roger of Wendover, 'and bottomless whirlpools swallowed them all up, treasure, horses, plate and men.'

The most famous aegre to hit the town of Boston on the west shore of the Wash was immortalized in 1863 by local poet Jean Ingelow in her ballad 'High Tide on the Coast of Lincolnshire, 1571'. The verse epic caught exactly the taste of the Victorian reading public, influenced by Tennyson, for wild and doomy romanticism. The poet imagines the coming of an aegre – the first hints from nature that something is in the air:

And there was nought of strange, beside
The flight of mews and peewits pied
By millions crouch'd on the old sea wall.

The narrator's daughter-in-law, Elizabeth, wanders happily with her two children over the meadows down by the sea, calling to her cows. While the sea wall breaks, the bells in the tower of Boston Stump ring out a warning, and the son frantically dashes around in search of his sweet young wife and babies. Ingelow described the clash of tides as the incoming sea meets the out-rushing River Lindis:

A mighty eygre rear'd his crest,
And uppe the Lindis raging sped.
It swept with thunderous noises loud,
Shap'd like a curling snow-white cloud,
Or like a demon in a shroud.

The townspeople spend the night on the roofs of their houses, while the bells ring out and a livid red beacon shines from the tower to guide the sailors rowing from roof to roof to rescue the victims. Elizabeth arrives home, carried lifeless on the flood to her husband's door, still clutching her babies; then she drifts back down the river to the sea.

A fatal ebbe and flow, alas!
To manye more than myne and mee;
But each will mourn his own (she saith);
And sweeter woman ne'er drew breath
Than my sonne's wife, Elizabeth.

137. GIBRALTAR POINT, LINCOLNSHIRE

Maps: OS Explorer 274; Landranger 122

Travel: A52 to Skegness. On the seafront turn right and follow coast road south for 3½ miles to Gibraltar Point. Park car here (OS ref. 555582).

Nearest railway station: Skegness (4 miles)

Coming east, you travel for more than 20 miles through completely flat land with never a contour in it. The rise of the grassy dunes at Gibraltar Point comes as a relief, a suggestion that there may be hills with valleys beyond. It is a shock to top the dunes and find the level North Sea stretching to the horizon.

As a natural barrier between sea and land, Gibraltar Point's dunes have been building for the past 300 years or more. The shelter they offer, the nutrition they supply and the different habitats they provide have produced such a rich flora and fauna that the whole 3-mile run of dunes and shore has been declared a National Nature Reserve, and also a Special Protection Area for birds.

It is hard to do justice to the richness of wildlife here, but some star attractions are the flowers of the oldest, most inland-sited dunes. A fine turf has developed on their lime-rich sand, supporting species often associated with chalk downland, such as the frothy yellow lady's bedstraw, cowslips and tiny white-flowered meadow saxifrage. Bright nail-polish-pink lesser centaury decorates the freshwater marshes of the reserve. The blue stars of sea aster and pale pink flowers of sea milkwort flourish on the saltmarshes at the seaward and southern edge of the reserve (these southerly marshes are still growing), where plants have to be tough and resilient to withstand the salt spray and fierce wind.

The chief fame of Gibraltar Point, however, rests on its birds. This is one of the few places in Britain where little tern can breed unmolested. In spring and autumn migrating birds fly through, stopping to refresh themselves on their incredible journey across the world. Huge numbers, clouds of birds in their tens of thousands, may 'fall' on the Point at any time during these seasonal movements. Enormous numbers are the order of the day, too, among the waders that feed on the tidal muds; it's quite common to see 5,000 or 10,000 dunlin in the air or on the shore together. This is a place to come to be reminded of our ignorance and smallness in the face of nature.

138. SALTFLEETBY AND THEDDLETHORPE DUNES, LINCOLNSHIRE

Maps: OS Explorer 283; Landranger 113

Travel: A1031 from Cleethorpes towards Mablethorpe. There are seven car parks along the reserve – at Saltfleet, Sea View Farm, Rimac, Sea Bank Farm, Theddlethorpe St Helen, Crook Bank (OS ref. 489893) and Mablethorpe North End.

The Lincolnshire coast is one of the quietest in the east of England, and the stretch between Cleethorpes and Mablethorpe is beautifully remote, windswept and lonely. The great dune system here runs for 5 miles along the shore, and as you walk these dunes the outside world fades away.

For escapist rambles with only nature for company, come in winter when the brent geese flock to the freshwater marshes, shelduck feed on the saltmarsh and wigeon swirl in the sky. Fieldfares, blue-headed cousins of the thrush, arrive for the winter and feed on the berries of the hawthorn scrub. Spring and summer are the time for flowering plants – lemon-yellow mouse-ear hawkweed with dandelion-like flowers and hairy leaves, startlingly blue viper's bugloss (another with hairy leaves), and pink storksbill with the long-beaked fruit that gives the plant its name.

Whitethroat and linnet breed in the buckthorn and hawthorn scrub, the former warbling a fluid little song, the latter pouring out the string of bubbling notes that caused its ancestors to be caged and hung in Victorian dining rooms. Skylarks nest on the saltmarshes, far from interference; and down in the pools of the freshwater marshes at nightfall you can hear the grating, burping mating calls of natterjack toads, a rarity in Britain that thrives on this lonely coast.

139. TETNEY MARSHES, LINCOLNSHIRE

Maps: OS Explorer 282; Landranger 113

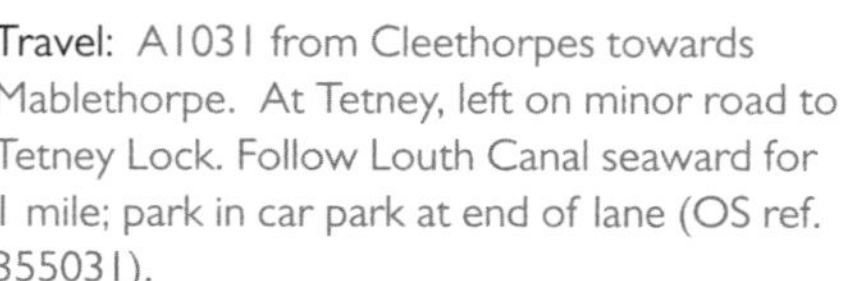

Travel: A1031 from Cleethorpes towards Mablethorpe. At Tetney, left on minor road to Tetney Lock. Follow Louth Canal seaward for 1 mile; park in car park at end of lane (OS ref. 355031).

Walking a circuit of the RSPB's Tetney Marshes Reserve gives you a grandstand view over the remote coastal landscape that

Tetney Marshes

constitutes this wild place. It's an enormous reserve, nearly 4,000 acres of the sort of land that nobody else wants: barren miles of tidal sand, sombre swathes of saltmarsh and big, bare fields over which skylarks pour out song, not pausing as they climb their aerial ladders. Autumn sees the marshes grow a handsome coat of sea lavender, brilliant purple-blue in strong sunlight. But in winter this is a bleak place under huge skies clamorous with packs of pink-footed and brent geese, where small fast hawks such as peregrine and merlin hunt the grasses.

Through the fields the disused Louth Canal approaches the shore. The canal was opened in 1770, and its seaward end, known as Tetney Haven, was busy for 150 years, dealing with coasting ships on the Humber, until advancing silt and declining sea trade put an end to it. Tetney Haven is your destination as you follow the snaking canal bank into an ever more desolate landscape. The sigh and roar of the sea on Tetney High Sands grows gradually louder, and as the twin banks flatten out into the estuary sands you see the two Humber forts standing stark on the horizon.

These big hexagonal forts loom in the tideway at high water. At the ebb, Bull Sand Fort, 3 miles out from Tetney Haven, stands with its feet still in the sea; but Haile Sand Fort, less than 1 mile away, rises from a flat bed of tan-coloured sand like a stranded dreadnought. The twin forts were built in

1915 to guard the mouth of the Humber, a job they did through two world wars. With their concrete shells and armour-plated hides, they look set to last out many centuries; freakish apparitions in the flat perspective of Lincolnshire's loneliest shore.

140. HUMBERSIDE CLAY PITS, LINCOLNSHIRE

Maps: OS Explorer 281; Landranger 112

Travel: A15 to south end of Humber Bridge. A1077 west ('South Ferriby') for ½ mile; right on minor road to T-junction (OS ref. 015230); left for 500 yards to Far Ings Nature Reserve car park and Visitor Centre on right (010229). Other clay-pits lie along the Humber, east of the bridge.

Nearest railway stations: Barton-on-Humber for Far Ings (1½ miles); also Barrow Haven and New Holland stations

The Great Lincolnshire Clay Rush is entirely forgotten now. But it was this nineteenth-century drive to satisfy the Industrial Revolution's demands for building materials that saw a string of clay-pits dug side by side in a line that stretched 6 miles along the south bank of the River Humber. At one time there were more than twenty brick and tile manufacturers along the shore, and the area was nicknamed Dawson City because fortunes could be made here as quickly as they could over in the Gold Rush-crazed North West USA.

Now that almost all the brickmakers are gone, the Humber clay-pits have flooded to become freshwater lagoons, and the birds have moved in. At Far Ings Nature Reserve at the western end of the pits, the lagoons are managed for wildfowl and other water birds – particularly that shy brown boomer among the reeds, the bittern. Teal arrive in winter, there are green-headed shoveler dabbling for seeds, and big dark marsh harriers sweeping over the reed-beds on uplifted wings.

Just upriver, the flat marsh islet of Read's Island is managed for avocet, the rare blue-legged waders which returned to breed in Britain in 1947 after many decades of absence. About 100 pairs nest here, something approaching 10 per cent of the UK population. Now their island, like so many other low-lying features along the Humber, is threatened by flooding. The hope is that, rather than disappear as they did before, the Humber avocets will re-establish themselves on islets that stand higher out of the water in the newly created wetlands at Alkborough Flats (see below), some 5 miles up the river. At present their fate is anybody's guess.

141. JULIAN'S BOWER AND ALKBOROUGH FLATS, LINCOLNSHIRE

Maps: OS Explorer 281; Landranger 112

Travel: From A15 at Barton-on-Humber (south end of Humber Bridge), left on A1077 through South Ferriby. At the third of three turnings on right to Winteringham, go round sharp left bend; in 300 yards, right through West Halton to Alkborough. Brown 'Julian's Bower' sign points to car park; path to Julian's Bower (OS ref. 879215).

Nearest railway station: Scunthorpe (9 miles)

This beautiful and enigmatic circle of ancient turf maze, 40 feet across, lies canted westwards at the 140-foot-high crest of a north Lincolnshire escarpment known simply as the Cliff. It has recently been returfed and reopened to the public. As

Alkborough Flats

little is known of the derivation of the curious name of Julian's Bower as of its original function. Possibly it was named in honour of Julius, son of Aeneas the Trojan prince. Legend says it was Julius who introduced mazes to Rome, whence Romulus had them imported into England. Was the maze at the crest of the Cliff cut by Benedictine monks from the monastery at nearby Walcot to symbolize the soul's pilgrimage? Or did druids create it before Christians ever set foot in Britain, as some tales tell? And what were those mysterious 'games' which the young men and women of Alkborough indulged in here each May Eve, before Victorian prudery put an end to them?

One can only stand, speculate and stare. The view is immense, stretching 60 miles from the green whalebacks of the Lincolnshire Wolds to the Pennines. Down on the levels closer at hand, two broad rivers come sinuating through the agricultural plains – the Trent, at the end of its 170-mile journey from Staffordshire, and the Ouse, completing its wanderings from the Yorkshire hills.

Just at the foot of the Cliff the confluence of the Trent and Humber is bounded by Alkborough Flats, a wide nose of land reclaimed from the rivers. The flats are a patchwork of colours – ice blue, dark and light green, long glinting slabs of ochre and brown. Until 2005 they were all farmland; now, in a bold move like that on Wallasea Island in Essex (see p. 119–20), their sea wall has been breached and they are reverting to mudbank, sandflat and saltmarsh. This is not just a scheme to create 1,100 acres of habitat for wild birds, though it has achieved that. The Humber is becoming increasingly liable to flooding as sea levels rise. 'Hard' features such as the city of Hull and the great docks at Immingham have to be protected by maintaining sea defences, and the flooding of the farmland of Alkborough Flats is a quid pro quo. The sea must break in somewhere; better here, where it can benefit wildlife, than further downriver in the vulnerable haunts of man.

5

WALES

When the professional romantic George Borrow (an East Anglian Saxon who passionately wanted to be a Welsh Celt) finally published a long, boastful and exhilarating account of his journeys on foot across the length and breadth of Wales, he called it *Wild Wales*, and with good reason.

BACK IN 1862 Wales, with its mountainous interior and lack of decent roads, was seen by those well-heeled enough to travel for pleasure as one of the most untamed corners of Britain – notwithstanding the fact that heavy industry was already ripping up the valleys, fouling the rivers and besmirching the skies of south Wales.

I have followed in Borrow's 10-league footsteps all over Wales, from the summit of Mount Snowdon to the plunging drama of Pistyll Rhaeadr Waterfall, from the bogs and springs of misty Plynlimon to the former industrial valleys around Merthyr Tydfil, where heavy industry has all but vanished and nature is returning with remarkable speed. 'Wild' has many nuances in Wales. The black, unvegetated ledges of abandoned slate quarries in the north still carry a stripped and brutalized appearance, while nature has worked on the coal-mine slag heaps in the southern valleys to the extent that they now look more like grassy or wooded hillocks than industrial wastelands. A former setting for heavy industry, either greened-over like a landscaped and planted pit heap, or still open and raw like a slate mine, can feel as wild as a more conventionally untamed place, a mountainside or sea coast.

Industry of one sort or another has left its mark throughout the country on both landscape and people. Out where the coal and slate seams did not run, it was the hard and relentless taskmaster agriculture that held sway. The moors and hills of rural Radnorshire and Montgomery, at the heart of mid-Wales, are crossed by seldom-frequented drove roads and lonely paths. Dangerous and demanding as these were for the cattle drovers, farm labourers and itinerant craftsmen who travelled them, I walk them today with huge pleasure in the way the track unrolls before me, the wild charges of the weather as it gallops in from the darkening horizon, and the exhilaration of hurdling one hill after another. These are also the delights and rewards of wandering the Welsh Borders along the rollercoaster bank and ditch of Offa's Dyke, on whose hilltops I love to stand and stare west into Wales, admiring once again the ingenuity with which the Mercian surveyors sited their earthwork more than 1,200 years ago to keep the wild Welsh under the constant observation of a civilized eye. In contrast stand the high mountains of Snowdonia, difficult of access, majestically harsh of aspect, among which I could easily have selected enough wild places to fill this chapter exclusively.

Being Wales, there are great stories, too: the jealous outlaw who cut off the hand of his lady-love; the Victorian 'holy fool' who built a monastery in the wilds; the couple who shared their honeymoon with 30,000 gannets; and the farmer who lost his beautiful fairy wife beneath the waters of an enchanted lake.

Above: Creigiau Eglwyseg (p. 184). Below: near Pistyll Rhaeadr (p. 182)

LINKS

- Offa's Dyke National Trail (www.nationaltrail.co.uk/offasdyke; www.offasdykedemon.co.uk): Black Mountains (Pen Allt-Mawr), Capel-y-ffin, Gospel Pass (southern end); Castell Dinas Bran, Creigiau Eglwyseg, World's End (northern end)

NATIONAL PARKS

- Brecon Beacons: www.breconbeacons.org
- Pembrokeshire Coast: www.pcnpa.org.uk
- Snowdonia: www.snowdonia-npa.gov.uk

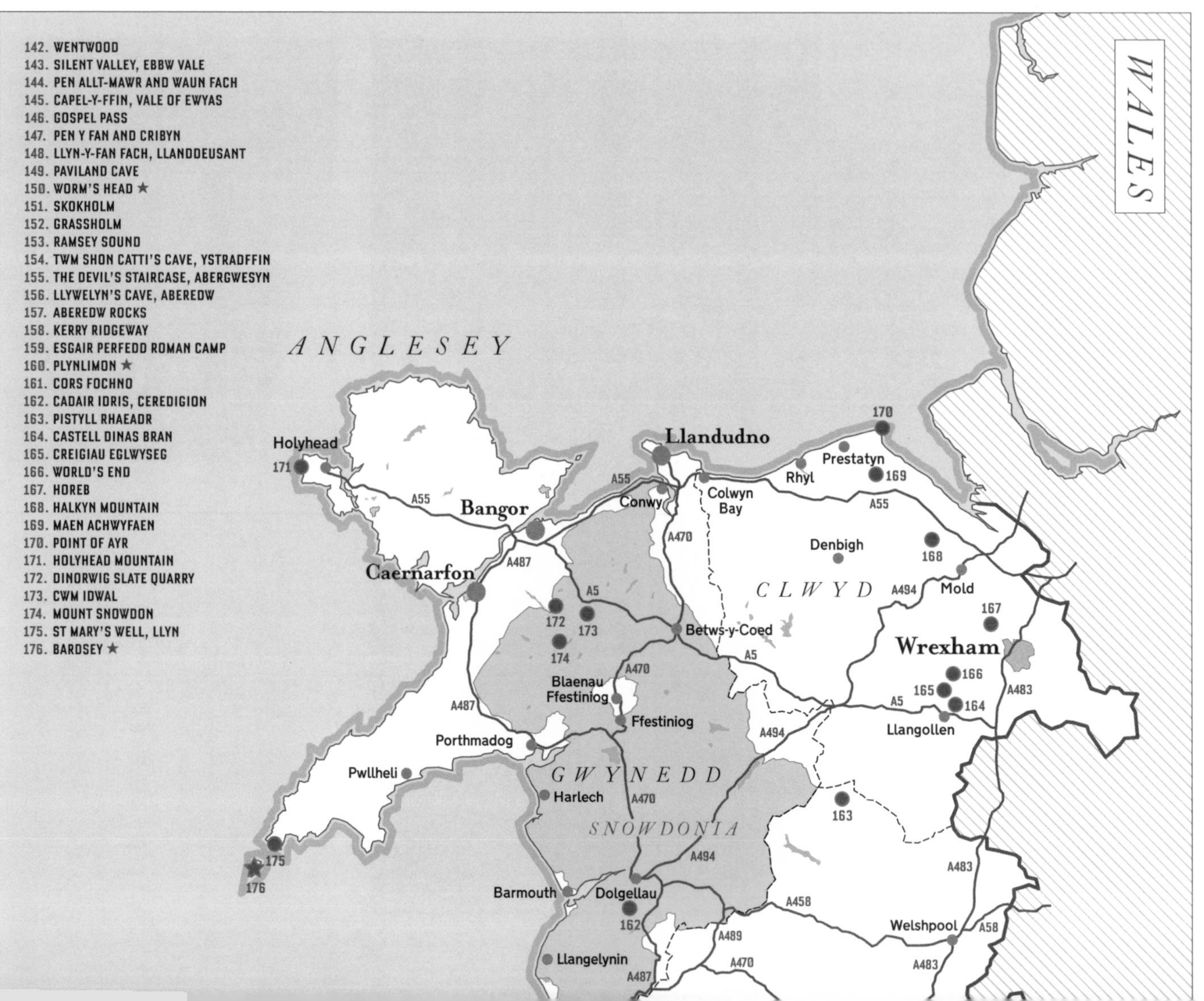
WALES
142. WENTWOOD
143. SILENT VALLEY, EBBW VALE
144. PEN ALLT-MAWR AND WAUN FACH
145. CAPEL-Y-FFIN, VALE OF EWYAS
146. GOSPEL PASS
147. PEN Y FAN AND CRIBYN
148. LLYN-Y-FAN FACH, LLANDDEUSANT
149. PAVILAND CAVE
150. WORM'S HEAD ★
151. SKOKHOLM
152. GRASSHOLM
153. RAMSEY SOUND
154. TWM SHON CATTI'S CAVE, YSTRADFFIN
155. THE DEVIL'S STAIRCASE, ABERGWESYN
156. LLYWELYN'S CAVE, ABEREDW
157. ABEREDW ROCKS
158. KERRY RIDGEWAY
159. ESGAIR PERFEDD ROMAN CAMP
160. PLYNLIMON ★
161. CORS FOCHNO
162. CADAIR IDRIS, CEREDIGION
163. PISTYLL RHAEADR
164. CASTELL DINAS BRAN
165. CREIGIAU EGLWYSEG
166. WORLD'S END
167. HOREB
168. HALKYN MOUNTAIN
169. MAEN ACHWYFAEN
170. POINT OF AYR
171. HOLYHEAD MOUNTAIN
172. DINORWIG SLATE QUARRY
173. CWM IDWAL
174. MOUNT SNOWDON
175. ST MARY'S WELL, LLYN
176. BARDSEY ★
ANGLESEY
Holyhead
Llandudno
Prestatyn
Rhyl
Colwyn Bay
Conwy
Bangor
Caernarfon
Denbigh
Mold
CLWYD
Wrexham
Betws-y-Coed
Blaenau Ffestiniog
Ffestiniog
Llangollen
Porthmadog
Pwllheli
GWYNEDD
Harlech
SNOWDONIA
Barmouth
Dolgellau
Welshpool
Llangelynin
A55
A470
A487
A5
A494
A483
A458
A489
A58

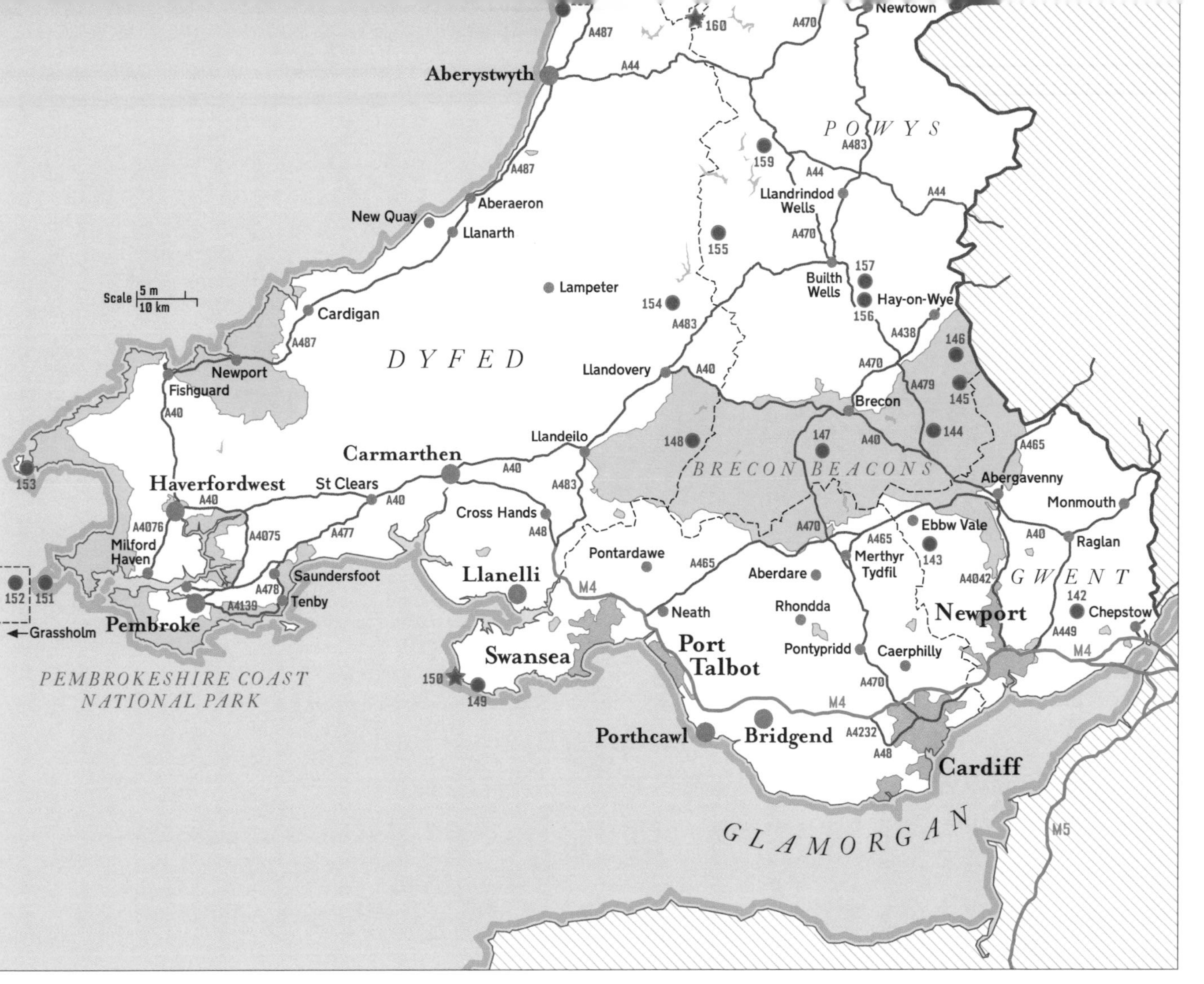
Newtown
A487
160
A470
Aberystwyth
A44
P O W Y S
A483
159
A44
A44
A487
Aberaeron
Llandrindod Wells
New Quay
Llanarth
A470
155
157
Builth Wells
Lampeter
Scale 5 m 10 km
154
Hay-on-Wye
Cardigan
156
A483
A438
146
A487
D Y F E D
A470
Llandovery
A40
Newport
A479
145
Fishguard
Brecon
A40
144
Llandeilo
148
147
A40
A465
Carmarthen
B R E C O N B E A C O N S
153
Haverfordwest
St Clears
A40
A483
Abergavenny
A40
A40
Monmouth
A4076
Cross Hands
A4075
A477
A48
A470
Ebbw Vale
Milford Haven
A465
A40
Raglan
Pontardawe
Merthyr Tydfil
143
Saundersfoot
A465
Aberdare
A4042
G W E N T
A478
Llanelli
M4
142
152
151
A4139
Tenby
Neath
Rhondda
Newport
Chepstow
Grassholm
Pembroke
A449
Port Talbot
Pontypridd
Caerphilly
M4
Swansea
PEMBROKESHIRE COAST NATIONAL PARK
150
149
A470
M4
Porthcawl
Bridgend
A4232
A48
Cardiff
G L A M O R G A N
M5

142. WENTWOOD, GWENT

Maps: OS Explorer 14; Landranger 171

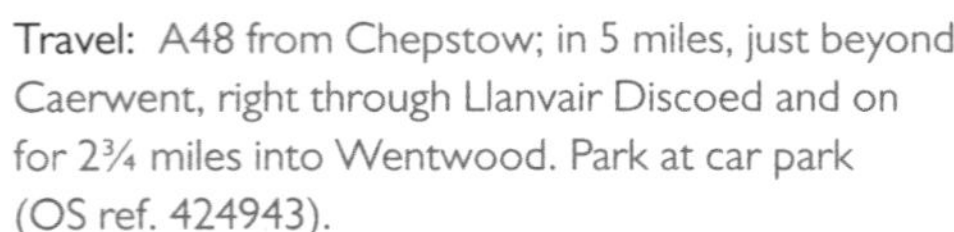
Travel: A48 from Chepstow; in 5 miles, just beyond Caerwent, right through Llanvair Discoed and on for 2¾ miles into Wentwood. Park at car park (OS ref. 424943).

'A dismal derelict waste, an upland hell and the bleakest of monuments to man's suicidal folly and cupidity.' That was how the country writer and poet Harold Massingham saw the ancient forest of Wentwood when he visited it in 1952 near the end of his life. Massingham had some justification for his gloom – most of Wentwood had been felled ten years previously during the Second World War, and what remained was mostly Forestry Commission conifers in dense, forbidding ranks. The venerable wood, relic of a great hunting forest that stretched in the time of the Romans from the Usk to the Wye, had been coppiced for building timber and cut for iron-smelting charcoal all through the Middle Ages, but conifer planting from the late Victorian era onwards had thoroughly compromised its ancient character by the date of its wartime destruction.

However, not all the great forest had been done away with. Deep among the conifers were centuries-old oaks and beeches, medieval forest banks full of violets and wood-sorrel, and dense cover where spotted woodpeckers, dormice and butterflies still found refuge. And now that the Woodland Trust has bought up a good chunk of Wentwood – the Trust purchased 870 acres in 2000 – a long-term plan of replanting, restoration and proper management as ancient woodland is already under way.

The paths among the trees are confusing, but that only adds to the magic of walking here. Kestrels dash in and out of the fringes, buzzards leave their treetop nests and circle overhead, mewing; woodcock dart from cover to cover, though you'll have to be quick to spot these. Come in spring and the ground under the trees is a mass of bluebells, with drifts of wild daffodils nearer the open light. It is as if the wildlife of Wentwood has only been biding its time, and will increase and flourish as the old forest comes back to health and wellbeing, a monument to something good in man's cross-grained nature.

143. SILENT VALLEY, EBBW VALE, GWENT

Maps: OS Explorer 166; Landranger 161

Travel: From A465 Heads of the Valleys road, A4046 south through Ebbw Vale towards Abertillery. A mile south of Waun-Lwyd, turn left (signed 'Cwm'). Pass church on your left; in 200 yards left (brown 'Nature Reserve' sign), over crossing streets and up long rise of Cendl Terrace (unsigned) for ½ mile to car park (signed) on right (OS ref. 187060). Duckboard trail from car park leads to gate and path into Reserve. Yellow, Blue and Red trails offer a choice of routes.

Nearest railway station: Rhymney (6 miles)

Silent Valley is a little leafy world apart, tucked away above the main valley of Ebbw Vale in the high side cleft of Merddog. When the steelworks of Ebbw Vale and the coal mines all along the valley were in full swing during the nineteenth and twentieth centuries, the beechwoods of Cwm Merddog were a refuge and retreat for the steelworkers, the pitmen and their families.

Silent Valley

These days the River Ebbw no longer runs black. The old mine sites have been flattened and the towering slag heaps resemble grassy hillsides. Heavy industry is all but gone from the South Wales Valleys. Now designated a Local Nature Reserve, the ancient beechwoods of Cwm Merddog and Coed-tyn-y-Gelli – both Sites of Special Scientific Interest – well deserve the name of Silent Valley.

Following the colour-coded trails through Silent Valley, you walk bombarded by birdsong. Song thrushes, chiffchaffs and warblers are loud in the spring and summer. Pied flycatchers nest in these woods. Woodpeckers cackle and the fluting songs of blackbirds are there all year round, along with the echoing *cronk-cronk!* of ravens above the 1,800-foot crest of Mynydd Carn-y-Cefn. This ridge blocks out half the eastern sky, adding to the valley's atmosphere of isolation.

The stream of Nant Merddog flows noisily in a rocky bed under fantastically gnarled beeches, mossy pollards that have overshot into wild shapes. Pale greeny-grey old man's beard lichens trail from the branches, indicators of unpolluted air – a remarkable change in the environment of the valleys over the past half century. These trees form the highest and just about the most westerly naturally seeded beechwoods in Britain. Some of the trees are well over 300 years old, and were mature long before industry came to ravage the surrounding valleys.

The scars of the coal mines that once straggled along the cwmside have mostly healed, though once up above the woods you can still find black diamonds of coal chips glinting through the grass and heather. The green hillside is a great place to sit and stare down the valley, enjoying the sound of the mountain wind sighing and roaring in the treetops below.

144. PEN ALLT-MAWR AND WAUN FACH, BLACK MOUNTAINS

Maps: OS Explorer OL13; Landranger 161

Travel: A40 from Abergavenny to Crickhowell; right up Llanbedr road. In 1¾ miles pass Llanbedr turning (OS ref. 234203) and continue ahead for 1½ miles to parking place on sharp bend at Neuadd-fawr (235229).

Pen Allt-Mawr, the Peak of the Big Cliff, is a splendidly wild height among many on the south-western edge of the Black Mountains. These old red sandstone mountains, covering 80 square miles of country to the east of the Brecon Beacons, should really be called the Black Ridges, since it is four great ridges that comprise them. Hatterrall, Fawddog and Gadair form successive ripples in the landscape as the crow flies south-west across the range. The final ridge of Allt-Mawr, the highest and most southerly, looks down on Crickhowell and the upper Usk Valley. This last is the only one that resembles a conventionally peaked mountain; and at 2,360 feet Pen Allt-Mawr, in spite of its name, is not even the highest summit in the range. That honour belongs to a boggy, flat-topped eminence 4 miles north that carries the appropriately downbeat name of Waun Fach – Little Moor.

You can climb Pen Allt-Mawr straight up from Crickhowell by way of the much-quarried lump of Table Mountain at 1,480 feet, with its Iron Age hill fort of Crug Hywel (Hywell's Tumulus) that gave Crickhowell its name. It's another 800 feet of uphill puff to reach Pen Cerrig-calch, Limestone Peak, at 2,300 feet, and from here a long ridge takes you gently north to Pen Allt-Mawr in 1½ miles. Up here the wind seethes through heather and grass, wheatears flirt their white rumps and black-headed stonechats with white cheek-flashes perch on the tips of the heather to chip out their characteristic call like two stones clicking together. Pause to catch your breath, because the view from the top is quite stunning, west across the twin humps of Pen Tir and Mynydd Troed towards the Brecon Beacons and the leonine head of Pen y Fan (see pp. 168–9), east to the Gadair Ridge and on back to the upturned bowl of Blorenge and the curious peak of the Sugar Loaf near Abergavenny.

Northwards, the ridge you are on skirts the head of the deep, sometimes shadowed valley of Cwm Banw, and marches on, narrowing to a famous meeting place of tracks at a cairn above Mynydd Llysiau, the Mountain of Herbs, before the track swings north-east near Pen Trumau and climbs in ever wetter and boggier conditions to reach the open, empty and truly wild moor of Waun Fach at 2,660 feet. Scarcely a triumphal trumpet-blast of a summit, this is nevertheless the highest place in the Black Mountains.

Back at the crossroads of tracks near Pen Trumau, a path descends into the wooded valley of Grwyne Fechan to bring you back to Crickhowell via Neuadd-fawr and a long 3 miles of country lane. This is a huge day, a 17- or 18-miler for tough and self-reliant hillwalkers with lots of stamina and skill with a map and compass – especially if the mist comes down. It will test you and tire you, but it will show you the highest, wildest and most magnificent face of the Black Mountains, one you cannot get to know in any other way.

145. CAPEL-Y-FFIN, VALE OF EWYAS, BLACK MOUNTAINS

Maps: OS Explorer OL13; Landranger 161

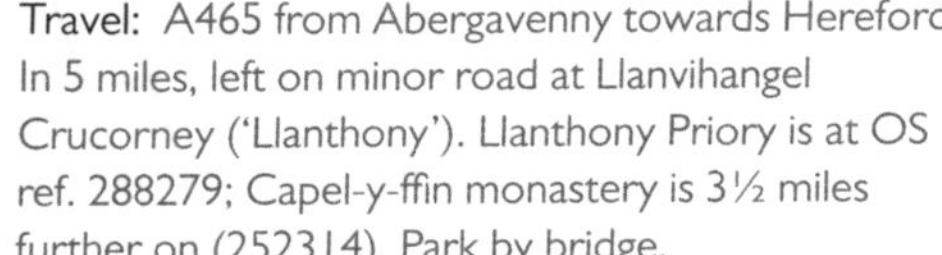
Travel: A465 from Abergavenny towards Hereford. In 5 miles, left on minor road at Llanvihangel Crucorney ('Llanthony'). Llanthony Priory is at OS ref. 288279; Capel-y-ffin monastery is 3½ miles further on (252314). Park by bridge.

There is something both wild and other-worldly about Capel-y-ffin, for it lies far down in the hollow of three hills with half the sky shut out, and holds only a simple chapel, a farmhouse and the ruins of a church. It is enough to climb the steep path above the Vision Farm on to Offa's Dyke on the crest of Hatterrall Ridge, or the other way to the skyline at Chwarel y Fan, and look down from 1,500 feet above the tiny cluster of buildings to see how enclosed and shut off the community is, held fast deep in the trough of the Vale of Ewyas, a hidden valley that has attracted solitaries and hermits throughout the centuries.

One of these was Father Ignatius, the name taken by the Reverend Joseph Leycester Lyne, a hot-to-handle fundamentalist and charismatic preacher, who arrived in 1870 with a handful of followers, much against the will of the established church, to found a new Benedictine monastery named Llanthony Tertia. The church they built still stands, though precariously, for the monks were amateur builders and did not know how to put the stones together with a mason's skill. The lives they led here were austere in the extreme: everything they ate they had to grow themselves; they wore heavy, hooded black habits with knotted scourge cords; and part of their rule was to undergo ritual humiliation at each other's hands – being spat at and trampled on, begging for their food and other privations.

Somehow the community lasted until Father Ignatius's death in 1908. Things fell apart quickly after that, and within a couple of years the monks had gone to other, more orthodox monasteries. In the 1920s sculptor and part-time satyr Eric Gill established one of his quasi-religious communities in the monastery house above the church for a few years; they scandalized the locals with naked open-air bathing and rumours of 'goings-on'.

Just across the valley lies the farm known as the Vision – a homage to an apparition of the Blessed Virgin Mary that appeared to one of the monks of Llanthony Tertia, then to local children and finally to Father Ignatius himself and a couple of hard-headed Vale of Ewyas farmers. The statue that stands today in the driveway to the ruined church shows the spot where the figure of a veiled woman, surrounded by a coruscation of light, was seen lifting her hands in blessing before slipping through a bush and vanishing from sight.

146. GOSPEL PASS, BLACK MOUNTAINS

Maps: OS Explorer OL13; Landranger 161

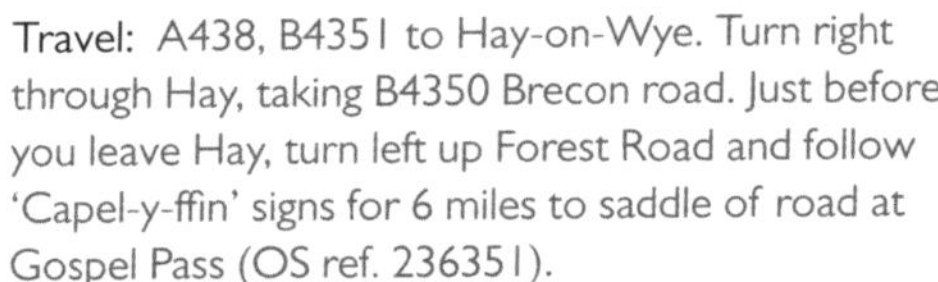
Travel: A438, B4351 to Hay-on-Wye. Turn right through Hay, taking B4350 Brecon road. Just before you leave Hay, turn left up Forest Road and follow 'Capel-y-ffin' signs for 6 miles to saddle of road at Gospel Pass (OS ref. 236351).

From Hay-on-Wye a long mountain road climbs slowly and steadily into the north-west corner of the Black Mountains. Gradually you leave the wide lowlands behind and enter wild highlands. It is a good 5 or

6 miles to the summit of the Gospel Pass at nearly 1,800 feet, and the country becomes progressively harder, colder and more rocky. As the road winds up across the lumpy hills, the imposing down and outward curve of Hay Bluff starts to loom ahead, paired by the rocky brow of the Twmpa, otherwise known as Lord Hereford's Knob. These two imposing bluffs are the ends of the two great snaking ridges, Hatterrall and Ffwddog, that enclose the Vale of Ewyas and throw their shadows down it.

'Bwlch' is a good word to know in this high part of the world. It means a pass or a place to get through, and the Gospel Pass is a superb example – Bwlch-yr-Efengel, the Pass of the Evangelist. Stop here and enjoy the view back over the Wye Valley to the far hills of central Wales, and also the prospect forward into the dark Vale of Ewyas. Either side of you, long mountainsides sweep up to the Bluff and the Knob. This is a lonely and uplifting place.

The chances are that Gospel Pass was named in memory of a preaching tour undertaken in the spring of 1188 by Baldwin of Exeter, Archbishop of Canterbury, to whip up fervour and finances for the Third Crusade. But a nicer version has the Apostle Paul and Jesus's hot-headed lieutenant Peter pausing up here on their way to convert the heathen Welsh after the two saints, having set out from Rome for Spain, had been blown off course into a British harbour by a storm. Paul was all for pressing on into the wild depths of the Black Mountains, but Peter did not really fancy either the surroundings or the company. He broke away and went down into the more agreeable country of the Golden Valley to the north of the Black Mountains, where he consecrated a well by releasing into its waters a great carp which he caught himself in the River Dore, a golden chain around its neck. Meanwhile the ominous valley of Ewyas swallowed his erstwhile companion. What happened to the stern, unbending Paul in the shadow of the Black Mountains, no one recorded.

147. PEN Y FAN AND CRIBYN, BRECON BEACONS

Maps: OS Explorer OL12; Landranger 160

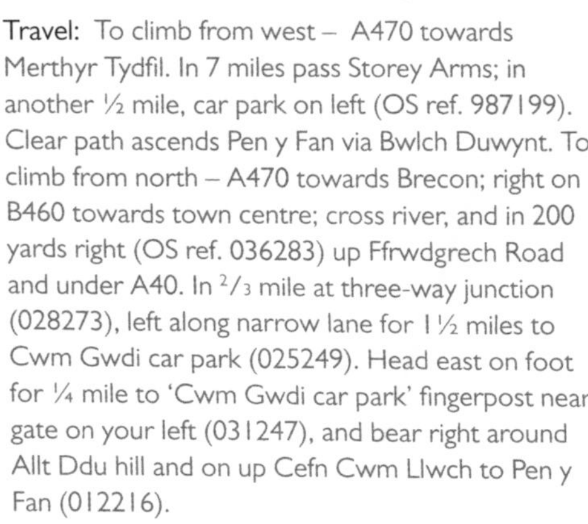

Travel: To climb from west – A470 towards Merthyr Tydfil. In 7 miles pass Storey Arms; in another ½ mile, car park on left (OS ref. 987199). Clear path ascends Pen y Fan via Bwlch Duwynt. To climb from north – A470 towards Brecon; right on B460 towards town centre; cross river, and in 200 yards right (OS ref. 036283) up Ffrwdgrech Road and under A40. In ⅔ mile at three-way junction (028273), left along narrow lane for 1½ miles to Cwm Gwdi car park (025249). Head east on foot for ¼ mile to 'Cwm Gwdi car park' fingerpost near gate on your left (031247), and bear right around Allt Ddu hill and on up Cefn Cwm Llwch to Pen y Fan (012216).

The flat-topped and high-shouldered Brecon Beacons are irresistible magnets for walkers. The four main summits – Corn Ddu, Cribyn, Fan y Big and Pen y Fan – spread out from black walls of cliffs and great sweeping corries. They are impressive fells in their own right, they are shapely and characterful, and they can be climbed by anyone with a bit of stamina. Children love to scamper up them, and walkers of riper years can make it to the top of Pen y Fan, summit of the range at 2,906 feet, at a steady pace. Best of all, the reward for getting to the top is a really fine view, back over lovely farmlands to the north and on into high, wild country to the east and west.

Climbing from the west is a straightforward push towards the great rounded wall of Pen y Fan, the most impressive of the four. From the north you climb the back of the 'hand' between the first and second fingers, with Pen y Fan rearing ahead in a fine dark peak and Cribyn beyond it as a stepped pyramid from which tremendous, horizontally striated cliffs fall 1,000 feet into the sheep-dotted depths of Cwm Sere.

On the peak of Pen y Fan you gaze around at the enormous view – getting on for 100 miles of Wales and the Border country laid out at your feet. Unless, of course, the mist is down ... Cwm Ddu, Cribyn and Fan y Big are all easily accessible from Pen y Fan by way of the ridge path that links them all. Choose an early morning midweek, early or late in the year, and the chances are you will share these shapely peaks, their cliffs and screes, their tiny lakes and cold, sweet-water rills with no one but the wheatears and the sheep.

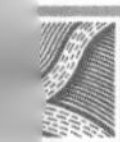

148. LLYN-Y-FAN FACH, LLANDDEUSANT, NEAR LLANDOVERY, CARMARTHENSHIRE

Maps: OS Explorer OL12; Landranger 160

Travel: From Llandovery, A4069 through Llangadog towards Brynamman. 3 miles south of Llangadog, left on minor road to Twynllanan. In village, turn right, then in 50 yards left (brown 'Youth Hostel' sign). Keep ahead on this road for 1½ miles to pass chapel at Llanddeusant, and follow 'Llyn-y-Fan' sign for another 1½ miles to car park area just beyond Blaenau Farm (OS ref. 799238). Follow track up to Llyn-y-Fan Fach (803218).

Llyn-y-Fan Fach

The Afon Sawdde flows out of the beautiful high lake of Llyn-y-Fan Fach, deep in the northern flanks of the tumbled upland known as the Black Mountain (not to be confused with the range of ridges called the Black Mountains to the east). The Sawdde itself is a channelled river, its flow regulated by a series of spillways and weirs in the narrow valley that climbs to the lake. A complex of tanks by the weir-houses halfway up the track holds young brown trout, their glossy backs flashing in the depths.

Up at the top a striking landscape: the arrow-headed Llyn-y-Fan Fach lying in a tall corrie, backed by the rugged wall of Bannau Sir Gaer, whose cliffs stand striped with dark bands of rock. Away to your left rises the high beak of Fan Brycheiniog, its promontory of Fan Foel raised like the upturned prow of a ship. The Black Mountain hills are covered with short pale grasses, rippling like corn in the wind. Ravens and buzzards are often seen circling overhead.

There is no formal path around the stony shore of Llyn-y-Fan Fach, but it is easy to pick out a circuit that passes under the cliff wall at the shadowed southern end. Look carefully among the cat's-paws of wind ripples on the surface and you may catch a glimpse of the fairy Lady of the Lake.

The story tells how a young farmer was watching his sheep beside the lake when a beautiful woman emerged from the waters. After an initially fruitless courtship she finally accepted him with the warning that, should he strike her three times without good reason, she would return to the lake and never more be seen. The marriage was a happy one for the farmer, and produced three sons. But in spite of all his efforts, he could not prevent the curse from coming to pass. Once he gave his wife a push to hurry her up when they were late for a christening, once he grabbed her by the arm to stop her crying at a wedding, and the third time he gave her a slap when she burst into hysterical laughter at a funeral. True to her promise, she turned without a word and went back to Llyn-y-Fan Fach. The farmer tried to follow her, but was too late, and had to watch as his fairy bride disappeared for ever.

The three sons grew up to be the Meddygon Myddfai, the Physicians of Myddfai, famed throughout Wales for their skill in healing – thanks to their fairy blood, so everyone said.

149. PAVILAND CAVE, GOWER PENINSULA

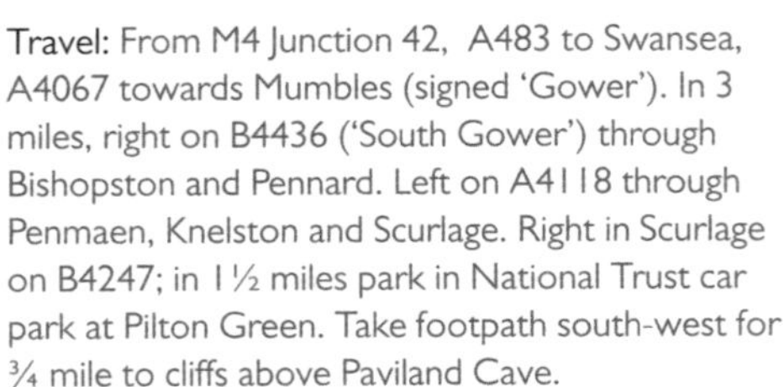

Maps: OS Explorer 164; Landranger 159

Travel: From M4 Junction 42, A483 to Swansea, A4067 towards Mumbles (signed 'Gower'). In 3 miles, right on B4436 ('South Gower') through Bishopston and Pennard. Left on A4118 through Penmaen, Knelston and Scurlage. Right in Scurlage on B4247; in 1½ miles park in National Trust car park at Pilton Green. Take footpath south-west for ¾ mile to cliffs above Paviland Cave.

NB: Paviland Cave (OS ref. 437858) is on private property, and like all the Gower caves should not be entered without consulting the National Trust at Little Reynoldston Farm, Reynoldston, Gower SA3 1AQ (tel: 01792 390636).

The coast of the Gower Peninsula is honeycombed with caves. Some are full of bats and seabirds; some echo only to the waves at high tide; others are resonant with history. The best-known is Goat Hole, better known as Paviland Cave, which opens a mouth more than 30 feet high in the most inaccessible and cave-ridden section of the Gower cliffs, between Port-Eynon and Worm's Head (see opposite). Paviland Cave is a fine cleft, faintly lit by a roof crack. Here in 1823 the Reverend William Buckley excavated from the cave floor a headless, half-eroded skeleton covered in red ochre staining, along with some items of ivory and a number of seashells pierced for use as a necklace. Buckley knew of contemporary theories that a world had existed before Noah's Flood, but he discounted them. His belief was that he had found the remains of a woman – a scarlet woman, literally and figuratively – who had 'comforted' the Roman soldiers in a nearby garrison and had been buried by them in the cave after her death. The find became known by the romantic title of the 'Red Lady of Paviland'.

A later, and more scientific, excavation in 1912 by anthropologist Professor William Sollas, and subsequent carbon dating and other analyses, brought a different story to light. The 'Red Lady' turns out to have been a man, a healthy male about 5 foot 8 inches tall and weighing perhaps 11 stone, with a liking for shellfish as well as hunted game, who was buried in Goat Hole cave some 25,000 years ago. It was a time of worsening climate, approaching the zenith of the last great Ice Age, when the southern edge of the ice was only a few miles north of the Gower coast. Judging by other finds – bone needles, flint blades, ornaments of mammoth tusk ivory – the cave was visited often over a long period. The status of the 'Red Lady' as an important person, perhaps a shamanic priest, is confirmed by the red ochre dressing of his bones. Gower, with the menacing ice at hand and a temperature not far off unbearably cold, would have seemed as much of a wild place to southern folk then as northern Siberia does today – a suitable place to lay one who had himself gone on into the most mysterious place of all.

150. WORM'S HEAD, GOWER PENINSULA

Maps: OS Explorer 164; Landranger 159

Travel: From M4 Junction 42, A483 to Swansea, A4067 towards Mumbles (signed 'Gower'). In 3 miles, right on B4436 ('South Gower') through Bishopston and Pennard. Left on A4118; in 7 miles, right in Scurlage on B4247 to Rhossili. Park in car park opposite Worm's Head Hotel (OS ref. 415880). Walk ahead past National Trust Information Centre, following track and descending to cross causeway. Follow path round south side of Inner Head, across Devil's Bridge (389877), round south side of Low Neck, out to Outer Head.

NB: Causeway is rough and jagged. It is only accessible safely for 2½ hours each side of low water, and takes at least 15 minutes to cross. Tide times posted in National Trust Information Centre (tel. 01792 390707). Please do not climb Outer Head between 1 March and 31 August, to avoid disturbance to nesting birds.

The old Norsemen who sailed to the Gower Peninsula found a line of tidal islets that stretched 2 miles out from its western tip, with the hump-backed profile of a sea serpent. They named it 'Wurm', the Dragon. On the map Worm's Head exactly resembles a mythical beast, with a blowhole for a nostril and the wave-cut arch of the Devil's Bridge for an eye. On the ground, too, the dragon resemblance is striking, with the blunt-faced Outer Head rearing 200 feet out of the waves beyond the disjointed members of Low Neck and Inner Head.

It is a rough and potentially dangerous scramble and stumble across the upended slabs of the causeway to the islets. Here at low tide you will find some of the best rock-pooling in Britain – delicate pink weed like coral, branched brown carrageen moss, and the filmy green 'leaves' of sea lettuce, along with edible and fiddler crabs, ragworms, sea-mice and tiny pug-faced fish. Tear yourself away and walk on past the rusty old ship's anchor to clamber on to the grassy slope of Inner Head where thrift, sea campion and white-flowered scurvy grass all nod in the sea wind. Seaward of here you scramble across the square arch of the Devil's Bridge and

cross another causeway on to the suddenly towering nape of Outer Head. Here in rough weather a blowhole shoots a spout of water 50 feet into the air with a hiss like a whale.

Outer Head is notable for its nesting seabirds in summer. Find a perch well out of sight of the cliffs; you won't be out of sound or smell, for the stink of guano and the noise of squabbling kittiwakes and fulmars reach you wherever you squat. Razorbills splash ecstatically in the sea, thrumming their stubby wings. Puffins hurry by in a blur of wings, as busy and preoccupied as portly brokers in the City. Great black-backed gulls bully the gannets and herring gulls. It's a mesmerizing sound, smell and spectacle. If you are not alert to the passing time you may, as Dylan Thomas once did, get cut off by the tide. The young poet had to wait on the promontory for the water to go down, and so will you.

151. SKOKHOLM, PEMBROKESHIRE

Maps: OS Explorer 36; Landranger 157

Travel: M4, A40 to Haverfordwest; B4327 towards Dale. 'Skomer and Skokholm' signs through Marloes to NT car park at Martinshaven (OS ref. 760089).

Boat trip: Half-hour crossing from Martinshaven.

NB: Check access and overnight stay availability before setting out (www.westwildlife.org/skokholm)

Romantics love Skokholm. This slip of pink sandstone, 2 miles south of Skomer across the treacherous tides of Broad Sound, is only a third of the size of its sister island. Skokholm (pronounced 'Skoe-k'm') accepts only a tiny handful of visitors at a time, a fraction of the numbers that Skomer receives. It still retains much of the air of dreamy isolation that arch-romantic Ronald Lockley so loved in 1927 when he came to fulfil a boyhood fantasy, living a simple and adventurous life on a remote island. Lockley stayed thirteen years, surviving countless escapades and hardships, and left having written a bestselling account of his life there, *Dream Island*.

The hand of Ronald Lockley is still evident in the timbers, ceilings and floors he built in the island's then dilapidated farmhouse, and the figurehead and steering wheel he salvaged from the wrecked coal boat *Alice Williams*. Lockley was a practical romantic. He was also a first-class observer of nature, carrying out the first scientific investigation into the private life of the Manx shearwater, the remarkable seabird whose current nesting population of about 165,000 pairs on Skokholm and Skomer forms more than half its world numbers. Skokholm's turf is riddled with burrows, nearly 100,000 of them, belonging to shearwaters, puffins and rabbits. The shearwaters spend the spring and summer in these waters, but are gone by early October to their wintering station off the Atlantic coasts of South America.

By day the adult shearwaters are out at sea, fishing. At night, however, Skokholm comes thrillingly alive with them, so it's worth staying overnight if you can. Standing at midnight beside the lighthouse, you find shearwaters rushing past from every quarter of the compass. The wind hisses in their wings. Some fly so close that they brush against your hair and clothes. As each shearwater approaches its burrow, it sends out a wheezy, frantic sounding call to its waiting chick: 'Poppa's-*here!* Poppa's-*here!*' Shearwater legs are placed too far back on the body for efficient walking; so, once landed, the parent bird strains and rows itself forward with stubby wings and beak. One last hoarse cry of 'Poppa's-*here!*' and the shearwater heaves itself into its hole and away from the light of your torch. As you stand and listen, you can hear the coos and squeaks from underground as parent and chick are reunited – a very moving moment in the dark.

152. GRASSHOLM, PEMBROKESHIRE

Maps: OS Explorer 36; Landranger 157

Travel: M4, A40 to Haverfordwest; B4327 towards Dale. 'Skomer and Skokholm' signs through Marloes to NT car park at Martinshaven (OS ref. 760089).

Boat trip: 1 ½ hours from Martinshaven. No landing. Sailings: www.dale-sailing.co.uk; www.thousandislands.co.uk.

From the boat heading west from the Pembrokeshire mainland, Grassholm is no more than a blob on the seaward horizon. During the hour-long crossing the 22-acre island resolves itself into a white-topped wedding cake. Forty thousand pairs of gannets produce a serious amount of guano, and the effect of the whitened rocks, crammed tight with large white seabirds, is dazzling in the extreme.

Early in the twentieth century there were 6,000 pairs here. Since then the colony has flourished mightily. When the birds took over the visitor viewing platform in the late 1990s, the RSPB, owners of Grassholm, issued a permanent ban on landing. It would be hard to find a toehold, anyway, among the jostling, beak-stabbing, expostulating gannets. The day will surely arrive when the birds will have expanded their roosts into every corner of the island. Until then a few guillemots and shags are permitted to live there, on sufferance.

Ronald Lockley of Skokholm Island (see opposite) honeymooned on Grassholm with his bride, Doris, in July 1928. During their stay the happy couple were subjected to repeated peckings and drenchings in regurgitated fish oil – not every young newlywed's dream. But all was sweet to the Lockleys, as Ronald remembered in *Dream Island*: 'All night long the north wind soughed and sighed, saying, "It is well, I blow softly; no other wind dares me. Sleep thou, thy boat is safe, the moorings are listless in the calm water …" '

153. RAMSEY SOUND

Maps: OS Explorer OL35; Landranger 157

Travel: M4, A40 to Haverfordwest; A487 to St David's; minor road (signed) to St Justinian's. Park here (OS ref. 724252) for ferry to Ramsey, or to walk south along cliffs overlooking Ramsey Sound.

Ferry to Ramsey: www.ramseyisland.co.uk.

After years of staggering along uneconomically as a hand-to-mouth farming operation, the 2-mile-long island of Ramsey was bought by the RSPB in 1992 and is now managed as a highly successful nature reserve with choughs and kittiwakes, dolphins and seals. The mile-wide strip of Ramsey Sound that separates Ramsey from the Welsh mainland, however, remains what it has always been – wild water.

Saint Justinian, a fifth-century Breton hermit and notable misogynist, was one of the few people ever to have crossed Ramsey Sound without a bumpy boat ride. He simply walked across, carrying his own head, which had just been cut off by three of his disgruntled monks. On another occasion the saint was lured into the middle of the Sound by three demons pretending to be boatmen. Luckily Justinian realized that only devils could be as ugly as this trio, and thwarted them by quoting from Scripture, whereupon they turned into a flock of crows and flew away.

Ramsey Sound has always been a place of ill omen, and walking along the island cliffs above the channel at mid-ebb you can see why. The Sound is the site of one of the most ferocious tide races in Britain. Even in calm weather there is a continuous roaring noise, a churning and rumbling. A curving highway of white water runs in the centre of the channel, forging irresistibly north at 20 miles an hour or more. Canoeists love to play with the tide, charging the jets of foam that spurt up from the Bitches reef, then letting their flimsy vessels slide into the central string, to be swept in a few minutes out of the Sound and into the wider sea. This main race is flanked by comparatively calm water, but even here are eddies, side currents, whirlpools and backwaters.

Former residents of Ramsey told of winter in the Sound in the days of sail-and-oar crossings when navigating that mile of water could involve an exhausting physical and mental battle that lasted all morning. The unpredictable violence of Ramsey Sound meant that island farmers could never guarantee to get their produce to market, and island dwellers never knew whether they were to be marooned for days or even weeks at a time. It is rare to find a stretch of water in Britain so powerful, so temperamental and intimidating; but Ramsey Sound is such a place.

154. TWM SHON CATTI'S CAVE, YSTRADFFIN, CARMARTHENSHIRE

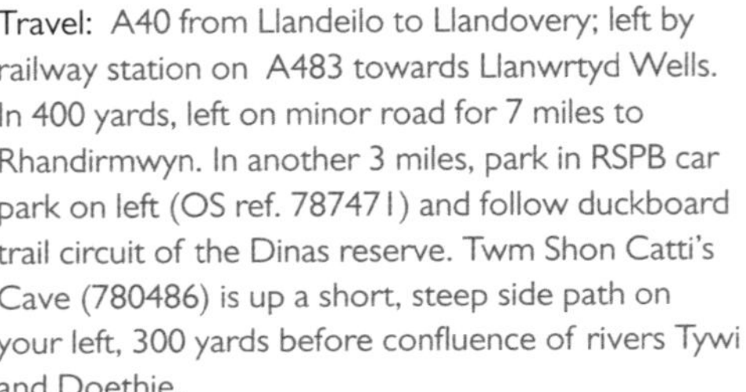

Maps: OS Explorer 187; Landranger 146 or 147

Travel: A40 from Llandeilo to Llandovery; left by railway station on A483 towards Llanwrtyd Wells. In 400 yards, left on minor road for 7 miles to Rhandirmwyn. In another 3 miles, park in RSPB car park on left (OS ref. 787471) and follow duckboard trail circuit of the Dinas reserve. Twm Shon Catti's Cave (780486) is up a short, steep side path on your left, 300 yards before confluence of rivers Tywi and Doethie.

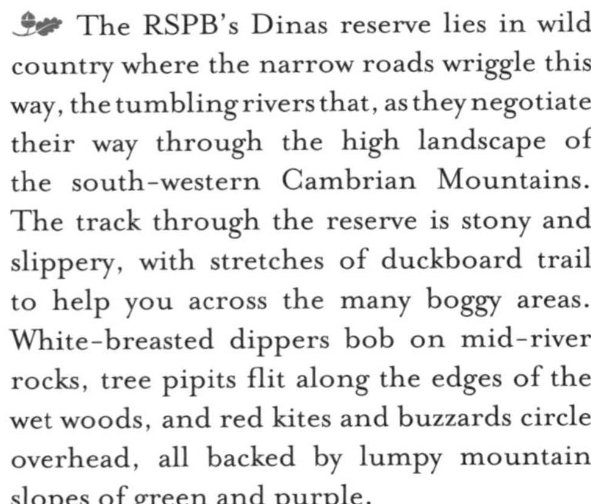

The RSPB's Dinas reserve lies in wild country where the narrow roads wriggle this way, the tumbling rivers that, as they negotiate their way through the high landscape of the south-western Cambrian Mountains. The track through the reserve is stony and slippery, with stretches of duckboard trail to help you across the many boggy areas. White-breasted dippers bob on mid-river rocks, tree pipits flit along the edges of the wet woods, and red kites and buzzards circle overhead, all backed by lumpy mountain slopes of green and purple.

Twm Shon Catti's Cave lies up a steep, slippery track. It's a low, narrow hole, half filled with fallen rocks, hidden away in its wooded slope above the rushing and roaring River Tywi: a suitably wild and romantic setting for the hideout cave of one of Wales's best-loved heroes, Twm Shon Catti – in others words, Tom Jones, son of Catherine. This illegitimate peasant boy, born into the Wales of lawless Tudor times, became a thief to provide for himself and his mother.

Twm would steal from the rich to feed the poor, sell the cattle he'd stolen back to their owners, and make himself agreeable to his victims with jokes and songs even as he robbed them. He was a man of wild deeds in love, too. He fell for the girl who was due to inherit Ystradffin, the farm just across the mountain from his cave, and swore his passion to her. On being refused, he made his way by night to the farm and pleaded his suit at her window. When the girl put out her hand, Twm seized it and swore he'd cut it off if she did not agree to be his wife. She indignantly refused once more, whereupon the robber suited deed to word, causing the blood from his lady-love's gashed wrist to spurt up and splash her bedroom ceiling – where its stain was a great talking point and showpiece for generations afterwards.

It seems that the lady responded to this rough wooing. Stories say that Twm gained her (and Ystradffin and its broad acres and 2,000 head of sheep), quit his cave hideout on the mountain, became respectable and died a rich man, mayor of Brecon and Justice of the Peace – a wild man tamed by love, or money.

155. THE DEVIL'S STAIRCASE, ABERGWESYN, POWYS

Maps: OS Explorer 187; Landranger 147

Travel: A483 from Llandovery to Llanwrtyd Wells; cross River Irfon, turn left for 5 miles through Llanwrtyd hamlet to Abergwesyn. In Abergwesyn turn left towards Tregaron; in 2½ miles, Devil's Staircase rises steeply.

In snow or ice, hard rain or mist the Devil's Staircase is a real challenge. This very steep piece of road climbs in tight zigzags beyond the valley-bottom hamlet of Abergwesyn, laboriously rising 450 feet to the summit of Abergwesyn Pass. As is the way with steep roads, going down the Devil's Staircase can be an even more difficult task, with your car appearing to tip forward and try to dig its bonnet into the tarmac. It's a brave cyclist who doesn't dismount on his way down, and even walkers face problems if it is wet or slippery underfoot. Yet this was the way the drovers came every spring, come rain, shine or storm, as they drove the black Welsh cattle east at 2 miles an hour towards the fattening pastures of lowland England.

From early medieval times onwards these hills were a through route for Welsh-bred livestock. Thirty thousand cattle or more went east each year. Hogs and sheep travelled, too, and great flocks of geese, their webbed feet tarred to harden them for the road. The cattle wore specially shaped iron shoes, to which they objected so violently that they had to be thrown upside down by strong men who would tie their legs together before the shoes were put on. The pigs had their trotters shod in woollen socks with leather soles, a kinder-sounding arrangement.

A drove comprised between 100 and 400 cattle, moved along by up to eight men and their dogs. They reckoned to cover 15 or 20 miles a day, and might walk well over 200 miles to their destination. The drovers wore heavy homespun and broad-brimmed hats, and soaped their brown-paper leggings against the weather and the soles of their stockings against blisters. They often slept out of doors with the animals, or in the outhouses of farms whose sign of welcome to drovers was a spinney of three Scots pine trees. With his ragged beard and weather-stained clothes, a drover might look like a wild man or an outlaw, but in fact he was generally a sober and reliable person who exercised huge responsibility looking after other men's fortunes on the hoof, bringing those fortunes, converted into gold coins, back to his clients, often carrying other commissions, messages and mail between the cattle breeders and dealers, the graziers and the small-town bankers who formed his network of business contacts.

Park in the wild moorlands beyond the Devil's Staircase, abolish the conifer forests with a stroke of the imagination, and you can picture those long, slow-moving trains of beasts and their attendant men and dogs, the dust and mud and bruising stones of the hard road they followed.

156. LLYWELYN'S CAVE, ABEREDW, NEAR BUILTH WELLS, POWYS

Maps: OS Explorer 188; Landranger 147

Travel: From A470 Brecon–Builth Wells road, follow 'Aberedw' signs on to B4567 and minor road to Aberedw; park near church. Follow road east out of village on foot, forking right just past Seven Stars pub, for ½ mile, descending to bridge over Afon Edw. Ahead up 'No Through Road' lane for 50 yards; hairpin back to the right through first gate (OS ref. 086470) up stony track for ¼ mile. At top of rise it bends left, then right and through a gate. Cave is in the low cliffs to your right (084468).

Nearest railway station: Builth Road (7 miles)

The steep land between Llandeilo Hill and the east bank of the River Wye is sheep country; sloping fields where flocks graze, hedges and fences are reinforced against intrusion by the animals, and small farms lie scattered across the hillsides. The hills run from green pastures in the valley bottoms to rough brackeny moorland on the tops. A feature of the Silurian rocks that outcrop here above the river is the way in which their narrow sandwiches of strata form long horizontal cliffs dozens of feet high, burrowed here and there with caves. Nowadays the terraces or steps between one level of cliffs and the next are grassy fields, the cliffs themselves thick with ash, oak and birch, but back in the thirteenth century the area was a wild tumble of forest where a hunted man could find refuge in a cave and be fairly sure of escaping detection by enemies – if he remained unbetrayed.

Llywelyn's Cave

That was the situation of Llywelyn ap Gruffydd, Prince of Wales, in the winter of 1282. Grandson of Llywelyn ap Iorwerth – Llywelyn the Great, medieval Wales's most effective ruler and champion of Welsh political freedom – Llywelyn ap Gruffydd had been forced to pay homage to King Edward I in 1277 after initially refusing, and had forfeited almost all the lands he had previously won from the English. In 1282 he and his brother, Daffyd, rose against Edward. The king responded with a devastating push into Wales, chasing Llywelyn into Snowdonia and harrying him south again. In December the garrison at Builth denied the fugitive prince sanctuary. He spent a night in a cave among the rocks above the Wye, and next day was killed in a skirmish at nearby Cilmeri. The head of Llywelyn the Last was cut off and paraded in London, and the final effective hopes of Welsh autonomy extinguished.

Llywelyn's Cave is unmarked among the ash and birch trees, but a prominent fence post and a stone slab bridge across a ditch give a clue to its whereabouts. Views are splendid, looking north across the deep valley of the Afon Edw. The cave entrance is formed by a low, narrow slit in a cliff face hung with moss and pennywort. The interior, with a stone-flagged floor, is wide and high enough for a man to hide in. Here in the rocks, his lair concealed by a boulder rolled across the cave opening, the last truly Welsh Prince of Wales spent his final night on earth.

157. ABEREDW ROCKS, POWYS

Maps: OS Explorer 188; Landranger 147

Travel: From A470 Brecon–Builth Wells road, follow 'Aberedw' signs on to B4567 and minor road to Aberedw; park near church. Follow road east out of village on foot, forking right just past Seven Stars pub, for ½ mile, descending to bridge over Avon Edw. Ahead up 'No Through Road' lane for 50 yards, hairpin back to the right through first gate (OS ref. 086470) up stony track. Follow this past Llywelyn's Cave (see above) and on up to go through gate by Pantau Farm (ruin). In 10 yards track curves right, but keep ahead on grassy path that climbs through a defile to a pool. From this saddle dip down to follow path under Aberedw Rocks.

Nearest railway station: Builth Road (7 miles)

Walk from the ruined farm of Pantau up through a rocky gully with only the curve of the skyline ahead of you, and it is a wonderful shock to reach the pool at the top of the path and see the grand sweep of Aberedw Rocks in front. Even then these tall cliffs, piled in horizontal strata of siltstone and sandstone as they were laid down some 430 million years ago, are not in full view until you have descended from the saddle and rounded the corner. Like dark grey teeth the rocks curve through a half-circle, facing west across the valley of the River Wye, hung with long creepers of ivy and blotched with green lichen. In the shadows under the pass it seems the place for an ambush.

The setting for Aberedw Rocks is bare moorland of gorse patches and bracken

Aberedw Rocks

slopes, tuffets of heather full of green mosses and clumps of blue-grey usnea or old man's beard lichen. Wind and lark-song seem constant features of the scene. The view is enormous, due south to the hump of the Brecon Beacons 15 miles away, with the Black Mountains in the south-east. This was a favourite place for Victorian romantics to come and get a taste of an easily accessible wild landscape, and they did not come any more romantic than the diarist curate of Clyro, Francis Kilvert, who mused nostalgically on 13 April 1875:

> *Oh, Aberedw, Aberedw. Would God I might dwell and die by thee. Memory enters in, and brings back the old time in a clear vision and wakening dream, and again I descend from the high moor's half encircling sweep and listen to the distant murmur of the river as it foams down the ravine from its home in the Green Cwm, its cradle in the hills. Once more I stand by the riverside and look up at the cliff castle towers and mark the wild roses swinging from the crag and watch the green woods waving and shimmering with a twinkling dazzle as they rustle in the breeze and shining of the summer afternoon, while here and there a grey crag peeps from among the tufted trees ... Oh, Aberedw, Aberedw.*

158. KERRY RIDGEWAY

Maps: OS Explorer 216; Landranger 137

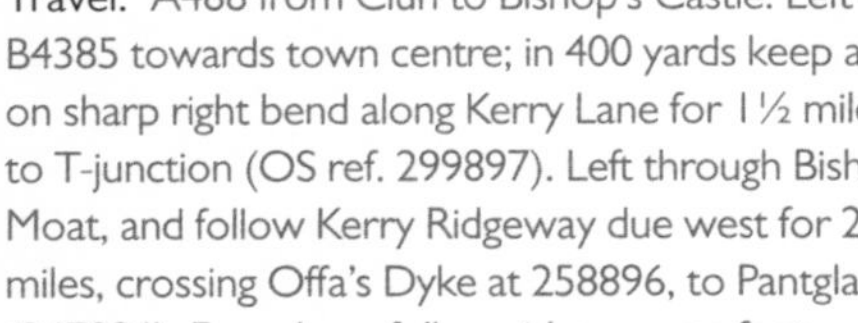

Travel: A488 from Clun to Bishop's Castle. Left on B4385 towards town centre; in 400 yards keep ahead on sharp right bend along Kerry Lane for 1½ miles to T-junction (OS ref. 299897). Left through Bishop's Moat, and follow Kerry Ridgeway due west for 2½ miles, crossing Offa's Dyke at 258896, to Pantglas (247896). From here follow ridgeway on foot.

Up across the wild highlands of the Kerry Hills runs the oldest road in Wales. Under the title of 'Kerry Ridgeway' it connects the Powys village of Kerry and the Shropshire town of Bishop's Castle; but this ancient track continues for many miles further into England. In former times it was the traditional through route between the two countries, a prehistoric highway across the Cambrian Mountains. The Kerry Ridgeway has many guises: a forest path, a deeply rutted moorland track, a farm lane, a high-banked road. Its straight course, a purposeful advance across some of the loneliest back country in Powys, and the way that it keeps to the high ground with far views in all directions, hint at its use over a very long time. No one knows exactly how long, but it certainly pre-dates the stone circle, the Bronze Age round barrows and the Iron Age hill fort that lie along its course.

The old straight track makes a bleak walk on a day of high wind and rain, or when the mist is down and the trees drip on a still morning. That is when one thinks with admiration of the drovers who used the Kerry Ridgeway, going at the snail's pace of

Kerry Ridgeway

cattle on the move, exposed to all weathers as they walked the beasts east towards England and the lowland fattening pastures. On either side bare moorland rolls away, partly cloaked in dark conifer plantation these days, but back then open and treeless. Farms lie tucked away in crevices of these brown, rolling moors, but for travellers crossing them – now as then – there is no shelter. The only comfort is in the unswerving course of the Kerry Ridgeway. Follow me, it indicates, and you will be down in kinder country sooner or later.

159. ESGAIR PERFEDD ROMAN CAMP, POWYS

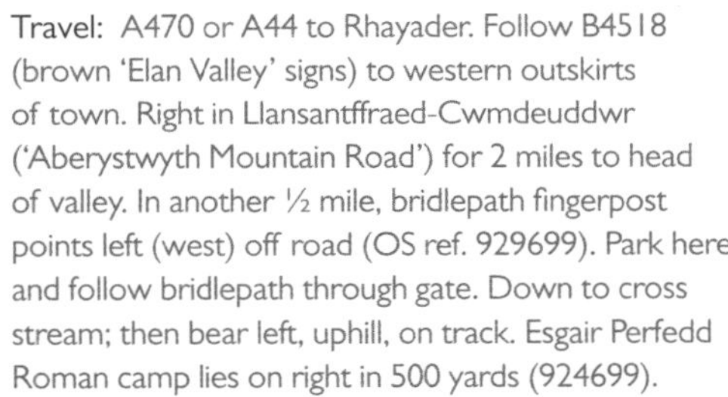

Maps: OS Explorer 200; Landranger 147

Travel: A470 or A44 to Rhayader. Follow B4518 (brown 'Elan Valley' signs) to western outskirts of town. Right in Llansantffraed-Cwmdeuddwr ('Aberystwyth Mountain Road') for 2 miles to head of valley. In another ½ mile, bridlepath fingerpost points left (west) off road (OS ref. 929699). Park here and follow bridlepath through gate. Down to cross stream; then bear left, uphill, on track. Esgair Perfedd Roman camp lies on right in 500 yards (924699).

The moors north-west of Rhayader offer a very bleak landscape indeed. There are no trees up here. Shallow bogs lie among pale grasses dried by the constant wind that shakes them. Heather and moss clumps make up the rest of the vegetation. There is the kind of enormous sky you associate with the flatlands of East Anglia rather than mid-Wales. Roman soldiers halted here some time around AD 74–80 to dig and mound a marching camp. What they thought of their surroundings isn't difficult to guess – and being hardened squaddies, they probably

Esgair Perfedd Roman Camp

did not keep their thoughts to themselves.

You can scarcely avoid such fantasies as you walk the old moor track over to Craig Goch reservoir. Long before the lake comes in sight you will have passed along the southern boundary bank of Esgair Perfedd camp, almost certainly without noticing it. You need a careful eye, allied with some dry or frosty weather and a low sun, to spot the 15-acre rectangle that has left only a ghost print in the moor grass. A Roman half-legion built it in a few hours on a temporary halt as they marched west into Ceredigion on campaign. No casual kipping on the moor for these warfare experts; they dug a ditch and mounded a wall to create a tight, secure fort where 4,000 men could pitch their tents and sleep safe from attack. Even for a halt of one night it was worth the trouble. The Romans had been in Britain for less than forty years, and took nothing for granted in the outlands of what was still a very wild country.

160. PLYNLIMON, POWYS

Maps: OS Explorer 214; Landranger 135

Travel: A44 from Ponterwyd towards Rhayader; in 2 miles, park at Castell Dyffryn Inn on left. A track leads north by the east side of Dyll Faen forest to reach the summer of Plynlimon in 3½ miles (about 1,650 feet of climb). From the summit, source of Rheidol is north-east above Llyn Llygad Rheidol (OS ref. 793872 approx.); source of Wye is east, about ⅔ mile, at 801872 approx.; source of Severn is about 2½ miles north-east at 820898 approx.; source of the Gwarin is 1¼ miles north-east at 806378 approx.

Plynlimon is without question one of the wildest mountains in Powys. Not particularly impressive as a peak, not very shapely or even clearly defined, its rocky crest at 2,467 feet overlooks a huge swathe of brown, lumpy moorland where cliffs plummet to lakes, springs burst out of sodden hillsides and great blankets of dreary, semi-eroded bog hold all the water that so frequently falls on Plynlimon, releasing it to form a multitude of streams and three of Wales's most important rivers – Severn, Wye and Rheidol. All three have their sources in an area of less than 2 square miles, to the north and east of Plynlimon summit, and it is one of the greatest wild walks in Wales to reach and have a drink from all three.

That was what George Borrow arrived to do when he ascended Plynlimon in 1854 while wandering on a foot journey that would produce his great and cranky book *Wild Wales*. Borrow was in love with himself and his own cleverness. He knew a lot, but not as much as he fancied. And it is pretty clear from a careful reading of his book that he was sadly led astray on Plynlimon by a smooth-talking guide.

To get to the source of the Rheidol you scramble precariously a little way down a precipitous slope north-east of the summit to find a lichen-hung pool of water tumbling into the beautiful lake of Llygad Rheidol. The source of the Wye lies two-thirds of a mile east of the summit, at the head of a dramatically deep, east-going cleft. As for the Severn, that great river rises in a pool in the middle of a waste of sloppy, slippy bog nearly 3 miles north-east of Plynlimon's peak – not the place any guide with a too-clever-by-half client would go, if he could see a way out of it.

The local shepherd that George Borrow engaged at the Castell Dyffryn Inn took him faithfully to the source of the Rheidol, though Borrow insisted on descending the crags to the lake shore, telling the guide: 'It is not only necessary for me to see the sources of the rivers, but to drink of them, in order that in after times I may be able to harangue about them with a tone of confidence and authority.' He was also guided accurately to the source of the Wye, where he took off his hat and sang a 'pennillion' in praise of Plynlimon. But when it came to slogging a path to the bog where the Severn whelms, the guide brought his client to a spring he thought would look prettier and be more likely to appeal to a *saesneg* (an Englishman) – and would also save him time and trouble.

'A little pool of water some 20 inches long,' was Borrow's description, 'six wide and about three deep ... covered at the bottom with small stones, from between which the water gushes up.' That is nothing like the Severn source – but it does exactly describe the spring of the Gwarin stream only half a mile from the Wye source. Borrow never knew he'd been tricked, the shepherd got his fee and a pint of ale back at the inn – and everyone was happy.

161. CORS FOCHNO, CEREDIGION

Maps: OS Explorer 23; Landranger 135

Travel: A487 from Machynlleth towards Aberystwyth; right at Tre'r-ddol on B4353 to Ynyslas Visitor Centre.

Nearest railway station: Borth (2 miles)

Cors Fochno, known to generations of geography and botany students as Borth Bog, is one of the treasures of west Wales. Lying along the south shore of the Dyfi Estuary a few miles north of Aberystwyth, these 3 square miles of estuarine raised bog are the largest such area in Britain. Over the years parts have been drained and reclaimed for agriculture, other sections cut for peat fuel. Yet the heart of Cors Fochno has remained as nature intended, a level, waterlogged mass with tuffets of green sphagnum providing shelter for the beautiful, delicate pink bog rosemary, a plant that is a graceful dancer in every sea wind, and for insectivorous plants such as great sundew. The former peat banks, cut into squared ramparts like miniature fortifications, now support scrub and fir woodland.

Cors Fochno is one piece in a mosaic of habitat which has seen the Dyfi Estuary designated a UNESCO Biosphere Reserve, the only one in Wales. The other pieces are the estuary itself, a wonderful resource for wading birds with its mudflats and broad sandy foreshore, and the Ynyslas sand dunes that line the estuary mouth and nurture a tremendously varied wildlife that includes voles, rabbits and the predators that feed on them – foxes, stoats and polecats. The wild violets of the dunes feed the caterpillars that will develop into dark green fritillaries with leopard-spotted wings, and the grasses support colonies of gatekeeper butterflies whose big black spots, one on each wingtip, mimic a pair of staring eyes to scare off predators.

Dunes and estuary shores, though rich habitats, are not uncommon around the British and Irish coasts. It is this big, relatively intact coastal bog that is the star. Otters find good hunting along the ditches and shelter in the woods; Welsh mountain ponies roam freely, and the wide skies overhead are cut by buzzards and red kites, and sometimes by the dark bullet whizz of a peregrine. The bog is in fact mostly water – if you jump up and down you can feel the ripples spreading outwards – and is best explored by venturing out along the boardwalks laid over this intricately balanced, intermeshing world.

162. CADAIR IDRIS, CEREDIGION

Maps: OS Explorer 18; Landranger 124

Travel: Climbing from north side: A470 to Dolgellau, left to cross Afon Wnion, right at T-junction along minor road for 3 miles to car park on right at Tynant (OS ref. 698153). From south side: A487 from Machynlleth towards Dolgellau; car park on left in Minffordd (732116).

Cadair Idris may be only 2,928 feet high – not even a Munro in Scottish terms – but this is a most impressive mountain. The Chair of Idris rises over the valley of the Afon Dysynni a little inland of Barmouth, a great rugged mass of rock whose full force you catch as you view it across narrow, shadowy

Tal-y-Llyn Lake. All these mountains round about were quarried for slate to pour into the Moloch mouth of the Industrial Revolution, and there is something slate-hard and dark about the hanging corries and cliffs that face east around Penycadair, the summit of Cadair Idris.

The two best-known approaches to the summit are from north and south. From the south you start at Minffordd and go steeply up to reach the jewel of the mountain, Llyn Cau (Secret Lake), in its tight black prison of 1,000-foot crags. A hard upward slog and you have topped them and are looking dizzyingly down on the lake; another 300 feet and you stand on Penycadair, Peak of the Chair.

You can reach the peak from near Dolgellau in the north by a longer and easier climb that has the merit of bringing you suddenly to the brink of the amphitheatre in which Llyn Cau lies, a dramatic moment hard to rival.

The adventurous way off the peak is via the Fox's Path, a famous and breathtaking descent that plunges 600 feet down a slope of loose rocks and scree to the shore of Llyn-y-Gadair, another dark lake under mighty cliffs.

163. PISTYLL RHAEADR, POWYS

Maps: OS Explorer 255; Landranger 125

Travel: A5 to Oswestry; B4580 to Llanrhaeadr-ym-Mochnant. In village, follow brown 'Pistyll Waterfall' signs up single track road for 4 miles. Car park at end of road (OS ref. 074295); walk forward ¼ mile to Pistyll Rhaeadr waterfall.

As you walk up the road from the car park towards Pistyll Rhaeadr waterfall, the faint

Pistyll Rhaeadr

rustling of the fall grows rapidly louder. Even during a dry spell you are aware that a mighty waterfall is close at hand. After prolonged heavy rain, or in conditions of snowmelt, there is something properly fear-inspiring about the waters of the Afon Disgynfa as they hurl themselves to destruction from the heights of the Berwyn Hills.

From the footbridge at the base of the falls, you gaze up at the numbing spectacle of 240 feet of furiously tumbling water. Pistyll Rhaeadr crashes down unimpeded from its upper lip in a straight fall of well over 100 feet, thundering into a pool from which it jets out again through a natural rock arch and seethes on down into the basin at its foot. The spray puffs and smokes out through the arch, and blasts of icy air sweep round the footbridge. The fall roars and hisses, battering the rocks like an ogre. No hellfire sermon could be more salutary than the raw power of Pistyll Rhaeadr, uplifting the spirit even as it pulverizes the ego.

George Borrow, the indefatigable East Anglian wanderer and marvellously imperfect scholar who would have given his right arm to have been born a Welshman, came to see the fall in 1854 when he was walking through Wales on the journey that would give rise to his eccentric masterpiece of travel writing, *Wild Wales*. He thought it exceeded all the remarkable cataracts in Britain for altitude, beauty and grace – though he would have liked 'nature in one of her floods' to sweep away 'the ugly black bridge of rock'. A local woman told him how she had seen a Russian visitor wriggling like an eel across the bridge.

'What shall I liken Pistyll Rhaeadr to?' wondered Borrow. 'I scarcely know, unless to an immense skein of silk agitated and disturbed by tempestuous blasts, or to the long tail of a grey courser at furious speed.'

After viewing the fall, Borrow went to a farmhouse to drink buttermilk and found a poem about the fall written in the visitors' book in Welsh, 'which though incorrect in its prosody I thought stirring and grand'. He made up a translation on the spot:

Foaming and frothing from mountainous height,
Roaring like thunder the Rhyadr falls;
Though its silvery splendour the eye may delight,
Its fury the heart of the bravest appals.

164. CASTELL DINAS BRAN, DENBIGHSHIRE

Maps: OS Explorer 256; Landranger 117

Travel: A5 from Shrewsbury to Llangollen. Cross River Dee; right on A539 ('Ruabon'). In 1¾ miles, left on minor road (OS ref. 241424) via Trevor Uchaf; in 1½ miles, park near gateway to Castell Dinas Bran (222430). Climb steep path to castle ruins.

Nearest railway station: Ruabon (6 miles); Llangollen (Llangollen Railway)

The ancient stronghold of Castell Dinas Bran dominates the town of Llangollen, which curls along the River Dee at its feet. It is not only the abrupt rise of the 1,050-foot knoll that draws all eyes, but also the jagged drama of the summit ruins outlined against the sky.

The castle that the Princes of Powys built and garrisoned on the hilltop was not a fortunate place for them. Gruffydd Madog lost it to Llywelyn the Last in 1257, regained it soon after and promptly died. His son Madog lost it to the English in 1276, got it back the following year, and almost immediately he, too, died. The castle fell into disuse, never properly demolished, never properly refortified.

The climb to the castle is steep, but the reward is a most awe-inspiring view, north to the banded crags of Creigiau Eglwyseg (see below), west to Snowdonia (see pp. 192–3), and south over Llangollen to the towering wall of the Berwyn Hills, with the River Dee snaking in a ribbon of silver 900 feet below. This is a wonderful place to sit among the broken arches and shattered walls, dreaming of Myfanwy Fechan, the beautiful but scornful ice maiden who walked abroad in scarlet robes with queenly gait, all bowing before her. The bard Hywel ap Eynion Llygliw cried to her in verse:

O bid me sing, as well I may,
Nor scorn my melody in vain,
Or 'neath the walls of Dinas Bran
Behold me perish in my pain.

165. CREIGIAU EGLWYSEG, DENBIGHSHIRE

Maps: OS Explorer 256; Landranger 117

Travel: A5 from Shrewsbury to Llangollen. Cross River Dee; right on A539 ('Ruabon'). In 1¾ miles, left on minor road (OS ref. 241424); this soon hairpins left and runs for 3 miles under Creigiau Eglwyseg. Park neatly where road bears away from crags near Rock Farm (218453); continue on foot along the crags themselves on Offa's Dyke Path National Trail for 2 miles through Eglwyseg Valley to World's End (see opposite) and beyond.

Nearest railway station: Ruabon (6 miles); Llangollen (Llangollen Railway)

When violent earth movements occur, they can result in spectacular landscapes. Part of what made the north Wales town of Llangollen such a popular resort for nineteenth-century holidaymakers was the extraordinary landscape of Creigiau Eglwyseg, or Church Rocks, overwhelming, impressive and strange, yet conveniently set on the town's

Creigiau Eglwyseg

doorstep. North of Llangollen the face of the countryside is dominated by a great sloping wall of 300-foot crags, a convex lateral bulge 5 miles long that is itself broken into several successive brows of out-thrust rock facing west and separated by deep, shadowy gullies. Creigiau Eglwyseg are not only eye-catchingly shaped and impressively tall; they also glow in wonderful shades of orange, grey and blue when the setting sun bathes them in evening light. Victorian strollers loved the crags, and the Panorama Walk along the top became a firm favourite.

Nowadays you can drive half the length of Creigiau Eglwyseg on a bumpy country road. The best way to appreciate them, though, is to take the Offa's Dyke Trail and follow the northern section through the ever-narrowing Eglwyseg Valley – Church Valley, named after the Cistercian abbey of Valle Crucis, which stands in splendid ruin in the meadows below. The limestone bluffs of Creigiau Eglwyseg billow like sails with a stiff easterly behind them, their feet lost in great downward-spreading fans of scree. It is no wonder they show so many colours to the world. Coal, iron, lead and copper are just some of the minerals hidden within and mined over the centuries.

What is really remarkable about this landscape is the violence of the mighty landslip along the fault line of the valley that tore it in two. So powerful was that event that the whole of the eastern part of the valley was jerked 5 miles further east, to where it now outcrops above Froncysyllte in rocks very similar to these. Creigiau Eglwyseg is a landscape in which a walker feels properly dwarfed.

166. WORLD'S END, DENBIGHSHIRE

Maps: OS Explorer 256; Landranger 117

Travel: A5 to Llangollen; cross River Dee. Left on A542 towards Ruthin; pass Valle Crucis Abbey, and in 1 mile turn right on steep minor road. Follow it by Plas Yn Eglwyseg (OS ref. 216462) and Ty Canol (221475) to pass World's End Farm (228479).

NB: World's End is private property.

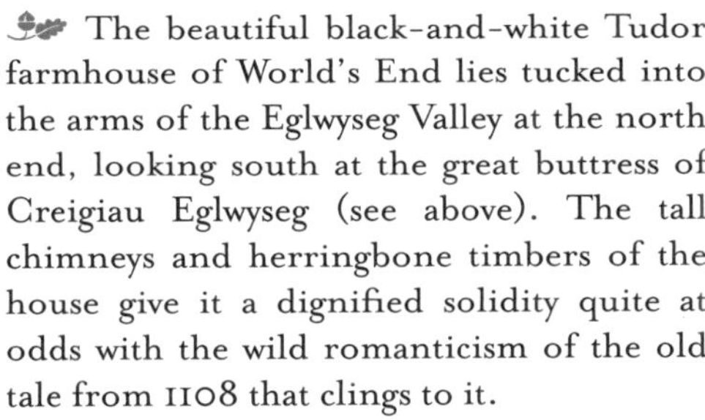

The beautiful black-and-white Tudor farmhouse of World's End lies tucked into the arms of the Eglwyseg Valley at the north end, looking south at the great buttress of Creigiau Eglwyseg (see above). The tall chimneys and herringbone timbers of the house give it a dignified solidity quite at odds with the wild romanticism of the old tale from 1108 that clings to it.

Owain ap Cadwgan, Prince of Powys (1111–16), owned a hunting lodge at World's End where the present farmhouse stands. Owain was a hot-headed and impetuous warrior, and by all accounts he brought those characteristics to his lovemaking, too. It happened that the young man heard tell of the charms of Nesta, the 'Helen of Wales' and wife of the Norman baron Gerald of Windsor. She had been King Henry I's concubine, and had been married off to Gerald, the Constable of Pembrokeshire, when the king had finished with her. Impulsive Owain determined to have her for his own. Gathering a band of armed ruffians, the prince rode the length of Wales to Cilgerran Castle, Gerald's stronghold. Having caused maximum confusion by setting fire to the castle, Owain grabbed Nesta and her two children, swung them on to his horse and escaped at full gallop, leaving the hapless husband to escape the conflagration by sliding down his own vile garderobe or lavatory chute and dropping into the moat in his nightshirt.

Beautiful Nesta does not seem to have objected to this behaviour by Prince Owain. He took her and her children back to his hunting lodge at World's End, and there the two lovers nested together. But they did not enjoy each other for long. King Henry, furious at the insult to his Constable, seized the lands of Owain's father, Cadwgan, setting off a series of battles and burnings across the countryside. The old man ordered his son to return Nesta to her husband, and this Owain reluctantly did – then fled across the water to Ireland and did not return until the fuss had died down.

Gerald of Windsor said nothing, but he had neither forgiven nor forgotten. He had to wait years for his opportunity, but at last the day came when he and Owain ap Cadwgan found themselves on the same side in battle. The Norman got himself alongside Owain, bided his time until they were on their own, and then slew his hated rival. Revenge for the garderobe incident, and the passionate affair at World's End, was a dish that Gerald tasted cold, and found all the sweeter for it.

167. HOREB, FLINTSHIRE

Maps: OS Explorer 256; Landranger 117

Travel: A541 from Wrexham towards Mold. In 4 miles pass through Caergwrle; in another ½ mile, at start of dual carriageway, left (OS ref. 297586) to Horeb. Park neatly in village. Horeb Chapel (286579 – NB: private property) is up a short lane on right as you leave Horeb for Llanfynydd.

Nearest railway stations: Hope or Caergwrle (both 1½ miles)

In the shadow of the Mountain of Hope stands the Holy Mountain, Horeb. Close at hand is Mount Zion, while Babylon, Babell and Sodom are not far away. The miners, quarrymen and ironworkers of nineteenth-century Wales were staunch chapel-goers, and around the industrialized valleys and heavily dug and delved uplands of Flintshire and Denbighshire they named many of their settlements after places they had heard of in the fiery preaching of their ministers.

Horeb lies north of Wrexham, out in the back country where the early nonconformist preachers tended to find the readiest ground to sow what was then thought of as revolutionary seed. Horeb Chapel was built during the nineteenth century for dissenters of the Calvinistic Methodist denomination – Presbyterianism of a very Welsh character, with plenty of eloquence and plenty of culture.

Horeb was only one island in a populous archipelago of nonconformism across this part of north Wales. In a 1905 survey, the parish of Caergwrle alone was reported to have nineteen chapels – including Horeb – of seven denominations. Here were chapels with resounding biblical names: Bethel and Sion, Moriah and Carmel. Relations between denominations could be tetchy, not to say petty. Daniel Owen, tailor and novelist of Mold, caught the mood in his novel *Gwen Tomos*:

> *If there are lead mines or coal-pits in the vicinity, one will usually find two, three or even four small chapels. In some places two chapels exist within a stone's throw of one another, eyeing each other jealously. It is a frequent sight to see two neighbours who agree on all matters except religion, passing each*

other on Sundays to attend a chapel a considerable distance away, having rejected one nearer, because the one had too much water and the other too little.

Back in the days when untutored Welshmen worked on the mountains at harsh, dangerous jobs in wild conditions, the little chapel at Horeb had 125 'adherents'. Today it has none, and is now a private house in a sought-after village in a most desirable location.

168. HALKYN MOUNTAIN, FLINTSHIRE

Maps: OS Explorer 265; Landranger 116

Travel: From A55 Junction 32a, right on B5123 into Pentre Halkyn; left in 200 yards towards Babell and Caerwys. In ½ mile, left towards Rhes-y-cae. Pant-y-pwll-dwr Quarry is on right of this road. Park anywhere and wander at will.

NB: Take care – many old mining shafts, some in poor repair!

Unseen and unsuspected as you drive across Halkyn Mountain, the giant limestone quarry pit of Pant-y-pwll-dwr (Hollow of the Pool of Water) lies on your left hand beyond a rickety fence and a line of bushes. Shaped like an elongated heart half a mile across, the same from north to south, hundreds of feet deep, it is an almighty hole. Galleries and ledges cut the cliffs into geometric shapes, all verticals and horizontals. Smoking quarry buildings stand on the northern rim. At the bottom lies an ice-blue pool.

This man-made chasm opens at the centre of the wide upland of Halkyn Mountain, a moor landscape that has been mined since the Bronze Age. It is a dark, bleak piece of country, strewn with heather, gorse and wind-stunted thorn trees. The Romans

Halkyn Mountain

mined lead here and so did every generation after them. Halkyn lead went on to medieval church roofs. Landowners of the seventeenth and eighteenth centuries opened up new mines and made fortunes. The London Lead Company pumped out old workings with new steam pumps and continued to mine. The last lead mine closed in 1958, but the stone quarrying still goes on.

The legacy of all these hundreds of years of lead mining lies all around. The moorland is cut into hollow and holes, lumpy with the grassed-over spoil heaps of lead mines and covered with rocks. Mining settlements are widely scattered, and scattered in themselves: Pwll-clai, for example, whose cottages with sloping roofs and tiny windows lie haphazardly distributed wherever the miners built them along the mountain road. As for what lies below the ground, that is a whole fantastic labyrinth of its own.

Just north of Pentre Halkyn, the Glan-yr-afon Inn stands on a crossroads outside the mining settlement of Dolphin. Locals will tell you about the Sea Level Tunnel, started in 1897, that took sixty years to complete and eventually ran 8 miles inland to the lead mines at Cadole near Mold. It sounds like a public bar yarn, but it is true. They also assert that from the bottom of a shaft just below the pub, one can see daylight out in the estuary, a pinprick of light 3 miles away. You just need to be mad enough to go down there and look.

169. MAEN ACHWYFAEN, FLINTSHIRE

Maps: OS Explorer 265; Landranger 116

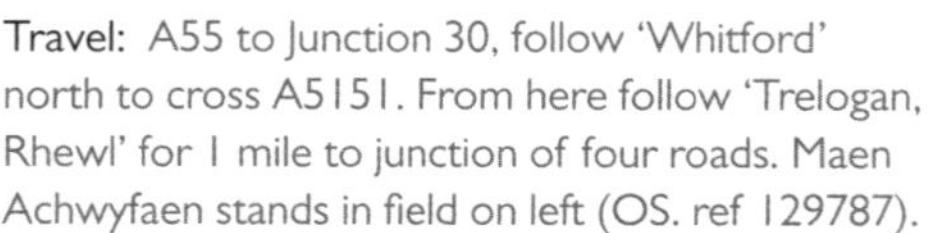

Travel: A55 to Junction 30, follow 'Whitford' north to cross A5151. From here follow 'Trelogan, Rhewl' for 1 mile to junction of four roads. Maen Achwyfaen stands in field on left (OS. ref 129787).

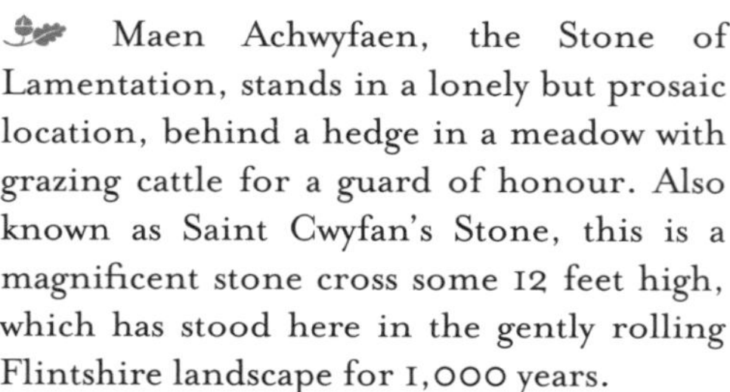

Maen Achwyfaen, the Stone of Lamentation, stands in a lonely but prosaic location, behind a hedge in a meadow with grazing cattle for a guard of honour. Also known as Saint Cwyfan's Stone, this is a magnificent stone cross some 12 feet high, which has stood here in the gently rolling Flintshire landscape for 1,000 years.

The top of Maen Achwyfaen is carved into a wheel cross with a big protruding boss, the shafts incised with an intricate interlaced pattern. This interlacing, very characteristic of Northumbrian carved crosses of the same era, is repeated in various forms all over Maen Achwyfaen. Each side is divided into panels – on the west a lot of writhing interlacing and a circular motif, on the east an elaborate X-shaped symbol and a figure like a demon with pointed ears and bandy legs.

The thinner edges of the Stone of Lamentation are carved, too, and if the sun casts the right angle of shadow you can make out on the south side a round-headed figure brandishing a spear and trampling on a serpent or dragon.

The north edge appears to show a horse-like creature with eight legs, walking vertically up the shaft. If this is so, it gives a very intriguing twist to the Christian monument. The Norse god of war, Odin, possessed an eight-legged horse called Sleipnir, a wonderful beast who could outrun any other horse, and who could also gallop his master in shamanic trances over the sea and through the air, creating thunderstorms as he passed. Could the Norse carver of the great cross of Achwyfaen have sneaked a pagan beast into the design? Not just any beast, but Odin's own enchanted warhorse – what a fine and provoking fancy.

170. POINT OF AYR, DENBIGHSHIRE

Maps: OS Explorer 266; Landranger 116

Travel: A548 from Prestatyn towards Mostyn. In 2½ miles, left at roundabout ('Talacre, Beach') through Talacre to Talacre Warren car park (OS. ref 125848).

Nearest railway station: Prestatyn (5 miles)

What with its gas-processing terminal, the holiday resort town of Prestatyn just to the west and the vast redundant steel and ironworks in sight at Shotton, not to mention the tall white turbines of the North Hoyle wind-farm whirling 5 miles offshore, the choice of the Point of Ayr, Wales's most northerly mainland point, as a wild place could seem a little strange. But half an hour among the sand dunes or along the shoreline, and all man-made intrusions diminish to spots on the horizon.

Approaching westward up the long straight shore of the Dee Estuary, it seems all mud in the bay. Coming east from Prestatyn, it is golden sand. The dividing line is the hooked Point of Ayr, a sand-spit that is slowly forming with saltmarsh and mudflats developing in the crook of its arm. Here and on the sandy tideline to the west is a wonderful high-tide roost for waders – knot and dunlin in large flocks, curlew and redshank stalking solo as they stab their long beaks into the flats. In the winter duck-watchers get their fill of pintail with chocolate-coloured heads and long, thin pencil tails, and of neat little teal with their shiny green eye-stripes and dashing flight. In spring the black and bar-tailed godwits stop over on their migration flights north, and this is also the time to walk in the dunes along the point to find whinchat and stonechat in the scrub bushes and be dazzled by outpourings of skylark song overhead.

Point of Ayr

Down by the tideline stands a solitary, salt-scabbed lighthouse, and lingering here with binoculars at migration time you can see seabirds passing over the water – kittiwakes near the shore, large white gannets further out on crook wings, and occasionally a group of little brown Leach's petrels skimming the sea on their way to breed on the North Atlantic islands. It comes as a shock to emerge from behind the binoculars and the protective shield of concentration to find the workaday world still in place, dog-walkers on the sands and the glittering arms of the wind turbines semaphoring on the northern horizon.

171. HOLYHEAD MOUNTAIN, ISLE OF ANGLESEY

Maps: OS Explorer 262, 263; Landranger 114

Travel: A55 to Holyhead; left on minor roads (brown signs) to South Stack car park (OS ref. 211819).

Nearest railway station: Holyhead (3 miles)

Holyhead Mountain stands proud of the generally flattish landscape of Anglesey, a handsome, craggy rock at the outer tip of Holy Island – itself a projection of the west coast of Wales's biggest island. When you traverse the slopes of the mountain and arrive at South Stack, descending 400 steps and crossing the girder bridge to stand beside the white stalk of the lighthouse on its black little hummock of rock in the sea – you feel as if you have come to the edge of the world.

Holyhead Mountain itself carries a fine Iron Age hill fort on the summit, well worth the climb for the ambience and the stunning views 50 miles north to the Isle of Man, the same distance west to the Wicklow Hills across the sea in Ireland on a clear day. Down at the foot of the mountain, just beyond the car park, lie the circles of twenty Iron Age huts, together with the little rectangular spaces that were once the villagers' ironworking shops. There is something very poignant about these circles linked by paths, a wind-bitten subsistence village whose inhabitants farmed the clifftops and carried out a dangerous harvest of guillemot and kittiwake eggs on the cliff ledges.

The seabirds still gather here in early spring to nest and rear broods. Guillemots and kittiwakes have other neighbours and rivals for perching space: razorbills, cousins of the guillemots, whose thick nutcracker of a bill has a distinctive white stripe; puffins; red-legged choughs, a rare species which is making a comeback along Britain's loneliest cliffs and island coasts. Birds of coastal heaths breed a few hundred yards inland: handsome little meadow pipits that sing reeling songs as they ascend and descend like skylarks, their larger and darker relations the rock pipits, and stonechats with black skullcaps who warble and scold in flight between their perches.

It is a long descent down to the lighthouse on South Stack, but worth it for the view back up to the mountain and, in dirty weather, the thrill of flying spray from storm waves beating at the stack's grey cliffs.

172. DINORWIG SLATE QUARRY, SNOWDONIA

Maps: OS Explorer 17; Landranger 115

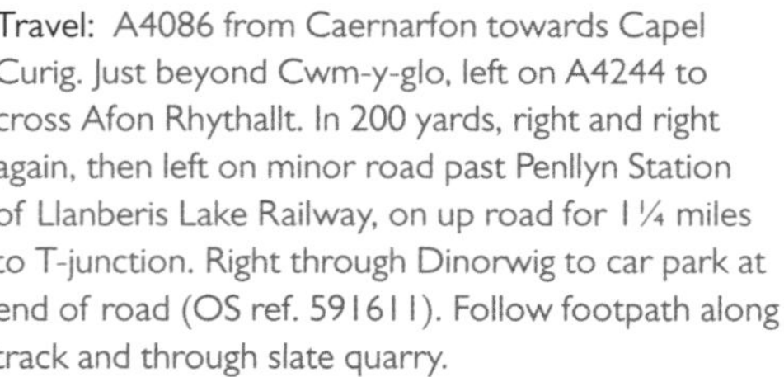

Travel: A4086 from Caernarfon towards Capel Curig. Just beyond Cwm-y-glo, left on A4244 to cross Afon Rhythallt. In 200 yards, right and right again, then left on minor road past Penllyn Station of Llanberis Lake Railway, on up road for 1¼ miles to T-junction. Right through Dinorwig to car park at end of road (OS ref. 591611). Follow footpath along track and through slate quarry.

Nearest railway station: Gilfach Ddu station, Llanberis Lake Railway (1 mile)

Dante would recognize Dinorwig Slate Quarry complex straight away. The concentric levels … the black walls … the poisonous lakes … it looks like Hell. And it must have felt like Hell to the 3,000 or so men who worked the quarries in their Victorian heyday. Now a deathly quiet

Dinorwig Slate Quarry

pervades the galleries and drifts, broken only by the croak of a raven or clatter of falling stones dislodged by a sheep or feral goat. Back then the whole area was loud with industry, a smoky cauldron of work and danger where men hung on ropes over 100-foot drops to hack out the rock face, or breathed in slate dust to exacerbate their silicosis as they blasted, hammered and split up to 100,000 tons of slate a year.

Come to Dinorwig on a day of rain and heavy cloud to see the quarries at their starkest. A footpath runs south-east through a good portion of the 800-acre site, and you can get a most dramatic overview from the path that runs parallel to the southern perimeter. Vast banks of spoil descend the mountainside in steps, the horizontals separated by long diagonal slopes. Stone ribs run downhill between the banks, as if the Great Wall of China had been miniaturized and reinstalled in sections among the Welsh mountains. Galleries 150 feet deep plunge to startlingly coloured pools. There is nothing natural here, unless you raise your eyes beyond the quarries and focus up to the rocky peak of Elidir Fach and its senior crest, Elidir Fawr.

Some of the quarrymen came from as far away as Anglesey, walking the 10 or 15 miles to Dinorwig each Sunday afternoon to spend the week on site, sleeping in the men's rough cold-water barracks. They were skilled workers, but they lived damp, dirty, hungry and highly dangerous lives. They roofed Industrial Revolution Britain, and much of the rest of the developed world. In 1969, after 200 years of intensive production, it all came to an end, leaving a landscape so tortured and alien it looks as if it will never recover.

173. CWM IDWAL, SNOWDONIA

Maps: OS Explorer 17; Landranger 115

Travel: A5 from Capel Curig towards Bangor. At Pont Pen-y-benglog at head of Llyn Ogwen, park at Idwal Cottage (OS ref. 649604). Follow trail south past Llyn Idwal into Cwm Idwal.

For sheer drama and a spectacular approach, it is hard to beat Cwm Idwal. Walking south up the path from the valley road with the long lake of Llyn Ogwen glinting behind you, the first sight of Llyn Idwal's dark, rippled water and the majesty of the mountain scenery beyond

Cwm Idwal

is breathtaking. The slopes leading up to the Glyder peaks, Glyder Fach and Glyder Fawr, wrinkle in the distance; between them and the lake, a pair of huge shadowy corries hang as if suspended on an invisible thread. The bigger, deeper and darker of these two giant scoops in the mountains, Cwm Idwal, runs back to the slit of Twll Du, the Devil's Kitchen, where the rock is squeezed up, over and down again, a petrified episode in the gigantic subterranean convulsions that shaped the Snowdon mountains.

You can reach the lower part of the Devil's Kitchen quite easily, and this is the place to look for some of the very rare arctic-alpine plants that have been living here since shortly after the glaciers retreated. Cwm Idwal was the first National Nature Reserve to be designated in Wales, partly thanks to this phenomenal richness of northern flora – for example, the beautiful starry saxifrage rising on a slender stalk, with tiny blood-red dots of anthers showing against the pure white of the petals, or the vivid, tiny flowers of purple saxifrage; also another pinky-purple beauty, cushion-like clumps of moss campion. Raise your eyes from these close-focus treasures to see a raven or a chough cruising across the valley, then look around at the landscape rearing skyward at your back – this is Welsh mountain heaven.

174. MOUNT SNOWDON, SNOWDONIA

Maps: OS Explorer OL17; Landranger 115

Travel: Mount Snowdon (OS ref. 610544) lies towards the south-east of a long isosceles triangle of roads, with A498 Beddgelert–Pen-y-Gwryd as the south-west to north-east base, and the other two sides formed by A4088 Pen-y-Gwryd–Caernarfon and A4085 Caernarfon–Beddgelert.

Nearest railway station: Summit station, Snowdon Mountain Railway

There are some mountains that maintain their dignity, no matter how famous or popular they are. Yr Wyddfa, the Great Tomb, is one. Snowdon, as the *saesneg* know it, is not only the highest mountain in Wales at 3,559 feet; it is also a national symbol, visible 100 miles off, always dominant as you approach it, always an element of challenge and mystery in the dark corries and clefts that surround its peak. Snowdon has been thoroughly walked over, quarried, run up and picnicked on. It is no Everest; you can reach the top without moving a muscle while sitting in one of the miniature carriages behind a puffing locomotive of the Snowdon Mountain Railway. Yet Yr Wyddfa is still a properly wild place, as anyone who has climbed it in mist and rain can testify.

Of the seven main routes up the mountain, those from the west – the converging Rhyd Ddu (OS ref. 571526) and Pitt's Head (577514) paths, plus the Snowdon Ranger track (565551) – are among the easier ascents, pleasant bumpy climbs with a sweaty push towards the end. From the north the Llanberis path (581594) simply follows the mountain railway track. It is the other three that put you most in touch with the wild face of Snowdon. The Miner's Track and the Pyg Track come at Snowdon from the east, starting from the same spot (647557), and then diverging through a wilderness of lakes at different levels, with the brow of the mountain always frowning down on them. The cliffs of Crib Goch hem these paths in on the north, increasing the sense of grandeur as they climb to converge above Glaslyn Lake.

The Watkin Path from the south is the longest ascent, and can be the toughest, depending on conditions. It is a steep and curving way, at first following a slate-miner's path to the bleak ruins of their barracks, then a long slog up a zigzag track to the saddle of Bwlch y Ciliau, where you are hit by a sudden opening of the lakes and peaks of the Snowdon Horseshoe. A thousand feet below lies Llyn Llydaw, a deep inky blue, the Pyg and Miner's tracks threading its shores. Crib Goch, Glydr Fawr and Glydr Fach, sharp-peaked Lliwedd on your right hand – a magnificent mountain view, as bracing as a slap in the face after the sombre valley that has enclosed you so far. Legend tells how King Arthur's sword Excalibur lies in the dark waters of Llyn Llydaw; some say he sleeps here under a cairn, others that he was borne away by the ladies of the mountains after falling to an enemy bowman at Bwlch y Saethau, the Pass of the Arrows.

Climbing the pass you come to the final precipitous and slippery scramble to the summit. Cardigan Bay curves south-west to vanishing point. A shadowy Isle of Man and the Llyn Peninsula, Cadair Idris (see pp. 181–2) in the south, Anglesey and the Menai Straits to the north. Below is a land of mountains, corries, lakes, crumpled walls of rock where walkers climb and climbers crawl – an enormity of wilderness, open at your feet.

175. ST MARY'S WELL, LLYN, GWYNEDD

Maps: OS Explorer 253; Landranger 123

Travel: From M6 Junction 10a or 11, M54 and A5 to Betws-y-Coed, A470/487 to Porthmadog; A497, A499 to Llanbedrog; B4413 to Aberdaron. Do not cross bridge in village, but keep forward uphill for ½ mile to staggered crossroads (OS ref. 165267); left for 1¾ miles to park car neatly at end of road (143255). Keep forward on footpath downhill to right of Mynydd Gwyddel, looking to your right till in 300 yards you spot square grassy foundation banks of St Mary's Church (140253). Continue down right bank of stream to cleft in clifftop and steep, uneven steps down to rocky shore. St Mary's Well is 30 yards to right under overhang (138252), reached by scramble along rocks.

NB: A low-tide excursion only; potentially dangerous.

The scramble along the rocks of Trwyn Maen Melyn, the Cape of the Yellow Rock, to reach the holy well of St Mary is an exciting and potentially dangerous one. You descend a narrow, eroded stairway of steps cut out of the cliff until you can see your goal only 30 yards off, a triangular slit in the rocks under an overhang. You can even see the water within, foamy with the last salt wave to splash into it. But getting to the well is a problem. The ancient catwalk along the rocks is slippery with weed, and only a few inches wide. The receding tide washes it every few seconds. Handholds in the rock face are few and far between.

For a fit and well-rested twenty-first-century visitor it is a tricky little test, with the chance of falling into the sea if you are not careful. For a medieval pilgrim to Bardsey (see oppsite), exhausted, starving and in a state of trembling excitement, the scramble out to Ffynnon Fair, the well of St Mary, was a hazardous venture. But it was also a necessity – not only physically (the well was the source of fresh drinking water at the end of the thirsty journey to the tip of Llyn), but also spiritually. The Blessed Virgin herself had ridden down to the well on her pony when she visited the church of St Mary on the cliffs above; there were the imprints of the pony's hooves, sunk in the rocks around the well, for all to see. A sip of the water brought a blessing. Better still if you could hold a mouthful without swallowing it while you climbed the cliff and ran three times round the church, for then you would be granted your heart's desire.

Green weed lines the rim of the cleft, and the sea intrudes into the well at high tide. But the water remains sweet and fresh, a cool and faintly mineral mouthful. You can sit there like countless thousands before you, sipping and praying and looking out across the tide races of the sound to the green hump of Bardsey.

176. BARDSEY, GWYNEDD

Maps: OS Explorer 253; Landranger 123

Travel: From M6 Junction 10a or 11, M54 and A5 to Betws-y-Coed; A470/A487 to Porthmadog; A497, A499 to Llanbedrog; B4413 to Aberdaron.

Ferry to Bardsey: Bardsey ferry (www.bardsey.org) leaves from Porth Meudwy (OS ref. 164255), 1½ miles south-west of Aberdaron.

History clings like sea mist to Bardsey, the Island of the Saints. Less than 2 miles long from tip to toe, it lies a couple of miles south-west of the very tip of the Llyn Peninsula and is one of the loneliest spots in Wales, with the solitary Bardsey Island Trust warden its only full-time resident. But once the island was thronged, tight-packed with pilgrims for whom it was the final stage on a journey to the ultimate resting place of Heaven. Three pilgrimages to Bardsey and its monastery, where St David was reputed to have died in AD 589 aged 146, ranked equally with one to Rome, and tens of thousands of earthly voyagers made the hazardous crossing of storm-prone and tide-ripped Bardsey Sound in hope of finding a humble grave in the sanctified ground of the 'very porch of Paradise'.

The Bardsey boat brings you into the island jetty past grey seals hauled out like slugs on the rocks and ranks of white-shirted guillemots and razorbills lining every crevice of the cliffs. From the landing place you can wander freely over the sheep-nibbled pastures of the island, round the remains of the monastery with its tiny chapel in the heart of a ruined tower, or up over the back of Mynydd Enlli, the 'mountain of Bardsey', as the 550-foot island hill is called.

In the nineteenth century Lord Newborough, owner of Bardsey, selected one of the islanders to be King of Bardsey, and furnished him with a crown, a treasury and an army – a brass coronet, a silver box and a wooden soldier. The king was appointed to keep law and order on the remote island, a function he fulfilled until 1926, by which time most of the islanders had decided to move to the mainland and say goodbye to a life of constant struggle, cut off from the mainland and exposed to frequent mists and gales. Life for the warden and the occasional summer residents is no easier today. Bardsey is a tough place – that was part of its attraction for the 20,000 penitents who are reputed to lie buried here. From the top of Mynydd Enlli you can look back across the turbulent sound to the cliffs from which the pilgrims set off on the final stage of their journey to the 'Gate of Paradise', and down along the steep heather cliffs of Bardsey to the rock faces in whose caves hermits would hole themselves up, to watch and pray unto death.

GLOUCESTERSHIRE, OXFORDSHIRE, NORTHAMPTONSHIRE, WARWICKSHIRE, WORCESTERSHIRE, HEREFORDSHIRE

THE SOUTH MIDLANDS

Though wild places are widely spread across the southern region of the English Midlands, individually they tend to come small-scale.

THERE'S LITTLE HERE that is of a big and impressive order: no grand uprising of mountains, no dramas of sweeping moorlands. Herefordshire has its red earth and lush grazing meadows, Worcestershire the single upthrust spine of the Malvern Hills, Warwickshire a corner or two of undulating Cotswolds, before things roll out east into the gentle grasslands of Northamptonshire. The theatrical aspect of the wild comes most into play in the west when the River Severn throws an occasional, spectacular tantrum and leaves its bed to invade the surrounding countryside. For the most part, these South Midlands wild places politely suggest you should abandon the car or the bicycle and take a stroll – into this tangly old wood, through wildflower meadows, to the brink of this pond. These intimate, close-at-hand landscapes require a little time and a measure of quiet to reveal these aspects, but it is worth taking the time to get to know them.

The South Midlands are founded on limestone and ironstone, and the landscape is pitted with hundreds of disused quarries. In Twywell Gullet and Collyweston Quarries I kneel and crawl among cowslips and orchids, my focus not more than a foot from the end of my nose, as it is when I lie stomach down and heels up in the traditionally managed hay meadows of Coombe Hill or Draycote. These sites and many more like them are now nature reserves, painstakingly and expertly looked after by local Wildlife Trusts – the unpaid, unsung and invaluable guardians of so much that is wild in these islands.

Much of the South Midlands's wildness is historical. This countryside has seen many bloody skirmishes down the centuries, but few as uncompromisingly ferocious as the Wars of the Roses battle that took place outside the Gloucestershire town of Tewkesbury, within walking distance of the village where I grew up. In the field now called the Bloody Meadow as many as 2,500 men died in a wholesale slaughter, and I have sensed since boyhood an eerie and haunting atmosphere in this seemingly tranquil grazing meadow. This same mood hangs over the quiet fields of Salcey Green, flanking the M1 motorway in Northamptonshire, where a famous and brutal single-combat battle between two bare-knuckle bruisers resulted in the death of one and the flight of the other.

Above: the White Horse at Uffington (p. 208). Below: the Severn Bridge and estuary (p. 200).

Exploring the South Midlands I find the wild hiding behind the mask of the everyday: in the flooded pits of Otmoor, where otters slip from willow to willow; in the bryony necklaces that string the hedges of Pack and Prime Lane and the Ridgeway; or out on a bleak winter day on the precarious walkways of the old Severn Bridge, where pintail and greylag geese take flight above the chocolate islets of mid-river mud, unseen by the drivers of lorries and cars rumbling 100 feet above their flightpath.

LINKS

- Ridgeway (www.nationaltrail.co.uk/ridgeway; www.ridgewayfriends.org.uk): Uffington White Horse, Wayland's Smithy, Ridgeway near Watlington Hill
- Severn Way (www.severnway.com): Severn Bridge, Coombe Hill meadows, Bloody Meadow at Tewkesbury
- Offa's Dyke (www.nationaltrail.co.uk/offasdyke; www.offasdykedemon.co.uk): Craswall Priory, Hergest Ridge

THE SOUTH MIDLANDS
GLOUCESTERSHIRE, OXFORDSHIRE, NORTHAMPTONSHIRE, WARWICKSHIRE, WORCESTERSHIRE, HEREFORDSHIRE
177. SEVERN ESTUARY
178. FOREST OF DEAN
179. HETTY PEGLER'S TUMP
180. WOODCHESTER MANSION
181. COOMBE HILL MEADOWS
182. BLOODY MEADOW
183. ROLLRIGHT STONES
184. WAYLAND'S SMITHY
185. UFFINGTON WHITE HORSE
186. PACK AND PRIME LANE AND DOG LANE
187. THE RIDGEWAY NEAR WATLINGTON HILL
188. WYTHAM GREAT WOOD ★
189. OT MOOR
190. THE BATTLE OF SALCEY GREEN
191. SALCEY FOREST
192. TWYWELL GULLET
193. GREEN MEN, CHURCH OF ST MICHAEL AND ALL ANGELS, WADENHOE
194. OLD SULEHAY
195. BEDFORD PURLIEUS
196. COLLYWESTON QUARRIES
197. DRAYCOTE MEADOW
198. RYTON WOOD
199. UFTON FIELDS
200. SNITTERFIELD BUSHES
201. PIPER'S HILL
202. SHRAWLEY WOOD
203. WORCESTERSHIRE BEACON
204. CHURCH OF ST MARY AND ST DAVID, KILPECK ★
205. CRASWALL PRIORY
206. EARDISLEY FONT
207. GREAT OAK OF EARDISLEY
208. HERGEST RIDGE
209. CROFT AMBREY HILL FORT
Birmingham
Kidderminster
Bromsgrove
WORCESTERSHIRE
Droitwich
Worcester
Leominster
HEREFORDSHIRE
Great Malvern
Evesham
Hereford
Ledbury
Ross-on-Wye
Gloucester
Cheltenham
Stroud
Cirencester
Chipping Sodbury
Yate
Bristol
GLOUCE

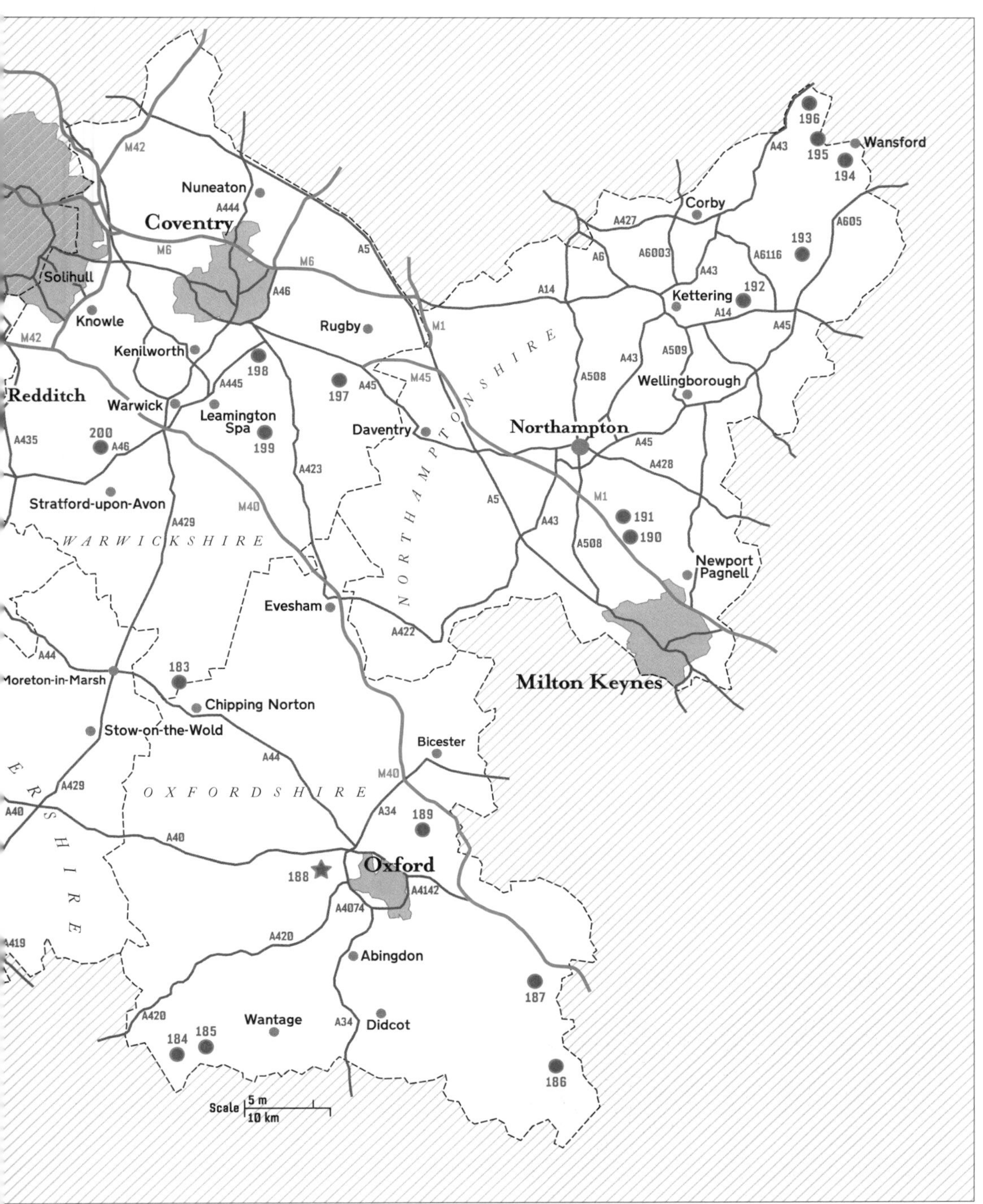

Coventry
Nuneaton
Solihull
Knowle
Kenilworth
Redditch
Warwick
Leamington Spa
Rugby
Daventry
Stratford-upon-Avon
WARWICKSHIRE
NORTHAMPTONSHIRE
OXFORDSHIRE
Northampton
Kettering
Corby
Wansford
Wellingborough
Newport Pagnell
Milton Keynes
Evesham
Moreton-in-Marsh
Chipping Norton
Stow-on-the-Wold
Bicester
Oxford
Abingdon
Wantage
Didcot
183
184
185
186
187
188
189
190
191
192
193
194
195
196
197
198
199
200
Scale
5 m
10 km

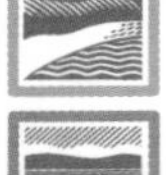

177. SEVERN ESTUARY, GLOS.

Maps: OS Explorer 167; Landranger 172

Travel: M4 to M48, Junction 1. Bear left at roundabout ('A403, Severn Bridge Maintenance Unit'); in 100 yards, right across central reservation (brown 'St Augustine's Vineyard' sign). Park along this road. In 100 yards (OS ref. 571891), right up side road ('Severn Way' and 'Footpath Chepstow' signs). In 200 yards blue 'cycleway' sign points left up access road on to bridge footpath/cycleway.

The Severn Estuary is a wild place whatever the tide. On a rising tide the mudflats and sandbanks disappear one by one under a flood of salt water, and the oystercatchers and herring gulls fly to the muddy margins of the river to continue their feasting on shellfish and invertebrates. On the ebb these same features are revealed as a veil is drawn away, drying to purple, tan and russet. There is a constant rush and gurgle as the great drain of the estuary sucks fresh water from the hills and meadows of England and Wales into the Bristol Channel.

This unstoppable power is best appreciated close to, on the floodbank footpath that runs upriver from the old Severn Bridge. But to gain a grand impression of the frontier between two countries, step out along the walkway that clings to the shoulder of the bridge as it makes the 2-mile crossing high in the air between the English and Welsh shore. The older of the two Severn Bridges was opened in 1966, a graceful link between the ancient rival countries with its two tall towers resembling gateways. From far out over the water the southward view is of its younger counterpart, opened in 1996, some 4 miles downriver. A glance over the side of the old bridge shows you the remnants of the landing stage at Old Passage, where cars would queue, seemingly for ever, for the ferry in pre-bridge days.

Out here, 120 feet above the water, the full majesty of the estuary is revealed, with its red-and-white striped cliffs, its vast but shapely curves, and the great width of the channel it has carved. The one feature of the river that is diminished when viewed from this aerial perch is the mini-tsunami called the Severn Bore, a salt-water surge that pushes up the tidal river and forces its crest high over the outflowing fresh water. To savour that to the full you must go 20 miles upriver to a place like Weir Green at the end of a straight stretch of the Severn, preferably on a moonlit night. A low roar announces the advent of the bore, followed by a stir in the air and a slapping, sucking noise as the tidal wave rushes towards you. Spray bursts around you as the bore sweeps by, sighing and seething, dragging a train of deep furrows as if ploughing the river. If the projected hydroelectric barrage is ever built across the estuary, King Bore will pass no more.

178. FOREST OF DEAN, GLOS.

Maps: OS Explorer OL14; Landranger 162

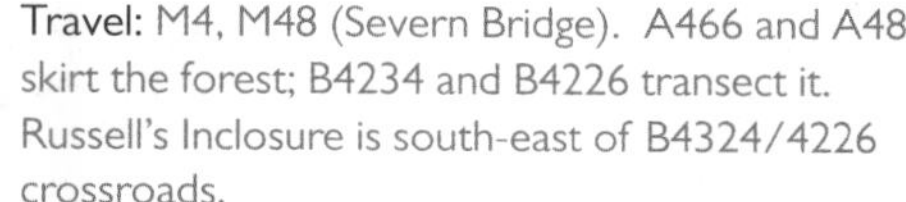

Travel: M4, M48 (Severn Bridge). A466 and A48 skirt the forest; B4234 and B4226 transect it. Russell's Inclosure is south-east of B4324/4226 crossroads.

Nearest railway station: Lydney

What you make of the Forest of Dean depends on the season you visit it, and whom you meet there. In spring the forest is a place of translucent green, full of light and birdsong; in summer it seems to breathe heavily as its streams dry and the birds fall quiet; in autumn every clearing and forest road flickers with the constant diagonal fall of scarlet and gold leaves. In a cold winter the place gains mystery, its frozen ponds creaking, its innermost corners sealed in absolute silence.

Forest of Dean people – 'Foresters' – are funny folk, according to their neighbours; insular, inward-looking, uneasy with strangers, and very jealous of their curious historical rights and customs, such as the right to open and work a coal mine, or to graze their sheep pretty much where they choose. Yet have yourself invited below ground into one of the tiny mines, or get into conversation with one of the elected Verderers with their ancient duty to preserve 'vert and venison', the plants and animals of the forest, and it is possible to see how

the place, so full of dark depths, silences, subtle shades and glints of light, moulds its inhabitants.

The Forest of Dean covers some 35 square miles, with the River Wye and the broad estuary of the Severn on two of its borders. Like all ancient woodlands in Britain, the forest has lived through enormous change. The coal and iron that underlie it have led men to strip it of its trees, either wholly or in part, many times over the past two millennia. The Romans dug here. So did the Saxons. Early medieval squatters led a life of poaching, coal mining and cattle grazing while their noble superiors enjoyed the use of the forest as a hunting preserve protected by stern laws. Iron mining, with its inexhaustible consumption of trees for charcoal-making, saw thousands of acres felled. At one time during the Civil War of the mid seventeenth century, the forest landowner Sir John Winter was cutting down 100,000 trees a year, and more than once in the nineteenth century it was stripped almost completely bare. Yet at the same time it has been continually replanted, restocked and restored to tree cover over the centuries. Some of its squat hollies and knotted oaks are several hundred years old; they have been left untouched, by chance, across all those years.

Russell's Inclosure in the heart of the forest is a good place to go. Inclosures were banked and fenced off to save their trees from the teeth of rabbits, sheep, cattle and pigs. Within its boundaries Russell's Inclosure contains 300-year-old oaks, conifers planted in the twentieth century by the Forestry Commission, wetland trees such as willow and alder around the stream bogs, and the two fine, large Cannop Ponds that powered Parkend Ironworks.

Frogs, butterflies, dragonflies, birds and insects thrive, as do the fallow deer. Best of all, you can walk ten minutes into the inclosure and find yourself, literally, lost in the forest.

179. HETTY PEGLER'S TUMP, GLOS.

Maps: OS Explorer 168; Landranger 162

Travel: From M5 Junction 13, A419 towards Stroud; in ½ mile, right at first roundabout to Eastington. Left through Frocester; in 2 miles, left on B4066 towards Uley. In 600 yards, park by reservoir on left (OS ref. 792999). Please leave gates clear. Hetty Pegler's Tump is signed 'Uley Long Barrow' across the road.

Nearest railway station: Stonehouse (5 miles)

When the Dobunni tribe of Britons built their magnificent hill fort of Uley Bury around 500 BC overlooking the vale of the River Severn, the grassy hillock of Hetty Pegler's Tump had already been standing just along the ridge for well over 2,000 years. What did the Dobunni make of the chambered tomb of their distant ancestors?

Hetty Pegler's Tump

Maybe they venerated it. Or perhaps the east-facing doorway had become blocked, the great stones of the interior unsafe, and they did not spare the long mound a second glance.

During the seventeenth century the land around the monument was the property of Henry Pegler, and it was his wife, Hester, who lent her pet name 'Hetty' to the tump. You must crawl under its mighty lintel like a supplicant; the doorway is less than 2 feet high. Upright monoliths, the gaps between them filled with drystone walling, support the huge flat capstones of the roof and form a passage into the heart of the tomb. Five burial chambers open off the corridor, two each side, one at the far end. Excavations in 1821 and again in 1854 unearthed several skeletons in the chambers and the passageway. The cold, damp stone presses down, weighty and powerful. Whoever built this tomb had permanence in mind.

180. WOODCHESTER MANSION, GLOUCESTERSHIRE

Maps: OS Explorer 168; Landranger 162

Travel: From M5 Junction 13, A419 towards Stroud. In ½ mile, right at roundabout through Eastington and Frocester. Continue to B4066; left for ½ mile, to turn right (OS ref. 795014), following 'Nympsfield'. In ¼ mile, left (brown 'Woodchester Park' sign) down track; park in car park at end (799014). Walk down valley drive for ⅔ mile to Woodchester Mansion (809014).

Open days and access details: www.the-mansion.co.uk

Walking down the secret valley of Woodchester Park and coming across Woodchester Mansion for the first time is not so much like discovering the palace of the Sleeping Beauty as entering the realm of Count Dracula. Approaching at dusk, you half expect an ancient manservant to be standing at the door with upraised lantern and sinister leer under the empty black windows and the grotesquely carved rainspout gargoyles. Woodchester Mansion is nothing if not Gothic, glowering and ominous among its dark trees in the shadows of its seldom-seen valley. Yet this is not what William Leigh had in mind when he bought the landscaped estate of Spring Park near Stroud in 1845.

Having demolished the classical Georgian house that stood in the valley, Leigh engaged an untried twenty-one-year-old local architect, Benjamin Bucknall, to design a fabulous new neo-Gothic mansion. But what was it for? William Leigh never lived there, and the house never even approached a habitable state. His son occupied a few rooms briefly, but the huge half-finished pile in the damp and sunless valley never attracted him back once he had moved away to get married. Woodchester Mansion stood empty from the start, dozens of rooms filled with stone carvings and embellishments, empty fireplaces hanging halfway up walls, the vaulted drawing room like a monastic chapter house, the great chapel with its rose window, winding stairways and rib-vaulted cellars, with the builders' wooden ladders left propped against the walls and their scaffolding and ropes still in position. A farmer kept his cattle in the dining room for a while, local schoolchildren had lessons in the echoing rooms, and during the Second World War the mansion housed a school evacuated from Birmingham. Then it stood empty once more. Stroud District Council bought it in 1986, and in 1992 the Woodchester Mansion Trust took on its preservation on a 99-year lease.

A visit to this great but lifeless house is

almost bound to be eerie. Hound and eagle gargoyles snarl at you outside, the black windows stare at you like so many blind eyes. Inside it is even stranger: leaves, fruit, faces, Green Men and flowers spring from the stone vaulting and cornices, from the stone casings around stairs that lead nowhere and doors that open on to nothing.

Coombe Hill Meadows

181. COOMBE HILL MEADOWS, GLOUCESTERSHIRE

Maps: OS Explorer 179; Landranger 162

Travel: A38 from Gloucester towards Tewkesbury; at Coombe Hill, where A4019 bears right to Cheltenham, turn left by Swan Inn down Wharf Lane. Park at foot of lane (OS ref. 876272); walk through gate into Coombe Hill Meadows.

There are two distinct seasons on Coombe Hill Meadows – wet and dry. During the dry months of late summer the ground cracks, the wild flowers shrivel away and a hot, heavy silence hangs over the fields and old canal. It seems incredible then that, only three months before, these large meadows between the A38 and the River Severn were bursting with flowers, loud with birdsong and seething with insect and animal life. To create this Sleeping Beauty awakening each spring, Coombe Hill Meadows undergo a period of winter flooding that astonishes visitors with its drama and anarchy.

These fields formed a wide common of marshes and pools, grazed in summer and flooded by the River Severn each winter, until the coal canal was built in 1796 and the area subsequently drained. The pools and marshes dried out, but the floods came every year notwithstanding. The meadows were managed on the traditional Lammas principle – cut for hay in summer, grazed and dunged in autumn, flooded in winter, allowed to grow in spring. Then came the intensive farming regime of the latter twentieth century with its chemical 'improvement', deep drainage and several cuts of grass a year. The ragged robin, willowherb, yellow loosestrife and marsh marigolds disappeared, the great flocks of lapwings and snipe went elsewhere, the hares and water voles vanished.

Now they are back, thanks to the purchase by Gloucestershire Wildlife Trust of 223 acres of the meadows, and their designation as a nature reserve. Walking the banks of the canal today you hear the plop of fish and hoarse, piping bark of moorhens. In spring the fields are dotted white and pink with milkmaids, in summer with the bold, deep pink of ragged robin. Yellow and purple loosestrife heads grow tall along the newly created pools and flashes, and overhead tumble flickering black-and-white multitudes of lapwings. Visit in winter, and the meadows wear their other wild complexion, as gunmetal sheets of water spread to the horizon. Dark lines on the floods show the shape of drowned hedges where willows and field maples stand in their own reflections. This lasts for a week or two; then the Severn falls back into its bed, having laid a rich silty foundation for the renewed life of the coming spring.

182. BLOODY MEADOW, TEWKESBURY, GLOUCESTERSHIRE

Maps: OS Explorer 190; Landranger 150

Travel: From M5 Junction 9, A438 into Tewkesbury; A38 towards Gloucester. Pass Tewkesbury Abbey; in ¼ mile, after left bend, right ('Council Offices') down Lincoln Green Lane. Bloody Meadow is 200 yards on right – park near map and descriptive plaque (OS ref. 888318).

For a quiet green field, the Bloody Meadow carries a heavy freight of savagery. Carpeted with dandelions and bounded with hedges of creamy may flowers, it looks as peaceful as can be. Yet this calm field was the scene of unbridled butchery during one of the most brutal and vindictive battles in the history of England.

The struggle between the Houses of York and Lancaster for the succession to the English throne had already been going on for sixteen disastrous years when King Edward IV of the House of York closed with the Lancastrian forces of his rival, Queen Margaret of Anjou, on 4 May 1471 on what was then called the Gaston field. Margaret's army, commanded by the Duke of Somerset, was hurrying towards Wales to gather reinforcements there. Edward was determined to catch and prevent them. Both armies had marched hard, Edward's men more than 30 miles the previous day; but once in sight of each other both found energy for battle. The Yorkists had fewer men but they had more cannon, and far more confidence – they were the pursuing army, and they had won a crushing victory only a few weeks before at the Battle of Barnet.

Somerset had his men drawn up in a good defensive position, and he was the first to go on the attack, charging at the centre of Edward's line. But Edward had hidden a couple of hundred men in some trees near by. They came in from the side against the oncoming enemy; and when Edward counter-attacked, the combined movements forced the Lancastrians to give ground, to falter and then to flee. It turned into a rout, with the Yorkists chasing their panicked enemies through the streets of Tewkesbury. In a meadow beside the river the fugitives were caught and mercilessly slaughtered, while many more drowned as they tried to struggle across the ford.

The Duke of Somerset and many of his lords were dragged from sanctuary in Tewkesbury Abbey. On 6 May they were summarily tried, then publicly executed. Somerset himself was beheaded in Tewkesbury market square. Margaret of Anjou was captured and eventually sent into exile; her eighteen-year-old son, Edward, Prince of Wales, whom she had hoped to place on the throne, was killed on the field of battle, probably after being captured. Her mentally ill husband, the deposed King Henry VI, was murdered a few days later in the Tower of London, where he was being held captive, and King Edward IV reigned in comparative peace until his death twelve years later.

The Bloody Meadow is not the only poignant battle site in Tewkesbury. The sacristy door in the abbey is plated with rough strips of metal, jaggedly cut and crudely painted over. They are chunks of armour, picked up from the battlefield and displayed like this as a reminder of how sanctuary was violated in the bloody aftermath of that terrible engagement.

183. ROLLRIGHT STONES, OXON./WARWICKSHIRE BORDERS

Maps: OS Explorer OL45 or 191; Landranger 151

Travel: A3400 from Long Compton towards Oxford; in 1¼ miles, right on minor road towards Little Rollright; parking lay-by beside Rollright Stones (OS ref. 296309).

So many mists, both ancient and New Age, have gathered around the Rollright Stones that it has become impossible to see them dispassionately. The prosaic, stumpy, weathered stones beside a country lane give way to the legend of the arrogant king and the witch, the stones that dance and the stones that drink, the lines of energy and the cosmic force fields. Mainstream archaeology may not care for them, but such more or less playful interpretations of this monument have had currency much longer than sober fact-finding.

The Rollright Stones fall into three parts. Just inside Oxfordshire stands a magnificent circle of seventy-seven stones, probably erected around 2500 BC. Another group of five stones stands 400 yards to the east; these formed the chamber of a tomb that pre-dates the circle by up to 1,000 years. Finally a solitary stone, the largest, rises by itself on the Warwickshire side of the road.

The Neolithic tomb chamber is a solid cold fact. However, nothing is known of the purpose of either the circle or the solitary stone. That has not stopped interpreters doing their best down the ages. Ley-line intersections and channels of energy are detected in the circle and round the standing stone by present-day dowsers and druids. But it is our forebears who came up with the most outlandish theories. The solo stone, a fine monolith, stands bent into a shallow 'S' shape, the product of the superstitions of former passers-by who would chip off a piece to carry with them as a good-luck charm. Legend says this is a king who wished to rule all England, and for his arrogance was turned to stone by a witch with a ringing curse:

King of England thou shalt not be;
Rise up, stick, and stand still, stone,
For King of England thou shalt be none –
Thou and thy men hoar stones shall be,
And I myself an eldern tree.

The hoar or ancient stones of the circle are the King's Men. As for the five weather-beaten monoliths of the tomb, they are the Whispering Knights, plotting against the king or murmuring a charm as they lean their heads confidentially together. Local girls would come to press their ears to the Whispering Knights and hear them breathe the name of their future husbands. But they knew not to be around the stones at midnight. That was the hour when the Whispering Knights would go down to the brook to drink, while the King's Men joined hands to dance in a circle. Any mortal rash enough to view such things would be sure either to die on the spot, or to go home a gibbering lunatic.

184. WAYLAND'S SMITHY, OXON.

Maps: OS Explorer 170; Landranger 174

Travel: From M4 Junction 15, A346 towards Marlborough. In ½ mile, left on minor roads by Badbury, Liddington, Upper Wanborough, Hinton Parva, Bishopstone and Idstone to Ashbury. Right in village on B4000 ('Lambourn'); in ¾ mile, park where Ridgeway National Trail intersects road (OS ref. 273843). Turn left along Ridgeway for ¾ mile to Wayland's Smithy on left (281854).

Bold and bloody-handed Wayland, the lame Viking hero who worked in the forge of the gods, left a long shadow on the ridge that overlooks the Vale of White Horse. The ancient tomb that lies there, and the trackway beside which it looms, were several thousand years old by the time the Norsemen and their fierce mythology came to Britain. Somehow it was the name and ghostly presence of the blacksmith that settled on the stone monument, so mysterious to men lacking a scientific culture to provide them with facts and figures.

The great Neolithic burial chamber, its entrance guarded by massive upright stones, lies in a ring of beeches just off the Ridgeway. It was completed over a period of several hundred years, with a southern stone-lined passageway and burial chambers being added around 3500 BC to the original stone-paved mausoleum built into an elliptical mound. Altogether the remains of twenty-two humans have been excavated from the tomb, fourteen from the earlier phase (very mangled, as if the stone-lined roof had fallen in on them), and eight from the southern chambers.

What Wayland had to do with such a structure is hard to fathom. Perhaps the tomb was seen as an entrance to the other world, or maybe it was connected to the joyfully cavorting chalk figure near by, the White Horse of Uffington (see p. 208). Wayland, unlucky fellow, had been lamed by King Niduth and incarcerated on an island to prevent him taking his iron-making talents elsewhere. In retaliation the crippled smith killed both the sons of Niduth, drank from their skulls, raped their sister and flew away to Valhalla on wings of wax and feathers, Icarus-style, pausing only to make sure the king knew exactly what he had done.

Wayland's Smithy

Smiths were secretive folk who held the intricacies of their craft close. The art of turning rock into metal and metal into tools and weapons was too valuable to its practitioners to be broadcast. Later travellers along the Ridgeway knew that anyone who left his horse and a silver coin at Wayland's Smithy could return for the steed and be sure to find it magically shod. But Wayland himself stayed forever unseen in the shadowy labyrinth of his forge. Visiting the Smithy on a dark day, wind whistling in the ring of trees, the power and mystery of this place is tangible.

185. UFFINGTON WHITE HORSE, OXON.

Maps: OS Explorer 170; Landranger 174

Travel: From M4 Junction 15, A346 towards Marlborough. In ½ mile, left on minor roads by Badbury, Liddington, Upper Wanborough, Hinton Parva, Bishopstone and Idstone to Ashbury. Keep ahead on B4507 for another 2½ miles; opposite left turning to Woolstone, right up lane to parking place on left (OS ref. 293866). Walk on up lane to Ridgeway National Trail; turn left along it for ½ mile, then left down path to White Horse (301866).

Why the White Horse of Uffington was cut out of the turf just along the ridge from Wayland's Smithy (see p. 207), no one knows. In one sense, it isn't hard to guess. As a piece of artwork, an expression of pure delight in the grace and power of a prancing horse, you could not find anything more perfect, either today or back when it was created in the middle Bronze Age. Perhaps that was justification enough.

The 365-foot-long horse, a sublime display of the somewhat specialized art of leucippotomy, the cutting of white horses in chalk turf, lies on the crest of its hill at the highest point of the downs. It is the oldest of all the chalk-cut horses of Britain. In the 1990s a process known as optical stimulated luminescence measured how long the soil beneath the chalk had been hidden from sunlight, and came up with a date of between 1200 and 800 BC. That put paid to the old story that King Alfred had caused it to be cut here in AD 871 to celebrate his great victory over the Danes at the Battle of Ashdown. But plenty of other tales still attach to the White Horse.

Anyone who stands in the eye of the horse (but don't, please!) can get their heart's desire by closing their eyes and turning round three times clockwise. The horse is in fact a mare, and has an invisible foal with her. Mother and offspring go down by night to graze the slope called the Manger, then descend into the vale below to drink at the wells of Woolstone, which the horse herself formed by stamping on the ground. Once every 100 years she jumps up and gallops across the sky to be shod in Wayland's Smithy by the lame blacksmith of the gods.

Some say that the horse is no horse at all, but the dragon slain by St George. There below lies the flat-topped knoll called Dragon Hill, and anyone can see for himself the bald patch on the summit where the saint spilled the monster's blood – what more proof could you possibly need?

186. PACK AND PRIME LANE AND DOG LANE, OXFORDSHIRE

Maps: OS Explorer 171; Landranger 175

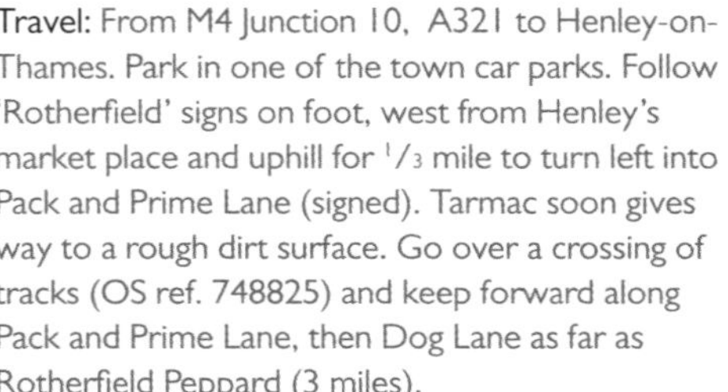

Travel: From M4 Junction 10, A321 to Henley-on-Thames. Park in one of the town car parks. Follow 'Rotherfield' signs on foot, west from Henley's market place and uphill for 1/3 mile to turn left into Pack and Prime Lane (signed). Tarmac soon gives way to a rough dirt surface. Go over a crossing of tracks (OS ref. 748825) and keep forward along Pack and Prime Lane, then Dog Lane as far as Rotherfield Peppard (3 miles).

Nearest railway station: Henley-on-Thames

Pack and Prime Lane and Dog Lane

The countryside of south-east Oxfordshire develops long dry valleys as it approaches the River Thames, and several of these lead west from Henley-on-Thames. The old track that runs between Henley and Rotherfield Peppard sticks to a low ridge, although the views from the lane are restricted now by thick, overgrown verges that would have been grazed back when animals were driven this way. One stretch goes under the name of Pack and Prime Lane and was an important route to the ford (from the twelfth century onward, the bridge) across the Thames at Henley.

The days of the packhorse trains and itinerant pedlars are long gone, and the old lane lies very quiet in its tunnel of holly trees, oak, ash and horse chestnut. Long-tailed tits and goldcrests swing in the hazel tops, and green woodpeckers give out cackling calls like bursts of mocking laughter as they swoop away up the lane. In spring the broad verges are thick with bluebells and speedwell. Further west the old track grows boggier and changes its name to Dog Lane; and here springtime quite appropriately spreads a display of dog's mercury under the trees. Later in the year two plant cousins put on a great show side by side – the white flowers of white dead-nettle, and the buttery yellow ones of yellow archangel. White dead-nettle used to be known as Adam-and-Eve-in-the-Bower, a charming name for a charming conceit, for if you look under the hood you will see our biblical progenitors lying together in the form of twin pollen-rich stamens.

187. THE RIDGEWAY NEAR WATLINGTON HILL, OXFORDSHIRE

Maps: OS Explorer 171; Landranger 175

Travel: From M40 Junction 6, B4009 to Watlington. In village centre, left towards Christmas Common; in 2/3 mile, park near the intersection of Ridgeway National Trail and road (OS ref. 698940). Turn left along Ridgeway.

There are plenty of stretches along the Ridgeway National Trail in which the 7,000-year-old road follows the traditional siting of ancient highways – along the crest of the chalk downs, with far views out to where threatening weather or strangers might appear. This section of Britain's best-known prehistoric track, however, runs at the base of the Chiltern escarpment, a wonderful straight way which skirts the out-thrust feet of a succession of hills, Britwell, Watlington, Pyrton and Shirburn, ancient and resonant names for deep dimples in the face of the Chilterns.

Here the lie of the road is all about the shelter it receives and the far prospect it

The Ridgeway

affords: shelter from the east, courtesy of the 300-foot bank of the hills, and prospect to the west over a gently descending landscape. The Ridgeway forms a narrow track which soon broadens, its surface of flint, clay and chalk deeply scored by farm traffic, off-road vehicles, mountain bikes and walkers' boots. After rain it becomes a sea of mud, puddles the colour of milky coffee filling every rut. In summer it bakes, cracks and grows dusty.

This is how all country roads used to be before tarmac drew the sting of the seasons. Hereabouts the Ridgeway runs confined in a green corridor of hazels, yew trees and spindle between verges thick with buttercups and blue spikes of self-heal. Modern laws of trespass keep travellers to the one line. But it was a different matter in older times, up on the highlands where the track had no sideways constraints. When winter rains turned the Ridgeway into a river of mud many feet deep, travellers would detour more and more widely in search of firm footing. In places the old track spread a mile from verge to verge. Men and beasts could become immovably stuck. Wheeled transport was out of the question. Venturing the Ridgeway meant taking your life in your hands. What our ancestors put up with on their winter journeys makes a mockery of our own pleasant strolls along the old road as, better fed and better shod than they ever were, we pussyfoot round the puddles.

188. WYTHAM GREAT WOOD, OXON.

Maps: OS Explorer 180; Landranger 164

Travel: A34 from Abingdon to Oxford; at Peartree roundabout on north-west outskirts, right on A44 towards city centre. In ½ mile, at roundabout with A40, take 4th exit (between A44 south and A40 west) on minor road through Upper and Lower Wolvercote. Park in Trout Inn car park on right just before narrow bridge (OS ref. 484093). Please ask permission and give the Trout Inn your custom. On foot, cross two narrow bridges, then turn right along south bank of Thames ('Thames Path' fingerpost). Go under A34; ahead across field to Wytham Mill; follow footpath signs to gate into Wytham Great Wood (467092).

NB: Permit to explore Wytham Great Wood from the Conservator – tel: 01865 726832.

As a large piece of mixed woodland, some of it ancient and all of it ecologically priceless, Wytham Great Wood would be a national treasure in any case. What makes these 600 acres of trees on their sloping ground above the River Thames unique is their status as the basis for long-term scientific research. Wytham Great Wood belongs to Oxford University and has been intensively studied for many decades; it is probably the most carefully recorded and monitored wood in Britain. The wood consists of three types of habitat: ash and sycamore woodland that has colonized what used to be farmland or wood pasture; ancient woodland that is mostly hazel coppice with great gnarled old oak standards; and areas that have been planted over the past 200 years. These woods nurture over 200 species of fungi, 800 of butterfly and moth, and over 1,000 different types of beetle – also a flora of more than 500 plant species. This kind of richness and diversity is unparalleled in British woodlands.

Nightingales are often heard producing their thrillingly resonant fluting song. Firecrests with their white headband and flame-like orange poll are occasional visitors, and woodcock can be seen on the fringes of the wood from time to time, performing their slow, jerky roding flight to reinforce their territorial claims. Collapsed trees are generally left to rot where they fall, producing an insect feast for the birds. Thick green moss and masses of old man's beard smother the soft, flaky timber of the dead trees.

Wytham Great Wood

Though the murmur of the A40 trunk road reaches this far, it is soon overlain, as you go deeper into the wood, by the noise of millions of leaves stirring and twigs rubbing together in the canopy above. The gentle susurration enhances the atmosphere of stillness, even of melancholy.

189. OT MOOR, OXFORDSHIRE

Maps: OS Explorer 180; Landranger 164

Travel: From M40 Junction 8, A40 towards Oxford. At roundabout with A420 and A4142, turn right on minor road signed 'Crematorium' to meet B4027. Left, and in 100 yards right to Beckley. Pass Abingdon Arms pub and continue for 100 yards ('No Through Road'). Bear left (OS ref. 566112) along Otmoor Lane to car park (570126).

Nearest railway station: Islip (4½ miles)

A quarter of Ot Moor was drained for crop farming after the Second World War, and most of the rest was threatened with destruction by road-building in the 1980s when the proposed route of the M40 ran right through the site. So it is a feather in the cap of conservation and of the wild places of this country that this great circular wetland in its ring of hills should still be intact, while the motorway roars by to the north and arable farming sterilizes other swathes of Oxfordshire elsewhere.

In 1980, when Government plans to build the Birmingham–Oxford section of the

Ot Moor

M40 directly across Ot Moor were revealed, there was an outcry among conservationists, orchestrated by Friends of the Earth – and also among lovers of Lewis Carroll, who maintained that the clergyman-writer had been inspired by the squared-off surface of Ot Moor to create Alice's adventures in the chessboard world of *Through the Looking Glass*. A field in the path of the proposed motorway just north of Ot Moor was named 'Alice's Meadow' and bought by the local Friends of the Earth who sold it to their supporters in over 3,000 separate plots, helping delay the construction of the road as they lodged appeals against the compulsory purchase of each tiny square. This and other actions and publicity campaigns eventually persuaded the road-builders to select a less environmentally sensitive route.

When the RSPB bought Ot Moor in 1997 it saw its potential for restoration as one of the richest and most extensive wetlands in the Midlands. It is a remarkable thing to descend from the intensively farmed 'highlands' 200 feet above into the controlled wilderness of reed-beds, scrubby wet woods, lush meadows and wide fleets of water. The RSPB owns nearly 600 acres of this wet lowland and is looking to buy more. Reed-beds have been restored, ponds created, irrigation and drainage balanced. Rough pale grass and thorn trees intersperse the damp acres. In pollarded willows and osiers sit the big haphazardly shaped stick nests of herons. Clay mud squelches underfoot on the paths between the bird hides. Bird numbers have increased dramatically since the RSPB took over; teal and wigeon overwinter in large numbers, along with russet-winged gadwall and big flocks of tufted duck with their white body flash and crest hanging far back on the head like a 1980s rock star's mullet. Ringed plover have appeared on Ot Moor, and there have been reports of the extremely rare corncrake breeding and calling from the grass that is left uncut till late in the year. If so, it would set the seal on the restoration and preservation of Ot Moor, a wild place rescued from destruction.

190. THE BATTLE OF SALCEY GREEN, NORTHAMPTONSHIRE

Maps: OS Explorer 207; Landranger 152

Travel: From M1 Junction 15, A508 to Roade. Left on minor road to Hartwell; right towards Hanslope. At Long Street, left to reach M1. From the motorway bridge (OS ref. 803492) there is a good view south to Hanslope, east to the fields of Salcey Green.

Salcey Green lies very quiet these days, an area of green fields whose only disturbance comes from the rush and roar of the M1 traffic hurtling by on the western edge. A tamer and gentler place is hard to imagine. But these mild acres were the setting on 2 June 1830 for a desperate battle – not a confrontation between armies, but a duel with bare fists. The protagonists were the Glaswegian pugilist Alexander McKay, 'The Highland Hercules', and his opponent Simon Byrne, 'The Emerald Gem', from Ireland. Their heavyweight bare-knuckle contest, illegal then as now, was for a purse of £200, a small fortune.

The two men were originally to fight outside the Watts Arms in the nearby village of Hanslope, across the border in Buckinghamshire, but the parish constable, Thomas Evans, was sent there to stop them. The landlord's lovely niece, Rosamund, distracted the officer's attention by displaying her charms in a kilt. McKay escaped out of a window and was whisked across the county border to Salcey Green where the magistrates were more disposed to turn a blind eye. So the two men squared up in front of a crowd of thousands. Forty-seven rounds later, McKay had been beaten unconscious. He was bled in the ring, then taken back by carriage to the Watts Arms, a jolting ride that worsened his condition, and he died of a brain haemorrhage in an upstairs room at the pub at nine o'clock that night. When the news of the Highland Hercules's death reached Scotland there were anti-Irish riots in Glasgow and Dundee in which seven people died. Simon Byrne was arrested in Liverpool as he tried to flee the country. At his subsequent trial for murder he was acquitted – his well-to-do backers made sure that he was represented by the best lawyers money could buy.

Three years later the Emerald Gem met the same end he had dealt to Alexander McKay, smashed to death by James 'The Deaf 'Un' Burke in a ninety-nine-round fight that lasted more than three hours. These terrible events led to the rules of boxing being tightened and a measure of protection afforded the combatants.

The Highland Hercules lies in Hanslope churchyard under a poignant inscription:

Strong and athletic was my frame,
Far from my native home I came
And bravely fought with Simon Byrne,
Alas but never to return.
Stranger, take warning from my fate
Lest you should rue your case too late:
If you have ever fought before,
Determine now to fight no more.

191. SALCEY FOREST, NORTHANTS.

Maps: OS Explorer 207; Landranger 152

Travel: From M1 Junction 15, A508 south towards Milton Keynes. In 1 mile, left ('Courteenhall, Quinton'); at T-junction in Quinton, right ('Hartwell, Quinton Green'). In 1¾ miles pass Salcey Forest sign on left; in another ¼ mile, left at another Salcey Forest sign into car park (OS ref. 794517). From car park follow waymarked and colour-coded trails through Salcey Forest.

Walking the swaying aerial walkway of Tree Top Way, children glimpse how it must feel to be a buzzard or kestrel, soaring at treetop height. The slatted walkway rises gently from the floor of Salcey Forest to a crow's-nest lookout some 70 feet up in the pine tops. It is like being rocked in a fragrant green sea. Views of the surrounding countryside impinge a little to the north where the edge of the forest is only a few hundred yards off, but staring south you

Salcey Forest

are looking at a solid mass of trees (with a hole in the middle, admittedly) that runs away for the best part of 2 unbroken miles. In the thoroughly farmed, comprehensively deforested Midlands, this represents an awful lot of wildwood.

Salcey Forest is what remains of one of the Norman royal hunting forests. It is managed for visitors, from tiny tots pedalling their first tricycles along the child-friendly Elephant Walk to groups of serious ornithologists out to spot treecreepers, siskins or lesser spotted woodpeckers in the depths of the forest. You can get away from the crowds – themselves a rare phenomenon, except on Bank Holidays – simply by plunging in among the old oaks and ash trees. There are some monster individual trees to admire, some of them now toppled by storms and left prone to house and feed forest insects. Wrens reel out their chittering little lines of song, and long-tailed tits go swooping across the clearings.

The Elephant Pond up near the Tree Top Way is a favourite place for frogs to lay their eggs, the water in spring becoming alive with hundreds of wriggling tadpoles. In 1942, at the height of the Second World War, elephants actually worked in Salcey Forest. They were pressed into service as haulers of timber, and were ridden to work by Sabu the Elephant Boy, a Hollywood star who was over in England making a film of *The Jungle Book* with Zoltán Korda. The Elephant Pond was where the patient beasts were taken at the end of their daily labours to let off steam with a good muddy wallow.

192. TWYWELL GULLET (SSSI), NEAR KETTERING, NORTHAMPTONSHIRE

Maps: OS Explorer 224; Landranger 141

Travel: Leave A14 between Kettering and Thrapston at Junction 11, and take minor road towards Cranford St John. In 100 yards, turn right (brown sign: 'Twywell Hills and Dales'), up track to car park (OS ref. 938771). Map ahead on stone plinth directs you to Twywell Gullet. Other footpaths explore the 'Hills and Dales' left by ironstone quarrying.

The bumpy land known as Twywell Hills and Dales conceals its secrets cleverly. It's not until you are below ground level that you appreciate the extent of the man-made gorge of Twywell Gullet. This mile-long canyon, shown on the OS map twisting north-eastwards like an earthworm, sinks you as far into the ground as a railway cutting. Yet Twywell Gullet was never a through route to anywhere. It was excavated by a giant Ruston steam shovel to get at the iron ore that lay deep in the oolitic limestone of north-east Northamptonshire.

It's hard to think of a more destructive business than quarrying – the ripping up of unbroken ground, the explosions, the demolition of a landscape, the dirt and dust, and the final abandonment, leaving a deep wound in the body of the earth, the raw rock exposed and an almighty mess for someone else to clear up. In the case of the Twywell quarries, however, land restoration had actually been part of the plan from the outset. The delvings formed a series of parallel gullets or quarry canyons, dug in sequence as each seam of iron ore became exhausted and the heaped-up spoil from each newly dug gullet was used to infill the previous one. The final trench in the sequence was left unfilled when quarrying ceased at Twywell in 1948, and it was nature that half drowned this final gullet with water and began to reclothe the cut rock.

The soil of this region is sparse over the underlying beds of oolitic limestone – a circumstance that breeds a rich flora. The approach to Twywell Gullet is carpeted with the tiny purple flowers of ground ivy, releasing pungent herby smells when the leaves are squeezed between finger and thumb. Exposed faces of rock carry the deep pink and green 'bubbles' of stonecrop, and down in the gullet there are tiny, intensely sweet wild strawberries to pick and savour. The coarsely bristly stems of viper's bugloss push up blue flowers between scattered boulders, and you'll find early purple and spotted orchids at the edge of the scrub willows and hawthorns.

The quarried rock lies in thick layers along the sides of the gullet, now powdered white with leached mineral salts and netted over with a gauze of spider webs. Warblers in the scrub bushes send out their scribbly little songs. Everything is quiet at the bottom, and the background murmur of bees and wood wasps overlays all man-made sounds.

193. GREEN MEN, CHURCH OF ST MICHAEL AND ALL ANGELS, WADENHOE, NORTHAMPTONSHIRE

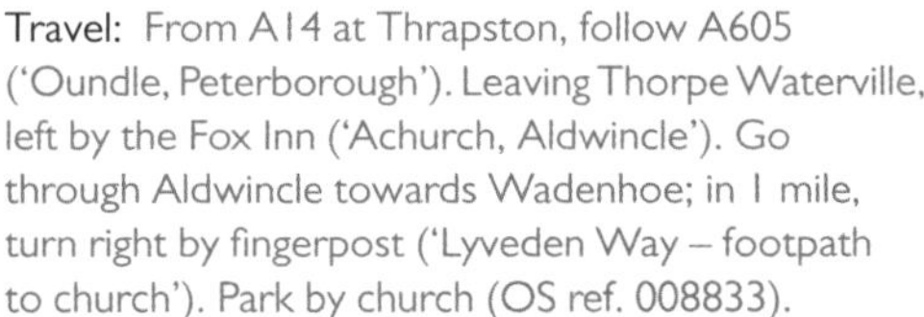

Maps: OS Explorer 224; Landranger 141

Travel: From A14 at Thrapston, follow A605 ('Oundle, Peterborough'). Leaving Thorpe Waterville, left by the Fox Inn ('Achurch, Aldwincle'). Go through Aldwincle towards Wadenhoe; in 1 mile, turn right by fingerpost ('Lyveden Way – footpath to church'). Park by church (OS ref. 008833).

The Church of St Michael and All Angels stands with its Saxon-looking tower in a peaceful, flowery graveyard at the end of a grassy ridge above Wadenhoe, the very picture of a peculiarly English calm and sobriety.

Outside, high on the south wall, a pair of

gargoyles with identical pig-like snouts stretch their mouths with both hands to facilitate the vomiting of rainwater. In the north porch a Green Man looks down through a layer of whitewash – a taster of his thirteenth-century brethren within. The twin corbels each side of the chancel arch are remarkable. On the north is a personage tugging at the corners of his mouth in echo of those outside. Opposite him is a Green Man with a mocking, monkish fringe, his lumpen peasant face completed by a misshapen right eye and a bulbous nose. Thick, crudely carved foliage shoots from his mouth, curving upwards to meet his clumsy bangs of hair.

The figure carved on the west face of the font is stranger still. A sly, fawnish face, small and triangular, sprouts a pair of huge horns that stretch halfway back around the bowl and terminate in curlicues of foliage. As a figure to underpin the ceremony of baptism, with its explicit rejection of the world, the flesh and the Devil, it is odd indeed. The impish, pagan face and unbridled horns are more suggestive of the cult of the Celtic pagan god Cernunnos than anything Christian. Quite some initiation for the innocent babies of Wadenhoe.

194. OLD SULEHAY, NORTHANTS.

Maps: OS Explorer 227; Landranger 142

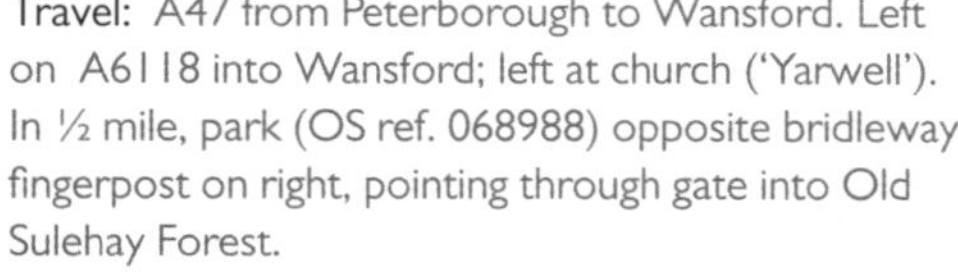

Travel: A47 from Peterborough to Wansford. Left on A6118 into Wansford; left at church ('Yarwell'). In ½ mile, park (OS ref. 068988) opposite bridleway fingerpost on right, pointing through gate into Old Sulehay Forest.

Nearest railway station: Wansford, Nene Valley Railway (2 miles)

This is a beautiful piece of ancient woodland above the Nene Valley – not just a block of trees, but a forest in the sense of a mosaic of habitats. Old Sulehay itself is a good example of overshot coppice, in which very old oak, ash and field maple stools have outgrown themselves and shot out mighty limbs to tangle in the canopy 50 feet up. Nuthatches push hazelnuts into cracks in the bark to hold them steady while they split them open. Under the trees the ground is a deep carpet of oak and hazel leaves, scattered in autumn with enough crab apples to make a lifetime's WI jelly. Spring sees a haze of bluebells and wide drifts of white wood anemones around the feet of the distorted old pollard oaks.

Out beyond the west end of Sulehay lies the abandoned limestone quarry called Stonepit, now partially grassed over, where cowslips flourish in spring and the startling blue flowers of viper's bugloss show up with psychedelic intensity against the pale crumbly soil. Handsome iridescent green tiger beetles scurry over the sandy patches, and lizards bask on the hot bare surfaces of limestone blocks still lying where they were left when the quarry closed in the 1970s. Next to the quarry lies Ring Haw, another piece of mixed woodland and grass, where venerable holly trees and pink-berried spindle thrive in the shade on lime-rich soil. Cowslips flourish here, too. Ring Haw's conglomeration of small sunny glades, thick tangles of wild jungly scrub and open meadows give it the feeling of a forest in miniature all by itself.

195. BEDFORD PURLIEUS, NORTHANTS.

Maps: OS Explorer 227; Landranger 141, 142

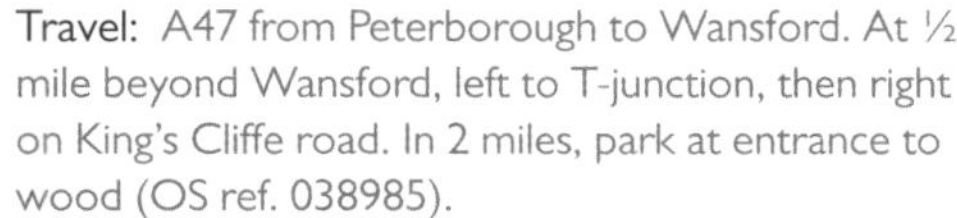

Travel: A47 from Peterborough to Wansford. At ½ mile beyond Wansford, left to T-junction, then right on King's Cliffe road. In 2 miles, park at entrance to wood (OS ref. 038985).

Nearest railway station: Wansford, Nene Valley Railway (4 miles)

In medieval times the Royal Forest of Rockingham covered a huge area of northern Northamptonshire, but no one except foresters and royal hunting personages was allowed free movement within it. These days most of the forest has been felled and the remnants are too widely separated to form a coherent picture. One piece remains in good shape, though, and everyone is allowed – in fact, encouraged – to wander where they like.

Bedford Purlieus lies west of Peterborough in gently rolling country bounded by the River Nene. The wood is founded on soil that contains elements both alkaline and acid, so the plant life – and therefore the butterflies, birds and animals it supports – is incredibly rich. Fly orchids grow in late spring; these plants of lime soil have remarkable brown flowers that look exactly like stout little gentlemen with waxed handlebar moustaches, dressed in capacious breeches and neat white waistcoats. Sinister-looking pink-flowered toothwort rises from its footing in the roots of hazels, its host tree. It gets its name from the sharply toothed capsule into which the flower fits. Other flowers are deadly nightshade with large and temptingly glossy, blackcurrant-like and very toxic fruits, lovely white lily of the valley, and columbine, whose purple flowers hang modestly like bells from a slender stalk and resemble a flock of doves with their beaks all held together and long wings gracefully trailing behind them.

Bedford Purlieus

Bedford Purlieus is a haven for bats – not only the white-bellied Natterers, but also the accurately named long-eared bat, whose ears are almost as long as its body, and the uncommon barbastelle, whose squashed-up face looks like a cross between a bulldog and a mountain goat. If you prefer flying creatures to be more conventionally attractive, there are white admiral and silver-washed fritillary butterflies, along with many other species that thrive in such ancient and well-kept woodlands.

196. COLLYWESTON QUARRIES, NORTHAMPTONSHIRE

Maps: OS Explorer 234; Landranger 141

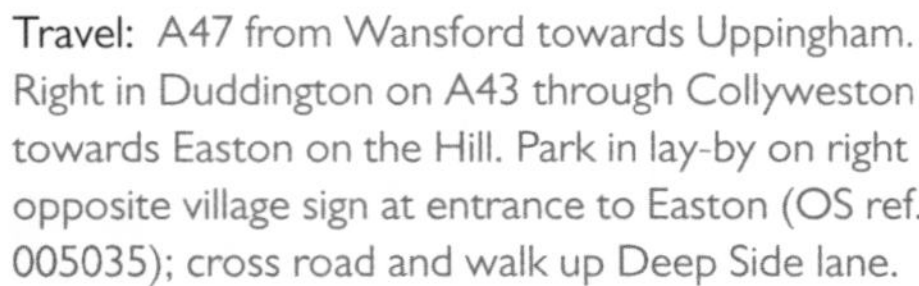

Travel: A47 from Wansford towards Uppingham. Right in Duddington on A43 through Collyweston towards Easton on the Hill. Park in lay-by on right opposite village sign at entrance to Easton (OS ref. 005035); cross road and walk up Deep Side lane.

Nearest railway station: Stamford (2½ miles)

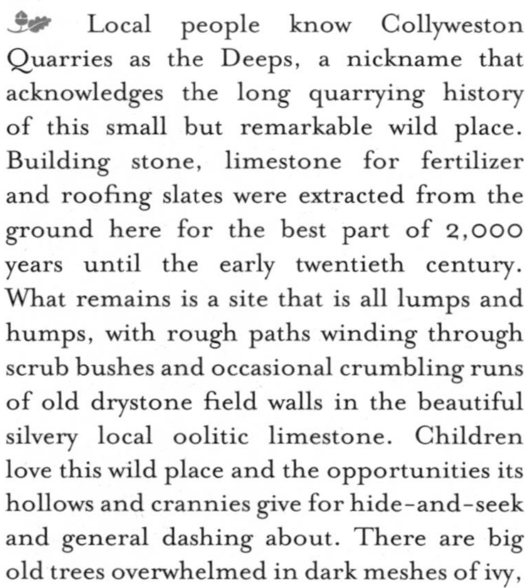

Local people know Collyweston Quarries as the Deeps, a nickname that acknowledges the long quarrying history of this small but remarkable wild place. Building stone, limestone for fertilizer and roofing slates were extracted from the ground here for the best part of 2,000 years until the early twentieth century. What remains is a site that is all lumps and humps, with rough paths winding through scrub bushes and occasional crumbling runs of old drystone field walls in the beautiful silvery local oolitic limestone. Children love this wild place and the opportunities its hollows and crannies give for hide-and-seek and general dashing about. There are big old trees overwhelmed in dark meshes of ivy, and open areas of grassland which in spring are covered in yellow sheets of rockrose and cowslips, and later dotted with the stumpy little pink cones of pyramidal orchid.

This limestone grassland of Collyweston Quarries is a rare habitat these days, having been reduced throughout Northamptonshire since the mid twentieth century to about one-fifth of its previous extent. More than 200 species of wild flowers have been recorded thriving on the lime-rich ground, including the hardy little plant dyer's greenweed, whose yellow flowers were used in the medieval dyeing trade to give a fine green colour to wool. Clustered bellflower pushes its purple flowers together in a tight bunch for a midsummer show, while dodder trails its scarlet strings and pom-poms of pink flowers up the shoots of scrub trees. It is really worth bringing a good flower book and a hand lens to Collyweston Quarries; there's enough floral fascination here to entrance beginners as well as experts.

197. DRAYCOTE MEADOW, WARWICKS.

Maps: OS Explorer 222; Landranger 140

Travel: M45 towards Coventry, then A45 for 1 mile; left on B4453 ('Princethorpe'). In ¼ mile, left down lane ('Draycote'). In ¾ mile pass under railway bridge; parking area and entrance to meadow are immediately on your left (OS ref. 449706).

Draycote Meadow is, quite simply, the best wildflower meadow in a county where meadows are rare. Where all the fields round about have had their ecological richness destroyed by late twentieth-century intensive farming practices, Draycote Meadow survives as 'unimproved' grassland – rather a downbeat term for a meadow managed in the

Draycote Meadow

traditional way. It is grazed in autumn, and cut for hay only in summer after the flowers have set seed. A bridleway and path allow you to cross the two meadows with their ancient hedges that make up the site.

The surface of Draycote Meadow is corrugated with furrows and ridges, remnants of the medieval system of strip farming which allotted everyone both good and bad land in turn. The bumps and hummocks show that the meadow has remained unploughed since the Middle Ages, so its wildflower communities are extremely long-established.

Early purple orchids and milkmaids or lady's smock in all shades of pink, purple and white are spring favourites here, along with drifts of cowslips. A little later, green-winged orchids make their appearance, delicate little flowers with a greenish tinge to the twin 'ears' of their hoods. Then comes the tall parrot-beaked yellow rattle, so called because its dried seed heads make a rattling sound in a breeze. The trailing pink flowers of ragged robin are out in damp patches of the meadow around the same time, and there are two very uncommon types of fern which look rather like pale green arum lilies – the hooded little adder's tongue, and moonwort with rudimentary green leaves and a spike to which cling what appear to be a number of tiny red-brown parcels, the pinnae or spore-carrying bodies. Once upon a time country folk would place a sprig of moonwort in their purses to attract further silver. But that was in older and more innocent times.

198. RYTON WOOD, WARWICKSHIRE

Maps: OS Explorer 221; Landranger 140

Travel: M45/A45 to Ryton-on-Dunsmore; left on A445 ('Bubbenhall'). Go over A423 roundabout, and in 1 mile a brown 'Ryton Pools Country Park' sign points to car park (OS ref. 374728). Pick up a Ryton Wood Trail guide leaflet at Information Centre and follow waymarks.

Nearest railway station: Coventry (6 miles)

The 200-acre ancient woodland of Ryton Wood is an excellent place for children. There is a playground, café and shop, and the guide leaflet for the trail through the wood is tailored for young explorers. Ryton Wood has certainly been growing here on its low ridge south of Coventry for 1,000 years, and there may well have been a wood here since broadleaved trees began to recolonize Britain as the post-Ice Age climate warmed up around 7500 BC. Oak, elm and small-

Ryton Wood

leaved lime were the chief trees of these early forests, and though Dutch Elm disease put paid to the elms in the 1970s the other two still flourish. The limes have traditionally been coppiced here, and there are enormous coppice stools up to 7 or 8 feet across, many hundreds of years old.

The ground is carpeted with bluebells and patched with wood anemone in spring, and the ancient ditches and banks that cross the wood are lined with primroses and violets. Perhaps the greatest delight, however, are the butterflies. White admirals congregate around blackberry bushes where coppicing has made a clearing in the wood canopy to let sunlight in. The flicker of their black-and-white wings in the light and shade is mesmerically beautiful.

Woodcock nest here, but with their speckled brown-and-white colouring and habit of keeping very still and under cover by day, they are horribly hard to spot. Your best chance will be around the edge of the wood at dusk when the spring mating season is on, and the males are carrying out their remarkable roding display, a jerky territorial flight accompanied by grating grunts and squeaky cries, once seen never forgotten – but seldom seen.

199. UFTON FIELDS, WARWICKSHIRE

Maps: OS Explorer 221; Landranger 151

Travel: A425 from Leamington Spa towards Southam; at roundabout by church in Ufton, turn right ('Ufton Fields'). In 1 mile car park on left beside wood (OS ref. 378613).

Nearest railway station: Leamington Spa (5 miles)

What is now the superb flower-rich reserve of Ufton Fields was once – and not so long ago – a place ripped apart and then abandoned. In the early 1950s the white lias under the ground was extracted for use in cement-making, a quarrying process that left the land furrowed as well as hollowed. The devastated site lay empty and naked, ripe for reclamation by plants and birds, a process that happened almost imperceptibly until scrub and coarse grass had smothered most of the workings. These are now carefully controlled and managed for orchids, delicate pink common centaury, mats of rich yellow bird's-foot trefoil and other flowering plants, and for a wide range of birds (goldcrest, bullfinch, yellowhammer) and

Ufton Fields

butterflies (common blue, marbled white, peacock and the moth-like, unflatteringly named dingy skipper, with its gently furry, subtly patterned brown-and-cream wings). The old ridges are nibbled by a population of remarkably large, dark-coated rabbits.

Pools have formed in the crevices and these are a tremendous resource for water-based creatures. Little grebe nest on floating piles of weed, reed buntings in the reed-beds. Some of the pools are breeding grounds for newts, which resemble enormous leeches with four stubby legs sticking out sideways. They speed over the silty bottom of their home pool, then swim up as if climbing an invisible mountainside to snatch a morsel from the surface and wriggle back down, leaving a single momentary bubble on the water.

200. SNITTERFIELD BUSHES, WARWICKSHIRE

Maps: OS Explorer 205; Landranger 151

Travel: From Junction 15 on M40, take A46 towards Stratford-upon-Avon. In 1½ miles, leave at Snitterfield turning. Turn right into Snitterfield and follow this minor road towards Bearley. In 1½ miles, just after left bend, car parking space is on the left (OS ref. 200603).

The ancient wood of Snitterfield Bushes, covering some 123 acres, is only a remnant of what was once a sprawl of semi-natural woodland four or five times as big. A glance at the map shows the 'pointing finger' shape of a wartime aerodrome immediately to the west. It was the building of this that destroyed the heart of the old wood and drove a half-mile wedge between its two surviving fragments. Some of the old tarmac aerodrome paths still exist deep in the undergrowth, and wartime utility bricks make up some of the wood's substratum, contributing their nutrients to the already lime-saturated clay on which the trees are founded.

A fine time to walk the perimeter path is on a late evening in spring. Just-awoken bees and flies keep up a constant, soporific background hum, and warblers and tits sing the sun down from the tangled depths. Roe deer move quietly among the trees, and the old wood banks and path boundaries lie thickly spattered with a really astonishing display of primroses and violets.

Snitterfield Bushes has plenty of old trees. There are sections kept coppiced by volunteers; other parts where trimmed limbs of oak and ash lie neatly stacked. There are clearings where the sunlight strikes down, and scrubby patches where the deer lie up. The woodland is rich in flora later in spring, too, when the delicate greeny-white bells of Solomon's seal and the spidery flowers of herb paris are seen. And you may be lucky enough to spot the black-and-white flicker of white admiral butterflies as they fly up and down the sunny paths of the wood.

201. PIPER'S HILL, WORCESTERSHIRE

Maps: OS Explorer 204; Landranger 150

Travel: From M5 Junction 5, A38 towards Bromsgrove. In Wychbold, right ('Hanbury') along Church Lane, and left ('Stoke Prior') to pass under railway, then right across canal ('Hanbury') to meet B4091. Right for ¼ mile to car park on right (OS ref. 957652).

Nearest railway station: Bromsgrove (4 miles)

Piper's Hill Wood

Piper's Hill is a fine example of a wood pasture, rather a rarity in Britain today. Such places were common land, used by the locals who enjoyed rights of estovers (picking up dead wood) and pannage (allowing their pigs to eat the fallen acorns). The trees had to be kept pollarded, their lower limbs cut back so that men and animals could move freely among them. The older and bigger specimens were left to grow to enormous size and provide plenty of shelter, not to mention dead wood to gather for fuel.

Since the nineteenth century Piper's Hill has remained ungrazed and unused, and has developed into widely spaced woodland. Some of the older trees are absolutely enormous and very distorted; they stand like war veterans, great oaks alongside sweet chestnut and beech pollards, some decapitated or disembowelled by lightning and storm winds. In the presence of these very senior trees – some are 400 years old or more – you feel awed and dwarfed.

No human skin, however aged, is as pitted and corrugated as the bark of these ancient oaks. The crooks of their limbs are saggy and pachydermous. Some stand defiant with green crowns, sprouting leaves from crevices in their trunks in lieu of branches long gone; others have shed their skins completely and are transfigured in ghostly pallor, dead in themselves, but still alive with insect movement and birdsong. Even in death they feed and shelter countless thousands of dependents. Owls, nuthatches, spiders, woodlice, red ants, wood wasps, grubs and centipedes and a host of fungi. They are extraordinary entities, and the natural order is being reversed for their benefit – far from being superseded by younger, fitter and taller trees, it is those upstarts that are felled to let the veterans through into sunlight.

202. SHRAWLEY WOOD, WORCS.

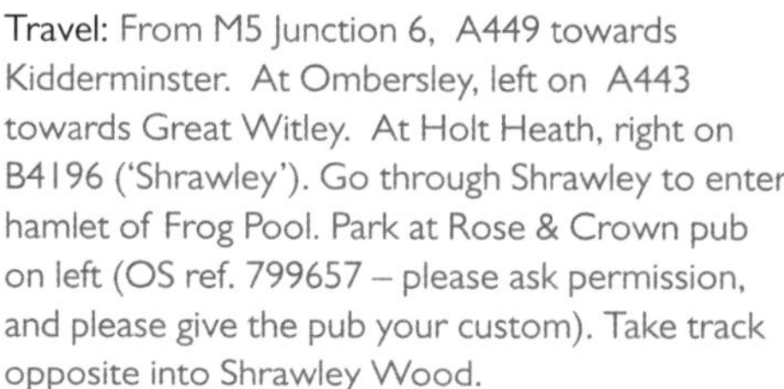

Maps: OS Explorer 204; Landranger 138

Travel: From M5 Junction 6, A449 towards Kidderminster. At Ombersley, left on A443 towards Great Witley. At Holt Heath, right on B4196 ('Shrawley'). Go through Shrawley to enter hamlet of Frog Pool. Park at Rose & Crown pub on left (OS ref. 799657 – please ask permission, and please give the pub your custom). Take track opposite into Shrawley Wood.

Shrawley Wood is a place of streams and pools, of squelchy paths and ponds with frogs, copses where blackcaps pour out fluid bursts of song so joyful you can scarcely believe it is all about territory and machismo. This is a rare piece of ancient wildwood – semi-natural, since its native small-leaved limes (uncommon in such numbers in this part of the world) have been coppiced since at least medieval times, but thoroughly wild, operating as a single organism made up of thousands of interdependent plants and creatures.

The wood is founded on acidic sandstone soils, with alkaline flushes on some of the slopes. The flora is very rich and varied – apart from the springtime bluebells and anemones that first claim attention, there are tall enchanter's nightshade, lily of the valley and the purple-blue bells of giant bellflower; also spreading bellflower, a smaller and more uncommon bellflower cousin with a wide spray of flowers, and the graceful, feathery wood fescue, a grass that is becoming rare in this country. Walk down towards the large fleet of water at the eastern edge of the woods, and in the damp stream-softened ground you may find large bittercress flowering in summer, another rarity, with eyelash-like purple anthers making a fine contrast to the four white petals.

In woods of such dampness autumn is a rich time for fungi: over 400 species have been recorded here. Kingfishers flash electric blue along the rivulets at the margins of the wood, and the plump black dipper with its white chest has been spotted on stones in midstream.

Worcestershire Beacon

203. WORCESTERSHIRE BEACON, MALVERN HILLS, WORCESTERSHIRE

Maps: OS Explorer 190; Landranger 150

Travel: From M5 Junction 7, A44 towards Worcester; left on A4440 for 3 miles to Powick Hams; left on A449 to Malvern; right on B4232 to West Malvern. Park above Brewers Arms pub (OS ref. 764457). Take uphill track ('The Dingle'), a stiff short climb to saddle; right here to reach summit indicator on Worcestershire Beacon (769452).

Nearest railway station: Great Malvern (1 mile)

To appreciate the spectacular Malvern Hills, you have only to view them from below, preferably from due east or west. They are miniature mountains, capped with crystalline volcanic granites that are the oldest in England, perhaps 1,000 million years old. They rise steeply from the flat Severn countryside where Worcestershire meets Herefordshire. 'Some term them the English Alps,' said Celia Fiennes in 1696. 'They are at least two or three miles up and are a Pirramidy fashion on the top.' Two or 3 miles up is a bit rich – Worcestershire Beacon, the summit of the range, only reaches 1,395 feet – but they swoop and soar, heading due south and north with no outliers to disturb their symmetry. They have a grandeur that far outstretches their actual compass, which is not much more than 7 miles in all.

Choose a bright day with lots of wind and a storm building far off, letting plenty of scudding light along the range and filling the sky with dramatic movement. The climb to the summit is short and sharp. Once up, helped by the toposcope or direction indicator erected in 1897 to commemorate Queen Victoria's Diamond Jubilee, you can pick out features in a landscape that stretches at least 120 miles and covers fifteen counties. This is one of the great prospects of England. The Cotswolds edge the flat Worcestershire plain in the east, with Bardon Hill in Leicestershire 60 miles off in the north-east. The prow-like profiles of the Black Mountains rise over the Welsh border in the south-west, the hump of Mendip in Somerset more than 60 miles to the south. The Clee Hills whisper for attention in the north-west.

In benign weather this panorama makes you shout and sing. On a threatening day it strikes you silent, standing buffeted by the wind in the tense hour before the storm strikes, watching its shadow slowly advance and absorb the land, blotting up the light to release it in diagonal stabs of silver and grey. This is what we climb hills for.

204. CHURCH OF ST MARY AND ST DAVID, KILPECK, HEREFORDSHIRE

Maps: OS Explorer 189; Landranger 161

Travel: A465 from Abergavenny towards Hereford; in Wormbridge, right to Kilpeck. Car parking spaces outside St Mary's Church (OS ref. 445305).

In the tiny village of Kilpeck, the Church of St Mary and St David is the acknowledged gem of a devoutly religious and wildly pagan sculptural movement of the late twelfth century. People come from all over the world to marvel at the red sandstone carvings round the windows and doors, under the eaves and in the chancel arch – artistry fired by an imagination that nowadays would be seen as completely over the top.

Hugh of Kilpeck, the royal forester who commissioned Kilpeck church in the 1130s, had most probably been on pilgrimage to Santiago, Rome and elsewhere, like many of his social equals. Even if he hadn't, he would surely have picked up tips on their sculptural styles from the other Norman lords of the Welsh Borders: the arrogant Payn fitz John (he died with a Welsh javelin through his head), Ralph de Baskerville, Lord Hugh Mortimer of Wigmore and his chief steward Oliver de Merlimond, who certainly did go on pilgrimage around this time to Santiago de Compostella.

These rich and sophisticated lords were obliged to build castles to subdue the termagant Welsh. Mindful of their souls, they also built churches, and these reflected their founders' power and prestige through the sublime craftsmanship of what has become known as the Herefordshire School of Sculpture. The masons and sculptors of

the Herefordshire School worked on nearly fifty churches over four counties. Their uninhibited carvings crop up all through the Welsh Borders in the pink sandstone churches of Herefordshire, Worcestershire and Gloucestershire: soldiers in ribbed tunics with egg-shaped heads and elastic limbs, bug eyed beasts – especially dragons – of every crazy shape and sort, all entangled in savage tendrils of foliage. We know little of the master craftsmen of the movement. But two shadowy figures do emerge from the mists, their work distinguishable from that of their fellows – the wildly expressive 'Chief Master', and the subtler and more restrained 'Aston Master'. Both worked at Kilpeck.

The south door of St Mary and St David's would itself be worth a long journey to see. Dragons, symbolic of the devil, writhe up and down the jambs. Long-faced warriors in peaked caps and ribbed clothes stand enmeshed in tendrils. A Green Man spews strappy foliage from his mouth above the east door jamb, while his brothers thrust their heads out from the frame of the west window. Over the doorway a semi-circular tympanum shows a stylized Tree of Life framed by beasts, birds and humans cavorting and contorted. A band of corbels runs right round the church under the eaves, and every stone is carved with some humorous or grotesque figure – a dog and rabbit straight out of Walt Disney, pigs and lions, a muzzled bear with two human heads in its mouth, a sheela-na-gig displaying her scalloped sexual parts with gusto. Inside the church, the riot of stone carving continues unabated.

205. CRASWALL PRIORY, HEREFORDSHIRE

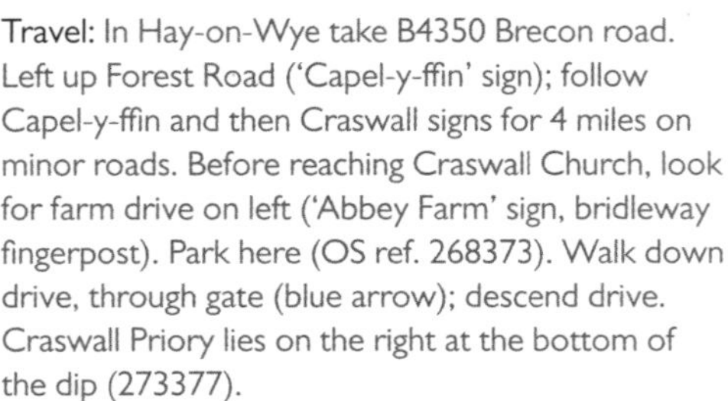

Maps: OS Explorer OL13, Landranger 161

Travel: In Hay-on-Wye take B4350 Brecon road. Left up Forest Road ('Capel-y-ffin' sign); follow Capel-y-ffin and then Craswall signs for 4 miles on minor roads. Before reaching Craswall Church, look for farm drive on left ('Abbey Farm' sign, bridleway fingerpost). Park here (OS ref. 268373). Walk down drive, through gate (blue arrow); descend drive. Craswall Priory lies on the right at the bottom of the dip (273377).

Craswall Priory was established around 1225, more than 100 years after the great Black Mountains monastery of Llanthony Priory was founded by Augustinian monks in the Vale of Ewyas, half a dozen miles south as the crow flies. Llanthony became a rich and powerful landowner in a wide district of the mountains and beyond. Craswall was different. Sited in strict isolation at the bottom of a constricted valley in the headwaters of the River Monnow, the priory was founded by monks of the severe Grandmont Order, rare in Britain, who observed a rule far more withdrawn and harsh than their brothers-in-Christ in the adjacent valley.

The austerity of their mode of living seems reflected in the ruin of their abbey church, which lies half sunk in the ground, easy to miss on the way to Abbey Farm. Yew trees are clamped by their roots to the walls. Sheep wander in and out at will. The valley sides press in, claustrophobic and even sinister in mist or rain.

The priory buildings have been excavated, but now lie in complete neglect. Cloister and chapter house to the south are all but

Craswell Priory

absorbed back in the earth, though the shape of the abbey church itself is clear to see. Its broken walls of roughly shaped purplish stones stand well above head height – a long, narrow, undecorated church, whose hillocky nave leads east to a rounded apse. Here are the crudely built altar, a blocked doorway with a pointed arch and another recess with a rounded frame, and in the south wall a piscina complete with bevelled bowl and sink hole.

There is something at once profoundly peaceful and melancholy about these ruins, lying forgotten and gently crumbling in their remote valley. The Grandmont monks founded the priory in the wildest spot they could find; and now their handiwork, the church where they worshipped and the buildings they lived in, are humbly and silently dissolving back into the ground they were raised from.

206. EARDISLEY FONT, HEREFORDSHIRE

Maps: OS Explorer 201; Landranger 148

Travel: Eardisley is on A4111, 5 miles south of Kington. St Mary Magdalene Church stands beside the road.

The Church of St Mary Magdalene in Eardisley is a fine building, but its other attractions pale beside the magnificent work of art in which the parish babies have been baptized for some 850 years. Eardisley's font is a product of that most extraordinary twelfth-century flowering of artistry in ecclesiastical stonework which we know as the Herefordshire School of Sculpture (see pp. 225–6). As such, it stands comparison with anything at Kilpeck, Shobdon or the other showpiece places. Positioned just inside the south door of the church, it is lit by timed switch so there is plenty of time to admire each detail.

Eardisley Font

There are three main groups of figures. Nearest the door two pop-eyed warriors with beards and pointed moustaches, trapped in a thicket of tendrils, battle it out. Each man wears a ribbed woollen tunic, nipped in at the waist with a sash. The soldier on the left raises a sword to stab his opponent, who has in fact already got the upper hand – he has thrust a spear clean through his enemy's thigh. Stage right, a holy man has his back to the fighters and is watching a vigorous tableau of salvation. A sturdy, wild-eyed Christ runs towards him at full pelt, brandishing a crucifix in his right hand. Christ's left hand is clamped round the wrist of a small, haloed figure, whom he is tugging with enormous force from a grasping maze of tendrils – tugging so heartily that the little stone feet of the saved man are flying through the air.

The tendrils curl all the way round to the back of the font, where they part to form a frame for a magnificent lion with a mane that falls in rows of curls like a judge's wig. Here perhaps is the clue to the riddle of the carver's message. Man is born in a state of original sin. He is capable of behaving as savagely to his fellow man as any lion. Only Christ and the sign of the Cross in baptism can purge the wildness of his nature and save him from the snares of Hell.

207. GREAT OAK OF EARDISLEY, HEREFORDSHIRE

Maps: OS Explorer 201; Landranger 148

Travel: A438 from Hay-on-Wye to Hereford; left at Willersley on A4111 towards Kington. At far end of Eardisley, left at Tramway Inn ('Woodseaves') for ¾ mile to Hurstway Common. Brown 'Great Oak' sign points to Great Oak of Eardisley (OS ref. 300497).

The twelfth-century master craftsman who sculpted the wonderful font for St Mary Magdalene Church in Eardisley (see above) gave full rein to his skill in the carving of curling, smothering tendrils of foliage. They represented the entangling snares of Hell. But there is something more to them – a suggestion of the fear and panic that lurked for medieval men deep in the heart of the forest.

The great forest that filled the Wye Valley at that time was a source of ambush and danger for Norman lords and their men, as the Welsh sought to repel their advance into Wales. It seems extraordinary now, wandering through this countryside of scattered woods and well-tended farmland, that so much of it lay so thickly wooded. Almost all has been tamed, cut down to clear the land or for raw materials or fuel. A few survivors of that wildwood remain, though, and one of the most striking is the Great Oak of Eardisley.

The Great Oak stands at the crook of a lane outside Eardisley. It is a monster tree, its limbs knotted and contorted by wind, drought, axe blows and lightning strikes. It grips the earth with knuckled roots as if it means to hold its ground no matter what. The oak was once calculated to be over 100 feet tall, but is now only house-high. Its girth, measured on New Year's Day 1999, was 31 feet. It looks rock solid. But walk round the back and you find that the Great Oak is a shell, a rind of bark hollowed out by time and fire into whose heart you can easily step.

Somehow the Great Oak raises the energy each spring to push out a fresh crown of green. How long has it been standing here, doing that? This tree was mentioned in the Domesday Book of 1086. It was over 200 years old when the Eardisley font (see above) was carved with its tangle of tendrils. It must be approaching its 1,000th year, if it has not already celebrated its first millennium and embarked on its journey to the next.

208. HERGEST RIDGE, HEREFORDSHIRE

Maps: OS Explorer 201; Landranger 148

Travel: From M5 Junction 7, A44 west through Bromyard and Leominster to Kington. From west edge of town follow 'Offa's Dyke' signs along Offa's Dyke Path National Trail, over back of Hergest Ridge (4-mile walk to Gladestry). Hergest Court (OS ref. 282554) is 1 mile south-west of Kington on Brilley Mountain and Rhydspence road.

The great 5-mile green whaleback of Hergest Ridge straddles the border between England and Wales and forms an ancient east–west route between the two countries. Offa, eighth-century King of Mercia, knew that whoever controlled the heights of such a hilly landscape would dominate the land. When he had his mighty defensive earthwork built along the border between AD 778 and 796, he ordered it to be sited so as to command every hill and ridge that had a view into Wales. Walking the ridge today along the Offa's Dyke Path, you look out across the same landscape as the Mercian border guards kept watch over – steep hills rolling out of Wales like waves, and breaking on the lowlands of the Border country.

Up on the back of Hergest Ridge lies the

huge triangular slab of rock that locals called the Whetstone. Stories say that infected sufferers during the Black Death epidemic of 1348–50 would place their money on the stone and withdraw, leaving the coast clear for merchants to pick up the coins and leave bushels of grain in their place. Perhaps the Whetstone is really the 'wheat-stone'.

Another pungent local tale concerns Thomas Vaughan, a fifteenth-century lord of this countryside who lived at Hergest Court just under the south-east face of Hergest Ridge. Black Vaughan, as he was known, seems to have been a terror to everyone. Commanding a Yorkist force at the Battle of Banbury in 1469, he was captured by the victorious Lancastrian army and beheaded. His ghost made its way back to the Borders and caused so much trouble that thirteen parsons gathered in Presteigne church to exorcise it. When Black Vaughan materialized in the middle of the ceremony, twelve of the clerics collapsed in fright. The thirteenth, however, was cool and collected enough to reduce Black Vaughan to the size of a fly and shut him up securely in a snuffbox. This was then thrown into the pool at Hergest Court. Box and spectre stayed at the bottom of the pool for 100 years, until by an unlucky chance they were dredged up. The ghost of Black Vaughan contrived to escape from its miniature prison, to haunt Hergest and the nearby countryside forever more in the form of a gigantic black hound.

209. CROFT AMBREY HILL FORT, HEREFORDSHIRE

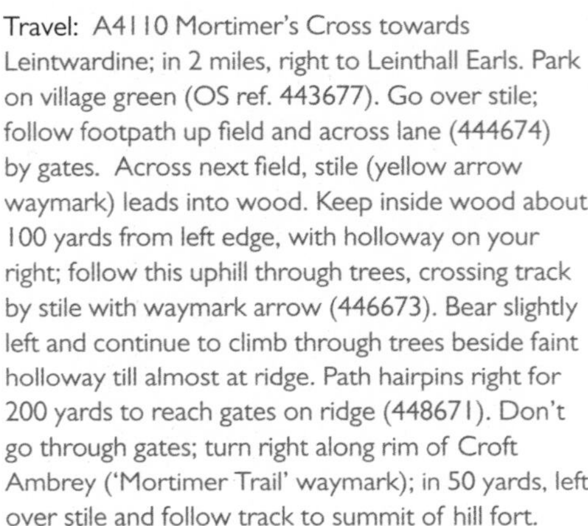

Maps: OS Explorer 203; Landranger 137

Travel: A4110 Mortimer's Cross towards Leintwardine; in 2 miles, right to Leinthall Earls. Park on village green (OS ref. 443677). Go over stile; follow footpath up field and across lane (444674) by gates. Across next field, stile (yellow arrow waymark) leads into wood. Keep inside wood about 100 yards from left edge, with holloway on your right; follow this uphill through trees, crossing track by stile with waymark arrow (446673). Bear slightly left and continue to climb through trees beside faint holloway till almost at ridge. Path hairpins right for 200 yards to reach gates on ridge (448671). Don't go through gates; turn right along rim of Croft Ambrey ('Mortimer Trail' waymark); in 50 yards, left over stile and follow track to summit of hill fort.

Croft Ambrey is one of the most impressive Iron Age hill forts on the Welsh Borders. The configuration of its hill means that it is not the conventional circular or rectangular shape, but a teardrop, with its point facing east and a steep drop on the northern flank. There are several ways to reach Croft Ambrey, but climbing up through the woods from Leinthall Earls on the north gives a sense of drama, with the shape and extent of the fort hidden until the last moment.

Archaeologists carried out a wide-ranging excavation of Croft Ambrey in the 1960s, and it's thanks to their patient discovery and interpretation that we have an unusually detailed picture of the stronghold's history. It was founded around 550 BC with ramparts 17 feet high, shortly after the concept of fortified hilltops as places to live and be safe was introduced along the Welsh Borders. Rectangular buildings, rather than the

Croft Ambrey Hill Fort

conventional round ones, were built back to back along narrow laneways that followed the contours of the hill. Their wooden posts were renewed many times over the centuries, so they were obviously meant to be permanently sited. Around 390 BC foreigners arrived in the region, bringing with them the clever new idea of fortifying the vulnerable gateways with stone-lined guard chambers with in-turned entrances. These were incorporated, and the whole place enlarged to encompass almost 9 acres of the hilltop. Fire was a problem thereafter, probably applied by enemies; the gateway guardrooms were burned out and rebuilt on more than one occasion. They were in use for over two centuries, but were then abandoned and left to fall in. Were they too susceptible to attack, or was the need to keep them manned and repaired no longer pressing?

Corn and the remains of cattle have been found inside the fort, along with pottery jars with chevron-patterned rims dating from 250 BC. There could well have been as many as 500 people living on the hilltop – a thriving, reasonably secure township, until the arrival of the Romans in the area in AD 49. Almost simultaneously, Croft Ambrey was deserted. The people could either have been ordered or driven out, or perhaps they felt more secure from other tribes and more able to expand on to lower, better land, now that there was a common enemy and master.

There are some magnificent old trees on the summit of the hill – giant yews, tremendous ancient oaks and beeches, a witchily warped field maple, a storm-shattered larch in the close embrace of an ash tree. A rampart standing almost to its original height guards the south perimeter. The view from the top is sensational, dozens of miles of Border country laid out like a lumpy relief map. Fourteen counties are said to be in view. This was the prospect that brought such a sense of security to the people of Croft Ambrey hill fort. Friend or foe, to prepare for their arrival it was necessary to be able to see them coming, and the further off the better.

7

SHROPSHIRE, STAFFORDSHIRE (*inc.* WEST MIDLANDS), DERBYSHIRE, LEICESTERSHIRE, RUTLAND, NOTTINGHAMSHIRE

THE NORTH MIDLANDS

The English Midlands are perhaps the least likely region, in most people's minds, to conceal any wild places. The North Midlands, as represented by the gentle countryside just north of Birmingham, the rolling Shire country, and the big making-and-mending cities of Birmingham, Coventry and Leicester, seem so thoroughly tamed by canals and motorways, by plough and seed drill, by civic engineer and bricklayer, that it's hard to imagine any scintilla of the uncultivated in these well-calibrated and well-regulated surroundings.

YET THE NORTH Midlands is where anyone on a journey north first begins to get a hint of higher and wilder country than has yet been on show. Moving up the western flank of the region, where Shropshire butts up against the Welsh Borders, the ground lifts into broken hills – the artificial slopes and ledges of the much-quarried Clee Hills, and beyond them the whaleback rise of the Long Mynd with its deep, secret 'batches' or clefts and its outlandish crest, the rugged and natural outcrops of the Stiperstones. You could get lost here, in the shadows of a batch or in the demon grasp of Wild Edric the Saxon, who rides out on witchy nights. Geographically the contrast between the west and east of the region is striking, with gently rolling farmlands replacing the uplands. Yet here, too, I discover flashes of the wild in sly elfin faces peeping through stone foliage in an Anglo-Saxon church frieze, or in

Left and below: Prior's Coppice (p. 262). Above: The Roaches (p. 245–6)

the shape of a fox half glimpsed among oxlips and early purple orchids in an old ironstone quarry – not to mention the Bottle-Kicking and Hare Pie Scramble that distributes bumps, bruises, glory and pie in equal measures among the villagers of Hallaton each Easter Monday.

North of Birmingham the heaths and woods of Cannock Chase give way to the high moors of the Peak District. There are fantastic shapes in the weather-contorted limestone of the White Peak, but it is in exploring northwards around the gritstone landscape of the Dark Peak, on Bleaklow and Big Moor, that you will sense the first rigour of a proper northern wildness.

NATIONAL PARK

- Peak District: www.peakdistrict.gov.uk

THE NORTH MIDLANDS

SHROPSHIRE, STAFFORDSHIRE (*inc.* WEST MIDLANDS), DERBYSHIRE, LEICESTERSHIRE, RUTLAND, NOTTINGHAMSHIRE

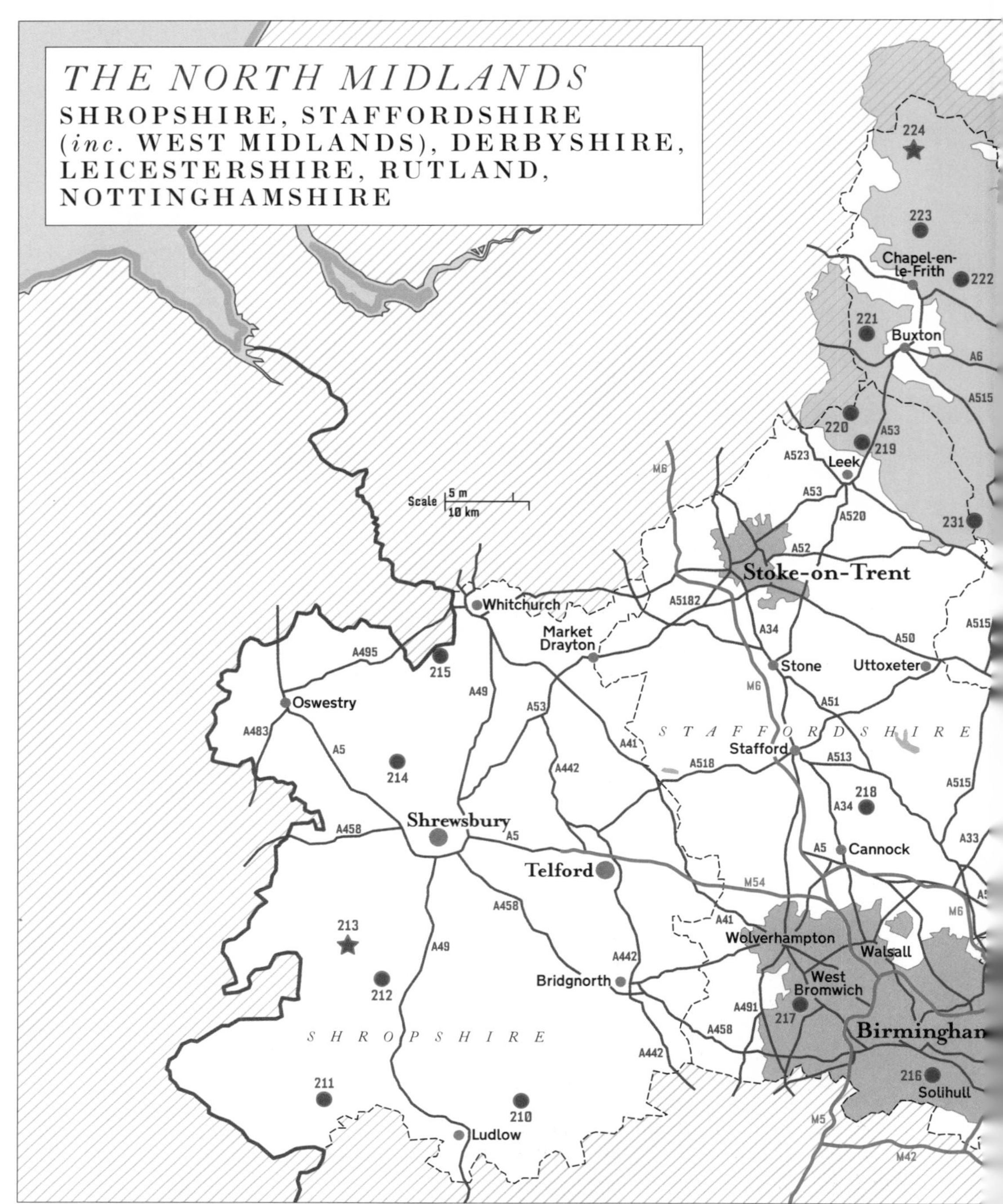

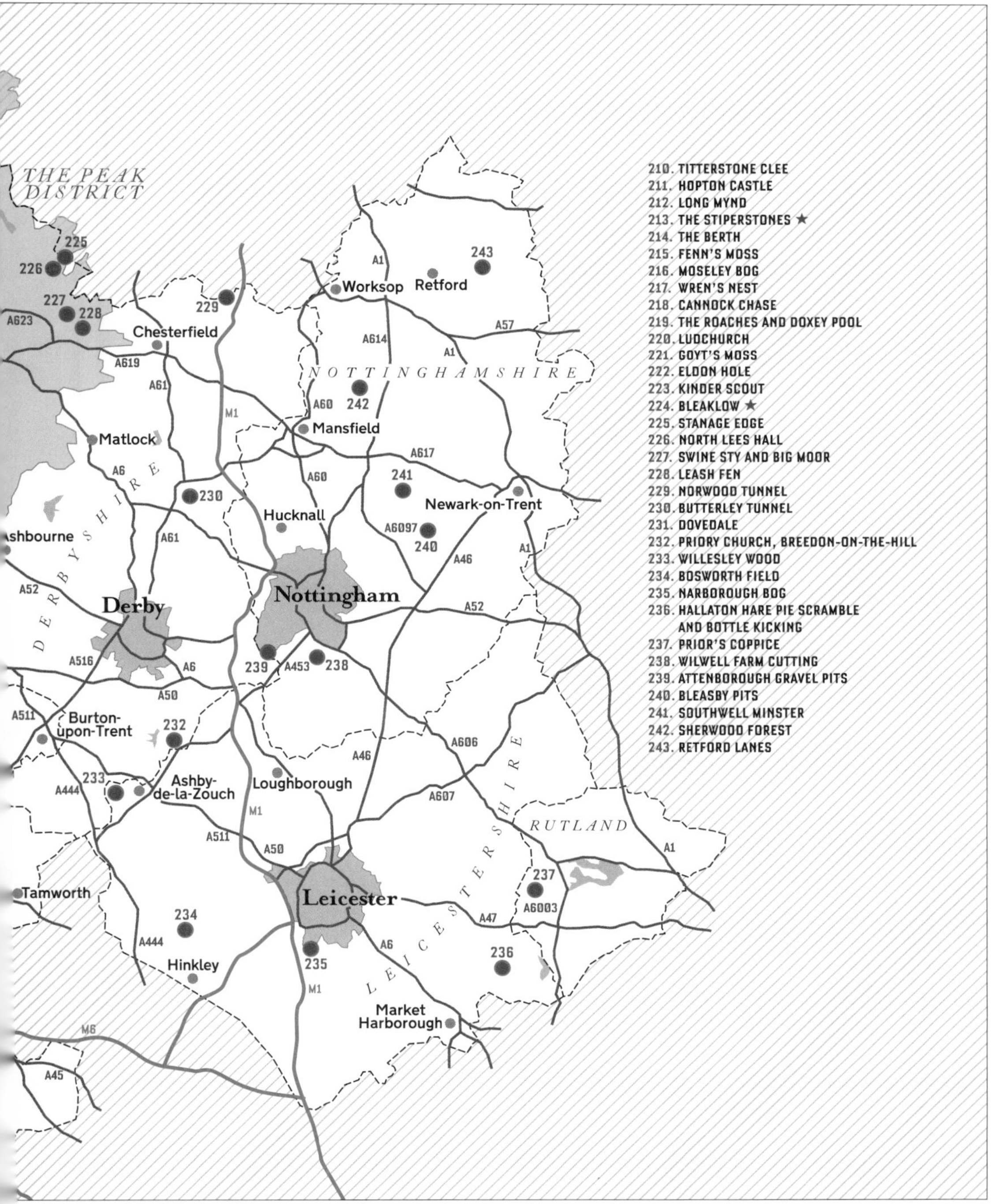
210. TITTERSTONE CLEE
211. HOPTON CASTLE
212. LONG MYND
213. THE STIPERSTONES ★
214. THE BERTH
215. FENN'S MOSS
216. MOSELEY BOG
217. WREN'S NEST
218. CANNOCK CHASE
219. THE ROACHES AND DOXEY POOL
220. LUDCHURCH
221. GOYT'S MOSS
222. ELDON HOLE
223. KINDER SCOUT
224. BLEAKLOW ★
225. STANAGE EDGE
226. NORTH LEES HALL
227. SWINE STY AND BIG MOOR
228. LEASH FEN
229. NORWOOD TUNNEL
230. BUTTERLEY TUNNEL
231. DOVEDALE
232. PRIORY CHURCH, BREEDON-ON-THE-HILL
233. WILLESLEY WOOD
234. BOSWORTH FIELD
235. NARBOROUGH BOG
236. HALLATON HARE PIE SCRAMBLE AND BOTTLE KICKING
237. PRIOR'S COPPICE
238. WILWELL FARM CUTTING
239. ATTENBOROUGH GRAVEL PITS
240. BLEASBY PITS
241. SOUTHWELL MINSTER
242. SHERWOOD FOREST
243. RETFORD LANES
THE PEAK DISTRICT
NOTTINGHAMSHIRE
DERBYSHIRE
LEICESTERSHIRE
RUTLAND
Worksop
Retford
Chesterfield
Mansfield
Matlock
Hucknall
Newark-on-Trent
Ashbourne
Derby
Nottingham
Burton-upon-Trent
Ashby-de-la-Zouch
Loughborough
Leicester
Tamworth
Hinkley
Market Harborough
A1
A57
A614
A623
A619
A61
M1
A60
A617
A6
A6097
A46
A52
A516
A453
A50
A511
A606
A607
A444
A47
A6003
M6
A45

210. TITTERSTONE CLEE, SHROPSHIRE

Maps: OS Explorer 203; Landranger 138

Travel: From A49 Ludlow bypass, A4117 towards Cleobury Mortimer. In 4 miles, left through Dhustone and on up road to car park near summit of Titterstone Clee (OS ref. 594776).

Nearest railway station: Ludlow (5 miles)

There is no getting away from the fact that Titterstone Clee is a weird-looking hill. It appears to have been dumped upside down out of a sandcastle bucket, for its natural configuration is pulled out of shape by levels and terraces jutting out of its flanks, and by greened-over spoil banks that nose out like the hulls of upturned ships. From the flattened top rise 'golf balls' and 'mushrooms', the radar devices of a civil aviation air traffic station.

As you get closer to the summit, you begin to see lakes set in amphitheatres of blasted rock, massive stone and concrete bunkers, platforms and abandoned buildings. There is a striking air of abandonment, obsolescence and desolation, and a breathtaking 50-mile view. Only the occasional flash of colour as a walker crunches up one of the sheep paths offers reassurance that the everyday world is still there.

This alien landscape is the result of centuries of coal, iron ore and copper mining, along with the quarrying of the dark basalt that caps the underlying sandstone. The hamlet of Dhustone below is not only built of this grim rock but also derives its name, 'black stone', from it. The cottage ruins on the slopes of Titterstone are where miners set up as squatters on small parcels of land, sinking one- and two-man pits and hoping for a lucky strike. The faint indentations of holloways scar the common and the lower slopes – these were the 'strakerways' down which the miners' wives carried coal from the pits in baskets on their backs.

211. HOPTON CASTLE, SHROPSHIRE

Maps: OS Explorer 201; Landranger 137

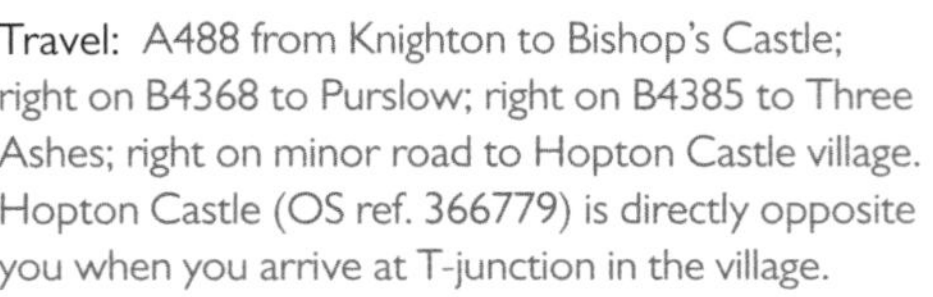
Travel: A488 from Knighton to Bishop's Castle; right on B4368 to Purslow; right on B4385 to Three Ashes; right on minor road to Hopton Castle village. Hopton Castle (OS ref. 366779) is directly opposite you when you arrive at T-junction in the village.

NB: Hopton Castle is private property.

Nearest railway station: Hopton Heath (1½ miles)

Hopton Castle is a place whose history, largely obscure, has been shot through with colour due to one extraordinary incident. Not that mass murder was anything out of the ordinary throughout the turbulent centuries of Border strife between the Welsh and English, but what happened at Hopton Castle during the Civil War took place long after military action between the two countries had come to an end, and even in the context of the Civil War, when antipathy between opponents grew especially sharp, this episode remains particularly barbaric.

The old Norman keep as it stands above its stream today is a modest grey stone structure, overgrown and looking tottery. Its walls, however, were built 10 feet thick, and when a Royalist force arrived to besiege the castle in 1644 the thirty-three members of the Roundhead garrison succeeded in holding off the attackers for three weeks. Offered quarter, the chance to surrender and be allowed to leave unmolested, they refused – a brave gesture of defiance, but a

poor decision. The rules of siege stated that there could be no mercy for defenders who had refused quarter, because the prolonging of the siege and its likely end in a storming of the stronghold would lead to casualties among the besiegers that could have been avoided. So it proved in the case of Hopton Castle, which eventually fell to the Royalist attackers after they had brought cannon up to pound it.

What happened then gave rise to two opposing stories. According to the Royalists, they shot the prisoners; but the Roundhead version was far worse: they claimed that the captives were tied back to back and thrown into the moat, having been hamstrung to prevent them swimming. It amused the victors to watch the maimed men struggle for life, each man striving to push his partner under the water in his own desperation to keep on top and so continue to breathe. One man only was spared this humiliating and appalling end – the garrison commander, Samuel More, who was taken to Hereford Castle and later exchanged for a Royalist prisoner.

Atrocious war crime, or baseless propaganda? It scarcely matters. The story persists, and the grey castle continues to cast its shadow in the quiet green valley.

212. LONG MYND, SHROPSHIRE

Maps: OS Explorer 217; Landranger 137

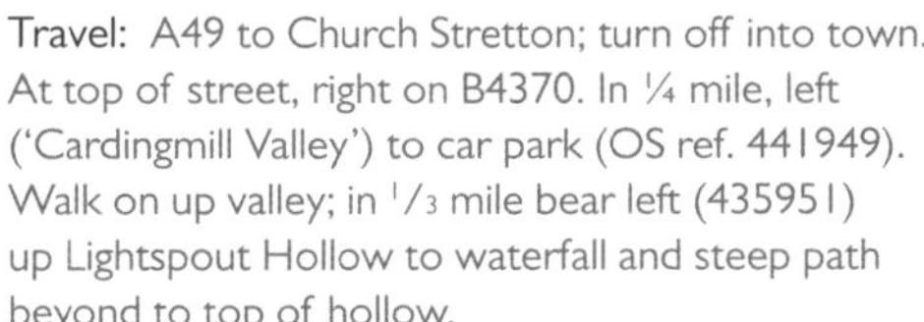

Travel: A49 to Church Stretton; turn off into town. At top of street, right on B4370. In ¼ mile, left ('Cardingmill Valley') to car park (OS ref. 441949). Walk on up valley; in ⅓ mile bear left (435951) up Lightspout Hollow to waterfall and steep path beyond to top of hollow.

A man crawled through thick snowdrifts down the cleft of the Lightspout Hollow on

Long Mynd

a winter afternoon in 1865, nearer dead than alive. He had no boots, no gloves and no hat. He was snow-blind, frost-bitten and bruised from head to toe. The man was Donald Carr, rector of Woolstaston, and he had been out for twenty-four hours in the worst blizzard in living memory.

The Long Mynd, the elongated whaleback of upland hills and moor that lies north and south on the Shropshire border with Wales, attracts threatening weather. It is an uncompromising height of dark vegetation, stunted trees and sudden steep drops into secret valleys. In the kind of snowfall and blasting gale conditions experienced by the hapless Reverend Carr, it becomes deadly. His tremendous account of the ordeal, written to raise money for Woolstaston church restoration funds, was entitled with admirable modesty *A Night in the Snow*. Some night. Some snow.

On 29 January 1865 Donald Carr set out through thick snowdrifts to take a service in the moorland hamlet of Ratlinghope, 4 miles away across the hills. On the way back 'a furious gale came on, driving clouds of snow and icy sleet before it.' Mr Carr soon realized he had lost his way. Darkness was coming on, the blizzard getting worse all the time. He began to stumble and lose his footing, falling down one ravine after another:

> *I found myself shooting at a fearful pace down the side of one of the steep ravines, a fearful glissade down a very precipitous place, and I was whirled round and round in my descent, sometimes head first, sometimes feet first, and again sideways, rolling over and over.*

Carr kept going all through the night, continually falling down and forcing himself up and on, fighting the seductive but fatal desire to lie down and fall asleep. Day dawned, but accurate navigation was still impossible. A thick fog lay over the Long Mynd, and in any case the clergyman was now snow-blind. He blundered into the top of the Lightspout Valley at last, having lost his scarf, hat and gloves, and fell over the waterfall, somehow escaping serious injury. Then he lost his boots.

> *They do not seem to have become unlaced, as the laces were firmly knotted, but had burst in the middle, and the whole front of the boot had been stretched out of shape from the strain put upon it whilst laboriously dragging my feet out of deep drifts for so many hours together, which I can only describe as acting upon the boots like a steam-power boot-jack.*

He stumbled on, walking in his socks on gorse bushes but feeling no pain, his feet completely numbed. At last the exhausted man staggered into the bottom of the Cardingmill Valley and came upon a group of children, who ran away screaming. 'Doubtless,' deadpanned Reverend Carr, 'the head of a man protruding from a deep snow-drift, crowned and bearded with ice like a ghastly emblem of winter, was a sight to cause panic.'

Donald Carr was in severe danger of losing his frost-bitten fingers, but he saved them by rubbing them with cold water for many hours on end. This remarkably tough and sanguine man waited for the gorse prickles to work themselves out of his feet and hands, wrote his little book, and then seems simply to have put the whole terrifying experience behind him.

213. THE STIPERSTONES, SHROPSHIRE

Maps: OS Explorer 217; Landranger 137, 126

Travel: A488 from Bishop's Castle towards Shrewsbury; in 7 miles, right on minor road for 2 miles through Shelve to T-junction (OS ref. 354988). Right for ½ mile to the Bog field centre (356980); left here on minor road (brown 'Stiperstones' sign) towards Bridges. Keep left in ¾ mile; in another ⅓ mile, park in Stiperstones car park (369977) and follow footpath up to Stiperstones.

Many wild places rely on special conditions of weather and light for their atmosphere, the Stiperstones in particular. On mild sunny days there may seem nothing especially wild about these quartzite outcrops on their west Shropshire hilltop. But wreathe them in mist, or in the sinister flickering light of an evening lightning storm, and it is easy to see why they have an ominous reputation.

Cranberry Rock, Manstone Rock, the Devil's Chair, Scattered Rock and Shepherd's Rock: the five craggy tors stand in line astern. They are super-hard quartzite, formed of sandstone under giant pressures and temperatures 500 million years ago, then pushed aloft by the upthrust of volcanic action. They stand in an area now carefully preserved and controlled to help it become a glorious 7-mile stretch of purple heathland once more. The Stiperstones seem alien in the heath, though this does not explain why they have such a hold on the local imagination.

The centrepiece of the group is the Devil's Chair, and most of the legends concern it. They say that the Devil was flying over from Ireland with an apronful of stones, intending to block up Hell Gutter, when his apron

The Stiperstones

strings slipped and the load tumbled to earth to form the Chair. A portion fell away to make the Devil's Window, through which only the bold dare to creep – those who do may come to good or ill, and there is no predicting which. When mist hides the Chair, the Devil is enthroned there waiting for the Stones to sink into the earth, an event which will cause the ruin and end of England.

Other tales concern Wild Edric, the Saxon warrior lord who meets all the ghosts, witches and wizards of Shropshire at the Stiperstones on the winter solstice. Lady Godiva can be heard wailing and mourning as she rides her spirit horse along the Stones by night – her punishment for going hunting when she should have been at church. And then there is Slashrags the tailor, who met the Devil near Cranberry Rock. Old Nick asked the tailor to make him a suit. But Slashrags had spotted the stranger's cloven hooves and long tail, not to mention his 'strong sulphurious smell'. So the canny tailor stalled the Devil, agreeing to meet again at the Stiperstones in seven days. He returned with Mr Brewster the parson, and when Old Nick caught wind of a holy man he vanished in a puff of brimstone, giving out a shriek that could have wakened the dead.

214. THE BERTH, NEAR BASCHURCH, SHROPSHIRE

Maps: OS Explorer 241; Landranger 126

Travel: A5 from Shrewsbury towards Oswestry; right on B4397 through Baschurch; in another ¾ mile, green lane on left leads near the Berth earthwork and pool (OS ref. 430236).

NB: The Berth is on private property, and there is no public access, but you can get a view of the pool and mound from this green lane.

For obscurity of siting and history, the Berth takes some beating. This large earthwork, shaped like an ampersand, lies near Baschurch in gentle farmlands. These low lands would have been marshes back when the Berth was built, in the centuries before the Romans came to Britain. A lower earthen ring is surmounted by a flat-topped, grassy mound, now partly fallen away and clothed with elder bushes. Two promontory arms reach out from this mound, one north-east to terminate in a small circular earthwork, the other south-east to disappear on the brink of a pool shawled in willows and alders, water lilies spread across its surface. The Berth was probably an Iron Age fort, built on top of one of the drumlins, or mounds of rubble, left behind by a melting glacier at the end of the last Ice Age.

The shape of the Berth remains unexplained; as it is a listed monument, English Heritage have so far refused to allow the mound to be excavated, on the grounds that it would permanently damage the site. In 1906 a workman found a bronze cauldron here, perhaps evidence of the Celtic custom of throwing valued vessels into lakes to honour their gods. Naturally, the history of the Berth that archaeology has failed to supply has been plentifully supplemented by myth and legend. According to these the Berth was the site of Pengwern, capital of the princedom of Powys during the Dark Ages and the seat of its court – a Welsh Camelot, in fact, and Welsh Dark Ages history has a dashing hero to rival King Arthur in Prince Cynddylan the Brave.

This whole area around Baschurch was the site of burial for the kings of Powys in the seventh century, when Cynddylan the Brave was killed defending Pengwern from the English during an epic battle in the marshes. Local stories say that a great prince lies buried under a mound on the south slope, his men lying under another near by. The links with the Arthurian story – a heroic king defending a kingdom from alien invaders, his death in a marshland battle and subsequent burial in a holy place – are obvious. Is the Berth the site of 'many-tower'd Camelot'? It seems a fair thought to ponder as you gaze across the dark pool to the old green mound.

215. FENN'S MOSS, SHROPSHIRE/ WALES BORDERS

Maps: OS Explorer 241; Landranger 126

Travel: From A41 Whitchurch bypass, B5476 south towards Wem. In 1¾ miles, right in Tilstock on minor road through Hollinwood to Platt Lane crossroads (OS ref. 514364). Go over, and in 300 yards turn left to find two car parks, one in ½ mile at 504360, the other ¾ mile further on at 493354. Pick up a Reserve leaflet, and follow Mosses Trail on foot.

Nearest railway station: Prees (4 miles)

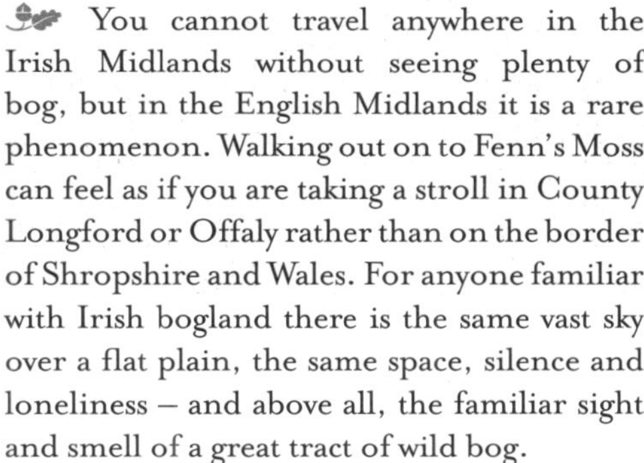

You cannot travel anywhere in the Irish Midlands without seeing plenty of bog, but in the English Midlands it is a rare phenomenon. Walking out on to Fenn's Moss can feel as if you are taking a stroll in County Longford or Offaly rather than on the border of Shropshire and Wales. For anyone familiar with Irish bogland there is the same vast sky over a flat plain, the same space, silence and loneliness – and above all, the familiar sight and smell of a great tract of wild bog.

Fenn's Moss is just one of five neighbouring bogs or mires – the others are Bettisfield, Wem, Whixall and Cadney Mosses – which together make up one big Site of Special Scientific Interest (SSSI). They are 'raised bogs', level plateaux of waterlogged sphagnum moss building up a dense mattress on top of a thick layer of black peat. These bogs formed on acidic ground scraped bare by Ice Age glaciers, where vegetation dries but is very slow to rot. Sphagnum can hold up to twenty times its own weight of water, so the mosses are sodden, sopping places. Silver birch scrub, bracken and heather, cranberry and cross-leaved heath all grow, a stern landscape of sombre colours. Fenn's, Whixall and Bettisfield Mosses together form a National Nature Reserve (NNR), and are crossed by a number of specially maintained Mosses Trails which you can follow on foot.

Fenn's Moss

The mosses seem always to have been cut for peat, originally as fuel and later for horticulture. Raised bogs are living and growing organisms, so some of the evidence of early activity has been swallowed up, but as you squelch along the black peat trails you can distinguish between the various states of the mosses. Here are the neatly squared hollows where 'Whixall Bibles' were cut – turves as small, square and black as Bibles. Here are the irregular banks left by small-scale domestic cutting; there lie the great shallow scars of machine harvesting. All these forms of destruction are now either in the process of being reversed (commercial cutting stopped in 1990) or are already being repaired by nature.

During the Second World War the wide, empty central plain was the site of a Strategic Starfish decoy, an arrangement of combustibles that could be set alight to fool German aeroplanes into bombing the area under the impression they were attacking the burning docks of Liverpool. On the northern edge stands the gaunt old skeleton of the peatworks, complete with its vast pressing and milling machines.

It seems incredible that the mosses could have survived such a long and varied attack by man, but they have. And now that they are designated and managed as SSSI and NNR, you have a better chance than ever of spotting kingfishers and raft spiders along the ditches and pools, breeding curlew and snipe in spring and summer, short-eared owls flapping stiffly on long wings in winter, and big flocks of white-fronted geese spending the dark months far from the stormy chill of their native Greenland.

216. MOSELEY BOG, BIRMINGHAM

Maps: OS Explorer 220; Landranger 139; Birmingham A–Z, p. 91 (5E)

Travel: Sarehole Mill car park (OS ref. 099818) is on Cole Bank Road (B4146), between A34 Stratford Road and Wake Green Road. After visiting Sarehole Mill, cross stream from car park and keep ahead with hedge on left to cross Wake Green Road into Thirlmere Drive. Take second right up Pensby Close; follow it round to left, and entrance to Moseley Bog is on your right (095819).

Nearest railway station: Hall Green (1 mile)

Moseley Bog

If your children (or you) long to follow in the footsteps of Frodo Baggins and his hobbit companions, here is a chance to venture into the miry depths of the Old Forest, home of the jolly sprite Tom Bombadil and lair of that most sinister of treacherous trees, Old Man Willow. When J. R. R. Tolkien, creator of these weird and wonderful beings, was a small boy, living at 264 Wake Green Road in Birmingham, he and his brother would play for hours, day after day, around Sarehole watermill and the neighbouring Moseley Bog. There seems little doubt that the adventures young Tolkien had there, and the fantasies he spun around the willow groves and winding streams on what was then the rural outskirts of the city, bore fruit later in the Old Forest of *The Lord of the Rings*.

It is quite remarkable how this dell of thick woodland, ringing with birdsong and carpeted with bluebells in spring, has survived in the heart of the city. Vigorous campaigning by local enthusiasts in the 1980s beat off approaches by developers who would have built houses here. Paths lead you deep among thickets of carr woodland, past black peaty pools, reed-beds and bog patches. On cold autumn mornings when mist fills the hollow, the willows raise trunks and limbs so eerie in shape that there is no mistaking the origins of Old Man Willow, nor those of the Nazgûl or Ringwraiths when you hear the shriek of a passing crow.

217. WREN'S NEST, DUDLEY, WEST MIDLANDS

Maps: OS Explorer 219; Landranger 139; Birmingham A–Z, p. 54 (1D)

Travel: There are thirteen access points to Wren's Nest; a convenient one is beside the Caves pub in Wrens Hill Road (OS ref. 936922). Numbered Location Posts and information boards are dotted along the main footpath, which runs south from the Caves to make an anticlockwise circuit of the Wren's Nest.

NB: To visit Seven Sisters cavern, contact Senior Warden: www.naturalengland.org.uk.

Nearest railway station: Tipton (1 ½ miles)

The industrial Black Country town of Dudley might seem an unlikely place to be mounting a bid for a UNESCO European Geopark designation, but Dudley contains a most remarkable carboniferous limestone hill. In 1954 the Wren's Nest was designated Britain's first National Nature Reserve, because of its 'exceptional geological and palaeontological features'. Along with the hill's deep-rooted industrial heritage, these features prompted the Wren's Nest designation as a Scheduled Ancient Monument in 2004. The UNESCO bid (unresolved at the time of writing) seeks official recognition of the mile-long hill as unique in Britain.

Wren's Nest

The Wren's Nest rises like a reef from a sea of houses, smothered in trees yet with the scars and holes of extensive quarrying still to be seen. It was this quarrying for limestone to use as flux in ironworks blast furnaces (20,000 tons a year at the height of the Industrial Revolution) that exposed so many rock faces and cave walls, home to a fabulous treasure of fossils laid down some 400 million years ago when Dudley lay in the warm, shallow water of a tropical sea. These tall, smooth planes of rock, some still carrying the print of rippling waves, greet you as you walk a circuit of the hill. The carboniferous limestone is packed with delicately branded crinoids or sea lilies, twin-shelled marine creatures known as brachiopods, and the woodlouse ancestors called trilobites whose star turn, the beautiful ridged *Calymene blumenbachii*, used to be collected by the quarrymen and sold as 'Dudley Bugs'.

It is not just fossils that have given the Wren's Nest its special status. The limestone quarrying produced a unique row of seven caverns with open mouths, separated from each other by precarious pillars of stone left by the quarrymen, all canted at the steep angle of the limestone strata. Eight of the fifteen species of British bats have been noted here. Watching them flying into the hole they use as a portal, like a cloud of smoke being sucked into the hill, is an unforgettable spectacle. Similarly, the flora has flourished since quarrying stopped in the 1920s, and now includes delicate purple autumn gentians, bee orchids and the fuzzy blue buttons of small scabious.

As for what lies under the hill, that is another extraordinary feature – the Wren's Nest canal tunnel system, 3 subterranean miles of it like a Black Country 'Mines of Moria', complete with wharves, branches, passing bays, basins and a tramway system. All now abandoned, the Wren's Nest administration team dreams of revitalizing it to bring visitors here from the Dudley Canal Trust at the Black Country Museum, over in Tipton.

218. CANNOCK CHASE, STAFFORDSHIRE

Maps: OS Explorer 244; Landrangers 127, 128

Travel: West side of Cannock Chase accessible from M6 Junctions 13 and 12; east side from A460 Cannock–Rugeley; south from M6 Toll Road; north from A513 Rugeley–Stafford. There are many parking places round Cannock Chase.

Nearest railway stations: Rugeley (north-east, 2 miles); Stafford (north-west, 5 miles), Penkridge (west, 3 miles)

Cannock Chase

Cannock Chase

The 26 square miles of Cannock Chase have been well described as 'the lungs of the Black Country'. Although this wide area of heath and forest lies beyond the northern fringes of the industrial region, it has always been a vital recreational resource for the people of the dozen or so crowded and busy towns nearby. Joggers, cyclists, walkers and families with picnics rely on the Chase. Yet there remain many lonely stretches of heath, boggy hollows and tracts of woodland, so that you can walk here on a weekday and feel as if you have the place to yourself.

The Bishop of Lichfield had Cannock Chase as his hunting preserve in Norman times. Since then the Chase has been thoroughly exploited. It was grazed and harvested for firewood, then Industrial Revolution iron-makers set up blast furnaces and felled trees to feed them. Sand and gravel extraction rumbled on for centuries. Where the trees were cut and the shoots grazed too short to grow, a broad lowland heath developed. This is the landscape you see today: tracts of heather, bracken and silver birch scrub, cowberry and bilberry and their rare cross-bred offspring, the hybrid or Cannock Chase berry. Staffordshire has lost nine-tenths of its heath in the last 200 years, but here it thrives and is even being reinstated in some places.

219. THE ROACHES AND DOXEY POOL, STAFFORDSHIRE

Map: OS Explorer OL24; Landranger 119

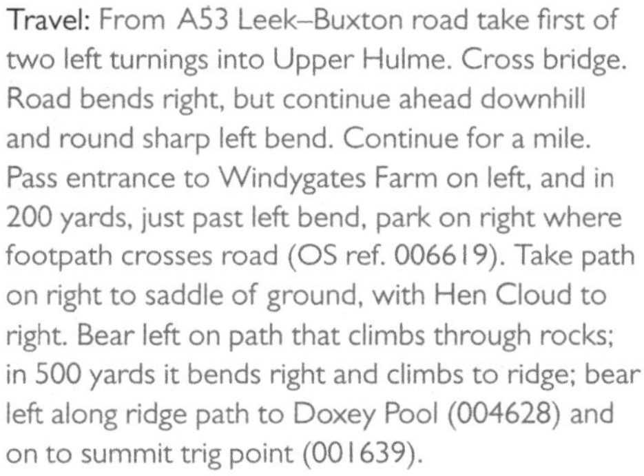

Travel: From A53 Leek–Buxton road take first of two left turnings into Upper Hulme. Cross bridge. Road bends right, but continue ahead downhill and round sharp left bend. Continue for a mile. Pass entrance to Windygates Farm on left, and in 200 yards, just past left bend, park on right where footpath crosses road (OS ref. 006619). Take path on right to saddle of ground, with Hen Cloud to right. Bear left on path that climbs through rocks; in 500 yards it bends right and climbs to ridge; bear left along ridge path to Doxey Pool (004628) and on to summit trig point (001639).

Nearest railway station: Buxton (10 miles)

The Roaches of the Staffordshire moorlands are a wonderful example of millstone grit at its grittiest. This rough escarpment, tremendous in appearance but less than 2 miles long, bares its teeth to the south-west – teeth of coarse grey sandstone, some of them thin blades, some great thick blocks. This is a superb stretch of rock which contains within its small compass some formidable challenges for rock climbers.

Walkers can start with the short climb from the saddle to the crest of Hen Cloud, a southern outlier. Then it's a swoop back down to the saddle and a scrambly climb north through house-sized outcrops canted at 40 degrees in a mirror image of Hen Cloud. Here you get a great impression of the famous 'breaking wave' illusion created by the angle at which the strata of the Roaches lie. The separate formations appear as a line of giant waves on the point of bursting to the north-east.

The path winds in and out of the rocks

The Roaches and Doxey Pool

and up to the ridge, where the prospect opens over a dour, dark heather moorland, beautiful and exhilarating in sunshine, grim and threatening in mist or foul weather. Views west and south across Tittesworth Reservoir and the rolling plain are enormous and uplifting.

The path reaches Doxey Pool in a hollow under sentinel rocks. The pool's shore is of silvery sand, gritstone pulverized by washing and weathering. In the peat-dark waters live two ghouls with a propensity for luring nice young men to their doom – or delight – in the depths. One is a lithe and beautiful mermaid; the other, a notorious hag named Jenny Greenteeth, a monster with green hair and skin who haunts lakes and meres all over Europe under different names, soothing her victims to sleep with caresses from her sharp talons and then devouring them with her long green teeth.

220. LUDCHURCH, STAFFORDSHIRE

Maps: OS Explorer 268; Landranger 118

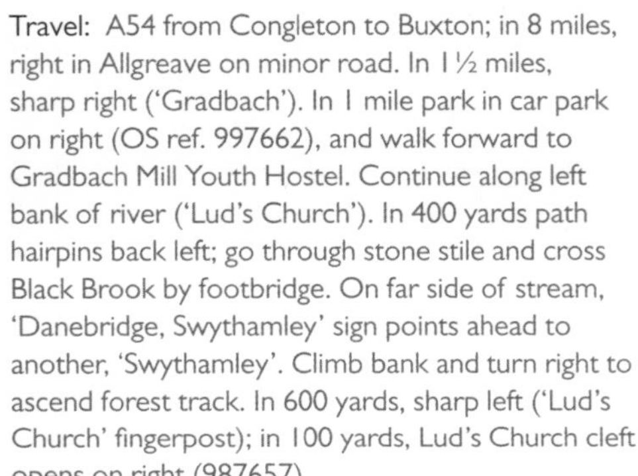

Travel: A54 from Congleton to Buxton; in 8 miles, right in Allgreave on minor road. In 1½ miles, sharp right ('Gradbach'). In 1 mile park in car park on right (OS ref. 997662), and walk forward to Gradbach Mill Youth Hostel. Continue along left bank of river ('Lud's Church'). In 400 yards path hairpins back left; go through stone stile and cross Black Brook by footbridge. On far side of stream, 'Danebridge, Swythamley' sign points ahead to another, 'Swythamley'. Climb bank and turn right to ascend forest track. In 600 yards, sharp left ('Lud's Church' fingerpost); in 100 yards, Lud's Church cleft opens on right (987657).

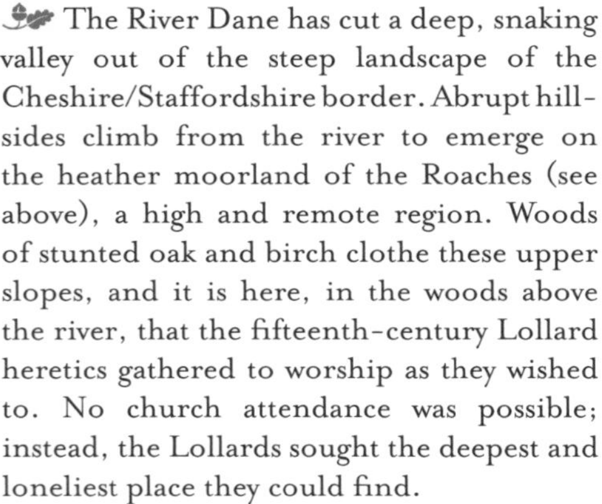

The River Dane has cut a deep, snaking valley out of the steep landscape of the Cheshire/Staffordshire border. Abrupt hillsides climb from the river to emerge on the heather moorland of the Roaches (see above), a high and remote region. Woods of stunted oak and birch clothe these upper slopes, and it is here, in the woods above the river, that the fifteenth-century Lollard heretics gathered to worship as they wished to. No church attendance was possible; instead, the Lollards sought the deepest and loneliest place they could find.

The Lollards were united in their burning desire for religious freedom and the right to worship in plain English rather than stifling Latin. They were a century too early in their nonconformism. The attitudes that would lead to the establishment of the Church of England in the following century were such anathema to the English Catholic Church of the time that the Lollards were imprisoned or killed whenever they were caught. The safe haven they found in the rocks above the River Dane could have been made for the

Ludchurch

purpose – a dark slit in the hillside only 3 feet wide that leads steeply down to the floor of a natural cleft with walls 60 feet high, twisting into the hill for a quarter of a mile in right-angle bends, concealed from all outside eyes. The floor of the canyon is a quagmire; the walls are hung with mats of moss, liverworts, pennywort and luxuriant ferns. A dank, dripping, cold cleft in the earth, silent but ready to echo to any sound, a refuge or a trap, depending on happenstance.

Other stories attach to Lud's Church cleft as naturally as the ferns to the wet rocks: Friar Tuck giving Holy Communion here to Robin Hood; Bonnie Prince Charlie spending a night of discomfort and despair; Squire Trafford of Swythamley Hall pulling his horse up on the bank, then cursing so savagely that he terrified the beast into leaping the chasm. And here is the Green Chapel of *Sir Gawaine and the Green Knight*, where gentle Gawaine was put to the test:

Hit had a hole on the ende, and on ayther side,
And overgrowen with gras in glodes aywhere,
And all was holw inwith ...
'Wee! Lord!' quoth the gentyle knight,
'Here myght aboute mydnight
The Devel his matynes telle.'

221. GOYT'S MOSS, DERBYSHIRE

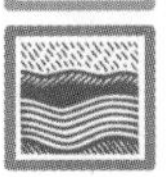

Maps: OS Explorer OL24; Landranger, 119

Travel: A537 from Buxton towards Macclesfield. Just after A54 diverges for Congleton, turn right off A537 ('Derbyshire Bridge only') on moorland road. Right at T-junction in ½ mile ('No Through Road'); in 300 yards, on sharp bend, park in car park (OS ref. 019716). From car park bear right up stony road. In ½ mile cross Berry Clough; in another 200 yards, at top of next rise, left over stile (027722) and walk north on moor path for ¼ mile to cross an east–west path 300 yards east of Berry Clough (026727). From here continue north on to the Access Land of Goyt's Moss.

Nearest railway station: Buxton (2½ miles)

Goyt's Moss has nothing particular by way of especially notable attractions. It is simply a perfect example of the Pennine upland moor which the Countryside and Rights of Way (CROW) Act of 2000 has opened for the pleasure of walkers. A wide, puddled track leads east across the moors from the car park, cobbled for horseshoes and animal hooves to get a better grip. Stone-walled and wide enough to allow two laden wagons to pass each other, the track runs between verges twice as broad, good indicators of a very old road. Walking down

Goyt's Moss

it, the roar of the A537 soon fades under the rush and whistle of moor wind.

To your left, vast tracts of moor roll away in pale grass and darker heather, rising to the long edges of Cat's Tor and Shining Tor beyond the deep cleft of Goyt's Clough. Soon you turn off the road and follow a grassy path through the heather along a breezy ridge. There are glimpses of Buxton to the east, but the elegant spa town seems a million miles removed from this bleak moor. Larks sing out overhead, grouse cackle Go-back! Go-back!, and from Errwood Reservoir comes the faint cackle and whoop of waterfowl. You dip in and out of Berry Clough before walking north over trackless Wild Moor. Plunge into one of the hidden, nameless cloughs that lead north and it is as if the outside world has entirely ceased to exist.

222. ELDON HOLE, DERBYSHIRE

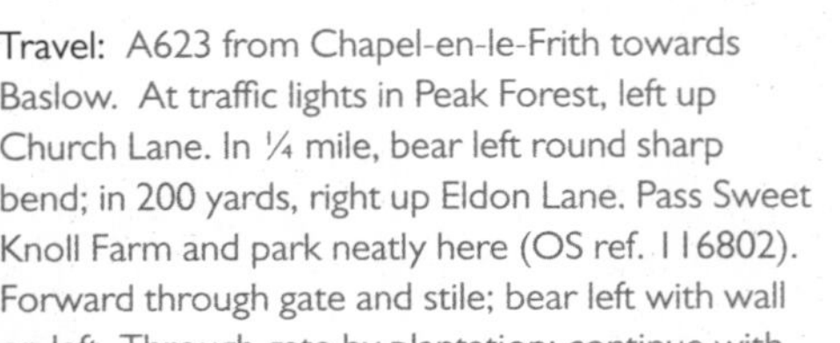

Maps: OS Explorer OL1, OL24; Landranger 110, 119

Travel: A623 from Chapel-en-le-Frith towards Baslow. At traffic lights in Peak Forest, left up Church Lane. In ¼ mile, bear left round sharp bend; in 200 yards, right up Eldon Lane. Pass Sweet Knoll Farm and park neatly here (OS ref. 116802). Forward through gate and stile; bear left with wall on left. Through gate by plantation; continue with wall on left, following track to Eldon Hole (116809).

Eldon Hole has a narrow rocky mouth, a gash in the green hillside that can be seen from a long way off. The largest pothole in the Peak District, it is fenced off to prevent sheep and cattle falling in, but a stile admits you to the very brink where a hollow basin allows you to crouch in comparative safety and peer over the edge. Beware! A slip here would be fatal – particularly as the hole, according to local tales, is bottomless. The walls fall away into the hill some 15 feet apart, narrowing as they pass out of sight about 100 feet down. Mosses, ivy and liverworts blanket the rock; ferns and spurges sprout in the damp crevices. A few metal rings fixed far down in the rock walls glint out of the depths, legacy of some intrepid potholer.

How deep is Eldon Hole? In 1697 Celia Fiennes wrote that you could throw a stone in and hear it strike the sides for a long time. Daniel Defoe in the early 1720s declared it 'a frightful chasm, or opening in the earth ... it has no bottom, that is to say, none that can yet be heard of.' Measured in 1780 by the first person actually to descend (voluntarily), the hole was declared to be 269 feet deep. That did not inhibit the story-makers, though. There is something fantastic about such a mighty crack in the ground, perhaps the knowledge that our own death is only a step away, or maybe the very evident connotations of the damp, bushy cleft – a nuance obvious to our ancestors long before Sigmund Freud came on the scene. Locals knew that anyone foolhardy enough to venture down it on the end of a rope would either be scorched in the fires of Hell, or would be drawn up again a madman. 'What Nature meant,' mused Defoe, 'in leaving this window open into the infernal world, if the place lies that way, we cannot tell. But it must be said, there is something of horror upon the imagination, when one does but look into it.'

223. KINDER SCOUT, DERBYSHIRE

Maps: OS Explorer OL1; Landranger 110

Travel: A624 from Glossop towards Chapel-en-le-Frith; in Hayfield, left to Bowden Bridge car park (OS ref. 049869). Continue ahead on foot up Kinder Road; by Kinder Reservoir zigzag left, then right (052883) along White Brow, ascending William Clough to cross Pennine Way National Trail at Ashop Head (063902). You can make a superb 9-mile circuit by turning right and following Pennine Way south along Kinder Edge by Kinder Downfall (083889), then on to turn right at Edale Cross (077861), down Oaken Clough and Coldwell Clough.

Nearest railway station: New Mills (4 miles)

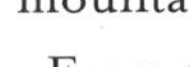 Kinder Scout is a wild place on two counts – first, as a classic piece of high, windswept and rain-sodden moorland; second, as the scene of the most famous confrontation in rambling history, a face-off that led to the eventual enshrinement in law of a walker's right to roam freely over mountain, moorland and heath.

From the valley path above Kinder Reservoir, Kinder Edge appears as a high green wall on your right hand, a circle of crags forming its ramparts. This prospect both captivated and tantalized the thousands of young workers of Sheffield and Manchester in the 1930s. After a long week's graft in their factories or offices on low wages and with pinched living conditions at home, the only affordable pleasure they had to look forward to was rambling in the countryside at weekends. Yet the empty moors around Kinder Scout belonged to the Duke of Devonshire, whose gamekeepers were under orders to repel any trespassers. The ramblers – especially the young communists and socialists of the British Workers' Sports Federation – didn't see why so much open land should be kept for the exclusive pleasure of a handful of grouse-shooters on a handful of days each year.

The long cleft of William Clough rises like a rocky staircase to Ashop Head. This was where a party of ramblers some 500 strong was headed when they set out on a well-advertised Mass Trespass on Sunday 24 April 1932. They came up the hillside spread out in a long wave, in order to frustrate the gamekeepers and a posse of water company bailiffs who were waiting to turn them back. Most of the confrontations occurred on Nab Brow, just to the west of William Clough. Newspaper reports the next day spoke luridly of hand-to-hand combat, busted crowns and broken limbs. But those ramblers who were there say that the only damage was a twisted ankle incurred by one of the keepers, and that most of the encounters ended with the gamekeepers simply being shoved aside.

Kinder Scout

Up on Ashop Head the Manchester ramblers met another party of trespassers who had come from Sheffield. Ashop Head is a fine wild spot, a sedgy saddle of ground under the peak of Scout End. From here you can do in perfect legality what the trespassers could not: climb up to the cairn on Scout End, and then walk the whole length of Kinder Edge, looking out on heavenly views across the plains of Cheshire and South Lancashire towards the Welsh hills. Or you can march on east across Kinder Scout itself, a maze of peat hags, bogs and trackless heather over which the Pennine Way used to flounder until it was relocated to Kinder Edge.

As for the Manchester ramblers, six were arrested after the crowd had dispersed, and four received jail sentences for riotous assembly. There was widespread indignation at their treatment. The publicity surrounding the Mass Trespass increased awareness of the open access cause, and led to the formation of the Ramblers Association in 1935. Sixty-five years of lobbying followed, before the Countryside and Rights of Way (CROW) Act of 2000 opened these places to all. Kinder is the place to stand and appreciate it.

224. BLEAKLOW, DERBYSHIRE

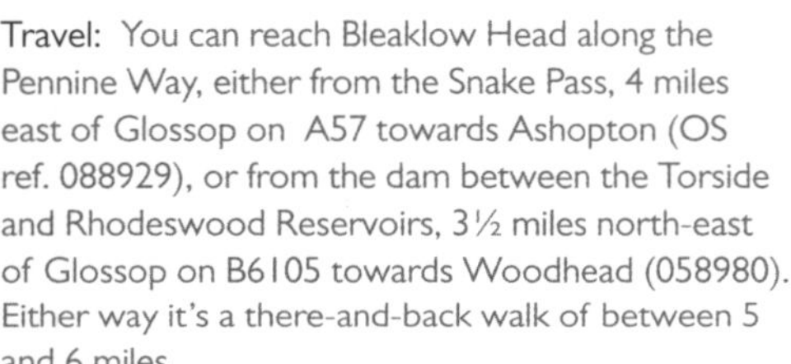

Maps: OS Explorer OL1; Landranger 110

Travel: You can reach Bleaklow Head along the Pennine Way, either from the Snake Pass, 4 miles east of Glossop on A57 towards Ashopton (OS ref. 088929), or from the dam between the Torside and Rhodeswood Reservoirs, 3½ miles north-east of Glossop on B6105 towards Woodhead (058980). Either way it's a there-and-back walk of between 5 and 6 miles.

Nearest railway station: Glossop

'Nature in the raw,' says the master maker of walking guidebooks, Alfred Wainwright, of Bleaklow in his *Pennine Way Companion*. 'An inhospitable wilderness of peat bogs. Nobody loves Bleaklow. All who are on it are glad to get off.'

This is a fairly justifiable view of Bleaklow if you have followed the Pennine Way across it in mist, rain or other dirty weather. 'This section,' warns Wainwright, 'is commonly considered the toughest part of the Pennine Way. It is certainly mucky, too often belaboured by rain and wind, and weird and frightening in mist. But cheer up. There is worse to follow.'

Bleaklow's moor encapsulates the Pennines at their wildest. You need to be good with a compass and map if you are planning to stray far off the Pennine Way. The whole of Bleaklow is now Access Land, and therefore open to anyone to walk where he or she pleases. There are staked paths that wander across the wilderness – for this is a wilderness, where the hand of man lies hardly at all. But to get to remote parts such as Grains in the Water or White Stones is a serious undertaking. Lashing rain and driving mist can descend very quickly and leave you stranded a long way from the nearest road.

Walking the Pennine Way to Bleaklow Head in powder snow on a clear winter's day is a fine way to appreciate this wild moor. The streams in Hern Clough and Torside Clough are half frozen into spun glass, the grass crunches under your boots and mountain hares in coats of creamy white sprint for cover. The Wain Stones, a pair of gritstone boulders whose adjacent faces have been so carved by wind and rain that they resemble a kissing couple, sparkle with mica fragments as they lean together out of the snow. Bleaklow Head when you get to it is a bit of a disappointment as a summit, marked only by a weather-beaten wooden post stuck into a cairn of rubbly stones. But at 2,060 feet it is the highest place on the moor, and your reward is a tremendous view encompassing Holme TV mast, Black Hill, Black Tor in the east, the long ridge of Kinder Scout in the south (see pp. 249–50), and Manchester in the south-west with a sluggish yellow shawl of pollution pulled over its head. Out here in the middle of Bleaklow, on this winter day, you stand and breathe air that is as cold, sweet and pure as the moors can make it.

225. STANAGE EDGE, DERBYSHIRE

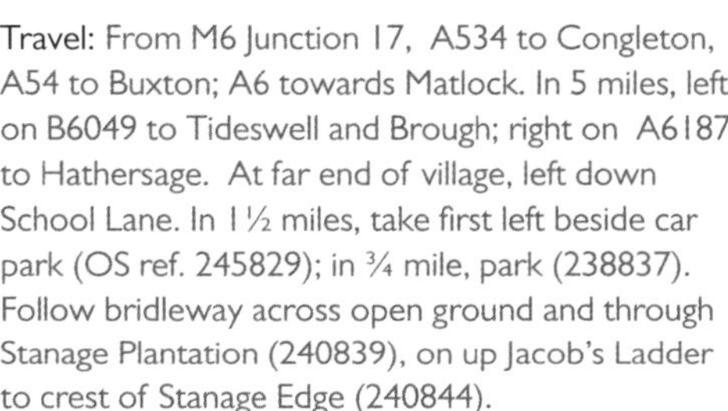

Maps: OS Explorer OL1; Landranger 110

Travel: From M6 Junction 17, A534 to Congleton, A54 to Buxton; A6 towards Matlock. In 5 miles, left on B6049 to Tideswell and Brough; right on A6187 to Hathersage. At far end of village, left down School Lane. In 1½ miles, take first left beside car park (OS ref. 245829); in ¾ mile, park (238837). Follow bridleway across open ground and through Stanage Plantation (240839), on up Jacob's Ladder to crest of Stanage Edge (240844).

Nearest railway station: Hathersage (2½ miles by footpaths)

Of all the gritstone edges on the Peak District Moors, Stanage Edge is probably the most popular and best frequented. It's easy to understand why. Here are 4 miles of superb crags, a dark wall of rock 80 to 100 feet high forming a majestic south-westerly curve, bleak moors beyond, and with gloriously beautiful lowlands at its feet. The rough adhesive gritstone, weathered into vertical and horizontal cracks, might have been forged specifically with climbers in mind. From its edge are mind-boggling views. From its wall ascend thermals ideal for hang-gliding and paragliding. It is within easy reach of the million city-dwellers of Sheffield and Manchester. So if you want a place of solitude, somewhere to be face to face with nature and with no one else, Stanage Edge on a weekend of decent weather is not really the place to go.

But come here in lowering cloud or on a murky day of threatened rain and you will see the lonely, frightening side of Stanage Edge. The gritstone darkens, as does the heather and the peaty soil, and if you stride along the full length of the ramparts in a chilly Pennine blow you'll find that walkers are few and far between. The wind streams the pale grasses of White Path Moss and Friar's Ridge so that it looks as if the whole moor is in motion. You can head out along the Roman road called the Long Causeway towards Redmires Reservoirs, or make the long circuit via Burbage Rocks and the craggy, flat-topped hillocks of Higger Tor and Carl Wark. No matter where you head to, these rocks and moors are electrically exhilarating on a wild day – the wilder, the better.

The rocks of Stanage Edge are also famous throughout the introverted, macho and phenomenally athletic world of climbing. The legendary Joe Brown and Don Whillans, both Manchester boys, cut their teeth on these harsh crags, and any northern climbers worth their salt come to climb the gullies of Goliath's Groove or Agony Crack.

226. NORTH LEES HALL, DERBYSHIRE

Maps: OS Explorer OL1; Landranger 110

Travel: From M6 Junction 17, A534 to Congleton. A54 to Buxton, A6 towards Matlock; B6049 via Tideswell and Brough to A6187; right to Hathersage. Footpath via St Michael and All Angels Church (OS ref. 234818) and Cowclose Farm (234829) to North Lees Hall (235834).

NB: North Lees Hall is private property.

Nearest railway station: Hathersage (1½ miles)

Approaching North Lees Hall along the footpath from Cowclose Farm you see the old house at its most impressive, backed by the edge of the high gritstone moorlands of north Derbyshire. This three-storey tower, square and imposing, was built in the 1590s for merchant William Jessop. The hall appears to be all tower; it is not until you have passed it on the stony path that you see the rest of the range crouched below and behind the tower. There are large stone-mullioned windows. The house exudes an air of security and solidarity, not of the grimness that attaches to other tower houses – Northumbrian pele towers, for example – in similarly wild upland settings.

The old hall struck a chord with Charlotte Brontë when she came walking this way in 1845, while on a visit to her best friend, Ellen Nussey, in nearby Hathersage. The parson's daughter from the West Yorkshire moors absorbed the image of the tower, and took note of the local landowning name of Eyre. When Charlotte returned to Haworth Parsonage, *Jane Eyre* began to take shape. On a misty night in Charlotte's teeming fancy, young Jane would approach Thornfield, the house where the saturnine Mr Rochester dwelt with his stark-mad wife: 'It was three stories high, of proportions not vast, though considerable; a gentleman's manor-house, not a nobleman's seat: battlements round the top gave it a picturesque look.'

Those battlements were the setting for one of the wildest scenes in literature. At the end of the book Jane arrives once more at Thornfield Hall, to find it a fire-blackened ruin. She hears from the landlord of the Rochester Arms how poor mad Mrs Rochester made her final appearance on the roof of Thornfield Hall:

> *'She was on the roof, where she was standing, waving her arms above the battlements, and shouting out till they could hear her a mile off ... She was a big woman, and had long black hair: we could see it streaming against the flames as she stood ... Mr Rochester ascended through the skylight. We saw him*

approach her; and then, ma'am, she yelled and gave a spring, and the next minute she lay smashed on the pavement.'

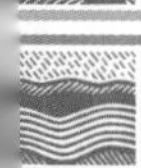

227. SWINE STY AND BIG MOOR, DERBYSHIRE

Maps: OS Explorer OL24; Landranger 119

Travel: A623 Chapel-en-le-Frith towards Baslow; left at Calver; cross River Derwent and turn immediately left. Don't take left-hand of two roads, but keep ahead ('Curbar Lane'). In 1 mile, round sharp right bend; in another 1/3 mile, park in Curbar Gap car park at top of hill on left (OS ref. 262747). Walk through gate on right of car park ('Access Land'); follow track round corner of wall. Look right to see several walled fields across a valley; head for the top right-hand corner of these (288751). From here bear right (three-way fingerpost); Swine Sty is to your left in 200 yards. Return and follow escarpment of White Edge north for 2 miles to the Hurkling Stone (287778).

Nearest railway station: Grindleford (5 miles)

The gritstone moors of Derbyshire are deceptive, often smuggling their treasures away behind a dip in the land or beyond a wall of crags. Swine Sty's seven circles are hidden below bracken and heather, and it takes a sharp eye and a bit of time to tease out the shapes of the late Stone Age settlement from the surrounding landscape. Stones stick out here and there from the horseshoes of grass that betray their locations. The people of Swine Sty made polished rings of shale and delicate flint tools; they grew crops, too, in fields whose boundaries they made from the stones they cleared from the land. The bog, encroaching as the climate worsened some 4,000 years ago, put paid to these fields, though the settlement continued to be occupied for 1,000 years more.

Swine Sty and Big Moor

The path that takes you north from Swine Sty up the escarpment of White Edge gradually reveals the long flank of the aptly named Big Moor to the east. This is all Access Land open to the walker, a brown-and-cream upland that sweeps away to low horizons. Out in the moor, gritstone outcrops stand sculpted by the wind and rain. The Hurkling Stone at the northern end of the edge is the most dramatic, a great boulder perched precariously on a column. The coarse surface of these outcrops is rough to the touch and adhesive enough to hold a slippery boot-sole well. The cracks in the gritstone are filled with wind-blown peat in which heather, mosses and tiny scarlet-tipped lichens flourish, miniature rock gardens in a wide barren landscape.

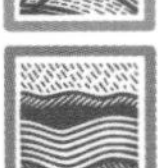

228. LEASH FEN, DERBYSHIRE

Maps: OS Explorer OL24; Landranger 119

Travel: A621 Baslow towards Sheffield; in 2 miles, right ('Cutthorpe, Chesterfield'). In 1½ miles, just before Clod Hall Farm, look for field gate on right and walker's gate opposite it on left (OS ref. 294728). There is just room to park on the verge here. Go through walker's gate on left and follow overhead wires. At second pole turn left along watercourse into the heart of Leash Fen.

Nearest railway station: Chesterfield (6 miles)

Leash Fen is very tough going underfoot. This great flat bog of heather, gorse and coarse grass is composed of tussocks that are hard and stumbly in dry conditions, heavy and sticky after rain. The whole fen is waterlogged, and is becoming more so as dams are inserted to maintain the water levels and attract frogs, dragonflies and water voles to the brimming ditches and ponds. Black peat underlies the tussocks, with long cushions of brilliant green star moss breaking up the endless sombre pale brown of the vegetation. Further away the fen is fringed by scrubby wood of silver birch, hazel and alder. Curlew are heard bubbling, snipe zigzag away. Rarities occur here: a great white egret – extremely rare in Europe – has been spotted flying low over the fen.

Leash Fen is a place to walk cautiously, a sedgy, sodden, secretive wetland, silent and deserted. It may indeed hold secrets, for there have always been tales of a town sunk under the fen.

When Chesterfield was gorse and broom,
Leash Fen was a market town.
Now Chesterfield's a market town,
Leash Fen is but gorse and broom.

Leash Fen

There certainly were Iron Age townships on the moors near by. In the 1830s workers digging a drain across Leash Fen unearthed pottery and pieces of worked oak; and recently a core taken from the fen suggested that crops were being grown and animals grazed here from the second to the first millennium BC. Now that Leash Fen is a nature reserve, though, the possibility of a full-scale excavation of this strange place seems remote.

229. NORWOOD TUNNEL, DERBYSHIRE

Maps: OS Explorer 278; Landranger 120

Travel: From M1 Junction 31, A57 towards Sheffield. At first roundabout, left ('Clowne, Wales') on A618. In 1 mile pass under railway bridge; next left ('South Anston') across M1 into Wales village. Right by war memorial to pass church. Where road bends sharp left and right, your footpath continues ahead beside

High Cottage (OS ref. 477825 – fingerpost). Park just beyond at gates of cemetery, and follow path. It soon dips to turn right under M1. On far side bear right, then left along field edge ('Cuckoo Way' arrows). At corner of wood (475819) keep ahead along field edge. Disused canal and tunnel entrance are visible down to your left in the wood.

Nearest railway station: Kiveton Bridge (1½ miles)

Within traffic murmur of the M1 this eerie site lies in a hollow inside a wood, a piece of eighteenth-century man-made technology staggeringly sophisticated for its day, now run completely wild. Ground ivy, moss and wild garlic blanket the banks and bluebells smother the floor of the abandoned cutting that the navvies dug, and warblers perch to sing on the fallen tree boughs that stick up out of the black water of the canal basin at the entrance to Norwood Tunnel.

The Chesterfield Canal was built in the 1760s to carry iron ore from the Peak District mines to the ironworks, and lasted for the best part of 200 years. For the second half of its life it was a dead man walking, starved of investment and trade by the coming of the infinitely more successful railways. As with Butterley Tunnel on the Cromford Canal (see below), the Norwood Tunnel, 2,895 yards long, was always the suspect part of the operation; it was built without a towpath so that bargees had to 'leg' through, lying on their backs and pushing the boat along by shoving at the tunnel walls and roof with their feet. When the roof collapsed in 1908, no money could be found to repair it. The canal limped on, cut in half but still just alive, until complete closure in the 1950s.

The surface of the canal, no more disturbed by narrowboats, lies green and thick with algae, occasionally furrowed by water boatmen and pond skaters. Rotting branches rise from the still, treacly water, giving the hollow the appearance of a swamp. Brambles and strings of ivy hang off the brickwork of the tunnel mouth, and in the silence of the wood you can now and then hear a soft, echoing 'plop' from inside the hill as another stalactite or fragment of brick detaches itself in the dark.

Norwood Tunnel

230. BUTTERLEY TUNNEL, DERBYSHIRE

Maps: OS Explorer 259; Landranger 120

Travel: From M1 Junction 28, A38 towards Alfreton. In 2½ miles, left on B600 ('Somercotes'). In 1 mile, right into Leabrooks; in ½ mile, left through Riddings. In ¾ mile where road bends sharp left, keep ahead for ¾ mile into dip, and park at Newlands Inn (OS ref. 423513). Please ask permission and give the pub your custom. Just beyond pub, turn right along footpath into canal cutting to reach Butterley Tunnel mouth (422513).

Nearest railway station: Alfreton (4 miles)

Butterley Tunnel lies deep in the trees in a basin choked with silt, its two stepped spillways still trickling water into the cutting. When the Cromford Canal opened in 1794 this 2,966-yard-long tube through the hill carried all manner of industrial goods – limestone, lead and iron for the factories, cotton for the mills – with a speed and efficiency that horses and heavy carts could not match. The Butterley Ironworks was sited above the tunnel; the cannon and cannonballs it made would be lowered through shafts directly into the barges waiting below for onward transportation.

After fifty years the Cromford Canal became obsolete. The railways, with their hugely greater speed and carrying capacity had stolen the show. When the Butterley Tunnel roof collapsed in 1900 the tunnel was closed; another fall in 1907 sealed its fate. The run-down and truncated canal ghosted on until complete closure in 1944. Now its cutting and basin are full of wren and garden warbler song, a forest of hart's tongue ferns droops from the tunnel face, and kingfishers fly in and out of the rusty grille that secures it. Sycamore suckers force the stones and bricks apart in a silent, motionless struggle of which there can be only one winner.

Butterley Tunnel

At the top of the spillway the reservoir that fed the canal is now a wide bowl of wet marshland full of reedmace and great willowherb. Marsh marigolds cluster the rim, and swallows hawk low over the water. It is as peaceful as can be in these woods where nature is completing her triumph over the works of our forebears (see Norwood Tunnel, pp. 254–5).

231. DOVEDALE, DERBYSHIRE/ STAFFORDSHIRE BORDERS

Maps: OS Explorer OL 24; Landranger 119

Travel: A523 or A515 from north, A52 from east or west, to Ashbourne. From here follow brown 'Dovedale' signs through Thorpe to Dovedale car park (OS ref. 147509). Follow footpath north into Dovedale.

Dovedale is the showpiece dale of the White Peak, a dramatically deep and sinuous cleft with Derbyshire on its east rim and Staffordshire on its west, from whose depths rise pinnacles of naked rock 100 feet tall and more. The River Dove has cut this great gorge, wearing gradually down through the limestone. The Dove is a gentle, sparkling trout stream, the lovely lazy fishing river that so powerfully attracted the London ironmonger Izaak Walton in the mid seventeenth century. Walton immortalized this aspect of the Dove in his classic guide to fishing, philosophy and the art of good living, *The Compleat Angler*. But the Dove can be hawkish, too, after prolonged heavy rain, becoming a thunderous sluice of brown floodwater that causes the pinnacles of Dovedale to tremble and rushes many feet higher than the footpath through the dale.

Dippers are a great feature of this lively river, perching on stones with their brilliant white bibs bobbling up and down before diving in to walk upstream underwater in search of grubs and other river invertebrates. The waterside path runs north to rise to the bald rock outcrop of Lover's Leap, scene of a tragedy in July 1761 when Dean Langton of Clogher – perhaps showing off to his companion, Miss La Roche – urged his horse too near the edge and fell off. The clergyman was killed; the lady survived with shock and bruises. Her long hair, becoming entangled in a bramble, brought her up short as she fell. The horse walked away unhurt.

There is a fine view from Lover's Leap over to the Staffordshire bank and the rock pinnacles known romantically as the Twelve Apostles. Upriver the sharp teeth of Tissington Spires rise against the sky from the Derbyshire rim of the gorge. Walking on up the dale you pass the 40-foot arch of Reynard's Cave and the twin hollows of Dove Holes.

There are several side dales on the Staffordshire bank by which to climb out of Dovedale. Hall Dale is the pick of them, with cowslips and early purple orchids on the slopes in spring. Or you can walk on up to the division of the dale into Biggin Dale and Wolfscote Dale, both superb, sinuous clefts that gradually ease you up to ground level some 400 feet higher than when you started at the foot of Dovedale, 7 spectacular miles to the south.

232. PRIORY CHURCH, BREEDON-ON-THE-HILL, LEICESTERSHIRE

Maps: OS Explorer 245; Landranger 129

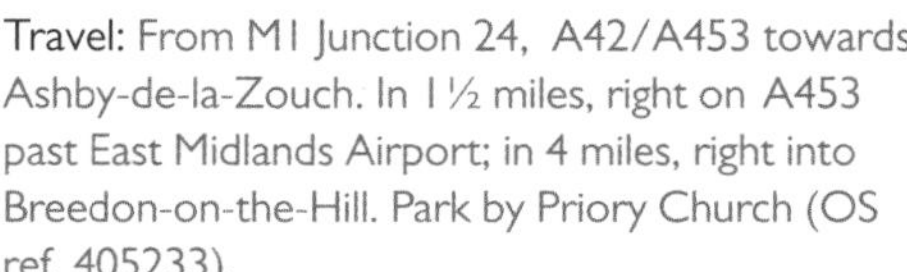

Travel: From M1 Junction 24, A42/A453 towards Ashby-de-la-Zouch. In 1½ miles, right on A453 past East Midlands Airport; in 4 miles, right into Breedon-on-the-Hill. Park by Priory Church (OS ref. 405233).

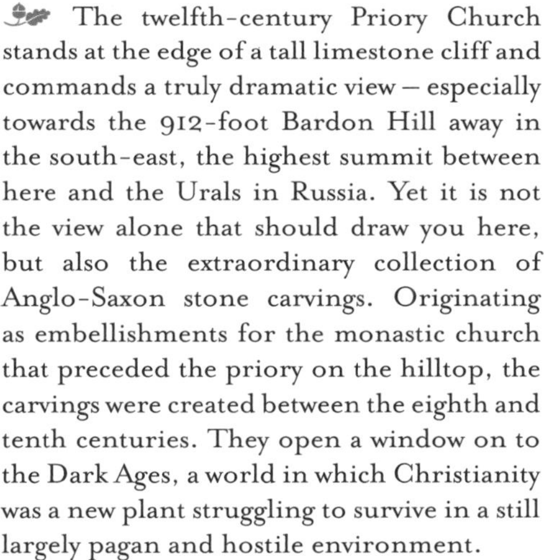

The twelfth-century Priory Church stands at the edge of a tall limestone cliff and commands a truly dramatic view – especially towards the 912-foot Bardon Hill away in the south-east, the highest summit between here and the Urals in Russia. Yet it is not the view alone that should draw you here, but also the extraordinary collection of Anglo-Saxon stone carvings. Originating as embellishments for the monastic church that preceded the priory on the hilltop, the carvings were created between the eighth and tenth centuries. They open a window on to the Dark Ages, a world in which Christianity was a new plant struggling to survive in a still largely pagan and hostile environment.

We know nothing of the carvers, not even if they were local lay people or monks, or if they were commissioned from elsewhere. Their work was certainly inspired by the great contemporary Celtic monastic illustrators from the north, who were producing such masterpieces as the Lindisfarne Gospels (see pp. 364–5). But also among the carvings we also find the staring eyes so characteristic of Byzantine art. The Anglo-Saxon kingdom of Mercia in which Breedon lay was at the zenith of its power at that time, and the elaborate, costly and sophisticated artworks of the newly established monastery reflected that.

Many of the carvings form a frieze that runs in segments along the nave. Warriors and huntsmen step through the leaves, some openly, some lurking. Long-tailed birds peck at bunches of grapes; others strut and display before each other, flapping their wings and walking on tiptoe. Fabulous gryphon-like beasts disport themselves with beaks as sharp as shears. Mounted warriors spur with spears towards a group of troll-like figures on foot. A beautiful lion grins as he raises a spring-shaped tail. A naked Eve, her long hair trailing down her back, reaches for a fruit from the Tree of Knowledge while Adam looks on.

In contrast stand other figures under arches – a wide-eyed Virgin, obscure saints bearing scrolls and books, all rather stiff and formal compared with the woodland charivari of the frieze. The highest expression of order and calm comes with the lovely carving of the Breedon Angel, sited between two windows in the tower chamber, probably from around AD 800. The angel gives a Byzantine blessing with the ring finger of the right hand touching the thumb tip. The wings are folded to fit under an arch, and one foot peeps out from under the heavy folds of robes. Woodland frolics would be unthinkable in the presence of such a serene, authoritative figure. Yet angels themselves are a pretty wild idea.

233. WILLESLEY WOOD, LEICESTERSHIRE

Maps: OS Explorer 245; Landranger 128

Travel: M42, A42 to Junction 12; on B4116 follow 'Ashby' and 'Willesley'. On right-hand bend on southern outskirts of Ashby-de-la-Zouch, left ('Willesley') for 1½ miles to crossroads. Turn left ('No Through Road') and park here (OS ref. 336146). Willesley Wood lies on both sides of the road.

Willesley Wood might currently look like a very eco-friendly municipal park, but it is a modern phenomenon, a wild place in the making. Even now, strolling along the newly mown pathways between ranks of saplings, glimpsing the newly created lake between the willow and cherry stems, you could believe you were in some edge-of-town estate gifted to the corporation by a rich benefactor. This must have been how the parks at Blenheim Palace or Holkham Hall looked a couple of decades after being landscaped by Capability Brown.

The wood is part of the National Forest, a great scheme to restore to nature a long swathe of industrially scarred countryside through the Midlands. Deep coal mining went on here from the early Middle Ages until the 1880s, and opencast thereafter until 1953. Parts were ancient woodland reduced by clearance and grazing to heathland; other parts were under crops or grass. In the 1980s, collapsing mining levels underground produced a large hollow on the surface, which filled and became a lake. The stage was set for the National Forest to begin planting, and the process was enriched and taken forward when the Woodland Trust bought 140 acres of the site.

Plantings include wild cherry, goat willow,

Willesley Wood

pedunculate and sessile oak, dog rose and guelder rose, blackthorn and buckthorn, silver and downy birch – all native English species. Birds flock here: blackcaps and treecreepers in the trees, grasshopper warblers and yellowhammers round the margins, great crested grebe and reed bunting around the lake. Garlic mustard, marsh marigold, harebells, marsh thistle and southern marsh orchid all thrive. What at present still looks rather new and thin will soon become a dense, rich, wild ecosystem in its own right.

234. BOSWORTH FIELD, LEICESTERSHIRE

Maps: OS Explorer 232; Landranger 140

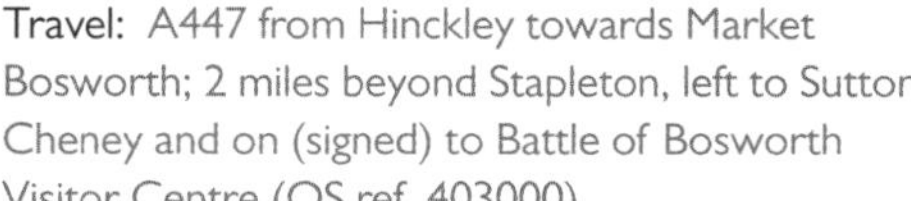

Travel: A447 from Hinckley towards Market Bosworth; 2 miles beyond Stapleton, left to Sutton Cheney and on (signed) to Battle of Bosworth Visitor Centre (OS ref. 403000).

Nearest railway station: Hinckley (7 miles)

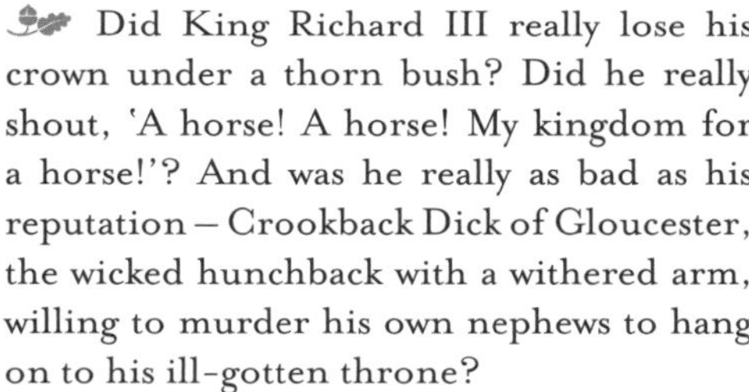

Did King Richard III really lose his crown under a thorn bush? Did he really shout, 'A horse! A horse! My kingdom for a horse!'? And was he really as bad as his reputation – Crookback Dick of Gloucester, the wicked hunchback with a withered arm, willing to murder his own nephews to hang on to his ill-gotten throne?

How much of his reputation is down to William Shakespeare's inventiveness, and how much to Tudor propagandists trying to put a better gloss on their paymasters' claims to kingship, is hard to disentangle. More than 500 years after the events of 22 August 1485 on Bosworth Field, the story is great food for thought as you walk the fields and woods where the Battle of Bosworth was fought to decide who would rule England – either King Richard III of the House of York, or Henry Tudor, Earl of Richmond, of the House of Lancaster. The two factions had been fighting the Wars of the Roses for the previous thirty years, a time of terrible slaughter and misery throughout the country. But this battle would settle the issue once and for all.

Henry Tudor had brought 5,000 men with him on his march from Wales to London to claim the throne. King Richard, riding out from Leicester to stop Tudor in his tracks, had an army more than twice that size; but 4,000 of these were followers of the powerful Stanley brothers, who had not yet made up their minds which side to back. Although Richard held the high ground, his initial charge failed to break through the Lancastrians, who had been hastily pushed together to form a wall of men. The Duke of Norfolk, one of Richard's most important leaders, was killed in this attack, demoralizing some of the royal army. Now Henry spurred towards the Stanleys, who were watching from the sidelines, to beg their support. Richard thought he saw his chance and led a charge towards the Tudor party. But the Stanleys decided at that moment to throw in their lot with the Lancastrians, and rode down to attack the king. In the fighting, Richard was knocked off his horse and killed. Whether or not his crown rolled under the proverbial gorse bush, it seems fairly certain that it was found on the battlefield and placed on the victorious Henry Tudor's head after the royal army had been put to flight.

What happened then has been hotly contested. It seems likeliest that Richard's body was stripped naked, perhaps defiled, and then slung ignominiously across the back of a horse and displayed to the public as proof that he was well and truly dead. He was then buried in the monastery of the Grey Friars in Leicester, whence his bones were disinterred at the Reformation fifty years later and thrown into the River Soar.

It seems unbelievable today, gazing around this gently rolling English landscape, that over 1,000 men – nine-tenths of them Richard's supporters – died here in one afternoon. A contemporary ballad tells of the fearful sights and sounds of this hack-and-smash battle, which secured peace for the following century:

Then they countred together sad & sore;
archers they lett sharpe arrows fflee,
they shott guns both ffell & ffarr,
bowe of vewe bended did bee ...

Then our archers lett their shooting bee,
with ioyned weapons were growden ffull right;
brands rang on basenetts hye,
battell-axes ffast on helmes did light.

There dyed many a doughtye knight,
there under ffoot can they thringe;
thus they ffought with maine & might
that was on HENERYES part, our King.

235. NARBOROUGH BOG, LEICS.

Maps: OS Explorer 233; Landranger 140

Travel: At M1 Junction 21, bear right and take slip road immediately on left; then follow B4114 to Narborough. Through traffic lights; on along dual carriageway, over B582 roundabout with pub (Toby Carvery at time of writing) and on. Just before motorway overbridge, left ('Recreation Ground') to park at Narborough Sports & Social Club (OS ref. 548982). Entrance to nature reserve is at far right corner of football pitch.

Nearest railway station: Narborough (1 ¼ miles)

From a distance Narborough Bog resembles a big untidy wood. It's only on entering it that you appreciate the scope of the site, the mature trees, streams, ponds, scrub, reed-beds, carr woodland and herb-rich meadows. The M1 rushes by only a field away, but here are kingfishers nest-building, grass snakes gliding through the warm meadow grass among milkmaids and meadowsweet, and small heath, common blue and orange-winged gatekeeper butterflies. Huge overshot willows stand split under their own weight, their shattered trunks providing insect food for greater spotted woodpeckers and tree creepers. Cowslips and meadow saxifrage spatter the grassland. Lying on the fringe of an industrial city, this place is a jewel, full of colour and movement.

The reed-beds stretch over many hundred yards, their dying reeds falling into the watercourses and ponds along with leaves and twigs from the overhanging trees. This sodden detritus is piling up to form a new blanket of peat to add to the several feet which already underlie Narborough Bog – a striking example of a natural process that you can actually observe in operation.

236. HALLATON HARE PIE SCRAMBLE AND BOTTLE KICKING, LEICESTERSHIRE

Maps: OS Explorer 233; Landranger 141

Travel: A47 from Leicester towards Uppinham; right at East Norton to Hallaton. Park near Berwick Arms pub and follow footpath behind, south across brook and next field to Hare Pie Bank, a hollow in the ground near far corner (OS ref. 786960).

Hallaton has been described as 'the most pagan village in Leicestershire', and the Easter Monday ceremonies of the Hare Pie Scramble and Bottle Kicking certainly seem to bear that out. There is unbridled dressing up and ritual feasting, followed by a muddy, sometimes bloody free-for-all in the fields, followed by more drinking and munching. Underneath the jollity, ale-quaffing and thumping lie Christian roots of charity and thanksgiving, but this is an occasion for a good blast of wildness just the same.

Legend says that it was two ladies who gave the rector of Hallaton a parcel of land in thanksgiving for their escape from a rampaging bull when a hare ran across the animal's path and diverted it. The rector in his turn agreed to provide a church service, a sermon, two dozen penny loaves, a 'quantity of ale', and two hare pies each Easter Monday – rather an ironic way of thanking the creature who saved them. So says myth, but the hilltop on which events unfold today was a ritual site back in pre-Christian days, and was also the site of the medieval chapel of St Morrell. Clearly some kind of ritual play has been going on at Hallaton for a very long time.

Today's ceremonies take the form of a church service attended by the Warrener and Breadmaid in medieval costume, followed by a procession during which the famous hare pie and the Breadmaid's basket of penny loaves are distributed to the crowds. Everyone then adjourns to the field at the top of the village and congregates at Hare Pie Bank, the site of medieval St Morrell's Chapel. Here the rest of the hare pie is hurled into the crowd. Then it is the turn of the Bottle Kickers. The three bottles – one-gallon ale casks, two full of beer and one a solid dummy – have previously been blessed in church and decorated with ribbons. One is now thrown into the air three times, and as it touches the ground for the third time a struggling mass of men descends upon it.

The rules of Bottle Kicking are few. The men of Hallaton compete against those of the neighbouring village of Medbourne, although any onlooker can join in if foolhardy enough. The bottles can be thrown, passed, carried or even kicked (unwise – they are heavy), and the object is to get them across the stream nearest either village. Each bottle is employed in turn, and the winning team is the first to score two points. Everyone becomes gloriously muddy. The injured are removed quickly and the game continues. Bottle Kicking can easily go on until dusk or later. At its conclusion both teams congregate at Hallaton Buttercross and drink the bottles dry.

Plenty of pie, ale, mud and rough-and-tumble. Our Iron Age ancestors would undoubtedly have rolled up their sleeves and plunged in.

237. PRIOR'S COPPICE, RUTLAND

Maps: OS Explorer 234; Landranger 141

Travel: A47 to Uppingham roundabout; take A6003 north towards Oakham, turning immediately left through Ayston to Ridlington. Bear right on outskirts of village and continue north for 1½ miles. Left here ('Braunston'); in ½ mile, park (OS ref. 839054) where track leads off on left ('Leighfield Lodge, No Through Road'). Prior's Coppice is 500 yards down this track on right.

Nearest railway station: Oakham (4 miles)

Wild flowers flourish in Prior's Coppice in astonishing numbers and variety, and

Prior's Coppice

they make a springtime visit to this ancient piece of woodland a wonderful treat. Prior's Coppice may very well be thousands of years old; its trees have been cut and harvested, allowed to grow for ten years or so and then cut again, for so many centuries that some of their stools or base structure measure more than 10 feet across. Most woods like this were cut down completely and removed by our ancestors to make way for crops, but the slopes on which this wood lies were too steep for unsophisticated agriculture – so steep that you will find some of the rides hard to negotiate after rain, when water sluicing downhill turns them into mud slides. Thickets of primitive jointed horsetails and thin spikes of sedge, both water-loving plants, grow along the margins of these rides.

Deep in the coppice in spring are bluebells and sulphurous clumps of primroses. Delicate little wood forget-me-nots on hairy square-section stems push their milky blue flowers into sunlit patches. One of the beneficial effects of coppicing is to allow more sunlight into the wood; common spotted orchids thrive here, as do wood anemones further into the shade. Later in the year a graceful and uncommon orchid cousin, violet hellebore, raises spikes of pale greeny-mauve flowers from purple-coloured leaves. This late-summer season is the time to spot the beautiful pearl-pink flowers of broadleaved hellebore, another very uncommon plant nurtured in this remarkable place.

Wilwell Farm Cutting

238. WILWELL FARM CUTTING, NOTTINGHAMSHIRE

Maps: OS Explorer 260; Landranger 129

Travel: Going south on Nottingham Ring Road (A52), leave at A60 ('Loughborough'). In 1 mile, right on B680 through Ruddington, back towards city. Just before you go under ring road, bear left up slip road and park here (OS ref. 568352). Walk forward, bearing left by mobile phone mast; follow path, and entrance is in the trees, 100 yards on your left.

This conversion, beautifully done by the Nottinghamshire Wildlife Trust, has transformed a disused railway cutting into a nature reserve. Immediately upon descending into the cutting you are sunk in a quiet green world, and it's easy to forget that you are right on the doorstep of one of the Midlands' largest and busiest cities. Walk down through a tangle of bluebell woodland to the old trackbed where the Great Central Railway ran between 1898 and 1969, to find a long grassy path with meadows and carr woodland on one side, a high grassy embankment on the other.

The land beside the tracks remained uncultivated throughout the railway's lifetime, and now grows a beautiful flora of the kind that used to be widespread in English hay meadows – notably orchids. Green-winged orchids grow in the upper and lower meadows near the reserve entrance in May, and there is often a display of several thousand southern marsh orchids; a small colony of bee orchids, too.

Further along the trackbed silver birch and willow flourish in boggy ground, and here the water glints a startling electric blue, iridescent from leached minerals in the soil. Willow and birch leaves lie several feet deep in places, building up a rich layer of mulch. The scrawly song of tree pipits and long-tailed tits fills this marshy, whispering little world. Other birds of Wilwell Farm Cutting include owls – long-eared, tawny and white-faced barn owls – hobby and merlin hunting the banks, both corn and reed buntings. The reed buntings shelter and nest in the sparse beds of reeds that grow gracefully curved, 7 or 8 feet tall, along the wet ditches of the cutting. The reserve's bird species list approaches 100, and will undoubtedly pass that. This is a small, tightly packed treasure chest of wildlife, tucked away where only those in the know can find it.

239. ATTENBOROUGH GRAVEL PITS, NOTTINGHAMSHIRE

Maps: OS Explorer 260; Landranger 129

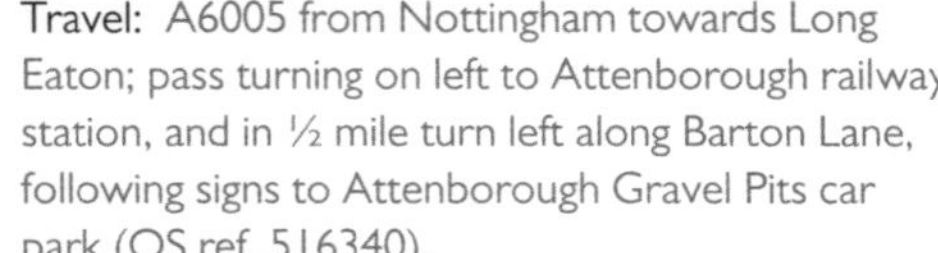

Travel: A6005 from Nottingham towards Long Eaton; pass turning on left to Attenborough railway station, and in ½ mile turn left along Barton Lane, following signs to Attenborough Gravel Pits car park (OS ref. 516340).

Nearest railway station: Attenborough

In and of themselves, Attenborough Gravel Pits are not especially wild. A string of large gravel quarries along the valley of the River Trent, just south of Nottingham, they were worked from 1929 until 1967, by which time Nottinghamshire Wildlife Trust had already established its first nature reserve here. Gravel is still extracted in the locality, and while there's no disguising the industrial past of what have now become a series of bird-haunted lakes, this is a very popular nature reserve, with bird hides and wheelchair-friendly paths.

What is special about this place is the feeling of exposure once out among the lakes, on the narrow causeways between such wide and windblown stretches of water. You can venture out along these causeways in two or three locations, or stick to the curving walkway along the eastern boundary where it snakes between the pits and the River Trent. Such an expanse of water so far inland attracts large numbers of birds of passage in the autumn, while in the winter playing host to many species in flight from colder conditions further north – teal, wigeon, the aptly named goldeneye, ruddy-headed pochard with their red eyes, and bulky goosanders with long hooked bills and white waistcoats. Spring sees ospreys passing through on the lookout for large fish, and when the dragonflies hatch there are little bustling hunters such as merlin and hobby to dash after them across the water.

Attenborough is not all about big water; there are reed-beds, too, areas of scrub where warblers nest, and wet meadows along the river covered in marsh and meadow flowers.

240. BLEASBY PITS, NOTTINGHAMSHIRE

Maps: OS Explorer 271; Landranger 129

Travel: A612 from Nottingham towards Newark-on-Trent; in 7 miles bear right into Goverton. Right here ('Bleasby') to park at Bleasby Station (OS ref. 709499). In another 100 yards, right along footpath, dog-legging past school and following waymarks for ⅓ mile to reach railway line. Bear left beside it for 300 yards to reach the gravel pits.

Nearest railway station: Bleasby

The valley of the River Trent north of Nottingham is a classic flood plain, a low-lying corridor a mile or so wide on the river's west bank. Gently undulating country forms its western boundary, while to the east a sharp 100-foot escarpment rises directly from the river bank. When the Trent floods there is only one way the water can spill – out to the west along the plain. Over millennia it has spread a rich layer of fertile soil on top of the thick beds of gravel laid down here after the last Ice Age. As a result the whole area is caught between two industries: farming and gravel quarrying. So much gravel has been taken from this region that the farmland between the villages and the river resembles a line of glinting mirrors when seen from the eastern bank on a sunny day.

The best time to appreciate this curious, man-made landscape is towards nightfall in the depth of a hard winter. As you crunch over frosty fields towards the great pits south and west of Bleasby, long lines of ducks fly in before you. The chatter of teal and whistling calls of wigeon are audible long before you come in sight of the flooded pits. Great crested grebe, tufted duck and long flotillas of mallard ride quietly, subdued by cold and the dusk. Barn owls ghost over the fields, and swirling clouds of starlings rush from one hedgerow treetop to another as they decide where to drop down for the night. The sight of another human is rare along these paths at such an hour and season; everything is geared to nature and the unchanging rituals of birds settling at dusk.

241. SOUTHWELL MINSTER, NOTTINGHAMSHIRE

Maps: OS Explorer 271; Landranger 120

Travel: A612 from Nottingham to Southwell. Park near Southwell Minster (OS ref. 701538).

Nearest railway station: Fiskerton (2 miles)

'By my blude,' quoth James I, flushed with pride over his new kingship of England, as he clapped eyes on Southwell Minster for the first time in 1603, 'this kirk shall justle with York or Durham, or any other kirk in Christendom!' The minster is one of the most beautiful churches in England, so James's encomium was spot-on. How much time the newly crowned monarch took on his whistle-stop tour to inspect the thirteenth-century chapter house is hard to say, but if he had more than a cursory peek it is amazing that he didn't single it out for praise. This octagonal room in rosy stone, vaulted but with no central pillar to interfere with its perfection, contains the medieval era's most exquisite stone carvings of foliage, fruits and flowers. To walk its stone glades and thickets is to be transported to the wildwoods of Plantagenet England.

The leaves, stems and fruits look as intricate and as sharply detailed as the day that they were carved. Here are instantly identifiable trails of ivy and hops, sprays of oak and vine, sprigs of apple, hawthorn and blackberry. If you insert a chip of mirror behind the carvings, you can see that the detail is as fine at the hidden back of the pieces as it is at the front. Perfection could be seen by the eye of God, if not of man.

From the shelter of this riot of forest leaves peep out animal and human figures – a pig gobbling acorns; a merman, sly-eyed and wild, with his tail curled round behind his head; a pair of Green Men, one a fine fat merchant, his neighbour a gross, blunt-nosed brute, leaves erupting from his mouth and the crown of his head. Puritan zealots chopped off a lot of stone noses, hands and mouths – you can see the diagonal and horizontal sword cuts. Luckily they could not deface them all; there were simply too many. So we have been left this wonderful, subtly didactic, wild and funny treasure.

242. SHERWOOD FOREST, NOTTINGHAMSHIRE

Maps: OS Explorer 270; Landranger 120

Travel: A616 Ollerton towards Sheffield; in 1¾ miles, left on B6034. Alternatively, A6075 Ollerton towards Edwinstowe; in 1¾ miles, right on B6034. Both ways (brown 'Sherwood Forest Country Park' signs) lead to car park (OS ref. 627676). Walk to Visitor Centre. From here Blue Trail leads to Major Oak (621679); Green Trail to a 1¾ mile circuit; Red to a 3½-mile round walk.

Thanks to a certain bow-slinging gentleman in Lincoln green and his woodland companions, a walk in Sherwood Forest is at once strangely familiar and ineluctably romantic. This is a wild place greatly and poignantly reduced from the early medieval days when Robin Hood and his Merrie Men had 100,000 acres of greenwood to roam – woodland cover which had existed here since the retreat of the glaciers 10,000 years before. Not that Sherwood Forest was an unbroken mass of trees even then; it was a royal hunting forest, with farms, commons, scrub and wetlands scattered among the woods. Most of it was open woodland, cleared for grazing under the big old trees, which were pollarded or trimmed of their lower branches to allow the pigs and cattle room to wander.

These days the forest is split into several relatively minor blocks of woodland. The Sherwood Forest Country Park itself, based on the Visitor Centre north of Edwinstowe, maintains some 450 acres as

Sherwood Forest

a National Nature Reserve. Reduced it may be, but within these bounds are snippets of acid grassland and lowland heath (haunts of lizards and slow-worms), patches of wetland, and of course a wide area of thick tree cover. At the heart stands the Major Oak, the daddy of them all with a girth of 35 feet, its gnarled limbs propped on crutches, a vast wrinkled structure with the dignity and presence of an ancient bull elephant. The Major Oak could be 1,000 years old – some say 1,500. Certainly it could have dropped an acorn on Robin Hood's hat; it must have been at least 200 years old when (or if) the legendary outlaw was robbing the rich to feed the poor.

There is generally a bit of a scrum of visitors around this venerable tree. Take one of the forest paths beyond, putting a fold of ground or two between you and the crowds, and you will find silence and serenity again, with time and elbow-room to seek out and admire some of the other tremendously bulbous and characterful oaks of the forest. These ancients can harbour hundreds of species of beetles, wood wasps and spiders. Moths lay caterpillars in the bark and on the leaves, woodlice and millipedes thrive on the rotting wood, dozens of types of bird from treecreepers to woodpeckers live in and feed on the trees. Ferns, mosses and lichens sprout on them; their acorns feed squirrels and badgers. They are the house, the larder and the launching pad for most of the wildlife of this diminished but still magical forest.

243. RETFORD LANES, NOTTINGHAMSHIRE

Maps: OS Explorer 271; Landranger 120

Travel: A638 or A620 to Retford. Follow A620 out of town towards Gainsborough. To join Lovers' Walk, Howbeck Lane or Red Flats Lane, turn right in 2½ miles into Clarborough and park (OS ref. 734836). Alternatively, continue along A620 for another 1½ miles to park (746848) and turn right down Blue Stocking Lane.

The survival of a whole complex of old tracks and lanes in the countryside just east of the town of Retford is astonishing. Generally such old-fashioned country roads are either laid with tarmac and made to bristle with warning signs and other road furniture, or they are blocked up, fallen in and forgotten. Somehow in this obscure corner of north-east Nottinghamshire they have not only continued to exist – they are also still in use. But not much, admittedly.

Take a stroll down Lovers' Walk in Clarborough, a back lane that is as broad, stony and muddy as country lanes used to be before the advent of motor cars. Just east, Howbeck Lane and Red Flats Lane diverge; they do not retain these names long, for Howbeck Lane slips into Muspit Lane as it makes north-east towards the village of North Wheatley, while Red Flats Lane becomes High House Lane and then Springs Lane on its 3-mile course east to Sturton-le-Steeple. As for the high-falutin' Blue Stocking Lane, it runs south to garner the altogether more down-to-earth style of Rathole Lane before borrowing Caddow Wood's name as it passes by to become Caddow Lane.

These wonderfully named lanes are the backbone on which the agricultural, social and recreational relationships of this 5-square-mile rural backwater were built up. No villages developed, no towns grew up around their crossroads; they simply came into being to funnel people between isolated farms and their fields. Primroses and celandine line them in spring, blackbirds and chaffinches nest in their hedges. In winter they lie thick with waxy mud in dark red folds like clotted cheese. Horseshoe prints, boot-sole marks and bicycle-tyre treads are the main spoor to compete with hare, rabbit and fox prints, though 4x4 drivers occasionally snarl by in a spatter of mud. Along the eastern horizon rolls an eternal bank of steam from the giant cooling towers of West Burton power station, looking for all the world like the aftermath of some titanic burning or battle, an eerie note in this 'Bermuda Triangle' of the East Midlands.

8

YORKSHIRE

Yorkshire is the largest, widest and most diverse county in England. Small wonder that the distribution and range of wild places inside its boundaries is enormous.

THREE OF THE four Ridings of Yorkshire (as the regions of the county are traditionally styled) are surprisingly little known. South Yorkshire is often stigmatized as the industrial area pinched between Sheffield and Doncaster, which most of us hurry through to get to somewhere better. Yet here you can find high moors, newly opened to the public, and the remarkable Thorne Moors near Doncaster, where nature is reclaiming wide areas of old peat diggings. West Yorkshire gathers around the celebrated Brontë Moors near Haworth. But there are other wild places here, too. The Industrial Revolution was seeded in the moorland valleys with their fast-flowing rivers and in the ever-expanding towns and cities that soon sprang up there – fertile ground for salvationist religion to take root in. Around the moors you will still find the isolated farms in overgrown fields where the early Methodist preachers would whip barns full of weavers and farm labourers into states of religious frenzy. The East Riding, filling the much-overlooked south-east corner of the county, has wide old commons and undulating wolds that are explored by few outsiders, and a dead-flat coastal hinterland leading to a lonely shore where 40 miles of black clay cliffs, bookended by the fragile sandspit of Spurn and the half-abandoned houses of Ulrome, lie at the mercy of rising seas and storms.

North Yorkshire is the focus and hub for visitors. This Riding could comfortably swallow the other three and still have room for more, though its population is the smallest of all. It possesses two National Parks, while the others have none. The wild Pennine Hills march up its western flank, and walkers on the Pennine Way National Trail march with them over rugged fells towards the even wilder moors of Durham and Cumbria. In the Yorkshire Dales National Park, beyond the gentle green 'inbye' meadows of the valley bottoms, are caverns and potholes, remote terraces and little-visited valleys such as West Stones Dale and Walden. Out east roll the sombre peat moorlands of the North York Moors National Park, haunted by signs and symbols of the lead and iron mines that once scarred their long dark backs. The splendid cliffs of the North York coast bear the marks of alum, jet and ironstone mining, too, and layer upon layer of fossils, from fish scales and dinosaur teeth to delicate leaves and submarine plants, remnants of aeons of geological upheaval.

Left: Spurn Head (p. 272). Above: Howden Moor (p. 299). Below: Rosedale Moor (pp. 282–3).

LINKS

- Pennine Way National Trail (www.nationaltrail.co.uk/pennineway; www.penninewayassociation.co.uk): Brontë Moors, Gordale Scar, Pen-y-Ghent, Cam High Road, Great Shunner Fell, Tan Hill Inn
- Dales Way (www.dalesway.org.uk): The Strid, Grassington Moor, Langstrothdale
- Coast-to-Coast (www.coast2coast.co.uk): Rosedale Moor, Spaunton Moor, Farndale Moor, Hasty Bank
- Cleveland Way National Trail (www.nationaltrail.co.uk/clevelandway): Whitby, Stoupe Brow, Peak Alum Works, Filey Brigg

NATIONAL PARKS

- North York Moors: www.visitnorthyorkmoors.co.uk
- Yorkshire Dales: www.yorkshiredales.org.uk

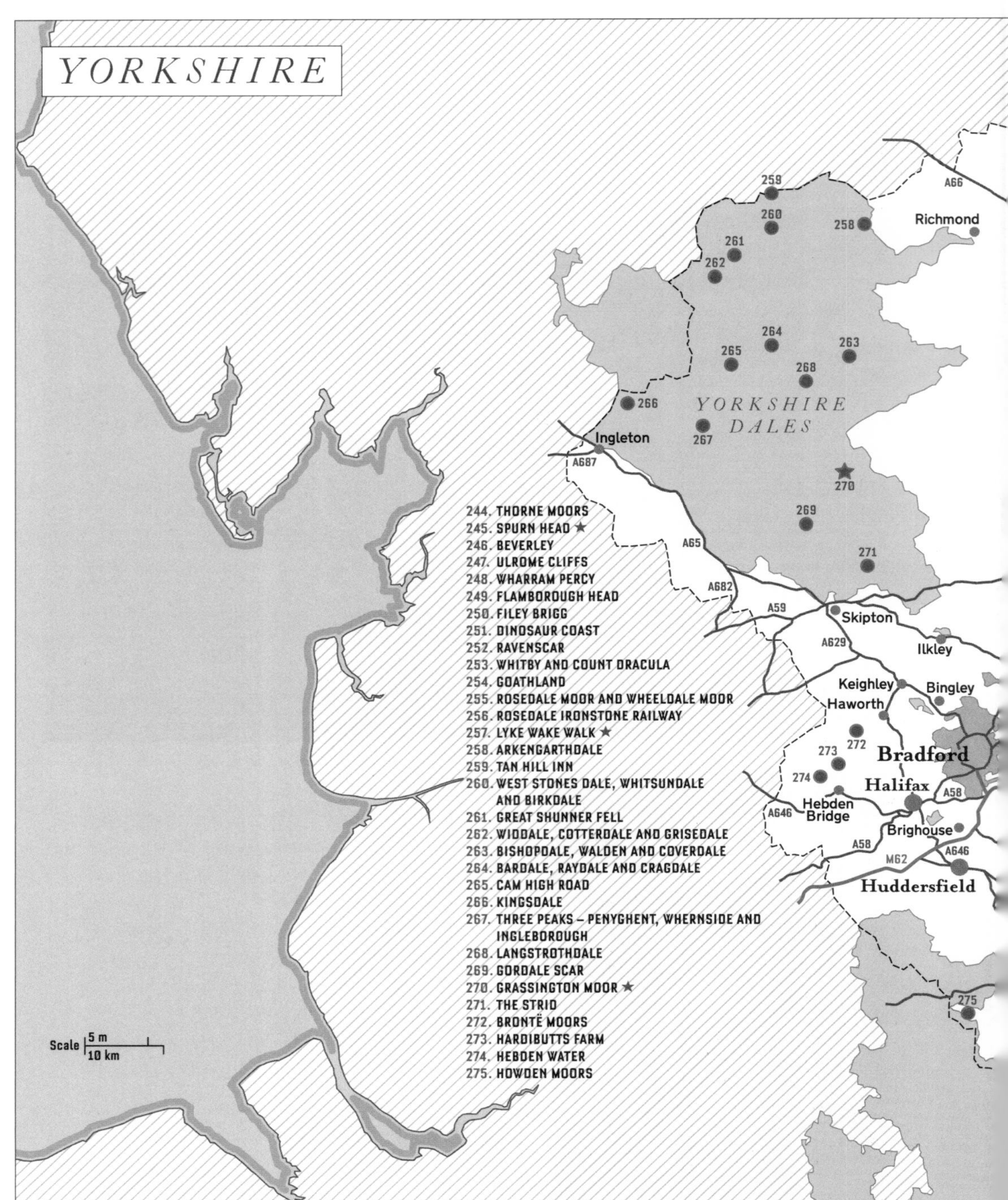
YORKSHIRE
YORKSHIRE DALES
259
260
258
Richmond
A66
261
262
264
265
263
268
266
267
Ingleton
A687
270
269
A65
271
A682
A59
Skipton
A629
Ilkley
Keighley
Bingley
Haworth
272
273
274
Bradford
Halifax
A58
A646
Hebden Bridge
Brighouse
A58
M62
A646
Huddersfield
275
244. THORNE MOORS
245. SPURN HEAD ★
246. BEVERLEY
247. ULROME CLIFFS
248. WHARRAM PERCY
249. FLAMBOROUGH HEAD
250. FILEY BRIGG
251. DINOSAUR COAST
252. RAVENSCAR
253. WHITBY AND COUNT DRACULA
254. GOATHLAND
255. ROSEDALE MOOR AND WHEELDALE MOOR
256. ROSEDALE IRONSTONE RAILWAY
257. LYKE WAKE WALK ★
258. ARKENGARTHDALE
259. TAN HILL INN
260. WEST STONES DALE, WHITSUNDALE AND BIRKDALE
261. GREAT SHUNNER FELL
262. WIDDALE, COTTERDALE AND GRISEDALE
263. BISHOPDALE, WALDEN AND COVERDALE
264. BARDALE, RAYDALE AND CRAGDALE
265. CAM HIGH ROAD
266. KINGSDALE
267. THREE PEAKS – PENYGHENT, WHERNSIDE AND INGLEBOROUGH
268. LANGSTROTHDALE
269. GORDALE SCAR
270. GRASSINGTON MOOR ★
271. THE STRID
272. BRONTË MOORS
273. HARDIBUTTS FARM
274. HEBDEN WATER
275. HOWDEN MOORS
Scale
5 m
10 km

Whitby
253
251
257
256
254
255
252
Catterick
Northallerton
NORTH YORK MOORS
Scarborough
Thirsk
Pickering
250
Filey
Malton
Norton
Ripon
Flamborough
249
Bridlington
YORKSHIRE
248
Knaresborough
Shipton
Harrogate
Driffield
247
York
Wetherby
Tadcaster
Market Weighton
Beverley
246
Leeds
Hull
Castleford
Withernsea
Batley
Wakefield
Dewsbury
Pontefract
Goole
Easington
244
245
Barnsley
Bentley
Dodworth
Doncaster
Wombwell
Mexborough
Chapeltown
Rotherham
Sheffield

244. THORNE MOORS, SOUTH YORKSHIRE

Maps: OS Explorer 279; Landranger 111, 112

Travel: From M18 Junction 6, A614 towards Goole; in ½ mile, right ('Moorends') to T-junction. Right over level crossing into Moorends; left down Grange Road and park at bottom (OS ref. 700158). Walk on along roadway past barriers, with Thorne Colliery football club pitch on right, to bottom of road; left by pylon to T-junction (705161). Bear slightly right to cross road; follow track east past north side of Thorne Colliery site to cross brick footbridge (711161), then metal footbridge ('Thorne Moors' sign) into Humberhead Peatlands NNR. Follow yellow route around the reserve.

Nearest railway station: Thorne North (2 miles)

The flat moorland region north-east of Doncaster is rich in natural resources, particularly coal (now uneconomic to extract) and a thick layer of peat. The peat of these moors has been harvested for many years for the horticulture industry; but that, too, is an industrial process with no future now that there has been a growth in awareness of the value of peat moorlands as wildlife habitat. They are also recognized as having an important role in the global-warming process with regard to two of the most significant greenhouse gases. Peat bogs produce vast amounts of methane, but release very little of it if they remain uncut. They also absorb carbon dioxide very effectively. So the bleak and apparently barren stretches of moor that lie east of the River Don have been designated the Humberhead Peatland National Nature Reserve. Managed by Natural England, they are being looked after as they never were before.

The reserve forms a darkly shaggy oasis at the heart of an enormous desert of intensively farmed crops and devastated peat extraction moors. Modern intensive peat extraction is on its last legs at Hatfield Moors just to the south, a hellish flatland of sour, black nothingness stretching to the horizon and beyond. Nothing darker, emptier or more ruined could be imagined. It seems incredible that this was the aspect until the 1990s of Thorne Moor, now an endlessly varied patchwork of bog, grassland, birch and willow scrub, glinting fleets of water, open heath and fertile ditches, all under an immense dome of sky, Orchids, butterflies, dragonflies, birds and insects thrive out here. Nightjars nest on the heath, nightingales in the woods. It takes constant hard work on the part of Natural England, emptying and refilling water levels, cutting scrub and planting indigenous species, always mindful of the balance of nature – will raising the water table to maintain the mire disturb the nightjars who need dry heath to nest on? Such are the delicate checks and balances operated by some to retain the wild moors that others all but destroyed.

245. SPURN HEAD, EAST YORKSHIRE

Maps: OS Explorer 292; Landranger 113

Travel: M180, A15 to Hull; A63, A1033 east to Patrington; right on B1445 to Easington; minor road to Bluebell car park, Kilnsea (OS ref. 417158). Walk 4 miles south to tip of Spurn Head (397105); return same way.

Spurn is a most extraordinary place – a thin line of sand and pebbles, knitted together with spiky marram grass and rare plants, that runs out more than 3 miles into the sea to the blunt extremity known as Spurn

Spurn Head

Head. On the map the promontory looks likes the snout of an anteater hanging down across the mouth of the River Humber from the south-eastern tip of Yorkshire. On the ground it seems like the loneliest place in the world, a gently curving green breakwater somehow defying the efforts of storms and tides to turn it into a string of islands.

Walking south down the long line of the spit you'll notice spatters of colour where the plants of Spurn thrive in the hostile environment of salt spray and gales. The telephone cables that shadow the road sing a high-pitched note in the constant wind and belly out between their single line of wooden posts. Sheep and rabbits nibble away at the grasses, leaving a cropped sward where yellow bird's-foot trefoil and lady's bedstraw can grow, along with the purple cones of vanilla-scented pyramidal orchid. Fine sand drifts have formed a rampart along the road, which snakes and swerves to find solid ground between dunes spattered over with big papery wild roses.

The North Sea pounds the eastern side, eroding each attempt to thwart it. The remnants of former defences rot and rust democratically together: iron and wooden stakes chewed by salt into totem poles, piles of concrete slabs that nature has plastered with wind-blown sand and seeded with marram grass to form low cliffs. On the west stretch huge expanses of tidal mud and sand, a larder both for wading birds such as redshank and dunlin, and for the dark-bellied brent geese that come to spend the winter here. Birdwatchers revere Spurn for the millions of small birds on migration that make landfall on the spit each spring and autumn.

Down at Spurn Head you'll find the old towers of two abandoned lighthouses, a coastguard post and a community of hardy lifeboatmen and their families who live out here all year round in the teeth of wind and waves. The shore lies littered with a curious mosaic of stones, angle irons, concrete and chalk blocks, bricks smoothed to pebbles, all rounded by the gentle mockery of the sea.

246. BEVERLEY, EAST YORKSHIRE

Maps: OS Explorer 293; Landranger 107

Travel: From M62 Junction 38, B1230 to Beverley. Park in town centre. From Tourist Information Centre (OS ref. 036395) bear right through Wednesday Market, along Highgate to Beverley Minster (038393). Leaving minster by north door, right to Eastgate; right to Wednesday Market. Just before TIC, left down Well Lane; right along Cross Street past County Hall; left along Toll Gavel, through Saturday Market to St Mary's Church (032398). From St Mary's, continue along left pavement of North Bar Within; through North Bar archway; on along North Bar Without for ¼ mile. By police station, left down Norfolk Street on to Westwood Common (025401).

Nearest railway station: Beverley

Somehow Beverley has managed to stave off the blandness that afflicts so many old market towns, and has retained its tremendous character. This is a lively place with a sense of its own style and history, epitomized in the magnificent thirteenth-century minster church. And here, as so commonly in the great churches of Britain, the medieval masons delighted in introducing a dark greenwood weirdness into their wonderful stone carvings.

There's a nice sense of mischief about the exterior work on Beverley Minster, from the line of scowling and gurning Green Men who underpin the west window, to the grinning sprites that carry dignified prelates on their stone heads. Inside the church the parade of grotesques includes a howling demon with prickly body and tangled beard; a grimacing woodwose, or wild man-beast of the woods, with a huge knotted club and a baby dragon in his grasp; and a Mass-going couple whose chaste embrace is overseen by an enormous, lecherous-looking goat. A Green Man stares bug-eyed from a pillar capital in the nave, mouth agape and teeth bared with the effort of spewing an enormous tangle of giant oak leaves and acorns.

Pilgrim rabbit, St Mary's Church, Beverley

Beyond Beverley's wide Saturday Market place rises St Mary's Church, another breathtakingly beautiful building in whose details the stone carvers allowed their artistic and religious sensibilities full play; their irony and their impudence, too. Naturally the Green Man appears, half-choking in oak leaves on a porch capital, grimacing through gold leaf from a roof boss. Perhaps even in this fierce guise he is supposed to be seen in some kind of Christian context – the fruitful word of God, perhaps. But there are other beings present who are less easily rationalized. Where on earth or under it are the harelipped wolfman and the porcine lion with the chimpanzee ears, both grinning fiendishly from the south doorway, supposed to fit in with 'gentle Jesus, meek and mild'?

247. ULROME CLIFFS, EAST YORKSHIRE

Maps: OS Landranger 107; Explorer 295

Travel: From A165 south of Bridlington, take B1242 ('Skipsea'). In 1½ miles, left by Ulrome West End church; continue to end of road and park here (OS ref. 175571).

Nearest railway station: Bridlington (8 miles)

Cliff Farm is still here – just. It teeters on the very brink above Ulrome Sands. With less than 5 feet of ground between its eastern wall and the cliff edge, it seems a miracle that the farmhouse continues to stand. Already the storm waves of winter break against its seaward wall. At some time in the next few years, probably during a torrential downpour or on a wild winter night with the sea beating

at the crumbling cliffs of Holderness, Cliff Farm will crack and tumble into the sea. Meanwhile its inhabitants cling on, proud of their survival in the face of the inevitable. This is the coast to visit to be reminded of the brute force of the sea around us.

Towards the end of the last Ice Age, melting glaciers left behind the materials that form the shaky cliffs of Holderness – clay, boulders and mud, never the most stable of components. The sea has been eating at them ever since. Each winter it burrows another 30 feet or so inland, swallowing the low cliffs in scoops that crenellate the edge of the land like a First World War trench. The mud is as glutinous as Flanders muck, too, flowing out of the cliffs in fan-shaped extrusions after heavy rain.

A whole string of villages that stood along this coast have been taken by the sea. Farms, roads, field walls and barns have all gone over the edge, though various methods have been tried to keep the sea at bay. At Ulrome East End, just north of Cliff Farm, the cliffs have been shored up and the clifftop caravan park underpinned with three storeys of large concrete cylinders. Their curved surfaces are supposed to break up the force of the waves, though evidence of former, failed efforts lies sprawling on the shore – concrete slabs in Dali-esque shapes, lumps of iron, stone blocks with their hard edges washed away.

248. WHARRAM PERCY, EAST YORKSHIRE

Maps: OS Explorer 300; Landranger 100,101

Travel: A64 to Malton; B1248 'North Grimston' to Wharram-le-Street. At ¼ mile past the village, right (OS ref. 867653) on minor road ('Burdale, Thixendale' and brown 'Wharram Percy' sign) to Wharram Percy car park. Follow footpath from bottom-left corner down to Wharram Percy.

Nearest railway station: Malton (8 miles)

Archaeologists have given us an astonishingly detailed picture of Wharram Percy during its lifetime. We know, for instance, that the longhouses – homes for the villagers and also for their cattle – on

St Martin Church, Wharram Percy

the edge of the plateau above the ruined St Martin Church had wooden cruck frames built inside the walls to carry the weight of the thatched roofs. We are aware that the site was occupied since long before the Romans came to Britain, and that the village, whose heyday was in the late thirteenth century, was carefully planned, designed to maximize use of the land and the river, with its watermill. Nitrogen isotope analysis of the 700 skeletons excavated from St Martin's graveyard shows that comparatively few infants died, probably because they were breastfed until the age of two, and that sophisticated skull surgery allowed a man with a fearsome head wound to live many years after his operation.

Many villages in England were deserted after the Black Death plague of 1348–50, but Wharram Percy was not one of these. The village continued its life for another century and a half before the people were evicted and the houses taken down to make way for more profitable sheep. This is a tale heard over and over again in the Scottish Highlands (see pp. 409–10, 411–12 and 437), but it brings you up short to contemplate it here in the fertile wolds of East Yorkshire.

Now, all that is really left is the Church of St Martin, down near the river, where the villagers' bodies were packed away under the ground. The church is an English Heritage property, and its carvings retain some of the humour and originality of the medieval minds that conceived them. On the north wall of the nave appear two opposing faces: a round-cheeked soul in a wimple, and a perky-looking woman, half smiling between the two coiled earpieces of a ram's-horn headdress. I wonder if George Lucas ever visited Wharram Percy, for here is *Star Wars'* Princess Leia, to the life.

249. FLAMBOROUGH HEAD, EAST YORKSHIRE

Maps: OS Explorer 301; Landranger 101

Travel: A165 from Scarborough towards Bridlington; left on B1229 to Flamborough. Park in village (OS ref. 226705). Walk south from Flamborough church on footpath to cliffs at Beacon Hill, then make anticlockwise circuit of the Head itself via lighthouse and North and South Landing, returning inland from Thornwick Bay.

The village of Flamborough sits isolated on the great peninsula of Flamborough Head, and this wonderful but windy place is all about the mighty ramparts of chalk cliff that buttress it. They are loud with gulls and gales, exhilarating with the crash and thump of the waves. Tides here are ferocious, and unpredictable even to the fishermen – over 1,000 years they have developed a specially shaped coble, or fishing boat, with narrow stern and bulging waist for ease of launching and handling in the treacherous tide rips close in under the cliffs.

The coast path runs along the top, very close to the edge in parts. From here you can look down on tide eddies swirling and sucking in and out of the caverns they have burrowed in the feet of the cliffs, the deep blue and grey of the inshore water lightened to intense turquoise where the seabed lies littered with white chunks of chalk.

There are plenty of seabirds here, but the most remarkable gatherings are on the ledges of Bempton Cliffs a mile up the coast. The sight, sound and smell of around a quarter of a million guillemots and gulls, puffins and razorbills, fulmars and kittiwakes – mainland Britain's largest breeding colony of seabirds – is an experience hard to forget. Travel-writer H. V. Morton crouched on the edge of these cliffs on a bright spring

Flamborough Head

morning in 1927, watching Sam Leng, the egg-gatherer of Bempton, 'swing, four hundred feet below, a tiny, sprawling figure poised perilously above the angry waves, the birds screaming round him as he worked his way from ledge to ledge gathering the bright blue and green eggs'.

The impetuous townee, a true romantic if ever there was one, was so entranced by the sight that in a mad moment he volunteered for duty:

> *An idiot desire to collect a guillemot's egg with my own hands possessed me, so that in a rash moment I asked to be allowed to go over the top. To my surprise and horror, he agreed. I could not draw back ... I found myself on an almost perpendicular ledge of rock. I felt like a fly on a ceiling. Something gave way, leaving me swinging at the end of the rope. I struck a piece of chalk with my foot, which broke away; I watched it fall, down, down, down, through a flight of gulls, through a cloud of kittiwakes, down, down into the distant steaming sea.*

Morton had himself pulled up 'in an agony of self-contempt', and waited while Sam Leng collected another sackful of guillemot eggs. 'At that moment,' confessed the failed adventurer, 'I would rather have done that than have received a chestful of decorations.'

250. FILEY BRIGG, NORTH YORKSHIRE

Maps: OS Explorer 301; Landranger 101

Travel: A165 from Bridlington to Filey; right on A1039 through town to seafront. Left along seafront for 300 yards, then road bends inland again. Follow it to turn right (OS ref. 116812) into Filey Brigg Country Park. Park here and follow Wold Way path on to Filey Brigg.

Nearest railway station: Filey

The Dinosaur Coast (see below) runs south for some 35 miles from Captain James Cook's home village of Staithes along a stretch of some of the finest and most fossiliferous cliffs in Britain, to end at the definitive full stop of Filey Brigg. The Brigg stretches out into the North Sea, a solid bar of chalky grit 700 yards long standing in defiance of the waves that are so dramatically eating into the soft black clays of the coast further south (see pp. 274–5). Weathering has produced a curious effect of vertical skin-like wrinkles, as if the Brigg were a mammoth's trunk laid on the water. Yet the cliffs, too, are slowly eroding, releasing showers of stones and fragments of ancient corals to tumble to the beach and be washed from the long seaward scars of Spittall Rocks.

The Romans built a signal station on Filey Brigg, a splendid vantage point out in the sea, and the underwater structure on the south side of the promontory, known as the Spittalls, has been identified as a Roman harbour. A little imperial discipline might have been a good thing for the rambunctious fishermen of Filey around the turn of the nineteenth century, when they and their wives became notorious for their swearing, drinking and harsh treatment of Christian proselytizers venturing to the town to save their souls. It took a spiritual hard man, 'Praying Johnny' Oxtoby, to break through the flung stones and showers of rotten skate. When he came to Filey in 1823, Praying Johnny was up on his soapbox before the wild men and women of the town had time to marshal their defences. They fell to their knees, shivered and quaked, roared and cried for salvation. A fellow preacher who witnessed this Daniel in the Lion's Den reported: 'In answer to the earnest breathings of his soul, a whole assembly has been moved as the trees are moved when shaken with a strong wind. A mighty shaking has been felt, and a great noise heard, amongst the dry bones.'

251. DINOSAUR COAST, NORTH YORKSHIRE

Maps: OS Explorer OL27, 301; Landranger 94, 101

Travel: A171 and A165 connect Whitby, Scarborough and the Dinosaur Coast. A174 reaches the northern section, Whitby to Staithes. The well-waymarked Cleveland Way National Trail runs the whole length of the Dinosaur Coast, with numerous side-tracks down to the shore.

Information: www.dinocoast.org.uk

Nearest railway stations: Whitby, Scarborough, Filey

The name 'Dinosaur Coast' tells only part of the story, hinting at the geological and palaeontological riches of the 50 miles of coast that stretch south from Staithes on the Cleveland border to the long wrinkled promontory of Filey Brigg (see above). This coast is made up of magnificent cliffs rising to 600 feet at the summit of South Cheek near Ravenscar, interspersed with rounded bays whose floors, exposed at low tide, are composed of 'scars' – strata of rock tipped on end and milled flat by the action of the sea. These tilted layers tell of the violence wreaked by vast subterranean upheavals, a history in which sandstorms have obliterated the land, rivers have fertilized it anew, tropical seas have flooded it, earth convulsions have hoisted it high, wind and weather have ground it down.

Tall dark cliffs of shaly limestone around

Whitby and Robin Hood's Bay, full of the bones of fish lizards, shell-shaped fossils of ammonites and delicate sea lilies, are all that's left of the deep warm sea that lay here around 200 million years ago. Further south the cliffs lighten in colour to show where the land, once more above the sea after the passage of another 50 million years, lay as a sandy desert.

The prints of dinosaur feet are found in the sandstone of the cliffs, interspersed with thin layers of mudstone laid down during the floods of a great river that flowed here, trapping and fossilizing the evergreen leaves of primitive fern-like plants. Down around Scarborough the prominent Castle Headland shows orange-and-cream layers of sandstone and limestone from later times, when the land had been plunged beneath another tropical sea rich in bullet-shaped belemnites, sea snails and bivalves, corals, fish and the paddle-footed plesiosaurs that hunted them – all this wildlife preserved in its component parts in the layers of rock. South again the cliffs dip and then rise towards the great rounded nose of Flamborough Head, many hundreds of vertical feet of solid white chalk composed of the shelly corpses of countless trillion tiny sea creatures. They inhabited yet another warm, shallow ocean towards the end of the age of the great dinosaurs, along with sea urchins, sponges and sharks whose minutely serrated, T-shaped teeth are found along the beaches after storms.

Finally, a scatter of rugged alien boulders along the shores and a spreading of clay around Filey Brigg and other places show how the coming of the Ice Ages some two or three million years ago dragged blankets of ice up to a mile thick across both sea and land, the latest but undoubtedly not the last act in this extraordinary drama played out and recorded along the cliffs of North Yorkshire.

252. RAVENSCAR (PEAK ALUM WORKS), NORTH YORKSHIRE

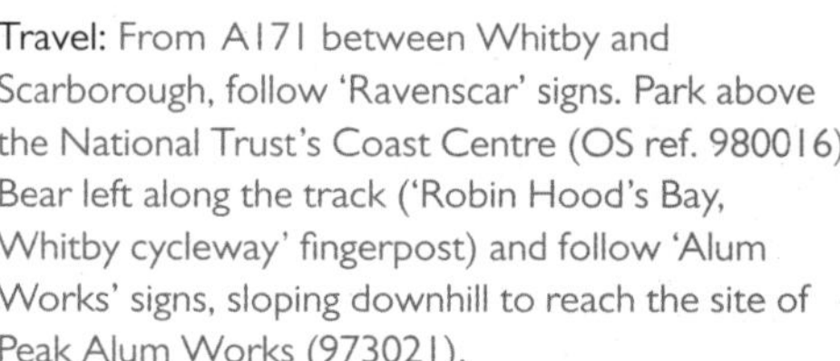

Maps: OS Explorer OL27; Landranger 94

Travel: From A171 between Whitby and Scarborough, follow 'Ravenscar' signs. Park above the National Trust's Coast Centre (OS ref. 980016). Bear left along the track ('Robin Hood's Bay, Whitby cycleway' fingerpost) and follow 'Alum Works' signs, sloping downhill to reach the site of Peak Alum Works (973021).

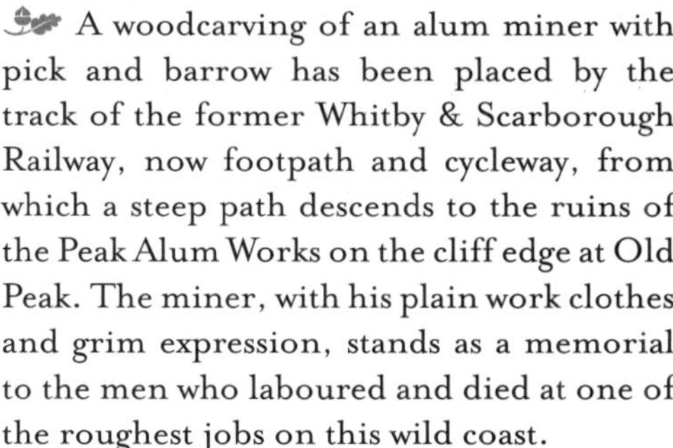

A woodcarving of an alum miner with pick and barrow has been placed by the track of the former Whitby & Scarborough Railway, now footpath and cycleway, from which a steep path descends to the ruins of the Peak Alum Works on the cliff edge at Old Peak. The miner, with his plain work clothes and grim expression, stands as a memorial to the men who laboured and died at one of the roughest jobs on this wild coast.

The site of the Peak Alum Works, cared for by the National Trust, is sparse enough. Some broken stone walls, a couple of stone-lined pits and some spoil heaps coated with gorse and bracken are all that remain on the cliff. But reading the interpretation boards and gazing around the curve of the bay, imagination soon supplies the story – especially in winter, with no one else about. Alum mining was a tough, dirty and exhausting business, carried out on lonely coasts where the North Sea weather was liable to turn nasty at any time.

Ravenscar

Before the introduction of modern chemicals, alum was a very important product. The textile trade fixed dyes with it, papermakers used it to bind the paper fibres together, and tanneries needed large quantities to make stiff leather more pliable. Alum production was no sinecure. Shale had to be quarried, a labour-intensive business: 100 tons of shale produced only around 1 ton of alum. The grey rock was burned in a clamp for nine months until it had turned pink, then soaked in water to produce a solution of aluminium sulphate. The solution was boiled, cooled and mixed with an alkaline agent – burned kelp seaweed (for its potassium content) and/or stale human urine (ammonia) collected from nearby towns. The noxious liquid then settled, and eventually produced crystals of alum, which were powdered for use by industry.

The cliff of Old Peak was perfectly situated to accommodate this complicated and long-drawn-out process. From the alum works ruins you can see the dark scoops of the alum shale quarries in the cliff faces inland, and the huge gorse-grown spoil heaps below them. In the deep cleft beside the works trickles the stream that supplied water to the site, and below on the shore – a maze of treacherous 'scars', or stubs of rock, at low tide – is the place where vessels landed cargoes of potash and urine, and loaded the precious alum for onward transmission. Ruins, quarried cliffs and rugged bay are silent witnesses to the unsung generations of alum miners who slaved here and died of poisoning, overwork, industrial illness or accident.

253. WHITBY AND COUNT DRACULA

Maps: OS Explorer OL27; Landranger 94

Travel: A171 to Whitby.

Nearest railway station: Whitby

Pack your garlic and high-collared cloak if you're bound for Whitby. There's no region of England more steeped in tales of ghosts, ghouls and hell-hounds, 'gabbleratchets' or spectral dogs that bark news of impending death from the sky, hobs that haunt farms, moor witches, and a white lady seen at the windows of the ruined abbey, standing so strikingly on the skyline above Whitby's harbour.

When Irish writer Bram Stoker heard the yarns of the superstitious Whitby fishermen in the 1880s, the seeds were sown for the creation of that most suave and deadly fiend, Count Dracula. In Whitby you can follow, step by step, the nefarious doings of the vampire count in the three gripping chapters of *Dracula* that Stoker set in the town.

In the lobby of the Royal Hotel hangs a photograph of Bram Stoker, heavily bearded and intense-looking. From the cliff outside there's a fine view across the harbour to St Mary's Church and Whitby Abbey on the opposite headland. Mina Murray, Stoker's heroine, stayed with her friend Lucy Westenra in the Crescent, now East Crescent, a pretty little arc of houses just back from the cliff. Mina must have had remarkable eyesight; from this spot she was not only able to distinguish Dracula dining off the neck of her friend in the graveyard of St Mary's, but could even make out the red spots glowing in the count's eyes.

Across the harbour is the sandbank under Tate Hill where one of the novel's strangest scenes takes place – the arrival of the storm-driven schooner *Demeter*, travelling from the Russian port of Varna, her dead captain lashed to the wheel. Then comes Count Dracula's escape from the wreck in the shape of a wolf, and the terrorizing of the town begins. A Russian schooner, *Dmitry*, from the port of Narva, was actually wrecked on this very bank in a storm in 1885; with the transposition of a few letters in the names, Stoker had all he needed for his epic wreck scene. At the far end of cobbled, atmospheric old Church Street on the east side of the harbour, the 199 Church Steps climb to St Mary's Church on the cliff above. Up these steps sprang Dracula in vulpine guise, seeking refuge in the graveyard. Mina Murray, too, ran up Church Steps one night, to find her sleepwalking friend Lucy slumped in her nightgown on a churchyard seat. 'Something dark stood behind the seat where the white figure shone, and bent over it.' And what were those two little red spots on Lucy's fair white neck ...?

It's said that the inspiration for *Dracula* came to Stoker as he wandered through St Mary's graveyard. There is a fine collection of gravestones up here, some eaten by wind and rain into uncanny shapes. And St Mary's Church itself is a queer place, a humpy, ancient church filled with a forest of old box pews, an immense three-decker pulpit and several railed galleries, all installed by Whitby shipwrights. The whole building has a nautical, foreign feel to it, a little outlandish and decidedly strange. On the ridge behind St Mary's stand the gaunt and beautiful ruins of Whitby Abbey, towards which Dracula would flit in bat shape after dining with, and on, Lucy Westenra. Finally – prosaic end – it was from Whitby railway station, by the 9.30 p.m. goods train to King's Cross, that the ghastly Transylvanian bloodsucker travelled inside his sinister box of mould, in search of fresh victims in other places ... Sleep well, my pretties ...

254. GOATHLAND, NORTH YORKSHIRE

Maps: OS Explorer OL27; Landranger 94

Travel: A169 from Whitby towards Pickering; in 5 miles, right on minor road to Goathland (OS ref. 834014).

Nearest railway station: Goathland, North York Moors Railway (www.nymr.co.uk)

In the heart of the northern sector of the North York Moors lies Goathland, a proper moorland village where sheep graze the rough grass and heather of the common land between the scattered houses. This is a place that vigorously celebrates the old tradition of Plough Monday, when young men in rural parishes all over Britain would drag a plough round their village on the Monday following 6 January (Twelfth Night), asking for alms and drinking plenty of beer, in commemoration of the first plough to break the soil following Noah's Flood. Mean persons, or those the ploughboys didn't like, would get their gardens and lawns ploughed up. In Goathland today it is all about the Plough Stots, the longsword dancing team who parade the village in pink-and-blue tunics, singing a verse which seems half-song, half-threat:

We're Goodlan Pleeaf Stots com'd ageean
All decked wi' ribbons fair,
Seea noo we'll do the best we can
An' the best can deea neea mair.

This kind of genial ritual perhaps helped to drive out a more malevolent kind in former times, for Goathland was a known haunt of witches. Anyone might be a witch. The best way to find out was to stick a cow's heart full of pins and roast it on the fire at midnight, then listen for the agonized screams of the witch whose heart would be scorching within her. Goathland even had its own family of witches, the Piersons. Awd Nanny and Young Nanny Pierson were the most feared of the clan. It was well known that Awd Nanny had the power to turn herself into a hare, like every self-respecting sorcerer.

Once, a young Goathland ploughboy fell in love with his landlord's daughter. Soon the girl's legs became paralysed. She discovered that her father, hoping to put the honest but impoverished suitor off, had paid Awd Nanny Pierson to cast a spell on her. The young man promptly consulted another practitioner of arcane arts, who prescribed a mixture of holy water and witch's blood to be applied to the sufferer's feet. The lover loaded his gun with a silver bullet and kept watch on Awd Nanny, waiting for an opportunity. When he saw her turn herself into a hare, he sent the silver bullet through the beast, collected its blood and applied it to the crippled legs. His girl sprang up into his arms, and shortly thereafter into the marriage bed. Huzzah!

255. ROSEDALE MOOR AND WHEELDALE MOOR, NORTH YORKSHIRE

Maps: OS Explorer OL27; Landranger 94

Travel: At Kirkbymoorside on A170 between Pickering and Helmsley, take minor road signed 'Hutton-le-Hole, Ryedale Folk Museum'. In

Hutton-le-Hole pass Folk Museum and turn right ('Lastingham'). In ¼ mile, left ('Rosedale'). Cross Spaunton Moor and descend Chimney Bank (very steep!) into Rosedale Abbey. Cross road in valley bottom and continue ('Castleton'), then take first right ('Egton'). In just under 2 miles cross Hamer Bridge; in another 1 ¼ miles, park in lay-by beside Public Bridleway signs near a 'road bumps' sign (OS ref. 744995).

Nearest railway station: Glaisdale (6 miles)

The Lyke Wake Walk long-distance path (40 miles from Osmotherley to Ravenscar – see pp. 284–5) crosses from White Moor on to Rosedale Moor at the lay-by. Bear west from the road along the boggy track across Rosedale Moor, or east across White Moor into Wheeldale Moor, and you enter a landscape of great desolation. The high moor is a forbidding place. The monks of Rosedale Abbey marked the travellers' tracks across these North Yorkshire moors by erecting large, easily seen stone crosses – with good reason. Mists, fierce winds and heavy rain frequently sweep across the landscape. In winter snow can lie thick. Even in summer, when the black heather turns green and the peat bogs dry out, the moor can seem a purgatorial place where it is easy to get lost and lose courage.

The eighteenth- and nineteenth-century lead miners who worked here in the harshest conditions imaginable left a legacy of spoil heaps all over the moor, now smothered in heather. The mine heaps and bare horizons seem daunting in their bleakness and the stark, admonitory finger of the standing stone known as Blue-Man-i'-th'-Moss only adds to the sense of isolation. Yet there is beauty here, too. Crystals of mica from the underlying acid sandstone lie in glittering white handfuls

Rosedale Moor

among the bent grass and tuffets of sedge. The blanket of heather is interspersed with clumps of mosses, some as smooth as velvet, others in individual stars, and with cushions of tiny lichens in pale green trumpets and bright scarlet match-heads. Grouse thrive on the heather shoots, often bursting away from underfoot with shrieks of *Go-back! Go-back!*, or ticking like erratic alarm clocks as they try to locate a mate.

256. ROSEDALE IRONSTONE RAILWAY, NORTH YORKSHIRE

Maps: OS Explorer OL26; Landranger 93, 94

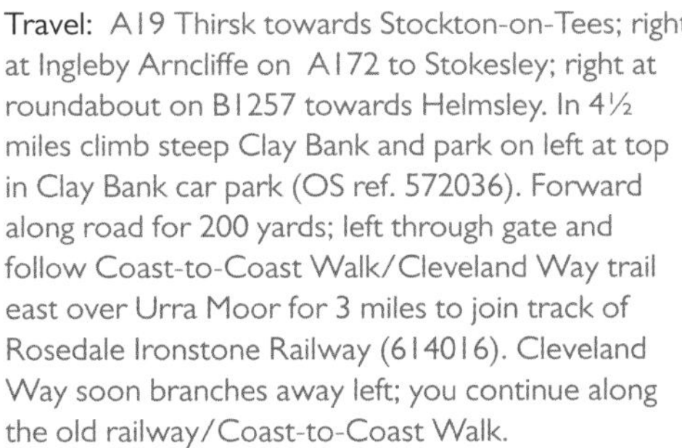

Travel: A19 Thirsk towards Stockton-on-Tees; right at Ingleby Arncliffe on A172 to Stokesley; right at roundabout on B1257 towards Helmsley. In 4½ miles climb steep Clay Bank and park on left at top in Clay Bank car park (OS ref. 572036). Forward along road for 200 yards; left through gate and follow Coast-to-Coast Walk/Cleveland Way trail east over Urra Moor for 3 miles to join track of Rosedale Ironstone Railway (614016). Cleveland Way soon branches away left; you continue along the old railway/Coast-to-Coast Walk.

The Rosedale Ironstone Railway was a most remarkable achievement. The 10-mile railway line, opened in 1861, ran from the ironstone mines at Bank Top above Rosedale Abbey, all the way west over the bleakest moors in North Yorkshire, to plunge down the 1-in-5 Ingleby Incline to more conventional railway connections 900 feet below. Apart from that fearsome incline the little railway hugged the contours all the way, sticking to the very edge of the moors as it skirted the rim of the deep valley of Farndale. At first things went well, and ore in scores of thousand of tons was shifted each year. But eventually the ore business became unprofitable, and the line closed in 1929. There in imprint on the moor it has stayed, a trackbed green in parts, in other places black and gritty, which snakes past the ruins of its operators' houses and fragments of plant.

To join the Rosedale railway line you strike out on the track of the Lyke Wake Walk (see below) across Urra Moor, a wild stretch of open moorland dotted with turf-covered grouse butts between which the grouse in ironic chorus cry *Go-back! Go-back!* The old railway track when you reach it is the best of guides in any weather up here on the roof of Middle Head, Blakey Head and High Blakey Moor. It swings and snakes, now on embankments, now through cuttings, eating up the miles of level walking through a desolate landscape that is a mixture of ancient mineral excavation and unblemished moorland. At the Lion Inn at Blakey the Lyke Wake Walk and Coast-to-Coast Walk swing off north, while the old trackbed turns south-east for the Bank Top ironstone mine ruins some 5 miles away, high above Rosedale Abbey. It is a strange juxtaposition, this ultimate expression of man's control over nature still clinging bravely on to its footprint in the wide moor where nature is slowly and steadily bringing its obliteration nearer to completion.

257. LYKE WAKE WALK, NORTH YORKS.

Maps: OS Explorer OL26, OL27; Landranger 93, 94, 99, 100

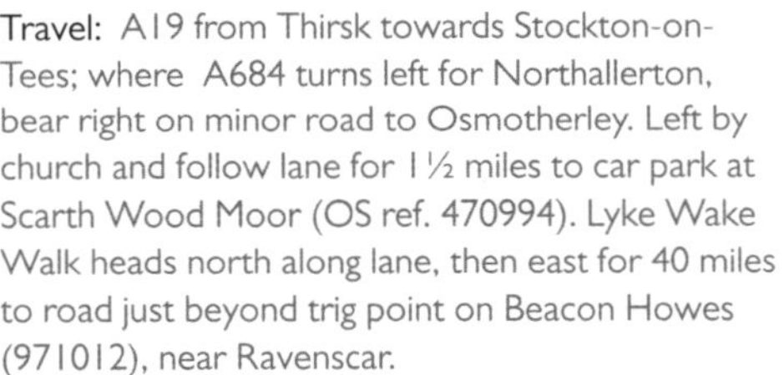

Travel: A19 from Thirsk towards Stockton-on-Tees; where A684 turns left for Northallerton, bear right on minor road to Osmotherley. Left by church and follow lane for 1 ½ miles to car park at Scarth Wood Moor (OS ref. 470994). Lyke Wake Walk heads north along lane, then east for 40 miles to road just beyond trig point on Beacon Howes (971012), near Ravenscar.

NB: The Lyke Wake Walk is extremely tough. It crosses bleak and exposed moorland, and is for very fit, experienced and confident hillwalkers. All details on the New Lyke Wake Club's website: www.lykewake.org.

Nearest railway station: Northallerton (7 miles from Osmotherley)

This yah neet, this yah neet,
— Ivvery neet an' all,
Fire an' fleet an' cannle leet,
An' Christ tak up thy saul.

So sing the Witches and Dirgers, the Masters, Mistresses and Doctors of the New Lyke Wake Club when they gather for their annual Wake. The singers are no ordinary mortals; in fact, many of them would claim they are no mortals at all, but souls who have passed through a particularly harrowing purgatory. To become a Witch or Dirger you must have accomplished the Lyke Wake Walk, a 40-mile traverse of the North York Moors, within twenty-four hours. The walk, devised by local farmer Bill Cowley, who thought it would make a fine challenge, crosses some of the toughest and wildest country in the north of England, a succession of windswept, open moors whose names remain stamped on the psyche of all who complete the trek – Holey Moor, Cringle Moor, Urra and Farndale, Jigger Howe and Stony Marl. Sticky, sloppy peat, bedded on sandstone, underlies the heather and coarse grass of these moors. In poor weather, in spite of modern attempts to surface its worse sections, the Lyke Wake Walk route becomes a black morass. Then the walkers – souls on their way to purgatory, according to their dirge – have good cause to recall whether or not they have been generous to their fellow man in life:

If ivver thoo gav owther hosen or shoon,
– Ivvery neet an' all,
Clap thee doon, an' put 'em on,
An' Christ tak up thy saul.

Bud if hosen an' shoon thoo nivver gav neean,
– Ivvery neet an' all,
T' whinnies'll prick thee sair ti t' beean,
An' Christ tak up thy saul.

Approaching the end of the walk, the aspirants cross Eller Beck Bridge on the A169 Pickering–Whitby road, a moment of relief from the boggy moors. Their souls, though, must cross 't' Brig o' Dreead'. If they have been free with their 'siller an' gowd' in life, they will find good footing on the bridge; if not, then they will fall off into 'Hell fleeame'.

There is one more big obstacle for the Lyke Wake Walkers to confront – the final 7-mile slog across High Moor and Stony Marl Moor. To bodies and spirits chilled and soaked to the bone, not to mention well blistered around the feet, this last stretch can seem like a form of Hell. The souls of the departed, though, having escaped the flames of Hell by crossing the Brig o' Dreead, now have to face those selfsame flames once more:

If ivver thoo gav owther bit or sup,
– Ivvery neet an' all,
T' fleeames'll nivver catch thee up,
An' Christ tak up thy saul.

Bud if bite or sup thoo nivver gav neean,
– Ivvery neet an' all,
T' fleeames'll bon thee sair ti t' beean,
An' Christ tak up thy saul.

The idea of the departed one's actions in life rebounding on the soul in death is central to most religions. But the notion of linking it to the exhausting and hazardous trudge across the wild North York Moors is truly salutary – especially for those hardy souls who win through to the heavenly moment when they reach the triangulation pillar on Beacon Howes and need take not one step more. Unless they are going for a double crossing. Or a treble. In which case they turn straight round and plunge out across Stony Marl Moor once more. Eternal punishment …

258. ARKENGARTHDALE, NORTH YORKS.

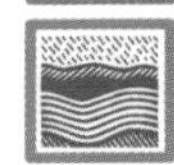

Maps: OS Explorer OL30; Landranger 92

Travel: Arkengarthdale is signed 'Langthwaite' from B6270 at Reeth in Swaledale. The road loops up through the dale to the Tan Hill Inn (OS ref. 896067).

Many people know Swaledale, wilder and more northerly than the gentler Wensleydale, but not so many know Swaledale's offshoot of Arkengarthdale, far lonelier and bleaker than its parent. The two dales between them produced 6,000 tons of lead a year at the height of the lead-mining industry in the seventeenth and eighteenth centuries. Spoil rubble patches, old levels and shafts, the bare ground of 'hushes'; all mark Arkengarthdale, but do not disfigure it.

A moorland road curves north up the dale from Reeth, passing the attractive settlement of Langthwaite, its atmospheric Red Lion pub tucked away in a diminutive village square below the bridge. There are no other hostelries in Arkengarthdale apart from the Red Lion and the nearby C.B. Inn; not even at Booze, a high-perched hamlet established by Methodist lead miners, and better reached on foot than by car.

The grey-and-pink spoil heaps of the lead mines ride out from the lower hillsides, some lightly sprinkled with grass, others as naked and repellent of plant life as when they were formed by the miners. As for the hushes, those hill becks whose water was dammed and then released to wash away the vegetation and reveal the ore beneath, their channels remain as torn and naked as ever. This is a landscape of industrial dereliction, tumbled and bare, that throws into greater relief the hard beauty of the moors that cradle it. Here and there you will spot the black hole of a mine level, its entrance neatly framed in dressed stone, a flooded, fern-sprouting tunnel into the heart of the hills. Through such scenes the road climbs on past Low and High Eskeleth, past the handful of houses at Whaw – wonderful raw-edged names – to run over bleak moors to the Tan Hill Inn (see below), the highest pub in England at 1,732 feet.

259. TAN HILL INN, NORTH YORKSHIRE

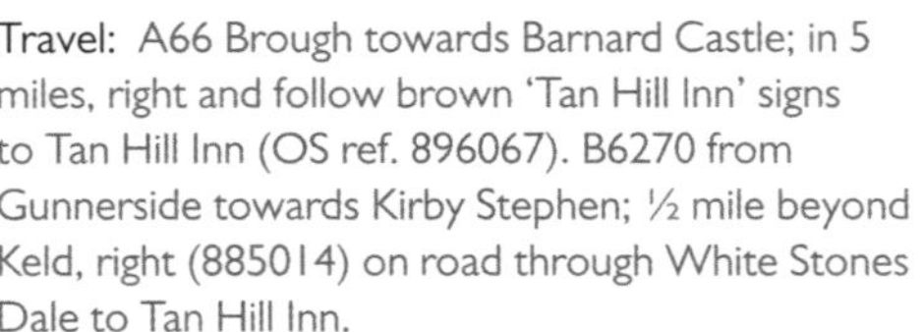
Maps: OS Explorer OL30; Landranger 91

Travel: A66 Brough towards Barnard Castle; in 5 miles, right and follow brown 'Tan Hill Inn' signs to Tan Hill Inn (OS ref. 896067). B6270 from Gunnerside towards Kirby Stephen; ½ mile beyond Keld, right (885014) on road through White Stones Dale to Tan Hill Inn.

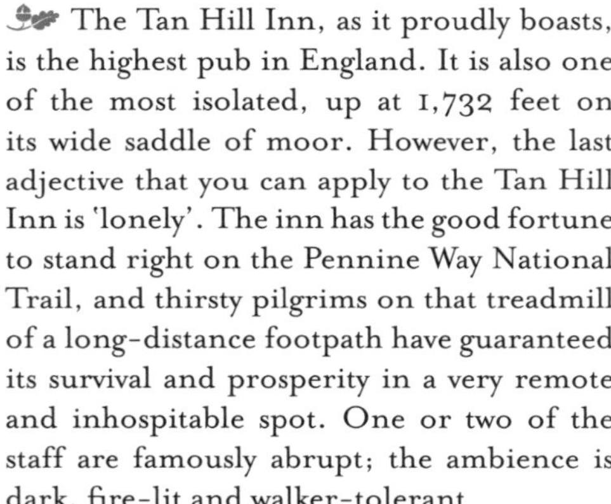
The Tan Hill Inn, as it proudly boasts, is the highest pub in England. It is also one of the most isolated, up at 1,732 feet on its wide saddle of moor. However, the last adjective that you can apply to the Tan Hill Inn is 'lonely'. The inn has the good fortune to stand right on the Pennine Way National Trail, and thirsty pilgrims on that treadmill of a long-distance footpath have guaranteed its survival and prosperity in a very remote and inhospitable spot. One or two of the staff are famously abrupt; the ambience is dark, fire-lit and walker-tolerant.

This plain stone building is Georgian, but there has been a hostelry of sorts here for many centuries. The Tan Hill Inn stands at the meeting place of North Yorkshire, Durham and Cumbria. What is now the Pennine Way was a packhorse trail and the drover's route on the way south out of Scotland, and a warm, dry place of resort was a necessity in such a bleak spot. Trade declined from that source with the improvement of roads and the advent of railways in easier locations at lower levels, but was kept up by the coal miners who worked small pits all over the moors around the inn. Their derelict shafts still pit the surroundings, some unguarded and highly dangerous.

Miners and packmen have gone; now it is the turn of the Pennine Way walkers to

Tan Hill Inn

haul their weary and weather-beaten bodies in at the door, no doubt drawn by Alfred Wainwright's foot-of-the-page comment in his *Pennine Way Companion*: 'Never was a pint better earned.' Reluctance to face out into wind and rain along the next stretch of the trail can be attributed to the pithy Wainwright-ism at the foot of the following page: 'Penance for sins.'

260. WEST STONES DALE, WHITSUNDALE AND BIRKDALE, NORTH YORKSHIRE

Maps: OS Explorer OL30; Landranger 92

Travel: B6270 from Gunnerside towards Kirkby Stephen; ½ mile beyond Keld, right (OS ref. 885014) on road through White Stones Dale to Tan Hill Inn (see above). Whitsundale is accessible on foot from bridge across the River Swale (871014 – 'Raven Seat' fingerposts) 1½ mile west of Keld on B6270; this road continues north-west up Birkdale towards Kirkby Stephen.

The road from Swaledale through West Stones Dale runs between wildflower haymeadows rich in buttercups, cranesbill and meadowsweet. Stonecrop, soft mosses and vetches colonize the stone walls. Peewits, snipe and curlew call from the wet fellsides. This is a beautiful little dale; and so is Whitsundale just to the west. A path rises from the B6270 road by the abandoned buildings of Smithy Holme to run north above the very steep and narrow dale – more of a miniature gorge than a dale, with high cliffs flanking the waterfalls and sinuous curves of Whitsundale Beck. At Ravenseat, a cluster of farm buildings a long mile up the dale, you cross the beck and return by the other bank.

Birkdale, through which the Swaledale road runs towards Kirkby Stephen, is the bleakest and moodiest of all the dales – treeless, forbidding dun-coloured moorland, set with peat bogs and dilapidated old stone barns. Birkdale Tarn lies hidden just north of the road; once you have climbed up to it, you will be the focus of attention of the hundreds of black-headed gulls that breed here. It is a good spot to linger, sitting by the steely lake and looking out across a landscape of great though sombre beauty.

261. GREAT SHUNNER FELL, NORTH YORKSHIRE

Maps: OS Explorer OL30; Landranger 98

Travel: A684 Sedbergh towards Hawes; just before reaching Appersett, 1 mile from Hawes, turn left to Hardraw. Park in the village (OS ref. 867912). Follow Pennine Way for 4½ miles up to Great Shunner Fell summit cairn (849973). Another 3 miles of descent leads to B6270 in Thwaite (889984).

You can scarcely get lost ascending

Great Shunner Fell. For all this mighty moorland shoulder's breadth and length (it covers about 20 square miles, according to Alfred Wainwright's *Pennine Way Companion*), the Pennine Way National Trail has been in steady use for nearly half a century, and all those years of tramping by what must amount to millions of boots have worn a very visible path in the moor grass and heather. The Way is marked hereabouts by great solid cairns of stone, so even in murky weather you have pretty reliable navigational aids. That said, there is something about Great Shunner Fell that saps more energy than many another far harder and higher hill, whether it is the gentle but persistent upward climb of over 1,500 feet from Hardraw, the immensity of not very much to look at in the foreground, or how the vastness of the prospect means bad weather always seems to be in view. I suggest bringing plenty of chocolate.

A rutted old miners' track leads between stone walls up Bluebell Hill and on to the grassy, sedgy moor. Then it is simply a steady upward climb, with views growing wider all the way. The miniature ramparts of peat hags make black lines near and far; wheatears flirt their white rumps (demonstrating how they got their sadly bowdlerized country name of 'white-arse') and in spring and summer the mournful calls of curlew and golden plover bubble across the moors. Up at the summit you stand at 2,349 feet, higher than anything else for many a mile. The views are panoramic – the twin fells of Ingleborough and Penyghent in the south; Nine Standards Rigg 5 miles to the north; the great rough dome of Cross Fell 10 or more miles beyond that; a long tumble of moors around Swaledale in the east; Whernside (see pp. 291–3) and the jagged and toothy silhouette of the Lake District off in the west. This is an absolutely breathtaking view of rough northern country. Pray for a fine day to appreciate it all.

262. WIDDALE, COTTERDALE AND GRISEDALE, NORTH YORKSHIRE

Maps: Explorer OL2, OL19; Landranger 98

Travel: B6255 runs through Widdale, from Ingleton on A65 Settle–Kendal road (OS ref. 682732) to Hawes on A684. Cotterdale (842921) and Grisedale (770903) are each signed north off A684 between Hawes and Sedbergh.

Widdale rises north-east from Ingleton without a name – locals call this part of the dale 'Chapel le Dale', after its sole village. Limestone outcrops scar the dale sides. There are impressive show caves at White Scar, where an eighty-minute underground walk lets visitors see what water can do to limestone in the way of caverns and stalactites. As you near the dale head the twenty-four arches of the Ribblehead Viaduct on the Settle & Carlisle Railway come dramatically into view, with the great hulk of Whernside and the lion-head profile of Ingleborough guarding the dale on each flank. Once past the viaduct you enter Widdale proper, a stretch of splendidly bleak moorland that reaches all the way down to the busy little market town of Hawes.

A couple of miles west of Hawes a side lane rises from the A864 Sedbergh road, marked 'Cotterdale only'.

Three Halls, two Kirks and a King –
Same road out as goes in.

So ran the old rhyme about Cotterdale when

the Halls, Kirks and Kings were farming families in this isolated dale. From the summit of the lane you get a wonderful view up the broad, short valley with its scattered stone barns and cluster of houses at the end. Up there, sombre blankets of conifers press down on the hamlet of Cotterdale. Some of the houses are spick-and-span holiday conversions; others are crumbling.

Grisedale, four miles further west, had its moment of fame a couple of decades ago when *The Dale that Died* became a book and TV documentary hit for Barry Cockcroft. He detailed how the dale farmers had one by one given up and left this lovely but remote valley. When the red-hot Methodist preacher and fiddle player Dick Atkinson was striding the Grisedale fells in argument with the Devil in the 1880s, there were enough families in the dale to make up 'Dick Atkinson's Disciples', a passionately evangelical bunch. Today the farmer at Mouse Sike is the only one still tending the wildflower hay meadows and the sheep in this haunting, beautiful valley.

263. BISHOPDALE, WALDEN AND COVERDALE, NORTH YORKSHIRE

Maps: OS Explorer OL30; Landranger 98, 99

Travel: B6160 runs the length of Bishopdale between A684 Leyburn–Hawes road (OS ref. 028888) and Buckden in Wharfedale. Walden is signed 'Walden only' from the top of West Burton village green (017866). Coverdale is signed 'Carlton' from West Witton on A684 (063884).

These three neighbouring dales run parallel, north-east to south-west, between Wensleydale and Wharfedale. Thoralby and Newbiggin at the northern foot of Bishopdale are two farming hamlets; Thoralby has the George, a small and typically Dales-style pub, friendly and uncomplicated. At Newbiggin, the Town Head Farm buildings show two carved lintel stones dated 1670 and 1690 – worth stopping for. As you go south between stone walls on Bishopdale's valley road, you can admire many fine traditional longhouses, the house and barn built all of a piece under the same roof, a style initiated by the Norsemen when they settled the Dales 1,200 years ago. The road rises to Kirkstone Pass at 1,400 feet, before tipping steeply down to Buckden.

The road in Walden (strictly speaking, it is not called Waldendale) divides soon after leaving West Burton. The left fork takes you on for 3 miles high above the east side of the dale, while the right meanders up to the intriguingly named Kentucky House. Both are dead-end lanes, so the only possible reason for penetrating this quiet and secluded little dale is to get out of the car sooner rather than later and climb one of the signposted tracks up on to the moor. Here you'll find nesting curlew, plenty of sheep, and wonderful wide views over the green cleft of Walden Beck.

Coverdale, the most easterly of these three dales, contains two splendid pubs: the Forester's Arms at Carlton, a noted eating house, and higher up the dale the admirably welcoming and 'unimproved' Thwaite Arms at Horsehouse. The straggly, narrow road was once the main through route for London–Richmond coaches, though the notorious 1 in 4 slope of the road at Park Rash above Kettlewell always made travel here a nerve-racking business. Coach horses were changed at the Thwaite Arms, still a pub at which to get enthusiastic and opinionated views on Coverdale affairs past and present. Near the summit of the road stands the craggy old Hunter's Stone: the monks of Coverham Abbey erected it as a skyline waymark, and inscribed it with a cross as a blessing for intrepid travellers.

264. BARDALE, RAYDALE AND CRAGDALE, NORTH YORKSHIRE

Maps: OS Explorer OL30; Landranger 98

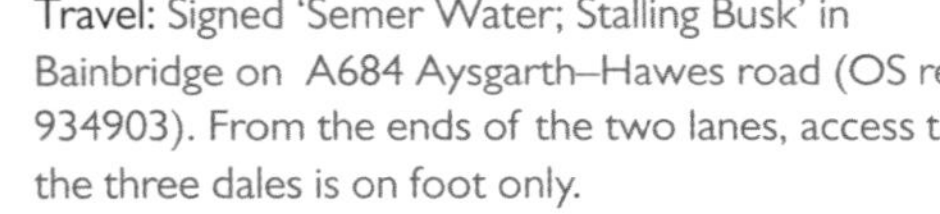

Travel: Signed 'Semer Water; Stalling Busk' in Bainbridge on A684 Aysgarth–Hawes road (OS ref. 934903). From the ends of the two lanes, access to the three dales is on foot only.

These three tight little dales join at Marsett, a lost-and-gone farming hamlet. Here their three becks combine to form the River Bain, a short tributary flowing north to join the River Ure in Wensleydale. Very few Wensleydale tourists turn up the two narrow lanes that flank the Bain; those that do are mostly making for the pretty lake of Semer Water, where troops of mendicant ducks pester all comers. Legend says that a fabulous city lies beneath the lake waters, drowned by the curse of a vengeful angel disguised as a beggar who had been roughly turned away from the city. And fact supports at least part of the tale: when the level of Semer Water was lowered in 1937, traces of ancient lake dwellings came to light.

But follow these lanes beyond the lake either to Stalling Busk, a cluster of houses on the hillside, or to Marsett, down in the dale bottom, and you will find superb scenery and peace and solitude. From Stalling Busk rough stony tracks rise to curve across the roadless moorland slopes above the empty Cragdale. From Marsett, whose name derives from the Norse word *saetr*, a 'summer pasture', you can stroll through beautifully kept pasture and hayfields to Raydale House, or strike out from the bridge along the right bank of Bardale Beck into the narrow, lonely valley of Bardale.

265. CAM HIGH ROAD, NORTH YORKS.

Maps: OS Explorer OL2; Landranger 98

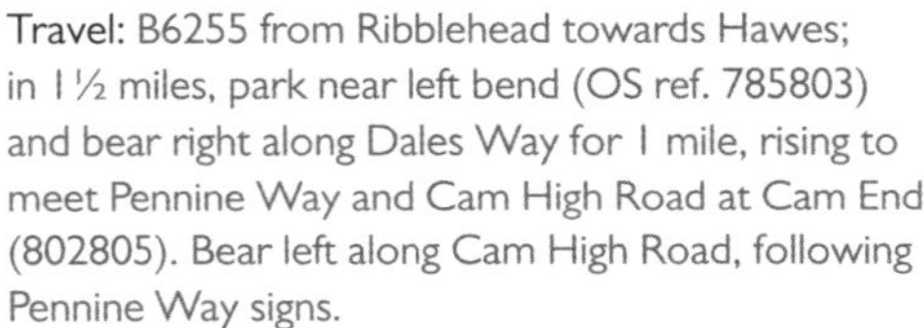

Travel: B6255 from Ribblehead towards Hawes; in 1½ miles, park near left bend (OS ref. 785803) and bear right along Dales Way for 1 mile, rising to meet Pennine Way and Cam High Road at Cam End (802805). Bear left along Cam High Road, following Pennine Way signs.

Nearest railway station: Ribblehead (1½ miles)

The landscape around Cam Fell has no dramatic aspects, but it is fantastically wild and exhilarating to walk in. The broad hill backs of Cam Fell and Dodd Fell trend north-east from Ribblesdale towards the wide green pastures of Wensleydale, nearly 10 miles of bleak uplands, carrying on their backs a high road that was once a Roman marching track heading for the fort at Bainbridge. The Romans built their Pennine highway as they did all their roads: with precision and pragmatism. Cleverly sited to have clear views all round, keeping just off the ridge itself, the Roman road was paved with stones and built 5 yards wide with a camber to let the rainwater – then, as now, a feature of any journey through the Pennines – flow off the trackway and into the flood ditches. Later generations resurfaced the old road, ran a continuous boundary of stone walling along each flank, and christened it Cam High Road. Packhorse trains used it, and eighteenth-century horsemen and wagons

travelled its rough surface on their way from Yorkshire into Lancaster.

For 2½ miles the Pennine Way National Trail takes advantage of Cam High Road, and this stretch from Cam End north-east to Kidhow Gate is the most atmospheric: a broad track, stony in the dry and miry in the wet, with beautiful grassy stretches now in the process of being reduced to mud by off-road vehicles. But where people once tramped the old moorland road out of necessity, now they do so for the pleasure of high and wild surroundings.

266. KINGSDALE, NORTH YORKSHIRE

Maps: OS Explorer OL2; Landranger 98

Travel: A65 from Kirby Lonsdale towards Settle; left on B6255 towards Ingleton; in 300 yards, left through Thornton in Lonsdale, where minor road beside church (OS ref. 686736) rises through Kingsdale towards Dent. For Yorda's Cave (705791), park on right at bottom of rise opposite a gate, with Kingsdale Beck on far side of dale. Go through gate and climb to right of cleft. Through another gate, and Yorda's Cave is on your left.

NB: A torch is useful in Yorda's Cave.

Kingsdale rises north-east from the Greta valley, a long straight dale with wonderful limestone crags each side. Near the lonely farm of Kingsdale Head stands the threadbare Yorda's Wood, its trees sheltering the low black mouth of Yorda's Cave. Here Norse legend sited the lair of Yorda, a giant with a penchant for stamping about and swallowing the local infants. You'll need a powerful torch and waterproof boots to explore the cave, a fair-sized cavern with a roof 30 feet high in places. It runs back 130 feet into the hill, full of the rushing and splashing of a stream that

Yorda's Cave, Kingsdale

falls at the far end. After heavy rain the floor can be awash, but this is the time when the sound of the fall grows to a thunder, and the ambience that gave birth to tales of an ogre comes to the fore. Candlelit tours of Yorda's Cave became all the rage for nineteenth-century Romantics.

Above the cave you can turn left to follow the Turbary Road, an old turf-cutter's track running south high above Kingsdale with spectacular views into the dale. It passes several magnificent and fearsome potholes, including one with the highly poetic and onomatopoeic name of Jingling Pot.

267. THREE PEAKS – PENYGHENT, WHERNSIDE AND INGLEBOROUGH

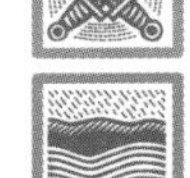

Maps: OS Explorer OL2; Landranger 98

Travel: M6 to Junction 36; A65 to Settle; B6479 to Horton-in-Ribblesdale. Various alternative paths join the three peaks of Penyghent, Whernside and Ingleborough. Contact the Penyghent Café (tel: 01729 860333) in Horton-in-Ribblesdale for details of the walking circuit.

NB: The Three Peaks Walk is a proper challenge,

involving 24 miles of tough, tiring walking and 5,000 feet of ascent. It is for fit, determined and experienced hillwalkers only. Take full hillwalking gear, food, drink.

Nearest railway station: Horton-in-Ribblesdale

The Three Peaks Walk is a single day's long sharp shock. At the Penyghent Café in Horton-in-Ribblesdale walkers clock in before they commence their early-morning ascent into purgatory. The café is also the haven to which they return towards nightfall, peat-stained and sore-footed, to a warm welcome and pint mugs of strong tea. The statistics can be simply told: you walk a circuit of about 24 miles, climbing around 5,000 feet on the way, taking in the three peaks of Penyghent (2,273 feet), Whernside (2,419 feet) and Ingleborough (2,373 feet). The idea is to do it in under twelve hours, thereby entitling yourself to wear the badge and tie of the Three Peaks of Yorkshire Club, and to display its small but coveted certificate.

Penyghent, the first fell to tackle if you walk the route anticlockwise, looks like a sleeping lion, its muzzle and paws extended to the south. Like Whernside and Ingleborough, its limestone bulk is capped by millstone grit, hard, sparkling stuff. You snake your way up beside limestone walls, out of green pastures and up to the heights among slippery dark gritstone clints. At the summit stands an OS triangulation pillar, very often swathed in mist. It is a steepish drop down; then you leave the stone-pitched paths so well maintained by the National Park wardens, to embark on a long boggy slog through the quaking quagmires of Black Dub Moss.

Finally, smeared with peat and soaked in beck water, you struggle on to the road at Lodge Hall, a noble old farmhouse with '1687' inscribed over the door. Beyond curves the mighty Ribblehead Viaduct of the Settle & Carlisle Railway, its twenty-four arches marching in step across a wide wet valley. You pass long green hummocks and trenches in the grass – these are remnants of the shops, huts and hospital of the army of railway navvies, at times 3,000 strong, who camped here while they were building the viaduct. The persevering, dogged spirit of Victorian railway engineering reached a kind of zenith with the construction of the Ribblehead Viaduct. It took six years, during which the navvies rioted, randied, drank, fought, achieved incredible feats with shovel and barrow, and died in droves from disease and accidents. The year of the viaduct's completion, 1875, stands emblazoned in gold above the central arch. Further along the track you cross the railway above the mouth of Blea Moor tunnel. Navvies burrowed the tunnel under the moor with dynamite and pickaxe; the spoil they excavated still lies in high heaps above Blea Moor, as bleakly beautiful a spot as any in the Pennines.

Climbing up the interminable spine of Whernside there is a good view south to the sphinx-like profile of Ingleborough, the third of the three peaks. The path over the soft bog is surfaced with flagstones salvaged from mill floors. Put your head down and trudge up into the mist to reach Whernside's triangulation pillar – the highest spot in Yorkshire at 2,419 feet – some 15 miles out from Horton-in-Ribblesdale. Two down; one to go.

The descent from Whernside is fiendishly

steep, but a gentle stroll through green sheep pastures follows. Unfortunately Ingleborough provides a nasty sting in the tail for anticlockwise walkers. From a distance the mountain looks no more difficult to climb than Penyghent. But as you approach over Black Shiver Moss, realization dawns: after walking 20 toughish miles, you are now expected to climb an almost sheer, 500-foot scree face. Somehow you scramble up, and steer for the final trig point. All around are the hut circles and crumbled walls of the Iron Age tribes who regularly took refuge up here. In one corner lie the broken remnants of a rest house, built in 1830 for climbers; it was demolished by over-refreshed revellers on the very day it opened.

Down in Horton-in-Ribblesdale, after clocking in at the Penyghent Café, sip your mug of celebratory tea and revel in a feeling of immense satisfaction, while you plan a return trip to climb the peaks in a more leisurely manner and savour everything you missed this time out.

268. LANGSTROTHDALE, NORTH YORKS.

Maps: OS Explorer OL30; Landranger 98

Travel: From M6 Junction 37, A684 via Sedbergh to Hawes; right on minor road through Gayle for 10 miles to pass down Langstrothdale to Church of St Michael and the George Inn at Hubberholme (OS ref. 924782).

Of the various dales that send tributaries into Wharfedale, Langstrothdale is the northerly extension down which the infant River Wharfe rushes over innumerable shallow falls into its namesake dale. Bronze Age people left their burial circle of stumpy stones by the Wharfe halfway up Langstrothdale, and later Norsemen settled here and gave their names to the farmsteads that still stand along the river – Deepdale, the house at the bottom of the valley; Beckermonds, the house at the mouth of the becks; Yockenthwaite, Eogan's farm. The long stone dwellings built all of a piece with the cattle byres echo the Norse longhouses that preceded them. Back then Langstrothdale was so thickly wooded that people said a squirrel could go the length of the dale and never set foot on the ground. He would have to be a champion jumper today – the sycamores and thorn trees are reduced to thin patches along the river and the high terraces of outcropping limestone.

Up above Yockenthwaite a green road runs along the limestone balcony to reach lonely Scar House, a quiet enough place these days, though what scenes of excitement and fervour there were in 1652 when George Fox, the Nottingham shoemaker's apprentice, arrived alight with religious ecstasy, fresh from his transformative revelations on Pendle Hill (see p. 312). In those days, when nonconformist sects were outlawed and forbidden to gather, Scar House became a great clandestine meeting place for the Friends in Truth, who were to become better known as the Quakers.

Hubberholme lies below at the dale foot where Langstrothdale becomes Wharfedale. Here you'll find the very characterful George Inn beside a handsome bow-backed packhorse bridge, and the dark little Church of St Michael in whose churchyard are scattered the ashes of J. B. Priestley, writer and champion of the working man. In the shadows of the church beside the old rood loft (carved in 1558, when no one knew whether it was safer to stick with the old Catholic religion or to throw in their lot with the new Church of England), you can find a scurry of little playful mice carved into the oaken pews by their maker, the celebrated woodcarver Robert Thompson.

269. GORDALE SCAR, NORTH YORKS.

Maps: OS Explorer OL2; Landranger 98

Travel: A65 from Skipton towards Settle. At Gargrave, right; in 1 mile left ('Malham'), through Airton to Malham. Park in village car park (OS ref. 900627). Follow Gordale Lane for 1 mile to Gordale Bridge (913635); bear left off lane to follow footpath through Gordale Scar.

Gordale Scar bites down through the limestone upland plateau north of Malham, a stunning piece of geological freakery. All this area lay under a mile-thick sheet of ice during the last Ice Age, and when the great melt took place the unleashed waters sliced through the soft limestone to create a great canyon with walls that rise nearly 200 feet in places. Into this you step from the farm lane like a Lilliputian into the fold of a Brobdingnagian piecrust. A twisted, compressed central 'staircase' of tufa, or crystallized limestone, rises between the walls and forms a cascade for Gordale Beck. It is worth scrambling up beside the first waterfall, for craning your head back you will see overhangs of rock at the lip of the Scar that hint at the previous existence of a roof.

Follow the rough, rocky bed of Gordale Scar as it takes a great anticlockwise bend, and beyond the waterfalls you will reach the upper section. The path climbs to the left and tops out in a grey sea of limestone pavement spattered with wild flowers, high above the bed of the gorge, which runs on northwards for another mile to meet an ancient Roman road and camp foundations in the uplands.

Gordale Scar was exactly the kind of craggy, rugged natural feature so beloved of the Romantic movement of the early nineteenth century. J. M. W. Turner painted it around 1816, but the most dramatic depiction, painted at roughly the same time as Turner's, is James Ward's *A View of Gordale*, an overwhelmingly dark and wild scene – a deep burrow in the psyche as much as in the earth.

270. GRASSINGTON MOOR, NORTH YORKSHIRE

Maps: OS Explorer OL2; Landranger 98

Travel: M65, A56, A59 to Skipton; from A65 Skipton bypass, B6265 to Threshfield and Grassington. Park in car park beyond bridge; walk into Grassington. At top of town (OS ref. 003642) follow Moor Lane for 1¼ miles to Yarnbury (015659), then Old Moor Lane and footpath on to Grassington Moor.

The great thing about Grassington Moor, apart from its beauty and emptiness, is the fact that you can walk there at all. Only in May 2005, when the provisions of the CROW Act of 2000 were implemented in Wharfedale, were members of the public legally allowed to take their first steps away from the public rights of way that skirt this huge area of Pennine upland. Grassington Moor is the most accessible section of some 25 square miles of open moor that was formerly crossed by just one footpath. Now it is everyone's right – subject to a few limited and temporary sporting and conservation restrictions – to wander where they will.

What do you find when you have climbed the long stony trod of Old Moor Lane and emerged on the open moor 600 feet above Grassington? At first a track snakes you through a desolate area of abandoned lead mines – great spoil heaps, wind-ruffled pools, broken buildings. Then you see the shoulder of Great Whernside raised over the skyline to the north, white with snow in winter. Walk up over low cliffs of limestone, across the crumbling walls of the high sheepfolds, until the last walls are behind you and the gently rising ground leads you over the skyline of Bycliffe Hill. Even here there are disused mine shafts, pink-and-grey mounds of lead-mine spoil and the hummocks of walls that once sheltered miners. Stand and marvel at the hardiness of those men in this bleak landscape, even as you wince at the thought of the poverty that drove them up here week after week. Out on Grassington Moor top it is all stream-cut land of bog and moss, where huge shake holes open and puny streams trickle down the gradual slopes – Crag Grainings, Straight Grainings and Old Stones Dike, draining out of Featherbed Moss and the lonely lake of Priest's Tarn. You may never get this far, and if you do you will be wet and plastered to the knee. But anywhere you roam up here will put you nose to nose with nature in the raw.

271. THE STRID, NORTH YORKSHIRE

Maps: OS Explorer OL2; Landranger 104

Travel: M65, A56, A59 to Skipton and Bolton Bridge; left on B6160 past Bolton Abbey. In another 2 miles, car park on right (OS ref. 059564). Walk down path through woods to the Strid (064564).

NB: Please take great care near the Strid – the rocks are very slippery.

Nearest railway stations: Skipton (7 miles); Embsay or Bolton Abbey stations (Embsay & Bolton Abbey Steam Railway: www.embsayboltonabbeyrailway.org.uk)

The woodland paths of the Bolton Abbey Estate in lower Wharfedale have been free of access to all since the rector of Bolton Abbey, the Reverend William Carr, laid out 30 miles of footpaths in the early nineteenth century. They became a refuge for countless West Riding mill hands, who flocked by train and charabanc to the sinuous bends of the River Wharfe in its beautiful limestone bed. Here among the beech, oak and sycamore they could unwind and escape the smoke, noise and overcrowded streets of the industrial towns where they lived and worked all week. To such constrained folk, leading such unnatural lives, the woods and river seemed wild enough in themselves, and there was one genuinely untamed and thrilling feature to cap all the rest – the turbulent narrows of the Strid.

You know when you are nearing the Strid by the noise, a hissing among the trees. After heavy rain when the water race is at its most powerful the rushing noise is accompanied by a deep drumming vibration, so that you

The Strid, River Wharfe

are prepared for something mighty to be waiting round the bend. The Strid appears as a gash of white in the green of the woods. In this section of the Wharfe's bed a string of caverns has collapsed, leaving their roofs open to the sky but preserving their hollow chambers each side of the narrows. The river, under enormous pressure after rain, forces its way through the narrow waist of rock, scouring round the chambers and shaking the hollows underground. It sluices dramatically, charged with dissolved peat from further up the dale, as glassy brown and thick with bubbles as boiling sugar – a compelling spectacle of fury.

The narrows look temptingly easy to jump across, but the rocks are slippery with treacherous green lichen. Stories say that those who fall in to their deaths are later seen rising from the water in the likeness of a white horse. Over the years many have tried the leap, and many have been swallowed and drown. As locals will tell you, no one who fails the leap has ever had a second go.

272. BRONTË MOORS, WEST YORKS.

Maps: OS Explorer OL21; Landranger 103, 104

Travel: From M62 Junction 24, A629 to Barcroft; left on B6033 ('Hebden Bridge'); in ¼ mile, right on B6142 to Haworth. Park in village car park; walk up hill to church and Brontë Parsonage (OS ref. 029372). Follow public footpath signs to Haworth Moor, taking Cemetery Road to a T-junction (016365). Cross on to track ('Brontë Waterfalls') for 1½ miles to Brontë Bridge, Chair and Falls (999358). From here follow 'Top Withins' signs for 1¼ miles to reach Pennine Way National Trail; left for 300 yards to Top Withins ruins (981354).

Nearest railway stations: Haworth, Keighley & Worth Valley Railway (www.kwvr.co.uk)

Top Withins and the Brontë moors

The parsonage in the village of Haworth, where the three Brontë sisters sat to brood and write at the dining-room table, is now a world-famous museum. Yet the rampant inspiration that produced their literature seems hard to fit within the compass of such narrow, respectable walls. Wandering through the parsonage, admiring Charlotte's long-sleeved dresses, Anne's collection of Scarborough pebbles and Emily's sketchbook, it is difficult to credit that dark Mr Rochester, drunken Arthur Huntingdon and the demonic Heathcliff took shape here in the minds of such confined and inexperienced young women. It is out on the puddled moor paths, looking over wind-whipped heather towards dark clouds boiling on the skyline, that the source of their power and inspiration becomes clear, for the Brontë sisters adored this wild countryside and wandered it at will. Their old nurse, Tabitha Aykroyd, told them its fairy, ghost and goblin tales; these, together with the bleakness, wild weather and harsh beauty of the landscape, helped give birth to *Jane Eyre*, *The Tenant of Wildfell Hall* and, most sensationally, *Wuthering Heights*.

Walking out across the moors by way of the Brontë Bridge and Falls of Sladen Beck, a favourite destination of the sisters, you can reach the Pennine Way and the hard black walls of the ruined farmhouse, Top Withins:

> *One may guess the power of the north wind, blowing over the edge, by the excessive slant of a few stunted firs at the end of the house; and by a range of gaunt thorns all stretching their limbs one way, as if craving alms of the sun. Happily the architect had the foresight to build it strong; the narrow windows are deeply set in the wall, and the corners defended with large jutting stones.*

It is not an absolute certainty that Emily modelled Heathcliff's dark and rugged lair of Wuthering Heights on Top Withins Farm, but the isolated farmhouse on the moor was well known to her, and its lonely aspect and setting make it the most likely candidate. Sitting by the ruin and staring over the wide expanse of land before you, you can picture the savage dogs, surly servants and cheerless chambers of Wuthering Heights, the horror of Cathy crying for admittance and rapping on the windows with her bleeding hands in the snowstorm. Arching over all is the relentless will of that passionate lover and hater, Heathcliff, embodiment of the wild spirit of the moors.

273. HARDIBUTTS FARM, WEST YORKS.

Maps: OS Explorer OL21; Landranger 103

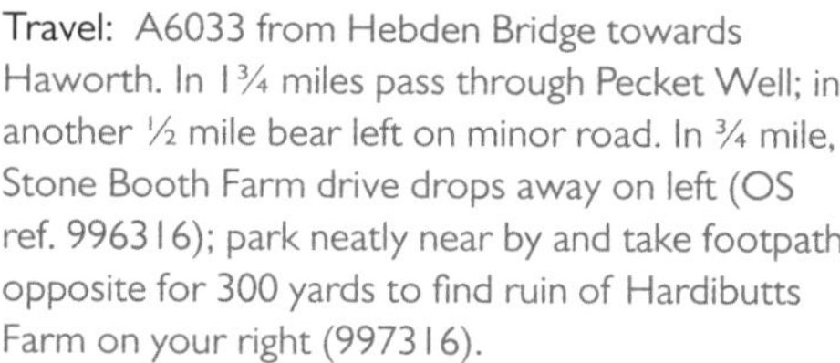

Travel: A6033 from Hebden Bridge towards Haworth. In 1¾ miles pass through Pecket Well; in another ½ mile bear left on minor road. In ¾ mile, Stone Booth Farm drive drops away on left (OS ref. 996316); park neatly near by and take footpath opposite for 300 yards to find ruin of Hardibutts Farm on your right (997316).

NB: Hardibutts Farm is on private land.

Nearest railway station: Hebden Bridge (3½ miles)

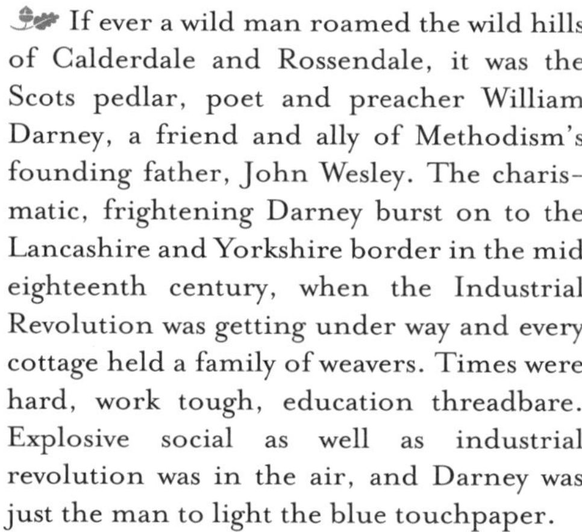

If ever a wild man roamed the wild hills of Calderdale and Rossendale, it was the Scots pedlar, poet and preacher William Darney, a friend and ally of Methodism's founding father, John Wesley. The charismatic, frightening Darney burst on to the Lancashire and Yorkshire border in the mid eighteenth century, when the Industrial Revolution was getting under way and every cottage held a family of weavers. Times were hard, work tough, education threadbare. Explosive social as well as industrial revolution was in the air, and Darney was just the man to light the blue touchpaper.

The Scotsman's rantings and his roams across the moors came vividly to life in Glyn Hughes's 1982 novel, *Where I Used to Play on the Green*, in which Darney appears as a 'good-looking rough man, huge, with a big red beard and hair'. Often threatened, chased, pelted with stones and ducked in streams, Darney was an outcast, a ragged bugaboo figure to frighten good Protestant children, yet he found a rapt audience in this district. He worked as a clog-maker, but his real business was to stride the hills and valleys with a sack of self-penned poems, hymns and religious tracts, preaching in out-of-the-way barns where his congregation of weavers, miners and farmhands would cram in, falling to their knees under the onslaught of Darney's rhetoric. He overwhelmed them with bursts of hellfire, glimpses of Heaven and fierce admonishment, until they burst out with: 'I'm saved, Brothers! Sisters, I'm saved!'

The ruin of Hardibutts Farm, where Darney often came to preach, stands in a field beside the old road over the moors from Hebden Bridge to Keighley. The roof is in shreds, the walls full of holes. Through the stone-mullioned farmhouse windows you can see the great stone fireplaces where the Methodist pioneers would warm themselves after their long wet journeys. And round at the end you can make out the butt end of the barn where Darney's fiery preaching set the brushwood of nonconformism so spectacularly alight across these hills and dales.

274. HEBDEN WATER, WEST YORKSHIRE

Maps: OS Explorer OL21; Landranger 103

Travel: From M65 Junction 9, A646 to Hebden Bridge. Left on A6033 towards Haworth; in ¾ mile, left to park at Hardcastle Crags car park (OS ref. 987292). Follow red-and-white, then red waymark poles down to the river's edge, then upstream past Gibson Mill (973298), crossing river here, then recrossing to right bank in 1 mile by footbridge beside weir and stone hut (973309). Cross side beck by stone bridge, and bear right through stone wall gap. Climb steep path on left bank of beck to reach farmyard (974313). Turn right by Walshaw Cottage along stony lane; follow this for 1½ miles to Shackleton (983295), where footpath fingerpost points right down walled field track. Cross stile at bottom; bear left and down through woodland for ⅓ mile to reach car park.

Nearest railway station: Hebden Bridge (1½ miles)

In the latter half of the twentieth century, what wasn't all muck and clatter in the industrial West Riding of Yorkshire seemed deserted and derelict: mills, textile factories, tall chimneys and terraced houses under bleak moors, a working landscape bitten savagely by recession. Though the old industrial towns have smartened up their fine Victorian buildings and their nightlife, lonely country still lies all around – much of it, like the deep cleft of the Hebden Water, right on the doorstep of the valley-bottom towns.

The Hebden Water comes down from the Brontë moors, and something of their wild spirit comes, too, especially after heavy rain. The rocky, muddy path beside the river winds under the oaks, pines and sycamores that clothe the steep sides of Hebden Dale. Hebden Bridge, the mill town lying at the foot of the dale, has cleaned its old black buildings to reveal the creamy colour of their sparkling gritstone, and these days it's hard to believe that the town and the narrow ravine of Hebden Dale were once the scene of grimy, smoky industry, lying under a permanent pall of smoke and loud with the roar of looms. The swift-flowing Hebden Water itself once powered a whole string of mills. Halfway up the dale stands Gibson Mill, built at the turn of the nineteenth century, when to lavish fine neoclassical architecture on an industrial building deep in an obscure dale seemed perfectly normal, a natural expression of aspiration and prosperity.

After a couple of miles you thread the rocky outcrops of Hardcastle Crags and scramble steeply up to reach the grim dark house of Walshaw. From here a lane high at the brink of the ravine loops back towards Hebden

Bridge, passing the isolated moorland farms of Lady Royd and Shackleton with their wide views over windswept country. It was in such lonely outposts that John Wesley and his colleagues would preach to congregations of farmhands and textile weavers, at that unbridled time when the Methodists' fervent eighteenth-century religious revival was beginning to run like wildfire throughout the industrial north.

275. HOWDEN MOORS, SOUTH YORKS.

Maps: OS Explorer OL1; Landranger 110

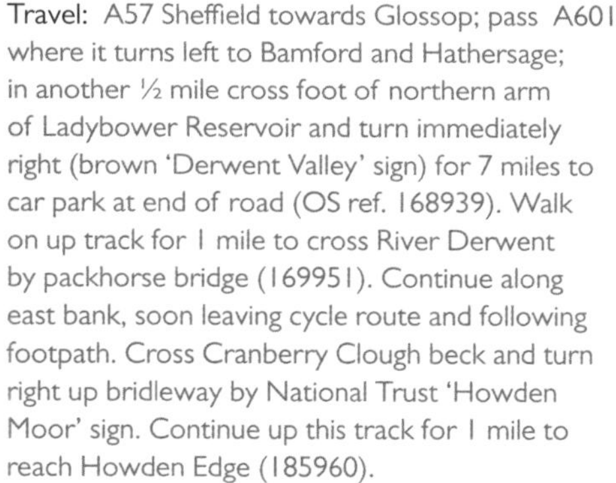

Travel: A57 Sheffield towards Glossop; pass A6013 where it turns left to Bamford and Hathersage; in another ½ mile cross foot of northern arm of Ladybower Reservoir and turn immediately right (brown 'Derwent Valley' sign) for 7 miles to car park at end of road (OS ref. 168939). Walk on up track for 1 mile to cross River Derwent by packhorse bridge (169951). Continue along east bank, soon leaving cycle route and following footpath. Cross Cranberry Clough beck and turn right up bridleway by National Trust 'Howden Moor' sign. Continue up this track for 1 mile to reach Howden Edge (185960).

The placid metallic sheet of Derwent Reservoir is your guide into the cleft of the Howden Moors. Once beyond the marshy north end of the lake, the forestry plantations that have flanked your approach fall away and you emerge into a lonely valley that narrows as it swings to the west. Sharp shoulders of hills are cut against the skyline – Ronksley Moor to the left, and up on your right hand the ridge of Long Edge and the rounded dome of Little Moor Top. The bracken banks are sombre green in summer, fox-red in autumn. Swaledale sheep with white noses forming a circle in black faces

Howden Moors

watch you distrustfully from the shade of twisted old thorn trees.

You can gain height without any great effort, walking the narrow track along the rim of Bull Clough with the rugged tor of the Bull Stones up ahead. Two hundred feet below, Bull Clough beck rushes and hisses like a high wind in pine tops. Now the track swings north-east and Howden Edge appears as a long, pale wall along the skyline. The path leads unerringly to the crest, and you will find yourself walking forward, suddenly on level ground, to the triangulation pillar on Margery Hill and a breathtaking view across an immense tableland of stream-sodden bog. Here are cloughs and groughs, gutters and dikes and springs, all names for the innumerable threads of water unravelling from Howden Edge and adding their trickles to the giant sponge of blanket bog that has been accumulating up here since well before the Romans came to Britain.

CHESHIRE, MERSEYSIDE, LANCASHIRE, CUMBRIA

THE NORTH-WEST

For many people the North-West of England is defined by the Lake District. This superb region of beautiful lakes scattered among small mountains or fells, modest in height (only Scafell Pike tops 3,200 feet) but tremendous in scenery and character, contains some very untamed places; but the wildness of their aspect tends, more than most of England's high country, to depend on weather conditions, and on how many other people are beside you at the time.

THE 885 SQUARE miles of the Lake District National Park receive around 10 million day visits a year – a statistic that seems to foreshadow queues on all footpaths and crowds on every peak. Yet very few stray far from the car parks and low-level paths. Places only a few minutes from the main walking routes are seldom crowded, and even the walkers' honey-pot spots you can have pretty much to yourself if you pick a weekday out of the holiday season. Get out among the western valleys to peaks like Bow Fell or splendid scree slopes like those above dark Wast Water, and you will be able to savour a proper taste of the wild – especially if you are experienced and well-equipped enough to venture out in mist, rain, gale or snow conditions. The guide, philosopher and friend at your side come rain or shine should most definitely be Alfred Wainwright, doyen of walking authors, with his classic and never-bettered series of guidebooks in seven volumes, *A Pictorial Guide to the Lakeland Fells*.

William Wordsworth, high priest of Lake District Romantic poetry, is the other author whose shadow lies long and fulsome over Lakeland. But there are plenty of rugged places outside the magic circle of Wordsworth Country. The eastern ranges of Lancashire and Cumbria contain some of the most rough and remote angles of the Pennine hills and moors – Pendle Hill, Saddleworth Moor, the hidden folds of the Howgill Fells. And the settlements that huddle in the steep valleys, former mill towns such as Clitheroe and Nelson, Blackburn and Burnley, with their gritstone buildings now sparkling after decades of being coated in

Wast Water (p. 324)

black oxidized grime, make excellent bases for exploring the moors above them.

Much of this country is accessible on foot via an excellent if demanding National Trail, the Pennine Way, and also along Alfred Wainwright's much-loved Coast-to-Coast Walk. Supposedly tame little Cheshire has its tales of wizardry around Alderley Edge and its places where nature encroaches on industrial landscapes or coexists with them. And the coasts of Cumbria, Lancashire and Merseyside, with their vast skirts of sand and mudflats, their wide muddy estuaries and long stretches of sand dunes, have a wild aspect that few passers-by on the M6 motorway would even suspect.

LINKS

- Coast-to-Coast (www.coast2coast.co.uk): St Bees and Whitehaven cliffs, Honister Pass, Helvellyn and Striding Edge, High Street, Whitsundale
- Pennine Way National Trail (www.nationaltrail.co.uk/pennineway; www.pennineswayassociation.co.uk): High Cup, Cross Fell
- Alfred Wainwright's ***A Pictorial Guide to the Lakeland Fells*** (www.franceslincoln.com; www.wainwright.org.uk): Helvellyn (Book One), High Street (Book Two), Eskdale + Bowfell, Scafell Pike, Wast Water + Illgill Head (Book Four), Innominate Tarn + Haystacks (Book Seven)

NATIONAL PARKS

- Lake District: www.lake-district.gov.uk

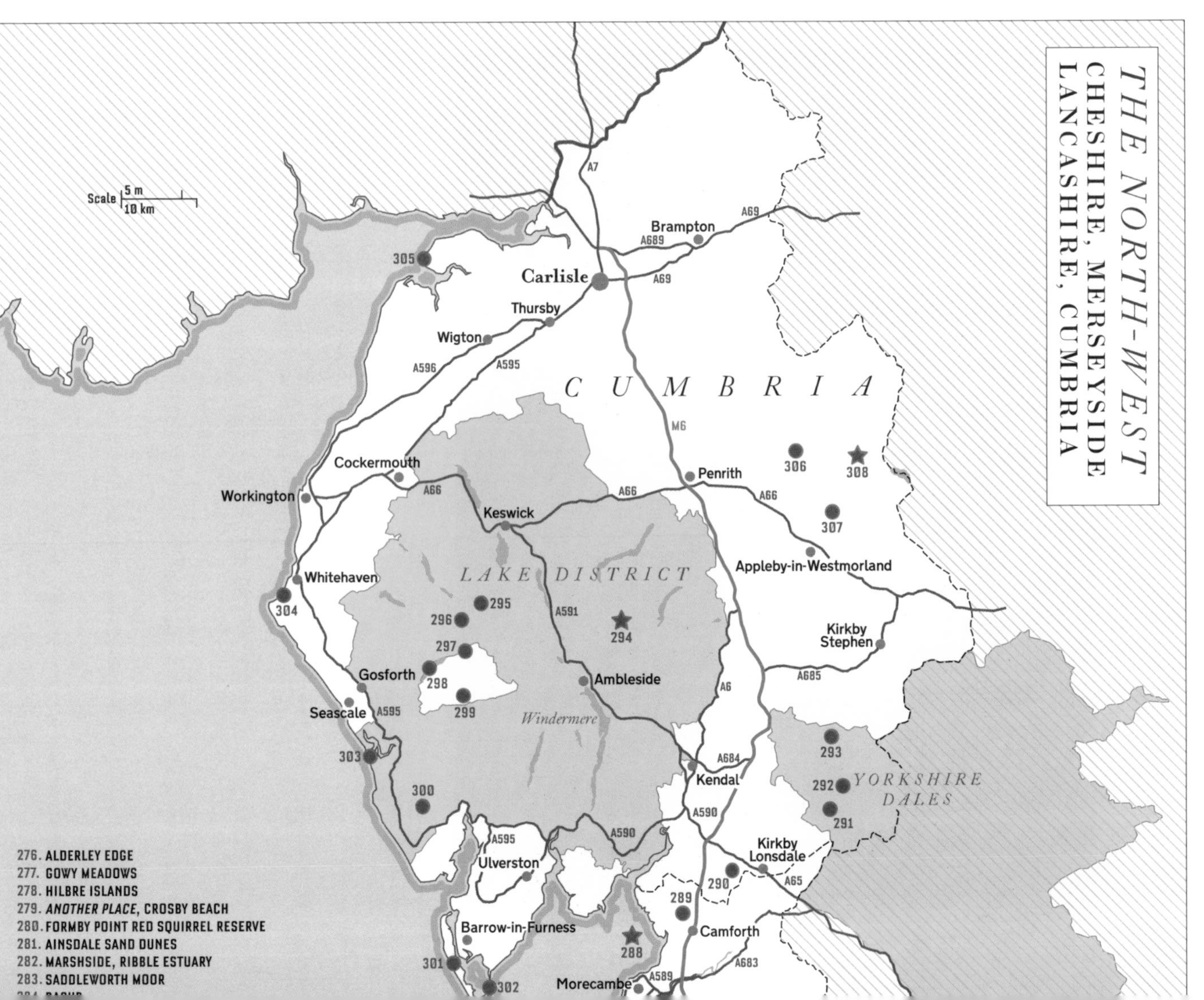

THE NORTH-WEST
CHESHIRE, MERSEYSIDE
LANCASHIRE, CUMBRIA
CUMBRIA
LAKE DISTRICT
YORKSHIRE DALES
Windermere
Scale 5 m 10 km
Carlisle
Brampton
Thursby
Wigton
Penrith
Appleby-in-Westmorland
Kirkby Stephen
Cockermouth
Workington
Keswick
Whitehaven
Gosforth
Seascale
Ambleside
Kendal
Kirkby Lonsdale
Ulverston
Barrow-in-Furness
Camforth
Morecambe
A7
A69
A689
A595
A596
A66
A591
A6
A684
A685
A590
A65
A683
A589
M6
305
306
307
308
304
295
296
297
298
299
294
303
300
293
292
291
290
289
288
301
302
276. ALDERLEY EDGE
277. GOWY MEADOWS
278. HILBRE ISLANDS
279. ANOTHER PLACE, CROSBY BEACH
280. FORMBY POINT RED SQUIRREL RESERVE
281. AINSDALE SAND DUNES
282. MARSHSIDE, RIBBLE ESTUARY
283. SADDLEWORTH MOOR

285. PENDLE HILL
286. WHITENDALE, FOREST OF BOWLAND
287. SAMBO'S GRAVE AND LUNE ESTUARY
288. MORECAMBE BAY ★
289. WARTON CRAG
290. HUTTON ROOF CRAGS
291. DENTDALE, BARBONDALE AND DEEPDALE
292. DENT VAMPIRE'S GRAVE
293. CAUTLEY SPOUT
294. HIGH STREET ★
295. HONISTER CRAG
296. INNOMINATE TARN
297. SCAFELL PIKE
298. WAST WATER
299. ESKDALE
300. SWINSIDE STONE CIRCLE
301. WALNEY ISLAND
302. PIEL ISLAND
303. ESKMEALS SAND DUNES
304. SALTOM BAY
305. CARDURNOCK FLATTS, SOLWAY FIRTH
306. CROSS FELL
307. HIGH CUP
308. MOOR HOUSE NATIONAL NATURE RESERVE ★
LANCASHIRE
GREATER MANCHESTER
MERSEYSIDE
CHESHIRE
Fleetwood
Catterall
Barnoldswick
Clitheroe
Colne
Nelson
Burnley
Kirkham
Preston
Blackburn
Accrington
Leyland
Chorley
Southport
Burscough
Rochdale
Formby
Ormskirk
Wigan
Bolton
Oldham
Salford
Crosby
Bootle
St Helens
Manchester
Birkenhead
Liverpool
Warrington
Heswall
Runcorn
Wilmslow
Ellesmere Port
Northwich
Alderley Edge
Macclesfield
Chester
Middlewich
Winsford
Sandbach
Crewe
Nantwich

276. ALDERLEY EDGE, CHESHIRE

Maps: OS Explorer 268; Landranger 118

Travel: B5087 from Macclesfield towards Alderley Edge; pass the Wizard of Edge Inn on right, and in 400 yards look for parking bay on right with fingerpost 'To The Edge' (OS ref. 855778). Path leads to steps down into trees; turn left for 100 yards to find wizard carved in rock face on your left, above stone trough (855780).

Nearest railway station: Alderley Edge (1 mile)

This sandstone escarpment rears above the north Cheshire plain, its high brow riddled with old mine levels and crowned with woods. Children love this place – particularly if they have been well primed with a reading of *The Weirdstone of Brisingamen*, Alan Garner's masterly retelling of a hoary local fable. The story of the farmer and the wizard is a great one, with plenty of King Arthur and Hans Christian Andersen resonances, and Garner uses it brilliantly as a springboard for a wonderfully witchy tale.

A well-to-do farmer from Mobberley is riding his beautiful white mare to sell her at market when he meets an old man on Alderley Edge. The farmer refuses to sell the mare to the stranger, who calmly tells him that there will be no bidders for her that day, and he will meet him again in the evening on the way home. Sure enough, the farmer fails to sell the mare. Riding home disgruntled, he meets the old man, and this time agrees to sell him the horse. Farmer and mare are taken to a high outlook, where the old man strikes the rocks with his stick. They burst asunder, to reveal a pair of gates deep in the ground. The wizard (for such is the old man) leads the farmer and the mare through them to a chamber full of treasure deep under the Edge. Here an army of knights lies asleep. There is a milk-white mare for every knight save one. The wizard thanks the farmer for providing the missing mare, and tells him that at England's hour of greatest peril, the knights will all awake and ride their white steeds to save the day. Then he fills the farmer's pockets with gold, and the lucky man returns through the great gates to the upper world. Try as the farmer does during the ensuing months and years to rediscover the gates that lead to the treasure chamber, he never succeeds.

The Wizard of Alderley Edge

You can find the huge crack that the wizard struck into the rock at Stormy Point (OS ref. 861777), and the wizard himself staring solemnly down from a ferny rock face some 400 yards along the path to the west. Finish up your supernatural exploration at the Wizard of Edge Inn, just along the road to Macclesfield (859772).

277. GOWY MEADOWS, CHESHIRE

Maps: OS Explorer 266; Landranger 117

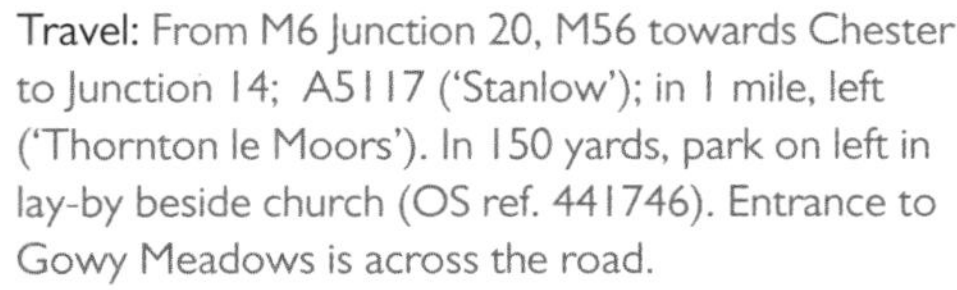

Travel: From M6 Junction 20, M56 towards Chester to Junction 14; A5117 ('Stanlow'); in 1 mile, left ('Thornton le Moors'). In 150 yards, park on left in lay-by beside church (OS ref. 441746). Entrance to Gowy Meadows is across the road.

Nearest railway station: Stanlow (2 miles)

Gowy Meadows is a supreme marsh and wet meadow habitat in the making. At first glance, though, the site appears no more than a succession of rather scruffy fields with the monstrous Stanlow oil and chemical plant peering over their shoulders. Appearances are deceptive, though. Cheshire Wildlife Trust rents Gowy Meadows from the plant's owner, Shell UK Ltd, and the conservation work they are carrying out here not only benefits the specialized wildlife of the meadow, but also helps safeguard the industrial complex itself. A win–win situation, as all parties involved like to point out.

Historically Gowy Meadows acted as washes or flood plains, harmlessly dispersing the winter flood water from the adjacent River Gowy. But these wetlands were drained centuries ago and converted to year-round cattle grazing. They lost their ability to act as flood defences, and their wildlife was greatly impoverished. However, a couple of cloudbursts that flooded the Stanlow refineries and chemical manufactories at the turn of the twenty-first century – and the bad press caused by the resultant leaks and pollution – persuaded Shell to lease the meadows and let Cheshire Wildlife Trust oversee their restoration as flood land. The process of blocking drainage in winter to allow the meadows to flood has resulted in a huge increase in overwintering birds attracted to the new fleets of water – wigeon and teal, shoveler and pintail among them. Water levels are lowered in summer to permit grazing. Lapwing, snipe and other wetland birds breed here now; water voles have established a colony (which has to be carefully protected from the winter floods); dragonflies and butterflies are returning in large numbers; otters have been seen on the margins of the River Gowy. The beautiful twin-lipped yellow flowers of bladderwort push up from the deeper ponds, while the shallow water is spattered through the summer with the tiny white stars and five-lobed leaves of ivy-leaved crowfoot.

Walking here you are never out of sight of pylons, chimneys and flare stacks. Yet the giant's chemistry set on the skyline impinges hardly at all among such wildlife riches.

278. HILBRE ISLANDS, MERSEYSIDE

Maps: OS Explorer 266; Landranger 108

Travel: From M53 Junction 2, A553 to Hoylake; A540 to West Kirby. Brown 'Marine Lake' signs to Dee Lane; crossing is from foot of slipway (OS ref. 210868). Tide times are displayed here.

NB: Crossing is over 2 miles of tidal sand, following a prescribed dog-leg route to avoid gutters, weaver fish, etc. Hilbre Islands are cut off by tide for 2½ hours either side of high water. Before crossing, seek advice from Wirral Country Park Visitor Centre: tel: 0151 6484371; www.visitliverpool.com/site/wirral-country-park-p7711.

Nearest railway station: West Kirby (¼ mile)

An expedition to the Hilbre Islands is not to be undertaken lightly. They lie in the sands of the Dee Estuary 1 mile or so out from the Wirral shore. The largest of the three islets, Hilbre, is only a few hundred yards long, and there are few creature comforts – no fresh water, for example, and no public lavatories. But the hour's walk from the seafront promenade at West Kirby out across the sands is a walk into heaven for anyone who savours seabirds, seals, strange history and unbounded solitude.

Hilbre, Middle Eye and Little Eye lie in line abreast, alone in a vast saucer of sand that glints at low tide with subdued tints of silver. Until the great melt at the end of the last Ice Age the three sandstone knolls were joined to the Wirral shore. In clear sunshine they gleam green and red; in foul weather they glower in black, indigo and dun, remote and dour, yet always alluring. Walking out to them you round the tiny slip of Little Eye, treading over inch-thick plates of sandstone compressed into a dusky red sandwich topped with a green salad of coarse grass. Then you splash past Middle Eye, dotted with the round pink heads of thrift. The 'big sister' island, Hilbre, carries a load of buildings on its back – a bird observatory; the old Telegraph House, home to the operators of the nineteenth-century optical telegraph that relayed messages between shore and ship; a ruined lifeboat station; a handful of holiday homes. Yet these don't detract from the lonely aspect of the island, nor from the sense – if you stay over between tides – of thrill as the sea advances up the sands to surround you.

The islands are a famous port of call and staging post for migrating and overwintering birds, especially waders. The giant larder of the Dee Estuary feeds 30,000 oystercatchers, nearly 20,000 knot and many thousand dunlin each winter, along with redshank, curlew and lapwing, not to mention duck and geese in their tens of thousands. Birdwatchers brave the discomfort of winter gales to trudge out here in order to catch sight of Leach's petrels, divers and skuas. Land birds, too, call on Hilbre in enormous numbers during spring and autumn migration: swallows, martins, pipits, warblers, goldcrests, finches. Grey seals haul out on the nearby sandbanks.

The pale light of dawn is a wonderful scene-setter for a falling tide on Hilbre. Look out on a world of infinitely subtle shades of grey, brown and silver. The outgoing tide coils seaward along snaking channels. Seals roll and flap lazily, and 10,000 turnstones, plovers and oystercatchers step fastidiously among the glinting pools and dark dots of worm-casts, each throwing its tiny spear of shadow across the sands.

279. *ANOTHER PLACE*, CROSBY BEACH, SEFTON COAST, LANCASHIRE

Maps: OS Explorer 275, 285; Landranger 108

Travel: M57 or M58 to Aintree; A5036 to Crosby; follow brown 'Another Place' signs to seafront. Car park by Marine Lake (OS ref. 318973).

Nearest railway stations: Blundellsands & Crosby (½ mile), Waterloo (1 mile)

The naked man, up to his knees in the incoming tide, stares intently out to sea as if he expects something apocalyptic to come marching out of the waves at any moment towards the Sefton shore. His dark brown body is sand-spattered and crusted with salt, his face blank and unemotional behind the rusty tear tracks down his cheeks. All along the broad northward stretch of Crosby Sands

Another Place, Crosby Beach

his ninety-nine brothers stand sentinel, some in the sea, some on the sands, devouring the western horizon with empty eyes. Wandering along the beach from one to another, lining up your glance with theirs, the prospect widens as far as the mountains of Snowdonia and the fells of Lakeland.

Together the 100 iron men compose an installation which its originator, sculptor Antony Gormley of *Angel of the North* fame, calls *Another Place*. Locals have grown proud and fond of the salt-stained, motionless men who hold their stance in tideways and on sandbars, maintaining their seaward vigil of disturbing intensity through sun, rain and windstorms. They direct a visitor's gaze, too, beyond the mundane world of the beach and the docks, out into the width of the 'unplumb'd, salt, estranging sea'.

280. FORMBY POINT RED SQUIRREL RESERVE, SEFTON COAST, LANCASHIRE

Maps: OS Explorer 285; Landranger 108

Travel: From M6 Junction 26, M58 to Junction 7; A5207, A565 to Formby. At second roundabout, left on B5424 and follow signs to pass Freshfield station and reach Formby Reserve car park (OS ref. 280082).

Nearest railway station: Freshfield (¾ mile)

It was one of man's sporadic attempts to make something productive of the 'empty wilderness' of the Sefton Coast that brought into being a safe habitat for another of Britain's most endangered wildlife species. Local landowner Charles Weld-Blundell, hoping to stabilize the untameable dunes while also establishing a lucrative crop, planted groves of Scots and Corsican pine at Formby Point around the turn of the twentieth century. Nowadays the full-grown conifers, sombre in their dark, massed ranks, provide safe haven for a thriving population of red squirrels.

Britain's native squirrel, resident in these islands since the close of the last Ice Age, has been decimated over the course of the past 100 years by disease, loss of habitat and food sources, and relentless competition from its introduced American cousin, the grey squirrel. The pinewoods of the Sefton Coast, carefully wardened and maintained by the National Trust and Natural England, provide the smaller and more vulnerable red squirrels with the conifer seeds and the lack of competition they need.

Strolling the sandy paths of the Formby Reserve, it takes a little time to tune into the sudden sharp rustle of pine branches or scurry of movement on the forest floor that betray the presence of a red squirrel. Though living a cosseted life on the reserve has made them bolder than their counterparts fending for themselves in other parts of Britain, they are still shy creatures and easily startled. The best time to catch them is the lonely hour after sunrise when they patrol the treetops and the forest floor for food, their sharply pointed ear tufts cocked and their shiny blackberry eyes on eternal lookout. Or you can take your binoculars out to the woods of Ainsdale or of Raven Meols at dawn, and have the red squirrels and the whole wide world of woods, dunes and vast sand flats all to yourself.

281. AINSDALE SAND DUNES, SEFTON COAST, LANCASHIRE

Map: OS Explorer 285; Landranger 108

Travel: A565 to Ainsdale; Shore Road to Ainsdale Discovery Centre, the Promenade, Ainsdale seafront (OS ref. 297127).

Nearest railway station: Ainsdale (1 mile)

Ainsdale dunes

The Sefton Coast of Lancashire is a moody, temperamental paradise, a wild, unadorned coast, beautiful in all weathers. It forms a westward-bulging arc of vast beaches, pinewoods and rambling sand dunes that shift shape and character with every tide and storm off the Irish Sea. The coast runs from Crosby on the northern outskirts of Liverpool for 20 miles, curving outwards as far as the blunt nose of Formby Point before trending north-east past Ainsdale and Southport to lose itself in an enormous desert of sands, mudflats and saltmarshes that wheels eastwards to meet the estuary of the River Ribble. Crosby, Formby and Southport are all sizeable coastal settlements, but this is not at all a built-up tamed seaside environment. On the contrary – these are the most extensive sand beaches and the largest sand-dune systems in England, building here and eroding there, a dynamic coast always on the move, constantly resculpted by wind and sea. Some of the rarest plants and animals in Britain thrive in this harsh environment.

The shaggy, seemingly lifeless dunes of Ainsdale Sand Dunes National Nature Reserve, dun-coloured and sparsely vegetated, have had few advocates over the centuries for their beauty. But now these mountain ranges in miniature are coming to be appreciated as a priceless refuge for a variety of wildlife with a very specialized list of requirements, such as the natterjack toad. This scarce amphibian with the distinctive yellow stripe along its back can thrive only in warm, sandy soils near sea level, with shallow pools to lay its spawn in and safe shelter for winter hibernation. Heathlands and dunes are what it needs, but well over 90 per cent of all such UK habitat disappeared during the last century under the demands of intensive agriculture, building development and tree planting. The dunes of the Sefton Coast, especially those looked after by Natural England in the National Nature Reserve at Ainsdale, harbour a growing population of several thousand natterjacks, breeding in the warm temporary pools of the slacks or hollows that lie in the shelter of the dune peaks. Sit quietly among the dunes on a spring night after a rainstorm when the slacks are full, and you will hear the male natterjacks in their mating passion, enticing the egg-laden females with a display of masculine prowess as they send their calls, as hoarse as they are loud, echoing across the shallow waters.

282. MARSHSIDE, RIBBLE ESTUARY, LANCASHIRE

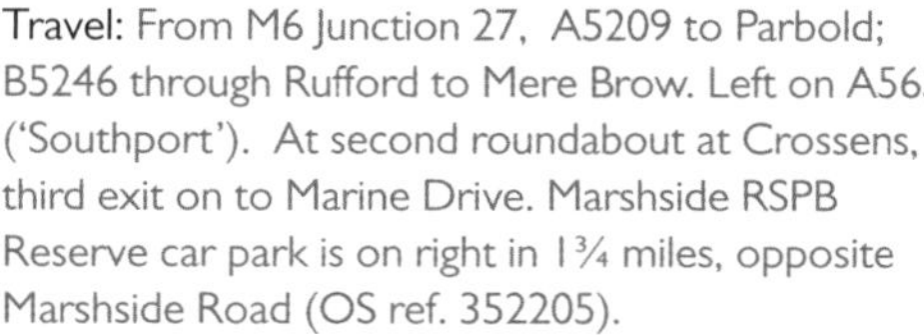

Maps: OS Explorer 285; Landranger 108, 102

Travel: From M6 Junction 27, A5209 to Parbold; B5246 through Rufford to Mere Brow. Left on A565 ('Southport'). At second roundabout at Crossens, third exit on to Marine Drive. Marshside RSPB Reserve car park is on right in 1¾ miles, opposite Marshside Road (OS ref. 352205).

Nearest railway station: Southport (3 miles)

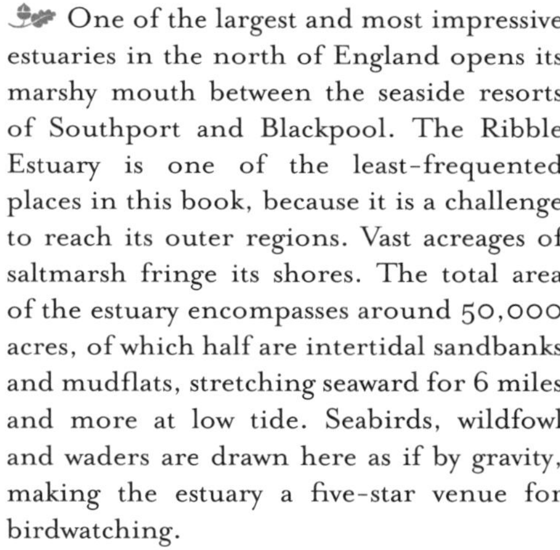

One of the largest and most impressive estuaries in the north of England opens its marshy mouth between the seaside resorts of Southport and Blackpool. The Ribble Estuary is one of the least-frequented places in this book, because it is a challenge to reach its outer regions. Vast acreages of saltmarsh fringe its shores. The total area of the estuary encompasses around 50,000 acres, of which half are intertidal sandbanks and mudflats, stretching seaward for 6 miles and more at low tide. Seabirds, wildfowl and waders are drawn here as if by gravity, making the estuary a five-star venue for birdwatching.

It is a fascinating experience to spend half a day between low and high tide at the RSPB's Marshside Reserve, just north of Southport. Wide swathes of this southern coast of the Ribble were reclaimed for agriculture during the nineteenth and early twentieth centuries, protected behind a long straight sea bank. The reserve lies inland of the flood defence on one of these reclaimed freshwater marshes, 250 acres of grassland now partially flooded again and managed as wet grassland for ducks, geese and waders. Blue-legged avocet breed here, as do lapwing and redshank; brown hares gallop off and stop dead still to assess you with constantly twitching nose. In winter pink-footed geese in their thousands throng the marshes.

Wading birds are free agents and acknowledge no boundaries. Towards low tide they stay far away on the rim of the sea at the edge of binocular sight, only very gradually hopping and flapping nearer the shore as the advancing tide covers their food banks and feeding stances. It is a 4-mile approach from the tideline to the sea bank, and by the time the sea is hard up against the land there are flocks of dunlin, godwit or plover close at hand that may be several thousand strong. Peregrines hunt the reserve, and it is a great thrill to watch one of these deadly, dark little falcons twisting and turning after a fleeing redshank or pigeon, before rising to stoop for the kill.

283. SADDLEWORTH MOOR, LANCASHIRE

Maps: OS Explorer OL1; Landranger 110

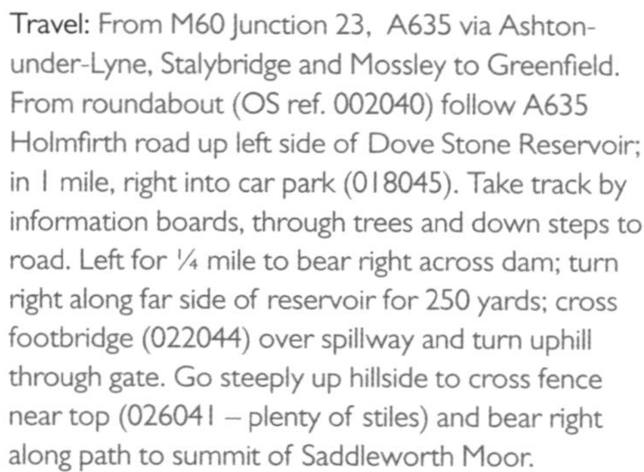

Travel: From M60 Junction 23, A635 via Ashton-under-Lyne, Stalybridge and Mossley to Greenfield. From roundabout (OS ref. 002040) follow A635 Holmfirth road up left side of Dove Stone Reservoir; in 1 mile, right into car park (018045). Take track by information boards, through trees and down steps to road. Left for ¼ mile to bear right across dam; turn right along far side of reservoir for 250 yards; cross footbridge (022044) over spillway and turn uphill through gate. Go steeply up hillside to cross fence near top (026041 – plenty of stiles) and bear right along path to summit of Saddleworth Moor.

Nearest railway station: Greenfield (2 miles)

It's a very steep climb up to the crags and heights of Saddleworth Moor, but worth every ounce of the effort. The view back

Saddleworth Moor

across Dove Stone Reservoir is superb, and facing forward you have all the wide wastes of the moor to wander.

The steep S-shaped valley of Dove Stone is a place of two industries – raising sheep, and storing water for the Tameside and Oldham areas. Since the implementation of the CROW Act of 2000, there's a third group of people involved with the valley and with Saddleworth Moor high above it – ramblers, who have always come here to walk the path, but who can now take advantage of their new right to roam over those exceptionally forbidding moors. This is some of the bleakest and most exposed land in England, guarded by fine grey gritstone bluffs. They stand four-square above you as you climb the slope from the reservoir through thick grasses and stumbly hags of peat, then up across a rough clitter of frost-shattered stones, abrasive and harsh underfoot.

Once on the top you can wander where you like – south along the edge by Great and Little Dove Stone Rocks, with great views over the reservoir to your right; north towards Saddleworth Moor proper, a dark height straddling beyond the deep cleft of Greenfield; or out east into a mess of spring-sodden ground where every tiny place's name ends in '-moss'. You need your wits about you if mist and rain descend. It is 2 miles as the rambler plods to meet the Pennine Way in the very middle of these empty hills; and when you have traversed the ground from Longdendale by way of Black Tor, Black Chew Head, Black Hill and Black Dike Head, you will have seen enough black peat mire to last you a lifetime.

284. BACUP, LANCASHIRE

Maps: OS Explorer OL21; Landranger 103

Travel: From M62 Junction 20 or 21, into Rochdale; A671 to Bacup. From roundabout in town centre, A681 towards Todmorden. Any side lane to the left leads uphill to meet old packhorse road running north-east. Turn right along it for a mile or so, to meet and turn left along Rossendale Way at Heald Top Farm (OS ref. 886253). Follow Rossendale Way north-west for 2 miles, then drop down into Bacup via the Irwell Sculpture Trail's old road (876259), or via Bacup Old Road (867262).

Bacup sits in a side cleft, the Rossendale Valley running east and west at its feet and the Irwell Valley carving north into the moors at its head. Steep green hills hem in the town, long a weaving centre but now reinventing itself as a very desirable place to live – especially for walkers, cyclists and riders who appreciate the web of old packhorse lanes that spreads up and out of the town, crossing the hills in all directions. Bacup has always been the natural place for travellers to descend from the moors above, and a glance at the map shows its hills threaded with hundreds of trackways – footpaths trodden by millhands from their homes to their place of work, and the narrow walled lanes up which strings of packhorses were led. Lines of cattle and sheep were driven here too, before the gentler inclines of roads engineered for wheeled traffic superseded them.

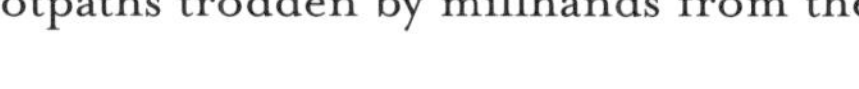

The high moors are visible from down in the valley, dun-coloured caps to the pastures of the hillside. Stone field walls and sheepfolds stripe the slopes as you climb steeply up Todmorden Old Road, rising between walls green with lichen from which other, narrower trods wind away between their own parallel walls. The hill slopes are riddled with springs of water, held and then released by the heavy sponge of the moors, and the old road is culverted every few yards to let the water by. Farms stand all of a piece with their outhouses, pierced with tall round arches to admit wagons. William Darney, the Scots pedlar and Methodist sermonizer (see pp. 297–8) came to preach at Heap Barn, a farm where horses were kept and sent down the hill to help pull heavy loads up the drag. A crudely carved date-stone on Greensnook cottages says '1704', but some of these old longhouses must pre-date that by a long way.

As you approach the open moor, forgotten mineshafts yawn, opening stony throats in the fields. The sedgy track that leads you along the edge of Todmorden Moor and Heald Moor is a limer's gate, a rough trail along which the packhorse leaders would bring strings of Galloway ponies laden with sacks of lime for the farmers to spread on their acid bog fields. Weather is wild up here, the views immense and the airy freedom as intoxicating as champagne.

285. PENDLE HILL, LANCASHIRE

Maps: OS Explorer OL41; Landranger 103

Travel: M65; A680, A59 for west side of hill, A682 for east side.

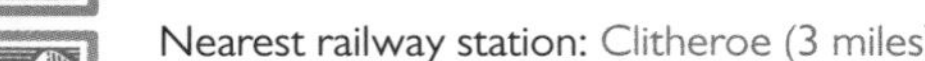

Nearest railway station: Clitheroe (3 miles)

For the most ill-reputed hill in England, Pendle owns a graceful shape. An outlier of the Forest of Bowland ranges, it rises from grassy pastures, its steep flanks puckered here and there with the shadowy clefts of gullies like the creases cut in a face on a sharp intake of breath. There is a brooding power to Pendle Hill, seen from below, especially when viewed from the west at dawn, the fawn moorland colours muted to blue-black and the rising sun behind the crest of the hill shooting a halo of rays through the bruise-coloured night mist clinging to the ridge. Pendle seems to gather its own weather. Storms close about it, rain lashes across and thunder cracks overhead when Bowland to the west and Trawden to the east are clear.

Maybe this sense of something ominous about Pendle Hill derives from the wildness of its reputation, which dates back to 1612. It was around the village of Barley, and particularly in nearby Malkin Tower under the shadow of the hill, that the Pendle Witches lived and were said to have cast their ill spells. These were no fairytale nasties, but real local men and women who were charged with having done at least seventeen victims to death by black magic. The worst of the lot were said to be Elizabeth Device and her mother, Old Demdike of Malkin Tower, along with a sorceress named Old Chattox and another known as Mouldheels. Lurid confessions of blood-drinking, effigy-burning and soul-selling were obtained after the so-called witches were arrested, and in 1612 ten of them were hanged in Lancaster Castle.

If you climb in sunshine to the top of Pendle Hill, accessible in its entirety as Access Land these days, and contemplate the 40-mile view, or sit beside the well where in 1652 the zealous young preacher George Fox received the inspiring vision that led him to found the Quaker movement – such fancies flee away. But let the mist gather, or sleety rain come rolling up from Bowland to blot out the light, and on the summit of the dark hill those famous hobgoblins and foul fiends are still not quite tidied away.

286. WHITENDALE, FOREST OF BOWLAND, LANCASHIRE

Maps: OS Explorer OL41; Landranger 103

Travel: From M6 Junction 33, A6 north towards Lancaster. In 1 mile, right in Galgate ('Abbeystead, Trough of Bowland'). Through Abbeystead; then bear right on Trough of Bowland road for 7 miles to Dunsop Bridge. Park in village car park across bridge (OS ref. 660503); return across bridge and in 100 yards turn right ('Private Road') to walk up road beside River Dunsop for 3½ miles to Whitendale (660550). From here continue up path beside Whitendale River for another 2 miles to reach Hornby Road (Roman road) at 662578.

The farmhouse and foresters' houses at Whitendale form a very remote settlement, and the wide bleak moors to the north offer a surfeit of harshly beautiful landscape. This is quintessential Forest of Bowland, full of secret clefts and hidden hollows, an area which was pretty much inaccessible to ramblers, except on a sparse number of public footpaths, until the Countryside & Right of Way (CROW) Act of 2000 opened most of it up. The medieval landowners' hunting rights in Bowland (transferred to shooting in later centuries) were rigorously upheld. Norman de Lacys gave way to

Whitendale

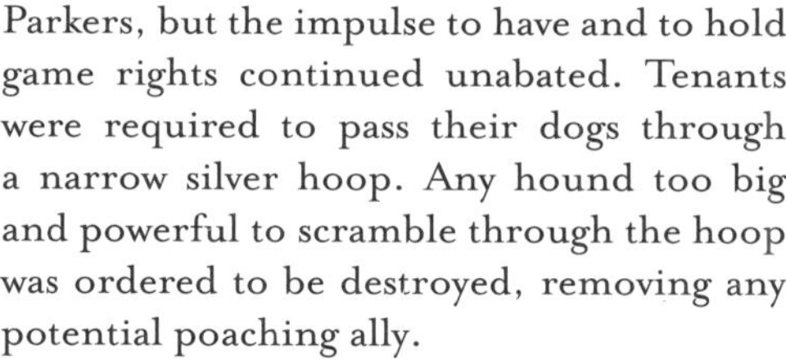

Parkers, but the impulse to have and to hold game rights continued unabated. Tenants were required to pass their dogs through a narrow silver hoop. Any hound too big and powerful to scramble through the hoop was ordered to be destroyed, removing any potential poaching ally.

The road to Whitendale from Dunsop Bridge is still a private one, and the only way to travel it is on Shanks's Pony. Deep side cloughs with steep scrambly flanks cut into the flanks of the dale and fold the hillsides as you bear north along the subsidiary and even narrower valley of the Whitendale River. Eagle owls nested and bred here early in the twenty-first century. These powerful birds with the upstanding 'ear' tufts stand over 2 feet tall, and fly with a wingspan of up to 6 feet; the females can weigh ten times as much as a barn owl, and are strong and determined enough to kill a young deer. Their nesting in Whitendale was a huge ornithological sensation, and a scarcely concealed worry to grouse-shooting tenants and others in the vicinity.

Beyond the farm the track rises beside the infant Whitendale River into strikingly lonely moorland, and follows the water almost all the way to meet the Roman road known as the Hornby Road, a splendid upland track that runs north–west and south–east as straight and purposefully as a Roman road should. You can follow it in either direction, hurdling the empty Bowland Hills for mile after mile, a highway through a high land.

287. SAMBO'S GRAVE AND LUNE ESTUARY, LANCASHIRE

Maps: OS Explorer 296; Landranger 102

Travel: From M6 Junction 34, A683 through Lancaster towards Heysham; left here to Overton; ahead at crossroads (OS ref. 437580) past Globe Hotel and on over causeway to Sunderland. Park on beach under wall (427562). From beach, follow pavement beside houses; right (427560) along the Lane to west side of peninsula; left along beach to Sambo's Grave (422559).

NB: Check tide times before you go (www.pol.ac.uk/ntslf/tidalp.html) – causeway is covered for 2 or more hours at high tide.

The River Lune flows south from Lancaster in a series of wide bends fringed by saltmarsh, the water at low tide cutting a narrow channel between wide mudbanks of chocolate and rose-pink. This is flat, moody country, an estuarine landscape narrowing to a peninsula where the sea spills over the roads at high water. Out at the tip, cut off at the flood, lies the tiny hamlet of Sunderland ('the divided place'). A handful of handsome houses stands on a quay at the edge of the peninsula beside a couple of sandstone warehouses. This was the port for Lancaster, built at the turn of the eighteenth century when trade with the New World was on the rise at the same time as the Lune was silting up. Oystercatchers pipe mournfully on the muddy tideline, and wagtails bob on the cobbled quay where the very first bales of raw cotton were landed from across the Atlantic in 1701. It is said that a million pounds' weight of cotton lay untouched on the Sunderland quay for a year because no one knew what this alien substance was.

Across the peninsula, in a corner of a lonely field, a grave marked 'Sambo' contains the remains of a young Afro-Caribbean man, probably a personal servant, who landed at Sunderland in 1736 and died shortly afterwards. The grave is kept well tended with fresh flowers and little offerings from local children. Sambo lies with his feet to the wide marshes and the long, low line of the river beyond, a solitary resting place. A plaque on his grave slab carries a touching elegy, composed by the Reverend James Watson in 1796:

Full sixty Years the angry Water's Wave
Has thundering dash'd this Bleak & barren Shore
Since Sambo's Head laid in this lonely Grave
Lies still and ne'er will hear their turmoil more.

Full many a Sandbird chirps upon the Sod
And many a Moonlight Elfin round him trips

Full many a Summer's Sunbeam warms the Clod
And many a teeming Cloud upon him drips.

But still he sleeps – till the awakening Sounds
Of the Archangel's Trump new Life impart
Then the GREAT JUDGE his Approbation founds
Not on Man's COLOR but his – WORTH of
HEART.

288. MORECAMBE BAY, LANCASHIRE

Maps: OS Explorer OL7; Landranger 97

Travel: From M6 Junction 34, A683 to Morecambe. For Sands Walk, M6 Junction 35A; right on A6 for 2 miles; left through Yealand Conyers and Yealand Redmayne for Silverdale.

NB: The Morecambe Bay Sands crossing is potentially extremely dangerous, and must be done only with the official Sands Guide on one of his group walks. Contact him via grangetic@southlakeland.gov.uk.

Nearest railway stations: Morecambe; Silverdale for Sands Walk

You won't find the designation 'Great Sands' in any tourist brochure or guidebook. But you will find the Great Sands, nonetheless, if you tear yourself away from the core of the Lake District and follow your nose southward to the sea. Here three ragged peninsulas hang from the rounded belly of the coast – the Cartmel peninsula, pushing south into Morecambe Bay between the rivers of Kent and Leven; the Furness peninsula, dividing the estuaries of Leven and Duddon; and the Millom peninsula, forming a westerly barrier against the open Irish Sea. What is remarkable about these three is the vast expanse of tidal sands they separate; sands that stretch as much as 10 miles from shore, that feed millions of wildfowl and are covered by incoming tides more quickly than an outsider would think possible.

There is a hard-edged beauty to this strange landscape. The Great Sands and their peninsulas are backed by the southerly fells of the Lake District. Views stretch for 100 miles over sea and mountains. Best of all are the gigantic sands themselves: their tides, their birds and their untamed beauty.

In the enormous wastes of Morecambe Bay, 117 square miles of sand lie exposed on the ebb. To reach the edge of the sea from the resort of Grange-over-Sands at extreme low tide, you would have to walk 10 miles out across the sands. Not that you would try any such thing on your own, because Morecambe Bay at low tide is one of the most treacherous places in Britain. Three rivers snake through the sands – the Kent, Leer and Leven – and they are unpredictable waters, especially the Kent, which has been known to switch from one side of the bay to the other in the space of a couple of days. Other hidden streams run under the sands, forming quicksands and soft sinking pits. Sandbanks appear and disappear, change shape, rise and fall from one tide to the next. Out in the middle you can get lost, disorientated, benighted, marooned on a sandbank amid rising waters. When the tide comes in it does so far more quickly than a panicking person can flee. On the night of 5 February 2004 a party of immigrant Chinese workers was caught by the tide, and twenty-one of them were drowned – the worst recorded single incident of tragedy among the hundreds of unwise or unfortunate victims who have been drowned in the bay over the centuries.

The Chinese workers were collecting cockles, which cling to the rocks and lie under the sands in uncountable millions. Along with mussels, shrimps and marine worms they make a great feast for the wading birds that throng here – knot, dunlin, curlew, godwit, oystercatcher. Much of the Great Sands foreshore is a dense green mat of saltmarsh. This is prime birdwatching territory, but it is a great place for walkers, too, though only under the careful guidance of the handful of local experts who know the intricacies of the sands inside out. Cedric Robinson, the official Sands Guide, is out in the bay at all hours, checking the 'brobs' or laurel sprig markers that he places to identify the safe routes across the sands. He leads parties of all sizes on walks across Morecambe Bay – a memorable experience, but emphatically not one to be undertaken by unguided walkers.

289. WARTON CRAG, LANCASHIRE

Maps: OS Explorer OL7; Landranger 97

Travel: From M6 Junction 35a, A6 towards Kendal for ½ mile, then left to Warton. At Black Bull Inn just before church, right up Crag Road and in 100 yards turn right into car park (OS ref. 496724). Follow path (badly marked) into trees from north-west corner of car park, through woods and up on to open summit of Warton Crag.

Nearest railway station: Carnforth (1½ miles)

The disused quarry where you park your car at the start of the walk to Warton Crag has taken a huge bite out of the southern flank of the limestone hill. The chakker of jackdaws and hoarse, deep cronk of ravens accompany you through the limestone woods, thick with anemones and bluebells in spring. The woods also breed a good crop of pignut, a cousin of the carrot whose frothy white flowers rise from a thick tuber hidden under the ground. Locally known in bygone days by the delightful names of yowie-yorlins or jocky-jurnals, pignut roots have a crunchy texture, a faintly peppery taste, and – apocryphally – an aphrodisiac effect.

Out above the trees you climb through levels of grassland and scrub up to a series

Warton Crag

of bare limestone ledges where bright yellow rockroses thrive, digging their long roots deep into the limestone cracks for nourishment and as stabilizers against the wind coming in off Morecambe Bay. On still, sunny days the limestone grassland and fringes of woodland are wonderful for butterflies – near the trees the rare high brown fritillary with its dramatic pattern of silvery-white and chocolate spots on a russet background, and out in the open the grayling with yellow wing blobs and the northern brown argus, whose caterpillars feed on the rockroses.

290. HUTTON ROOF CRAGS, CUMBRIA

Maps: OS Explorer OL7; Landranger 97

Travel: From M6 Junction 36, A65 towards Kirkby Lonsdale to first roundabout; right on A6070 towards Burton-in-Kendal. In 3 miles, left at Clawthorpe Hall Hotel (OS ref. 531775 – 'Clawthorpe'). Follow minor road for 1½ miles to summit of hill; park in bay here (552788). Go through kissing gate on right of road and follow path through scrub and up over Hutton Roof Crags.

Nearest railway station: Carnforth (6½ miles)

Natural limestone pavements were a diminishing habitat across Britain for many decades in the late twentieth century as opportunists ripped them up for garden rockeries. That sort of landscape vandalism has all but ceased now, and pavements such as those that spread across the top of Hutton Roof Crags are safeguarded for the very varied plant and insect life that relies on their combination of sun-warmed stone, shady cracks, damp hollows and a mixture of acid and alkaline surroundings.

The narrow road from the valley of the River Beta rises through hazel woods into a fine open upland. Walk up from the summit of the road across a surface of pitted, eroded and rain-sculpted limestone, cracked into deep oblongs as it was hoisted high from the shallow seabed where it was formed some 350 million years ago. Remnants of shell and coral fossils can still be made out in the rough grey rock. The shaded hollows are known as grykes, the domed islands of stone between them as clints. From the depths of the grykes, several species of fern push forth long, pale green tendrils in search of sunlight – notably the twisted spearblades

Hutton Roof Crags

of hart's tongue ferns, and the nationally scarce rigid-buckler fern, which looks very much like a delicate frond of bracken. Lily of the valley raises its beautiful fringed white bells from big sheath-like leaves; and there are other tiny floral bells, too, the crimson ones of dark red helleborine.

The higher you go across the limestone pavements, the broader the view, until you emerge above the highest band of scrub to see the peaks of the Lake District mountains walling in the sky to the west, and the vast silver-streaked saucer of Morecambe Sands stretching away south-west to the sea horizon.

291. DENTDALE, BARBONDALE AND DEEPDALE, CUMBRIA

Maps: OS Explorer OL2; Landranger 97, 98

Access: Dentdale curves roughly east-south-east, 3 miles south of and parallel to A684 as it runs through Garsdale from Sedbergh. Dent, the chief village, is signed from A684 at Garsdale Head, from Sedbergh, and from B6255 near the head of Widdale. Barbondale is signed 'Barbon' from A683 Sedbergh–Kirkby Lonsdale road. Deepdale is signed 'Ingleton' from the southern Dentdale road (1 mile east of Dent village)

Nearest railway station: Dent (4½ miles)

Dentdale is probably the best-known of all the hidden dales, thanks to the picture-postcard attractiveness of Dent village with its solid stone houses – some whitewashed in a style more characteristic of the Lake District than the Dales – packed tightly along narrow cobbled streets. Dentdale is a deep, impressive dale, well wooded, with stone farmhouses and barns scattered up the fell sides among trees. A narrow road, the verges thick with meadowsweet, runs east from the village along the north bank of the River Dee. An even narrower one, hardly wide enough for a car, ribbons along the south bank in parallel. As far as Lea Yeat the landscape is pastoral; then it becomes wilder as the lane climbs to the sinister dark arches of the Settle & Carlisle's Dent Head Viaduct. From the fell beyond there is a wonderful view back over the folded country.

The very steep and lonely valley of Barbondale cuts up from the Sedbergh–Kirkby Lonsdale road to reach Dentdale 1 mile west of Dent. The hard gritstones on the west flank of Barbondale were wrenched thousands of feet higher than their original bed when ancient subterranean upheavals created the Great Pennine Fault – hence their dramatic steepness. Barbondale is smothered in bracken, riddled with potholes and occupied by only a couple of farms: a solitary, moody dale. Deepdale is another such, running south from Dentdale under the looming west flank of Whernside (see pp. 291–3). The narrow open-sided road is gated against straying animals, so you have to get out of your car or off your bicycle every few minutes and look about you as the way rises into windswept moorland of sedge, thistles and stone walls, before curving over into a long descent through Kingsdale by way of Yorda's Cave (see p. 291).

292. DENT VAMPIRE'S GRAVE, CUMBRIA

Maps: OS Explorer OL2; Landranger 98

Travel: From M6 Junction 37, A684 through Sedbergh; in 1 mile, right on minor road to Dent. Park in town and walk to St Andrew's Church (OS ref. 705871). The grave of the 'Dent Vampire' lies flat on the ground on the south side of the church, immediately outside the porch.

Nearest railway station: Dent (4½ miles)

In the early eighteenth century remote communities such as Dent lay very much cut off from the mainstream of news and opinion. There were packhorse routes converging on the little town under its high moorland slopes, but rumour and superstition still tended to play as big a part in people's everyday thinking as any solidly verifiable news that the itinerant packmen and drovers might bring to town with them. Woe betide you if you were in any way 'other', in a manner which your neighbours could not justify or explain to themselves.

That was the situation of the unfortunate George Hodgson of Dent. 'Here lyes the body of George Hodgson', reads the inscription on his modest tombstone sunk in the ground just outside the porch of St Andrew's Church, 'who departed this life June ye 4, 1715, aged 94.' Although a respectable man whom everyone knew well, Hodgson sported a pair of long, sharp canine teeth that stirred a horrid suspicion among his fellow townsmen. The fact that he lived what was for those times an abnormally long life fuelled the talk. After he had died and been buried, several people swore they had seen him walking abroad. His body was exhumed and examined. The hair and nails had continued to grow, and the whole body seemed pink, healthy and uncorrupted. It must be true! George Hodgson was a vampire!

The tale has never left the town. The square hole in Hodgson's grave slab was almost certainly knocked in the stone to take a railing post – but every child in Dent knows perfectly well that that was the place where the stake was driven through the Dent Vampire's heart ...

293. CAUTLEY SPOUT, CUMBRIA

Maps: OS Explorer OL19; Landranger 98

Travel: From M6 Junction 37, A684 to Sedbergh; A683 towards Kirkby Stephen. In 4 miles, park on left beside Cross Keys Inn (OS ref. 698969). 'Cautley Spout' fingerpost points down bank and across footbridge; bear left along path, which swings right in ¼ mile into valley of Cautley Spout. With Cautley Holme Beck on your left, walk up valley to climb steep, partly pitched path beside Cautley Spout (682975).

The Howgill Fells are a secret range. Their best-known aspect is the western one you see from the M6 between Junctions 37 and 38, where they block in half the sky on your right in a series of tremendous rounded folds, as soft-looking and tempting as a stack of pillows punched into comfortable shapes by an invisible giant. Their eastern flanks are creased with deep clefts down which streams tumble from the high moors above, none more dramatically than Cautley Spout. The walk to the falls is a very popular one, but few visitors carry on to make the 600-foot climb up the narrow, steep zigzag path beside Cautley Spout.

The roar of the fall is heard, rustling and echoing throughout the narrowing valley,

Cautley Spout

but the full sight of it is hidden until you are nearly up at the end of the dale. The path climbs a gentle bank and then commences a stiff ascent. Climbing the track is an uneven business, rather like ascending a flight of neglected stone stairs – an effort which will have you breathing hard. The higher you climb the more of the fall is revealed. Lacy skeins of white water tumble from ledge to ledge down a great stairway of slippery black rock, overhung with rowan and birch trees that drink in the spray. At the very top the climb eases, and you can catch your breath and look back down the vertiginous cleft of the fall and over the Cautley Holme valley, a snaking beck its centrepiece, across the wider dale of the River Rawthey to the great rough upland of Baugh Fell.

Come here and savour this view on an evening visit, when the sun behind the fells casts immense inky shadows across the valley, or in the early morning, when the whole cleft is brilliantly lit and the falling water glitters in its plunge.

294. HIGH STREET, CUMBRIA

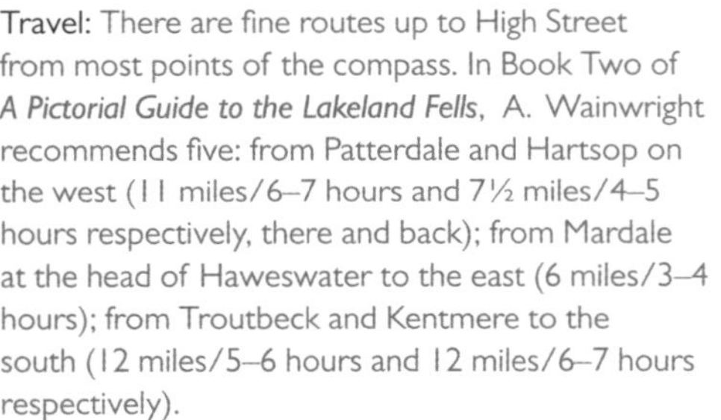
Maps: OS Explorer OL5, OL7; Landranger 90

Travel: There are fine routes up to High Street from most points of the compass. In Book Two of *A Pictorial Guide to the Lakeland Fells*, A. Wainwright recommends five: from Patterdale and Hartsop on the west (11 miles/6–7 hours and 7½ miles/4–5 hours respectively, there and back); from Mardale at the head of Haweswater to the east (6 miles/3–4 hours); from Troutbeck and Kentmere to the south (12 miles/5–6 hours and 12 miles/6–7 hours respectively).

NB: It is a fairly strenuous climb to High Street, and these timings are only approximate.

High Street sits in the middle of a great tumble of lonely fells and small lakes, 2 miles as the crow flies from the nearest road, but a good deal longer than that as the walker plods. No one who has climbed the 2,000 feet and more to reach it will fail to be enchanted with what they find. Up there on the spine of a long, slim north–south ridge, a Roman road threads its way with the grain of the mountains towards Penrith, some 15 miles northwards. The road is a walker's track today, and you can follow it for almost all its length. It is a splendid and reassuring thing to see it in front of you, leaping the crests and hurdling the summits.

All around the summit ridge of High Street steep edges drop away – in craggy cliffs on the east to the teardrop-shaped bowl of Blea Water (lakes are 'waters' hereabouts, not 'tarns'), in tremendous screes to the corrie and squeezed-in valley of Hayeswater on the west. Views are wild and wide, as far as the Pennine whalebacks in the east and Morecambe Bay's glint in the south. To the north is an ocean of wave-like peaks that include Skiddaw, Helvellyn and Scafell Pike.

As with so many of these wild places, an early start increases your chances of having High Street to yourself, walking freely across a high landscape that cannot have changed much since Roman soldiers built the road and marched its lonely miles.

295. HONISTER CRAG, CUMBRIA

Maps: OS Explorer OL4; Landranger 89

Travel: From M6 Junction 40, A66 through Keswick. Left on B5289 Borrowdale road; follow this through Rosthwaite and Seatoller, then up steep rise to Honister Pass. Park on left in Honister Slate Mine car park (OS ref. 225135). Visit Honister Slate Mine for underground tours, and climb Honister Crag path on the Via Ferrata.

Information: www.honister-slate-mine.co.uk

NB: Via Ferrata involves a steep climb using safety harness and helmets, with some tunnels and subterranean inclines.

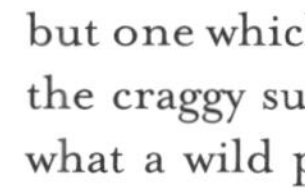

Slate has been mined up at the Honister Pass in the heart of the Lake District for many centuries. Though the industry still limps on, it is a shadow of what it was in its nineteenth-century heyday when quarrymen came from all over the region to work here. They left behind them a scene of devastation, but one which blends astonishingly well with the craggy surroundings. To appreciate just what a wild place this was to work, you can follow the miners' track up the narrow 45-degree pathway they cut in the naked face of Honister Crag.

A quick burst of instruction in the function of safety helmet and harness, and you are off, unclipping and reclipping your spring-loaded shackles each time the guide wire passes through the loop of a belaying bolt. The slate miners had no such safety gear; they began their daily grind by clambering up this mile-long flywalk in rain, snow or ice, slipping and sliding, always in danger of toppling off the edge. Glances over the side of the incline show you black crags plummeting sheer away to the thread of the pass road in the valley below.

The first part is the hardest as you teeter across a bridge composed of three iron rails with no handholds, then scramble by boot and fingertip up a series of ledges to the start of the incline proper. Slate fragments skid away underfoot from the slope in which rusty rails and rotten sleepers still lie embedded. At the top of the first section, 1,500 vertiginous feet above the road, you bore into the mountain through low-roofed tunnels where mist vapour rolls eerily,

Buttermere from Honister Crag

climbing up the throat of a steep railway incline to emerge through a rock mouth from which the tunnel exhales a chilly breath. Now you pass through the ruins of the stone bothies where the miners sheltered during the week – work and home were too far apart for many of them to return to their families each night. A roofless dynamite store stands as a reminder of another hazard of the miner's daily toil. Then you reach the top of the crag and walk forward to stand on the summit of Fleetwith Pike, lord of a stupendous view down the Buttermere Valley to Buttermere and Crummock Water, west through a gap in the fells to the Solway Firth and the Galloway Hills, east to Helvellyn's great bulk, and south to where Scafell and Lingmell peer round the hunched shoulder of Great Gable.

A bang and clatter from the opencast slate quarry away to your left is a reminder of the impact that industry had upon this peerless romantic landscape, and of the everyday dangers and hardships of the slate miners of Honister Crag.

296. INNOMINATE TARN, CUMBRIA

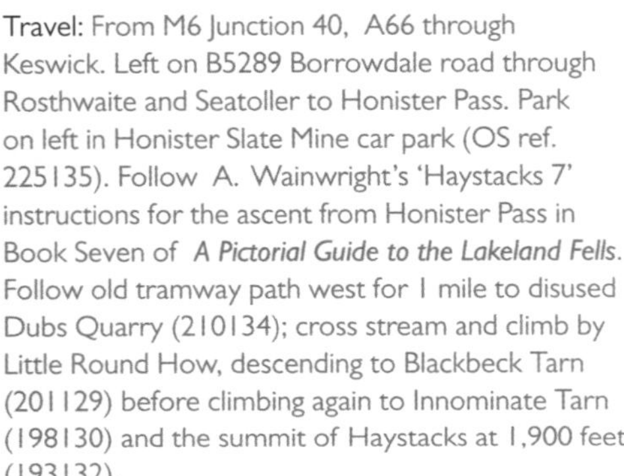

Maps: OS Explorer OL4; Landranger 89

Travel: From M6 Junction 40, A66 through Keswick. Left on B5289 Borrowdale road through Rosthwaite and Seatoller to Honister Pass. Park on left in Honister Slate Mine car park (OS ref. 225135). Follow A. Wainwright's 'Haystacks 7' instructions for the ascent from Honister Pass in Book Seven of *A Pictorial Guide to the Lakeland Fells*. Follow old tramway path west for 1 mile to disused Dubs Quarry (210134); cross stream and climb by Little Round How, descending to Blackbeck Tarn (201129) before climbing again to Innominate Tarn (198130) and the summit of Haystacks at 1,900 feet (193132).

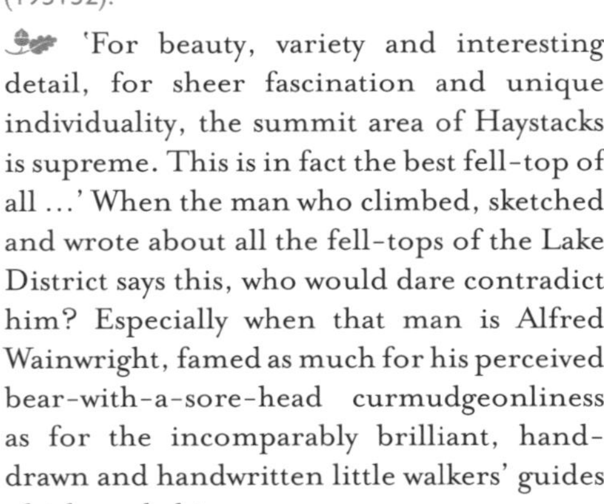

'For beauty, variety and interesting detail, for sheer fascination and unique individuality, the summit area of Haystacks is supreme. This is in fact the best fell-top of all ...' When the man who climbed, sketched and wrote about all the fell-tops of the Lake District says this, who would dare contradict him? Especially when that man is Alfred Wainwright, famed as much for his perceived bear-with-a-sore-head curmudgeonliness as for the incomparably brilliant, hand-drawn and handwritten little walkers' guides which made his name.

There is nothing peculiarly wild about either the top of Haystacks or the shores of the fell's 'baby' lake of Innominate Tarn. But this is the place to sit beside the cold little tarn, looking up at the rocky summit of Haystacks, and give silent thanks to the Blackburn-born accountant who transcended his poor-boy upbringing and myopic job to open the glories of wild Cumbrian country to anyone who could get their hands on one of his *Pictorial Guides to the Lakeland Fells*. At the time of his death in 1991, at the age of eighty-four, Wainwright had sold over a million copies of some sixty titles, and they have gone on selling since then in ever-increasing numbers. He mellowed a little as the years went by, but never lost the defensive carapace that guarded a very sensitive and shy inner man. He was hugely protective of his own privacy, liable to snub over-eager fans, and possessed some very strong and idiosyncratic views on the subject of walking in wild places. Walkers should not talk when out on the fells. Accidents happen only to clumsy or stupid people. Those who never walk alone lack gumption, or are plain daft.

Such views fed the curmudgeon myth. In private Wainwright could be, and often was, kind and generous. The supreme achievement of this complex and difficult man was to demystify the fells. His maps and directions gave everyone the confidence to get out there and enjoy it all. 'Fell walking is not a dangerous sport,' he urged, 'it's a pleasure. Fell walking isn't dicing with death; it is a glorious enjoyment of life.' As for the wild hills themselves, Wainwright wanted everyone to see them as friends.

The fells are not monsters, but amiable giants. You can romp over them and pull the hairs on their chests and shout in their ears and treat them rough, and they don't mind a bit. They are not enemies to be wrestled with. They are friends. Go amongst them as you go amongst friends.

On 22 March 1991 Wainwright's ashes were scattered, at his request, along the shores of Innominate Tarn. His final word on the subject in his autobiography, Fellwanderer, was laced with characteristic dark humour:

A quiet place, a lonely place. I shall go to it, for the last time, and be carried; someone who knew me in life will take me and empty me out of a little box and leave me there alone.

And if you, dear reader, should get a bit of grit in your boot as you are crossing Haystacks in the years to come, please treat it with respect. It might be me.

297. SCAFELL PIKE, CUMBRIA

Maps: OS Explorer OL4, OL6; Landranger 89

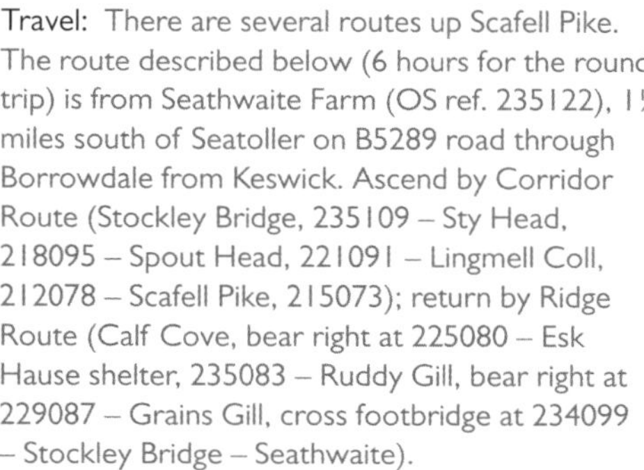
Travel: There are several routes up Scafell Pike. The route described below (6 hours for the round trip) is from Seathwaite Farm (OS ref. 235122), 1½ miles south of Seatoller on B5289 road through Borrowdale from Keswick. Ascend by Corridor Route (Stockley Bridge, 235109 – Sty Head, 218095 – Spout Head, 221091 – Lingmell Coll, 212078 – Scafell Pike, 215073); return by Ridge Route (Calf Cove, bear right at 225080 – Esk Hause shelter, 235083 – Ruddy Gill, bear right at 229087 – Grains Gill, cross footbridge at 234099 – Stockley Bridge – Seathwaite).

Other popular ascents are from Wasdale Head at the upper (north-east) end of Wast Water (187088), from Dungeon Ghyll Old Hotel at the upper (west) end of Great Langdale (286061) and from Brotherilkeld Farm car park at the upper (east) end of Eskdale (212011). These routes may take from 5–7 hours or more, there and back, depending on your fitness and weather conditions.

Excellent directions for all these ascents are in Book Four of A. Wainwright's ***A Pictorial Guide to the Lakeland Fells.***

NB: Scafell Pike is a serious mountain and needs to be treated with respect.

Scafell Pike may be lumped in with other Lake District heights as a fell, but it feels, and should be treated as, a proper mountain. England's highest peak (3,210 feet) is no grassy hummock, but a high head of bare rock with some formidable crags and screes, and one or two very deep ravines falling away from its upper shoulders. Climbing it is a rite of passage for everyone who loves the Lakeland fells, but no one finds a prettily composed subject waiting for a camera up here. Scafell Pike is a big, rough lump of a mountain. As Alfred Wainwright puts it in Book Four of *A Pictorial Guide to the Lakeland Fells*: 'The landscape is harsh, even savage, and has attracted to itself nothing of romance or historical legend. There is no sentiment about Scafell Pike.'

That said, there is all the romance of wet rock, clinking gills, flying mist and sudden revelations of gleaming black cliffs when – as is usually the case – you make the climb in grim weather. Seathwaite Farm is the wettest place in England, so the guidebooks say, and its cobbled yard makes a fitting place to set off from. Sour Milk Gill roars after rain, and this noise accompanies you across humpbacked Stockley Bridge and up the old green pony track to where Taylorgill Force thunders whitely down its channel. At the Sty Head pass there is a confusion of tracks; you swing left and then right, climbing on rock where bright green parsley fern and alpine club moss tell you that you are above the 2,000-foot mark. You inch across the slippery head of Piers Gill, a tremendous crack in the mountainside down which water tumbles with a snake-like hiss. This is a notorious accident black spot: in Victorian times a walker who slipped and fell here managed to survive for eighteen days on fruit cake and gill water. But you get past and trudge on up among the screes and boulders to Lingmell Coll, then over rock to reach the summit cairn. The view on a good day encompasses a great sea of Lakeland peaks, distant Pennine hills, the Cumbrian coast, perhaps the cone of Snaefell 50 miles west on the Isle of Man, and, reputedly, even a glimpse of Slieve Donard in the Mountains of Mourne, 100 miles west across the Irish Sea. But today the mist is down, and you can see no further than the summit cairn. No matter: the satisfaction of reaching the summit is stupendous.

298. WAST WATER, CUMBRIA

Maps: OS Explorer OL6; Landranger 89

Travel: From M6 Junction 36, A590 to Greenodd; A595 towards Whitehaven. At 2½ miles beyond Ravenglass, right to Santon Bridge; left, then right to Nether Wasdale and along north shore of Wast Water to pass Wasdale Hall (OS ref. 145045).

Walks: From here you can try two excellent ascents, both described in Book Seven of A. Wainwright's *A Pictorial Guide to the Lakeland Fells*:

(a) Middle Fell: at ¾ mile past Wasdale Hall, turn left along road to reach Greendale. Park neatly here (144056) and climb the path on your right, north beside Greendale Gill for nearly ½ mile to the 700-foot contour (343062), forking right here to aim north-east for the summit of Middle Fell at 1,908 feet (151072).

(b) Buckbarrow: continue past Greendale for 1 mile; 400 yards short of Harrow Head, park neatly (130055) and take path on your right between two plantations, climbing beside Gill Beck for ¼ mile to the 1,000-foot contour (131060) before forking right to reach the summit of Buckbarrow at 1,410 feet.

To walk the south shore of Wast Water under the Screes, drive the length of Wast Water's north shore and park beyond Overbeck Bridge (168068). Walk along road to upper end of lake, turn right from road across bridges, then right again along the shore (3 miles from end to end).

Wast Water is the Lake District's darkest, deepest and most mysterious lake. It is also the most confined of the large lakes, overhung on the south by the tremendous stony curtain of the Screes, a rocky downfall from the high ridge of Whin Rigg and Illgill Head that plunges dramatically 1,700 feet into the lake. The Screes form a truly rugged and impressive backdrop to the long, narrow mere of Wast Water. The lake is less than half a mile wide at its maximum breadth, but it goes down to a maximum depth of 243 feet. You could sink Queen Mary 2 in that narrow cleft so that not even her topmast would show above the surface.

Climbing the Screes would tax an expert mountaineer. You can walk the path (tricky underfoot) that runs below them, but these great sheets of stones are best seen in all their glory from across the lake. Wainwright's two suggested ascents lead to splendid views of the wild side of Wast Water – from Buckbarrow the mighty Screes themselves, and from Middle Fell the whole dark length of Wast Water laid out for admiration at your feet.

299. ESKDALE, CUMBRIA

Maps: OS Explorer OL6; Landranger 89

Travel: From M6 Junction 36, A590 to Newby Bridge and Greenodd, A5092 to Grizebeck, A595 to Ravenglass. In another 2½ miles, right off A595 to Santon Bridge; right through Eskdale Green and Boot to car park by Brotherilkeld Farm (OS ref. 213011). Pass Brotherilkeld and follow path on either bank of the River Esk for 2 miles to Esk Falls (226037). If river is in spate, return by same path; if water is low enough, ford river by stones and return down opposite bank. To continue to Bow Fell (NB: a long and strenuous walk), follow

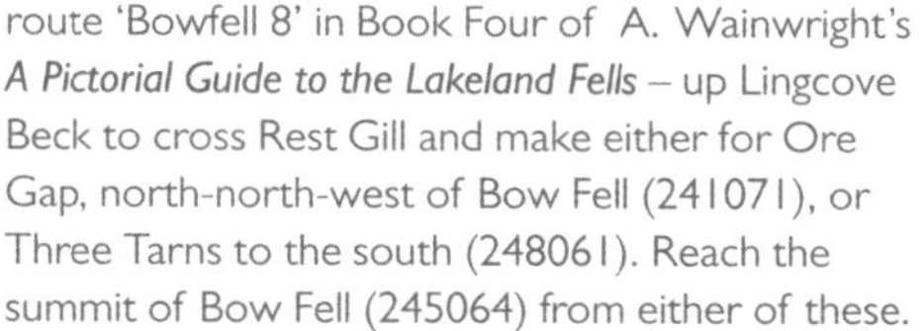

route 'Bowfell 8' in Book Four of A. Wainwright's *A Pictorial Guide to the Lakeland Fells* – up Lingcove Beck to cross Rest Gill and make either for Ore Gap, north-north-west of Bow Fell (241071), or Three Tarns to the south (248061). Reach the summit of Bow Fell (245064) from either of these.

Nearest railway station: Dalegarth (2½ miles from Brotherilkeld) on the Ravenglass & Eskdale Railway (www.ravenglass-railway.co.uk)

The south-western sector of the Lake District is one of the least visited, in spite of the lonely majesty of many of its fells and lakes. There are no major honey-pot attractions here, just the lure of the simple components of Lakeland – water, rock, wind and sky.

Upper Eskdale is one of the most rugged, naked and harshly beautiful dales, and the path that rises up its length beside the young River Esk is suitably rocky and narrow. You start beside Brotherilkeld Farm, established by the monks of Furness as a grange farm to supply their needs. Trust the Cistercians to find somewhere remote but beautiful. From here the path winds with the river, crossing mossy tributary becks of the Esk and climbing under the high grey brow of Yew Crags, with the corresponding heights of Brock Crag and Heron Crag leading the eye forward to the classic mountain cone of Bow Fell, standing high at the head of the valley. Esk Falls, when you reach them halfway up the dale, are revealed as a long, dramatic tumble of water in a succession of cascades.

From this wild and elemental place you can go on, if you have the stamina, beside Lingcove Beck and then steeply up the southern corrie of Bow Fell to reach its shoulders. A short section along either ridge will land you on the narrow, rocky top, almost 3,000 feet up, with tremendous views, notably a sea of tops to the north, a glimpse of Windermere to the south and, closer at hand, the pie-shaped hummock of Scafell Pike (see pp. 323–4) a couple of miles off, at 3,210 feet the highest point in all England.

300. SWINSIDE STONE CIRCLE, CUMBRIA

Maps: OS Explorer OL6; Landranger 96

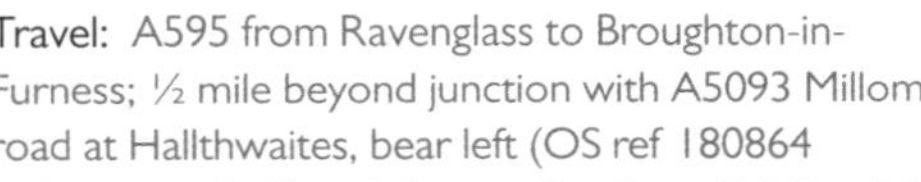
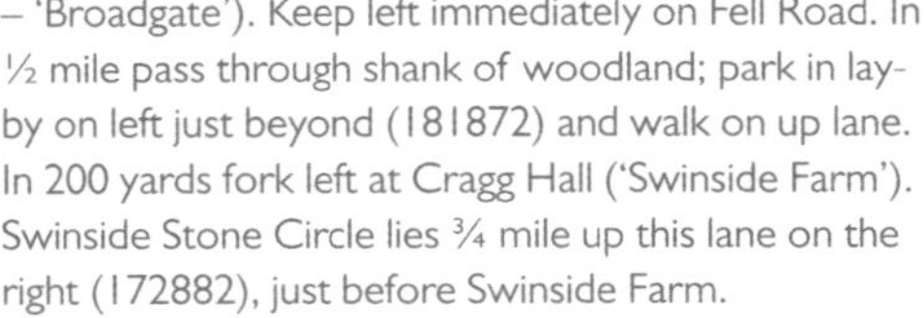
Travel: A595 from Ravenglass to Broughton-in-Furness; ½ mile beyond junction with A5093 Millom road at Hallthwaites, bear left (OS ref 180864 – 'Broadgate'). Keep left immediately on Fell Road. In ½ mile pass through shank of woodland; park in lay-by on left just beyond (181872) and walk on up lane. In 200 yards fork left at Cragg Hall ('Swinside Farm'). Swinside Stone Circle lies ¾ mile up this lane on the right (172882), just before Swinside Farm.

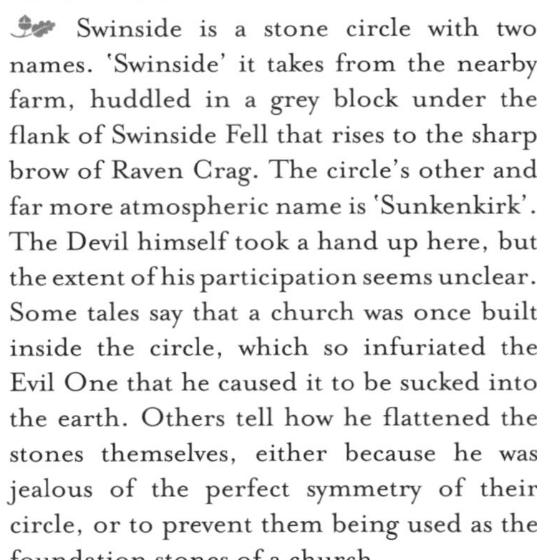
Swinside is a stone circle with two names. 'Swinside' it takes from the nearby farm, huddled in a grey block under the flank of Swinside Fell that rises to the sharp brow of Raven Crag. The circle's other and far more atmospheric name is 'Sunkenkirk'. The Devil himself took a hand up here, but the extent of his participation seems unclear. Some tales say that a church was once built inside the circle, which so infuriated the Evil One that he caused it to be sucked into the earth. Others tell how he flattened the stones themselves, either because he was jealous of the perfect symmetry of their circle, or to prevent them being used as the foundation stones of a church.

Whatever the truth is about the sunken church, the circle itself pre-dates Christianity by at least 3,000 years. Its fifty-five grey slate stones, blotched with lichen and distorted by many millennia of weathering, one or two banded with thin layers of white quartz, are positioned with their entrance facing towards the line of the sun on midwinter's day. The tallest, 10 feet high, stands in a tapering cone shape like a cloaked human figure, a striking presence in winter evening sunshine when it casts a long shadow on a field of powder snow.

301. WALNEY ISLAND, CUMBRIA

Maps: OS Explorer OL6; Landranger 96

Travel: A590 to Barrow-in-Furness and on to Walney Island. Right to North Walney, left to South Walney.

Nearest railway station: Barrow-in-Furness (2 miles)

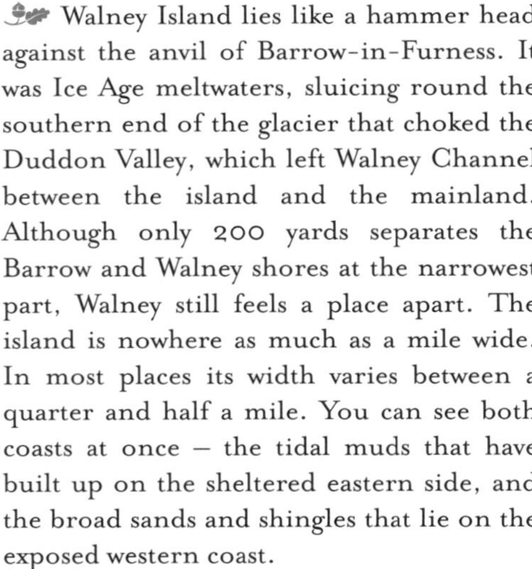
Walney Island lies like a hammer head against the anvil of Barrow-in-Furness. It was Ice Age meltwaters, sluicing round the southern end of the glacier that choked the Duddon Valley, which left Walney Channel between the island and the mainland. Although only 200 yards separates the Barrow and Walney shores at the narrowest part, Walney still feels a place apart. The island is nowhere as much as a mile wide. In most places its width varies between a quarter and half a mile. You can see both coasts at once – the tidal muds that have built up on the sheltered eastern side, and the broad sands and shingles that lie on the exposed western coast.

Walney is actually shaped more like a bow-saw than a hammer, with its northern and southern extremities hooked landward. These tips are completely different in character, but each is a nature reserve packed with wildlife interest. North Walney with its great landward apron of saltmarsh is a National Nature Reserve whose range of sand dunes and their slacks or damp hollows burst into flower each spring. Here you can wander and spot floral treasures: dune helleborine with tiny half-open flowers, and coralroot orchid, another plant with minuscule pale green flowers that colonizes dune slacks.

Down at South Walney it is all about nesting gulls – nearly 30,000, the vast majority of them lesser black-backs. They have settled in huge numbers around the old gravel pits, most now flooded, that exploited the shingle of the spit. If it is a stormy day and the flowers of North Walney don't appeal, you can settle down in a hide at the south end for a spot of sea-watching. Such conditions drive seabirds nearer to the land, and the reserve offers the chance of seeing large numbers of shearwaters, fulmars and gannets flying past.

Seabirds are not the only fowl to enhance Walney Island's reputation. Tummer Hill, an almost imperceptible rise in the marsh at the centre of the island, was the site of famous cockfights in the past. The most heavily wagered-on and bitterly disputed were those between the men of Biggar in the south and North Scale in the north. The old ballad 'The Charcoal Black and the Bonny Grey' charts the defeat of the black cock of Biggar by the grey cock of North Scale:

Now the black cock he has lost their brass,
And the Biggar lads did swear and curse
And wish they'd never come that day
To Tummer Hill to see the play.

302. PIEL ISLAND, CUMBRIA

Maps: OS Explorer OL6; Landranger 96

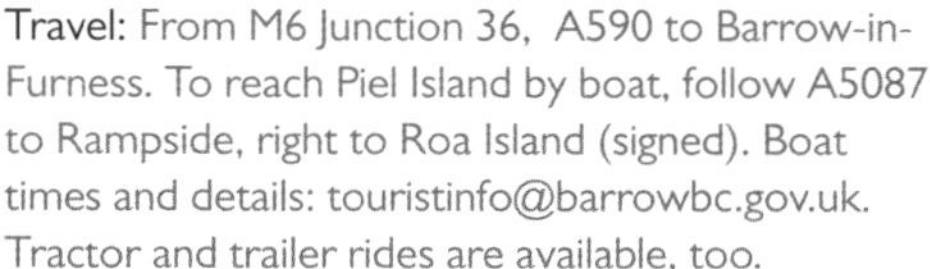
Travel: From M6 Junction 36, A590 to Barrow-in-Furness. To reach Piel Island by boat, follow A5087 to Rampside, right to Roa Island (signed). Boat times and details: touristinfo@barrowbc.gov.uk. Tractor and trailer rides are available, too.

NB: Walking to Piel Island is possible at low tides, but is potentially dangerous. It is essential to consult Barrow-in-Furness Tourist Information Centre beforehand – contact details as for boat.

Nearest railway station: Roose (4 miles)

Why not seek an audience with the King of Piel Island? You can walk over the sands to the tiny island at low tide, from the south end of the Isle of Walney beyond Barrow-in-Furness, or take a boat from Roa Island south of Barrow. The King of Piel is the honorary title given to the resident landlord of the Ship Inn, who is marooned in his minuscule kingdom each high tide – one of the strangest situations in Britain for a pub. The Ship is the loneliest and most atmospheric inn in the North-West. It shares the few windswept and storm-battered acres of Piel Island with a magnificent ruined castle, a pele tower or defensive stronghold built in the fourteenth century by the monks of Furness Abbey to safeguard their trading and smuggling activities. There are legends – of course – of a secret tunnel under the sands to Furness Abbey 5 miles away. It's certain that the island was a centre for smuggling right up until the nineteenth century; it was so conveniently situated a mile or so offshore in a location where anyone could be seen coming from a long way off.

Lambert Simnel, the hapless ten-year-old

pretender to the crown of England, landed here on 4 January 1487 with a contingent of Irish and Flemish troops, the first step on his journey to London to claim the throne. His backers, opponents of King Henry VII, gave out that he was the missing Earl of Warwick and rightful heir to the kingdom. By the time Simnel reached London he was a prisoner of the king. The rebels had been defeated in battle and were either dead, scattered or in custody. Heads rolled, but not that of Simnel – wise Henry pardoned him. He also kept him close by, appointing him spit-turner in the royal kitchen.

You can become a knight of Piel by sitting in the Ship Inn's ceremonial oak chair. And many do. Roddy Scarr, ex-King of Piel, put it this way:

"I love the island, simple as that. Collecting wood from the beach, looking after my wildfowl pond, fetching a few of the locals over for a pint and a game of cards. No bosses, no one to push me around. In summer we get the yachtsmen and visitors from the ferry; singsongs in the bar, no bother from anyone.

When I open my door at six in the morning and look out on the sands and the birds at sunrise, I know how lucky I am. I wouldn't go back ashore. No way."

Roddy 'abdicated' in 2006 for health reasons, and does in fact now live ashore. A new king has just been appointed – Steve Chattaway – who will be reopening the Ship in 2009.

303. ESKMEALS SAND DUNES, CUMBRIA

Maps: OS Explorer OL6; Landranger 96

Travel: A595 from Millom towards Ravenglass; just before Ravenglass, bear left in Waberthwaite on minor road through Newbiggin and on through viaduct. Park in lay-by just beyond (OS ref. 087943) and take footpath on to Eskmeals Reserve.

NB: Eskmeals is an MoD firing range. Please ring 01229 712200 before your visit to check the reserve is open. When yellow flags are flying, the reserve is closed.

Nearest railway station: Bootle (3½ miles)

The estuary at Ravenglass on the coast of west Cumbria is a complex place. The three rivers of Esk, Irt and Mite push out to sea together through mud and sand flats. The power of these mingled tide streams and the eternal influence of the west wind off the Irish Sea have mounded up huge ranges of sand hills on shingle spits both north and south of the estuary, a 6-mile wall of dunes pierced only by the outflow of the three rivers.

During the twentieth century something approaching 80 per cent of all marshy and sandy coasts in Britain were built over, turned into farmland or compromised by leisure users. Here at Drigg Sands and Eskmeals the coast lies unspoiled, and the natterjack toad has colonized it to an astonishing degree. Natterjacks are Britain's rarest and fussiest amphibian. The big toads with the greeny-gold eyes and the distinctive yellow stripe down their spines require a highly specific habitat in order to thrive and breed – warm sandy soil near the sea that is loose enough to dig burrows in, with close vegetation that they can negotiate with their short legs. They also need spawning pools that are shallow (natterjacks don't swim well, and can easily drown). These pools should ideally contain little plant food and should dry out from time to time, so as to make them unattractive to rival amphibians and also to dragonflies and water beetles that eat natterjack eggs and young.

Such conditions are fully met among the Eskmeal dunes south of the Ravenglass estuary; nevertheless the conservation workers who look after natterjack interests here face an uphill struggle. Too much rain and the pools and burrows flood; too little, and the pools dry out before the tadpoles can hatch, killing a whole year's brood. In spite of all the obstacles the Eskmeals natterjacks thrive, and the time to enjoy them is on a warm night in spring. The volume and resonance of the males' croaking is something to hear. They grate, they groan and they grunt. Reclining in the dunes surrounded by lovelorn natterjacks is rather like lying in a motel bedroom with too-thin walls. It makes you blink a bit.

304. SALTOM BAY, CUMBRIA

Maps: OS Explorer 303; Landranger 89

Travel: A595 to Whitehaven; park near harbour and follow cliff path south for 1¾ miles to triangulation pillar above Saltom Bay (OS ref. 962157). Alternative approach from St Bees (960118) north along cliff path for 4 miles.

Nearest railway stations: Whitehaven or St Bees

The red sandstone cliffs between Whitehaven and St Bees are wild enough, with an abundance of wild flowers and seabirds and tremendous uninterrupted sea views, but it is hard to appreciate just how splendid these natural assets are without a glimpse into the industrial past of the clifftops.

As you stroll south from the Georgian port of Whitehaven, up the cliff steps and past the little house where Jonathan Swift, author of *Gulliver's Travels*, lived as a child, it is tempting to think that this agreeable waterfront and its cradling headlands have always lain so peacefully looking out to the Irish Sea. But Whitehaven was built on heavy industry; the cliffs are full of coal, and the Lowther family, Earls of Lonsdale and owners of this area, spotted a good opportunity back in the seventeenth century when they invested in the harbour and laid out the town. Just near Jonathan Swift's house rises the Candlestick Chimney, a ventilation shaft for the Wellington coal pit in the cliffs below. In 1910 the Wellington was the scene of the worst disaster in Cumbrian coal-mining history, when an explosion and ensuing fire killed 136 men and boys underground. The Wellington pit closed in 1933, as did the Ladysmith and Croft pits further south. Where the Haig Colliery stood until 1984, an industrial museum now guides visitors through the story of coal mining in the area.

The last of the industrial clifftop sites south of Whitehaven is the most problematical, for here until 2007 stood the giant Marchon chemical works, a gross polluter of air, land and water. The fuming chimneys, square hoppers and packing plants sent out a strong soapy smell over the surrounding countryside, and would occasionally produce a white 'snow' that settled over everything. Marchon made the component chemicals for shampoo, bubble bath and soap flakes. The burn that poured over the cliffs in a waterfall used to be romantically foamy – not with bubbles of oxygen, but with soap bubbles, which turned the shore rocks black and slippery. A sluggish reef of suds lay offshore, covering the waters of Saltom Bay with a greasy film. Layers of coal spoil, also tipped over the cliff on the 'out of sight, out of mind' principle, put the black icing on the white chemical cake.

Whatever is planned for the Marchon site, and whatever actually happens to it, nothing will ever remove that image of ultimate industrial vandalism from the minds of those who witnessed it – nor the extra fillip they now get from the wild flowers, the seabirds and the fresh air that are once again the keynotes of these cliffs.

305. CARDURNOCK FLATTS, SOLWAY FIRTH, CUMBRIA

Maps: OS Explorer 314; Landranger 85

Travel: From M6 Junction 43, A69 into Carlisle; A595 ('Workington, Whitehaven') out of city centre, then right on B5307 through Kirkbampton and Fingland to Angerton. Right here to T-junction at Whitrigg; left through Anthorn to Cardurnock. Park and turn left along green lane beside telephone box (OS ref. 172588), down to shore.

NB: Carlisle Western Bypass is under construction at time of writing; when open, follow it from M6 to turn right along B5307 through Kirkbampton.

This is a bleak little place, out on a headland amid the vast sandflats of the Solway Firth. A great spider's web of radio masts rises just inland, like the poles of a circus Big Top still waiting for the canvas. Big box-like buildings of utility brick show where ammunition was stored and planes zeroed in for target practice during the Second World War. Yet somehow none of this impinges, adding only a sombre tinge to the atmosphere as you step from the low shelf of the saltmarsh on to the sands.

Cardurnock Flatts

Isolated islets of marsh lie in moats of seawater, their grassy hummocks pink with sea thrift. The sands stretch away north, west and south, level, firm and clean, without a single upstanding feature to anchor the sight until it lights on the bow-shaped hummock of Criffel 10 miles away across the Solway. Twice as far off in the south stands 3,000-foot Skiddaw, guardian of the northern Lakeland fells. This is a giant prospect in an utterly lonely, always windswept landscape, where a flashing bar of waves breaks on the outer edge of the flats with a low, threatening roar as the tide begins its mile-long gallop in across the sands.

306. CROSS FELL, CUMBRIA

Maps: OS Explorer OL31; Landranger 91

Travel: Cross Fell (OS ref. 687343) is a long walk from anywhere. The Pennine Way National Trail crosses the summit on its way between Dufton (8½ miles from Cross Fell) and Garrigill (9 miles). A bridleway from Kirkland (651326 – 3½ miles) meets the Pennine Way on the flank of Skirwith Fell (684352); you can turn right up the Pennine Way for 2/3 mile to the summit of Cross Fell from here. Another bridleway from Blencarn (640312 – 4 miles) meets the Pennine Way between Little Dun Fell and Cross Fell (697339); left here for 2/3 mile to the summit.

Cross Fell is unmistakable. A great round bastion of a hill with walls of steep scree dropping off the gently domed summit on all sides, it looks exactly like what it is, a king and a castle, the highest point on the Pennine Way at 2,930 feet. Cross Fell doesn't merit inclusion in a list of Munroes or peaks over 3,000 feet, but for Pennine Way walkers, and anyone venturing into the moorland fastness of Moor House National Nature Reserve (see p. 333), it is the place to aim for.

Coming up the Pennine Way from Dufton, you first hurdle the twin summits of Great and Little Dun Fell. The communications masts on Great Dun Fell may not be objects of beauty – Alfred Wainwright in his *Pennine Way Companion* apostrophized them as 'a monstrous miscellany of para-phernalia' – but they do aid direction-finding when there is no mist or low cloud. That is not often – Cross Fell is notorious as a magnet for bad weather, and has its own vicious wind, the Helm, which has been known to raise roofs and topple trees in Dufton and Garrigill. In fact the fell had such a reputation for lightning, storms and terrifying noises that local people used to know it as 'Fiend's Fell'.

The summit of Cross Fell, a featureless place of rock and sparse grass, offers an appropriately cross-shaped stone shelter to cower behind when wind and rain are blowing around. Of much more interest are the old mine levels that litter the flanks of the fell – you only need to walk a mile or two down the Pennine Way to come across plenty of them. Tunnels, open shafts, wet levels to let the water out and dry levels to let the miners in, old bothies and processing plants: their carefully shaped stone arches, wall angles and broken corners lie all around, lapped by a surf of stone fragments and chips of white quartz and purple-blue fluorspar, the by-products of lead mining. The London Lead Company operated dozens of small lead mines up here very profitably during the Industrial Revolution with its insatiable demand for building materials of all sorts; but the LLC is only one operator in a long chain of lead miners that stretches back to the Romans, who themselves may have simply continued what their British predecessors had started.

Nowadays the old levels, shafts and buildings lie forlorn, a legacy of those obscure men who worked and frequently died in grim conditions and all weathers up here on the comfortless slopes of Fiend's Fell.

307. HIGH CUP, CUMBRIA

Maps: OS Explorer OL19; Landranger 91

Travel: There are three main approaches to High Cup:

(a) from M6 Junction 38, B6260, or from Junction 40, A66 – both to Appleby-in-Westmorland (nearest railway station: Appleby). From town centre, minor road to Dufton; right at Town Head just before village, on minor road ('Murton'). In 2 miles, park neatly near Harbour Flatt farm (OS ref. 718232). Follow High Cup Gill up its valley on stony track. Keep left of rocky outcrop of Middle Tongue and continue for another 1½ miles to head of beck. Steep climb, then scramble up valley head – keep left of main scree – to High Cup rim (745262). (5 miles there and back – involves a short but potentially hazardous scramble up rocks.)

(b) follow Pennine Way National Trail from Saur Hill Bridge (854302), reached from Langdon Beck (853312) via B6277 and farm track opposite hostel (860303). This is a demanding trek, partly across wild moorland. (10 miles to High Cup, plus 4 miles into Dufton.)

(c) the easiest way is to follow the Pennine Way east for 3 miles from Bow Hall Farm on the eastern edge of Dufton (702251).

High Cup is so affectionately regarded by walkers that it has – literally – its own nickname. Technically speaking, High Cup Nick is the name of a sharp nick or cleft in the west face of the dramatic vee of cliffs that forms High Cup, but it is as High Cup Nick that the whole feature is known to almost everyone. Whatever its name, this extraordinary boat-shaped valley driven into the flank of Dufton Fell is a place one comes to with a huge sense of relief and pleasure, particularly if the approach has been from the east along the miry miles of the Pennine Way. It is no walk in the park to reach High Cup, but the rewards are great.

The valley's vertical black cliffs are part of the Whin Sill, that wedge of dark volcanic dolerite that runs across the country, surfacing every now and then in such spectacular manifestations as High Force Waterfall (see pp. 339–40), the crags that underpin Hadrian's Wall (see pp. 350–51) and the Farne Islands (see pp. 362–3). High

Cup is another splendid showing, its dark ramparts standing tall above the classic U-shaped dale of High Cup Gill. This valley was gouged out by a glacier and smoothed into its perfect rollercoaster hollow by 10,000 years of post-glacial weathering. The view down the dale over the Eden Valley to the outline of the Lake District fells 25 miles away, and the contrast between the pastoral beauty of the lowlands at your feet and the wild bleakness of the moors at your back, are simply breathtaking.

308. MOOR HOUSE NATIONAL NATURE RESERVE, CUMBRIA

Maps: OS Explorer OL31; Landranger 91

Travel: The upper half of Moor House NNR lies in very wild country, and can be approached only on foot or by bicycle.

From the west, three routes reach the ridge between Knock Fell and Great Dun Fell (OS ref. 717731): a bridleway from Milburn (661294 – 4½ miles), a miners' road from just north-west of Knock (676274 – 4 miles), and the Pennine Way National Trail from Dufton (692252 – 5 miles).

From the north-east, follow the Tyne Head road south from Garrigill (745415) for 2½ miles to end of tarred road beyond Hill House (757384), walk or bicycle from here on South Tyne Trail for another 3½ miles to cross River Tees into the reserve (760338). Continue along track up Trout Beck for 3½ miles to meet Pennine Way on shoulder of Great Dun Fell (716316).

Moor House National Nature Reserve is truly, impressively wild. This wide swathe of sodden bog and rolling moor lies west of Cow Green Reservoir in a region crossed by no motor roads and served by no villages. One or two determined sheep farmers still live and work here, but these 10,000 acres of bare, empty upland are left mostly to the curlew and snipe. Even to enter the reserve costs you plenty of time and physical effort, slogging up one of a handful of footpaths or old miners' trods from the comparative civilization of hamlets such as Milburn and Knock or the small villages of Dufton and Garrigill in the green pasturelands below. Exploring Moor House can hardly be achieved without getting thoroughly wet and mucky – much of the ground is water-laden sphagnum moss, much of the rest is black peat up to 10 feet thick, overlain with the fluffy white buds of cotton grass and with sparse heather. Most of it is Access Land, but few care to strike off the paths and tracks out into such a wilderness.

Moor House is the most thoroughly researched and examined piece of moorland in Britain. Scientific experiments that have been going on since the 1930s include investigation of the structure and ongoing development of peat bog, the effect of rainfall, of airborne pollutants and of change in the use of the land, of undergrazing and overgrazing, and of the inexorable progress of climate change. You can walk the old trackways without being aware of any of this, of course. Side by side with the science goes simple pleasure in the sound of snipe drumming in the spring air, the liquid calls of curlew and golden plover, the tremendous views off the tops of Knock Old Man and Great Dun Fell, and the tumultuous weather systems that come crashing through and rumble away, leaving everything – including walkers – soaked and refreshed.

10

DURHAM, NORTHUMBERLAND

THE NORTH-EAST

The North-East of England is terra incognita to many, a never-visited, occasionally visualized waste of coal-mining desolation, defeated industrial towns and wind-blasted moors. There is some truth in the stereotype, but wide varieties of wild places exist in this region. Times may have changed in the North-East in the last few decades, but the high moors of west Durham, the lonely Cheviot Hills and the cold and pristine sandy coast of Northumberland remain intact.

UP NEAR THE source of the River Tees the valley of Upper Teesdale is jewelled each spring with beautiful, delicate plants, arctic-alpine primroses and gentians which have clung on here, and nowhere else in the region, over all the millennia since the last Ice Age. The Tees's estuary at Teesmouth, some 80 miles to the east, is a very heavily industrialized place; yet here exists a fine coastal nature reserve and a carefully preserved urban marsh and wetland. Up in Northumberland are vast tracts of lonely hill country, the haunt of long-distance walkers on the Pennine Way, and many other little-known historic paths that criss-cross the Cheviot Hills. Here, too, lie peat moors blanketed in sombre black forests where the cheep of long-tailed tits and drip of rain seem to be the only sounds of life or movement. Down on the coast, beyond the windy beaches, the treeless, salt-sprayed basalt wedges of the Farne Islands rise a mile or so offshore. Bleak landscapes all.

Perhaps the most striking wild place of the region is the East Durham coast, where a series of bays loops along fine magnesian limestone cliffs cut through by denes or steep ravines. As a student at Durham University in the 1960s I would bicycle out to the coast for the freaky pleasure of exploring what seemed more moonscape than any terrestrial landform. Unlike the Northumbrian moors or the flowery heights of Teesdale, this was a landscape apparently blasted beyond hope of redemption by coal mining and colliery dumping – a blighted region

Bamburgh Castle (p. 362)

from which nature had been ruthlessly expunged. Yet after the coal mines closed in the late twentieth century, a breathtaking transformation began. These cliffs, denes and beaches, so drastically fouled only a few years ago, are already being encroached upon and recaptured by nature (with a little help from man) – a remarkable success story.

LINKS

- Pennine Way National Trail (www.nationaltrail.co.uk/pennineway; www.penninewayassociation.co.uk): High Force, Upper Teesdale, Upper Coquetdale, The Cheviot, Wark Forest
- Hadrian's Wall National Trail (www.nationaltrail.co.uk/hadrianswall; www.hadrians-wall.org): Housesteads, Windshield Crags to Walltown Crags
- Durham Heritage Coast Path (www.durhamheritagecoast.org): Castle Eden Dene, Easington Beach, Hawthorn Dene and Hive
- Northumberland Coast Path/North Sea Trail (www.northumberland-coast.co.uk): Coquet Island, Dunstanburgh Castle, Beadnell Bay, Farne Islands, Lindisfarne causeway

NATIONAL PARK

- Northumberland: www.northumberlandnationalpark.org.uk

THE NORTH-EAST
DURHAM, NORTHUMBERLAND

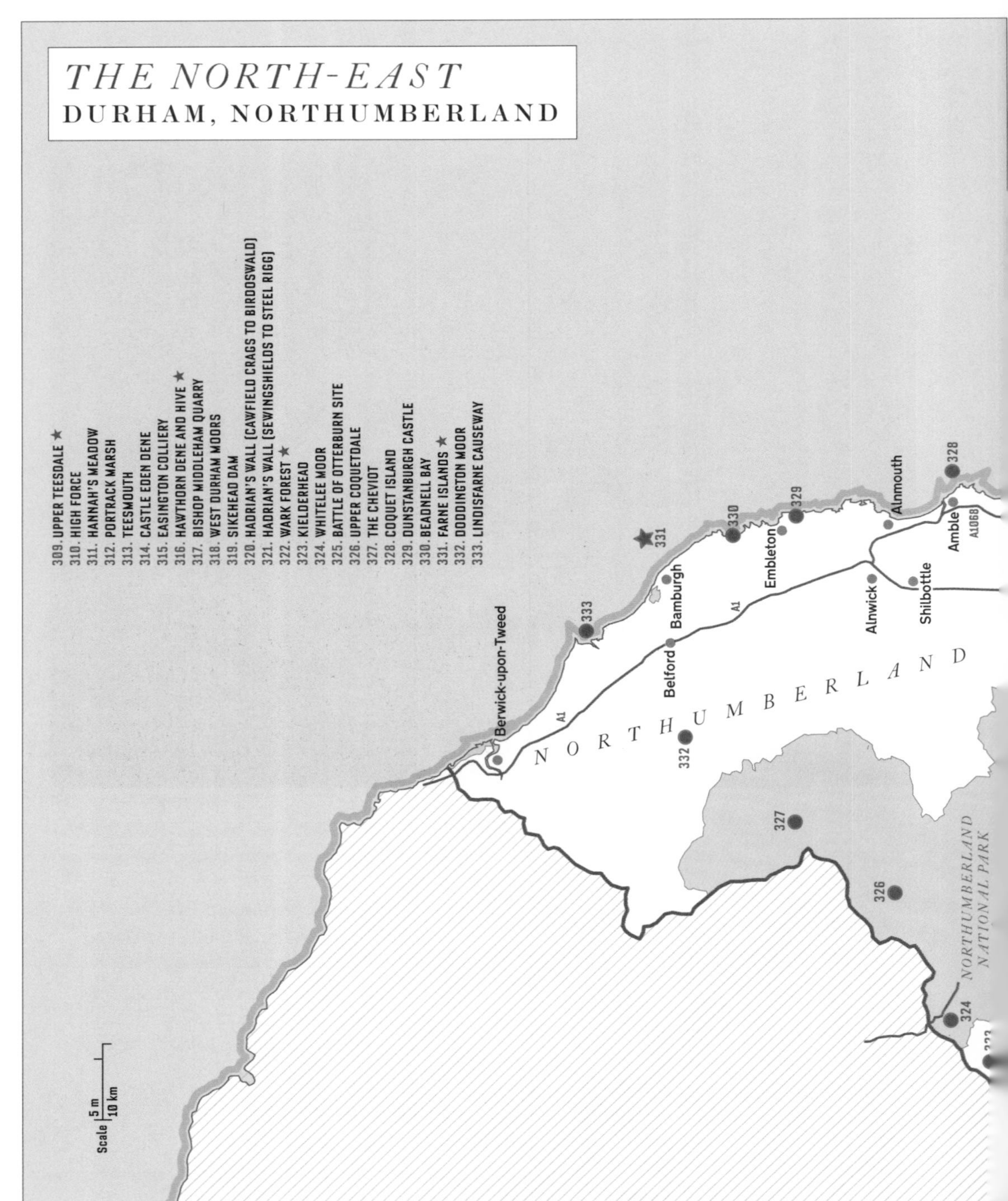

325
Otterburn
Kielder Water
Ashington
Newbiggin-by-the-Sea
Morpeth
A189
Bellingham
A68
A696
Blyth
Cramlington
322
Ponteland
A1
A19
North Shields
Newcastle -upon-Tyne
320
321
A69
Longbenton
Haydon Bridge
Hexham
Prudhoe
Blaydon
A194
A184
Whitburn
A19
A1
Washington
Sunderland
Consett
A692
Chester-le-Street
A693
Houghton-le-Spring
A167
Seaham
316
319
Castleside
A691
Langley Park
Easington
315
Durham
A1(M)
Peterlee
314
Stanhope
Spennymoor
318
Bishop Auckland
317
Sedgefield
A179
Hartlepool
DURHAM
309
310
A66
Newton Aycliffe
Greatham
313
A689
Redcar
A1053
311
Barnard Castle
A67
A688
312
Middlesbrough
Saltburn-by-the-Sea
A174
A171
Guisborough
Eaglescliffe
Darlington
A19
NORTH YORK MOORS

309. UPPER TEESDALE, CO. DURHAM

Maps: OS Explorer OL31, OL19; Landranger 92, 91

Travel: A1 to Scotch Corner, left on A66 to Barnard Castle, B6277 to Middleton-in-Teesdale; or M6 to Junction 38, right on A685 to Brough, B6276 to Middleton-in-Teesdale. From Middleton, B6277 towards Alston.

Upper Teesdale is a national treasure, a rare gem of landscape that is not only wildly beautiful, but also beautifully wild. The dramatic, twisting valley of the young River Tees, with its great waterfalls that tumble over steps in the river bed, its curving walls of clints and its high billowing peat moors, is a wonderful piece of landscape theatre, and from the Pennine Way National Trail you get a grandstand view of it all. But Upper Teesdale is also one of the wildest dales in the North, notable for the unique flora it sustains as much as for the golden plover, the lapwings and redshank that breed here. Spring is the time to come, a bright day in May after heavy rain when the Tees is a roaring torrent, the birds are sitting close and all the spring flowers are out. Spring gentians are the stars, clusters of delicate plants with trumpet-shaped flowers so intensely, royally blue that anyone glancing at them for the first time is liable to blink and look again. Bird's-eye primroses are another pearl. The intense mauve-pink of these gorgeous flowers on their tall graceful stems is in stunning contrast to the sulphur yellow of their more common and stubbier cousins. Kneel on the crunchy limestone to admire the pale yellow eye at the heart of each flower, and you will find yourself marvelling at the tenacity of these plants, fugitives from the intensive farming that has crushed out the wildflower life of so many British landscapes.

Upper Teesdale

It is the coarse, sandy-looking limestone around the River Tees that has enabled the spring gentian, the bird's-eye primrose, the little Teesdale violet and the delicate deep blue Alpine forget-me-not to survive for thousands of years up here, in their wild valley on the border of Cumbria and Durham. And the crystalline rock itself, evocatively named 'sugar limestone', owes its existence to the hot and irresistible intrusion of a tongue of boiling magma into the carboniferous limestone some 300 million years ago. The molten rock cooled slowly, but not before it had baked and crystallized the limestone in its immediate vicinity. The resultant sugar limestone provided the perfect mix of nutrients to nurture the plants of the tundra landscape that came into being hereabouts after the last glaciers had creaked and melted away.

Nowadays some 7,000 acres of Upper Teesdale are carefully managed as Moor House National Nature Reserve (see p. 333). The damp slopes and hollows of the Pennine moors, the sugar limestone, the pavements of limestone blocks and sheltered cracks, the acid patches of bog and the traditionally farmed hay meadows are recognized for what they are – a unique landscape in which flourish plants that are among our most senior floral residents, plant communities that are a throwback to that slowly unfreezing Britain. But attitudes towards conservation weren't always so enlightened. Cow Green Reservoir in Upper Teesdale is a beautiful stretch of water, but there was an enormous row when it was built in the late 1960s, flooding a valley which was one of the strongholds of the Teesdale violet and many other rare plants. The water needs of industrial Teesside were paramount, it seemed. Luckily the reservoir's construction didn't turn out to be the ecological disaster feared by conservationists. But one of its consequences, the regulation of the flow of the River Tees down the 200-foot rock staircase of Cauldron Snout, was bitterly regretted by those who loved the drama of the river in full and furious springtime spate, when it would thunder over the fall as if a plug had been pulled from the hills.

310. HIGH FORCE, CO. DURHAM

Maps: OS Explorer OL31; Landranger 92

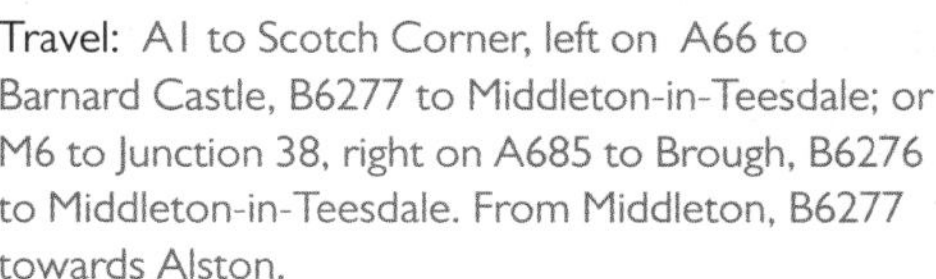

Travel: A1 to Scotch Corner, left on A66 to Barnard Castle, B6277 to Middleton-in-Teesdale; or M6 to Junction 38, right on A685 to Brough, B6276 to Middleton-in-Teesdale. From Middleton, B6277 towards Alston.

To view High Force from below, after 5 miles park on right at High Force Hotel (OS ref. 884287) – please ask permission and give the hotel your custom. Cross road, go through gate and follow path down to High Force (880284).

To view from beside the fall, after 3 miles park on right at Bowlees Visitor Centre (906282). Cross B6277; follow signposted field path to cross River Tees by Wynch Bridge (904279); turn right up the Pennine Way along far bank of Tees for 1 mile to reach High Force.

The time to come, without a shadow of a doubt, is after very heavy rain, especially in early spring with snow thawing off the fells of Upper Teesdale. The setting of England's biggest and most majestic waterfall is magnificent, an outspread landscape of wide green fields striped with stone walls, rising to purple moorlands. Through the fields hurries the River Tees, swollen from a shallow moorland river into a broad, powerful sluice, yellow with dissolved peat, that charges down its valley with a low thundering noise, carrying juniper trees, boulders and drowned sheep. Across its path lies the barrier of the Whin Sill, a great

High Force

tongue of volcanic magma which forced its way between more compliant rocks some 300 million years ago and cooled into a hard underground wedge of dolerite, 200 feet thick in places. Here in Upper Teesdale it outcrops in the form of a 70-foot step in the river bed, and it is over this dark cliff that the Tees plunges.

In times of spate High Force is a stunning sound and spectacle. The river approaches the lip of the falls as a feathery, tumbling mass of jostling yellow water that divides into two distinct cataracts before leaping into space, not so much falling as surging down its gleaming volcanic stairway. At the bottom the Tees crashes into a smoking basin over which a rainbow shimmers through a veil of finely misted spray.

311. HANNAH'S MEADOW, CO. DURHAM

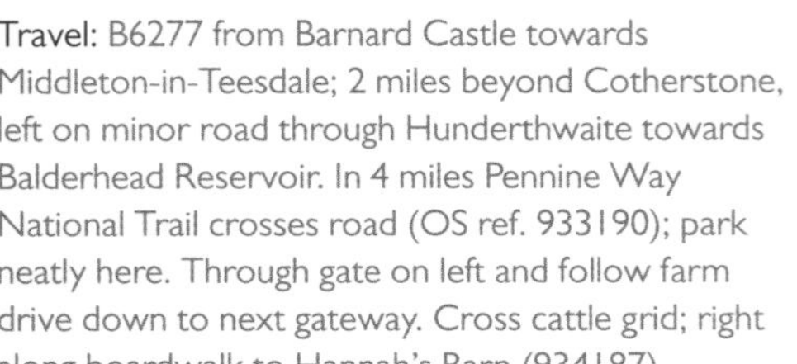

Maps: OS Explorer OL31; Landranger 92

Travel: B6277 from Barnard Castle towards Middleton-in-Teesdale; 2 miles beyond Cotherstone, left on minor road through Hunderthwaite towards Balderhead Reservoir. In 4 miles Pennine Way National Trail crosses road (OS ref. 933190); park neatly here. Through gate on left and follow farm drive down to next gateway. Cross cattle grid; right along boardwalk to Hannah's Barn (934187).

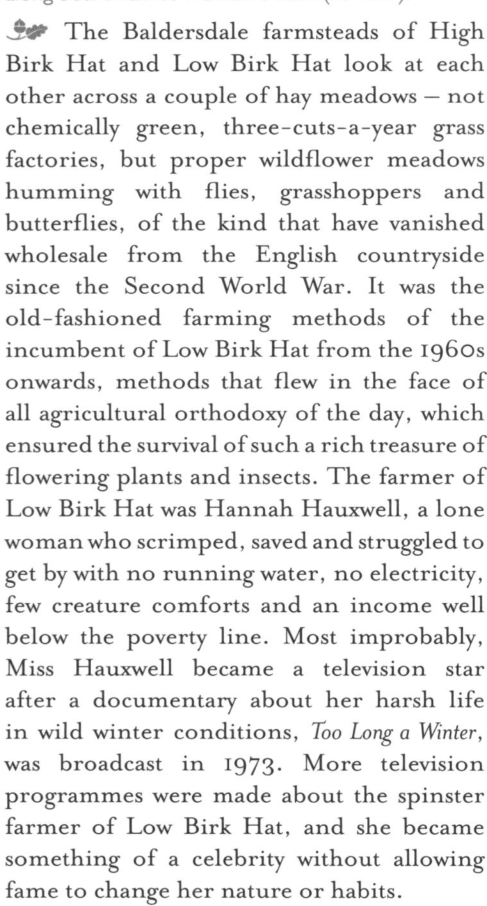

The Baldersdale farmsteads of High Birk Hat and Low Birk Hat look at each other across a couple of hay meadows – not chemically green, three-cuts-a-year grass factories, but proper wildflower meadows humming with flies, grasshoppers and butterflies, of the kind that have vanished wholesale from the English countryside since the Second World War. It was the old-fashioned farming methods of the incumbent of Low Birk Hat from the 1960s onwards, methods that flew in the face of all agricultural orthodoxy of the day, which ensured the survival of such a rich treasure of flowering plants and insects. The farmer of Low Birk Hat was Hannah Hauxwell, a lone woman who scrimped, saved and struggled to get by with no running water, no electricity, few creature comforts and an income well below the poverty line. Most improbably, Miss Hauxwell became a television star after a documentary about her harsh life in wild winter conditions, *Too Long a Winter*, was broadcast in 1973. More television programmes were made about the spinster farmer of Low Birk Hat, and she became something of a celebrity without allowing fame to change her nature or habits.

The hayfields that Hannah Hauxwell

farmed without the use of chemical fertilizers, pesticides or herbicides are now styled 'Hannah's Meadow', and are maintained by Durham Wildlife Trust in all their tremendous richness of wildlife. In the autumn sheep are put into the meadows and stay there all the winter, through the tupping season in November and on into lambing time. In spring they are removed and the grass grows on, along with the wild flowers. These months from April until July are the prime time to visit and admire the yellow balls of globeflowers, pink straggles of ragged robin and beaked blooms of yellow rattle; also nesting curlew and lapwing, and old-fashioned species of meadow grass such as the stiff little bottle-brush of crested dog's tail and the feathery spike of vanilla-scented sweet vernal grass. The meadows are mown in midsummer or a little later, and cattle then graze the 'fog', or late growth of grass, until it is time to introduce the sheep once more.

Hannah's Meadow

The cosy image of a traditional farmer in a lovely hayfield is belied by the reality of Hannah Hauxwell's daily grind on her high Pennine farm. After twenty-five years of lone work, and in spite of her television celebrity, life became too difficult as she grew older and more infirm. By the 1990s the farm and her beloved animals had been sold and she had left Low Birk Hat to live in less pinched circumstances not far away. She is still living there, but out of the public eye. The farmhouse was modernized for another occupant, the fields bought by Durham Wildlife Trust to be maintained in Miss Hauxwell's style.

Around Baldersdale and all through the Pennines are farms abandoned over the course of the late twentieth century as the old ways of life became impossible to sustain. The exhibition in Hannah's Barn about Low Birk Hat and its modest, heroic incumbent tell some of the tale: the rest is to be read among the ruins of lonely farmsteads and their unrecorded stories.

312. PORTRACK MARSH, TEESSIDE

Maps: OS Explorer 306; Landranger 93

Travel: A66 Darlington towards Middlesbrough; at A1130 turn, bear left and follow 'Tees Barrage'. In 200 yards cross roundabout and then Barrage; in 100 yards, right along Whitewater Way to Premier Travel Inn (OS ref. 464193). Park here and follow surfaced path by caravan park fence to information board; from here walk on to reserve.

Nearest railway station: Thornaby (1 ½ miles)

Back in the days before the Industrial Revolution, Portrack Marsh was a series of meadows and wetlands around the meanders of the River Tees in open country. Before the

Portrack Marsh

river was straightened to improve navigation, barges would be 'racked' – hauled bodily – round the tight bends by a strong man or a horse. The 1,100-yard Portrack Cut opened in 1831; taken in conjunction with another cut a little higher up the river made two decades before, it snipped as much as a week off the time a barge would take to make its way to the port of Stockton. By the mid nineteenth century the railways had done for the barges, of course, and the roads did for the railways by the end of the twentieth. By that time Teesside was a maze of iron and chemical works, the once clear Tees had become Britain's most grossly polluted estuary, and Portrack Marsh itself was the site of a huge waste incinerator (closed in 1996), followed by an enormous municipal rubbish dump (closed in 2001).

How such a poisoned and hopeless site, squashed in between industrial estates and the River Tees, could undergo a Cinderella-style transformation into a much-loved urban wild place packed with wildlife interest is one of the modest triumphs of the conservation movement. Walking the reserve paths nowadays you find a wide low-lying area of freshwater marsh and scrub cut across by big fleets of water. Ditches, wetland patches and wet grassland are the haunts of hunting dragonflies, of frogs and water voles. You may spot the startling blue streak of a kingfisher, or the sudden scurry followed by absolute immobility of a harvest mouse. Goldeneye, with their expressionless but beautiful presence, little grebe nesting in the reed-beds and wily urban herons are often seen. Duckboard trails carry you through half-sodden everglades of reeds and aquatic plants, where grasshopper warblers click and purr, all under a dramatic skyline of chemical towers and refinery plants.

313. TEESMOUTH, CO. DURHAM/ NORTH YORKSHIRE

Maps: OS Explorer 306; Landranger 93

Travel: A19 from Sunderland towards Teesside; at Billingham, left on A1185 for 3½ miles, then left on A178. Car park for Seal Sands is in 1 mile (OS ref. 509251). For North Gare continue another 2½ miles to turn right (525281) to car park at end of minor road (534282).

Nearest railway station: Seaton Carew (2 miles from North Gare car park, 4 miles from Seal Sands car park)

Teesmouth National Nature Reserve is a place of two halves – North Gare with its sand dunes and beach on the north side of Seaton-on-Tees Channel, and opposite it the solid square mile of tidal mudflats that bears the name of Seal Sands. What is most remarkable about this strange and compelling piece of coast is that the dune plants, the wading birds in their thousands and the basking seals look across the channel and the adjacent mouth of the River Tees at one of Europe's most monstrous coastal industrial complexes. The fact that so many rare, beautiful and sensitive plants and creatures can coexist with chemical, gas and oil plants, a nuclear power station and a vast steelworks, is testimony to nature's extraordinary resilience and adaptability, and also to the skill of Natural England in managing these highly pressurized sites.

From the North Gare car park you pass a collection of hummocks – not Bronze Age burial mounds, but old ash heaps from the fires that once evaporated sea salt – and reach a run of fine flowery dunes. In late spring look for marsh orchids in the damp slack hollows, and floods of yellow bird's-foot trefoil and brushy lady's bedstraw across the lime-rich slopes, as you walk south towards North Gare Sands. Here in winter large convocations of knot, the 'Canutes' or tideline waders of the coast, stand head to wind in winter. On the far shore of the Seaton-on-Tees Channel gleam the mudflats of Seal Sands, winter quarters for the handsome large shelducks with their knobbly scarlet beaks and rich chestnut breast-bands who sweep their bills from side to side across the muds as they hoover up tiny saltwater snails and other shelly creatures. Seal Sands also play host to their namesakes, both brown seals and the grey-coloured common variety, which resumed breeding and raising pups in summer here at the end of the last century after many decades of absence owing to pollution and disturbance.

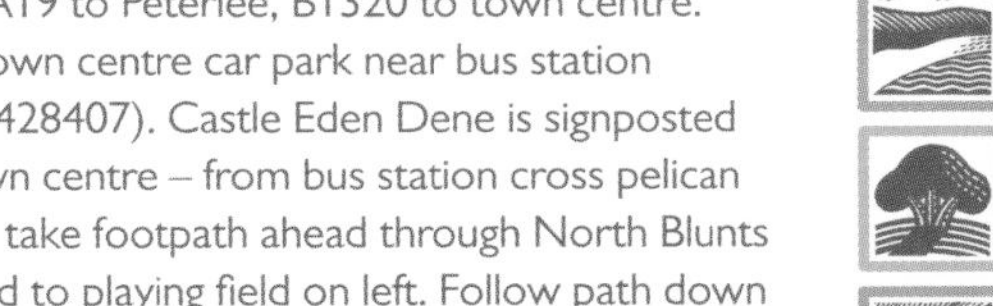

314. CASTLE EDEN DENE, CO. DURHAM

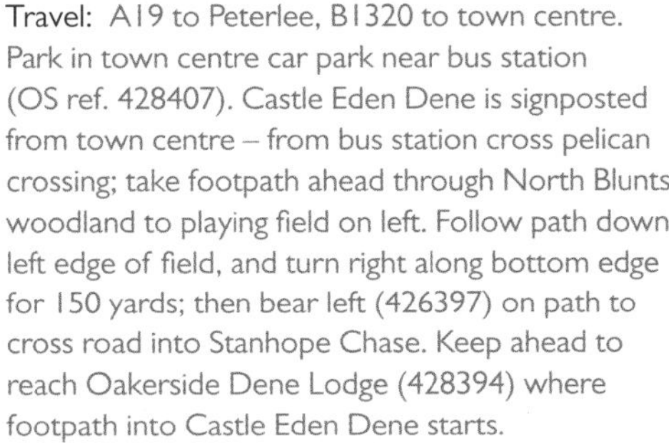

Maps: OS Explorer 308; Landranger 88, 93

Travel: A19 to Peterlee, B1320 to town centre. Park in town centre car park near bus station (OS ref. 428407). Castle Eden Dene is signposted from town centre – from bus station cross pelican crossing; take footpath ahead through North Blunts woodland to playing field on left. Follow path down left edge of field, and turn right along bottom edge for 150 yards; then bear left (426397) on path to cross road into Stanhope Chase. Keep ahead to reach Oakerside Dene Lodge (428394) where footpath into Castle Eden Dene starts.

Castle Eden Dene is a 3-mile-long ravine that has hardly been touched by the hand of man since the time of the last Ice Age. Trees and plants grow as exuberantly here as they did when wolves and bears roamed the land, and the steep, rocky dene sides are as impossible as ever to cultivate or to build on. So Castle Eden Dene survives as a National Nature Reserve, a precious fragment of original wildwood, the largest and by far the richest piece of ancient woodland in the North-East.

Stepping down the steep paths, sticky with clay after rain, you drop into a wonderful green tangle of oak, sycamore, ash and wych elm. Groves of solemn yew trees brood undisturbed. In May, the sharply sloping floor is a mass of bluebells, usurpers of the early spring colonizers, primrose clumps and sheets of wood anemones. Later on the bird's-nest orchid begins to raise its drab head, rather nondescript and colourless at first glance, revealing a beautiful heather-honey hue and scent on closer inspection.

The undergrowth of the dene is a maze of spindle and guelder rose, and provides shelter and food for a stunning array of bird species. Many kinds of warblers, tits and sweet-voiced blackcaps are here, as well as the crossbill with its distinctive bill, the two points crossed over to provide a suitable pick for winkling out conifer seeds from the cones. If you walk quietly and are prepared to stop still, you can enjoy the rare sight of red squirrels bouncing in the treetops and through the undergrowth here, one of their few remaining strongholds south of the Scottish Border.

The dene is not entirely filled with woodland. There are also patches of open grassland where the underlying magnesian limestone is close to the surface. In its crevices grows yellow rockrose, the foodplant of the Durham argus butterfly, a small brownish beauty with silver-edged wings that is unique to this wonderful and much overlooked coast.

315. EASINGTON COLLIERY, CO. DURHAM

Maps: OS Explorer 308; Landranger 88

Travel: A19 from Peterlee towards Seaham; in 1½ miles, right on B1283 to Easington Colliery. Park at foot of road near sharp right bend (OS ref. 437439); ahead on footpath to Easington Beach (444440).

Information: www.durhamheritagecoast.org

Up until the late twentieth century, a stranger arriving on the East Durham coast would be forgiven for thinking he had landed on another planet. Working collieries lined the cliffs, spewing their waste into the sea and on to the beaches. Aerial cableways, their chains of buckets dolorously clanking, spilled black, grey and orange rock, sludge and small coal, transforming the beaches and cliffs into a hellish landscape. Dark waves, thick with coal spoil and untreated sewage, fell sluggishly on black sands. Back then, there was a strange thrill to be had in wandering through such a scene of ruin and desolation.

Now, this formerly blighted coastline is a destination where walkers and wildlife enthusiasts flock, an area so rich in plant and bird life that it is an SSSI (Site of Special Scientific Interest) and an SAC (Special Area of Conservation), known as the Durham Heritage Coast. Such has been the energy put into 'Turning the Tide', the plan to restore the region after the last collieries closed in 1993, that these unlikely things have come to pass.

Between the neat little village of Easington and the coastal cliffs run the low herringbone ranks of grey slate roofs that herald the former mining village of Easington Colliery. If any ex-mining village epitomizes the physical character and the spirit of the East Durham coastal coalfield, it is this one: ranks of red-brick terraced houses, family-run shops, a community close-knit to the point of insularity. The pit closed in 1993. Unemployment has soared. Times are extremely hard. But the people are survivors. They remain tough, resilient and determined not to go under.

A gaunt memorial, the hollow metal shell of the pit cage, crowns the green swell of ground where the mine buildings stood. On the shore below, the beach is of pale creamy pebbles on tan sand, backed by dark red-and-yellow cliffs. During the working life of the colliery sea-coalers used to haunt the beach, collecting small waste coals in plastic sacks to sell for a few pennies around the houses or to burn on their own domestic hearths. Now they are all gone. The biggest challenge facing the 'Turning the Tide' project was winning local residents over. They regarded the beaches as their own. Once they saw the improvements begin, there was a great surge of interest and goodwill. It was the locals who volunteered their help to put in footpaths, clear the scrub and clean up much of the mess.

Observers who knew these East Durham beaches in coal-mining days find it impossible to reconcile the beauty of the scene today with what was there before. It is a small form of modern miracle: 12 miles of beautiful coast brought back from the dead.

Hawthorn Hive and minestone 'cliff'

316. HAWTHORN DENE AND HIVE, CO. DURHAM

Maps: OS Explorer 308; Landranger 88

Travel: A19 from Peterlee towards Seaham; in 1½ miles, right on B1283 through Easington; in ½ mile, left on B1432 to Hawthorn. Right at village crossroads to park by Stapylton Arms pub (OS ref. 420455). Footpath fingerpost points over wall and down field to enter trees of Hawthorn Dene.

Nearest railway station: Seaham (3½ miles)

The coast of East Durham is composed of coal-bearing magnesian limestone, a rock that has formed a range of fine tall cliffs but is still basically fragile. At the end of the last Ice Age meltwater from the dissolving glaciers rushed coastwards, cutting deep canyons through the soft rock, twisting and turning past harder obstacles on its way to the North Sea. These deep gullies, spaced a mile or so apart along the coast, became the natural outlet for springs; these formed streams, cutting ever deeper pathways to the sea. In this way were created the sheltered, steep-sided denes, or snaking coastal valleys, of East Durham.

Hawthorn Dene, the most northerly, cuts down to the sea from the village of Hawthorn a couple of miles south of Seaham. The dene is a nature reserve looked after by the National Trust, offering shelter, breeding places, food and concealment to a large number of tree, plant, bird, animal and insect species. Walking its narrow pathways in the half-light and silence under the sycamore and ash trees, you are in one of the wildest places this previously heavily industrialized area can show. Groves of massive old yews throw a sombre shade across the path. Drifts of wild garlic and wood anemones spatter the undergrowth white in spring. Bluebells and early purple orchids appear, as do the blue spikes of bugle and the curious flowers of herb paris with their black centres and long, thread-like stamens. Hawthorn Dene is a damp place, the trees catching and trapping mist and moisture to produce conditions in which ferns, liverworts, mosses and horsetails thrive.

Down at the bottom you descend steps to the beach of Hawthorn Hive. At first sight it seems as though a model-maker has been building a line of miniature cliffs along the beach, but these 4-foot-high 'cliffs' are streaked with chemical yellow and red, and contain strange fossils – lengths of conveyor belt, pieces of tin, glazed pipes. This is the so-called 'minestone' of the Durham coast, a scab of colliery waste as a legacy of the decades when such refuse was tipped into the sea and left to be washed back on to the shore. The coal mines that once stood shoulder to shoulder along the magnesian cliffs have all closed, and high tides and winter storms are sweeping away the minestone that still clings to the beaches. The harsh beauty of Hawthorn Hive is once more apparent, breaking through the filth that has masked it for 100 years.

317. BISHOP MIDDLEHAM QUARRY, CO. DURHAM

Maps: OS Explorer 305; Landranger 93

Travel: From A1(M) Junction 60, A689 towards Billingham; left on A177 ('Durham'). In 2 miles, left to Bishop Middleham. On far outskirts, right at crossroads (OS ref. 330320) up narrow lane; in 1/3 mile park in lay-by on left and go over stile on right (footpath fingerpost) past Durham Wildlife Trust sign, and follow woodchip path.

Magnesian limestone is uncommon in Britain, and County Durham has the lion's share of it. This limestone is partly

Bishop Middleham Quarry

composed of dolomite, a crystalline mineral very low in acidity, which encourages the flourishing of limestone flora – especially orchids. The old quarry on the outskirts of Bishop Middleham has not been worked since before the Second World War, and is now one of the best sites for beautiful limestone flowers in the North-East.

A path surfaced with woodchip takes you along the edge of a sheer precipice falling to the scooped-out hole of a working quarry. Glimpses into the basin show vast yellow sandheaps the size of hills, round which lorries and bulldozers grunt on slippery gravel tracks. The path turns a corner and leads down steps into the green tree-lined depths of the old quarry. The deep delvings are smothered in well-grown ash, sycamore, whitethorn, elder and blackthorn, more like a wood than an industrial site. Cranesbill, herb robert and dog's mercury grow here.

The path winds out of the trees into an open hollow hemmed in by pitted, crumbling cliffs – the working faces of the quarry. Yellow buttons of rockrose on the ledges provide food for the northern brown argus, a rare and handsome butterfly with a scalloped orange hem to its dark wings. In the magnesian limestone grassland of the quarry floor grow cowslips in spring, beautiful orchids later in the year – fragrant and pyramidal orchids, northern marsh orchids with their lustrous purple flowers, and the slender, aptly named dark red helleborine.

318. WEST DURHAM MOORS

Maps: OS Explorer 31, 307; Landranger 92, 87

Travel: A1 to Scotch Corner; A66 to Barnard Castle; B6277 to Middleton-in-Teesdale and on up Teesdale. B6278 runs from just east of Middleton to Stanhope in Weardale. A689 runs up Weardale. Moor road from Westgate goes north to Blanchland.

The moors are quiet these days, but from the mid eighteenth century they were loud and dirty with the business of the London Lead Company. The LCC was more than just a business enterprise. Quakers ran it, aiming to put their workers in the way of salvation as well as employment. The miners of Middleton-in-Teesdale were a rough lot, but their employers insisted on strict temperance. They set up a Sunday school; they gave the men the weekend off, and opened allotments where the miners could grow vegetables for a healthier diet. And they developed Middleton as a model industrial village in stone and slate.

Outside Middleton-in-Teesdale the narrowest of roads strikes north into the remote valley of the Hudeshope Beck. The names of the hills and their farms – Coldberry, Pikestone, Stonygill – sum up the bleakness of this cleft in the hills, whose slopes are scattered with farmsteads. The grass shines softly with a nap like velvet, and under it bulge old lead-mining spoil heaps, veined and lumpy like muscles under smooth skin. At the head of the dale you pull up under a miniature alp of mine spoil and walk out on the moor, to hear only sheep bleating, the trickle of water and a thin piping of wind in sedges.

Middleton Common and Langdon Common: the names may give a southerner the notion of a scrubby piece of village dog-walking land, but these commons are high, lonely swathes of bare brown moorland, streaming with wind-battered sedge clumps,

crossed by narrow, gated roads that ribbon between stone walls. You come down into Weardale chilly but exhilarated by the enormous moorland views and the racing skies.

Stanhope is the capital of Weardale, a compact little town strung out along the valley road. In the churchyard wall a niche holds the fossilized stump of a fern-like tree 250 million years old, standing like a column of rusty brown ironstone, tubular roots spread to grip some ancient swamp bed. Inside the church stands a pagan Roman altar, a stubby rectangle dedicated in blurred letters to Silvanus, god of the woods – strange relic of days when the moors were covered in virgin forest and men worshipped wilder gods.

When the lead- and iron-mining industries were in full swing during the eighteenth and nineteenth centuries, there were hard men around Stanhope. The harshness of the miners' lives is hard to credit these days. They drank too much on payday, smoked too much, lived mostly on bread and tea, earned £2 a month to feed a family of a dozen children, and choked to death before the age of fifty – mostly from diseases of the lungs such as pneumonia, silicosis and phthisis.

Exploring the moors north of Stanhope you find their landscape, knotted and lumped with old scar tissue: spoil heaps grassed over, gaunt mine buildings under rusty tin roofs lowering on the skyline, tramway beds snaking away over the heather and sedge. One old railway track now serves as a footpath, the Waskerley Way, wandering for several miles past pools and reservoirs, engine sheds and embankments. Cut by the wind and dazzled by the crisp light of the moors, it is easy to become mazed by the stark scenery and endlessly unrolling trackbed, and find yourself walking till nightfall.

319. SIKEHEAD DAM, CO. DURHAM

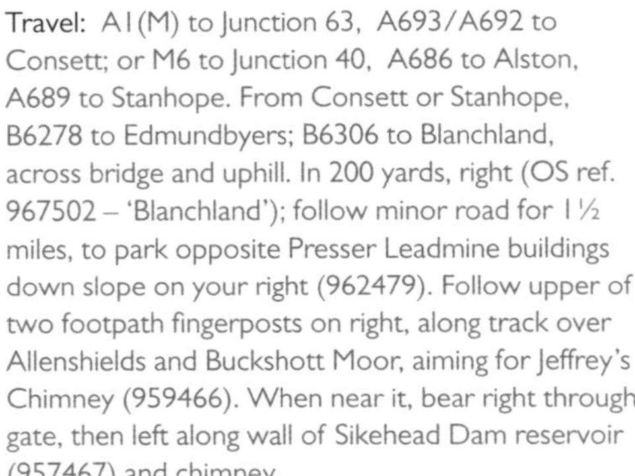

Maps: OS Explorer 307; Landranger 87

Travel: A1(M) to Junction 63, A693/A692 to Consett; or M6 to Junction 40, A686 to Alston, A689 to Stanhope. From Consett or Stanhope, B6278 to Edmundbyers; B6306 to Blanchland, across bridge and uphill. In 200 yards, right (OS ref. 967502 – 'Blanchland'); follow minor road for 1½ miles, to park opposite Presser Leadmine buildings down slope on your right (962479). Follow upper of two footpath fingerposts on right, along track over Allenshields and Buckshott Moor, aiming for Jeffrey's Chimney (959466). When near it, bear right through gate, then left along wall of Sikehead Dam reservoir (957467) and chimney.

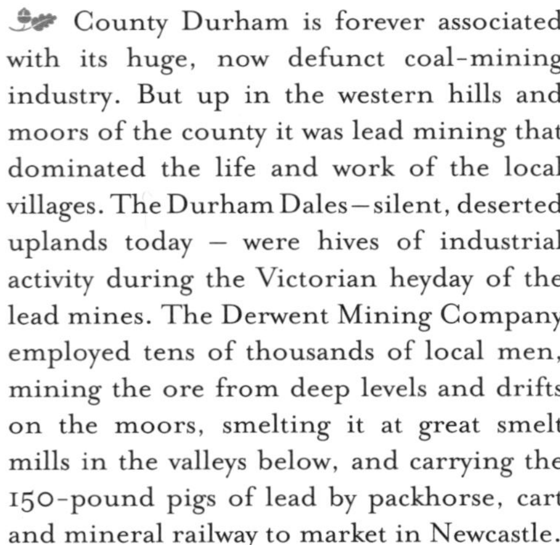

County Durham is forever associated with its huge, now defunct coal-mining industry. But up in the western hills and moors of the county it was lead mining that dominated the life and work of the local villages. The Durham Dales – silent, deserted uplands today – were hives of industrial activity during the Victorian heyday of the lead mines. The Derwent Mining Company employed tens of thousands of local men, mining the ore from deep levels and drifts on the moors, smelting it at great smelt mills in the valleys below, and carrying the 150-pound pigs of lead by packhorse, cart and mineral railway to market in Newcastle.

Though the Durham moors are crossed by a superb network of footpaths, they are still undiscovered and blissfully lonely walking country, a rare treat. Allenshields and Buckshott Moor, high on the roof of the country between Blanchland and Rookhope,

is all slopes and shoulders of rolling brown moorland, a vast sea of heather dipping to green walled inbye land. If you walk south-west across the moor, you will pass the Presser Lead Mine's pumping station with its squat chimney and pyramid roof. On the skyline ahead loom two tall stone-built smokestacks – the Sikehead Mine's pumping engine chimney, and the broken-topped Jeffrey's Chimney, which disgorged deadly lead vapour brought along a mile-long flue tunnel from Jeffrey's smelting mill far below. Each year some wretch would have to climb the interior of the chimney and scrape off the 'fume', the condensed lead vapour, for resmelting. 'We get from this a great quantity of lead,' noted the Derwent Lead Company's agent, 'sufficient to remunerate for the expenses of making the tunnel.'

On the south side of the moor the sloping track of an old industrial railway descends Bolt's Law Incline towards the slate roofs of Rookhope under the pale green bulk of Northgate Fell. Back in its lead-mining heyday Rookhope played host to hundreds of miners who would sleep during the week in unsanitary, overcrowded 'lodging shops' and walk across the moors to their home villages at weekends. The Boltsburn Mine was the most productive in England, and the Rookhope smelting mill clattered and fumed by night and day. Nowadays the little village on its curve of road is a quiet spot in a remote valley, hidden below the moors, where dams and chimneys and the deep shafts that litter the heather are all that remains to tell the brutal old tale.

320. HADRIAN'S WALL (CAWFIELD CRAGS TO BIRDOSWALD), NORTHUMBERLAND

Maps: OS Explorer OL43; Landranger 87

Travel: A69 Hexham towards Brampton; right on B6322 towards Haltwhistle; in 300 yards, right for 1¾ miles to cross B6318. In ⅓ mile park in car park on right (OS ref. 713666). Turn right to climb Hadrian's Wall National Trail to Cawfield Crags; then return and follow the wall for 7 miles to reach Birdoswald Fort.

NB: Hadrian's Wall Bus operates along the wall between Wallsend and Bowness during the summer.

Information: www.nationaltrail.co.uk/hadrianswall

Nearest railway station: Haltwhistle (2½ miles)

Hadrian's Wall is far and away the most splendid and evocative memorial that the Romans left us of their 400-year rule in Britain. Much of it was built to take advantage of the rollercoaster cliffs provided by that great dolerite fault, the Whin Sill. Climbing up above the flooded quarry pit at Cawfield Crags you get a wonderful overview of the landscape and of Hadrian's Wall itself, looking east over the ruin of Milecastle 42 to see the wall riding along its high petrified wave of dark stone crags.

After their successful invasion of Britain in AD 43 under Emperor Claudius, the Romans took several decades to subdue the natives. The northernmost boundary of the area over which they had control moved slowly up the island. Emperor Hadrian, coming to power in AD 117, ordered a stone wall 10 feet wide and some 15 feet high to be built from the Tyne westward for 45 miles, with a turf wall 20 feet wide at the base to run the rest of the way to the Solway. The wall as actually built was a slimmer construction, with a milecastle – a fortified gateway – at each mile, and two observation turrets between each of them. A great vallum, or ditch, 10 feet deep, ran on both sides of the wall, which was garrisoned by twelve major forts. Hadrian's Wall was not simply a means of keeping the Scots at bay; it was a grandstand for viewing what the northern savages were getting up to, and a launching-pad for aggressive military action against them. And it was a political statement, too: here is the northernmost boundary of our mighty empire. From this point outwards, the writ of civilization and the rule of law cease to run.

These days you can walk the Hadrian's Wall Path National Trail all along the wall, from Wallsend in Newcastle-upon-Tyne westward for 84 miles to Bowness on the Solway Firth. The superb 7-mile stretch between Cawfield Crags and Birdoswald is one of the finest, with the vallum's vast open vee of a ditch your companion for much of the way. Above Walltown Farm the wall stands up to 10 feet high, a broad band of stone laid across the landscape. Many of its stones have been robbed in the 1,900 years since it was built, and sharp-eyed walkers can spot them reused in field walls and farm buildings – also in the blank-eyed ruins of fourteenth-century Thirlwall Castle, built almost entirely of Hadrian's Wall stones.

There are more wall stones – including one inscribed in Latin: 'Fifth Cohort of the Century of Gellius Philippus' – in the buildings of Willowford Farm, where a magnificent section of Hadrian's Wall sweeps down a bank to the edge of the River Irthing. Beyond lies Birdoswald Fort with its fine gateways, its drill hall and its pair of stone-paved granaries big enough to feed a garrison of up to 1,000 of the mercenaries, conscripts and other flotsam and jetsam of the Roman empire, who shivered here on sentry duty, looking out over the wild lands beyond the bounds of the civilized world.

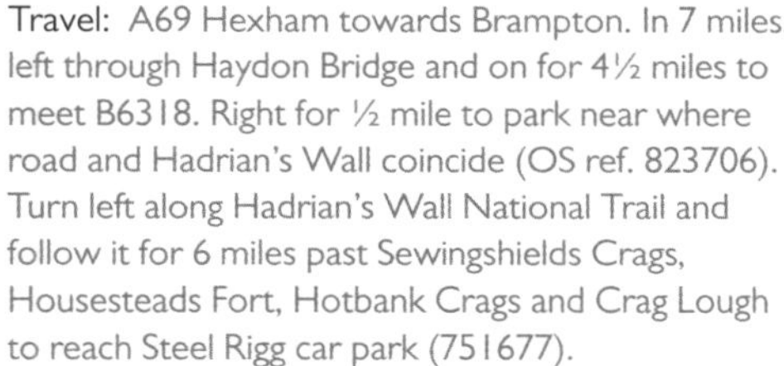

321. HADRIAN'S WALL (SEWINGSHIELDS TO STEEL RIGG), NORTHUMBERLAND

Maps: OS Explorer OL43; Landranger 87

Travel: A69 Hexham towards Brampton. In 7 miles, left through Haydon Bridge and on for 4½ miles to meet B6318. Right for ½ mile to park near where road and Hadrian's Wall coincide (OS ref. 823706). Turn left along Hadrian's Wall National Trail and follow it for 6 miles past Sewingshields Crags, Housesteads Fort, Hotbank Crags and Crag Lough to reach Steel Rigg car park (751677).

NB: Hadrian's Wall Bus operates along the wall between Wallsend and Bowness during the summer.

Information: www.nationaltrail.co.uk/hadrianswall

Nearest railway station: Haydon Bridge (5 miles)

Hadrian's Wall is the finest Roman monument we have in these islands – so important historically and culturally that it has been declared a UNESCO World Heritage Site. The ancient wall, built from AD 117 onwards as a northern boundary between the Roman empire and the uncivilized wilds beyond, was and remains an enormous feat of engineering.

When the Romans withdrew from Britain at the beginning of the fifth century AD to shore up their crumbling empire further south, the abandoned frontier forts decayed, along with the now ungarrisoned and useless wall. Over the centuries the structure was continually plundered for its conveniently cut and shaped stones. The wall could have disappeared completely. Large parts of it actually did so when a military road – now the B6318 – was built, after the Jacobite rebellion of 1745, on top of the eastern section of what remained. But even back then, antiquarians were interested in the remarkable old monument.

Hadrian's Wall National Trail runs beside the wall for its full 84-mile length. But for the first 30 miles the wall itself slips all but unseen through the landscape. Driving the rollercoaster of the old military road westward from Newcastle-upon-Tyne you can spot disconnected sections of wall and ditch running parallel in the fields alongside. The land begins to rise in extravagant shapes in the far distance – the breaking waves of the Whin Sill, a tsunami of dark basalt peaks petrified in the act of crashing northwards, which rush suddenly on the consciousness so thrillingly they can take the breath away.

At Shield on the Wall the road swings away from the line of Hadrian's Wall, and at the same point you forsake the car and join the trail for the first properly exciting stretch of walking. Beyond Sewingshields Wood the wall itself appears, a run of dark stone courses 5 feet high, clinging to the edge of the crags, the foundations of its meticulously spaced turrets and milecastles looming up with metronomic regularity. Follow its undulations all the way to Housesteads, where the most complete and best-displayed fort anywhere on the wall lies on the slope of the Whin Sill – a wonderful place to explore with its courtyarded commandant's house, fortified gateways, and multi-seater soldiers' lavatory with patent flush drains and all other Roman mod cons.

From here you walk on along the spine of the Whin Sill with dramatic views to the north over the big dark lakes of Broomlee Lough and Greenlee Lough. You pass high above rushy little Crag Lough and come to Steel Rigg, a natural break where the wall curls round the flank of a hill and you can stand and look back along the line of its lichened stones, still squarely and sharply cut after almost 2,000 years of wind and weather.

322. WARK FOREST, NORTHUMBERLAND

Maps: OS Explorer OL43; Landranger 87

Travel: A69 Hexham towards Brampton; 1¾ miles past Bardon Mill turning, bear right on minor road (OS ref. 754643); in ¾ mile follow road round sharp left bend and continue north for 1¼ miles to cross B6318 at Twice Brewed Inn. In another ½ mile, minor road passes through Hadrian's Wall at Steel Rigg (751676). Follow it for 1¾-miles to T-junction (726674); right here for 3 miles to park at edge of Wark Forest (724711). Turn right along dirt road here for a 1¾-mile walk past the communications mast at Hopealone (735718) to Hindleysteel farmhouse (747726).

Wark Forest is the southern extension of Kielder Forest (see p. 354), a mass planting of the Northumbrian uplands with quick-growing conifers that now covers well over 100,000 acres of formerly open moors. The forest was begun in 1926 as a reaction to a First World War crisis when the nation ran desperately short of timber and ancient and valuable woodlands had to be felled for trench boards and pit props. The main body has now become a popular leisure resort, and some of its overregulated coniferous drabness has been alleviated by amenity planting of broadleaved trees. Wark Forest, however, has retained its black-browed grimness in full measure.

Seen from the natural grandstand of Hadrian's Wall (see above), Wark Forest crouches low and dark, filling the northern horizon like a threatening wave. Approach-

Wark Forest

ing across the undulating plain, the wave of conifers grows gradually higher and darker until you walk into their shadow, bracing yourself for a cold shock. Pass the eerie skeleton of the early-warning communications tower at Hopealone (a splendidly mournful name), and follow the silent forest road until you come to another wraith of a place – the farmhouse of Hindleysteel, which stood among open fields with moors to the horizon all round until the trees of Wark drew near and sealed it into one tiny pocket in their immense, smothering blanket.

The verges of the forest track lie thickly cloaked in moss. Walk in among the conifers until the light fades behind you and the moss gives way to a dense carpet of pine needles, and you will find the trees drilled into ranks, their dark tops hissing, their light-starved lower limbs as pale and brittle as biscuit – a macabre sensation straight out of the Brothers Grimm.

323. KIELDERHEAD, NORTHUMBERLAND

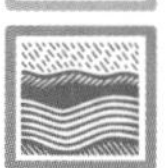

Maps: OS Explorer OL42; Landranger 80

Travel: From M6 Junction 44, A7 north to Canonbie; right on B6357 through Newcastleton to Saughtree; right on minor road to Kielder. Turn right at village (brown sign: 'Byrness via Forest Drive to A68'), bear left past Kielder Castle and follow 'Forest Drive' (modest toll charge). In 2 miles road bends right (651959); in another 1/3 mile park neatly near East Kielder Farm (657959). Take track on left, uphill to reach two gates in angle of stone wall. Continue north from here above East Kielder Burn for 2 miles to descend opposite Scaup Farm (664978). If you wish to continue, ford right-hand water, White Kielder Burn, just above ruin of Kielder Head Farm (666980) – use stones in burn for stepping stones. NB: If water is powerful or noisy after heavy rain, do not attempt to ford, but return to East Kielder Farm! Continue up path on west bank of Kielder Burn for another 3 miles to meeting of burns under Kielderhead moor (687009), and further if you wish.

The great lake of Kielder Water is beautiful, and the massed conifers of Kielder Forest impressive in their domination of a huge acreage of the Northumbrian hills. But when you have spent a few hours in the gloomy depths of this mighty Forestry Commission scheme, you might find yourself longing for the sight of something other than water and trees. At East Kielder Farm a walker's prayers are answered. The farm stands on a spur of moorland at the edge of the forest, and ten minutes after setting out along the northward path you have turned your back on the corduroy battalions and are striding over tussocks of rush and coarse grass towards long, bare shoulders of open hillside. These are hills where the wind blows cold and the sense of isolation increases with every mile. Walking here, you leave the modern world behind on the outskirts of the forest and enter the unreconstructed emptiness in which the reivers, or cattle thieves, and cross-border raiders of the past could operate unhindered.

Where the White Kielder and Scaup streams rush together to form the East Kielder Burn lies Scaup Farm, one of the loneliest in England, tucked down in the shelter of the hills, Kielder Forest's dark mass blocking its southward view and the narrowing valley of the White Kielder Burn filling half the sky to the north. Ford the burn upstream of the ruined farmhouse of Kielder Head, where a line of stunted alders, shaggy with lichen, lean over their own reflection in the water. A rough track leads you on north, no more than a sheep track these days, but once a great droving road over the hills to Byrness in Redesdale. Flat stones bridge the side burns, their backs hollowed by the tread of feet and hooves through the centuries.

A crumbling stone sheepfold has the remains of a hut built into one wall, where the shepherd would sleep by night and warm himself by day. Beyond this outpost the path runs through the heather high above the burn, past sheepfolds long disused. Soon the hillsides cease their rolling and curve together to form a dead-end valley of broad-breasted slopes 5 miles from the nearest tarmac road, hidden deep in the folds of Kielderhead Moor. Here the old drove road turns aside and climbs below the rock faces of High Crags to continue its lonely course over Girdle Fell and down into distant Redesdale.

324. WHITELEE MOOR, NORTHUMBERLAND

Maps: OS Explorer OL16; Landranger 80

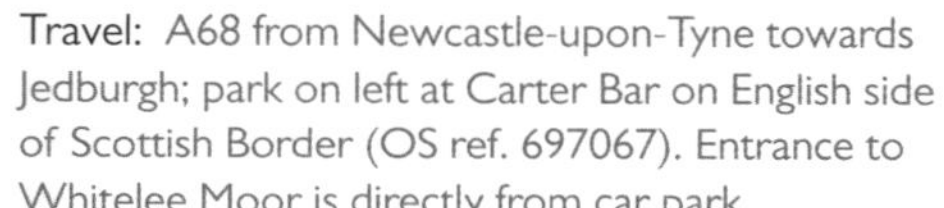

Travel: A68 from Newcastle-upon-Tyne towards Jedburgh; park on left at Carter Bar on English side of Scottish Border (OS ref. 697067). Entrance to Whitelee Moor is directly from car park.

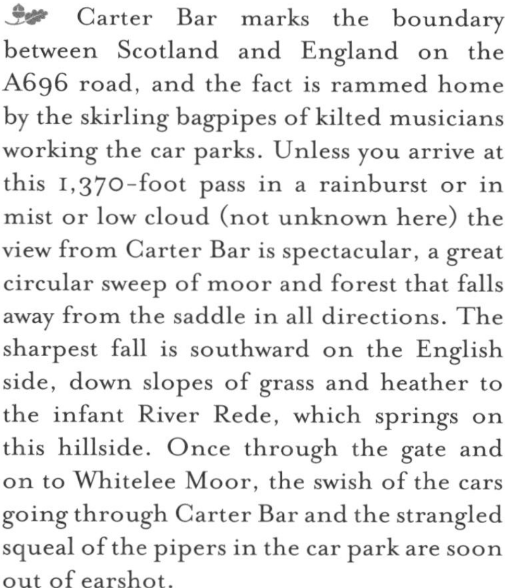

Carter Bar marks the boundary between Scotland and England on the A696 road, and the fact is rammed home by the skirling bagpipes of kilted musicians working the car parks. Unless you arrive at this 1,370-foot pass in a rainburst or in mist or low cloud (not unknown here) the view from Carter Bar is spectacular, a great circular sweep of moor and forest that falls away from the saddle in all directions. The sharpest fall is southward on the English side, down slopes of grass and heather to the infant River Rede, which springs on this hillside. Once through the gate and on to Whitelee Moor, the swish of the cars going through Carter Bar and the strangled squeal of the pipers in the car park are soon out of earshot.

There are over 3,000 acres of wild land in Whitelee Moor National Nature Reserve, some of it thick heather moorland where both red and black grouse live, some a patchwork of blanket bog rich in sphagnum moss, trickling with water and bright with dove's-feather tufts of cotton-grass. Look carefully and you can spot what look like small, unripe blackberries – these are the fruit of the cloudberry, but you'd need an awful lot of sugar and a drop of the hard stuff to make them palatable.

Whitelee Moor

Merlin and peregrine hunt these moors. You'll be fortunate to catch a daytime sight of the otters that are thriving down on the River Rede – more a chattering burn, really, as it tumbles down to Catcleugh Reservoir – but there are dippers to spot as they bob their white bibs on stones midstream. And if you are lucky, and quick with the binoculars, you may catch a summertime glimpse of another white-chested bird of the wild places, the ring ouzel, a blackbird cousin whose numbers are declining as the kind of lonely, undisturbed moorland – such as Whitelee – that it needs for nesting becomes harder and harder to find.

325. BATTLE OF OTTERBURN SITE, NORTHUMBERLAND

Maps: OS Explorer OL42; Landranger 80

Travel: A696 Newcastle-upon-Tyne towards Jedburgh; 1 mile beyond Otterburn village, brown sign points right to car park (OS ref. 877936). Walk forward through trees to Percy's Cross monument and information boards overlooking battlefield. To walk battlefield, return along A696 and turn left into Otterburn. In 350 yards bridleway on left leaves road and crosses battle site.

The mild green hills of Redesdale could not look more peaceful, rising north of Otterburn on the lazily winding River Rede. Only the blunt old obelisk, Percy's Cross, hidden in a conifer plantation, stands as a reminder of the momentous events that happened here. The monument should really be called 'Douglas's Cross', for it marks the spot where James, Earl of Douglas, was killed at the height of an affray in which his Scottish raiders were thrashing their English opponents – the Battle of Otterburn, one of the bloodiest set-tos in a very bloody part of the Border country.

The moon was clear, the day drew near,
The spears in flinders flew,
But mony a gallant Englishman
Ere day the Scotsmen slew.

The Gordons good, in English blood
They steep'd their hose and shoon;
The Lindsays flew like fire about,
Till all the fray was done.

The Percy and Montgomery met,
That either of other were fain;
They swakked swords, and they twa swat,
And aye the blood ran down between.

The Battle of Otterburn was not soon forgotten on either side of the Border. The English crown had been trying to subdue the termagant Scots for the best part of 300 years when, on a moonlit night in August 1388, an English force under Sir Henry Percy, son of the Earl of Northumberland (universally remembered, thanks to Shakespeare's portrait of him in *Henry IV Part 1*, as Harry Hotspur), caught up with a Scottish raiding party led by James, Earl of Douglas. The Douglas and Percy families, rival powers of the lawless Borders, had been at loggerheads for centuries, and the seemingly interminable war between England and Scotland gave them the perfect opportunity to get even with each other.

That August the Earl of Douglas had brought about 7,000 men across the Border and raided as far south as Newcastle, where, according to some accounts, he managed to capture Hotspur's pennant. Douglas then withdrew, well aware that the impetuous Hotspur would not be able to resist giving chase to retrieve his 'honour'. So it proved. Outside Otterburn, after a remarkably quick forced march, Hotspur's 9,000 Englishmen caught up with the Scots. Night was approaching, Hotspur's men were exhausted, and there had been no time to see how well or badly the enemy was sited – but hot-headed Percy decided to attack anyway. The Scots were positioned on the high ground, and a force under Sir Thomas Umphraville, Lord of Redesdale, soon overran their camp and plundered it. But a large number of Englishmen then simply deserted with what they had managed to grab. Douglas attacked the weakened English, who could not use their most effective weapon, the longbow, because it was night-time. Hotspur's men were routed, put to flight and slaughtered.

Nearly 2,000 English bodies were buried in and around Otterburn churchyard. Fewer than 100 Scots died, but among them was their leader, the Earl of Douglas – killed, according to legend, by none other than Harry Hotspur.

When Percy with the Douglas met,
I wat he was fu fain;
They swakked their swords, till sair they swat,
And the blood ran down like rain.

But Percy with his good broad sword,
That could so sharply wound,
Has wounded Douglas on the brow,
Till he fel to the ground.

Soon afterwards Hotspur was taken prisoner, and the engagement was over. Harry Percy, architect of his own downfall, was taken away with his brother, Ralph, to await ransom. Douglas was buried with honour in Montrose Abbey. As for the pennant that caused all the trouble – it was never seen again.

326. UPPER COQUETDALE, NORTHUMBERLAND

Maps: OS Explorer OL16; Landranger 80

Travel: A1 to Morpeth, A697 to Weldon, left on B6344 to Rothbury, B6341 ('Elsdon') through Thropton. In 2 miles, right on minor road through Sharperton and Harbottle to Alwinton. Continue past Rose & Thistle pub up 'No Through Road' for 6 miles to Windyhaugh; cross River Coquet and in 200 yards park on left opposite Windyhaugh Farm (OS ref. 864110). Follow track north past Lounges Knowe and Fairhaugh (875122) to Usway Burn and farm road to Uswayford (887145). Bear left to ford Usway Burn; climb to join Clennell Street (875157) and follow it up to cross the Border fence (871160). Left along Pennine Way National Trail for 1½ miles to Russell's Cairn at Windy Gyle (855152); cross fence and bear downhill to Trows farmhouse (855125) and then Windyhaugh.

NB: This is a 10-mile walk, not difficult but steep and tiring in places.

The Cheviot Hills billow and heave like a restless sea across the borderlands of England and Scotland. This is wet country, where a walker's boots are soon besmirched by sucking peat. Ruined farms and circular stone bields, or sheepfolds, offer the only shelter from the weather, which comes rolling up like gunsmoke from behind the high skyline. You can easily find yourself marooned on a hilltop between one cloud and the next, unsure if this is Great Standrop or Hedgehoe Hill, for the folds and upsurges of the Cheviots all look remarkably similar to a stranger's eye. In sunshine they show a quite stunning beauty as cloud shadows and brilliant sun-splashes chase across the slopes; but when the weather and the valleys darken and the first raindrops whirl by, the Cheviots take on a grim and even threatening aspect that echoes their history of Border battles, clan 'frays', bloody ambushes and cattle raids that ended with men hanging from trees and the burns running 'three days bluid'.

Many roads climb through the rolling Cheviots, none of them tarred – Salter's Road and Gamel's Path, the Roman-built Dere Street, the track known simply as The Street, and the wide green Clennell Street, old before the Romans ever came to Britain. Monks used these paths to travel between monastery and grange farm; so did sheep rustlers, cattle thieves, hooch-makers, salt-merchants, smugglers and bloody-handed men intent on no good. Today it is the peat-smeared walkers who share them with the occasional shepherd or a party of soldiers come from the training moors to the south.

The Street climbs from Alwinton, following the sinuous bends of the River Coquet past farms and hillsides with evocative names: Quickening Cote, Shillmoor, Bygate Hall. At the well-named Windyhaugh a long upward path brings you to Clennell Street above Uswayford, one of the remotest farms in the Borders, tucked under the protective wall of Bloodybush Edge. Who could fail to thrill to such names as these? In fair weather Clennell Street is a golden road over silvered hills; in foul, it becomes a black morass. Up at the Border you bear along the Pennine Way to Windy Gyle, 2,000 feet up, site of the murder of Sir Francis Russell in 1585. Russell, son of the Earl of Bedford and one of the deputy Wardens of the Middle Marches, had been trying to negotiate a settlement of yet another cross-Border grievance – Windy Gyle was recognized as a sort of demilitarized zone in that savage era before the Act of Union, and regular Truce Days were held where Scots and English could meet and sort out disputes. That arrangement did not save the earl's son from a bullet. The Bronze Age burial mound at Windy Gyle is named Russell's Cairn in his memory. But if each man, woman and child done to death in these grassy green hills was honoured with a cairn, the Cheviots would be a grey and stony range.

327. THE CHEVIOT, NORTHUMBERLAND

Maps: OS Explorer OL16; Landranger 74

Travel: A68 from Jedburgh towards Lauder; in 2 miles right on A698 ('Kelso'). In 4½ miles, right on B6401 through Morebattle towards Town Yetholm. In 3 miles, right on minor road (OS ref. 813266) for 6½ miles through Mowhaugh to Cocklawfoot (854186). Park neatly here. Follow Clennell Street track for 2 miles up to Border Gate (871160); left along Pennine Way National Trail for 3 miles to Cairn Hill (west top – 896194), and bear right on 1¼ mile detour to summit of the Cheviot (909205).

NB: This is a 13-mile there-and-back walk over difficult country, some of it steep, most of it wet and mucky, all of it exposed.

At 2,676 feet, the Cheviot is the highest summit in its namesake range of hills, and ought to command a most majestic view. Many walkers on the Pennine Way, having visited it in the course of the final purgatorial day of their epic of endurance, suspect that it does command such a view but will never know for sure, because the top of the hill was swathed in mist and/or driving rain when they got there. Very many more could not care less and never gave themselves the opportunity of finding out, because they were far too exhausted and fed up to drag themselves the extra 2½ miles there and back to find out. Those who do make it to the top on a fine day will probably take a cursory glance around before limping back, head down, to the treadmill.

The view from The Cheviot, it must be said, is not the finest in the Borders, but the Cheviot Hills themselves, rounded and deeply indented as they are, make a great deal of their comparatively modest height. Once up there, every height seems much like its neighbour, every cleft the same as the one beyond it – and all together give a striking impression of bare, exposed country, wild and unfrequented. You can see an awful lot of this from the top of The Cheviot, but not significantly more than from the Schil, say, or Beefstand Hill. The point about The Cheviot, quite simply, is that for a conscientious Pennine Way walker it is the straw that bids fair to break the camel's back.

The Cheviot

Such a walker has already foot-slogged a minimum of 240 miles on the way north from Edale in far-off Derbyshire, enduring rain, mist, wind, mud, tumbles, hunger, thirst, sunburn, both hyper- and hypothermia, and plenty of blind panic. The final day demands that the blistered feet and the empty energy reservoir carry the walker, complete with heavy pack, 29 miles in one non-stop stretch over just about the most difficult terrain – sloppy, hateful conditions and sheer isolation – of the whole adventure. The Cheviot lies in wait about 20 miles into this most testing of all Pennine Way days. Not on the path, but a futile, peat-sodden, bridge-too-far mile and a quarter off piste. Why walkers at their limits of endurance are required to make this detour is beyond questioning. Some do it; many don't.

Walking up from Cocklawfoot on a nice sunny day, of course – unblistered, unworried and fresh as a daisy – you will find The Cheviot a lovely hill with a splendid view, and wonder what all the fuss is about.

328. COQUET ISLAND, NORTHUMBERLAND

Maps: OS Explorer 332; Landranger 81

Travel: A1068 from Ashington or Alnwick to Amble. Park near harbour (OS ref. 268048).

Boat trips: (no landing) www.visitnorthumberland.com

Coquet Island lies so low off the old Northumbrian coal port of Amble that all you see of it from the harbour is the thin stick of the lighthouse tower at its southern point. But as the boatman steers out of Amble and across the mile of sea that separates mainland and island, you cannot help but be guided by the seabirds. Clouds of them – terns, puffins, gulls – circle round Coquet Island or come hurrying across the water around the boat. Coquet is an island dominated and defined by its seabird population, and as such it is one of the jewels in the crown of its owners, the RSPB.

Visitors are not allowed to land on Coquet Island. Before the RSPB took over in 1972 the island had only a few nesting pairs of birds; visiting boating parties had scared the rest away. Now the flat-topped island is crammed with up to 35,000 birds in the breeding season. Their webbed feet have stamped Coquet's 15 acres of turf into a yellow plateau, riddled with puffin tunnels and thick with nettles fertilized by the never-ending guano. The portly puffins with their rainbow bills and air of fussy self-importance are the boat-trip favourites (there can be up to 25,000 puffins resident on Coquet from May until July), but as a conservation refuge the island is especially important for its population of terns. Four of the UK species of these crook-winged screamers breed here in summer: common terns with scarlet beaks and legs; Arctic tern, rather similar but with shorter legs and a generally greyer look; sandwich terns with shorter tails and black beaks; and the rare pink-chested roseate tern, whose minute British breeding population – about 200 birds – is mostly concentrated here.

On the way back to Amble harbour it is worth keeping one eye over the side of the boat. Very often you will spot a gleaming mauve shape curvetting in the water – a dolphin, beautiful outrider of the North Sea.

329. DUNSTANBURGH CASTLE, NORTHUMBERLAND

Maps: OS Explorer 332; Landranger 75

Travel: A1 north past Alnwick; B6347, B1339 to Embleton. At 100 yards past school, left; in 150 yards, right; in 200 yards, left (OS ref. 234223) to Dunstan Steads Farm and on for 200 yards to shore car park (245224). Turn right along coast path for 1 mile to Dunstanburgh Castle (257218).

Nearest railway station: Chathill (4 miles from Embleton)

One feature dominates all others on the Northumbrian coast around Embleton Bay – the huge shattered ruin of Dunstanburgh Castle on its volcanic knoll a mile north of Craster. The pinnacles of the great gatehouse still tower 80 feet high, yet somehow the castle looks half its actual size until you get up close. Then the sheer scale of this fourteenth-century sea fortress, defended on two sides by cliffs and on the third by a man-made ditch dug through the solid rock, hits you fully. The castle was built in 1313–16 on the orders of Thomas, Earl of

Lancaster, an implacable enemy of his cousin King Edward II, and especially of Piers Gaveston, Edward's lover. When Edward left England in February 1308 to marry Princess Isabella of France and appointed Gaveston as Regent, Gaveston made the mistake of treating Lancaster – as he did the other senior courtiers – with flippant contempt, styling him 'Play-actor'. The Play-actor had the last laugh three years later, when he himself was Regent for an absent Edward II. Gaveston, a prisoner of Lancaster after a string of misdeeds, had his performance ignominiously cut short with an axe-blow. Lancaster met an identical fate ten years later, when Edward finally took his revenge on the powerful baron who had humiliated him and executed his friend and lover.

Leaning out from the gatehouse stair and gazing towards the blue humps of the distant Cheviot Hills, you might feel the cold breath of a ghost more wretched than Piers Gaveston. The legend of Sir Guy the Seeker relates how a homecoming crusader was caught in a fearful storm and took refuge in Dunstanburgh Castle. At midnight a giant woke Sir Guy and took him to a chamber where a beautiful princess lay in an enchanted sleep. 'Choose,' roared the ogre, pointing to a sword and a horn hanging on the wall. 'Choose rightly, and you will wake the maiden and have her for your wife.'

Sir Guy took down the horn, and on it blew a great blast. Instantly he sank into a swoon. When he awoke it was to find himself outside the gates of Dunstanburgh, condemned forever to tramp a circuit of the castle in spectral form and with an aching heart.

330. BEADNELL BAY, NORTHUMBERLAND

Maps: OS Explorer 340; Landranger 75

Travel: A1 Alnwick towards Berwick-upon-Tweed; in 5 miles, right on B6347 to Christon Bank; B1340 to Beadnell. Park near harbour (OS ref. 235288).

Nearest railway station: Chathill (4 miles)

The enormous empty sands and flowery

dunes of the Northumberland coast are justly trumpeted as a still-unspoiled national treasure. Thank God for the unswimmable coldness of the Northumbrian sea. If the water were 10 degrees warmer, this utterly delectable, unfrequented coast would have been developed out of all recognition long since. It is the emptiness of these beaches (in anything like a wind or on a crisp winter day you are likely to have them to yourself), the undeveloped nature of their low cliffs and sandhills, which lends them such a wonderful allure.

This shallow coast holds a string of harbour villages, and Beadnell, its big eighteenth-century yellow stone lime kilns dominating the seafront, is the place to begin a walk. The Northumberland coast encompasses a score of sizeable beaches, each one a curve of pristine sand, but none tops Beadnell Bay for symmetrical beauty. You can walk, run or go fly a kite on the firm sands, or venture along the boardwalks through the range of dunes that backs the beach – dunes spread in summer with clumps of sea pinks nodding to every tiny shift of wind, powder-blue sea holly flowers guarded by large prickly leaves, common spotted orchids and thickets of dramatically purple bloody cranesbill. The southern half of the sandhills is in the care of the National Trust, and during the breeding season the volunteers who staff the warden's hut in the dunes are only too keen to share their knowledge of the Arctic terns that incubate eggs among the marram grass tussocks. Arctic terns, black-capped and scarlet of beak and legs, are beautiful creatures, fantastically brave in defending their nests, and unbelievably far-ranging. It is hard to credit the journey they make each autumn, parents and youngsters both – some 11,000 miles to their winter quarters in Antarctica from this tiny patch of Northumbrian beach, to which they will unerringly return the following spring.

At the southern end of the beach the impossibly photogenic fishing hamlet of Low Newton-by-the-Sea lies under the buttercup headland of Newton Point, where the stone walls shelter families of weasels. If not threatened into flight by sudden movement or noise, these handsome little chocolate-and-white beasts are prone to stop and stand up on their hind legs to inspect you with eyes as black and shiny as elderberries.

331. FARNE ISLANDS, NORTHUMBERLAND

Maps: OS Explorer 340; Landranger 75

Travel: A1 from Alnwick towards Berwick-upon-Tweed; in 5 miles, right on B6347, then B1340 to Seahouses. Park at quay (OS ref. 219322).

Boat trip: www.farne-islands.com; www.lighthouse-visits.co.uk

Nearest railway station: Chathill (5 miles)

From the ramparts of Bamburgh Castle the view is sensational, out across an immense beach of dull gold and a surf of gently roaring waves to the grey basalt shelves of the Farne Islands, rising like monsters out at sea. This is very often the first sight a stranger catches of the Farnes, magnetic and irresistible.

The Farne Islands are the last seaward gasp of the Whin Sill, the ledge of basalt that also forms the river-bed step of High Force (see pp. 339–40) and the crags that uphold Hadrian's Wall (see pp. 350–52). The Farnes are low, craggy, treeless and windswept, the haunt of 100,000 pairs of breeding seabirds. Dark Ages people infested the islands with black-headed demons riding on goats. In the late seventh century St Cuthbert spent eight years in eremitic isolation on Inner Farne, dodging rocks hurled by evil spirits and resisting their most lascivious temptations. Countless lives have been lost on the wickedly concealed tidal rocks of the Wamses, the Harcars and the Wideopens, evocatively named groups of islets that make up the Farne Island archipelago.

The Shiel clan have been running trips from the fishing village of Seahouses to the Farnes for so long they have forgotten more about the seabirds of the islands than most twitchers would learn in a lifetime. Rocking to the swell of the ice-blue North Sea you can admire the guano-whitened cliffs of Staple Island, where chocolate-jacketed guillemots stand packed in their thousands on the ledges. Puffins skim briskly over the water on blurry wings. 'Busy lad, the puffin,' comments the boatman. 'Hereabouts we call him the Tommy-Noddy.'

You can land on Longstone to climb the red-and-white striped tower of the lighthouse from which Grace Darling and her father, William, the Longstone lightkeeper, made their brave dash in a rowing boat on the stormy morning of 7 September 1838. The Darlings managed to save only nine of the fifty-two souls aboard the paddle steamer *Forfarshire*, wrecked on Big Harcar, but the rescue made the twenty-three-year-old lighthouse keeper's daughter a national heroine. The Shiels spin the tense, romantic tale as they steer you down to Inner Farne. Here you land to savour a couple of hours on the island where St Cuthbert wrestled his demons. It is tempting to speculate whether those Dark Ages Northumbrians who populated Inner Farne with evil spirits did their visiting during the breeding season. Certainly the Arctic terns prove furiously resentful of human visitors then, excreting upon them and pecking with their needle-sharp scarlet bills until the interlopers are out of their territory.

Crouch close to the edge of the cliffs and you can enjoy the rare privilege of an intimate glimpse into the private life of the shag, a rather dashing bird of remote sea cliffs and islands. On Inner Farne they contest breeding space with thousands of guillemots and kittiwakes, and have to nest where they can. Shags are extremely handsome birds, seen close to. Their plumage is the subtlest of iridescent greens, their eyes coruscate with a brilliant emerald sparkle, and when they open their long hooked beaks they display throats of the most vibrant yellow. Judging by their dry cackles, they possess a sense of humour that Arctic terns lack. I tear myself away from their company with extreme reluctance. But time and tide and the Shiels wait for no man.

332. DODDINGTON MOOR, NORTHUMBERLAND

Maps: OS Explorer 340; Landranger 75

Travel: A1 from Newcastle-upon-Tyne to Morpeth; A697 to Wooler. Right on B6525 to Doddington. Park near telephone box (OS ref. 999325). Retrace steps to old cross and bear left ('Golf Club'); in 100 yards right over stile, and follow 'Dod Law' fingerpost on footpath that climbs to Shepherd's House (005316). Bear left on to Dod Law and Doddington Moor.

The coast of Northumberland is the county's acknowledged treasure. But Northumberland has another and entirely different landscape inland, the high and enticing range of the Cheviot Hills (see pp. 358–9). From far and wide the green line of the Cheviots beckons those with a taste for lonely country. For anyone with a mind to enjoy the sight of Cheviot but without the time to go there, Doddington Moor offers a grandstand view across the dead-flat valley of three rivers – the Glen, the Till and the Wooler Water – into the north-east flanks of the range. Doddington Moor has its own attractions, too. It holds the finest collection of neolithic and Bronze Age art in the region.

From Doddington village it is a steep haul up the breast of Dod Law, and near the top you reach what you least expect to find in such a high and remote location – a strongly built old shepherd's cottage, whose million-dollar view has preserved it from dereliction or demolition. Whoever lives up here commands the most marvellous view in Northumberland. Above the old house you climb to the summit at 492 feet, the rounded domes of Yeavering Bell, Humbleton Hill and others standing high across the valley.

Up here, in the face of that heavenly view, Stone Age and Bronze Age people buried their dead, erected ceremonial circles and pillars of stone, and scooped in the surface of the outcrop rocks the enigmatic markings known as cup-and-ring. You can find dozens of examples of these clusters of depressions, each 'cup' a bowl-shaped hollow the size of half an orange and surrounded by an incised ring. Some of the groups of markings seem to be marshalled inside oblong shapes, an aerial view of huts inside a palisade. Whatever the Northumbrians meant – if anything – by their cup-and-rings, there is no mistaking their inspiration in climbing up here to carve the rocks. You only have to look around at that breathtaking view to feel the same impulse, the irresistible call of a high view over a wild place, chiming with theirs across the millennia.

333. LINDISFARNE CAUSEWAY, NORTHUMBERLAND

Maps: OS Explorer 340; Landranger 75

Travel: A1 Alnwick to Berwick-upon-Tweed; 1½ miles north of B6353 left turning to Lowick, turn right at West Mains (OS ref. 053421) for 2 miles, to park at start of Holy Island causeway (079427).

NB: Check tide times: www.northumberlandlife.org/holy-island. The causeway is generally safe to cross between 3½ and 4 hours either side of low water, but prior checking on specific times is essential.

Holy Island Sands is a lonely place, especially with the North Sea tide closing in on you. If you stop your car halfway across the causeway and walk out through hanks of seaweed and drifts of cockleshells across the sands, you can climb up a barnacled ladder into one of the tall wooden refuge towers. From this rough grandstand you watch the steely blue water creeping nearer, cutting in around the southern cliff of Lindisfarne, the Holy Island, on its slow, inexorable journey to smother the tarmac causeway across the sands, along with anything – car, bicycle, beast or man – foolish enough to have got caught in the middle of the crossing. This is not a game you can play for very long. The danger of the tides on Lindisfarne causeway is

real enough, as many have found to their cost as they try and fail to race the oncoming sea.

If you want to savour the pleasure of solitude in a vast expanse open to the sky there is nothing to beat crossing Holy Island Sands, especially if you do it the hard way by forsaking your car on the mainland shore, rolling up your trousers and carrying your shoes and socks in your hand as you follow the barnacled poles that mark the ancient pilgrim path. For the seventh-century hermits and their successors who set up on the rock of Lindisfarne, the 'land of the Lindis stream', the tidal island with its skirt of dunes and basalt crag meant isolation in which to fast and pray, and safety from mainland marauders – though not from the Vikings, who sacked the fledgling monastery more than once. From this tiny slip of rock off the Northumbrian shore St Aidan and St Cuthbert spread the flickering light of Christianity throughout the North. Norman monks built the great dusky pink sandstone monastery that now stands in ruin next to the village, a focus for the pilgrims who still approach their journey's end by the ancient pole-marked route across the sands.

In the Heritage Centre on Holy Island you can admire computer-enhanced facsimile pages of the Lindisfarne Gospels, an illuminated book of unearthly beauty created on the island shortly after St Cuthbert's death in AD 687. Blue-headed dogs, dragons, beaked beasts and disarmingly smiling birds of prey emerge from forests of elaborately interlaced patterns. This wonderful book (the original is in the British Museum) journeyed with the monks when, under threat of death from Danish raids, they fled Lindisfarne in AD 875. They took the body of St Cuthbert with them, and – some say – were so clumsy in their haste and terror as they rowed to the mainland that they knocked the precious Gospels overboard.

Seen from the shoreline when the tide is up, the 'refuge box', a small shed on stilts for the safety of anyone stranded by the tide, appears to float like a square little ark on the water. It is easy to picture the fleeing monks halfway to the mainland, desperate with worry and now distraught, watching the jewelled book glint and turn below their boat. The ghostly singing of seals out on a rock or sandbar only enhances the desolation of the image. The men in the boat were not to know that the following morning they would find the Gospels lying on the shore, miraculously restored to them.

11

THE BORDERS AND CENTRAL SCOTLAND

It's no wonder that most people from south of the Border who start out in search of the UK's most extreme forms of physical and mental challenge in wild surroundings head for Scotland. There is so much more empty country here, so much more upland and outland.

THE HIGHLANDS NORTH-WEST of the Great Glen and the great scatter of islands to the west and north of the mainland (see 'North-West Scotland and the Isles') always seem to me to form a place apart. The rest of Scotland can be separated into two regions, Borders and Central. Although there are topographical differences – the rounded hills and grassy glens of the Borders are low and modest compared with the sharper mountain ranges and intervening valleys further north – the point where Borders gives way to Central, or where Lowlands shift into Highlands, is as much a matter of atmosphere as it is of geography.

The steep uplands and remote tangle of river glens that make up the Border country south of the Glasgow–Edinburgh line include the very wild and lonely back-of-beyond Galloway. The country further east and north, birthplace of Scotland's national poet, Robert Burns, is where Sir Walter Scott set many of his great historical novels that gave birth to the kilt-swishing, toast-drinking Jacobite scene. These beautiful hills are traversed by the Southern Upland Way, a long-distance footpath which will carry you as far as the rugged coast of Berwickshire and East Lothian. This Border is soaked in ancient blood from clashes between the English and the Scots, between one Border tribe and the next, and from religious persecutions down the centuries, especially of the Covenanters, seventeenth-century dissidents who were hunted mercilessly to their deaths.

Further north lie Loch Lomond and the Trossachs (the 'Highlands in Miniature'), mountainous country beloved of Victorian seekers of wild Romantic landscapes and the favourite destination of day travellers out from Glasgow and Edinburgh. Out towards the north-west you will find Rannoch Moor and the ominous hollow of Glencoe. North and east again stands the great arc of the Grampian Mountains, where the peaks and high plateau of the Cairngorms and the upthrust of the Monadhliath Mountains form this region's heartland, the wildest piece of high mountain country in Scotland.

Left: Meigle Pictish Stones (p. 398). Above: Spey Bay (pp. 407–8). Below: Glen Esk (pp. 402–3)

LINKS

- North Sea Trail (www.nave.no; www.northseatrail.org): From Berwickshire up most of the East Coast to Duncansby Head
- Southern Upland Way Long Distance Route (www.southernuplandway.com): Mull of Galloway, Range of the Awful Hand
- West Highland Way Long Distance Route (www.west-highland-way.co.uk): Dumgoyne and Campsie Fells, Ben Lomond, Falls of Falloch, Rannoch Moor, Glencoe, Ben Nevis
- Speyside Way Long Distance Route (www.speysideway.org): Speymouth, Abernethy Forest, offshoots to Cairngorms and Monadhliath Mountains

NATIONAL PARKS

- Loch Lomond and the Trossachs: www.lochlomond-trossachs.org
- Cairngorms: www.cairngorms.co.uk

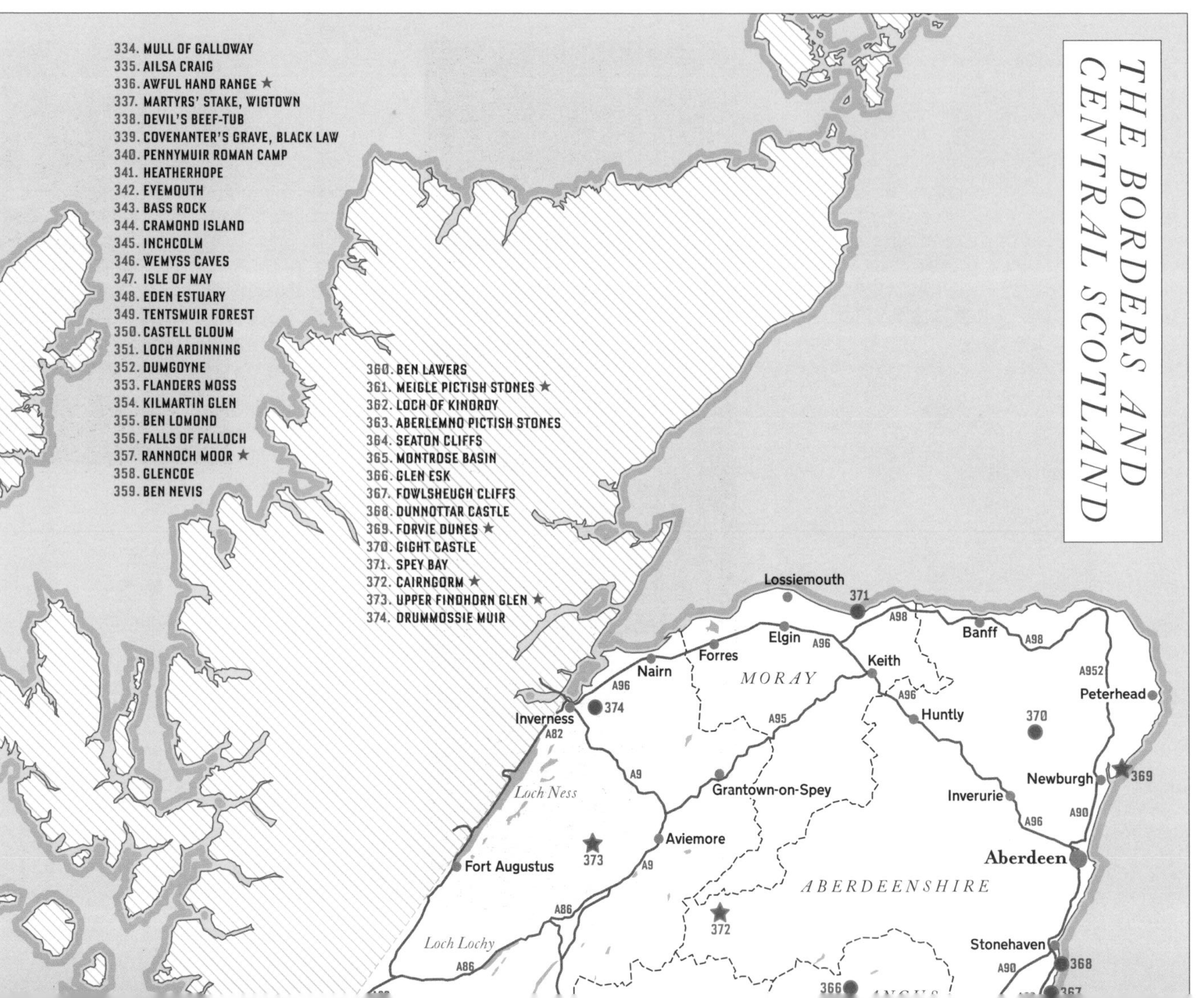
THE BORDERS AND CENTRAL SCOTLAND
334. MULL OF GALLOWAY
335. AILSA CRAIG
336. AWFUL HAND RANGE ★
337. MARTYRS' STAKE, WIGTOWN
338. DEVIL'S BEEF-TUB
339. COVENANTER'S GRAVE, BLACK LAW
340. PENNYMUIR ROMAN CAMP
341. HEATHERHOPE
342. EYEMOUTH
343. BASS ROCK
344. CRAMOND ISLAND
345. INCHCOLM
346. WEMYSS CAVES
347. ISLE OF MAY
348. EDEN ESTUARY
349. TENTSMUIR FOREST
350. CASTELL GLOUM
351. LOCH ARDINNING
352. DUMGOYNE
353. FLANDERS MOSS
354. KILMARTIN GLEN
355. BEN LOMOND
356. FALLS OF FALLOCH
357. RANNOCH MOOR ★
358. GLENCOE
359. BEN NEVIS
360. BEN LAWERS
361. MEIGLE PICTISH STONES ★
362. LOCH OF KINORDY
363. ABERLEMNO PICTISH STONES
364. SEATON CLIFFS
365. MONTROSE BASIN
366. GLEN ESK
367. FOWLSHEUGH CLIFFS
368. DUNNOTTAR CASTLE
369. FORVIE DUNES ★
370. GIGHT CASTLE
371. SPEY BAY
372. CAIRNGORM ★
373. UPPER FINDHORN GLEN ★
374. DRUMMOSSIE MUIR
Lossiemouth
371
A98
Banff
A98
Elgin
A96
Forres
Keith
Nairn
MORAY
A952
A96
A96
Peterhead
374
Inverness
A82
Huntly
370
A95
A9
Newburgh
369
Loch Ness
Grantown-on-Spey
Inverurie
A96
A90
Aviemore
373
Aberdeen
Fort Augustus
A9
ABERDEENSHIRE
A86
372
Loch Lochy
Stonehaven
A86
368
A90
366
367

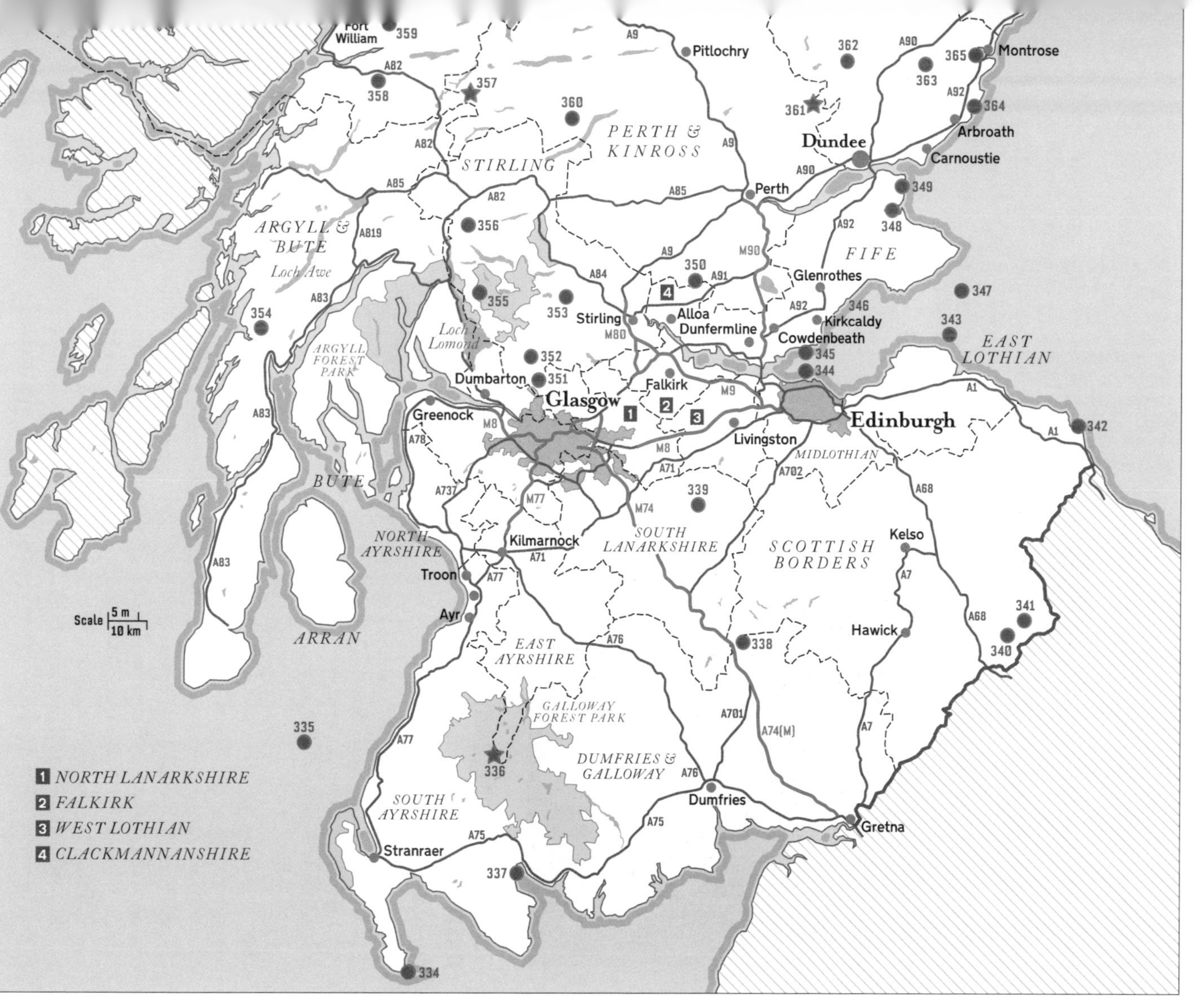
Fort William
359
Pitlochry
362
Montrose
365
363
358
357
360
PERTH & KINROSS
361
364
Arbroath
Dundee
Carnoustie
STIRLING
Perth
349
348
ARGYLL & BUTE
356
FIFE
Loch Awe
350
Glenrothes
355
353
347
354
Stirling
Alloa
Kirkcaldy
346
Dunfermline
343
Cowdenbeath
EAST LOTHIAN
Loch Lomond
352
345
ARGYLL FOREST PARK
344
Dumbarton
351
Falkirk
Glasgow
Edinburgh
342
Greenock
Livingston
MIDLOTHIAN
BUTE
339
NORTH AYRSHIRE
SOUTH LANARKSHIRE
Kelso
Kilmarnock
SCOTTISH BORDERS
Troon
341
Ayr
Hawick
ARRAN
338
340
EAST AYRSHIRE
GALLOWAY FOREST PARK
335
DUMFRIES & GALLOWAY
336
SOUTH AYRSHIRE
Dumfries
Gretna
Stranraer
337
334
A1
A7
A9
A68
A71
A74(M)
A75
A76
A77
A78
A82
A83
A84
A85
A90
A91
A92
A701
A702
A737
A819
M8
M9
M74
M77
M80
M90
1
2
3
4
Scale 5 m 10 km
1 NORTH LANARKSHIRE
2 FALKIRK
3 WEST LOTHIAN
4 CLACKMANNANSHIRE

Mull of Galloway

334. MULL OF GALLOWAY, DUMFRIES & GALLOWAY

Maps: OS Explorer 309; Landranger 82

Travel: M6 north to Carlisle, A74 Junction 22, A75 towards Stranraer. At 2 miles beyond Glenluce, left on B7084; A716 south to Drummore; minor road south to car park at Mull of Galloway (OS ref. 154304).

Galloway is the wildest and least accessible part of the entire Border region. Down in the south-west corner of Galloway, countless millennia of Irish Sea storms have pounded the coastal sandstone into a double-ended peninsula, the Rhinns of Galloway, a hammer head 30 miles long with Loch Ryan on the north and Luce Bay to the south. An hour's drive on bumpy, grass-grown back roads down the full length of the Rhinns peninsula, and you cross a narrow isthmus to climb a great cliff-girt promontory. At the outermost tip a lighthouse stands on a bare headland. This is the Mull of Galloway, the southernmost tip of Scotland, a blunt head of land with a brow of lichened cliffs and a collar of sea foam.

You can inch round the lighthouse and down a long, rickety flight of steps to an eyrie in the cliffs. Here an ancient foghorn still lies anchored to a semicircular rail, its bell mouth pouting out over a tumble of silvery, lichen-bearded rocks towards the boiling tide-rips off the Mull. Across a dark stretch of sea lies the jagged grey silhouette of the Isle of Man, its lighthouses winking conspiratorially. Far off in the west, where a faint outline of Ireland rises and falls, the hills of Down and Antrim stand along the horizon. This is a good place to shelter from the wind and call wild old tales to mind.

The Mull of Galloway lighthouse was built in 1828 by Robert Stevenson, and it was the architect's grandson and namesake, Robert Louis Stevenson, who based a stirring poem, 'Heather Ale', on a hoary story of this rocky outpost.

From the bonny bells of heather
They brewed a drink long-syne,
Was sweeter far than honey,
Was stronger far than wine ...

Stevenson, a magpie for old legend, had heard the tale of how the secret of the legendary Heather Ale was known only to two living souls – the last of the Picts, father and son. The King of Scots, desperate to know the recipe, hunted the pair as far as these clifftops. Brought to bay, so Stevenson relates, the father wheedled the king:

I dare not sell my honour
Under the eye of my son.
Take him, O King, and bind him,
And cast him far in the deep:
And it's I will tell the secret
That I have sworn to keep.

And then, after the boy has been thrown to his death, the old man leaps after him with the bold exit line:

Here dies in my bosom
The secret of Heather Ale!

335. AILSA CRAIG, SOUTH AYRSHIRE

Maps: OS Explorer 317; Landranger 76

Travel: A77 to Girvan.

Boat trip: www.ailsacraig.org.uk

Landing permits: South Ayrshire Council, County Buildings, Wellington Square, Ayr KA7 1DR (tel: 01292 612000; www.south-ayrshire.gov.uk)

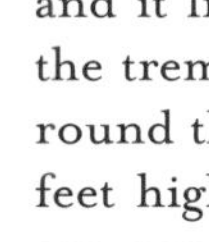

Coming south from Glasgow along the coast road, you glance out west to see a monstrous humped shoulder surfacing on the sea horizon. This first sight of Ailsa Craig – rose-coloured and gleaming in sunlight, or grim and sulky under rain in a slate-black sea – is breathtaking. The Craig is a solid lump of granite, a plug of solidified magma that once blocked the throat of a giant volcanic crater, now eroded and flooded by the sea. It may look impressive from the shore, but its full majesty is concealed by distance. Ailsa Craig rises over 1,100 feet, three times the height of the Bass Rock (see pp. 379–80), and it lies 8 miles out in the sea. Some of the tremendous columns of basalt that wall round the lower half of the rock stand 600 feet high. The ledges, cracks and crannies are occupied by screaming seabirds, part of the island's overall population of some 100,000 birds. A cruise round the Craig is an excellent experience, but landing on Ailsa Craig is a desert-island fantasy. It is a comparatively rare feat, being dependent on a favourable wind and tide. There are plenty of signs of human occupation, including the lighthouse (now solar-powered), the barracks-like quarters built in the 1880s for its keepers, the shattered stub of a castle, and a run of rusty railway tracks left by the quarrymen when blasting of the granite finally ceased. Ailsa Craig is probably best known as the source of the blue hone granite that is the finest material in the world for making curling stones, thanks to its dense texture and hard surface that takes a high polish. Granite for curling stones is still picked up from the old quarries, but now that the rock is an RSPB reserve no more shots are fired here.

As for those 100,000 seabirds, if you visit in late spring you will be dodging black-backed gull nests and trying not to walk on their eggs on your climb to the rocky summit with its superb sea and land views. More than half the bird population is made up of gannets – up to 40,000 breeding pairs of the big white seabirds with the ice-blue eyes. Other significant numbers: 12,000 guillemots, 1,000 of their streaky-beaked cousins the razorbills, and a tiny handful of black guillemots whose white wing-flashes show up startlingly in flight. A couple of thousand kittiwakes shrieking *'Ee-wake! Ee-wake!'* and a scattering of herring gulls, of portly puffins and stiff-winged fulmars; all nest here, too. The Craig seems alive with birds, so that as you look back on the

rock from the Girvan-bound boat you will marvel that you could ever have thought it a lifeless lump.

336. AWFUL HAND RANGE, GALLOWAY

Maps: OS Explorer 318; Landranger 77

Travel: A714 north from Newton Stewart for 10 miles; right through Glentrool village and on to car park at Bruce's Stone by Loch Trool (OS ref. 416803). Track signposted north to summit of The Merrick (2,766 feet) – 7 miles there and back.

The tumbled ranges of hills north of Wigtown, now designated the Galloway Forest Park, have had their lower slopes clothed in coniferous forests. Robert the Bruce, who in 1307 routed an English army on the banks of Loch Trool by rolling boulders down on top of them, would scarcely recognize the place. Yet the cragged peaks, lost lochs and valleys above the tree line are still bare places open to the sky, naked and elemental, as wild a landscape as you will find anywhere south of the Highlands.

Awful Hand Range

North of Loch Trool, the Range of the Awful Hand stretches five mountainous fingers across the breast of Galloway. Chief of these, The Merrick is the highest peak in the Lowlands of Scotland. A well-found track leads in 4 miles from Bruce's Stone up to The Merrick's 2,766-foot summit. Up where the shoulders of the hills roll clear of the tree blanket is a world of bare grey rock outcrops, slopes and crags covered with long golden blow-grass and darker clumps of heather. Bruce was hunted by bloodhounds across these hills, wading down the hill burns to confuse the scent. Red and roe deer, feral goats and half-wild sheep, golden eagle and mountain hare, snow bunting and rock pipit rule this high and lonely roost.

Under the bow-shaped peak of Mullwharchar lies Loch Enoch, remote and beautiful. Ice-cold water laps the shores of silver sand. A hill burn trickles, a sheep coughs, the wind whistles gently through a wire fence. This is the true heart of Galloway, harsh and sublime.

'You are here on a precarious sufferance,' noted Reverend C. H. Dick in his 1916 travel classic *Highways and Byways in Galloway and Carrick*.

> *Something in the wilderness is uneasy and resentful of your presence. It is patient, but has the latent possibility of capricious outbreaks, and you cannot tell when or how it may strike. Tramping over the moors, you have now and then the sensation of being watched by an alien intelligence, and you turn round as if to face an indefinable threat. You are glad to hear the croak of the raven that tells you that you*

are not quite alone. This is the effect of the place in fine weather. On a sunless day, when the clouds are low, you feel like a lost soul committed to some chill reach of eternity.

As the shepherds of the Awful Hand liked to say: 'Ony sauchle o' a body can write a book, but it tak's a man tae herd The Merrick.'

337. MARTYRS' STAKE, WIGTOWN, DUMFRIES & GALLOWAY

Maps: OS Explorer 311; Landranger 83

Travel: M6 north to Carlisle, A74 Junction 22, A75 towards Stranraer. At Newton Stewart, left on A714 to Wigtown. Turn left in town to park near church; continue down lane to shore and duckboard trail to Martyrs' Stake (OS ref. 437556).

From the grassy sea bank on the western shore of Wigtown Bay a duckboard trail leads out across a boggy, water-pocked grazing marsh to a granite memorial pillar, standing alone in a staked enclosure. Nowadays the tide scarcely ever reaches this spot, but back in the late seventeenth century, before its marginal land was reclaimed for agriculture, Wigtown Bay filled from shore to shore at each high water. That was the case on the May morning in 1685 when Margaret McLachlan, a woman of sixty-three, and a young girl of eighteen named Margaret Wilson were tied to stakes on this spot to drown in the incoming Solway tides. They were to suffer this horrible and lingering death on the orders of the man known as 'Cruel Lag' – Sir Robert Grierson of Lag, Steward of Kirkcudbright – for the crimes of 'nonconformity, disorderly behaviour, and absenteeism from church'. In other words, they were Covenanters.

Many independent-minded Galloway folk had signed up to the National Covenant

in 1638, pledging themselves to 'recover the purity and liberty of the Gospel as it was established'. These Covenanters, who wanted the Scots Kirk ruled by a lay hierarchy rather than bishops loyal to the English Crown, suffered desperate persecution for the next half-century. Three hundred of their ministers took to the heather and conducted illegal services in remote valleys, caves and cottages among the wild Galloway hills. When caught, the dissenters were shot or hanged out of hand by the dragoons who hunted them in company with local 'gentlemen'. Occasionally, as in the case of the two Wigtown women, the authorities felt it necessary to make an even more forceful point.

Margaret McLachlan's stake was driven into the mud further out from shore than that of Margaret Wilson. The teenager had to watch as her co-religionist drowned before her eyes. Then a dragoon was detailed to hold the young girl's chin up out of the water as the tide lapped round it. But when she still refused to recant, the soldier let her head fall forward, and she, too, was drowned.

A poignant gravestone in an enclosure in the graveyard of Wigtown parish church cemetery is inscribed with the names of the accusers, infamous forever more: 'Here lyes Margrat Lachlane who was by unjust law sentenced to die by Lago, Strachane, Winrame and Grhame and tyed to a stake within the flood for her adherence to Scotlands Reformation.'

Devil's Beef-Tub

338. DEVIL'S BEEF-TUB, DUMFRIES & GALLOWAY

Map: OS Explorer 330; Landranger 78

Travel: A74 to Moffat; A701 Edinburgh road north; on outskirts of Moffat, right on minor road for 3½ miles to Ericstane (OS ref. 073110). Park here carefully – farm traffic uses the lane. North on foot along farm road for 1 mile to Corehead (072125). Through first of two gates on right, round back of farm; follow 'Beeftub' signs, keeping to right of burn as you approach Devil's Beef-Tub.

"Ye must have seen it as ye cam this way: it looks as if four hills were laying their heads together, to shut out daylight from the dark hollow space between them. A d—d deep, black, blackguard-looking abyss of a hole it is, and goes straight down from the road-side, as perpendicular as it can do, to be a heathery brae. At the bottom, there is a small bit of a brook, that you would think could hardly find its way out from the hills that are so closely jammed round it".

Sir Walter Scott was a sharp-nosed collector of tales from his native Borders, and in Redgauntlet (1824) he recycled a story he had heard from the lips of its hero, an old Jacobite who had fought for Bonnie Prince Charlie in the disastrous 1745–6 Rebellion. The man had escaped from the dragoons taking him to imprisonment in Carlisle by hurling himself into the Devil's Beef-Tub as they passed it by. This was no small feat of bravery. The Beef-Tub is a sombre and overwhelming place, a declivity in the moors north of Moffat that plunges 500 feet between four hills to the infant River Annan. Entering the valley on a hillside path from Corehead Farm, you pass an old circular stone sheepfold and reach a parting of the ways. To the right a rough stony cleft rises to the 1,529-foot summit of Great Hill, while to the left opens the Beef-Tub proper. Another name for it is the Marquis of Annandale's Beef-Stand, a reminder of lawless days when the cattle thieves of the Johnstone family under their leader Lord Annandale would hide their stolen beasts in this remote hollow in the hills. It's easy to imagine that several thousand could be secreted here in the cleft, with grazing and water ready to hand.

In August 1685 a Covenanter (see below) named John Hunter was shot dead here by dragoons as he tried to run from them up the impossibly steep sides. High above, beside the A701 at the rim of the hollow, stands his memorial. You can stare down the brae into the Beef-Tub from here, imagining the somersaulting descent of Scott's hero:

"I slipped out my hand from the handcuff, cried to Harry Gauntlet, 'Follow me!' – whisked under the belly of the dragoon horse – flung my plaid round me with the speed of lightning – threw myself on my side, for there was no keeping my feet, and down the brae hurled I, over heather and fern, and blackberries ... I kept my senses thegither, whilk has been thought wonderful by all that ever saw the place; and I helped myself with my hands as gallantly as I could, and to the bottom I came".

339. COVENANTER'S GRAVE, BLACK LAW, SOUTH LANARKSHIRE

Maps: OS Explorer 344; Landranger 72

Travel: From Edinburgh, A702 Biggar road. At 3½ miles south of West Linton, right turn to Garvald. Park at farm (OS ref. 097492 – ask permission, please). Two ways to reach Covenanter's Grave:

(a) Follow footpath signed 'Covenanter's Grave' north-north-west for 3 miles to reach the grave (see below).

(b) Follow farm road via Medwynbank (098497) to Medwynhead (092514). Above farm, track with tall posts leads left to cross Medwin Water (089518). Adam Sanderson's house ruin lies below (088515 approx.). In ½ mile, right (082513 – fingerpost marked 'Covenanter's Grave') north-north-east up south flank of Black Law, following line of shooting butts. Aim for direction post on skyline. Covenanter's Grave (078528) lies just to right of post, almost at summit.

The heart of the Pentland Hills, south-west of Edinburgh, contains some good lonely country, including the bare hill of Black Law that rises over the hidden valley of the Medwin Water. Here during the late

Covenanter's Grave, Black Law

seventeenth century, as in many such secret corners of Scotland, the religious sect known as the Covenanters – Presbyterians who refused to accept a Church of Scotland ruled by bishops – would gather for illegal open-air services, or 'conventicles'. Attendance at a conventicle laid a worshipper open to persecution that might include fines, beatings, imprisonment or even summary execution. Any minister who was caught preaching at a conventicle was liable to be put to death.

On 27 November 1666 an encounter between Covenanters and Government forces took place at Rullion Green near Penicuik on the north-east slopes of the Pentlands. Against the heavily armoured dragoons, a peasant army lined up:

Some had halbards; some had durks;
Some had crooked swords like Turks;
Some had guns with rusty ratches;
Some had firey peats for matches;
Some had bows but wanted arrows;
Some had pistols without marrows ...

The dragoons mowed down the ill-armed countrymen. Fifty were killed on the field; many more were hunted and slaughtered, arrested and hanged, over the following weeks.

Beside the Medwin Water at Medwynhead under Black Law lies the broken shell of a stone-built house. It was here that the shepherd Adam Sanderson answered a thump on his door on the night of the battle. A desperately wounded fugitive, John Carphin of Ayrshire, wanted help, but would not come into the house in case his presence should bring trouble on the occupants. All he was able to gasp out before he died was, 'Bury me within sight of my Ayrshire hills.' Sanderson carried Carphin's body up Black Law and buried it near the summit with a view west between Bleak Law and the Pike to the distant hills of Ayrshire – an act of charity that set at risk his own life and liberty. Later the Black Law herd put up a memorial stone, discreetly lettered so as to be indecipherable to unfriendly eyes. But the story of the buried Covenanter persisted in the area. In 1817 one young farmer's son went so far as to dig up John Carphin's skull and coat buttons, a desecration that earned the lad a good belting from his outraged Presbyterian father.

The memorial stone that stands on Black Law today, inscribed with the facts of the burial, was erected in 1841. Adam Sanderson's original stone, crudely lettered 'UNONE [unknown] COVENANTER 1666', lies on the windowsill in Dunsyre Kirk a couple of miles from Garvald.

340. PENNYMUIR ROMAN CAMP, SCOTTISH BORDERS

Maps: OS Explorer OL16; Landranger 80

Travel: A68 north from Corbridge to cross Scottish Border at Carter Bar; in 3½ miles, first right on minor road ('Edgerston') through North Riccalton and Middlesknowes to park at Pennymuir by Roman camp explanation board (OS ref. 755143). Bear right at crossroads, and in 250 yards turn right over stile (757140) to find ramparts of Roman camp.

Arriving at Pennymuir after the long trek on minor roads and looking around at the moorland landscape – windswept, bleak and austerely beautiful – I didn't quite see what the fuss was about. Where was this Roman camp? Where were the ramparts marked out so boldly and clearly on the map? All that greets you on the ground is heather and sedge, the long valley of the Kale Water unrolling to the north, and the lumpy green upthrust of the rounded Cheviot outliers. It takes a little time to attune your eyes – and your imagination. After all, 2,000 years have passed, and the marching men never meant this temporary encampment to last. But it has survived, quite astonishingly well, under the heather and pale moor grass. It seems as though the Roman army could not build shoddily, even if it tried.

The entire rectangle of ramparts must be 700 feet long and half that wide, with side shoots and auxiliary boundaries. In fact there are two camps laid out on a grid, the larger of the two big enough to accommodate 5,000 men with their fighting and everyday gear, their baggage and animals – a Roman army marched on its stomach as much as any, and its meat had to march with it. The basic camp of ditches and turf walls was run

Pennymuir

up by the soldiers themselves, wielding the mattocks they all carried just for this. You could be safe for the night from the bloody savages of locals in a matter of a few hours. Erect your leather tent, take the meat off the hoof and put it on a spit in double-quick time, get a bellyful, roll yourself in your woollen cloak and Julius is your uncle – sleep like a baby until it is your turn for sentry-go. Next day, on southwards along Dere Street into the heart of the Cheviots, with eyes in the back of your head for the next twenty-four hours, looking forward to the safety, the women and the proper sit-down lavatories of the barrack forts on Hadrian's Wall.

341. HEATHERHOPE, SCOTTISH BORDERS

Maps: OS Explorer OL16; Landranger 80

Travel: A68 north from Corbridge to cross Scottish Border at Carter Bar; in 3½ miles, first right on minor road ('Edgerston') through North Riccalton. Pass Middlesknowes and Pennymuir (OS ref. 755143 – see above). Cross Kale Water; left at next crossroads for 3 miles to Hownam. Just before village, right up No Through Road (778189); park at Greenhill Farm and walk on up track to Heatherhope Reservoir (809167).

Heatherhope is one of the remotest farms in the Scottish Border country and is a meeting place for the Border Hunt, a gathering place for sheep at shearing time, and a talking place for anyone and everyone who passes and has the time to stop and shoot the breeze with the Heatherhope shepherd. This knowledgeable man spends much of his time walking his rounds on the hills above the farm, and can point you in the direction of some wonderful old paths and tracks into the inner fastnesses of Cheviot.

Passing Heatherhope and its reservoir, climb steeply above Philip Hope Burn to reach the ancient trackway called The Street a little short of the Border fence. Instead of carrying on up to the Border to join the miry trudgers on the Pennine Way National Trail, turn sharply to your left along The Street for an exhilarating 5-mile stride on the high tops back to Hownam. The wonderful views are not the only pleasure of this lonely walk; on the way you will pass a pair of hill forts, two among many that lie scattered across these hills.

At the fort on Sundhope Kip (OS ref. 816167) overlooking Heatherhope, twenty-three round hut foundations shelter inside a ring of four distinct ramparts built of rubble, with a long entrance passage that kinks in the middle – a device to slow down an intruder and obstruct the flight of his hurled spear or shot arrow. Two miles along The Street you can bear off left down Headshaw Hope to Greenhill; a mile more on the high road, though, and just before you take the plunge down the slope to Hownam another fine old fort looms on the hill ahead, the stronghold of Hownam Rings. There was a great stone wall around the top of the hill until, late in the first century AD when the Romans began to make their presence felt in the Cheviots, it was pulled down to make defensive ramparts like those on Sundhope Kip.

Heatherhope Reservoir

Did the warriors of Sundhope and Hownam fight the invaders fiercely? Or were they defenceless farmers, easily cowed? Who owned the bronze fingernail cleaner that was unearthed at Hownam Rings, the pots and jars, the iron knife, the inlaid armlet of yellow-and-white glass? What did these hill-dwellers think of the ancestors who raised a line of crudely shaped standing stones on the Hownam heights, 2,000 years before the ramparts were built? And how do we, walking the slopes of Windy Law, connect with them, and with our own forerunners, who said – and maybe believed – that the ancient monument was not a line of stones at all, but a gang of sheep shearers caught working on a Sunday and turned into rocks for their impiety?

342. EYEMOUTH, SCOTTISH BORDERS

Maps: OS Explorer 346; Landranger 67

Travel: A1 from Berwick-upon-Tweed towards Edinburgh; in 6 miles, right on A1107 to Eyemouth. Park on harbour (OS ref. 945644).

Nearest railway station: Berwick-upon-Tweed (8 miles)

The rolling cornfields north of Berwick-upon-Tweed look prosperous, a well-favoured farming landscape set with small villages. Only the ruins of fortified pele tower and castles hint at the bloody past of this Border country of the east coast. Men cut and hacked each other here for centuries without leaving a dent on this landscape; it is the sea that is master here. A cruel master, as they know only too well in Eyemouth, a dour stone fishing town huddled round a narrow harbour.

During a long, wary relationship with the sea, Eyemouth fishermen and their families have endured many losses in obscurity. But the calamity of 14 October 1881 hit the national headlines, when a hurricane-force storm fell on the fleet out of a clear horizon.

'The sky suddenly thickened with dark, heavy clouds,' recorded the local minister, Reverend Daniel McIver, in his book *Eyemouth: An Old-time Fishing Town*:

> *A fierce wind arose which was as wild in its fury as the calm was quiet; the sea began to heave its threatening bosom, like a man in whose heart passion was rising, and what with sudden darkness – it was then between eleven and twelve of the day – the shrieking of the hurricane as it drove at the creaking masts and ripping sails, and the thunderous roar of a boiling ocean, the poor fishermen thought that the Judgment Day had come.*

One hundred and twenty-nine of them drowned within sight of their families, gathered in horror along the shore, as their boats smashed on the Hurkers reef at the mouth of the harbour or piled into the cliffs. Five hundred women and children lost their loved ones and breadwinners. 'Eyemouth is a scene of unutterable woe,' lamented the *Berwickshire News*. 'The town has received a blow from which it will be long ere it will recover; the fleet is wrecked, and the flower of the fishermen have perished.'

Eyemouth Museum preserves a tapestry created by the townspeople in 1981 to commemorate the centenary of the disaster. Embroidered with images of fishermen overwhelmed by the storm, the fish they gave their lives to catch, and a radiant sunrise as a symbol of new hope, it makes a very poignant and moving memorial.

343. BASS ROCK, EAST LOTHIAN

Maps: OS Explorer 351; Landranger 67

Travel: A1 from Berwick-upon-Tweed towards Edinburgh; right at roundabout just past Dunbar on A198 to North Berwick. Park at Scottish Seabird Centre (OS ref. 554855).

Boat trip: www.seabird.org

Nearest railway station: North Berwick

The first-class Scottish Seabird Centre in North Berwick runs boat trips out to the Bass Rock, a plug of basalt rising 350 feet out of the Firth of Forth. The extraordinary sight of a dense cloud of gannets streaming to leeward off the Bass never fails to draw gasps from boat-borne visitors. The birds circle and circle as if incapable of fatigue. How they avoid mid-air collisions is a miracle, for there are individuals peeling off to return to their clifftop nests, and others arriving to join the ever-turning cartwheel of birds above the rock.

From down at sea level one hardly notices the noise that these 100,000 birds are making. But once ashore and trudging up the zigzag path to the summit, a rhythmical sound like the surging of a giant kettle on the boil begins to make itself heard. By the time you reach the viewing place near the summit it has swelled to a roar. The smell of the colony hits you next, a stench that makes you gag. Then the spectacle claims your attention. Gannets are big – 3 feet long, with a wingspan nearly twice that – and they are beautiful, with china-white body and inner wings, long pointed black wingtips, and a buff-coloured head from which protrudes that sharp grey beak. The eyes are a remarkable cold blue. Birds returning to their nests from fishing trips greet their mates with a thrusting together of heads, a rubbing of beaks and intertwining of necks. Gannets have soul.

As a human, you get used to being anathema to all wild birds. They shrink away, they run and hide, they take off. Not so with the Bass Rock gannets. There is simply no room for any gannet to shuffle sideways without inviting a stabbing from its neighbour's dagger of a bill. If a parent bird flies away, a black-backed gull will have its egg in ten seconds flat. So the gannets stay put, eyeballing the stranger, alert for catastrophe but intent on their own affairs. It is an extraordinary privilege to be looking in, from a distance of a couple of feet, on the everyday life of a wild creature – something to treasure as you make your way back down the path towards the boat, carrying with you like a keepsake a faint but fishy after-whiff.

344. CRAMOND ISLAND, EDINBURGH

Travel: A90 ('Edinburgh') from south end of Forth Road Bridge; in 3 miles, Cramond Island is signposted in Cramond village. Park near slipway (OS ref. 190770).

NB: Causeway open for 2 hours each side of low water – contact coastguard (tel: 01333 450666) for times. Allow 15–20 minutes for crossing causeway.

Nearest railway station: South Gyle (3 miles)

There are no boats to Cramond Island. You have to walk there from the south shore of the Firth of Forth along a tidal causeway that crosses gleaming mud and ribbed sandbanks, a crunchy carpet of mussels and winkles underfoot. The island is thickly coated with soft grass and wild flowers and possessed of magnificent views across the firth. At first glance it seems a green haven untouched by man. But once you have passed through the island's grove of willows and sycamores, traversed the rocky knoll of the summit and dropped down to the north shore, you discover just how thoroughly these islets of the Forth were fortified during the world wars of the twentieth century.

Here are concrete pillboxes, observation bunkers, gun emplacements and searchlight bases. The causeway trestles carried a power supply to the men who garrisoned Cramond Island. A couple of miles up the firth the great red dinosaur humps of the Forth Railway Bridge rise over the trees, with the naval dockyard at Rosyth in their shadow – prime targets for German bombers. Cramond Island and its sister islands of Inchgarvie,

Inchmickery and Inchkeith were perfectly placed to defend bridge and dockyard by spotting, illuminating and shooting down any attackers.

The world wars were not Cramond Island's only brush with violence. Back at the turn of the eleventh century, when Scotland was the Kingdom of Alba, the fabulously ruthless Malcolm mac Cineada was hacking his way to the throne by killing off all his rivals. It is rumoured that one sought refuge on the island – not the wisest choice of hiding place, with only one way on or off. Malcolm's brother arrived, crossed the causeway, hunted down the wretched fugitive and killed him here. Details are shadowy, but if the tale is true it was only one of many 'whackings' that Malcolm's supporters carried out to gain their man the throne. The following year he killed the reigning King Kenneth III and Kenneth's son Giric in battle, and once Kenneth's grandson had also been liquidated King Malcolm II settled down to a long and effective reign – until 1034, when he in his turn was murdered at Glamis Castle.

The peace of the island today, its remarkable views up and down the firth, its seals and seabirds going unconcernedly about their business, make the violence of the past feel unreal. Cramond Island is a secret shared among surprisingly few, considering its proximity to Edinburgh. It is easy to stroll out there in mid-afternoon, spend the time in seal-watching and lotus-eating, miss the tide and find yourself marooned till nightfall.

345. INCHCOLM, FIFE

Maps: OS Explorer 371; Landranger 65

Travel: Ferry from Hawes Pier, South Queensferry (M9, A90, then B924), or Newhaven Harbour, Leith (many buses from Edinburgh city centre).

Information: www.maidoftheforth.co.uk

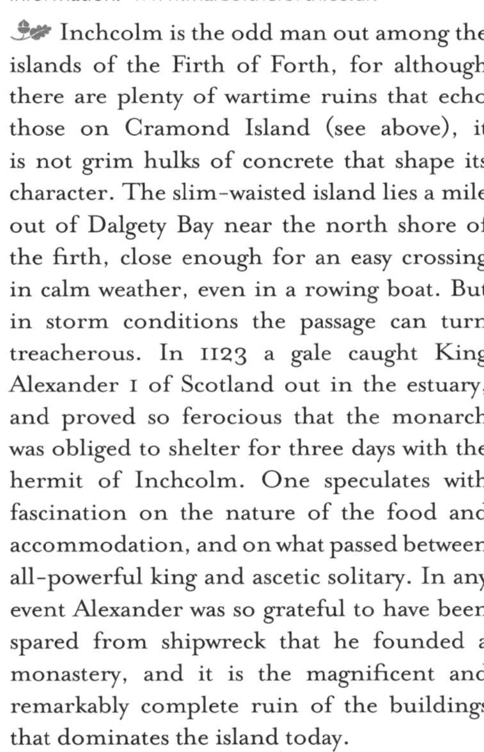

Inchcolm is the odd man out among the islands of the Firth of Forth, for although there are plenty of wartime ruins that echo those on Cramond Island (see above), it is not grim hulks of concrete that shape its character. The slim-waisted island lies a mile out of Dalgety Bay near the north shore of the firth, close enough for an easy crossing in calm weather, even in a rowing boat. But in storm conditions the passage can turn treacherous. In 1123 a gale caught King Alexander I of Scotland out in the estuary, and proved so ferocious that the monarch was obliged to shelter for three days with the hermit of Inchcolm. One speculates with fascination on the nature of the food and accommodation, and on what passed between all-powerful king and ascetic solitary. In any event Alexander was so grateful to have been spared from shipwreck that he founded a monastery, and it is the magnificent and remarkably complete ruin of the buildings that dominates the island today.

The monastery of Inchcolm suffered two English attacks in the fourteenth century, during which the soldiers looted the treasury and stole all the deeds and records. Trying to prove ownership of their far-flung lands and other possessions was a source of misery and fury for successive abbots. The monastery survived these events, but finally fell victim to the Scottish Reformation of 1560. The buildings became residences; later, in the eighteenth century, soldiers used them as a barracks. As a result of this continuous use the vaulted monastic offices and church and the cloister with its tremendously stubby, thick-necked arcade remain remarkably well preserved. A climb up the spiral stair is rewarded by a prospect across the whole island from the roof of the church tower.

During the Second World War a brick-lined tunnel was built through the spine of the island in order to carry stores to the line of searchlights sited on Inchcolm. Passing through the dark, damp tunnel, you emerge at the north end of the island to walk a circuit via the lighthouse. As you do, the permanent residents of Inchcolm are likely to give you a vigorous, not to say vicious, reception. Many thousands of pairs of lesser black-backed gulls lord it over the island during the breeding season, and will dive-bomb anyone who approaches their nests, close enough to draw blood with a jab of feet or beak. A stout stick waved over your head prevents the gulls from actually striking you, but they thoroughly test your nerves as they rush overhead with a hiss of wings, a furious scream and a distinct whiff of rotten fish.

Below and above: Wemyss Cave carvings

346. WEMYSS CAVES, FIFE

Maps: OS Explorer 367; Landranger 59

Travel: From M90 Junction 3, A92 to bear right at second Kirkcaldy roundabout, then left on A915 towards Windygates. In 1 ½ miles, right on minor road towards West Wemyss for ¾ mile, then left on A955 towards Methil. In 1 ½ miles, right down East Brae (brown sign) to seafront car park (OS ref. 342969). Follow shore path past caves.

NB: Some of the caves (clearly marked) are closed for safety reasons.

Nearest railway station: Kirkcaldy (6 miles)

The south coast of Fife is of soft red sandstone, perfect material for the sea to hollow out. The stretch of low cliffs east of Kirkcaldy is riddled with shallow caves, formed after the end of the last Ice Age when the land, relieved of the crushing weight of ice a mile thick, rose several scores of feet and exposed this friable rock to waves and weathering. People on the lookout for safe places to shelter soon began to inhabit the caves, and it must have been shortly after they took up residence that they began to cut pictures into the walls.

Many millennia of carvings must have been weathered and washed away. The earliest decipherable today could date back 5,000 years, but most of the antique depictions (there are plenty of more contemporary ones) were probably made in the time of the Picts, roughly corresponding to the Dark Ages. You can walk the shore to seek these out, though coal-mining subsidence allied to natural faulting weaknesses has made several of the caves unsafe.

The best cave for an untutored eye is Jonathan's Cave, the home back in the eighteenth century of a poor nail-maker who raised a family in this troglodytic hole. Passing through the entrance of rusty bars, you will find a cavern some 15 feet high that runs back 100 feet into the cliff, the green of lichens and white of leaching salts contrasting with the red of the sandstone and the blackening of age and of random fires. Mixed in with the 'Daz 4 Shaz' modern graffiti and the carved lovers' initials of more romantic times are the Pictish designs, impressionistic, powerful, bursting with life. A bull cavorts with lashing tail and forward-curving horns. A fish with a lateral line and fins and triangular tail like a salmon swims vertically upwards. A long-necked creature like a giraffe stalks on stubby legs. And two ghost-like human figures, half absorbed into the rock, confront each other, perhaps to dance, perhaps to fight. Something is etched in the rock between these naked Picts, the cause of their delight or else their anger, but the gulf of years and weathering is too deep even to guess what it might be.

347. ISLE OF MAY, FIFE

Maps: OS Explorer 371; Landranger 59

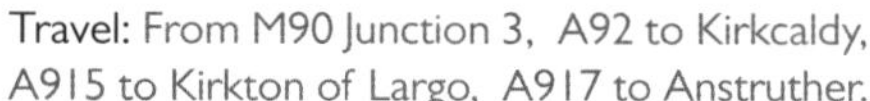

Travel: From M90 Junction 3, A92 to Kirkcaldy, A915 to Kirkton of Largo, A917 to Anstruther.

Ferry: www.isleofmayferry.com

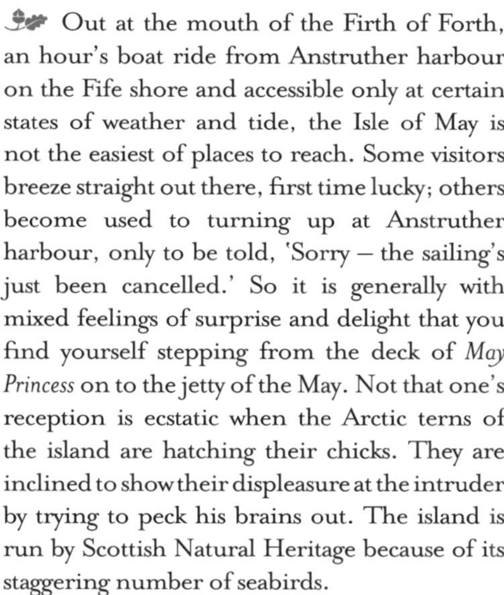

Out at the mouth of the Firth of Forth, an hour's boat ride from Anstruther harbour on the Fife shore and accessible only at certain states of weather and tide, the Isle of May is not the easiest of places to reach. Some visitors breeze straight out there, first time lucky; others become used to turning up at Anstruther harbour, only to be told, 'Sorry – the sailing's just been cancelled.' So it is generally with mixed feelings of surprise and delight that you find yourself stepping from the deck of *May Princess* on to the jetty of the May. Not that one's reception is ecstatic when the Arctic terns of the island are hatching their chicks. They are inclined to show their displeasure at the intruder by trying to peck his brains out. The island is run by Scottish Natural Heritage because of its staggering number of seabirds.

St Adrian was martyred by the Danes on the island in the seventh century. Since then the May has seen saints, murderers, smugglers and pirates, farmers and lighthouse keepers come and go, leaving behind them various signs and wonders of their tenancies – the ruins of the monastery founded by King David I in the twelfth century, a baronial castle of a lighthouse built by Robert Stevenson in 1816, the huge old cast-iron compressed air pipes that worked the foghorns, and a row of houses where the lighthouse keepers and their families lived, known as Fluke Street – 'believed to have acquired its name from a street of ill repute in Edinburgh', as the explanation board rather prissily puts it.

348. EDEN ESTUARY, FIFE

Maps: OS Explorer 371; Landranger 59

Travel: From M90 Junction 8, A91 ('St Andrews') through Auchtermuchty and Cupar. In another 6 miles at roundabout in Guardbridge, left on A919 Dundee road ('Leuchars'). In 200 yards, brown 'Eden Estuary' sign points right to car park (OS ref. 451193). Go through gate and follow path through park ('Eden Estuary') to Visitor Centre at far end. Return to road and turn right for ¼ mile to pass paper mill and cross Inner Bridge (450198); turn immediately right on to path along north bank of Eden Estuary.

Nearest railway station: Leuchars Junction (1 mile)

The River Eden's estuary runs east for 3 miles to reach the North Sea just north of St Andrews – in fact, the famous golf courses overlook it. But however crowded the links, once you are across Inner Bridge and past the huge old paper mill at Guardbridge, you share the whole gleaming vista of sandbanks, mudflats and wind-ruffled River Eden with the seals and wild birds. Few visitors and only a handful of locals walk here, so the wild creatures are less wary than in other, more frequented nature reserves.

The Eden reaches the sea through wide aprons of sand and mud which are crammed with tiny shrimps, molluscs, mud snails and lugworms. In addition to this, the birds that flock to the estuary ride at high tide on a river sheltered by the broad sandbanks and dunes at the river mouth and by a skirt of saltmarsh, the biggest in Fife. Autumn and spring migrations see thousands of waders passing through and stopping to stock up on food, some of them to stay on through the winter – redshank and oystercatcher, dunlin in large flocks, grey plover, whose white underwings show striking black 'armpits' as they fly off, twisting and turning, and the eye-catching black-tailed godwit who stands tall with a beautiful fiery red head and long pink bill.

Winter is a good time to prowl, well wrapped up with binoculars at the ready, to spot sea ducks wintering in the estuary: scaup with glossy green heads, white-faced and white-breasted eider, dark scoter and red-breasted merganser, whose bills are actually redder than their breasts. Summer, by contrast, is for the seals, who come ashore both to mate and to moult. If you are quiet and keep a reasonable distance, the sandbanks from Shelly Point seawards are a good place to observe common seals in their scores, doing what comes naturally.

349. TENTSMUIR FOREST, FIFE

Maps: OS Explorer 371; Landranger 59

Travel: A91 from St Andrews to Guardbridge, A919 towards Dundee. In 2 miles, sharp right into Leuchars; in 100 yards, left up School Hill to T-junction; left along Pitlethie Road, and follow 'Kinshaldy', then 'Tentsmuir Forest' to car park (OS ref. 498242).

Nearest railway station: Leuchars Junction (4 miles)

There are nearly 4,000 acres of sandy littoral under the pine trees of Tentsmuir Forest, and about half as much exposed as sand dunes along the fringes of the great blunt nose of a peninsula that pushes east between the Eden Estuary (see above) and the Firth of Tay. These large blocks of Forestry Commission conifers can seem thoroughly tame in their dark conformity and stillness. Not in the case of Tentsmuir Forest, however, where roe deer move

Tentsmuir Forest

among the slim Corsican pine trunks and red squirrels bounce through the wheel-spoke branches of Scots pines. Crossbills forage for seeds, their hooked beaks askew for the precise angle of leverage they need to extract kernel from pine cone.

Emerging from among the corduroy battalions, you find yourself in a wide world of dunes shaggy with marram grass and bright with pink of centaury, purple-blue of milk vetch and deep mauve of northern marsh orchid. Willow and alder scrub grows here around pools which fill and dry out in the dune slack hollows. Ragwort and rosebay willowherb show where the sand has been disturbed and has then resettled. The beautiful common blue butterfly makes a summer appearance, and there are usually seals to admire as they lie like exhausted nude bathers on sandbanks down on the southern point of the peninsula where it shades round into the Eden Estuary.

Out here on the peninsula shore you look back to see streams carving miniature canyons in the sands, and beyond them the forest hanging on the western skyline like a black wave about to break into the sea.

350. CASTELL GLOUM (CASTLE CAMPBELL), CLACKMANNANSHIRE

Maps: OS Explorer 366; Landranger 58

Travel: From M80 Junction 10 or M90 Junction 6, A91 to park in the town centre of Dollar. From the clock tower (OS ref. 963979) turn north up West Burnside and follow 'Dollar Glen' signs through Dollar Glen to reach Castell Gloum (Castle Campbell) – 962993.

NB: Parts of the path through Dollar Glen are steep and can be vertiginous.

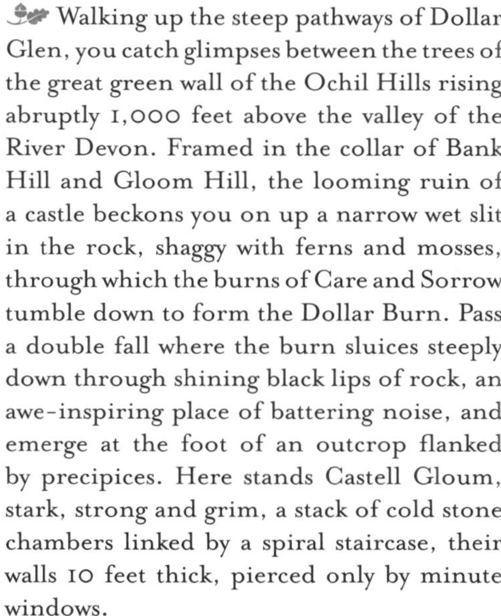

Walking up the steep pathways of Dollar Glen, you catch glimpses between the trees of the great green wall of the Ochil Hills rising abruptly 1,000 feet above the valley of the River Devon. Framed in the collar of Bank Hill and Gloom Hill, the looming ruin of a castle beckons you on up a narrow wet slit in the rock, shaggy with ferns and mosses, through which the burns of Care and Sorrow tumble down to form the Dollar Burn. Pass a double fall where the burn sluices steeply down through shining black lips of rock, an awe-inspiring place of battering noise, and emerge at the foot of an outcrop flanked by precipices. Here stands Castell Gloum, stark, strong and grim, a stack of cold stone chambers linked by a spiral staircase, their walls 10 feet thick, pierced only by minute windows.

The stronghold was built in the mid fifteenth century by the Earl of Argyll, Colin Campbell, who changed its name to Castle Campbell to reflect his own style and consequence. Before then it was known as Castell Gloum or Castle Gloom – originally Castell Glamair, from the Gaelic/Norse word for a chasm. Legend has a better story, suggesting that the nickname was bestowed in bitterness by a long-term resident of the castle's dungeons. Round Castle Gloom flow Care and Sorrow, a trio of names so splendidly mournful that they might have been coined specifically to darken the reputation of the ruin on the rock.

During the seventeenth century Castell Gloum was a refuge for Covenanters (see pp. 375–6 and 373–4). During the Civil War the Marquis of Montrose attacked the castle in the name of King Charles I. Failing to take it, he burned and ravaged the surrounding countryside instead. The stronghold was finally destroyed in 1654 during a raid by the Macleans, supporters of the Parliamentary cause; they fired it with burning arrows while the inhabitants were out looking for food. A century later it was a ruin.

Castell Gloum was mourned in an elegy by Carolina Oliphant, Baroness Nairne, a contemporary of Robert Burns (though she long outlived him) and a fine heroic poet:

Oh! Castell Gloom! thy strength is gane,
The green grass o'er thee growin',
On hill of Care thou art alone,
The Sorrow round thee flowin'!

Oh! Castell Gloom! on thy fair wa's
Nae banners now are streamin';
The howlit flits amang the ha's,
And wild birds there are screamin'.

351. LOCH ARDINNING, EAST DUNBARTONSHIRE

Maps: OS Explorer 348; Landranger 64

Travel: A81 north from central Glasgow towards Strathblane. 1 mile before Strathblane, parking lay-bys on both sides of road (OS ref. 563779). Follow numbered Nature Trail through the reserve on a surfaced path, wheelchair- and pushchair-friendly.

Nearest railway station: Milngavie (3 miles)

Loch Ardinning lies beside the A81 main road from Glasgow into the Trossachs. At first glance this Scottish Wildlife Trust Nature Reserve does not look like much of a candidate for a wild place. Traffic rushes by on the road, and the wheelchair-friendly tarmac path through the reserve has a suburban air. But once away from the road the noise of the cars and lorries quickly fades, and you find yourself in a closed world of dripping woodland, thick moor and rushy, sedgy loch.

In the sodden soils beside the loch edge grow the frothy pink-and-white flower heads of bogbean and the orange spikes of bog asphodel, along with the narrow leaves and ruddy-coloured shoots of bog myrtle.

The path runs on, screened from the loch by willows and alders, with dense purple heather moorland colonizing an old quarry and spreading up across the shoulder of the hill. Buttery yellow marsh marigolds dot the margins of the loch in spring, and bluebells grow in the shade of the trees. Later on, the pale blotched spikes of common spotted orchids rise from the grass. It's a rich palette of colours from spring to autumn, while in hard winters the shallow loch freezes over and every dried bulrush head and sedge clump is outlined whitely in frost.

Towards the bottom end of the loch the reeds and rushes peter out and Loch Ardinning is seen through gaps in the trees as an open stretch of water where tufted duck sail and dragonflies dart close to the shore. The trail loops back from here across moorland where blueberries vie for space with heather; their blue-black berries burst in the mouth in autumn to release a stab of flavour half sharp and half sweet. Walking here, with gleams of the loch below, it seems astonishing that the busy road lies only a few minutes' walk away.

352. DUMGOYNE, CAMPSIE FELLS, STIRLINGSHIRE

Maps: OS Explorer 348; Landranger 64

Travel: A81 north from central Glasgow to Strathblane; on towards Killearn. In 3 miles, park in lay-by on left, opposite buildings of Glengoyne Distillery (OS ref. 527828). Cross road (with care!); walk up gravel track beside cottages for ½ mile. Just before Blaircar Cottage, bear right through gate, then left through trees and on across grass towards Dumgoyne Hill. Cross two stiles and climb steeply to summit (541828). Continue east-north-east for 2 miles, gaining 500 feet more, to Earl's Seat (570838); or return same way.

The Campsie Fells lie just 10 miles due north of Glasgow, so it is surprising that they are not packed to the bulwarks with city folk out for a jaunt in the countryside. It is probably their steepness that saves them from being overrun. From the south and west they present a high green wall of seemingly breakneck slopes, interspersed with horizontal bands of purple rock that fall to impressive cliffs and screes – not strolling country at first glance. Once you are up there, on the undulating plateau that forms the heart of the Campsies, you find it's far less hard work than it appears from down below. Here is a circular tract

Dumgoyne, Campsie Fells

of high country some 7 miles from east to west and from north to south, wonderful to explore early or late in the day when you're almost guaranteed to have rocks, ravens and mountain flowers to yourself. But first you have to get up there.

A splendid but steep way into the Campsie Fells starts on the A81 from Glengoyne malt whisky distillery, whose sweetly pungent smell scents the air as you climb gently on a gravel track through coniferous forestry and then through woods of sycamore and oak, where the tree line falls away. Ahead rears the big crook-backed lump of Dumgoyne, a plug of hard volcanic matter left behind after the infinitely gradual erosion of its parent volcano. The green hill and its purple-grey cliffs and outcrops dominate the entire skyline, with the clear scar of the path to the summit rising steeply up the shoulder.

It is a breathless half-hour to the crest of Dumgoyne. The footfalls of millions of walkers have trodden steps in the tussocky grass of the slope, and up these you plod. Springs bursting out of the flanks of the hill form wet slicks of rushy bog, in which grow the orange spikes of bog asphodel and the daisy-like white composite flowers of sneezewort (an ancient specific against colds and flu). Further up the slope lie pale purple cushions of wild thyme, and the delicate blue trumpets of harebells.

Nearing the top you can bear left on to a narrow sheep track under cliffs, to curve clockwise around the dome of Dumgoyne; or continue up the steep and effortful path to the summit at 1,400 feet. From here there's a fine prospect east and north, over hill crests rounded, table-shaped or beast-backed, between Garloch Hill and the enjoyably named Clachertyfarlie Knowes (say it over to yourself; it's in jig time), to the high head and buttressing cliffs of Earl's Seat, at 1,896 feet the summit of the Campsie Fells.

353. FLANDERS MOSS, STIRLINGSHIRE

Maps: OS Explorer 365; Landranger 57

Travel: A81 from Aberfoyle towards Callander; in 3½ miles, right at Port of Menteith on B8034 for 3 miles to Dykehead. Left here for 1 mile to Ballangrew; park in farmyard (OS ref. 611985) and follow track out on to Flanders Moss.

Much of Flanders Moss is agricultural land of vast hay meadows interspersed with wet wood of alder and willow carr. The lumpy profile of the Trossach Hills stands to the north, while on the southern skyline run the sharp cliffs and bluffs of the Gargunnock and Fintry hills. The Moss itself is hemmed in, a saucer of ground in whose heart lies a great domed plateau of raised bog, the largest unbroken expanse of such bog in Britain, over 2,000 acres of sphagnum mosses, sodden peat and bright bogland flowers.

Raised bogs tend to occur in such bowl-like confines, where the water that constantly pours and trickles into the site from surrounding hills cannot find a way out, and stays to feed and swell the ever-absorbent sphagnum moss. Plants of the raised bog that you'll find here include white beak-sedge, with tight bursts of white flowers, insect-eating sundew, bog rosemary with its beautiful pink bells, and the cranberry, whose pink flowers give way to crimson berries that add a splash of colour in autumn. Heather blankets some of the

Flanders Moss

dry sections of Flanders Moss, while in the wetter parts the tiny ruddy-coloured catkins of bog myrtle in spring give way to the tall red spears of bog asphodel that push out an orange star flower for summer. It is the bog myrtle that acts as the food plant of the grey-and-yellow caterpillar of the Rannoch brindled beauty, a rather rare and very remarkable moth whose adult males possess handsome fern-like antennae and smoky grey wings, but whose females go wingless and resemble large furry beetles – once seen, never forgotten.

354. KILMARTIN GLEN, ARGYLL & BUTE

Maps: OS Explorer 358; Landranger 55

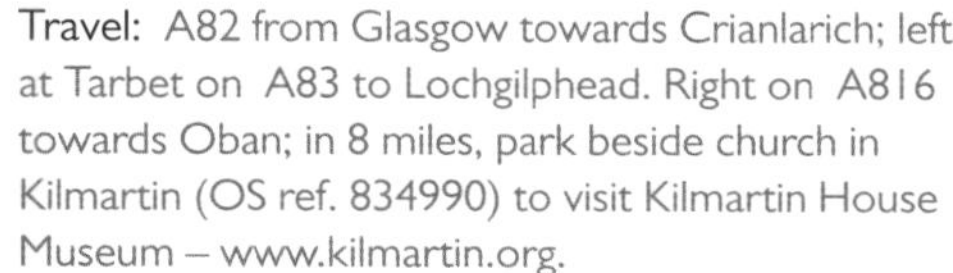

Travel: A82 from Glasgow towards Crianlarich; left at Tarbet on A83 to Lochgilphead. Right on A816 towards Oban; in 8 miles, park beside church in Kilmartin (OS ref. 834990) to visit Kilmartin House Museum – www.kilmartin.org.

For Nether Largie South cairn (828979), Temple Wood stone circle (826978) and Ri Cruin cairn (825971): return south from Kilmartin along A816, in 2/3 mile turn right ('Slockavulin'), and the three sites are marked off this road.

For Dunadd Fort, continue south along A816 for 3½ miles; Dunadd is signed to right. Park in car park by Dunadd farm and climb to summit (837936).

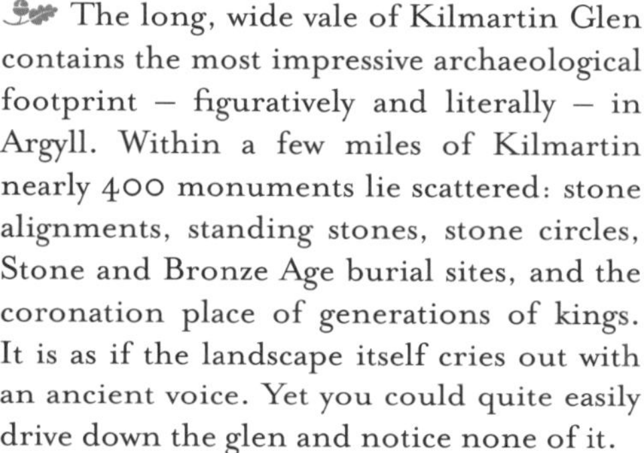

The long, wide vale of Kilmartin Glen contains the most impressive archaeological footprint – figuratively and literally – in Argyll. Within a few miles of Kilmartin nearly 400 monuments lie scattered: stone alignments, standing stones, stone circles, Stone and Bronze Age burial sites, and the coronation place of generations of kings. It is as if the landscape itself cries out with an ancient voice. Yet you could quite easily drive down the glen and notice none of it.

To help you interpret what you see on the ground, call into Kilmartin House Museum and browse the excellent displays that bring to life the prehistoric culture of this remarkable site, a landscape of continuous human engagement over 10,000 years. These people shot wild boar and red deer with beautiful little white flint arrowheads set with deadly barbs, and cleaned the skins with

scrapers made of the animals' own bones. They worked shale into necklace rings, polished until they glowed. The clay beakers and bowls they embellished with horseshoe and dogtooth designs might have come from the kiln of a modern artist-potter. They incised chosen rocks with circles, sunbursts, cup-and-ring dimples, ram's-horn spirals. When they died they were buried in cists, little lidded stone boxes that held their ashes, within great cairns hundreds of feet long, ships of death in which to voyage beyond this world.

The big cairn of Nether Largie South, some 5,000 years old, lies in a meadow, a big stone burial chamber submerged in a sea of millions of pebbles. Stone slabs flank the entrance and block off the far end; the roof is a line of huge slabs. Inside, more great kerbstones form the walls of the deep communal burial pit. Once there were four internal compartments, but their walls are long gone. Bowls and burned bones were excavated here. A couple of hundred yards off, the Temple Wood monument of thirteen standing stones encircles a square, box-like cist marooned in another great lake of pebbles. Half a mile to the south a grove of sycamores shelters the impressive chambered tomb of Ri Cruin, built perhaps 1,000 years later than Nether Largie South and used for individual burials in separate cists. It, too, lies in a vast mound of pebbles, mossy and green. In the centre a huge stone slab faces a kind of courtyard, while at the south end a slit of cist is open to the light so that you can peer down below the slab roof and make out carvings in the wall shaped like the blades of bronze axes.

These monuments were raised long before recorded history. The most evocative of all is the youngest, lying south of Kilmartin Glen itself, in the wide floodplain of the River Add known as Mòine Mhór, the Great Moss. The first Scots came to Mòine Mhór from Ireland around the turn of the sixth century AD to found the Kingdom of Dalriada. If you climb to the summit of the knoll of Dunadd, at the edge of the Great Moss, you will find the symbols of kingship they cut into the rocks there – the outline of a foot; a bowl-shaped indentation to symbolize the washing of kingly feet; a great humpbacked boar, the sign of royal lineage. From Dunadd summit the newly crowned rulers of the Dalriadic Kingdom could survey hills, marshes and sea as far as the blue hills of the Isle of Jura, then set their foot into the coronation footmark that faced east towards the rising sun.

355. BEN LOMOND, STIRLINGSHIRE

Maps: OS Explorer 364; Landranger 56

Travel: A82 from Glasgow towards Crianlarich; at foot of Loch Lomond, right in Alexandria on A811 for 8 miles to bear left on B858 into Drymen. B837 to Balmaha; minor road up east shore of Loch Lomond for 6 miles to pass Rowardennan Hotel (OS ref. 360983) and park in National Trust for Scotland car park just beyond. Continue along lochside road; in 1/3 mile fork right by entrance to Youth Hostel; pass NTS centre on right, then Ben Lomond Cottage. Cross stream just beyond cottage, and turn immediately right (360995) – before fork in road) up left bank of stream on narrow path through trees. Meet fence on your right and follow it north to pass below and left of Tom an Fhithich (361012). Climb on up zigzag track over Ptarmigan (358022) and follow clear ridge path round to right (north-east). At 363031 bear

Loch Lomond

right to climb some 600 feet up three rock 'steps' to summit of Ben Lomond (367028). Descend by obvious southward track, back to Rowardennan.

NB: This is a long and in parts strenuous circuit of 7 miles with an ascent of 3,192 feet. Ben Lomond is a serious mountain, and this 'back way' ascent is trickier in mist than the 'tourist ascent' route by which you descend.

Ben Lomond is the Glaswegian's Munro, a shapely 3,000-footer that beckons seductively across Loch Lomond to drivers on the Fort William road. There is a 'tourist path', broad and clear, that ascends the long, gently rising south ridge of the mountain, delivering walkers quite easily to the summit. The temptation for hillwalkers who climb and descend Ben Lomond this way on a lovely sunny day is to dismiss the mountain as tame. As with so many wild places, however, the character of Ben Lomond alters dramatically as the weather worsens. What appears a smiling green hill in sunshine seems to swell and darken when rain and wind are pushing across Loch Lomond.

A great way to enjoy a fine day and still taste the wilder side of Ben Lomond is to take the much steeper and more uneven path that ascends the mountain a mile to the west of the main route. You climb from the lochside through bracken and broom on hill slopes that are earmarked for replanting with native woodland. This is part of a massively ambitious scheme that will one day see the mountainsides between Loch Lomond and the Trossachs reclothed in the oak, birch, rowan, ash and alder that have been felled and grazed to near extinction over past centuries.

The zigzag path goes steeply up the flank of Tom an Fhithich, the Mound of the Ravens. Across slopes bright with harebells and shocking-pink lousewort you climb, looking across the ever-broadening water to the hooked peak known as the Cobbler. Over the rock-scabbed head of Ptarmigan knoll at 2,400 feet, where a sheen of mica makes the schist gleam salmon-pink and silky grey; round past a string of lonely dark lochans to cross the saddle of Bealach Buidhe, the Yellow Pass, and finally the 600-foot ascent of three sharp rock 'steps' to the crown of the mountain at 3,192 feet.

After the climb, the 100-mile view round the compass: the Campsie Fells in the south-east (see pp. 387–8), with the Ochils beyond them running down to the Firth of Forth and the Pentland Hills; the 'Highlands-in-miniature' of the Trossachs to the east with the peaks around Ben Lawers (see pp. 396–7) further away; 3,852-foot Ben More in the north overlooking Crianlarich and the Road to the Isles; out west a sea of mountains parting to reveal the Inner Hebrides and the

Paps of Jura (see p. 436). And to the south, in front of you all the way during your descent, the magnificent prospect of Loch Lomond, spattered with islets, spreadeagled in all its glory for your admiration.

356. FALLS OF FALLOCH, ARGYLL & BUTE

Maps: OS Explorer 364; Landranger 50

Travel: A82 from Glasgow past Loch Lomond towards Crianlarich; 2½ miles north of Inverarnan, brown Falls of Falloch sign points right into car park (OS ref. 334207). Follow footpath to Falls of Falloch (338208).

Nearest railway stations: Ardlui or Crianlarich (4 miles, either)

The path to the Falls of Falloch starts from a picnic place on the road from Loch Lomond to Crianlarich, so modestly placed among its screening trees that most motorists pass it by without registering its presence. So these splendid rapids and falls of the River Falloch, which would otherwise be crowded, retain their dignity. They are best visited very early or late in the day when mist is gathering or dispersing, or in a heavy frost or after snowfall, when the charging passage of the river along the narrow gorge of rapids and over its rock staircase becomes a striking drama of turbulent black against motionless white. The main fall tumbles in a natural rock amphitheatre, magnifying the roar of the river. Visiting in summer when the Falloch runs low, only the quern-like hollows in the rock pavements far above the level of the water, their basin bottoms spread with pebbles, tell you of the scouring power and fury of the river.

Dorothy Wordsworth came here with her beloved brother, William, and their great friend Samuel Taylor Coleridge in September, 1803. It must have been a wet summer, because Dorothy recorded in *Recollections of a Tour made in Scotland* how overwhelming she found the noise of the falls, even from her perch on the mountainside high above:

Falls of Falloch

> *The ascent was very laborious, being frequently almost perpendicular. It was one of those moments which I could not easily forget ... being at a great height on the mountain we sate down, and heard, as*

if from the heart of the earth, the sound of torrents ascending out of the long hollow glen. To the eye all was motionless, a perfect stillness. The noise of the waters did not appear to come from this way or that, from any particular quarter, it was everywhere, almost, one might say, as if exhaled through the whole surface of the green earth. Glenfalloch, Coleridge has since told me, signifies the Hidden Vale; but William says, if we were to name it from our recollections of that time, we should call it the Vale of Awful Sound.

357. RANNOCH MOOR, HIGHLAND

Maps: OS Explorer 385; Landranger 41, 42

Travel: A82 Tyndrum to Ballachulish passes over Rannoch Moor. A walk to Rannoch station (11 miles) from Corrour station (OS ref. 355664): cross railway line and take the rough road marked 'Tulloch Station 15 m'. In 1¼ miles, opposite Youth Hostel (371671) on Loch Ossian, bear right off road; immediately left (372669) on to grassy track eastward. Pass Meal na Lice on your right, keeping parallel with and above lochside road. After 1½ miles track swings south (marked 'Peter's Rock' on the map – 393670).

Continue south, then south-west on clearly defined track, passing ruin of Corrour Old Lodge after 4½ miles (408648) and crossing Allt Eigheach on footbridge after 7½ miles (435604). In another 1¾ miles, meet B846 road by Loch Eigheach (447578); turn right for Rannoch station (423579).

Nearest railway station: Corrour

Corrour is the remotest railway station in Scotland, marooned below the mountains at the northern edge of Rannoch Moor, 10 miles at least from the nearest tarmac road. This is one of the wildest and most forbidding places in the country. Striking east across Rannoch Moor you are greeted by a truly bleak scene: the rolling empty moor, bedded on peat up to 20 feet thick, stripped hundreds of years ago of the great Wood of Caledon, edged with inhospitable mountains and spattered with ragged lochs. The fugitives David Balfour and Alan Breck Stewart, fleeing from the redcoats, were trapped on Rannoch Moor by their creator, Robert Louis Stevenson, in *Kidnapped*, and found it a desolate place:

The mist rose and died away, and showed us that country lying as waste as the sea; only the moorfowl and the peewees crying upon it, and far over to the east, a herd of deer, moving like dots. Much of it was red with heather; much of the rest broken up with bogs and hags and peaty pools; some had been burnt black in a heath fire; and in another place there was quite a forest of dead firs, standing like skeletons. A wearier-looking desert man never saw …

Walkers on the West Highland Way learn a hard lesson about Rannoch Moor's notoriously fickle mists. So did the party of engineering experts who set out in January 1889 to walk the 40 miles from Spean Bridge to Inveroran across the moor. They became separated in a pea-souper that suddenly descended. Benighted and lost, with one of the party helpless with exhaustion, they had to be rescued. 'An inconceivable solitude,' wrote Dr John MacCulloch in 1811, 'a dreary and joyless land of bogs, a land of desolation and grey darkness.' The authors of the West Highland Way official guide, Bob Aitken and Roger Smith, remark drily of Rannoch Moor: 'In rain or snow with low cloud driving before a gale, it tends to promote the conviction that Hell need not be hot.'

358. GLENCOE, HIGHLAND

Maps: OS Explorer 384; Landranger 41

Travel: A82 from Glasgow to Fort William passes through Glencoe.

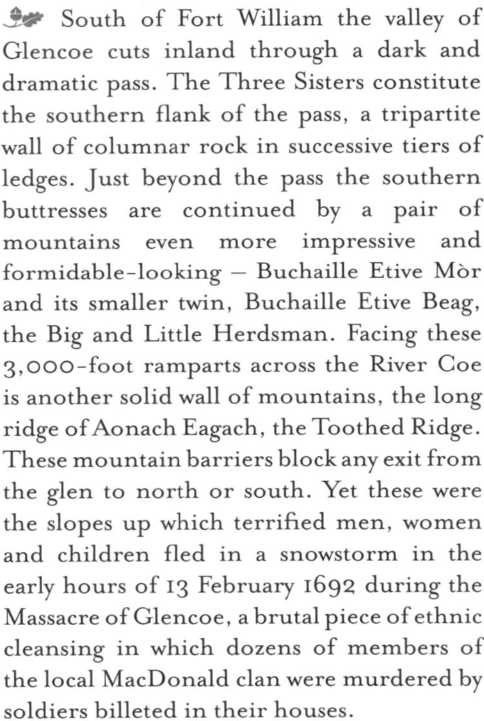

South of Fort William the valley of Glencoe cuts inland through a dark and dramatic pass. The Three Sisters constitute the southern flank of the pass, a tripartite wall of columnar rock in successive tiers of ledges. Just beyond the pass the southern buttresses are continued by a pair of mountains even more impressive and formidable-looking – Buchaille Etive Mòr and its smaller twin, Buchaille Etive Beag, the Big and Little Herdsman. Facing these 3,000-foot ramparts across the River Coe is another solid wall of mountains, the long ridge of Aonach Eagach, the Toothed Ridge. These mountain barriers block any exit from the glen to north or south. Yet these were the slopes up which terrified men, women and children fled in a snowstorm in the early hours of 13 February 1692 during the Massacre of Glencoe, a brutal piece of ethnic cleansing in which dozens of members of the local MacDonald clan were murdered by soldiers billeted in their houses.

The MacDonalds of Glencoe were no angels. These Catholic cattle thieves were as ready to raid and slaughter as the next Highland clan, and they had made a special point of robbing and killing the Campbells of Glenlyon, their long-term enemies. The cattle they stole were customarily hidden in Allt Coire Gabhail, the Hollow of Capture, a hidden refuge in a cleft between two of the Three Sisters. But since 1688 a new Protestant power had occupied the throne of Britain, in the shape of King William and Queen Mary of Orange. A new social order was pushing southern influence rapidly north of the Border, and such people as made up this small MacDonald community were seen by the authorities as backward, incorrigible and barbaric, to be brought to heel as savagely as was expedient. The Highland chiefs were ordered to swear an oath of allegiance to the new monarchs, with a deadline of 31 December 1691. Alastair MacDonald, 12th Chief of Glencoe, was late setting out for Fort William, and when he arrived a magistrate could not be found to hear his formal submission to the Crown. There was a delay in sending in the papers, finally sworn at Inveraray and in any case soon 'mislaid' by the authorities. It all added up to a perfect excuse to act rigorously against the troublesome, insolent men of Glencoe.

Glencoe

Although the brooding Pass of Glencoe with its tremendous lowering overhangs and crags is exactly the place a film company would choose for a setting, the massacre actually took place a little further west, where the landscape softens slightly towards the coast at Loch Leven, in and around the townships – hamlets, really – of Achnacone, Inverrigan, Carnoch, Invercoe, and also at Achtriachtan by the loch just west of the Three Sisters. The officer charged with carrying out the action, Captain Robert Campbell of Glenlyon, had had his men billeted in the Glencoe townships for a fortnight, living in the houses of the MacDonalds as their guests. A Highlander himself, Glenlyon knew how unbreakable were the rules of hospitality he was about to violate, even though the action would be against a clan he had reason to fear and hate. But the orders he received on behalf of King William on 12 February 1692 were crystal clear: 'They must all be slaughtered ... put all to the sword under seventy ... have a special care that the old fox and his cubs do upon no account escape your hands.'

At 5 a.m. the next day, at the height of a terrible blizzard, the soldiers attacked their sleeping hosts, killing thirty-eight out of about 300 – men, women and children, old and young, including the 'old fox', Alastair MacDonald. The survivors jumped half-naked from their beds and ran for their lives up the glen. Most of them made the 300-foot climb up to the refuge of Allt Coire Gabhail. When the soldiers marched away the next morning, the MacDonalds came down out of hiding to find dead bodies and burned houses all through the snow-choked glen.

The old fox's cubs did in fact survive the massacre. But the example made of the MacDonalds shocked other reluctant oath-takers into immediate obedience. Later the MacDonalds were allowed to return and live in Glencoe once more. There was a Commission of Inquiry which rapped a few knuckles. But the massacre had delivered a mortal wound to the Highland way of life in general, its death finally to be confirmed some forty years later in the awful aftermath of the Battle of Culloden (see pp. 411–13). The independent, cattle-raiding society of the clans was finished, and would never return.

359. BEN NEVIS, HIGHLAND

Maps: OS Explorer 392; Landranger 41

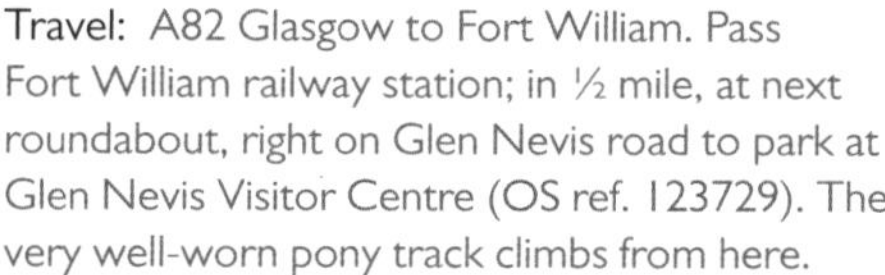
Travel: A82 Glasgow to Fort William. Pass Fort William railway station; in ½ mile, at next roundabout, right on Glen Nevis road to park at Glen Nevis Visitor Centre (OS ref. 123729). The very well-worn pony track climbs from here.

NB: This is a demanding ascent in terms of stamina – allow 6–8 hours or more to the summit and back, and wear weatherproof clothes and hillwalking boots.

Information: Get advice and weather forecast at: www.bennevisweather.co.uk/visitor_centre.asp

Nearest railway station: Fort William (2 miles)

At 4,406 feet Ben Nevis is the highest peak in Britain. It may be a minnow compared with Himalayan summits, but it possesses dignity, grandeur and a very individual character. Many of Britain's mountains are shapelier, some are more dramatic, but this senior partner of the UK's Big Three Peaks (Snowdon and Scafell Pike – see pp. 192–3 and 323–4 – are the other two) has a certain something, in addition to its surveyed superiority in height. This is the summit everyone wants to reach, to savour the thrill of being at the highest point in Britain.

Ben Nevis is a friendly, anyone-can-climb-it mountain, but it bites back hard at carelessness or disrespect. Nearly half a million people visit every year, about 100,000 set out to climb it, and dozens have to be rescued from its slopes and gullies because they have underestimated just how wild Britain's highest mountain can get. Ben Nevis has a well-earned reputation for sudden storms. Episodes of rain, low cloud, hill mist or strong winds are almost guaranteed on an ascent, and the pony-track path, the only viable route to the summit for non-mountaineers, can be snowed up until June. So set out from the Glen Nevis Visitor Centre knowing that you may meet almost any conditions between starting at sea level and reaching the top of the mountain.

The pony track, pitched with stones, is rather patronizingly known as the 'tourist path'. There is nothing technically difficult or demanding about it, but it eats up energy as you gain height. Hill torrents tumble over the path and crash on down out of sight. Out in the distance mountain peaks appear in every direction like the frozen waves of a dun-coloured sea. At 1,800 feet you skirt Lochan Meall an t-Suidhe ('little lake of the rounded hill where you rest'), generally known, somewhat optimistically, as the Halfway Loch. Here commences the second and stiffer part of the climb, crunching interminably back and forth up the elbows of track called the Zigzags. If you are lucky the mist parts, revealing glorious blue ridges and peaks far and near. In wind and driving mist, though, the full potential of the mountain for mischief is realized.

You will reach the summit with relief – perhaps with a sense of anticlimax, too, that the peak itself is not actually peak-shaped, but unrolls as a rocky plateau. It's always cold and generally snowy. An ark-shaped shelter built atop a 20-foot stone pedestal vividly demonstrates how deep the snow and frost can lie up here in winter. Hundreds may be on the summit to share this moment with you, or you may have the whole rocky wilderness to yourself. The view to all quarters is of range upon range of beautiful mountains, ink-shadowed valleys and intensely blue lochs. You stand and gaze, a tiny presence on the roof of Britain.

360. BEN LAWERS, PERTH & KINROSS

Maps: OS Explorer 378; Landranger 51

Travel: A9 from Dunkeld towards Pitlochry; in 8 miles, left on A827 through Aberfeldy and Kenmore. In another 12 miles, right up minor road towards Bridge of Balgie and Innerwick; in 1¾ miles, park on right at Ben Lawers Visitor Centre (OS ref. 610377) and follow the nature trail up to the shielings in Coire Odhar (614393).

Ben Lawers is upside down. The presence of the many wonderful arctic-alpine flowers that give this great rugged hump of a mountain its special character is explained by the fact that the oldest rocks, the lime-rich Ben Lawers schists, are on top, and the youngest, the marbles and limestones, are underneath – all thanks to a giant upheaval some 400 million years ago, which tipped the whole area on its head. From a lower region of mica schist studded with red crystals of garnet, on which acid bog has developed, you move up to higher levels of older rocks. These calcareous schists are the ones on which arctic-alpine plants thrive best, and as you climb higher up the mountain you find more and more of these delicate, colourful flowers, which have clung on here in the high grassland since they

arrived in the post-Ice Age era – mountain pansy and cerulean Alpine gentian, rock speedwell with its tiny scarlet eye in a blue face, springy cushions of yellow cyphel.

Ben Lawers has been thoroughly grazed for many centuries, first by cattle taken up to the high slopes in summer, and then by sheep from the eighteenth century, as the traditional Highland life was coming to an end. These grazing regimes have left a unique flora – acid, nutrient-poor grassland lower down with plants such as tormentil and frothy white heath bedstraw, birchwoods and taller flowers like lady's mantle and globeflower on ledges in the cliffs where nibbling teeth could not reach them; then mountain willow scrub, a rare habitat in Britain, and places where water rich in nutrients courses down to nourish beautiful white Scottish asphodel, sedges and yellow saxifrage with its pepper-red spray of sepals.

The National Trust for Scotland has established a big exclosure, or fenced-off area, on the mountainside around the Burn of Edramucky ('between the two streams where pigs are found') just above the Visitor Centre, and the nature trail around this grazing-free zone runs through beds and banks of exuberant flowering plants. Here are clusters of tiny eyebright, mats of pungent wild thyme, lemon-scented fern that you can pinch to release its sharp citrus smell, yellow saxifrage in large clumps among the rocks of the stream.

High on the hillside above, you come to Coire Odhar, the Yellow Hollow, watered by the Edramucky Burn and sheltered by the mountain, where the people would drive their cattle to summer pasture. The ruins of the sheilings, or summer houses built of mountain stones, lie deeply sunk in bracken and moss, their hearths and doorways still to be made out in the tumble of stone walls. Excavations have shown that these rough houses were in use from the fifteenth century onwards; but there is evidence in the shape of flint tools and ancient charcoal to suggest that the Yellow Hollow was occupied as far back as 7000 BC, by the very first hunter-gatherers to settle in Scotland after the glaciers had receded and the arctic-alpine flowers had begun to bloom.

361. MEIGLE PICTISH STONES, PERTH & KINROSS

Maps: OS Explorer 381; Landranger 53

Travel: From M90 Junction 11, A85 towards Perth. Do not cross bridge into town centre, but continue on A93 ('Blairgowrie'), forking right in 200 yards on A94 Forfar road through Scone and Coupar Angus to Meigle. Park near church (OS ref. 287445). Vanora's Mound is on north side of church. Wicket gate in south-west corner of churchyard leads to Meigle Museum (brown signs from village street).

This wild place is confined within four walls, in the somewhat antiseptic surroundings of a purpose-built, well-lit, clean and modern museum. But once you are absorbed in Meigle Museum's remarkable collection of Pictish carved stones, the wildest thickets of human imagination entangle you so mightily that it is a shock to step out into the 'real', contemporary world once more.

What is now the modest, middle-of-nowhere village of Meigle was highly important sacred and secular ground in the heyday of the Pictish civilization (see pp. 400–401) some 1,300 years ago. These warlike, religious-minded descendants of the Iron Age Scots had virtually no written language; instead, they recorded their mythologies and histories in vigorous, wildly expressive carvings in stone. One wonders whether news or even examples of Pictish carvings could have made their way south as far as the Welsh borders during the twelfth century, because the work of the Herefordshire School of Sculpture (see pp. 225–6 and 227–8) carries just the same wildness, the same importation of pagan strangeness, into Christian symbolism. Before exposure to Christianity around AD 600, Pictish and Celtic religious belief had a lot in common, siting gods in rivers and trees, investing both the spirit and the natural world with a startling capacity for violence. The pictographs on the stones set up in Meigle, carved between AD 550 and 850 as Christianity became absorbed by Pictish culture, tell of a fierce fighting society in a world thronged with savage animals and heavily armoured foes. Whether these slabs of pink local sandstone were grave-markers or boundary indicators, or served some other purpose, no one knows. A disastrous battle against Viking invaders in AD 839 saw much of the Pictish ruling class wiped out; only four years later the King of Dalriada (see pp. 389–90) grabbed the Pictish throne and lands to form the new amalgamated Kingdom of Alba. The culture, language and religion of the Picts faded away.

The tallest stone in the collection is a 10-

foot-high memorial to Vanora, a Pictish version of Queen Guinevere, who was torn to death by wild animals on the order of King Arthur after she had betrayed him with the dastardly Mordred. Vanora herself, according to tradition, lies under a grassy mound in Meigle churchyard; the memorial slab shows her being clawed and bitten by four lions with heavy manes. Crosses feature on many of the stones, intricately interlaced; one in the form of a Tree of Life is flanked by a seahorse and an eel locked in combat, while a snarling dog holds a huge-headed boar at bay. Another wild boar chews the face off a fallen hunter. Mythic beasts abound: animals with elaborately curly tails pinned with brooch-like bars; a composite monster known as a manticore with a human face, leonine body and scorpion tail; and a creature unique to Pictish art with a long platypus beak and a great curly horn.

The vigour of these animal figures is echoed in those of warriors with aggressively jutting beards, sporting beaked helmets with brave plumes, riding prancing, caparisoned horses. A cloaked hunter hastens to the chase, spear in hand. As well as war and sudden death the Pictish world has room for love, too – of a strikingly orgiastic nature, if the four intertwined figures on one of the slabs are doing what they seem to be doing. Sex, strife, impatient journeying, terror in the wilderness, faithful hounds and fearsome, shadowy foes: the Pictish world of these marvellous works of art seems remarkably close to ours.

362. LOCH OF KINORDY, ANGUS

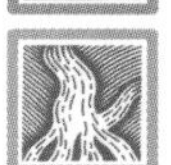
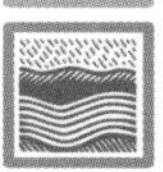

Maps: OS Explorer 381; Landranger 54

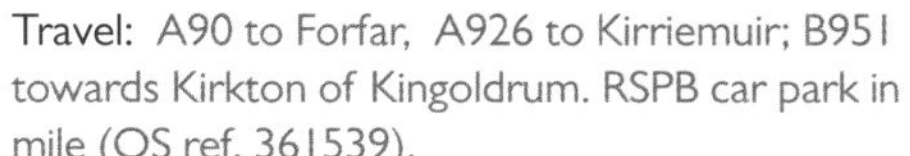

Travel: A90 to Forfar, A926 to Kirriemuir; B951 towards Kirkton of Kingoldrum. RSPB car park in 1 mile (OS ref. 361539).

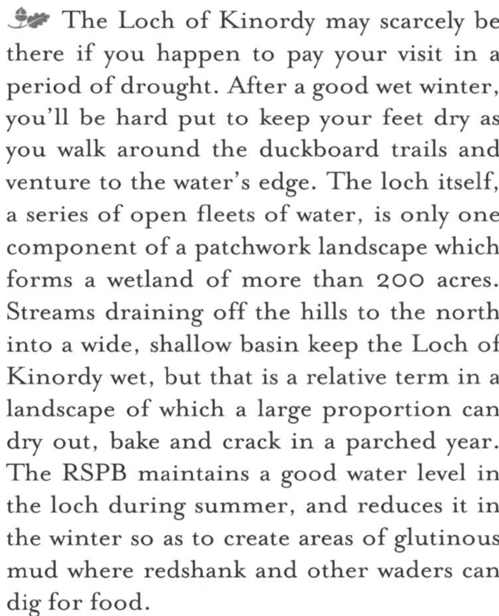

The Loch of Kinordy may scarcely be there if you happen to pay your visit in a period of drought. After a good wet winter, you'll be hard put to keep your feet dry as you walk around the duckboard trails and venture to the water's edge. The loch itself, a series of open fleets of water, is only one component of a patchwork landscape which forms a wetland of more than 200 acres. Streams draining off the hills to the north into a wide, shallow basin keep the Loch of Kinordy wet, but that is a relative term in a landscape of which a large proportion can dry out, bake and crack in a parched year. The RSPB maintains a good water level in the loch during summer, and reduces it in the winter so as to create areas of glutinous mud where redshank and other waders can dig for food.

In late spring the carr woodland and reed-beds shelter nesting sedge warblers, handsome little birds with marked white eyebrows and a song that explodes into an excited scribble of chuckles, whistles and exclamations, like a miniaturized starling. Summer sees the occasional dramatic visit by an osprey, a splendid fish eagle with white pate and breast that quarters the loch before descending and hitting the water, to fly off after a brief flurry with a fish dangling in the clutch of one foot. Pink-footed geese arrive in their thousands for winter, along with several duck species including goldeneye, wigeon and the dark-headed and creamy-breasted goosander, whose saw-edged bill grasps a fish just as securely as the osprey's claws.

I find this a fascinating place, with an atmosphere that changes day to day, perhaps best seen around dawn in early summer with warblers singing and the prospect of the thumping splash of an osprey to make you jump.

363. ABERLEMNO PICTISH STONES, ANGUS

Maps: OS Explorer 389; Landranger 54

Travel: A90 to Forfar, B9134 to Aberlemno. Turn right in village to find churchyard with stone (OS ref. 523556); roadside group is on right side of B9134, 300 yards further on (523559).

The idea of the Picts as a bunch of poison dwarves, with painted skin and bloodthirsty ways, does little justice to the people of the northern lands whose heyday coincided with the Dark Ages. 'Picts' was the collective name for a congeries of north-east Scottish tribes, farmers and horse-breeders by occupation, part pagan and part Christian by religion. Their language has been lost, but not their memories and dreams, for they carved fabulous beasts, lively depictions of human stories and a number of now indecipherable symbols into the surfaces of standing stones.

By the road just out of Aberlemno rises a tall slab carved with a richly decorated wheel cross whose arms are separated by four large bosses. On one side the shaft is flanked by a mass of interlacing which frames a pair of angels, their wings drooping and heads bent in conventional but touching gestures of sorrow. The reverse face shows a vigorous hunting scene, with men on horseback blowing long trumpets, and hounds leaping on to the backs of deer. Below the hunt a splendid centaur trots away with a great tree branch under his arm. The other stones are carved with symbols simple in execution but striking in effect – curly serpent shapes, two circles joined by a bar, zigzag flourishes, and what looks like a hand mirror and a comb, perhaps the trappings of priesthood.

The carved stone in Aberlemno churchyard is even more intriguing. The east face records one of the crucial episodes in Pictish history, the Battle of Nechtansmere on 20 May, AD 685. The Pictish alliance, long subservient to Northumbrian rule, had rebelled under their leader King Bruide, provoking the Northumbrian ruler King Ecgfrith to march north to crush them. The rival armies met at Dunnichen Moss, just east of modern-day Forfar, where Bruide and his foot-soldiers soon had the invaders trapped between Dunnichen Hill and the bog of Nechtansmere. Slaughter ensued, and the victorious Picts secured a breathing space in the succession of invasions of their territory. The sculptor shows the

Northumbrians on horseback with braided chin-beards, wearing shell-shaped helmets with elongated nose-guards. The long-haired Pictish warriors fight on foot with swords, shields and spears. In one panel a Northumbrian gallops his horse away in full flight, his round shield and short sword flying through the air as he hurls them aside in panic. The base of the slab shows the dying King Ecgfrith dropping his shield and crumpling backwards, while a death-raven darts forward to peck his throat out.

A civilization capable of producing a work of art such as this can hardly have been a primitive nest of barbarians.

364. SEATON CLIFFS, ANGUS

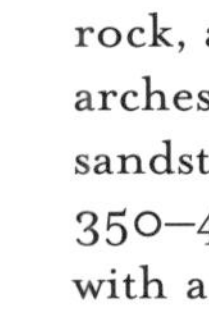

Maps: OS Explorer 382; Landranger 54

Travel: A90 to Dundee, A92 to Arbroath; park near harbour (OS ref. 642406). Continue on foot along Oldshorehead and Seagate, then promenade along Victoria Park to Whiting Ness (660412). From here follow Seaton Cliffs Nature Trail for 1½ miles to Carlingheugh Bay.

Nearest railway station: Arbroath

A short walk north from Arbroath offers the most spectacular section of weathered cliffs along the Angus coast. Seaton Cliffs are of red sandstone; but these coast ramparts, seen from out at sea as a formidably solid-looking wall of red rock, are in fact so soft that there are caves, arches, hollows and sea stacks. The old red sandstone that forms the cliffs, laid down 350–400 million years ago, is mingled with a conglomerate rock made of ancient pebbles stuck together; they were washed from far inland along a giant river delta that flowed through a lifeless desert.

On a fine day you will be able to see the tapering rocket shape of the Bell Rock lighthouse rising on the south-west horizon. The slim, sea-stained tower, built by the great lighthouse architect Robert Stevenson in 1807–11, appears to climb straight out of the sea. This is one of the most remote lighthouses in Britain, on one of the deadliest reefs. The seamen of the days of sail learned to fear the fierce storms of this coast, and it is those blasting North Sea gales and waves that have carved the outlandish features of Seaton Cliffs.

The Needle's E'e is a natural arch with a crack in its apex, part of the original fault that admitted the sea to gouge out a cave. Another example of a weakness exploited by the sea is the Mermaid's Kirk, an amphitheatre with a pebble floor that lies awash at high tide. Dickmont's Den is a great inlet bright with primroses in spring, the remnant of a sea cave whose roof eventually thinned to the point of collapse. Out on the shore stands the sea stack known as the Deil's Heid, a resting post for cormorants and guillemots, shaped like a bulging head with a crumpled, gurning 'face' rising from a bull neck that will one day be severed by the sea. Further along lies a headland with three distinctive hummocks, the Three Sisters; some know it as the Sphinx because of the leonine shape that weathering has given its many horizontal layers. Finally you skirt the wide scoop of Carlingheugh Bay and pass through the natural arch or elongated hole of the Dark Cave, a suitably outré conclusion.

365. MONTROSE BASIN, ANGUS

Maps: OS Explorer 382; Landranger 54

Travel: A90 to Brechin; A935 towards Montrose. In 5 miles bear right off road ('Bridge of Dun') past Mains of Dun Farm (OS ref. 669593); in 150 yards, park in car park on right (669591). Take green track opposite, walking below Mains of Dun, to join gravelled track. Follow it to cross embankment of disused railway (673590) and continue to pass 'Montrose Basin Local Nature Reserve' sign. In 200 yards, waymark post (675588) points left to Wigeon Hide (683590 – ½ mile) or forward to Shelduck Hide (676578 – ⅔ mile).

Infomation: Montrose Basin Wildlife Centre: www.swt.org.uk

Nearest railway station: Montrose (4 miles)

Walking the wide tidal inlet of Montrose Basin, your binoculars will grow red-hot with gazing at thousands upon thousands of wildfowl. At over 1,600 acres of mudflats, the basin's vast tidal inlet contains the muds in which live shellfish, worms, shrimps and snails by the uncountable million. The birds love it, either in the breeding and nesting seasons of spring and summer, the migration time of autumn when they make a refuelling stop here, or during the winter when northern ducks and geese come to spend the cold months close to an inexhaustible food supply.

It's not only birdwatchers who enjoy Montrose Basin. Anyone with a taste for big skies and melancholy will be captivated by this unfrequented area, so close to the ancient town of Montrose, yet unpolluted and with a lonely atmosphere all of its own.

Two well-sited hides give you the chance to observe all that's going on out on the mudflats – Wigeon Hide up on a 30-foot tower overlooking the marshes and the main basin, Shelduck Hide tucked into a bank on a creek. You're very likely to see eider duck, mute and whooper swans, curlew, redshank, and in winter clouds of wigeon and big flocks of pink-footed geese.

366. GLEN ESK, ANGUS

Maps: OS Explorer 395, 388; Landranger 44

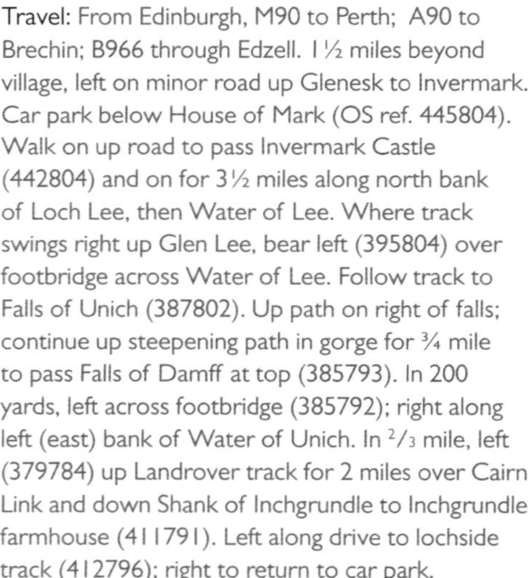

Travel: From Edinburgh, M90 to Perth; A90 to Brechin; B966 through Edzell. 1½ miles beyond village, left on minor road up Glenesk to Invermark. Car park below House of Mark (OS ref. 445804). Walk on up road to pass Invermark Castle (442804) and on for 3½ miles along north bank of Loch Lee, then Water of Lee. Where track swings right up Glen Lee, bear left (395804) over footbridge across Water of Lee. Follow track to Falls of Unich (387802). Up path on right of falls; continue up steepening path in gorge for ¾ mile to pass Falls of Damff at top (385793). In 200 yards, left across footbridge (385792); right along left (east) bank of Water of Unich. In ⅔ mile, left (379784) up Landrover track for 2 miles over Cairn Link and down Shank of Inchgrundle to Inchgrundle farmhouse (411791). Left along drive to lochside track (412796); right to return to car park.

They say that when God created the earth, He was so enchanted with the work that before He set it spinning into space He gave it a last loving pat. It was that celestial hand-print which formed the Glens of Angus. God's thumb marked out the River Tay, His four fingers the four glens of Isla, Prosen, Clova and Esk. As the poet John Angus expressed it:

Four fair green glens reach far into the west,
And of them all, the loveliest and best
Is Esk – Glen Esk, by loving gesture given;
God's little finger left the mark of heaven.

Glen Esk

The best way to admire God's handiwork is on a 10-mile ramble through the upper reaches of the delectable Glen Esk. First, though, the mark of wicked man, in the form of the gaunt ruin of Invermark Castle at the tail of Loch Lee. Jackdaws sail in and out of the windows of the fortified tower, built stark and strong in the bad old days of the 1520s when a Scots lord with any sense trusted neither foe nor friend. The front door of Invermark's grim stronghold is sited 15 feet above ground level. With the ladder pulled up and the squint windows manned, you could hope to sit out a siege until help arrived or frustration drove your enemy away.

Beyond castle and loch, splash across the Water of Lee and make for the Falls of Unich, a skein of white water tumbling out of a shadowed gorge below Craig Maskeldie. It marks the start of a 1,000-foot climb past pools and rapids, up and up on a zigzag path towards the lip of the cleft, passing rock ledges bright with yellow and purple saxifrage.

Up in the broad glen of the upper Unich you pass the rush and tumble of the Falls of Damff. Walking is squelchy. Tracks, rocks and open patches of moorland glitter with mica in sunshine. Away to the north the 3,000-foot crest of Mount Keen rises above all its sister peaks. Turn aside on a well-found track and follow it until it tips down the steep breast of the Shank of Inchgrundle. Just to the left curves the craggy corrie of Cairn Lick. At the foot of the cliffs lies the shadowed little lake of Carlochy, tucked away from all but hillwalkers' view on its high cushion of green glacial rubble, a jewel of a loch that – like so many other glories of the Scottish mountains – reveals its beauty only to those who venture on foot among the wide hills.

367. FOWLSHEUGH CLIFFS, ABERDEENSHIRE

Maps: OS Explorer 396; Landranger 45

Travel: A90 from Stonehaven towards Dundee; on southern outskirts of Stonehaven, left on A92 ('Montrose, Arbroath'). In 2½ miles, turn left (brown sign) to Crawton, and park just before start of Fowlsheugh Cliffs Reserve path (OS ref. 880798).

Fowlsheugh, 'the bird cliff', lives up exactly to its name. Here, just south of Dunnottar Castle (see pp. 404–5) the RSPB looks after a 2-mile run of magnificent red sandstone cliffs, deeply indented with sharp-edged bays and coves, their headlands rising 200 feet out of the sea. From puffin burrows in the thin clifftop turf among thrift and red campion, to kittiwake and fulmar nests on narrow cliff-face ledges, Fowlsheugh is alive with seabirds.

This is one of the largest seabird colonies

in Britain, an awe-inspiring spectacle and sound in early summer when the eggs are hatching and chicks are being reared by tens of thousands. The thin sandstone strata of the cliffs have been eaten by wind, rain, frost and waves into tiers of ledges, perfect for the construction of nests out of reach of predators. Though numbers fluctuate from year to year, there are generally 100,000 adult nesting birds at Fowlsheugh. About a tenth of these are kittiwakes, whose chicks can be seen squatting and shifting uncomfortably on their dusty, precarious-looking cracks of ledges. These youngsters with their short, rubbery black beaks, black neck rings and kohl-black eyes are guarded by mothers that open sharp yellow beaks to display scarlet throats as they warn off intruders, adding their screams to those of their eternally circling mates whose eerie cry echoes back from the red bowl of the cliffs.

Around 250 fulmars nest here, rearing their young on the higher ledges until September, by which time the kittiwakes and puffins are already gone to their wintering grounds further south. Fulmars enjoy a long lifespan in seabird terms – some can survive up to forty years, perhaps more – and they employ a defensive mechanism, as effective as it is unpleasant, that consists of squirting a bright orange fish soup over anything or anyone that threatens them. At Fowlsheugh, luckily both for them and for you, their nests are too far down the cliff face for the occupants to feel threatened enough to retaliate.

One of the largest British colonies of guillemots nests here, too, but their peak numbers of 70,000 or so have been in decline in the opening years of the twenty-first century. In common with many of our seabirds, guillemots rely mainly on sand-eels for food; and the North Sea population of these tiny, slender fish, estimated to be several hundred thousand million, has been tumbling year by year – perhaps through over-fishing, perhaps because they cannot withstand the rising sea temperature that is one symptom of climate change.

368. DUNNOTTAR CASTLE, ABERDEENSHIRE

Maps: OS Explorer 396; Landranger 45

Travel: A90 from Stonehaven towards Dundee; on southern outskirts of Stonehaven, left on A92 ('Montrose, Arbroath'). In 1 mile, follow brown 'Dunnottar Castle' signs to park above castle. Follow footpath to Dunnottar Castle (OS ref. 882839).

Nearest railway station: Stonehaven (3 miles)

On an impregnable crag overlooking the North Sea stands Dunnottar Castle, massive and formidable, on a site where some sort of fortification has been maintained since Pictish times. And no wonder: the promontory, a giant inverted pudding of conglomerate rock of pebbles and baked clay with which the castle appears all of a piece, falls 160 feet sheer to the sea on three sides. There are only two ways of approaching Dunnottar; one is across a narrow isthmus, which a couple of well-sited cannon could defend, the other is via a flywalk path which ends at a gate, also easy to defend against single-file invaders. If you want to dominate both sea and land, keep an eye on all that goes on near by while remaining safe from attack, and thoroughly intimidate all comers,

Dunnottar Castle

a great dark sea-girt castle like Dunnottar is exactly what you need.

The castle whose ruin dominates the crag today was built from the late 1300s onwards as a stark stronghold. In its early years it changed hands several times between English and Scots. When a measure of peace came to Scotland towards the end of the sixteenth century, after hundreds of years of internecine fighting and cross-Border battles, Dunnottar was extended into something approaching a domestic dwelling, though still strongly defended. The unyielding atmosphere is heightened as you draw near; the steep pathway to the crag is flanked by elliptical loopholes from which visitors could be kept covered until they had entered the gateway. Even then there are right-angle passages to stop the flight of bullets, murder-holes and trip-stones. The thick walls, echoing stone rooms and vaulted cellars only add to the sternly martial air. It is hard to imagine anyone having been comfortable or at ease in Dunnottar – certainly not the many wretches who found themselves forgotten in its dungeons.

Of these the Whig's Vault with its stone-lined barrel ceiling and end wall open to the elements retains the most ominous atmosphere, a grim undertone increased when you learn of the 122 men and 45 women who were incarcerated here in May 1685 because of their Covenanter faith (see pp. 373–4 and 375–6). They were simply left to rot for over two months, during which nine of them died of disease and starvation. A group of about twenty-five tried to escape by climbing out of the window and inching along a ledge in the crag, but two of them fell to their deaths and the rest were recaptured and punished with torture. Eventually the survivors were taken from the stinking dungeon, formally banished from the kingdom, and transported across the Atlantic – and all for their faith and conscience.

369. FORVIE DUNES, ABERDEENSHIRE

Maps: OS Explorer 421; Landranger 38

Travel: A90 from Aberdeen towards Peterhead; in 9 miles, right on A975 through Newburgh ('Cruden Bay'). In 1 mile cross River Ythan; on following left bend turn right into car park (OS ref. 004270). Follow tarmac path through gate to end of trees and turn left uphill across moorland into Forvie Dunes. Blue Route reaches beach at Forvie Kirk (021266) in ¾ mile, and turns clockwise to return; Red Route runs to the left for 2 miles to Collieston and the Stevenson Forvie Centre (036282).

In these islands sand has always been a rogue element, liable to blow around, to shift and stick at whim, to uncover bare rock or smother whole communities. That was the case at the mouth of the Ythan Estuary on the north Aberdeenshire coast in 1413, when a terrible sandstorm overwhelmed the fishing village of Forvie. All that remains of the settlement today is the stubby stone shell of the twelfth-century parish kirk, marooned in a sand dune.

The 1,800 acres of Forvie Dunes, sometimes known as the Sands of Forvie, are one of Britain's biggest dune systems. They began forming some 5,000 years ago as a series of sandstorms piled up sand on top of cliffs that already stood 100 feet above the sea. Some of these dunes are in never-ending movement, their alkaline content replenished by wind-blown fragments of seashell rich in lime, forming a characteristic *machair*, or seaside sward of flowers and grasses. Others in more sheltered locations have ceased to move and are fixed features, leached of their lime content. They underpin a beautiful coastal heath where red grouse thrive on the black fruit of crowberry. These heaths are also home to mainland Britain's largest colony of eider ducks. Up to 4,000 arrive from their winter sea stations further south, each female laying a clutch of four or five eggs in a nest among the heather and cross-leaved heath which she lines with her own down.

Turning back south from the Red Route through the dunes before you reach Collieston, you can explore the clifftops around Hackley Bay where the pink of thrift, white of sea campion and sulphur-yellow of primroses vie for attention in late spring. Further south, a mile or so beyond the ruin of Forvie Kirk, the largest colony of Sandwich terns in Scotland nests on the remote beaches around the outlet of the River Ythan alongside their cousins, the Arctic, common and little terns.

In winter short-eared owls quarter the dunes and heaths, looking for voles. Some Forvie Dunes connoisseurs prefer this season to all others, walking the dunes in the teeth of North Sea gales with nothing but their own thoughts for company.

370. GIGHT CASTLE, ABERDEENSHIRE

Maps: OS Explorer 426; Landranger 30

Travel: A90 from Aberdeen towards Peterhead; in 15 miles, left on B9005 through Ellon and Methlick towards Fyvie. 2 miles beyond Methlick, turn left into car park marked 'Braes of Gight Wood' (OS ref. 832399). Descend through forest on gravel track to bottom of slope; bear right across bridge over Burn of Stonehouse (832396) and continue. Track soon becomes grassy path, passes between old gateposts and enters field where Gight Castle stands (826392).

Gently crumbling in a thicket of nettles and rowan trees, Gight Castle stands forgotten in the corner of an Aberdeenshire meadow. It forms a peaceful, pastoral composition, but many cruel deeds were planned and carried out in its Great Hall, now half ruined above the vaulted cellars and the kitchen with its vast stone fireplace. The arrow-slits and gun-loops in the walls tell you that the Tudor era, when this stronghold was built, was turbulent and dangerous this far north. The headstrong Gordons who inhabited the Castle of Gight compiled one of the wildest family annals in

Scottish history. Their castle's abandonment followed the death of its final owner in a fall from his horse; he had acquired it in 1787 from the last Gordon to live there – Lord Byron's mother, Catherine Gordon, who had been forced to sell the family home to pay the gambling debts of her dissolute husband, Mad Jack Byron, a very bad hat.

The Gordons of Gight died by being drowned or murdered, by stabbing and shooting, in battles and accidents. Very few expired in their beds. The Gordon who accomplished that rare feat in 1605, William Gordon, the 5th Laird of Gight, was the worst of the lot. He was a tearing bully and a rakehell, who treated his neighbours as enemies and the neighbourhood as his own kingdom. He killed one man who was trying to prevent him fighting a neighbour, and another with whom he lost his temper. In 1587 he murdered his own brother-in-law. Four years later it was the Laird of Gight who struck the fatal blows to the face of the Bonny Earl of Murray, after a gang of Gordons he was with had set fire to Murray's castle in the dead of night and hunted its owner down by the telltale light of his blazing nightcap tassel.

As he got older, William Gordon became no wiser. In 1594 he took part in a great slaughter of Campbells, and was severely wounded in the battle. The following year he was excommunicated. But nothing seemed able to draw his sting. In the winter of 1597, up to the elbows in horse-thieving, he took a pack of cronies 'armed with hagbuts, pistols, jacks, steelbonnets, swords, gauntlets and other weapons' to beat up the legitimate owner of the stolen beasts. By 1601 he was attacking his neighbours again and trampling their crops. When a long list of accusations against the laird was sent by the Privy Council to the Castle of Gight, this terrible man tore up the document, mashed it into a bowl of soup and forced the messenger who had brought it to swallow it.

Musing on these fantastic goings-on as you contemplate the castle, you may hear a skirl of music from the ghostly piper who haunts the ruins. You might even catch a glimpse, as some say they have, of the De'il himself, feasting with the Laird of Gight. 'By the pricking of my thumbs, Something wicked this way comes.'

371. SPEY BAY, MORAY

Maps: OS Explorer 424; Landranger 28

Travel: A96 from Keith towards Elgin; leaving Fochabers, right on B9014 to Spey Bay. Park at Tugnet Ice House Museum (OS ref. 349654).

In the low water of a hot summer the River Spey enters the Moray Firth as a stately dowager enters a drawing room. The water in its pebbly, boulder-strewn bed finds passage through the shingle spits in dozens of separate streams. But in spring it is a different river entirely. The Spey becomes a headstrong schoolgirl. The shingle spits are overwhelmed, and the river simply throws itself at the sea in one solid surge. Scott Skinner's wonderful reel 'The Spey in Spate', all ecstatic leaps and runs, catches exactly this irresistible mood.

The Spey is one of the great salmon rivers of the Scottish Highlands. The Atlantic salmon that hatches in its headwaters and leaves it as a smolt a few inches long returns several years later as a regal fish weighing 30 pounds or more, its muscular flesh pink with the juices of the prawns it has gorged on out in the open Atlantic. The fish return to their native river to spawn, taking up to a year to travel upriver from the estuary to the redds, or gravel-bedded shallows, where the females lay their thousands of eggs and the males fertilize them in a milky cloud of milt.

Salmon do not confine their spawning runs exclusively to springtime, but to enjoy the spectacle of the big fish at their liveliest you should come to Tugnet in that promising season when winter is deciding if it is ready to move over and give way to spring. The first hint of warmer air brings snowmelt to the high Cairngorm and Monadhliath Mountains, 50 miles inland. Torrents of meltwater are released into dozens of tributary hill burns, all tumbling down to join the confusion of floodwater in the Spey itself. There is a continuous rumble from the river as it forges north-eastwards, flushed with ice-cold water and supercharged with bubbles. The incoming salmon are as stimulated and exhilarated by the oxygenated fresh water as if the Spey were running with champagne. They leap euphorically through the shallow press of water at the mouth of the river, hurdling the ripples, their shining silver backs half in and half out of the tide.

372. CAIRNGORM, ABERDEENSHIRE/HIGHLAND/MORAY

Maps: OS Explorer 403; Landranger 36

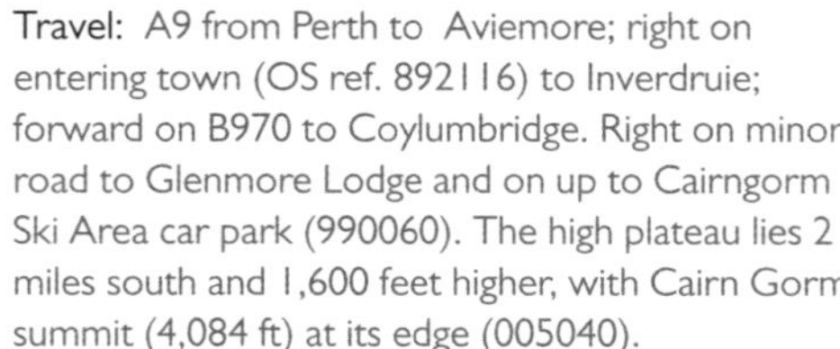

Travel: A9 from Perth to Aviemore; right on entering town (OS ref. 892116) to Inverdruie; forward on B970 to Coylumbridge. Right on minor road to Glenmore Lodge and on up to Cairngorm Ski Area car park (990060). The high plateau lies 2 miles south and 1,600 feet higher, with Cairn Gorm summit (4,084 ft) at its edge (005040).

NB: Cairn Gorm is a serious mountain, especially in winter when conditions on the high Cairngorm plateau can be Arctic. Rangers will advise on best route for climbing, depending on weather conditions.

Snow-holing: Snow-holing is for people who are physically fit, have experience of hillwalking in winter, possess plenty of stamina and determination, and can put in three hours' hard labour at the end of a tough day's mountain walking through snow. For snow-holing expeditions, contact www.scotmountain.co.uk

The Cairngorm Mountains rise over 4,000 feet, and their high plateau is subject to severe and prolonged spells of Arctic weather in winter. Spending a night in a self-dug hole in a snowbank is something you might have to do to save your life if benighted up there. You can also do it for pleasure, and you don't have to be a superhero to survive and even enjoy it. But you do have to take it seriously.

For all but extremely capable mountaineers, the only way to do this is to join a guided expedition such as those run by the Mountain Innovations company (see website, above). Part of the initiation ritual involves climbing the 4,084-foot peak of Cairn Gorm. But first comes the crash course in winter skills, up in the snowy

cleft of Coire Cas. This involves launching yourself down a steep snow slope, feet first and face first, on your front and on your back, with only an ice axe between you and oblivion. You also learn how to cut steps in snow, and how to walk in stiff boots and spiked crampons. These preparations are essential. One stumble at the head of a Cairngorm snowfield when wearing a pack laden with snow shovel and saw, ice axe, gas cylinder, crampons and sleeping bag, and, if you don't know exactly what to do, you can slide 2,000 feet faster than an express train, but without benefit of buffers when you hit the bottom.

Setting off for the expedition proper, you climb the snowy Fiacaill ridge to reach Coire Domhain's white hollow. The high Cairngorm plateau is an inhospitable place. Snow lies thick, the wind whips across, and visibility is down to 100 yards at times. It's cold. But the expedition leader navigates you unerringly, and by mid-afternoon you reach the selected snow-hole site in the high cleft above frozen and remote Loch Avon.

Everyone is cold and tired by now, and you groan inwardly at the prospect of having to cut your own accommodation out of a solid snowbank. But the work warms you up, sawing great blocks of snow, shovelling debris, sweating and cursing, digging and giggling. What you end up with is a crooked, crudely shaped apartment. It feels like home, and heaven, by the time you have crawled into your sleeping bag and had something hot to eat. Candles cast a magical blue light. Jokes, tall tales and jibes go the rounds, and so do the bottles of sleeping elixir.

It is not a comfortable night by any means, but the hard exercise and the whisky combine to poleaxe you till a ghostly blue dawn filters in through the doorway. Breakfast is a plastic bag of muesli and dried milk, moistened with a generous helping of boiled snow.

Struggling into half-frozen, sopping-wet outer gear and cold, damp boots is an ordeal no one finds pleasant. But body heat dries and warms clothes and footwear remarkably quickly. Emerging from your Arctic hobbit-hole, you may find yourself faced with anything from blue sky to white-out. If conditions are right you might set off to bag the second highest peak in the British Isles, 4,295-foot Ben MacDui. Otherwise you descend out of the wind and murk, through the snowfields and over the icy rocks, down into the real world once more.

Snow-holing is a hard, demanding experience, much more so than you might guess. You arrive back in the everyday world dog-tired, but feeling absolutely wonderful.

373. UPPER FINDHORN GLEN, MONADHLIATH MOUNTAINS, HIGHLAND

Maps: OS Explorer 417; Landranger 35

Travel: A9 from Perth towards Inverness; pass Aviemore and Carrbridge; in 6 miles, left on minor road towards Tomatin. Half a mile before Tomatin, left at Findhorn Bridge (OS ref. 804277) on single track road for 10 miles to park neatly at end of public road at Coignafearn Old Lodge (710180). Walk on along road for 3 miles to pass Coignafearn Lodge (680153); in 300 yards, left across River Findhorn and follow narrow glen of Elrick Burn.

Wildlife expeditions: www.speysidewildlife.co.uk

A few hours' snow in a Scots winter can spoil an awful lot of people's day. Roads and railways close, trees and power lines come down, paths across the mountains become impassable. But lovers of the shy wildlife of the Scottish Highlands welcome this cold manna from heaven. If you are going animal-tracking in the Grampian range in midwinter, a nice soft fall of snow before you set off is exactly what you want. As for a location – you may come across anything from red deer to golden eagles almost anywhere in the mountains, but a variety of habitat and altitude helps to boost your chances. The long glen of the River Findhorn, cutting north-east for 15 miles through the heart of the Monadhliath Mountains, has broadleaved woodland (bare at this time of the year, of course) as well as coniferous plantations, a winding, shallow river and many tributaries, field walls and rocks for shelter, river flats and high open mountain slopes. And it possesses a narrow motor road which, if not snowed up, carries you far up the glen before you have to get out and walk.

After a night of soft powder snow there will be plenty of tracks in the Upper Findhorn glen to follow. But first spotting and then identifying them is hard for amateur snowfield sleuths. You find a set of tracks in the snow of the River Findhorn's bank, leading up from the water's edge and following a side burn – five-toed tracks, clearly printed, with a faint groove running between them. Otter or mink? Or stoat, perhaps? Here is another, with a pair of large incurved dints side by side, a deer for certain. But what of these ones near by, with their four toe-pads and one heel-pad all in a neat line? Are they fox or dog, or a large cat, maybe – even a wild cat? Unless you have specialized skills and lots of experience, it is all guesswork.

Several organizations offer tracking expeditions with an expert guide. Speyside Wildlife, for example, lays on animal tracking and viewing in the open air that can feature golden eagle, red deer, mountain hare, otter, capercaillie, ptarmigan and red squirrel; or from a wildlife viewing hide by night, when sightings can include pine marten, roe deer, badger and many more nocturnal creatures. Uninstructed visitors can scarcely hope to see such a spread of wildlife without help of this sort.

A day out with a tracker sharpens the eyes and mind like magic. Once you have had the otter's rounded toes pointed out, and the drag-mark between its left and right prints where the heavy rudder has worn a groove, you find yourself looking for these signs. The two middle toes of the fox, set neatly together as opposed to the dog's splayed pair, and the cat's absence of tiny claw marks (it walks with claws retracted) are clues you can apply next day when you venture out tracking on your own – perhaps in the gully-like side glen of the Elrick Burn that wriggles off south of the Findhorn. The biggest thrill of the lot, and the hardest-earned, comes when you raise your eyes after they have been glued to the set of tracks you have been following, to see the creature itself up ahead: a set of slots leading to a sighting of a magnificent red deer stag with uplifted antlers, or two neat round front paw prints close together, with a pair of hind prints falling in line behind – the hopping gait of the mountain hare who now lies in full view a hundred yards away. His full winter coat of white glows with a faint but definite tinge of blue, his short ears are dark grey, his thickly furred and constantly twitching nose is a rich creamy colour, and his eyes are fixed on you in surprise and enquiry, an interloper in his crisp white kingdom.

374. DRUMMOSSIE MUIR (BATTLE OF CULLODEN), HIGHLAND

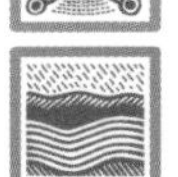

Maps: OS Explorer 416; Explorer 27

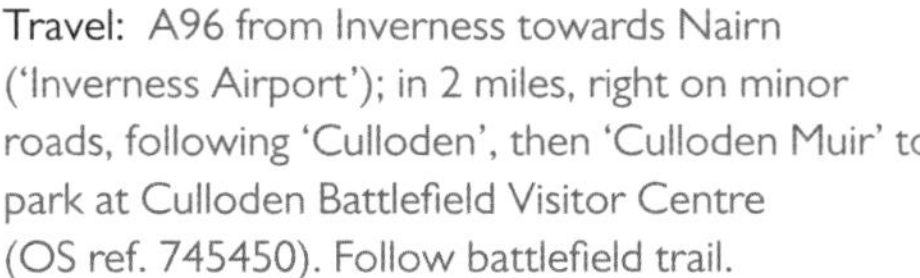

Travel: A96 from Inverness towards Nairn ('Inverness Airport'); in 2 miles, right on minor roads, following 'Culloden', then 'Culloden Muir' to park at Culloden Battlefield Visitor Centre (OS ref. 745450). Follow battlefield trail.

Nearest railway station: Inverness (4 miles)

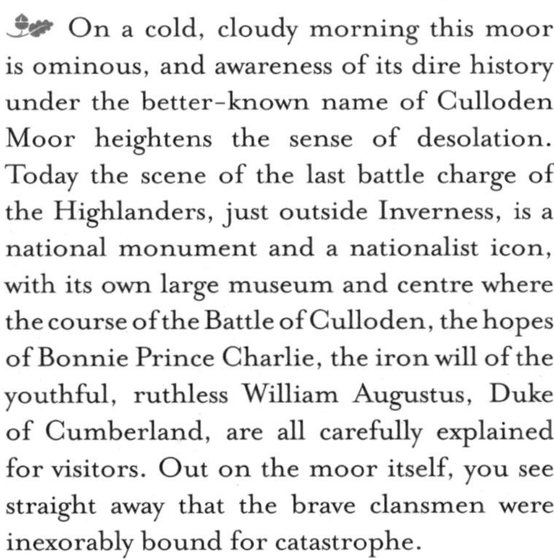

On a cold, cloudy morning this moor is ominous, and awareness of its dire history under the better-known name of Culloden Moor heightens the sense of desolation. Today the scene of the last battle charge of the Highlanders, just outside Inverness, is a national monument and a nationalist icon, with its own large museum and centre where the course of the Battle of Culloden, the hopes of Bonnie Prince Charlie, the iron will of the youthful, ruthless William Augustus, Duke of Cumberland, are all carefully explained for visitors. Out on the moor itself, you see straight away that the brave clansmen were inexorably bound for catastrophe.

'There could never be a more improper ground for Highlanders,' remarked Lord George Murray of the battlefield. This was a bare moor open to the elements, where men charging uphill with drawn swords towards a fixed line of trained professional soldiers could be blasted with artillery, picked off one by one or smashed en masse by disciplined volleys, then ridden down by galloping dragoons as they fled across the open ground. That is exactly what happened to the Highlanders on the morning of 16 April 1746.

The moor was soaked in rain and sleet

that morning. The Duke of Cumberland's men only had to stand still in rank; it was the Highlanders who had to charge through the sodden heather with wind, rain and sleet in their faces, into a storm of bullets and cannonballs. The king's army consisted of 9,000 dragoons and foot-soldiers; the clansmen numbered fewer than 5,000, having haemorrhaged supporters during a long and depressing retreat from England. It was the culmination of a disastrously flawed attempt by Charles Edward Stuart, exiled grandson of King James II, to seize the throne he thought was his by right. The 'Bonnie Prince' had marched almost to Derby before he and his ragtag army of loyal Highland clansmen, emigrés, Irishmen, English deserters and renegades were ignominiously harried back to Scotland, where Charles had raised his standard after landing from France in high hopes only nine months before.

The wild, screaming charge was the first, last and only weapon in the Highlanders' armoury. Once that had been beaten down, there was nothing to do but run for it. Cumberland wanted no mercy given to the rebels, and his men showed none. The fugitives were sabred and bayoneted wherever they were found. Some were mutilated, 'their privities placed in their hands'. Women and children who had followed their men to the battlefield were murdered there. 'The moor was covered in blood,' reported an English officer, 'and our men, what with killing the enemy, dabbling their feet in the blood, and splashing it about one another, looked like so many butchers rather than Christian soldiers.'

The brutality did not stop on Drummossie Muir, or in the streets of Inverness, where Highlanders looking for refuge were hunted down. After such a crushing victory, Cumberland knew he would not be held to account for stamping as hard as he liked on rebels who were seen as posing a serious threat to social and political stability. For months afterwards Cumberland's dragoons went through the Highland glens, burning, raping and killing. Houses were torched or dismantled, crops fired, cattle and sheep driven off, personal possessions looted, families forced into the hills with only the clothes on their backs. This 'Harrying of the Glens' sounded the long-drawn-out death knell of a clan system that was already in disarray.

One in three of Charles Stuart's army lost their lives at Culloden; one in 200 of the king's men. Hundreds of Highlanders were murdered in the aftermath, scores executed, thousands imprisoned and left to rot. Heavy penalties were imposed, and the hereditary jurisdiction of the clan chiefs abolished. It was the most brutal exhibition imaginable of victor's might being victor's right, and it sowed the seeds of irrevocable change in the Highlands.

Charles himself rode away from the shambles of Drummossie Muir, and after six months on the run was able to escape to the Continent by ship. He became a disappointed, melancholic drinker and gambler, and died in exile over forty years later.

Nearly thirty years after the battle James Boswell expressed the general feeling of Scotsmen when he wrote in his *Journal of a Tour to the Hebrides* of his own emotions on hearing Mr McQueen, landlord of the inn at Glenmorison, recount his own experience of charging with his fellow-Highlanders at Culloden:

As he narrated the particulars of that ill-advised, but brave attempt, I could not refrain from tears. There is a certain association of ideas in my mind upon that subject, by which I am strongly affected. The very Highland names, or the sound of a bag-pipe, will stir my blood, and fill me with a mixture of melancholy and respect for courage; with pity for an unfortunate and superstitious regard for antiquity, and thoughtless inclination for war; in short, with a crowd of sensations with which sober rationality has nothing to do.

12

THE HIGHLANDS AND THE ISLES

If there's one part of Britain more than any other that seems to sum up the spirit of the wild, it's the north and west of Scotland. The Great Glen that slashes diagonally from south-west to north-east is more than a geographical divide; it separates the popular playgrounds of the Trossachs, Cairngorms and Monadhliaths from less high but much harsher and more remote landscapes.

LOOKING DOWN FROM the heights of Wester Ross, or following the cavern-hollowed burns through arctic-alpine flower meadows in the shadow of great mountains such as Ben More Assynt, I have felt more genuinely uplifted and more dwarfed into insignificance than anywhere else in our islands.

The wedge of land that forms these outer Highlands tails out to the south-west in blunt-nosed, infrequently visited peninsulas. North of here the glens and mountains of Wester Ross and Easter Ross fill the centre of the long triangle, while up in the north stretch the empty bogland miles of the Flow Country and the bleak moors and black cliffs of the far north. This is all wilderness, with such beautiful but desolate spots as Loch Coire Lair in its high cradle above Glen Carron, the breathtaking shapes of Suilven and Canisp beyond Inverpolly, and the solid dark ramparts of the northernmost coast.

While the huge emptiness and scale of the western mainland seems overwhelming, the isles offer very different wild places in wild situations, isolated in the teeth of all that Atlantic and North Sea weather can throw at them. Yet however fantastic their shape, the island hills are far smaller in scale than their mainland counterparts, and seem more intimate than imposing. Out west of the mainland curve the twin island chains of the Inner and Outer Hebrides, Inner a random scatter of volcanic lumps, Outer a mighty arc. Beyond the north coast lies another pairing of archipelagos – the roughly circular collection of islands that makes up the Orkney Isles, and the ragged straggle of Shetland. My own first proper excursion among the islands in the early 1990s took me on a never-to-be-forgotten caper through all four of Scotland's island archipelagos. The rock and bog, the streaming Atlantic weather, the history of battles, feasts, famines and emigration, seemed matched by the driving energy of the tall tales, the stories and tunes that seethed like living things in every barn and back kitchen. It was magic – harsh, wild magic.

Above: The majestic Highlands. Below left: Strath of Kildonan (pp. 422–3), centre: Inverpolly (p. 431), below right: Loch Fleet (p. 420)

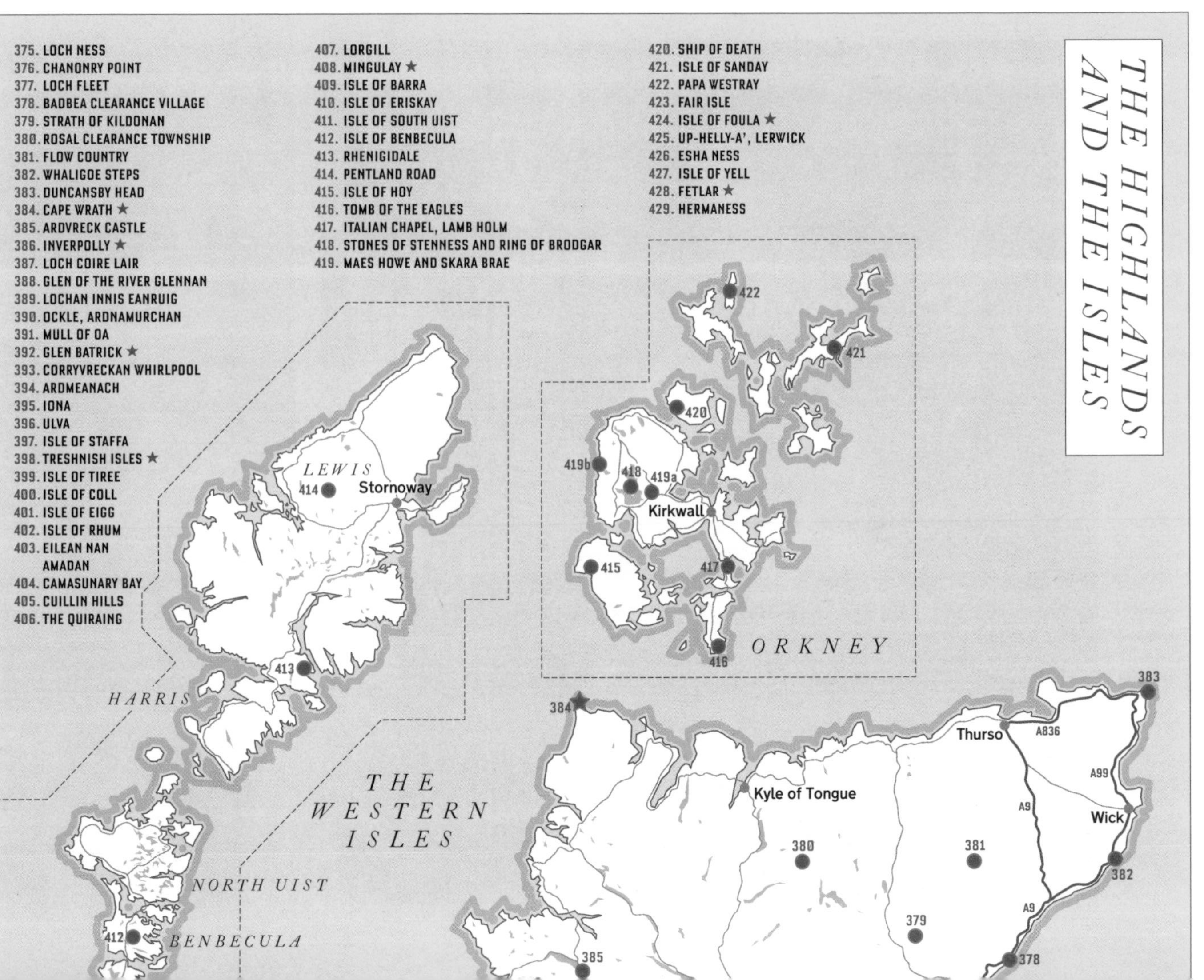
THE HIGHLANDS AND THE ISLES
375. LOCH NESS
376. CHANONRY POINT
377. LOCH FLEET
378. BADBEA CLEARANCE VILLAGE
379. STRATH OF KILDONAN
380. ROSAL CLEARANCE TOWNSHIP
381. FLOW COUNTRY
382. WHALIGOE STEPS
383. DUNCANSBY HEAD
384. CAPE WRATH ★
385. ARDVRECK CASTLE
386. INVERPOLLY ★
387. LOCH COIRE LAIR
388. GLEN OF THE RIVER GLENNAN
389. LOCHAN INNIS EANRUIG
390. OCKLE, ARDNAMURCHAN
391. MULL OF OA
392. GLEN BATRICK ★
393. CORRYVRECKAN WHIRLPOOL
394. ARDMEANACH
395. IONA
396. ULVA
397. ISLE OF STAFFA
398. TRESHNISH ISLES ★
399. ISLE OF TIREE
400. ISLE OF COLL
401. ISLE OF EIGG
402. ISLE OF RHUM
403. EILEAN NAN AMADAN
404. CAMASUNARY BAY
405. CUILLIN HILLS
406. THE QUIRAING
407. LORGILL
408. MINGULAY ★
409. ISLE OF BARRA
410. ISLE OF ERISKAY
411. ISLE OF SOUTH UIST
412. ISLE OF BENBECULA
413. RHENIGIDALE
414. PENTLAND ROAD
415. ISLE OF HOY
416. TOMB OF THE EAGLES
417. ITALIAN CHAPEL, LAMB HOLM
418. STONES OF STENNESS AND RING OF BRODGAR
419. MAES HOWE AND SKARA BRAE
420. SHIP OF DEATH
421. ISLE OF SANDAY
422. PAPA WESTRAY
423. FAIR ISLE
424. ISLE OF FOULA ★
425. UP-HELLY-A', LERWICK
426. ESHA NESS
427. ISLE OF YELL
428. FETLAR ★
429. HERMANESS
LEWIS
Stornoway
HARRIS
THE WESTERN ISLES
NORTH UIST
BENBECULA
ORKNEY
Kirkwall
Thurso
Wick
Kyle of Tongue
A836
A99
A9

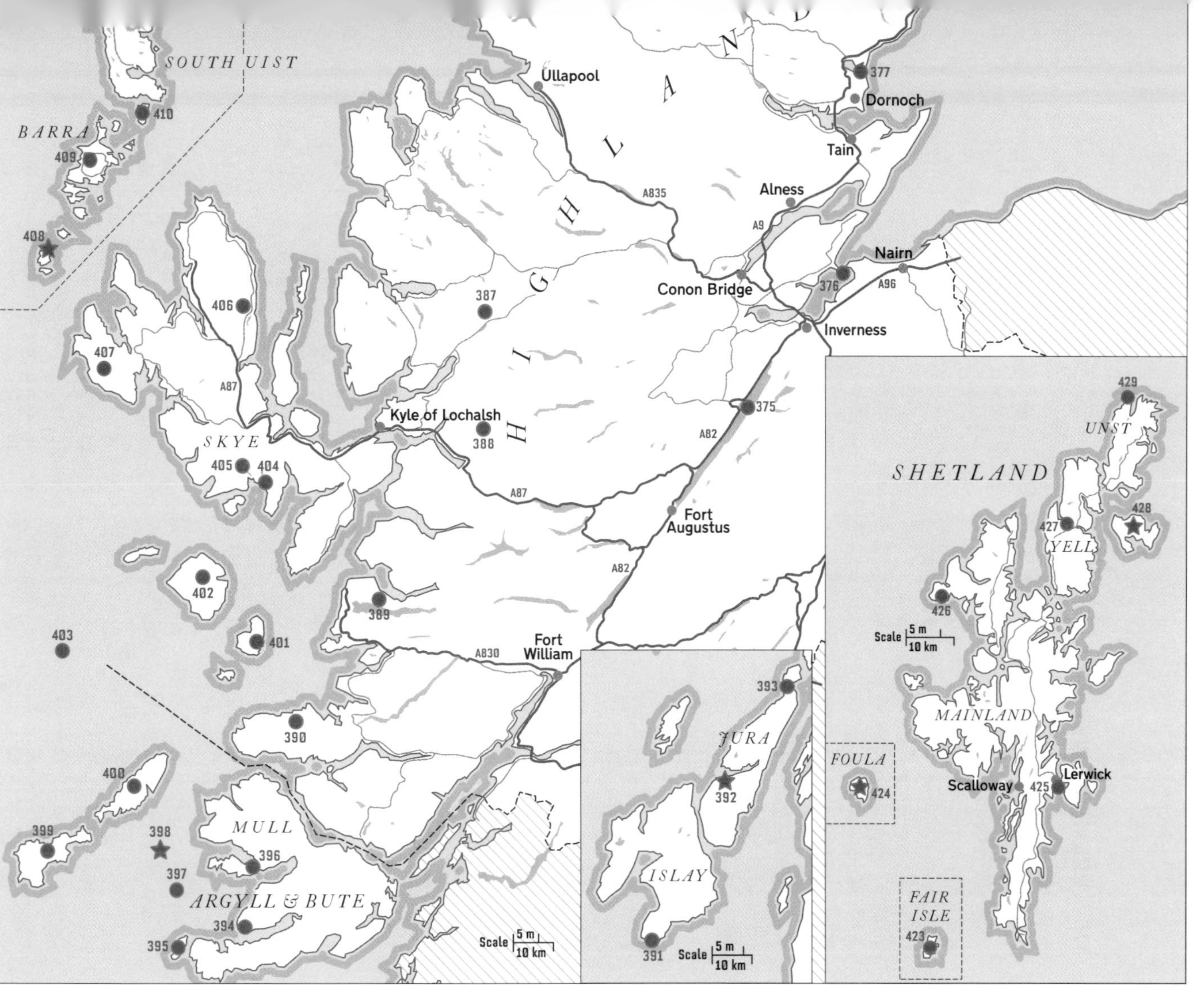
SOUTH UIST
BARRA
410
409
408
Ullapool
HIGHLAND
377
Dornoch
Tain
Alness
A835
A9
Nairn
A96
376
Conon Bridge
Inverness
406
387
407
A87
375
Kyle of Lochalsh
388
A82
SKYE
405
404
A87
SHETLAND
UNST
429
428
427
YELL
Fort Augustus
A82
402
389
426
Scale 5 m 10 km
403
401
Fort William
A830
393
MAINLAND
390
JURA
FOULA
424
400
392
Scalloway
425
Lerwick
399
398
MULL
396
397
ISLAY
ARGYLL & BUTE
FAIR ISLE
394
423
395
Scale 5 m 10 km
391
Scale 5 m 10 km

375. LOCH NESS, HIGHLAND

Maps: OS Explorer 392, 400, 416; Landranger 25, 34, 41

Travel: Loch Ness runs in a straight north-easterly direction from Fort William to Inverness. A82 accompanies it all the way, at first on the east bank, switching to the west at Fort Augustus where B862/852 takes over on the east bank. There is a Loch Ness Monster Centre at Drumnadrochit on A82, 14 miles south of Inverness. Boleskine House (NB: private property) stands above Boleskine Old Graveyard on B852 between Foyers and Inverfarigaig on the east bank, 18 miles south of Inverness (OS ref. 510221).

Nearest railway stations: Spean Bridge (south end), Inverness (north end)

Drumnadrochit Loch Ness Monster Centre: www.lochness-centre.com

Immensely long, narrow, cold and deep, nowhere much more than 1 mile wide, running 23 miles in a dead straight line, Loch Ness is a lake like no other. It fills the long groove of the Great Glen, a giant fault line that, since the Caledonian Canal was opened in 1823, has carried an unbroken thread of water between the North Sea and the Atlantic, making an island of the whole of the North-West of Scotland. This connection between Loch Ness and the sea, the chilly murkiness of its peaty waters, not to mention their depth – 754 feet at their deepest – means the legend of the Loch Ness Monster can never be entirely discounted. No one can see far enough into the loch to disprove it.

Legends of a great beast in the dark waters date back to the sixth century, when St Columba was said to have saved the life of a Pict who was being attacked by the monster. St Columba 'commanded it to go no further, nor touch the man, but go back with all speed. The monster was terrified, and fled more quickly than if it had been pulled back with ropes.' Many sightings followed down the centuries, with a flurry in the 1930s when motor cars brought tourists with cameras and willing imaginations. Hydrophones, sonar scans, submersibles, all have been employed in the hunt for Nessie, none with any tangible results. All alleged sightings agree that the beast possesses a small head on a long, sinuous neck and a grey body, perhaps up to 30 feet long. A 1975 photograph, blurred and grainy, that seemed to show a diamond-shaped flipper had eminent naturalist Sir Peter Scott declaring that the creature must exist and should be dubbed *Nessiteras rhombopteryx*, 'creature of Ness with diamond-shaped limbs'. All too soon it was pointed out that this was an anagram of 'Monster hoax by Sir Peter S.'.

Nessie is not the only creature to have spawned legends around the loch. In 1899 the 'wickedest man in Britain', dark magician and occultist Aleister Crowley, bought Boleskine House, sited on the east bank above the reputedly haunted Boleskine Old Graveyard. He used it as the setting for a magic ritual by which he hoped to summon his guardian angel. The evil spirits raised and released during the course of Crowley's fourteen-year tenure of Boleskine House drove servants mad, caused a local butcher to chop off his own hand, and left a legacy of unease that still persists today. Wild doings were also rumoured throughout the 1970s and 1980s, when Boleskine House was owned by rock god and Crowley enthusiast Jimmy Page. When Page sold up in 1992 much of the glamour and newsworthiness departed with him. Still in private ownership, the house guards whatever secrets it possesses behind a modest façade.

376. CHANONRY POINT, FORTROSE, HIGHLAND

Maps: OS Explorer 432; Landranger 27

Travel: A9 Inverness towards Wick; in 7 miles, right at Tore on A832 to Fortrose; right on minor road (signposted) to park at Chanonry Point (OS ref. 749556), near Brahan Seer memorial.

A rugged, weather-rounded block of granite, sparkling with chips of mica, stands on the promenade at Chanonry Point, a 2-mile promontory across the narrow throat of the Moray Firth 7 miles north-east of Inverness. The surroundings are lovely – the glinting waters of the firth, dolphins rolling in the constricted waters just offshore, big

blowy skies – but the only wildness here comes from a stumpy little monument commemorating an obscure, ill-educated person by the name of Coinneach Odhar Fiosaiche, Pale Kenneth the Seer. So little is known of Pale Kenneth, a native of the Isle of Lewis, that it is not even certain whether he lived in the sixteenth or seventeenth century. But his name and fame are still celebrated in the Highlands, for the Brahan Seer – he worked for the Earl of Seaforth on the nearby Brahan Estate – had the unnerving ability to see into the future.

Some say that Pale Kenneth received his gift through the medium of a fairy stone bequeathed to him by his mother. Be that as it may, he certainly impressed all around him with his predictions. These included foreseeing the Jacobite debacle of the Battle of Culloden of 1746 ('Drummossie! Your barren moor shall soon be soaked in the blood of the flower of the Highlands!'); the opening of the Caledonian Canal in 1822 ('Full-rigged ships shall sail east and west over the land behind Inverness'); and many disasters relating to bridges. He also predicted the fall of the House of Seaforth, and failed to keep it to himself – an error of judgement believed by some to have led to his gruesome death.

The other story goes that the seer was being questioned by Isabella, Lady Seaforth, about the health and wellbeing of her absent husband. Lord Seaforth was in fact in Paris in the arms of another woman, something Pale Kenneth could see but was understandably reluctant to reveal. She insisted, he prevaricated, until at last he blurted out that her husband was being 'entertained' by someone nicer and prettier than she. Lady Isabella flew into a towering rage and had the unfortunate seer hauled off and cooked alive on Chanonry Point in a spiked barrel of boiling tar. Truth, according to this tale, did not prove to be the best policy for Pale Kenneth.

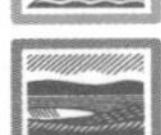

377. LOCH FLEET, HIGHLAND

Maps: OS Explorer 438; Landranger 21

Travel: A9 from Inverness towards Wick; entering Golspie, cross railway and turn next right (Ferry Road) to reach north shore of Loch Fleet. For south shore, turn right (OS ref. 771969) where A9 first meets the loch, ¾ mile before the Mound Causeway, and follow minor road along loch shore for 1¾ miles to car park near Skelbo Castle (794953).

Nearest railway station: Golspie (2½ miles)

The River Fleet once tumbled into the North Sea through an estuarine bay 3 miles wide. Since then the sand and shingle bar to the north of the river mouth has crept south to the point where it all but closes off the bay. The narrows that are left, a gap only 200 yards wide, seethe and roar with water at half-tide as the sea shoves inland and the river bullies its way outwards. This dynamic water action sweeps and scours, and has built up vast tan-coloured sandbanks inside the protective arm of the Ferry Spit promontory. Here oystercatchers, godwits and dunlin probe for shellfish and invertebrates, common seals lie hauled out and sea otters scamper at dawn and dusk. In winter the bay becomes a haven for pink-footed and greylag geese, down from Iceland for the cold months.

The seaward faces of the opposing spits have grown mountainous with sand dunes, in whose sheltered slack hollows grow orchids and bird's-foot trefoil, the globular blooms of purple milk-vetch and the delicate pink flowers of sea milkwort on tough shrubby stems. Butterfly lovers have a field day here with peacocks and graylings, the confusingly named dark green fritillary (it is a striking tiger-spotted orange) and the exceptionally beautiful olive-hued green hairstreak.

All these treasures are set in a frame of bulky, distinctive mountains – the hills of Creag an Amalaidh and Crock Odhar on the western shore, Mound Rock and Silver Rock to the north.

378. BADBEA CLEARANCE VILLAGE, NEAR HELMSDALE, HIGHLAND

Maps: OS Explorer 435; Landranger 19

Travel: A9 from Helmsdale towards Wick; in 6½ miles, car park on right (OS ref. 085204). Follow boardwalk footpath south for ⅓ mile to monument (088201).

Nearest railway station: Helmsdale (6½ miles)

Badbea lies on the south-west slope of the cliffs some 6 miles from Helmsdale, an utterly exposed location. Salt, spray and fierce winds blow across the site, the soil is so thin that the rocks poke through, and the cliff edge a few yards beyond the settlement falls 300 feet to the sea. It is not a place where you would want to establish a new community, but from 1793 onwards, when local landowners turned their tenants out of house and home and replaced them with more profitable sheep, that's exactly what happened. All over the Scottish Highlands the notorious Clearances were under way, and farming families from inland were on the move, to hardship on poor coastal lands, or to new lives in the New World. Those who came to Badbea from nearby Ousdale around 1802 were at least fortunate in having a well-disposed landlord. Sir John Sinclair was an agricultural improver who took a genuine interest in the welfare of his displaced tenants, encouraging them to form cooperatives and to work in coastal industries he funded, such as fishing, distilling and weaving. Ironically, he was also the man who first introduced the big Cheviot sheep to the Highlands, the animal that was soon to replace tenants all over Scotland.

Now, walking down the steep pathway to Badbea, you brush through gorse bushes and pass the rough boundary wall and ditch of the settlement. Stumps of stone form outlines of houses in the gorse and bracken, some with their chimney gables and hearths still intact. Badbea was a small settlement of a dozen families. They grew oats and potatoes in the thin earth that they broke with foot ploughs. Somehow the settlement limped on for a century, but the poor soil, the danger to children of the windy cliffs (mothers would tether their infants to sticks and bushes while they worked) and the isolation spelled the death of Badbea. By the turn of the twentieth century the place was silent and deserted once more.

In 1911 New Zealander David Sutherland set up the massive memorial that still stands on the cliffs. Sutherland's father, Alexander, was born at Badbea in 1806 and raised there before emigrating to New Zealand in 1839. David built his memorial on the site of the house of John Sutherland, otherwise known as 'John Badbea', who was removed to Badbea with his family from Ousdale as a child during the original Clearances, and died there in 1864. John Badbea, says the inscription, was 'loved for his Christian character and the charm of his personality and gifts' – a poignant tribute to read on this harsh, unpopulated cliff among the ruins of houses that saw so much suffering.

379. STRATH OF KILDONAN, HIGHLAND

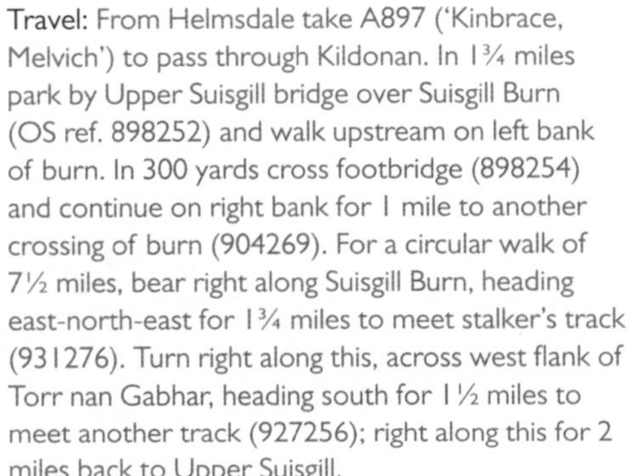
Maps: OS Explorer 444; Landranger 17

Travel: From Helmsdale take A897 ('Kinbrace, Melvich') to pass through Kildonan. In 1¾ miles park by Upper Suisgill bridge over Suisgill Burn (OS ref. 898252) and walk upstream on left bank of burn. In 300 yards cross footbridge (898254) and continue on right bank for 1 mile to another crossing of burn (904269). For a circular walk of 7½ miles, bear right along Suisgill Burn, heading east-north-east for 1¾ miles to meet stalker's track (931276). Turn right along this, across west flank of Torr nan Gabhar, heading south for 1½ miles to meet another track (927256); right along this for 2 miles back to Upper Suisgill.

Nearest railway station: Kildonan (2½ miles)

In 1868-9 more than 500 gold prospectors thought it worth making a long journey into the wilds of north-east Scotland, settling themselves into tented encampments beside the River Helmsdale and panning the streams for gold. They braved the wild weather, isolation, cold and hunger for a dream which brought riches to nobody and destitution to many. All told, about £10,000 worth of gold was retrieved from the Strath of Kildonan, most of it only poor-quality gold dust.

Today, the dream of the Sutherland Gold Rush lives on. At Baile an Or, the riverside location romantically or ironically named the Town of Gold by the prospectors, a notice proclaims that the Suisgill Estate allows anyone to pan for gold under certain conditions and obligations. A little further along the Suisgill Burn comes chuckling in from the north and you can follow a path thick with the two-pronged prints of deer slots into the hills. Cliff faces of white and orange above the Suisgill water shows where the gold-diggers hacked and hushed for glory. They would build a dam across a side burn, wait a while, and then release the pent-up water to flush away the ground in the hopes of revealing the precious flecks of gold. Turn aside here and you can follow the burn for a couple more miles into the moors, past hummocks of mining spoil.

Fragments of walls show where houses once stood, part of the community of Kildonan that was cleared in the early nineteenth century to make way for more-profitable sheep. 'The whole inhabitants of Kildonan parish,' recorded their young minister Donald Sage, 'with the exception of three families, nearly 2,000 souls, were utterly rooted and burned out. Many, especially the young and robust, left the country, but the aged, the females and the children were obliged to stay and accept the wretched allotments offered them on the seashore and endeavour to learn fishing.' This took place only fifty years before the Sutherland Gold Rush, but by that time the townships of Kildonan were no more than stones piled in the heather.

380. ROSAL CLEARANCE TOWNSHIP, STRATHNAVER, HIGHLAND

Maps: OS Explorer 448; Landranger 10

Travel: A836 Bettyhill towards Tongue; in 3 miles, left on B871 ('Syre'). At Syre bear left across River Naver on B871, then immediately right (OS ref. 696440) on rough track by river (green Forestry Commission 'Rosal Township, Strathnaver Trail' sign). In ¾ mile park (691427) and walk on along forest track for ²/₃ mile to path on left (686419) signed to Rosal.

Strath of Kildonan

Rosal township would have been entirely forgotten if it were not for a Strathnaver stonemason called Donald Macleod and his angry, seething account of the clearance of his native valley, *A History of the Destitution in Sutherlandshire*. As it is, Macleod's furious words have echoed down two centuries, making Rosal notorious and causing the heaps of houses to be regarded as a national monument to what was in effect a brutal act of ethnic cleansing. The clansmen and their families were ordered off the land by Patrick Sellar, the factor, or estate manager, of the landowner, the Countess of Sutherland, wife of the Earl of Stafford. She wanted to put the strath – and dozens like it in the 1,500 square miles of Scotland she owned – under sheep. The expanding Industrial Revolution cities of Britain were desperate for meat and woollen cloth, and there were enormous profits to be made from grazing land.

As Donald Macleod wrote:

Every imaginable means, short of the sword or the musket, was put in requisition to drive the natives away, to force them to exchange their farms and comfortable habitations, erected by themselves or their forefathers, for inhospitable rocks on the sea shore. The country was darkened by the smoke of burnings and the descendants were ruined, trampled upon, dispersed and compelled to seek asylum beyond the sea.

Burning parties came down Strathnaver on 13 June 1814 and evicted the people of several townships, including Rosal. Those who stayed by their houses watched them and their contents being torched. 'Some old men took to the woods and precipices,' said Macleod, 'wandering about in a state approaching to, or of, absolute insanity ... pregnant women were taken with premature labour, and several children died. To these events I was an eye-witness.' Patrick Sellar himself watched the burnings, and no mercy was shown. At Badinloskin an old woman had to be carried out of her house with her blankets ablaze after the building was set on fire while she was still inside.

The foundations of the houses of Rosal lie loosely scattered across their former fields in a clearing in the trees. You can make out the outlines of walls and hearths on the green grassy floors. An imaginative trail of display boards leads you round. It is a very well-presented visitor attraction, not especially wild in appearance. But Donald Macleod's words ring in your head as you look at the empty hills beyond the forest.

381. FLOW COUNTRY, HIGHLAND

Maps: OS Explorer 449; Landranger 10, 11, 17

Travel: The Flow Country is very roughly bounded by A9 Helmsdale–Wick–Thurso on the east, A836 coast road on the north, and A987 Helmsdale–Kinbrace and B871 Kinbrace–Bettyhill on the south and west. A897 Kinbrace–Melvich runs north through the middle.

Railway stations: Helmsdale, Kildonan, Kinbrace, Forsinard, Altnabreac, Scotscalder, Georgemas Junction and Thurso

RSPB Forsinard Reserve Visitor Centre (April–October) is at Forsinard station (tel: 01641 571225; www.rspb.org.uk/reserves).

In the Flow Country of northernmost Scotland there are about 1 million acres of blanket bog. This bog is 98 per cent water, yet you can walk across it. The underlying gneiss rock stops the sphagnum from rotting

Ben Loyal, Flow Country

down into soil. Starved of nutrients, all but the top few inches of the bog is dead material. The thin top layer sustains a diverse, close-knit and, owing to its shy, secretive nature, seldom-seen community of wild plants, animals and birds. To the untuned eye the Flow Country looks entirely devoid of wildlife. But ask permission of an estate owner, worker or crofter to spend the day out among the pools and peat hags of their land, and you have every chance of spotting red deer, greenshank, dragonflies and hen harriers, as well as an occasional otter, black-throated diver or wild cat. Startlingly coloured bog flowers and mosses, insect-devouring plants, golden plover and dipper, merlin and golden eagle: a cornucopia of Scottish natural life has been upended over the bogs.

To get a well-informed glimpse of its damp, seething heart you can't do better than walk out from the RSPB's Visitor Centre at Forsinard station into the 25,000 acres that make up its Forsinard Reserve. Here are self-guided trails, accompanied walks with a ranger, Wildlife Explorer packs for children, and more expert help and information than any amateur could possibly absorb. Out among the sphagnum tussocks, the peaty lochans and the heather hags, you marvel at how bursting with life are the seemingly sterile plains of this spellbinding place.

Altogether the peat lands here account for about 2 per cent of Britain's land surface, hemmed in by blocky mountain ranges and rough seas. This giant wilderness, its gently undulating surface pushed up here and there into hill peaks, has been getting on with its own natural business since before man put in any significant appearance. The cool wet climate keeps the bog moist and fills the countless thousands of lochans that wink from the dun cushion of the bog as you pass by in car or train. Only along the narrow straths, or valleys, do any settlements penetrate the interior: almost all the crofts and villages lie sprinkled along the perimeter. The Flow Country is crossed by one railway line, a couple of roads and a loose skein of tracks. If you want absolute loneliness, the Flow Country is the place.

It was also the place selected by investors in the 1980s and 1990s as perfect empty ground for the planting of conifers. Helped by grants, about one in ten acres of the bog were drained, ploughed, fertilized and planted up. This disastrous assault on Britain's most extensive wilderness and its dense, delicate web of wildlife has slowed now, but constant vigilance continues to be the watchword among Flow Country conservationists.

382. WHALIGOE STEPS, ULBSTER, HIGHLAND

Maps: OS Explorer 450; Landranger 12

Travel: A9/A99 from Inverness towards Wick. In Ulbster turn right towards the sea by the telephone box ('Cairn of Get' sign opposite). Park at end of roadway (OS ref. 320404). Walk along side of house next to sea, bear left round end of house and continue towards sea to top of Whaligoe Steps.

NB: www.scotland-index.co.uk/wick/whaligoe/steps1 contains excellent directions.

It is a steep and slippery descent down Whaligoe Steps, and a hard puff upwards if

you are not in condition. Imagine doing this in clumsy sea boots or in bare feet with a heavy creel of lobsters or fish on your back.

Whaligoe, or 'whale inlet', is a deep and narrow cleft in tall flagstone cliffs. The weather was so rough and the wind-driven seas so difficult in the jaws of the inlet that fishing boats would be winched up for safety and hung perpendicularly from ropes on the cliff face. The cliffs rise 200 feet, and to reach the curing shed at the cliff edge from the landing place the locals cut a zigzag path in the vertical rock face. David Brodie paid £8 to have flagstone steps laid in the path at the turn of the nineteenth century, and these were renewed from time to time. The stepped path opened up the inlet to serious fishing – from seven boats in 1808, capacity increased to thirty-five in 1855. But competition from bigger and more easily negotiated harbours such as Wick, Lybster and Helmsdale saw a decline in business, and Whaligoe soon reverted to a purely local haven. The steps remain – perhaps 330, perhaps 356 of them; it is impossible to distinguish step from natural ledge in many places.

'Every crab, lobster, herring and all species of fish had to be carried up on their backs in creels,' recalled Minnie Rye in 1967 of her childhood in Whaligoe at the turn of the century. 'The men and women both had to do this, but there was a resting place at each bend of the steps, where one stood and rested the creel and took a breather.'

Tread carefully down the cliff face, negotiating the sharp angles and thanking your lucky stars that this was not your daily lot. At the bottom of the cracked, uneven flight, step on to a grassy platform. Near by are the remains of an old stone fishing shed and the rusty winch that hauled up the boats. Kittiwake and herring gull cries reverberate around the cliffs that tower darkly overhead. A length of rusty chain, a few bolts, some ring-eyes in the cliff face and three little stone-built storage shelves are all that remains of the fishing station at Whaligoe.

383. DUNCANSBY HEAD, HIGHLAND

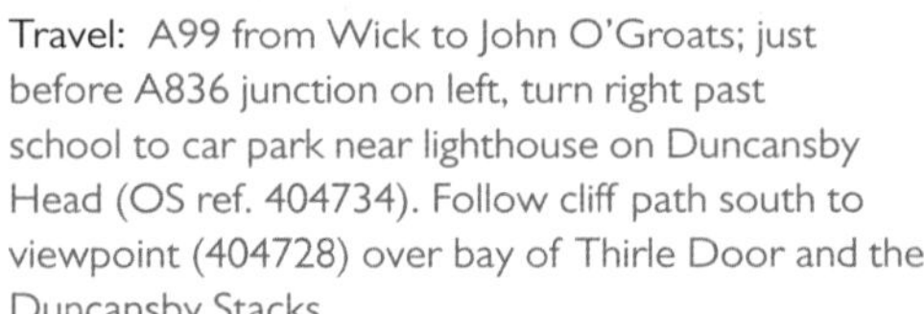

Maps: OS Explorer 451; Landranger 12

Travel: A99 from Wick to John O'Groats; just before A836 junction on left, turn right past school to car park near lighthouse on Duncansby Head (OS ref. 404734). Follow cliff path south to viewpoint (404728) over bay of Thirle Door and the Duncansby Stacks.

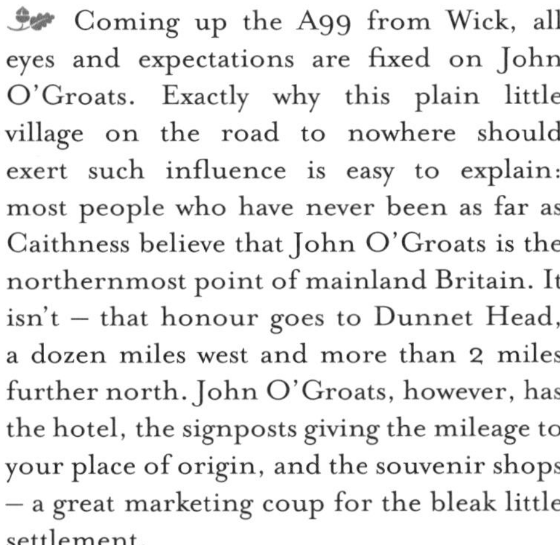

Coming up the A99 from Wick, all eyes and expectations are fixed on John O'Groats. Exactly why this plain little village on the road to nowhere should exert such influence is easy to explain: most people who have never been as far as Caithness believe that John O'Groats is the northernmost point of mainland Britain. It isn't – that honour goes to Dunnet Head, a dozen miles west and more than 2 miles further north. John O'Groats, however, has the hotel, the signposts giving the mileage to your place of origin, and the souvenir shops – a great marketing coup for the bleak little settlement.

Others think that John O'Groats is the furthest you can travel in a north-easterly direction. This, too, is a misapprehension. A minor road leads east out of John O'Groats, declining to a narrow way that undulates for the best part of 2 miles across a bulge of grassy headland to reach the lighthouse on

Duncansby Head

Duncansby Head. Here is the true end of the road, the outermost tip of Gaeldom and the whole 1,000-mile mass of the British mainland.

John Hillaby finished his epic walk across Britain in 1965 at this place, looking down from the clifftops on 'a flurry of water and black rock ... in the greenish twilight'. That is the time of day to come, with the light closing down on the Orkney Islands as they sail on the northern horizon, flat Stroma the nearest.

A footpath leads south from Duncansby Head lighthouse. Kittiwake echoes come up out of the deep cleft of the Geo of Sclaites as you pass its inner rim before reaching the clifftops overlooking Thirle Door. The bay is a scoop of boulders under fractured red sandstone cliffs. They have spawned the Stacks of Duncansby, layered sea stacks tapering to points like a pair of Turkish turbans. They stand out in the sea, their sides slimed pale green with guano, their ledges a shrieking mass of seabirds whose hysteria calms to a matter of grumbles and squawks as night sweeps out day from the eastern horizon.

384. CAPE WRATH, HIGHLAND

Maps: OS Explorer 466; Landranger 9

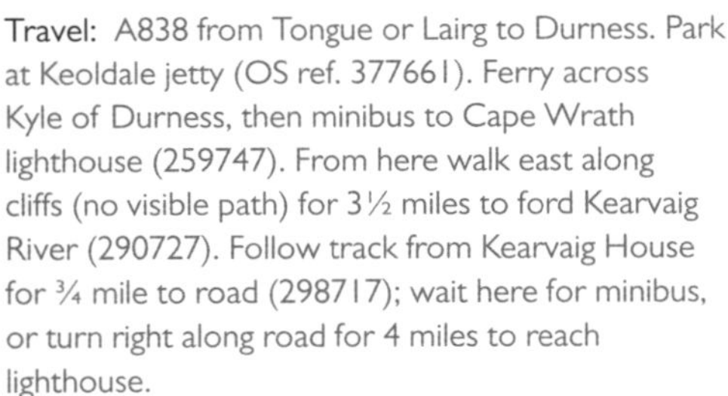

Travel: A838 from Tongue or Lairg to Durness. Park at Keoldale jetty (OS ref. 377661). Ferry across Kyle of Durness, then minibus to Cape Wrath lighthouse (259747). From here walk east along cliffs (no visible path) for 3½ miles to ford Kearvaig River (290727). Follow track from Kearvaig House for ¾ mile to road (298717); wait here for minibus, or turn right along road for 4 miles to reach lighthouse.

Ferry/minibus: Booking essential: tel: 01971 511343/511287; www.capewrath.org.uk.

NB: This is a demanding walk, over peat hags and rough moorland to Kervaig Bay, followed by a fording of the wide, shallow and fast-flowing Kearvaig River. The terrain is completely exposed and often very windy. Take proper hillwalking gear, and be prepared to get wet to the knees or beyond!

What wilder name could anyone imagine than Cape Wrath? Here at the north-western corner of mainland Britain, when the Atlantic waves crash and thump against the pink gneiss cliffs and a Force 10 gale screams over streaming grass and heather, it's easy to see how the headland got its name. Easy, but wrong. 'Wrath' derives not from the splendid old word for 'fury', but from the Old Norse word for 'cape', a turning point for ships. On sighting the great cliffs of the promontory the Viking longships would put their helms over, either to run south down the long and comparatively sheltered channel between the mainland and the Western Isles or, if returning home, to shape a course east through the Pentland Firth into the North Sea.

For travellers making the minibus journey out to Robert Stevenson's stumpy white

Cape Wrath

lighthouse, the road to Cape Wrath is a rough ride. It bumps and jolts through a treeless landscape of bog and moor grass, parts of it blasted by fire from naval shells, for the Cape is used from time to time as a target range. Once out at the headland tip you can walk south or east along the clifftops, and within ten minutes feel as though you're the only person left in the world. Cape Wrath is supremely lonely, a rolling moor that falls down pink-and-black cliffs to bays that seldom see a human footfall. Bog cotton, sphagnum and millions of pink and purple orchids; otters and seals playing in the tides; dark rock stacks shaped like cathedral towers; bearded lichens rippled by the wind; an ice-cold soaking in the Kearvaig River; intimations of bliss on the creamy sands of Kearvaig Bay – such are the delights of one of the wildest places in this book.

385. ARDVRECK CASTLE, INCHNADAMPH, HIGHLAND

Maps: OS Explorer 442; Landranger 15

Travel: A835 north from Ullapool; in 18 miles, left on A837; Ardvreck Castle on left, 1½ miles beyond Inchnadamph (OS ref. 240236).

The dungeon vault of Ardvreck Castle must have been a dark and comfortless hole in April 1650, when James Graham, Marquis of Montrose, was incarcerated there. The capture and brief imprisonment of 'gallant Montrose', staunch royalist and supporter of the Stuart cause, ranks as a betrayal according to the tenets of Highland hospitality; for Montrose sought sanctuary after the Battle of Carbisdale. Yet his host, Neil Macleod of Assynt, handed him over to his pursuers in exchange for £20,000 and 400 bolts of flour.

Ardvreck Castle is a ruin these days; the vaulted chambers open yawning black mouths beneath a stub of masonry, all that remains of the Macleod stronghold. Neil Macleod, betrayer of the fugitive Montrose, was already losing his grip on power in the locality when the hunted man arrived at his gates. The tale goes that Macleod himself was away from home, but had left his formidable wife, Christine Munro, in charge. Montrose had been back in his native Scotland from exile for less than a month, trying in vain to whip up support for his master, King Charles II, who had fled the kingdom the previous year after the execution of his father, King Charles I. Montrose may have been tricked into coming to Ardvreck after the battle; he was certainly received by Lady Macleod in the guise of friendship, before she either inveigled him into the dungeon and turned the key on him, or summoned his captors while he slept – stories vary.

The prisoner was marched away to Edinburgh, where he was quickly tried and condemned for treason. On 21 May Montrose was hanged at the Mercat Cross in Edinburgh, then disembowelled and dismembered. The castle on Loch Assynt did not survive its prisoner long – partly destroyed in 1672 during a fourteen-day siege by the powerful Mackenzie clan, a lightning strike in 1795 completed the devastation.

Two ghosts haunt the ruins. One, tall and grey, is either that of Montrose or of his betrayer. The other, seen weeping bitterly, is the beautiful daughter of a Macleod chief, perhaps Big Angus III himself. The Devil desired her so much that he offered his help in building the castle in exchange for her hand in marriage. But as soon as the battlements had been completed, the wretched girl threw herself to her death from them, rather than submit to the embraces of the Evil One.

386. INVERPOLLY, HIGHLAND

Maps: OS Explorer 439 (Stac Pollaidh), 442 (Suilven); Landranger 15

Travel: For Inverpolly National Nature Reserve, take A835 north from Ullapool; in 10 miles, left at Drumrunie on minor road signed 'Achiltibuie'. In 4 miles, park where road bends left, a mile before reaching Stac Pollaidh (OS ref. 127089), and take path to your right, over saddle by Loch Fhionnlaidh and down to Loch an Doire Dhuibh and mountain of Cul Mor (2,787 feet).

For Stac Pollaidh, continue along road for 1¼ miles to car park on left (108095); very steep path on right leads straight up to high saddle between east and west summits of Stac Pollaidh (2,009 feet).

For Suilven, A835/837 north from Ullapool to Lochinver. At 300 yards beyond Information Centre, left along minor road towards Glencanisp Lodge. After nearly 1 mile, park at fork in road (107220). Keep ahead past Glencanisp Lodge and on for 3¾ miles, aiming straight for Canisp Mountain. At 300 yards past Lochan Buidhe, bear right over footbridge across Abhainn na Clach Airigh (165202); in ¼ mile, where track bears left (167198), keep ahead towards Suilven. After a boggy mile, pass right-hand end of Loch a Choire Dhuibh (159187) and follow cairned track to left, up very steep cleft to top of Bealach Mór (158182). From here it is a scramble to your right to reach Caisteal Liath (153183), the summit of Suilven at 2,398 feet. Retrace your steps to Glencanisp.

NB: The Suilven walk is long and strenuous, nearly 12 miles there and back, with steep climbing and a little scrambling on Suilven – allow a good 8 or 9 hours. You are a long way from help in an emergency.

Inverpolly is a most wonderful wilderness, arguably the most bewitching in this book. There are red-throated divers in the lochans, golden eagles in the skies, otters in the rivers and red deer on the braes. Out on a ragged limb between the inland heights of Assynt and the open Atlantic, these are 26,827 acres of extremely lonely bog, loch, mountain and moor. The weather changes smear rainbows across the hills, amid

Stac Pollaidh

thunderous clouds and shafts of sun. This place is soaked in wild magic.

You can wander Inverpolly to your heart's content with map and GPS or compass. The path over from Linneraineach on Loch Lurgainn to the south brings you down into its heart, beside the vast expanse of Loch Sionascaig under the ledges of Cul Mor. The most breathtaking of views can be caught by climbing either of the two sandstone mountains that bookend the reserve. To the south is Stac Pollaidh, a tremendous, eroded crag that sweeps up above Loch Lorgainn.

To the north is Suilven, probably the most strangely shaped mountain in Scotland. A striated sphinx with two very distinct ends, the climb to the saddle between them is a hard sweat, but the scramble up the western, higher peak is not too hair-raising. The flat, grassy table-top of a summit is the perfect place to eat your picnic (you did bring one, didn't you?) and survey the broken, jumbled, glinting landscape.

387. LOCH COIRE LAIR, ACHNASHELLACH, HIGHLAND

Maps: OS Explorer 429; Landranger 25

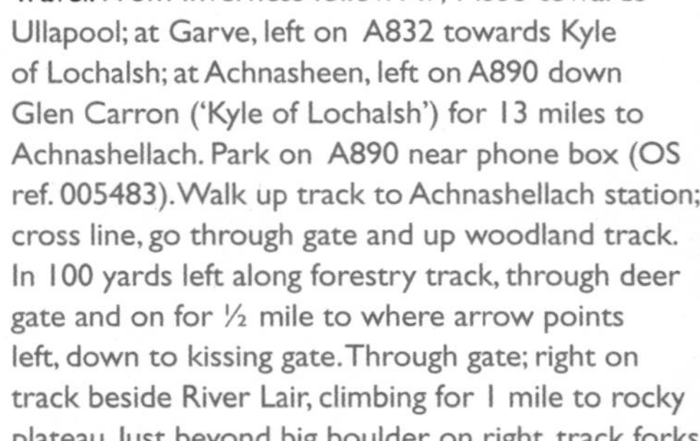

Travel: From Inverness follow A9, A835 towards Ullapool; at Garve, left on A832 towards Kyle of Lochalsh; at Achnasheen, left on A890 down Glen Carron ('Kyle of Lochalsh') for 13 miles to Achnashellach. Park on A890 near phone box (OS ref. 005483). Walk up track to Achnashellach station; cross line, go through gate and up woodland track. In 100 yards left along forestry track, through deer gate and on for ½ mile to where arrow points left, down to kissing gate. Through gate; right on track beside River Lair, climbing for 1 mile to rocky plateau. Just beyond big boulder on right, track forks at small cairn (990503). Left for 1 mile to reach foot of Loch Coire Lair (977508). Make circuit of loch and return.

NB: This 6-mile walk has some moderately steep parts and visits a wild, lonely part of the mountains. Hillwalking gear and boots advisable.

Nearest railway station: Achnashellach

The wide, steep-sided strath of Glen Carron cuts south-west through the mountains of Wester Ross, and Loch Coire Lair lies high above the strath floor, unseen by anyone except walkers, eagles and deer. Start the climb to the loch from the railway station at Achnashellach, one of the wettest places in Scotland and surely one of the most beautiful, the twin peaks of Fuar Tholl ('the cold one') and Carn Odhar ('the dun hill') standing as buttresses to the steep cleft of the River Lair. You climb north beside the rocky bed of the river, staring down between oak and rowan to where the Lair hisses and bounces among boulders far below the path.

Loch Coire

Enormous country unpeels itself as you reach a saddle 1,000 feet above Achnashellach. The view west is into a majestic horseshoe of tilted sandstone 750 million years old – Fuar Tholl, Sgurr Ruadh ('red rocky peak') like a shark tooth, and facing them Beinn Liath Mhor, the 'great grey mountain', its three humps streaked with dully gleaming patches of quartzite.

Below the slopes of the mountains you look down on Loch Coire Lair cradled in these rocky arms, remote and beautiful, a pear-shaped lake lying dark and glittering in its hollow. Burns rush down clefts in the mountain walls to feed the loch. You can walk round it – a tiring trek in ankle-deep bog – looking for sundews and orchids, bog asphodel, dwarf juniper, dragonflies and miniature frogs.

388. GLEN OF THE RIVER GLENNAN, DORNIE, HIGHLAND

Maps: OS Explorer 413; Landranger 33

Travel: A87 from Invergarry towards Kyle of Lochalsh. Pass Eilean Donan Castle; bear right before Loch Long bridge into Dornie. Pass Dornie Hotel and post office; continue for 1 mile to park at end of tarmac in Bundalloch (OS ref. 896276). Cross footbridge and turn right along track beside River Glennan for 2½ miles to head of glen (931279). Track climbs to pass, and descends to hamlet of Camas-Luinie (946283).

Visitors come in their many tens of thousands to photograph and admire the famous spectacle of Eilean Donan Castle on its promontory, reflected in the waters where Loch Alsh and Loch Duich join together at the foot of Loch Long. But few venture into the hinterland that rises to the east, a roadless upthrust of rough and craggy mountains

Glen of the River Glennan

running with a thousand mountain burns. The hills are rumpled and lumpy, as if the rocks are alive and struggling to emerge from their green-and-brown cocoon of grass, heather and peat hag. A foot track crosses this upland waste, running up the river of An Leth-allt into Coire Dhuinnid before striking steeply north over the roof of the mountains to Camas-Luinie on the River Elchaig. Tough and experienced hillwalkers go this way. Lesser mortals, or those who wish to see these mountains from the inside, can make for the glen of the River Glennan, which cuts east and west through the northern section of the massif.

The Glennan glen is impressively steep and narrow, its sides rising abruptly and rearing back to ridges 1,000 feet overhead. These slopes run in silhouette ahead of you as you forge through the glen, sloping into the depths at 40-degree angles, one behind the next. The boggy hillsides are quilted in purple heather, bright green sphagnum, dove-grey usnea lichen and pink dots of lousewort. Burns splash down in a series of miniature falls from the mountains, swollen after rain to bubbling torrents that soak the grass and encase your ankles in a cold spongy embrace. Up at the pass beyond the glen head, stand and catch your breath; a wonderful view opens to the east, the sinuous River Elchaig 700 feet below, another wilderness of jagged, alluring peaks beyond.

389. LOCHAN INNIS EANRUIG, NORTH MORAR, HIGHLAND

Maps: OS Explorer 398; Landranger 40

Travel: A830 from Fort William to Mallaig; 3 miles before reaching Mallaig, right ('Morar, Bracora') for 3 miles through Bracora to the end of the road in Bracorina (OS ref. 725927). Cross footbridge and stile beyond ('Stoup' fingerpost) and follow path up hillside for ¾ mile (737930) to Lochan Innis Eanruig. You can continue another 1½ miles to descend steeply to Stoul bay (755944).

North Morar's long, thin peninsula harbours no settlement larger than a hamlet until the ferry port of Mallaig. This is a back-of-beyond place, its spine a formless mass of ground between 1,000 and 2,000 feet high, flashing with lochs and lochans and heavy with waterlogged peat. Climb the narrow hill track from Bracorina on the south shore and you soon leave the coastal oak and birch groves for treeless upland. The steep, stony track, its course marked with rough cairns, becomes a rushing stream after rain. It passes bogs bright with the rabbit-tails of bog cotton and the pink dragon-heads of lousewort, running through patches of heather and bilberry as it gains height.

A wonderful view opens up near the top

Loch Innis Eanruig

of the climb. To the south stretches the steely inlet of Loch Morar, the deepest loch in Scotland at 1,000 feet, with a monster, Morag, to rival old Nessie (see p. 418). Out west across the sea lies the long bar of the Isle of Eigg, buttressed with the volcanic wall of the Sgurr. Compared with the drama of this prospect, Lochan Innis Eanruig slips modestly into view beyond the pass, a sheet of wind-flecked water, leaden grey, hidden in a hollow and cradled by purple-grey basalt hills. The pool is cold to the fingers, icy to the bare legs on a hot summer afternoon.

Climb the hillock behind the lochan to savour this silent place, muted, harsh and beautiful. The track winds on for another mile or so to tip abruptly downhill to Stoul; you can follow it, or simply sit out the hours in contemplation here.

390. OCKLE, ARDNAMURCHAN, HIGHLAND

Maps: OS Explorer 390; Landranger 47

Travel: A82 from Glencoe towards Fort William; 4 miles north of North Ballachulish, left across Corran Narrows of Loch Linnhe by Corran Ferry, then left on A861 to Salen. Left on B8007 through Glenborrodale. In another 8 miles, right (OS ref. 525665) on minor road; in 1/3 mile, right for 3 miles to Ockle (556704). Park near Ockle holiday cottages and follow stony track on foot. In 200 yards keep ahead at fork with house to your right, and follow track north to ruined croft house on shore (555713). Bear right along coast, a stiff scramble of nearly 3 miles (allow 1½–2 hours) to reach headland of Rubha Aird Druimnich (579729).

The long promontory of Ardnamurchan, sniffing west above the Isle of Mull like a bulbous nose, is one of the loneliest peninsulas in the deeply indented western flank of Scotland. Coming here for solitude and silence, I make for the north coast and the narrow moor road to Ockle. Bumping north beside the Achateny Water, it seems never-ending, but at last it decants me beside the watersplash over Allt Ockle near an array of old houses done up for holiday cottages.

The track passes through a gate and declines to a grassy meander, all sign of human habitation now shut away by the shoulder of the hill. I drop by curves and dips to a rocky bay hidden between the bare jaws of low cliffs. A crumbling croft house of two rooms open to the sky, a rusted anchor half buried under a boulder, a whispering haze of rushes and a stupendous view north to the Isle of Eigg 7 miles away. Daisies and tormentil spatter the grass, yellow lichen smears the rocks and the shore pools lie

thick with brown, emerald and crimson seaweed.

I turn east and scramble along the rocky shore for an hour or two, fording the hill burns where they come chattering down to the beach, poking around the many caves, to reach the 100-foot headland of Rubha Aird Druimnich, the 'high promontory of the ridge'. Here in this remote spot I sit and stare out at Eigg, with the high peaks of the Isle of Rhum smoking behind and the Hebridean sea sparkling in front.

391. MULL OF OA, ISLE OF ISLAY, INNER HEBRIDES

Maps: OS Explorer 352; Landranger 60

Travel: Ferry from Kennacraig, or by air from Glasgow (www.islay.co.uk). A846 from Port Ellen towards Bowmore; just after leaving Port Ellen, left (OS ref. 361458) on minor road past distillery, through Cragabus. Park at end of tarmac road at Lower Killeyan (285428), bear left on track to Upper Killeyan farm (280419) and keep forward for ¾ mile to monument on Mull of Oa (270415).

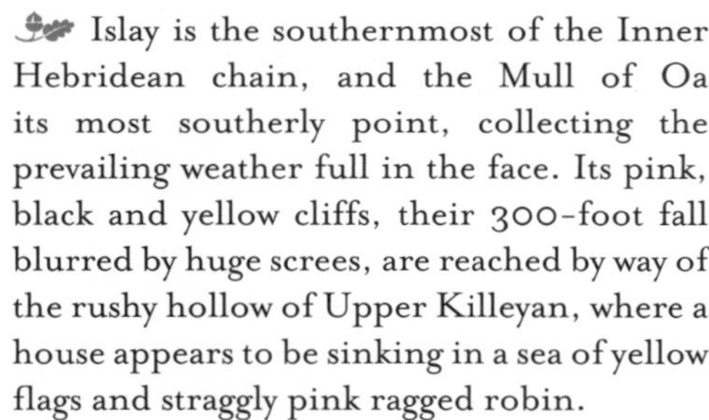

Islay is the southernmost of the Inner Hebridean chain, and the Mull of Oa its most southerly point, collecting the prevailing weather full in the face. Its pink, black and yellow cliffs, their 300-foot fall blurred by huge screes, are reached by way of the rushy hollow of Upper Killeyan, where a house appears to be sinking in a sea of yellow flags and straggly pink ragged robin.

Down on the edge of the cliffs stands a stark tower banded in dark and light stone. It looks like a lighthouse, but it is in fact a memorial to dark events, the wreck of two American troopships off Islay in 1918. HMS *Tuscania* went down with the loss of 266 lives on 5 February after being torpedoed 7 miles off the Mull of Oa by German submarine *UB77*, and HMS *Otranto* was lost on 6 October after a collision with another troopship that cost the lives of 431 sailors and soldiers. The windy cliffs of Oa are a suitably sombre place to contemplate these tragedies.

392. GLEN BATRICK, ISLE OF JURA, INNER HEBRIDES

Maps: OS Explorer 355; Landranger 61

Travel: Ferry from Port Askaig on Isle of Islay to Feolin Ferry on Jura (www.juradevelopment.co.uk). A846 through Craighouse and Leargybreck. In another 1½ miles park at foot of track to Glen Batrick (OS ref. 550732). Follow track north for 5 miles to Glenbatrick bay (517800).

NB: This is a 10-mile there-and-back walk over rough, boggy ground, with no shelter, refreshment or transport.

Jura is the loneliest island for its size in the whole Hebridean chain. Its human population of under 200 have 100,000 acres, 5,000 red deer, three quartzite cones of mountains, and a superb west coast to enjoy. In the whole of Jura there is just one road, and three tiny settlements. In 1946 George Orwell chose the island as a place of perfect solitude in which to write *1984*. He chose wisely.

Most of the island is composed of hard white quartzite, the sand of prehistoric seabeds which discourages plant growth and allows a reluctant covering of heather, bog and sedge. Near the waist of the island rise three eye-catching conical mountains called the Paps of Jura, a splendid challenge for hillwalkers. The track to Glen Batrick curves round their feet to the north, and offers a striking walk across the spine of Jura to a wild and lonely coast. Once you have threaded your way down the narrow defile of Glen Batrick itself and reached the single house on the shores of Glenbatrick bay, you will feel very far from civilization.

You can ramble east or west along the rocky bays and be virtually sure of seeing nobody. This is a shore of rock ledges, promontories and thick tracts of bog, interspersed with great pale sheets of pebbles backed by cave mouths, which can lie 100 feet or more above the shore. They are the shingle strands of the pre-Ice Age era. When the ice sheets of the last Ice Age finally receded northwards from Scotland, the land that had been weighed down so heavily for so long rose gratefully upwards. From these beaches marooned high over the sea there are stunning views over islets, sea and headlands. There are also 50 miles of roadless west coast to explore – a seductive prospect

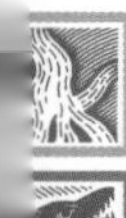
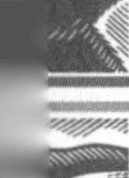

393. CORRYVRECKAN WHIRLPOOL, ISLE OF JURA, INNER HEBRIDES

Maps: OS Explorer 355; Landranger 55

Travel: Ferry from Port Askaig on Isle of Islay to Feolin Ferry on Jura (www.juradevelopment.co.uk). A846 through Craighouse and Leargybreck to Ardlussa, where tarmac ends (OS ref. 647878). Parking recommended here. From Ardlussa, a very rough road north for 8 miles (4×4 necessary if driving) passing Barnhill (705970 – NB: private residence) to reach end of road at Kinuachdrach (705987). Follow path north for 2 miles to top of Jura overlooking Corryvreckan Whirlpool (685022 approx.).

Whether St Columba prayed for the deliverance of one of his brethren from the dreaded whirlpool of Corryvreckan, or whether Breccán, grandson of Niall of the Nine Hostages, drowned in the maelstrom along with the crews of his fifty black currachs, will never be known. It is certain that George Orwell, his adopted son and two young relations almost came to grief here in August 1947 when the writer was living at Barnhill on the north end of the Isle of Jura. The Corryvreckan Whirlpool, the third largest in the world, is notorious for the wrecks it has caused, but Orwell thought he could tease it like a tethered beast. The suck of the eddy was so strong that it unseated the outboard motor of the party's little boat, and they only just managed to scramble on to the rock of Eilean Mór as the tide whirled them past it before the boat turned over and sank. Orwell and the children had to be rescued by boat from the shore.

The very rough road, suitable only for 4x4 vehicles, bumps and lurches north along the east coast of Jura towards the apex of the big island. Barnhill lies tucked down below the road. The house where Orwell wrote *1984* is a weather-beaten place crouching under a green slope. When he first arrived in 1946, Orwell stayed at Kinuachdrach, the most northerly house on Jura, where the road comes to an end. From there a path leads on over bog and heather to the brow of the island, from where you can see the whirlpool seething and swirling below.

Corryvreckan owes its existence to the presence of a hole some 650 feet below the seabed, and a pinnacle to the west of it that rises from the floor of the sound to within 100 feet of the surface. Strong tides push in over the hole, gaining a sucking force as they hit the east face of the pinnacle at around

8½ miles an hour. The water is squeezed upwards and shot forward. When the wind is from the west, forming a fist of resistance to the tide, a static wave can form that some observers have recorded reaching a height of 30 feet. You may be fortunate enough to see this, or a boat revolving like a propeller as it passes through the whirlpool. Red deer have been spotted swimming frantically against the tug of the tide as they attempt to reach Scarba from Jura, and one or two humans have succeeded in swimming the sound through the eddy, notably Orwell's one-legged brother-in-law, Bill Dunn, the first person to be recorded doing so. If you come towards the end of autumn you may even be lucky enough to spot the Cailleach Bheur, the blue-faced hag of winter, as she washes her plaid in Corryvreckan and spreads it on the hills as bleach-white snow.

394. ARDMEANACH, ISLE OF MULL, INNER HEBRIDES

Maps: OS Explorer 375; Landranger 48

Travel: Ferry from Oban, Kilchoan or Lochaline (www.isle.of.mull.com). A849 towards Kinloch, Bunessan and Iona Ferry. 1 mile before Kinloch Hotel, right (OS ref. 547292) on B8035 Gruline and Salen road. In 4 miles, left by converted chapel (491286 – 'NTS Burg') for 2 miles, past Tioran House, to NTS car park (477275). Continue on foot along track for 3½ miles to pass NTS bothy (425266); in another 1½ miles, reach top of ladder and descend to shore (404273). The Fossil Tree is another ⅓ mile along the cliffs, just beyond the second of twin waterfalls (402278). Return the same way.

NB: This is a 12-mile walk, there and back, with some fairly strenuous and narrow sections. The cliff ladder is about 20 feet high, an unguarded descent not for vertigo sufferers.

The middle and the wildest of the Isle of Mull's three west coast peninsulas is Ardmeanach, a place as rugged as any lover of rough country could desire. Its western face is dubbed the Wilderness, with good reason. Cliffs hem it in, caves pierce its flanks, crystalline columns of basalt buttress it. The seaward slopes are crammed with tiny, delicate wild flowers – eyebright, stonecrop, centaury, sea plantain, thyme, slender St John's wort. It is a place to go only if you are well-shod and sure-footed, with a good head for heights and no fear of being on your own. Feral goats crop the grass, golden eagles fly over the beaches, and seals, otters and porpoises play off its headlands. It is, quite simply, a foretaste of wild heaven.

The path from the National Trust for Scotland's bothy at Burg, on the south coast of the peninsula, is narrow, steep and slippery. So is the unguarded metal ladder by which, at your own risk, you descend the cliff face to the jumble of boulders on the shore. This is incredibly rich volcanic ground. The geological map of Mull looks like an explosion in a paint factory, with many and varied rock types cartwheeling out of a central nucleus, a giant volcano that erupted some 10 million years ago. Not only did it form the basalt columns so characteristic of the Mull cliffs and shores; it also fossilized a giant tree trunk which still stands 40 feet tall, moulded into the cliff face of the Wilderness. The black sludge of burned wood and the fine imprint of pine bark scales are preserved in the rock for you to find and marvel at.

395. IONA, INNER HEBRIDES

Maps: OS Explorer 374; Landranger 48

Travel: Ferry from Fionnphort, Isle of Mull (www.isle-of-iona.com).

Iona, St Columba's holy isle, is sacred ground, the place to which fifty Scottish kings were brought for burial, the fountain of Christian faith in Scotland and the focus of prayer and pilgrimage today. Iona has magical beauty, and a spiritual resonance recognized across the world. This is where the sixth-century Irish fugitive and saint Columba nursed the spark of Christian faith in the darkest days of the Dark Ages, to take it clear across Scotland in an all-consuming flame. As such, this 3-mile-long slip of an island is often crowded.

If you are looking for Iona's solitude it is best to spend the night here, to wait until the crowds have gone from the beautifully restored abbey and from the museum, with its remarkable high-relief tomb slabs of bygone Scots kings and chieftains. Venture out in the quiet of evening for a walk to the lonely north, west and south coasts. Down on the north shore the sands shine white, the sea glass-green. From Dun-I, the highest crag on the island, you can look east across the Sound of Iona to the pink granite cliffs around Fionnphort, west over miles of sea to the mountains of North Uist and Harris in the Outer Hebrides. Seeing these at sunset, outlined against a burning sun, you can easily understand how the legends arose of Atlantis and of Tir-na-nog, the Land of Youth, the lost isles of the blessed in the depths of the ocean.

The western beaches of Iona lie covered in pebbles of many hues – green, black, red and a striking mottled pink and white, the colours of immensely ancient gneiss. This volcanic rock, the fundamental material of the Outer Hebrides, is the oldest rock in Britain, laid down some 3,300 million years ago. It has made its way here to the beaches of Iona in the form of sea-smoothed pebbles.

A smattering of Gaelic brings a lot of pleasure in the Hebrides; and what you don't know, you can always guess at. Southwards along the west coast you walk by way of the Blest Place of the Red-Haired Lad, the Port of the Coward and Weeper's Rock, until you reach Port na Curaich, the Harbour of the Coracle, where Columba beached his skin-covered boat in AD 563, an exile in disgrace with the death of thousands of men on his conscience. Columba's unauthorized copying of a set of precious gospels had led to a condemnation by the High King of Ireland himself, a taking of sides by furious factions, and terrible bloodshed in a pitched battle in County Sligo. Appalled by the consequences of his plagiarism, Columba fled in self-imposed exile with a few companions. His penance was to bring more men to Christianity than he had caused to die that day. The Celtic Church he founded on Iona would last 1,000 years and exert its influence throughout the northern Christian world.

396. ULVA, INNER HEBRIDES

Maps: OS Explorer 374; Landranger 48

Travel: Ferry from Oban, Kilchoan or Lochaline to Isle of Mull (www.isle.of.mull.com). A848/849 to Salen; B8035 for 2½ miles towards Gruline; right on B8073 through Killichronan and on towards Tobermory. In 7 miles, left (OS ref. 451401) to Isle of Ulva ferry (www.ulva.mull.com/ferry). Wander at will on Ulva; all exploration is on foot. Free camping under strict rules: see website www.ulva.mull.com. All provisions, including water, need to be carried.

Ulva lies off the west coast of the Isle of Mull, separated from its big sister island by a sound no more than 200 yards wide. It seems impossible that such a narrow and shallow stretch of water could pose any dangers. Yet in 1774, only a year after Samuel Johnson and James Boswell had met him during their famous tour of the Hebrides, the young laird of the Isle of Coll, Donald Maclean, drowned in a sudden storm while trying to cross between Mull and Ulva. 'Young Coll', a noble savage as depicted by Boswell (see pp. 442–3), was not the only victim of the crossing to Ulva. Thomas Campbell's dramatic and romantic ballad 'Lord Ullin's Daughter' tells of Lord Ullin's pursuit of his runaway daughter and her lover, who attempt to make the passage on a wild night:

A Chieftain to the Highlands bound
Cries, 'Boatman, do not tarry!
And I'll give thee a silver pound
To row us o'er the ferry!'

'Now who be ye, would cross Lochgyle,
This dark and stormy water?'
'O! I'm the chief of Ulva's isle,
And this, Lord Ullin's daughter!'

Tossing spray, cavernous waves, two lovers clutched in each other's arms, a frail boat overwhelmed under Ulva's dark cliffs; wretched Lord Ullin frantic on the shore, bitterly regretting his actions and powerless to save his child:

'Come back! Come back!' he cried in grief,
'Across this stormy water;
And I'll forgive your Highland chief,
My daughter – O, my daughter!'

'Twas vain: the loud waves lash'd the shore,
Return or aid preventing;
The waters wild went o'er his child,
And he was left lamenting.

The explanation of how such a meek-seeming crossing could turn so wild is probably that the ferry to Ulva ran in former days from the cliffs of Gribun, a genuinely dangerous 3-mile crossing of storm-tossed waters. Not so now, but the facts need not detract from the romance of stepping ashore on one of Scotland's privately owned islands. Everything is kept deliberately low-key for the sake of wildlife and the essential loneliness of the isle, but you can walk a long, demanding circuit of trackless bogs and rocky shores. You can camp rough here, too, waking to the sound and sight of deer in the heather and sea otters on the shore, with every chance of watching the drama and power of a squall in the channel such as that which inspired Thomas Campbell to dream up his doomed, devoted lovers.

397. ISLE OF STAFFA, INNER HEBRIDES

Maps: OS Explorer 374; Landranger 48

Travel: Excursion boats from Ulva Ferry (tel: 01688 500241; www.turusmara.com) or Fionnphort (tel: 01681 700338; www.fingals-cave-staffa.co.uk), Isle of Mull – see www.scotland-inverness.co.uk/staffa.

Staffa is basalt's masterpiece in the Inner Hebrides. This flat-topped block of black rock casts a spell over everyone who visits it. Not much more than half a mile long, its main attraction, the giant opening of Fingal's Cave, possesses the size, shape and solemnity of a cathedral nave – 200 feet long, 50 feet high, flanked by pillars of basalt and with a mouth rising to close at the top in a cathedral's arch. The cave burrows gigantically into the southern point of Staffa, the focus of 99 per cent of all visits to the island.

Staffa is composed of three layers: a solidified mass of rocks and gas bubbles trapped in a petrified sludge of basalt at the base; a top layer that bulges out 100 feet above the sea like a black brain; and a central band of hexagonal columns 30 to 40 feet tall, hundreds of black pencils packed tightly together. Some of these columns stand completely vertical, others bend and twist sideways together. 'The grandeur of the whole structure is on such a vast scale,' wrote Thomas Nicol in 1931, 'that you cannot comprehend its meaning. When one attempts to describe it, words fail. Staffa stands alone as a wonderful example of Nature's craftsmanship veiled in solitary grandeur, a lone isle guarded by the great Atlantic swell.'

That swell washes the tour boats and the inflatables and sea kayaks of intrepid solo voyagers into the cave itself, where Felix Mendelssohn came during his Hebridean tour of 1829. Poor Felix was feeling horribly seasick, yet in the dark majestic depths of An Uamh Binn, the Cave of Melody, he received inspiration for his Hebridean Overture. Back on land he hastened to the piano in his lodgings in order to try out the wild sea melody washing round his head, only to be sternly chided by his host for playing music on the Sabbath.

398. TRESHNISH ISLES, INNER HEBRIDES

Maps: OS Explorer 374; Landranger 48

Travel: Excursion boat from Fionnphort, Isle of Mull (tel: 01681 700338; www.fingals-cave-staffa.co.uk or www.turusmara.com).

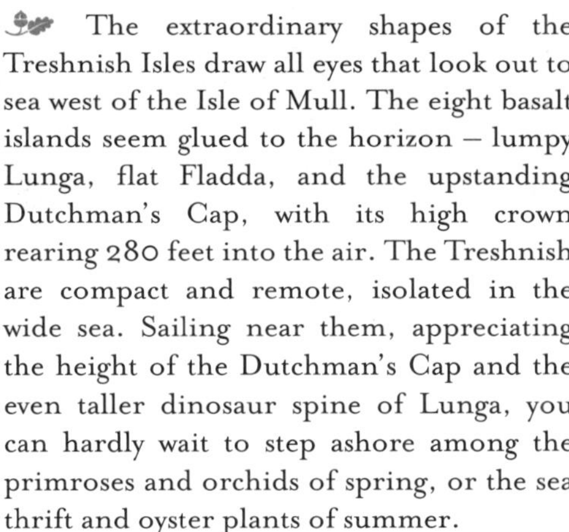

The extraordinary shapes of the Treshnish Isles draw all eyes that look out to sea west of the Isle of Mull. The eight basalt islands seem glued to the horizon – lumpy Lunga, flat Fladda, and the upstanding Dutchman's Cap, with its high crown rearing 280 feet into the air. The Treshnish are compact and remote, isolated in the wide sea. Sailing near them, appreciating the height of the Dutchman's Cap and the even taller dinosaur spine of Lunga, you can hardly wait to step ashore among the primroses and orchids of spring, or the sea thrift and oyster plants of summer.

Lunga was inhabited until the mid nineteenth century, and the ruins of houses remain. The chief island of the archipelago is home to breeding guillemots in their tens of thousands and to storm petrels that creep ashore by night, avoiding the attacks of piratical gulls. Atlantic grey seals congregate to breed and pup in the autumn, safe on these lonely outposts. Populations of black rabbits and house mice betray the human influence on the Treshnish; but since harsh conditions drove the last of the native islanders ashore, no one has braved the challenge of life in

Treshnish Isles

such a remote location. For summertime adventurers, though, flat on their backs among the orchids or dreamily contemplating the outline of Staffa and distant Coll and Tiree, a few hours out on the Treshnish Isles seems a precious chance to shrug off the world that is too much with us.

399. ISLE OF TIREE, INNER HEBRIDES

Maps: OS Explorer 372; Landranger 46

Travel: Ferry from Oban, or by air from Glasgow (www.scotland-inverness.co.uk/tiree).

Tir-i-odh, the Land of Corn, the scapula-shaped 'Granary of the Isles', lies at the trailing hem of the Hebrides. Flying in, you look down to see dark blue turn to milky turquoise, a tropical brilliance of clear water over white shell sand. Then you thump down on Tiree's airfield among sheets of ox-eye daisies and buttercups. Tiree, the most westerly of the Inner Hebrides, is low-lying and double-humped, crouched in the path of all the wind and weather the Atlantic can hurl in its direction. There is a photograph in one of the island's little museums of two weathermen leaning on the wind, their bodies slanted at angles inconsistent with the laws of gravity. Wild weather is as integral to this island as its orchids, celandines, yellow rattle and yarrow, and the unsullied white sands of its shore.

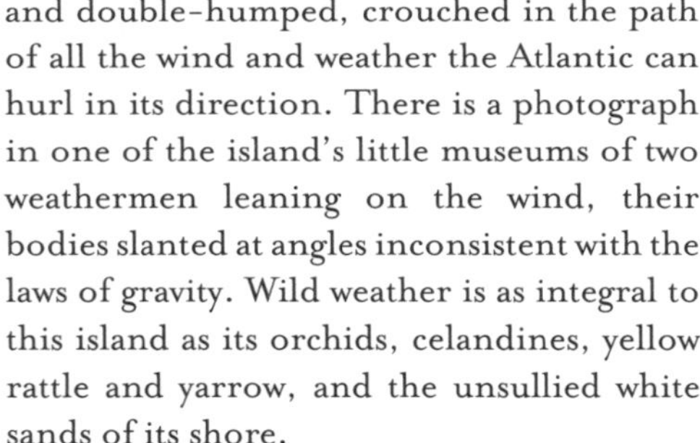

On Tiree there are beaches where the only footprints are those of sea otters, stubs of lookout towers 2,000 years old, and a west coast of crashing seas and seething gales. Arctic terns skim and twist over Loch Bhasapoll. The lime-rich shell sand, driven by the wind, has piled up over the millennia to coat the underlying granite – so barren and unproductive in the other Hebridean islands – with the richest of flowery meadows. At the western and most exposed end of the island the sand has all but buried the ancient Church of St Kenneth in grassy hillocks. These slopes decline to a shore of creamy sands, lichen-speckled rocks and a roaring green sea – a pristine, transcendent place.

400. ISLE OF COLL, INNER HEBRIDES

Maps: OS Explorer 372; Landranger 46

Travel: Ferry from Oban (www.isleofcoll.org).

The Isle of Coll and its sister island of Tiree (see above) lie together, the furthest west of the isles of the Inner Hebrides. Coll looks tremendously barren from the sea. On the ferry, especially if the wind and waves are up, it is easy to picture the storm-tossed arrival of the intrepid travellers Samuel Johnson and James Boswell in 1773 – an unplanned visit. They were forced to seek shelter on the island after being caught in a squall during their tour of the Hebrides. Luckily the helmsman of their boat was Donald Maclean, son of the laird of Coll, a highly competent young man who entertained the city slickers in his native isle for several days until the weather relented. Young Coll, as they dubbed him, was a beacon of hope in an island that was overpopulated and under-resourced. He was full of tremendous plans for the welfare of the island and its 1,000 inhabitants. To Dr Johnson he seemed the personification of the heroic savage:

> *... a noble animal. He is as complete an islander as the mind can figure. He is a farmer, a sailor, a hunter, a fisher: he will run you down a dog: if any man has a* tail, *it is Coll. He is hospitable, and he has an intrepidity of talk, whether he understand the subject or not. I regret that he is not more intellectual.*

It was a terrible blow to his island, and people, when the young man was drowned the following year while sailing between Mull and Ulva (see p. 440).

These days Coll is just as barren and lonely, but far poorer in population: at the 2001 census, 164 people were living there. This absence of human disturbance makes the island an ideal location for the conservation of the corncrake, a shy bird with a grating call – *Crex crex*, its Linnaean name. The corncrake is facing extinction in Britain because of modern agricultural practices that see cornfields and hay fields, its habitat and nesting place, cut short too early in the year for the bird to rear its chicks. The RSPB bought some 3,000 acres at the western end of Coll in 1992, and encourages its tenant farmers to continue traditional practices and allow hay and corn to grow until the infant corncrakes are fledged. As a result *Crex crex* is thriving, its numbers of calling males up from the initial twenty or so to near double that number.

Along with the corncrakes, you can enjoy the sound and sight of sedge warblers, grasshopper warblers, larks and pipits on Coll. Brown hares lollop the grasslands, seals and otters haunt the coasts. Weather systems race in from the Atlantic to soak or dry the island, darken or lighten its craggy slopes, then forge away landwards.

401. ISLE OF EIGG, INNER HEBRIDES

Maps: OS Explorer 397; Landranger 39

Travel: Ferry from Mallaig or Askaig (www.road-to-the-isles.org.uk/eigg). From Galmisdale walk south along the cliffs and shore to find Uamh Fhraing, the Massacre Cave, at OS ref. 475834. Take a torch!

The wedge-shaped Isle of Eigg sits under the right heel of the Isle of Rhum (see pp. 444–5), sheer cliffs 1,000 feet high forming a curtain at the northern end, the great volcanic whalehead of An Sgurr rising in the south. Eigg has endured many vicissitudes over the years, including a succession of more or less flamboyant and unrealistic owners, until the islanders themselves formed the Isle of Eigg Heritage Trust and bought the island in 1997. With its dramatic columnar basalt, wide boglands and remote beaches, Eigg is a very wild place. The wildest tale of all, though, concerns an incident in the winter of 1577, which saw every single islander murdered, save one.

On the southern shore, not far from Galmisdale, lies the Massacre Cave – in Gaelic, Uamh Fhraing, or the Cave of Francis. The entrance drops from an arch 20 feet high to a tiny hole, and you have to wriggle in on your belly. Once inside, torchlight shows a sizeable cavern where you can stand upright. In 1773, when Samuel Johnson and James Boswell visited, Uamh Fhraing was still full of skeletons. These days there are only ghosts in the black cavern in the cliffs.

A party of Macleods from Harris landed in Eigg, so the story goes, either to ravage the island – they were sworn enemies of the Macdonalds of Eigg – or because a storm had driven them there. Either way, they cornered and raped a number of Eigg girls. The male kinsmen of the victims managed to capture the rapists, and had their revenge by castrating them and setting them adrift in a boat at sea. When the raided raiders fetched up back in Harris, their clansmen filled several galleys and set off for Eigg to wreak revenge.

The Macdonalds, suspecting that the Macleods would come after them, gathered on the south shore, and the entire population of the island crawled into hiding in the Cave

Isle of Eigg

of Francis. One old woman who could not get in was left at large, and she was – rather remarkably – spared by the Macleods when they arrived in Eigg. After searching the island for three days and finding no one, the Harris men were reluctantly sailing away when one of them spotted footprints in freshly fallen snow on the shore. They had been made by a Macdonald scout, sent out to see if the coast was clear. The Macleods put into the bay and found the entrance to Uamh Fhraing, where they could hear the whispers and coughs of a large number of people inside. Realizing that it would be suicide to try to enter such a narrow passage, the raiding party simply built a fire in the cave mouth, covered it with green fuel, and drove the thick, choking smoke into the cave, where it 'smorit the haill people thairin to the number of 395 personnes, men, wife and bairnis'.

402. ISLE OF RHUM, INNER HEBRIDES

Maps: OS Explorer 397; Landranger 39

Travel: Ferry from Mallaig or Askaig (www.road-to-the-isles.org.uk/rum).

The great conical mountains of Rhum (sometimes spelled 'Rum') beckon a Hebridean traveller, always in view – or so it seems – on the sea horizon, usually streaming smoky cloud from their tips, as if in remembrance of the volcanic explosions that formed them. And it is mountains that remain in the mind when you leave and are staring back in regret from the Mallaig-bound ferry. Norsemen gave these peaks their evocative names: Askival, the Ash Tree Mountain; Hallival, the Rocky Peak; Ainshval, the Stronghold Mountain; Tralival, the Fell of the Trolls. Both names and shapes cast a wild, romantic spell, the kind of magic that induced the Bullough family to buy the island in 1886. Before the Bulloughs the owner had been Lord Salisbury, a benevolent laird; before him, Dr Lachlan Maclean, who had ruthlessly cleared Rhum of its 300 people in 1826, shipping them all to Nova Scotia and replacing them with 8,000 sheep.

Nowadays it is Scottish National Heritage who owns the island. Rhum is famous for its sea eagles, its rare mountain plants and its huge herd of red deer. You are free to wander the deep-cut glens and rugged mountains as you will; and everywhere you go there are reminders of the seventy-year reign of the Bulloughs. Most spectacular is turreted Kinloch Castle overlooking the bay, a fabulous fantasy castle built at the turn of the twentieth century, constructed of imported red Arran sandstone by a team of Lancastrian builders who were paid an extra shilling a day to please Sir George Bullough's fancy by wearing kilts on site. Here at Kinloch Sir George and his French divorcée wife, Monica, ruled in lairdly style, shooting, fishing and giving dancing parties in the few months of the year they were resident. Sir George, grandson of a clog-wearing Lancastrian mill machinery manufacturer, had a fruity reputation, burnished by tales of London showgirls shipped out to Rhum to entertain Highland regimental officers at wild weekend parties. He lies today with his father, John, and with Lady Monica in a splendidly over-the-top mausoleum, more like a Grecian temple with its pillars and pediments. In the hillside near by crumbles a semicircular mosaic of leaves,

flowers and a torch of life, the entrance to the sepulchre of John Bullough before his body was removed to the mausoleum. These fantastic and in some ways ridiculous structures stand as touching mementoes to the most extravagant and romantic lairdship that Rhum ever knew.

403. EILEAN NAN AMADAN, INNER HEBRIDES

Maps: Special supplements of OS Explorer 397 and Landranger 39, both available on island only.

Travel: A82 to Fort William, A830 to Mallaig and Isle of Skye; minor road to Aird of Sleat in extreme south of island, narrow track for 3 miles west to Point of Sleat. Boat leaves for Eilean nan Amadan 8 a.m. alternate Saturdays, returning 8 a.m. the following day (www.amadan.co.uk).

NB: If bad weather prevents return crossing you may have to stay on the island until next boat arrives. Bring all own food, drink, cooking gear, camping equipment (including lavatory paper) and rain-gear – no amenities on island. Please do not pick Erica malvidica – it is a protected species.

'Ma gheibh mi aon fhacal bhuat, buaillidh mi thu air an t-sroin ghoraich, Shasannaich!' is the traditional greeting as you step ashore. It means, 'A thousand greetings to the stranger', and is a welcome sound after the crashing of waves against the hull of the tiny ferry throughout the five- or six-hour sickening crossing from the Isle of Skye. Eilean nan Amadan, the Isle of Gulls, lies west of Eigg, Muck and Rhum, but unlike its neighbours it has no amenities and no modern facilities whatsoever. You need a strong stomach, a capacity for making the best of rain and cold wind, and a well-developed sense of humour to appreciate a stay on this uncompromising island. Being so far off the tourist track, the island has never had a hotel or guest house. Visitors are tolerated on the understanding that they are prepared to camp out in the often waterlogged fields. There is no electricity, no gas, no tap water. There are no roads and no cars. All the islanders have bicycles and cycle everywhere. This is not as easy as it sounds, for the topography of Eilean nan Amadan is not exactly cycle-friendly.

On the west coast lie the ruins of the Chapel of St Seumus. The saint arrived in AD 567, chased by pirates; he managed to run his coracle up to the cliffs, but as he leaped ashore he somehow got his leg wedged in a crevice. The pirates left him there to die, hanging upside down. Five days and five nights later, according to island lore, 'the virgins of the isle, finding the saint *in extremis*, both freed and comforted him as best they might'. This legend may have given the bleak bay beyond the chapel ruins its name of Camus nan Boireannaich Deonach, the Bay of Caressing Hands, though some say the name simply reflects the movement of the waves on the pebbly beach.

Apart from climbing Sgurr Dubh, the Dark Peak, and looking for the Chapel of St Seumus, you can also hunt for the rare heather *Erica malvidicus*, out of which the dozen islanders make heather whisky, a fatally potent brew. You will be urged to fortify your stomach with a dram before you step aboard the boat and steel yourself for the return crossing, the island blessing ringing in your ears: 'Thalla a h-amadain, fhaion 's na tig thu air ais!' – which translates roughly as: 'Farewell, stranger no more, and may you hurry back again!'

404. CAMASUNARY BAY, ISLE OF SKYE

Maps: OS Explorer 411; Landranger 32

Travel: From Kyle of Lochalsh, Skye Bridge and A87 to Broadford; left on B8083 to Elgol. Park in parking bays half way down the hill (OS ref. 519137) and return uphill to start of path on left ('Camasunary' fingerpost). In 200 yards keep forward ('Footpath to Coruisk' sign) on narrow path for 3 miles to Camasunary Bay (518186). Turn right up rough road for 2 miles to B8083 near Kirkibost (545172); right for 3 miles to Elgol.

NB: A 9-mile round walk. Elgol–Camasunary path is narrow, slippery and vertiginous.

Two features in particular make this teeter of a walk so entrancing: the presence of the hungry Hebridean sea 150 feet below your left elbow; and the extraordinary brooding shapes of the Black Cuillins hanging 3,000 feet in the sky directly ahead. As a dramatic backdrop to what is actually a pretty straightforward coast and hill walk, this is unbeatable.

Prevailing winds are from the west and south-west, and since this walk is up the western flank of the Strathaird peninsula you will get plenty of buffeting. However, the wind tends to blow you both up the path and in towards the reassuring hill slope on your right hand, so unless you suffer acutely from vertigo you should not have much difficulty negotiating the track, although it is slippery after rain and in places less than 6 inches wide. What you will get, in any and all weather conditions, is the sheer exhilaration of walking in some truly wild scenery. The two little white houses on Camasunary Bay, one at either end like a quarrelling couple, only enhance the majestic height and rough beauty of the mountains that hem them in.

The mesmerizing focus of Camasunary Bay beckoning at the end of the path is so strong that it comes as a shock to find, halfway there, the hidden bay of Cladach a' Ghlinne, the 'beach at the foot of the narrow glen'. Tucked away between two headlands, the lonely shingle strand is not visible until you are right on top of it.

Descending at last into the bay, the view back from Camasunary, over the hills of the Isle of Soay to the far-off mountain cones of Rhum, is one to linger over. You may also be looking forward to identifying some of the wild flowers that clothe the machair so thickly in such bright colours. Alas! They turn out to be plastic fish boxes, red, turquoise, orange and blue, cast up by storms in their tens of dozens. Among them roll the rusty metal and sea-frosted glass balls of ancient fishermen's floats, chalky cuttlefish skeletons, hanks of cable and tarry planks.

405. CUILLIN HILLS, ISLE OF SKYE

Maps: OS Explorer 411; Landranger 32

Travel: A87 from Broadford towards Portree; left at Sligachan Hotel on A863 towards Bracadale; in 5 miles, left at Glendrynoch Lodge on B8009 towards Carbost. In 1½ miles, left at Merkadale for 8 miles to Glenbrittle car park (OS ref. 410205). Retrace your steps to Glenbrittle Memorial Hut (411216) and bear right on eastward path that soon crosses Allt Coire na Banachdich. Leaving Eas Mor Waterfall on your left, climb path past Loch an Fhir-bhallaich (430208) to fork left (431208) into Coire Lagan. Bear steeply uphill here (437207) on a path to reach a little loch (444209) under Sgurr Mhic Choinnich. Return to Coire Lagan and keep ahead down the clearer path (431208) all the way to Glenbrittle shop, campsite and car park.

NB: This is a tough hike for experienced hillwalkers, climbing on rough ground from sea level nearly 2,000 feet into the high land just below the Cuillin peaks. Good walking boots, hillwalking gear, map and picnic/water are essential.

The Cuillin Hills exert tremendous influence on every visitor to the Isle of Skye. They are splendid and dramatic, strikingly coloured (red towards the east, black in the west and highest part) and very tall, with several 'Munro' peaks over 3,000 feet. Above all, they are jagged, especially the Black Cuillins, being formed of a particularly sharply weathering granite called gabbro, a rough dark rock. The Black Cuillins look as mountains should. They are iconic to the Isle of Skye; when their owner, Macleod of Dunvegan, put them up for sale for £10 million in 2000 to raise money for the repair of Dunvegan Castle's leaky roof, he provoked outrage across the climbing, walking, conservation and heritage communities.

A great way to penetrate the heart and soul of the Cuillins without too much sweat and effort is by way of the path from remote Glenbrittle that climbs east into a dark corrie between Sgurr Dearg, 'the red rocky peak' (3,235 feet), and Sgurr Alasdair, at 3,257 feet the tallest peak in the Isle of Skye. Ahead of you is the mighty rock wall of Sron na Ciche, and after you have passed the steely waters of Loch an Fhir-bhallaich and headed up through Coire Lagan your target is the vast dark skirt of scree that forms the Great Stone Shoot. Under this is a tiny lochan, still and sheltered in its mountain cradle. There may be the clink and scrape of a climber's progress high on the faces above you, but more likely than not you will have only cold wind, water and rock for company beneath the majestic gabbro crown.

'It's the far Cuillins that are putting love on me,' sang Harry Lauder, and anyone who has walked these rugged hills knows exactly what he meant.

406. THE QUIRAING, ISLE OF SKYE

Maps: OS Explorer 408; Landranger 23

Travel: A87 from Skye Bridge to Portree, A855 through Staffin towards Uig. You can approach the Quiraing two ways:

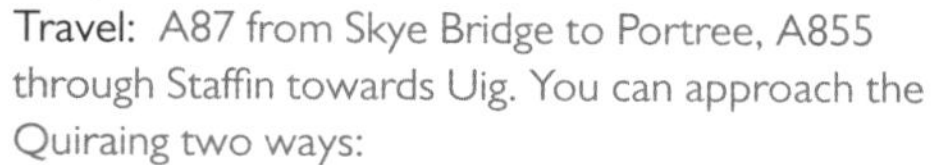

(a) 1 mile beyond Staffin, left up minor road ('Uig') to top of cliffs; two car parks here (OS ref. 440680 or 443682) from which you turn north for a mile to the Quiraing.

(b) Continue towards Flodigarry; in 2 miles park at foot of track on left (463710) and follow it uphill past Loch Langaig to reach the Quiraing.

Driving up the Trotternish peninsula, one feature claims the eyes and imagination to the exclusion of all else – the dark, dramatic curtain of rock that rises 2,000 feet and runs north for nearly 20 miles. It gives a walker itchy feet.

This wall of rock is solidified volcanic lava, the same outpouring that formed most of the isles of the Inner Hebrides some 60 million years ago. Twenty-four separate gushes of molten rock have been identified by geologists. So heavy was this geological topping that it cracked the sedimentary rocks below, causing giant landslides that left a vast cliff facing the sea. The mile-high ice sheets of the succeeding Ice Ages, grinding their unimaginable weight across the basalt, left a series of fantastic shapes, of which the free-standing, 160-foot-high Old Man of Storr is the best known and most photographed.

Ten miles north of the Old Man, the Quiraing looks out over Staffin and Flodigarry. The Quiraing was formed by the largest landslide known in Britain – and one of the most long-drawn-out, because there were at least five great slips here after the last Ice Age, dragging parts of the escarpment over a mile seaward. Most of the spectacular features of the Quiraing stand a few hundred feet from their parent cliff, towering stumps of basalt with varied names and shapes – the slim Needle, the flat-topped Table, the Prison with its cluster of turrets. The rapid weather changes so characteristic of Skye bring an endless succession of shifts in aspect to the Quiraing – melancholy in cloud, threatening under overcast skies, warm in sun shafts, dream-like under rainbows. Any English valley so generously provided with natural wonders would be signposted, safety-railed and tea-shopped to within an inch of its life. Not so in these lonely heights.

407. LORGILL, ISLE OF SKYE

Maps: OS Explorer 407; Landranger 23

Travel: A87 from Skye Bridge to Sligachan; left on A863 to Dunvegan. Just before entering village, left on B884 through Glendale. At ½ mile beyond Glendale, left ('Ramasaig') for 3½ miles to Ramasaig (OS ref. 164443). Park beside house and follow track past old farmhouse and on for 2 miles to Lorgill (175415).

The lazybed strips in the steep hill slopes are visible as soon as you leave the house of Ramasaig and strike out on foot for Lorgill. The long furrows of the lazybeds – ironic nickname – were dug by hand to receive the seed potatoes of the tenant cottagers who once farmed these slopes. They were manured with seaweed, sand, excrement and sooty thatch from the cottage roofs. Hard labour was required to make potatoes grow in the poor peaty soil; likewise to produce a crop of oats or a scrawny cow. Life in general was hard in the nineteenth century on the Isle of Skye; it had become much harder after the collapse of the traditional clan system following the 1745 Rebellion and the Battle of Culloden (see pp. 411–13). But the dozen or so poor families that lived in the broad glen of Lorgill did not suspect until the last moment that they were to be burned out of house and home, marched away with their possessions in their hands and herded on board a crowded ship. They were sent against their will across the Atlantic – not by their enemies, but by the agents of their own chief and landlord.

The track to Lorgill runs over an empty bog plateau. Basalt ledges lean seaward, and there are spectacular glimpses of the flat tops of Macleod's Tables to the east. All around the green strath are the shattered remains of houses, the ruins of stone animal pens and the faint print of Lorgill's village streets.

The strath of Lorgill is well watered, sheltered and covered in fine grass – perfect for sheep pasture. Those too old to be sent to Nova Scotia in 1830 were taken to the workhouse, and the houses in the well-favoured valley were burned. No one could ever return to Lorgill, and the strath went under the sheep.

408. MINGULAY, OUTER HEBRIDES

Maps: OS Explorer 452; Landranger 31

Travel: Ferry from Oban or South Uist, or by air from Glasgow or Benbecula (www.isleofbarra.com), to Barra. Boat trips to Mingulay: arrange through Castlebay TIC, Barra (tel: 01875 810336).

Hill you ho, boys; let her go, boys;
Bring her head round, now all together;
Hill you ho, boys; let her go, boys;
Sailing home, home to Mingulay.

If it had not been for a sentimental song written by Sir Hugh Roberton, founder of the Glasgow Orpheus Choir back in 1906, almost no one would have heard of Mingulay. As it is, with the 'Mingulay Boat Song' still current in choirs and classrooms, the magic of the wave-whitened Minch channel, the chanting oarsmen and the wives waiting on the island shore have entered the popular imagination, full of remote Hebridean mystery and romance. And Mingulay really is remote, stuck out at the tail end of the long Outer Hebridean island chain. It takes a good two hours of motoring through the long swells of the Sounds of Pabbay and Mingulay to reach the island from Barra, and the three green peaks of its mountains are visible a long way out.

You land on fabled Mingulay in a tiny bay of pale gold sand behind which the crumbling houses of the island's clachan, or village, lie drowned in drifts of sand and bracken. Mingulay's fishermen, farmers and families clung on here in their splendid isolation until the early years of the twentieth century. They existed on seabirds' eggs, boiled cormorants and puffins, rough porridge and greens. A trip to Barra, the nearest island with any services, meant 25 miles of rowing in an open boat; in winter, the journey had to be made through mountainous seas in the sounds. A population of 150 lived like this until 1910, when some of the men were jailed for trespassing on the island of Vatersay. It was their own landlord, Lady Gordon Cathcart, also owner of Vatersay, who pressed the charges – the men believed they had the traditional right to possess any land on which they could build a house in a single day and have the chimney smoking before nightfall. Lady Cathcart, who had entirely neglected the Mingulay community, was outraged by their insolence. This conviction was the end for the people of Mingulay, who packed up and quit the island in 1912.

Stone walls stand a few feet high in the clachan; doorways, hearths, chimneys and window frames can still be made out. Behind the ruined settlement a steep slope rises over the furrows of lazybeds, grass tussocks and orchid drifts, to a sharp ridge where the cliffs fall 800 feet sheer into the sea. Up here a vast prospect over the southern end of the Outer Hebrides spreads before you, green islands and blue seas, all empty and all beautiful.

409. ISLE OF BARRA, OUTER HEBRIDES

Maps: OS Explorer 452; Landranger 31

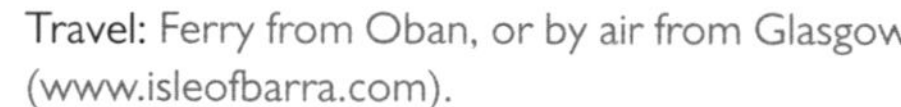

Travel: Ferry from Oban, or by air from Glasgow (www.isleofbarra.com).

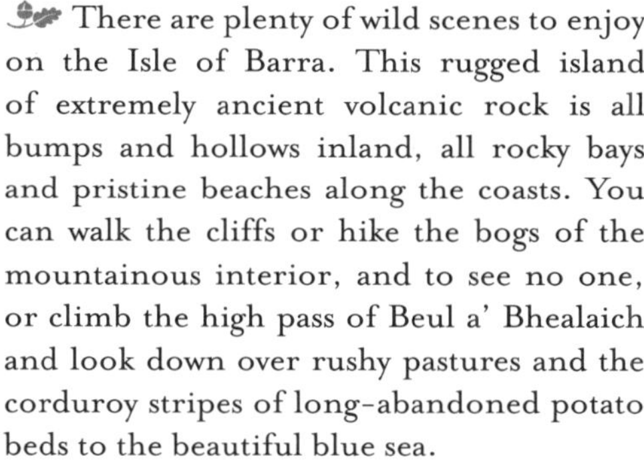

There are plenty of wild scenes to enjoy on the Isle of Barra. This rugged island of extremely ancient volcanic rock is all bumps and hollows inland, all rocky bays and pristine beaches along the coasts. You can walk the cliffs or hike the bogs of the mountainous interior, and to see no one, or climb the high pass of Beul a' Bhealaich and look down over rushy pastures and the corduroy stripes of long-abandoned potato beds to the beautiful blue sea.

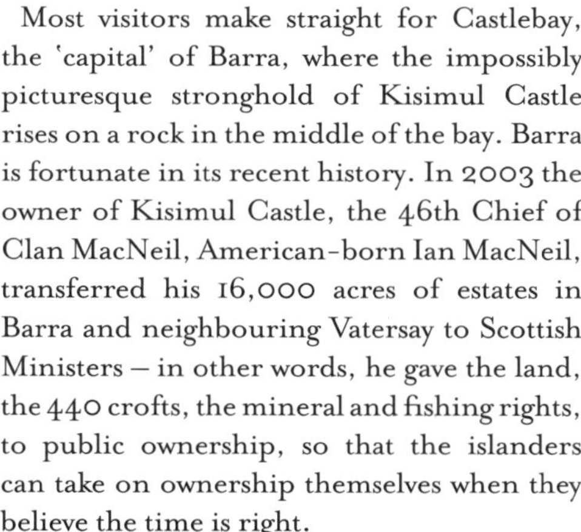

Most visitors make straight for Castlebay, the 'capital' of Barra, where the impossibly picturesque stronghold of Kisimul Castle rises on a rock in the middle of the bay. Barra is fortunate in its recent history. In 2003 the owner of Kisimul Castle, the 46th Chief of Clan MacNeil, American-born Ian MacNeil, transferred his 16,000 acres of estates in Barra and neighbouring Vatersay to Scottish Ministers – in other words, he gave the land, the 440 crofts, the mineral and fishing rights, to public ownership, so that the islanders can take on ownership themselves when they believe the time is right.

Ian MacNeil's generosity and public-spiritedness stand in stark contrast to the actions of a former owner, Colonel John Gordon of Cluny in Aberdeenshire, who bought Barra in 1838 from the bankrupt Roderick MacNeil, 41st clan chief. Gordon of Cluny turned out to be a ruthless landlord. By 1850 he was owner of the southern half of the Outer Hebridean archipelago, as far north as Benbecula, and proceeded to clear his lands of tenants in the most cold-blooded way possible. South Uist and Benbecula men were tied like cattle and removed humiliatingly in carts. In 1851 the men of Barra were summoned to a rent meeting on threat of a fine, where over 1,500 of them were grabbed, tied up, beaten if they resisted, and pushed on board emigrant ships bound for America. This treatment of unarmed, law-abiding tenants caused a stir, but the same kind of thing had been happening across the Highlands for the previous half-century. Sheep were more profitable than men – though in the case of Gordon of Cluny, he had already tried unsuccessfully to sell his chain of islands to the British Government for use as a penal colony.

410. ISLE OF ERISKAY, OUTER HEBRIDES

Maps: OS Explorer 452; Landranger 31

Travel: Ferry from Barra, or causeway from Ludag on South Uist (www.cne-siar.gov.uk/eriskay.htm).

Three miles long and shaped like a grinning troll's head with blunt nose and pendulous lip, the Isle of Eriskay looks east into the Sea of the Hebrides. The island's population has halved since the mid 1960s and now stands at about 130, but after decades of emigration and abandonment, Eriskay's future is beginning to look more promising with the opening of a causeway from South Uist.

Eriskay has two claims to fame, two stories to tell round its firesides. The first concerns the young man who landed on the island on 23 July 1745 along with seven companions, stepping ashore from the French ship *Du Teillay* at the spot now called Coilleag a' Phrionnsa, the Prince's Strand. Alexander Macdonald of Boisdale met the party, and advised them to go back home. 'Sir,' retorted young Charles James Stuart, 'I am come home.' Then Bonnie Prince Charlie left for the mainland, for his brief and thrilling advance into England, his ignominious retreat and disastrous defeat at the Battle of Culloden (see p. 411–13), and his five months on the run before another French ship took him away on 20 September 1746, into exile for ever more.

The second incident has been immortalized by Compton Mackenzie in his 1946 romp of a novel, *Whisky Galore!* It was a murky February night in 1941 when the freighter SS *Politician* ran aground on Eriskay. *Politician*'s was no ordinary cargo; she was carrying a quarter of a million bottles of first-class, untaxed Scotch whisky to America, a payment-in-kind for war materials from the US Government. The freighter was also loaded with Jamaican banknotes – worth several million pounds at today's rate – reputedly a contingency fund in case the Germans invaded Britain and the Royal Family were obliged to flee across the Atlantic.

Naturally the news of a wreck piled to the gunwales with money and the 'water of life' – both in drastically short supply in wartime Scotland – soon got around. As fast as the island men 'liberated' the cargo, willing hands hid it ashore. A game of hide-and-seek with the Customs and Excise forces followed, as did a year-long party. All jolly fun and games, the very stuff of a picaresque novel. What was not so amusing was the arrest, trial and imprisonment of several islanders for theft. They themselves claimed, perhaps disingenuously, that they were simply carrying out a legitimate act of personal salvage. Eventually the conscientious Customs man in charge of the case received permission to dynamite the ship and her alcoholic cargo – not before the islanders had extracted an estimated 24,000 bottles. As *Politician* and her contents exploded, island man Angus John Campbell spoke for all when he commented: 'Dynamiting whisky! You wouldn't think any man in the world would be as stupid as that.'

411. ISLE OF SOUTH UIST, OUTER HEBRIDES

Maps: OS Explorer 453; Landranger 31, 22

Travel: Ferry from Oban and Barra (www.undiscoveredscotland.co.uk/southuist/southuist/index.html); A865 from Benbecula.

You can hire a bicycle on South Uist, and that is probably the best way to explore this 20-mile-long island, its two wildly contrasting coasts, the rearing mountains of the east and the loch-raddled shores of the west. The eastern region of South Uist begins to climb in earnest about halfway across the spine of the island, rising in a graceful curve of rock to the peak of Beinn Mhor that tops 2,000 feet. The impression is of an east-rushing granite tsunami.

Five miles west, the landscape is so different that you might be on another island. With your back to the mountains you look out to a flat sea across a flat littoral, a mile or so broad, without a contour in it. Here the Atlantic wind comes rushing unimpeded, catching grains of lime-rich cockleshell and piling them into thick shelves along the north–south coast. Rich grass covers the shell sand, and pushing their roots

down through this green lawn to feed on the nutritious lime are dozens of flowering plant species. In the pure sea air of the island the colours are intense – yellow of bird's-foot trefoil and dandelion, delicate blue of speedwell and harebells, bright white bursts of daisies and eyebright, red and purple clover and wild thyme. The profusion can seem overwhelming.

Lie prone on the machair on an early summer's day, before the grazing cattle have levelled the flowering plants, and look through a gauze of colours to white, green and blue, beach, sea and sky. There is nothing but ocean between you and America.

412. ISLE OF BENBECULA, OUTER HEBRIDES

Maps: OS Explorer 453; Landranger 22

Travel: By air from Glasgow; A865 causeways from South and North Uist.

Benbecula is a most extraordinary island, perhaps the most extraordinary in all the Outer Hebrides. It lies almost completely flat, except for the 406-foot pimple of Ruabhal, its one hill. Entirely treeless, open to the weather from all quarters, the island is composed as much of water as it is of land. Thousands of lochs and lochans lie in ragged streaks in the dark green bog.

A long-abandoned trackway curves down from Ruabhal to the shore of Scarilode Bay. Here cattle were loaded on to boats and taken across the Minch at the start of epic droves across the West Highland mountain roads to markets in the east. An abandoned shieling, or shepherd's summer house, stands on a bank above the bay.

Benbecula is so tremendously flat that you would scarcely believe even a dog could go missing without being spotted. Yet in the summer of 1980, during the filming of an advertisement for Kleenex, an 8-foot-tall, half-ton grizzly bear named Hercules somehow went AWOL on the island and stayed that way for well over three weeks before being spotted swimming, shot with a tranquillizer dart, airlifted in a giant net bag and restored to his tearful owner, wrestler Andy Robin. Where had Hercules been hiding? He must have been under cover – perhaps in the Scarilode shieling. Wherever it was, it had evidently had a poor food supply. Hercules shed 20 stone during his time on the run, and was a sylph-like 34 stone when apprehended. After waking up he consumed 120 pints of milk and several dozen eggs before greeting his new and adoring international public.

413. RHENIGIDALE, ISLE OF HARRIS, OUTER HEBRIDES

Maps: OS Explorer 456; Landranger 14

Travel: Ferry from Uig, Isle of Skye or Lochmaddy, North Uist; A859 from Stornoway, Isle of Lewis (www.scotland-inverness.co.uk/harris.htm) to Tarbert. From ferry pier, drive towards town and in 200 yards turn right; from Stornoway direction, enter Tarbert, bear left towards ferry terminal and in 100 yards left. Follow this road (Main Street) from its junction with A868 (OS ref. 154000) for 2 miles through Oban and Urgha Beag to parking place (184004). Bear left along old road (trackway) for 3½ miles to Rhenigidale (228018).

NB: This is a rough track with some steep ascents and descents.

In 1989, the day they closed the school at Rhenigidale, the media descended on Harris. Television, radio and the newspapers could not get enough of the story: six-year-old Duncan Mackay, sole pupil; his mother, Moira, the one and only teacher; the approach of the tarmac road that the dozen inhabitants of Rhenigidale had asked for but were uneasy about; the end of an isolated way of life for the remotest village in the Outer Hebridges. Previously the only way in or out had been by boat or via a mountain track 4 miles long. In the event the school on the lonely inlet closed, young Duncan transferred to a primary school in Tarbert along with his mother, and the road reached Rhenigidale. And what then? Ruthless development of the one-time paradise, a rash of cheap housing, supermarkets, a disco, a marina and casino? Far from it. Rhenigidale stayed much the same, except for the odd car-borne tourist or fleet of cyclists. The hostel did a little better, the population remained around a dozen. All of which goes to show that a new road does not necessarily bring the world, the flesh and the Devil.

You can still walk the old mountain track over to Rhenigidale, a beautifully engineered path through a most heavenly landscape. Pale granite outcrops push through the grass and heather; the path dodges this way and that towards the skyline, then tips over to fold down on itself like a concertina, dropping at 1 in 2 to the foot of a burn on a deep sea inlet. Rhenigidale is not yet visible. Now the track rises again, curling over two more headlands before reaching a breathtaking viewpoint over Rhenigidale, a clutch of white-painted croft houses, silent and remote. Picture Kenny Mackay, father of Duncan and husband of Moira, who traversed the knee-cracking track every day for years in all weathers, fulfilling his role as Rhenigidale's postman. The path was engineered and maintained at great cost and trouble for Kenny Mackay and the few others who lived at Rhenigidale. The tarmac road, seen rising up the hillside beyond the settlement, cost hugely more, and was built as another political nod to the villagers. It has made life easier, but it siphoned off some magic all the same.

414. PENTLAND ROAD, ISLE OF LEWIS, OUTER HEBRIDES

Maps: OS Explorer 459; Landranger 8

Travel: A859 Tarbert ('Tairbeart') road out of Stornoway; in 1 mile, right on A858 Breasclete ('Breascleit') and Carloway ('Carlabhagh') road. In 3 miles, right (OS ref. 363338) along Pentland Road for 12 miles to Carloway.

You can drive the Pentland Road if you wish. But it is better to bicycle and best of all to walk this narrow ribbon across the waist of the Isle of Lewis. Only by travelling through the heart of Lewis at a slow pace, stopping every now and then to step off the road and walk out into the wilderness, will you arrive at a proper understanding of the desolation and lonely grandeur of this unique and brooding landscape.

See Lewis from the aeroplane and it seems half land, half water. Bog and loch, bog and loch for 50 miles. It is not a flat landscape; out among those long miles of moor and fleets of peaty water there are hills, rising far off in the bogs. Walk 3 or 4 miles north or south from the Pentland Road and it will take you a good couple of hours; everything squelches and sucks underfoot, where the ancient acid gneiss rock, formed 3,300 million years ago (the oldest rock in Britain, and some of the oldest in the world), prevents the poor vegetation from rotting down and holds it in suspense for the rain and countless springs to turn it into sloppy, barren bog. The silence is broken only by the seething of water and wind, the bleating of sheep and the sharp tick of pipits. In the apparently empty wastes live red-throated divers, golden plover, dunlin, otters. Merlin and golden eagle hunt the moors.

At the turn of the twenty-first century, plans were hatched to build the largest wind farm ever seen in Britain across the bleak bog along this lonely road. There were to be 176 turbines, each 450 feet tall, in clusters stretching more than 30 miles. Four million tons of rock would have been dug from the bog in quarries 40 feet deep. A hundred miles of road would have been built. And this was just the start of it. Many other wind-farm planning permissions were applied for. Lewis is just about the windiest place in Britain, and the opportunities for outside investors are obvious. Potential electricity production could equal that of two nuclear power stations. Altogether the plans envisaged 500 turbines at least. They would have been visible from almost everywhere in this low landscape. The RSPB vigorously objected on the grounds of danger and disturbance to birds, and the potential release of the greenhouse gases at present locked in the bogs. Local communities were opposed to the destruction, the disruption, the promises of jobs that might have come to nothing, and the visual intrusion.

The jury was out for years, while everyone waited. Then, in January 2008, the Scottish Government rejected the plans to build the Lewis wind farm. No one on Lewis has stopped holding their breath yet, though.

415. ISLE OF HOY, ORKNEY

Maps: OS Explorer 462; Landranger 7

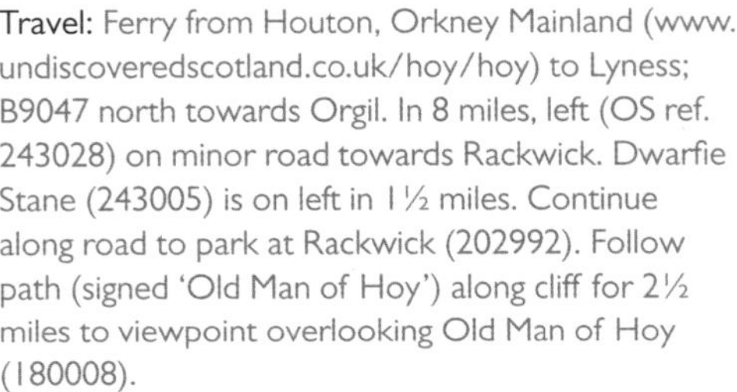

Travel: Ferry from Houton, Orkney Mainland (www.undiscoveredscotland.co.uk/hoy/hoy) to Lyness; B9047 north towards Orgil. In 8 miles, left (OS ref. 243028) on minor road towards Rackwick. Dwarfie Stane (243005) is on left in 1½ miles. Continue along road to park at Rackwick (202992). Follow path (signed 'Old Man of Hoy') along cliff for 2½ miles to viewpoint overlooking Old Man of Hoy (180008).

Though the Isle of Hoy is 10 miles long and 6 miles broad, there is only one road to follow north from the ferry jetty, and one narrow side road off that to take you across the island to the lonely hamlet of Rackwick, the only settlement on Hoy's east coast. On the way over to Rackwick, pull off the road after a couple of miles and make over the moor to your left, following a thread-like duckboard trail to reach the Dwarfie Stane. Wrinkled and grey like a slumbering elephant, the Dwarfie Stane lies some 30 feet long and 4 feet high. This is one of only two tombs in Britain cut out of rock, and when you have passed the big square stone that once blocked the mouth of the sepulchre and have crouched down into the central passage, you will see that the Dwarfie Stane holds two chambers, one either side, low rooms scooped out of the bare rock 5,000 years ago with bone and flint tools. It must have been achieved with the most enormous trouble and difficulty. Our more recent ancestors took the tomb to be a house built by a dwarf or a troll,

The Old Man of Hoy

and nowadays children adore playing house there.

You can also admire another example of stone-shaping on Hoy, this one by natural rather than human agency, reached via a slippery cliff path that leads out of Rackwick. The Old Man of Hoy raises his head almost level with the cliffs, his red face and green thatch a challenge to every rock-climber. A magnificent sea stack of sandstone, the Old Man stands footed on the shore, a couple of hundred yards from the cliff. Seabirds circle and nest in his crevices, climbers hang in cradles of ropes from his brow. Bent and thin, rearing dramatically 450 feet into the air, seamed and whittled by rain, wind, frost and sea, the Old Man of Hoy is one celebrity worth meeting.

416. TOMB OF THE EAGLES, SOUTH RONALDSAY, ORKNEY

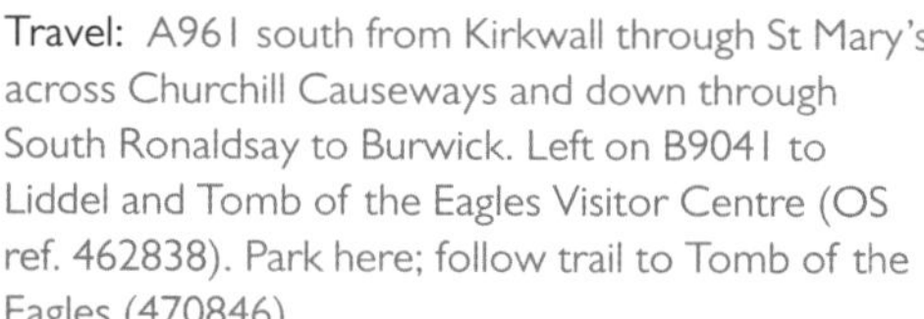

Maps: OS Explorer 461; Landranger 7

Travel: A961 south from Kirkwall through St Mary's, across Churchill Causeways and down through South Ronaldsay to Burwick. Left on B9041 to Liddel and Tomb of the Eagles Visitor Centre (OS ref. 462838). Park here; follow trail to Tomb of the Eagles (470846).

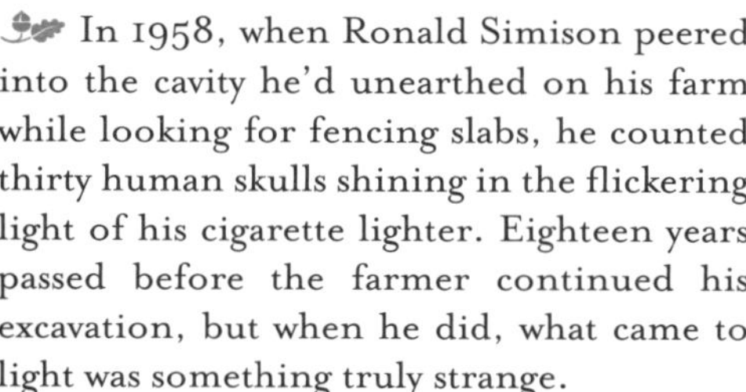

In 1958, when Ronald Simison peered into the cavity he'd unearthed on his farm while looking for fencing slabs, he counted thirty human skulls shining in the flickering light of his cigarette lighter. Eighteen years passed before the farmer continued his excavation, but when he did, what came to light was something truly strange.

Isbister Chambered Cairn, or the Tomb of the Eagles, as it is universally known, was built around 5000 BC for the interment of the bones of human bodies that had already been dismembered and cleaned of flesh and organs. The tomb-builders constructed their mausoleum carefully, drystone-walling it with stone slabs and creating three internal stalls and three side cells in which to store the remains of their dead. Along with the 30 skulls, Mr Simison discovered an enormous number of bones, some 16,000 altogether, the relics of 342 people, old, young, male and female. Analysis showed that these ancestral Orcadians tended to lose their children young, to suffer from spinal defects in their adult lives, and to die before they reached fifty.

What is really remarkable about the tomb – in use for nearly 1,000 years – was the material buried alongside the human remains. The excavators unearthed more than 600 bones of sea eagles, enough to compose eight of the big birds of prey, as well as seventy sea-eagle talons. They seem to have been inserted in the cairn towards the end of its active life. Sea eagles, or white-tailed eagles, as they are sometimes called, include carrion in their varied diet. Perhaps it was they who picked the bodies clean before interment, thus earning a berth in the 'ship of death'. Or perhaps they were simply revered for their 6-foot wingspan and majestic flight.

417. ITALIAN CHAPEL, LAMB HOLM, ORKNEY

Maps: OS Explorer 461; Landranger 7

Travel: A961 south from Kirkwall through St Mary's and over Churchill Causeway No. 1 on to Lamb Holm island. The Italian Chapel stands 300 yards on your left (OS ref. 488006).

The Italian prisoners of war who inhabited Camp 60 during the Second World War must have thought they had entered a particularly refined kind of northern Hell. It was freezing cold and windy most of the time, they seldom saw the sun, they were stuck out in the bleak waters of Scapa Flow, and they were 'encouraged' to build defence works for their enemies – the four Churchill Causeways that linked up the islands of Lamb Holm, Glims Holm, Burray and South Ronaldsay. At the start of the war a U-boat had slipped between the islands into Scapa Flow, anchorage of the British Home Fleet, and torpedoed the battleship *Royal Oak* with the loss of 833 men. The causeways were built to seal off the anchorage, though the Italians were persuaded that they were intended as amenities to allow easier access to Mainland for the islanders.

The lonely Italians, most of them devout Catholics, set about making their own chapel under the guidance of Domenico Chiocchetti, one of their number. They were allotted a couple of bare Nissen huts, and from scrap metal, driftwood, 'liberated' cement and paint they succeeded in creating a most moving and enduring work of art. The crow-stepped façade of the Italian Chapel leads into an interior meticulously painted to resemble a Renaissance chapel of the prisoners' own homeland. The barrel roof is 'tiled' with *trompe l'oeil* paintwork. The light fittings are made from Spam tins, the elaborate rood screen of wrought scrap iron, the tabernacle from delicately carved driftwood. Altar and rail are moulded concrete. Iron and brass candelabra were crafted by the prisoners, musical angels depicted on the roof of the sanctuary, and behind the altar Domenico Chiocchetti painted a beautiful Madonna and Child, copied from the holy medal he wore.

Chiocchetti stayed on to finish his chapel after the other prisoners went home at the end of the war, and after he returned to Italy he periodically revisited the chapel to carry out repairs until his death in 1999. Nowadays the building is preserved as a much-loved memorial, redolent of the extraordinary resilience of the human spirit.

418. STONES OF STENNESS AND RING OF BRODGAR, MAINLAND, ORKNEY

Maps: OS Explorer 463; Landranger 6

Travel: A965 from Kirkwall towards Stromness. In 10 miles, shortly after passing Maes Howe, right on B9055 towards Skara Brae. Stones of Stenness are on right of road in 1/3 mile (OS ref. 307125), just before crossing causeway between Loch of Stenness and Loch of Harray. Ring of Brodgar is in another mile on left of road (294133).

The Stones of Stenness rise on the brink of the sea loch of Stenness, four slender fingers capping a circle of grass. The height of the stones is astonishing; they are three times as tall as the component members of most other ancient stone circles, and instead of being weather-eroded and shapeless they stand graceful and shapely, slim structures of sandstone with sharply angled heads. The tallest stands 17 feet high. A little removed are the two lower stones, their heads close together as if forming a frame for the mighty mound of Maes Howe (see pp. 448–9), which lies three quarters of a mile off. Since the two constructions roughly equal each other in age – they were built around 5,000 years ago – it is tempting to make connections between them that may be purely fanciful.

A mile along the causeway, with the shimmering waters of Loch of Stenness on your left, is the Ring of Brodgar. When this remarkable monument was erected, several hundred years after the Stones of Stenness, there were sixty individual pieces forming a ring-shaped puzzle: sandstone blades of rock that resemble those of Stanley knives. These days twenty-seven of the stones remain upright, casting deep black shadows on a sunny dawn or at nightfall. The largest of the stones resemble a cloaked and hooded figure, its lowered head brooding over the others.

Some call the Ring of Brodgar the Circle of the Sun, the Stones of Stenness the Temple of the Moon. A local farmer in the early nineteenth century destroyed some of the Stenness stones, including the Odin Stone with its pierced hole through which young children were passed for good luck, and at whose foot lovers would plight their troth, clasping hands through the hole and swearing the Odin Oath. So solemn and binding was the promise that when the ruthless Orcadian pirate John Gow was hanged, drowned, tarred and gibbeted in London in 1725, the girl he had left behind in Stromness travelled all the way to the capital to touch the hand of the dead man and release herself from the oath she had sworn with him at the Stones of Stenness.

419. MAES HOWE AND SKARA BRAE, MAINLAND, ORKNEY

Maps: OS Explorer 463; Landranger 6

Travel: A965 from Kirkwall towards Stromness. In 9 miles, Maes Howe stands on right of road (OS ref. 318127). In 1 mile, right on B9055 past Stones of Stenness and Ring of Brodgar (see p. 459); continue for 6 miles, crossing A967 to reach Skaill; Skara Brae is signed to left (292187).

Follow the path towards the mound of Maes Howe, lying like a grassy upturned bowl in the fields. Stoop down, bend double, and squirm along 30 feet of low stone passageway into the darkness of the monument. Here, in the hollow heart of Maes Howe, stand and let your eyes adjust to the stark splendour of the finest chambered tomb in Europe.

Maes Howe is 5,000 years old. The builders constructed it so carefully of shaped blocks of sandstone that, as the guide tells you, it is impossible to slide a knife blade between the stones. Openings in three of the four walls lead to further recesses, where the shadows dance. The passage of five millennia seems to have had no effect on the interior of the tomb, its walls rising to a corbelled roof. But men did enter here, long after the chamber had ceased to be used for burial. Vikings broke in and scratched runes in the walls. Some boast of robbing the tomb of its treasure, while others more down-to-earth claims. 'These runes were carved by a champion rune carver,' says one. Another, scratched by a lovesick warrior, sighs, 'Ingibiorh is just so gorgeous!' A third is straight to the point: 'Thorni fucked; Helgi carved.' Standing among these 1,000-year-old graffiti in a chill, silent chamber more than five times as old, you feel the crushing power of cold, piled stone.

Maes Howe provides a glimpse of ancient Orcadian ways of death. North-west on the seashore lies Skara Brae, a window into the lives of the islanders 4,000 years ago. During excavations of the huddled stone houses, two female skeletons were found lying together on a stone bed, and beads were scattered along a passageway as if the wearer had broken them in headlong flight. The Neolithic village on the shore was overwhelmed by a sudden sandstorm, it seems. The details of the buildings are extraordinary; furniture made of stone slabs, room dividers, doorways, stone tables and chairs. There was even a form of cavity-wall heating, using the fermentation warmth given off by the settlement's midden and refuse heaps. The thinking is that perhaps this was a village for young people, a housing estate for early teens setting up home together, learning their responsibilities in the harsh and unforgiving conditions of the ancient world.

420. SHIP OF DEATH, ROUSAY, ORKNEY

Maps: OS Explorer 464; Landranger 6

Travel: Ferry from Tingwall, Mainland (www.visitrousay.co.uk). Left on B9064 to pass the tombs of Taversoe Tuick (OS ref. 426276), Blackhammer (414277) and Knowe of Yarso (404281), to reach Mid Howe Chambered Cairn (the 'Ship of Death' – 372307) and Broch (371308).

This is the best of all the Orkney archipelago's smaller islands for archaeological treasures. In a couple of hours you can cycle its 13-mile belt of road easily, but the best fruits of the archaeological crop all lie close together in a signposted 4-mile stretch off the south coast road, close to the ferry jetty.

The first of three neighbouring chambered burial cairns is Taversoe Tuick, a very rare double design with one tomb above the other, each with its own entrance – two chambers across a flagged floor upstairs, three below with a paved and walled tunnel leading to them from the hillside. A mile to the west is Blackhammer Cairn, into whose interior – a triangle of tessellated, unmortared stones – you step from a trapdoor in the roof. Blackhammer and Taversoe Tuick both date back 5,000 years; the green mound of the Knowe of Yarso, another mile up the hill, is perhaps 500 years younger. Here the long, boat-shaped interior was in use for 1,000 years; the remains of twenty-nine adults were found during excavation, seventeen having had their skulls carefully separated from their skeletons.

On a rocky shore at the west end of Rousay stands a 2,000-year-old broch, or Iron Age round tower, that was built on the cliff as a defensive stronghold. In its shadow lies the Ship of Death, or Mid Howe Chambered Cairn, housed in a covered gallery on the shore. This is a weighty and sobering place, built of rock and shaped like a ship, 100 feet long and divided into two dozen compartments, in each of which human remains were deposited. Mid Howe was probably used for well over 1,000 years, and was already 3,000 years old when the broch was built. Old tower and ancient tomb make a memorable pair, starkly outlined against sea and sky in their end-of-the-world location.

421. ISLE OF SANDAY, ORKNEY

Maps: OS Explorer 465; Landranger 5

Travel: Ferry from Kirkwall, Mainland, or by air from Mainland (www.sanday.co.uk).

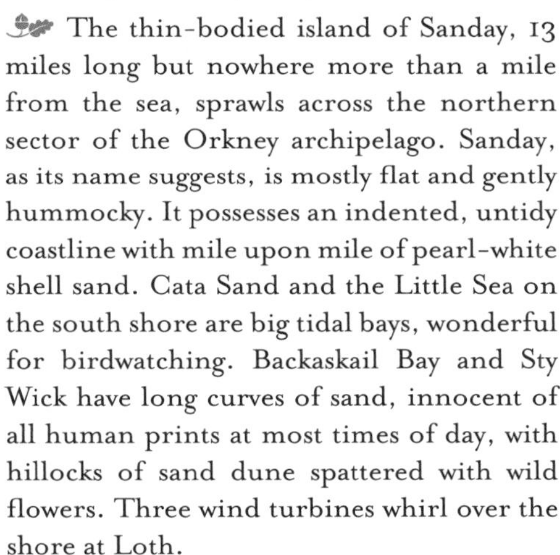

The thin-bodied island of Sanday, 13 miles long but nowhere more than a mile from the sea, sprawls across the northern sector of the Orkney archipelago. Sanday, as its name suggests, is mostly flat and gently hummocky. It possesses an indented, untidy coastline with mile upon mile of pearl-white shell sand. Cata Sand and the Little Sea on the south shore are big tidal bays, wonderful for birdwatching. Backaskail Bay and Sty Wick have long curves of sand, innocent of all human prints at most times of day, with hillocks of sand dune spattered with wild flowers. Three wind turbines whirl over the shore at Loth.

Out to the north the bay of Otters Wick pushes two long promontories north-east, ending in a curve of pebbly bay, the haunt of oystercatchers whose melancholy piping scatters on the wind. Long causeways of raised sand lead to the daisy-covered machair of Tres Ness and Els Ness. Out at the east edge of Els Ness stands what looks at first like a Pictish broch, or defence tower. Close-to it reveals itself as a burial chamber, one of those extraordinary tombs in which Orkney is so rich. Here at Quoyness all heads are obliged to bow on entry. A hands-and-knees crawl along a passageway leads into a tall stone chamber of carefully slotted stones, tapering upwards to a slab roof. The remains of fifteen people were found in the six cells that are burrowed into the walls.

422. PAPA WESTRAY, ORKNEY

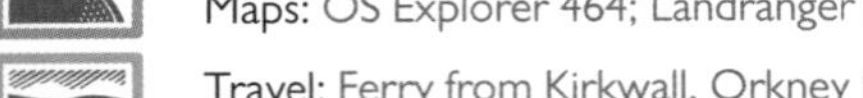

Maps: OS Explorer 464; Landranger 5

Travel: Ferry from Kirkwall, Orkney Mainland, or by air from Mainland (www.papawestray.co.uk).

Papa Westray, the Island of the Priests, lies right at the northern rim of Orkney. The two-minute plane hop from the neighbouring Isle of Westray is the shortest scheduled flight in the world. The last time I went to Papa Westray, the Birdie Man was getting married. It was the first wedding there for seven years and the fifty-odd islanders were not about to let slip the opportunity for a load of fun. The fog descended ten minutes after the plane had hopped down on to the island's grass airfield, and I was due to be sealed up in Papay (as locals call it) for at least the next forty-eight hours. Could I play any instrument? Oh, the guitar and the spoons, eh! Right, you'll be in the band, then, at the Birdie Man's wedding ceilidh tonight! OK!

The Birdie Man – the RSPB warden on seabird-haunted Papay – had been snared by one of the island girls. He couldn't wait to embrace his bride, but then she couldn't wait to dance the eightsome reel in her full white wedding dress. They managed both at the same time, many times that night, while we clapped and cheered and shot the bottle round. Next day I woke with sore fingers and a sorer head. Had I really played guitar, spoons and mouth organ all at the same time? It seemed so, from what everyone was only too delighted to tell me. It had been a mighty night.

Papay is only 4 miles long, but the birdwatching at the north end's RSPB reserve is magical. Fowl Craig is so raucous with kittiwake cries they call it Kitty City. I could hardly bear their echoing racket on the bleary morning-after, though I was impressed to see the Birdie Man out and about in the fog. But there was balm and quiet after the mist lifted later that day, down on the west coast at the Knap of Howar. The two oval houses that stand in a bank on the shore are beautifully fashioned, with stone walls, hearths, doorways, shelves, corn-grinding querns and room dividers. They looked as if the inhabitants had just popped out and might be back at any moment; but this pair of semi-detached residences was built 5,500 years ago, long before the Pyramids of Egypt. They are the oldest houses in Europe.

I sat in one of the ancient houses, looking west out of the door as the sun began to dip to the horizon. It was a time of absolute stillness, broken only by the scratching of claws on shingle as a sea otter, fur spiked with salt, ran purposefully across the strand and slipped away into the sea.

423. FAIR ISLE, SHETLAND

Maps: OS Explorer 466; Landranger 4

Travel: By ferry or air from Shetland Mainland (www.fairisle.org.uk).

It has always been a sickening boat trip to Fair Isle, jolting over the violent tide-rips of Sumburgh Roost for three hours or more. These days you can opt to buzz into the island by plane, banking low over tremendous cliffs before dropping down to bump along the short airstrip. Either way, you will land somewhere rare and strange.

Fair Isle sits 25 miles south-south-west of Sumburgh Head on the southernmost tip of Shetland Mainland, and 30 miles east-north-east of North Ronaldsay in the Orkney Islands – a long way from anywhere. This chunk of rock measures 3 miles from south to north, about half that from east to west. Impressive cliffs many hundreds of feet tall plunge into the sea and about 70 people live in croft houses and other low-standing dwellings, hunched against the wind on the high green saddle of the island.

Life for Fair Islanders is better now than it has been for centuries. The island is doing very well, thanks to the worldwide renown of its Bird Observatory and the constant stream of visitors it attracts. Fulmars, kittiwakes, puffins, gulls, guillemots, petrels and, especially, skuas are Fair Isle's staple species. They can be augmented at any time by almost any exotic incomer, blown into the island from the migratory routes that cross the northern heavens far above Fair Isle. The great skua – 'bonxie' to Shetlanders – nests in enormous numbers on the heather and peat moors and will not hesitate to attack and dive-bomb any intruder in its territory. On the cliffs it's the gracefully wheeling fulmars and kittiwakes that attract attention, and out at sea there are porpoises, dolphins and whales to spot. The islanders themselves are practical, hospitable people. A ceilidh in Fair Isle is an event to savour, the island's own traditional quadrilles and waltzes danced with vigour.

Visit Fair Isle in May at the time of 'simmer dim', when the light never fades out of the sky even at dead of night, and walk round the cliffs at 3 or 4 a.m. The slap of waves far off below and the sleepy complaining of seabirds are the only sounds. Stars and daylight glow together in the heavens. Climb to the 760-foot crest of Ward Hill and sit there to watch the early mist swirl off the moors and out over the sea. I can guarantee you'll never forget it.

424. ISLE OF FOULA, SHETLAND

Maps: OS Explorer 467; Landranger 4

Travel: Ferry from Walls on Shetland Mainland, or by air from Tingwall, Shetland Mainland (www.foulaheritage.org.uk).

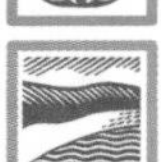

If Fair Isle (see above) is wild, Foula is even wilder and more remote – even though, technically speaking, the Island of Seabirds is a few miles closer to Shetland Mainland. Some 20 miles west of Walls jetty, pear-shaped Foula rises from the sea, its long back sloping up to the west into tremendous peaks that drop away into the sea – in the case of Da Kame, some 1,200 feet of fall, the highest sea cliff in Britain outside St Kilda, beyond the Outer Hebrides. The eastern side is low-lying, a green shelf by the sea from which the interior climbs and keeps on climbing. The western cliffs are the haunt of millions of sea-fowl; their constant presence and noise, not to mention the nutrition their meat and eggs provided for the Foula islanders in bygone days, gave the island its name.

It takes grit and bloody-mindedness to live on an island as remote and weather-dependent as Foula. Around thirty people manage it, maintaining the airstrip they built themselves in the 1970s, doing a little fishing, grazing the slopes with Shetland sheep. Foula is swept by winds laden with salt spray, and crofting is a hard life. But the harsh conditions and the uncertainties of communication and supply have bred people who are tough, extremely self-reliant, pragmatic and yet warmly hospitable. They barter and bargain, help out and get on with each other and with their few visitors in a manner that puts the outer world to shame. They have to, in order to survive out here.

Winter and its week-long gales and succession of gloomy days can be crushingly depressing, though lovers of truly wild weather and mood will find all they crave here at that season. But in summer the backs of the hills are flooded with orchids, the deep valley of the Dael flushes yellow with tormentil and marsh marigolds, the fulmars and skuas are back to mate and raise their chicks. That is the best time to come to Foula. Bring a bottle and a fiddle with you.

425. UP-HELLY-A', LERWICK, MAINLAND, SHETLAND

Maps: OS Explorer 466; Landranger 4

Travel: Ferry from Aberdeen or Orkney Mainland; by air from Aberdeen, Edinburgh, Orkney Mainland, Glasgow, Inverness.

Up-Helly-A' is celebrated on the last Tuesday of each January. All details: www.visitshetland.com.

The blurting and thumping of a brass band floats on the January wind through the narrow streets of Lerwick, stone-built capital of the Shetland Isles. Here they come – a double line of bare-kneed Vikings in horned helmets, scarlet cloaks and silver-plated armour, roaring as they march. At their head stamps the Guizer Jarl himself, the King of Up-Helly-A', splendidly bearded, raven wings on his helmet, shaking his war axe at we onlookers who line the streets ten deep. 'Aaah-oi!' he yells, and 'Aaah-oi!' we yell back.

These magnificent costumes have cost the wearers and their families hundreds of pounds and thousands of hours of work apiece, but a member of the Guizer Jarl's squad is a great man in Shetland on the last Tuesday of every January, and no one would think of skimping for Up-Helly-A'. Among the Norsemen rides a full-sized, dragon-headed war galley, grinning fiercely into the wind, her bulwarks lined with round shields. She is manhandled into the water. The Vikings climb on board. One or two fall over while doing so; it is only 10 a.m., but it has been a long day already for these once-a-year Lords of Misrule. A deep-throated song rises from their band. Which bloodthirsty celebration of heroic skull-splitting have they chosen? 'Zip-a-dee-doo-dah, zip-a-dee-ay, my oh my, what a wonderful day!' roar the Vikings, and everyone bursts out laughing.

Shetland's shout in the face of winter wasn't always so good-humoured. Back in the nineteenth century, masked gangs would roll blazing tar barrels through the narrow streets of Lerwick until they met another band; fighting and cracked heads would follow. Nowadays it is all a tremendously genial affair. The Guizer Jarl and his squad, on dry land again, march to the Town Hall and invade the council chamber, their swirling red cloaks and glittering armour sounding a note of fierceness among the civilized suits and ties. They drink a toast from a goblet fashioned like a war galley, and then comes a rendition of the Up-Helly-A' song, its bombast perfectly suited to the occasion:

Grand old Vikings ruled upon the ocean vast,
Their brave battle-songs still thunder on the blast;
Their wild war cry comes a-ringing from the past;
We answer it: 'Aaaah-oi!'

At nightfall the Lerwick streets are packed once more, the houses outlined in smoky red as the guizer squads march with paraffin torches, a flaring snake that flows along King Harald Street and enters the playing field, dragging the galley with the Guizer Jarl in her bows, brandishing his axe. She is hoisted on trestles, the Guizer Jarl raises a voice now hoarse to call for three cheers, and the torches rain down on the ship. We cheer ourselves sore and watch them fall in fiery arcs, filling the longship with flame. She roars and crackles in her death throes until the dragon head tumbles to the ground in a shower of sparks and lies flickering in the mud. Winter has been defied once more, and we will celebrate its death with drinking and dancing until dawn.

426. ESHA NESS, MAINLAND, SHETLAND

Maps: OS Explorer 469; Landranger 3

Travel: Ferry from Aberdeen or Orkney Mainland, by air from Aberdeen, Edinburgh, Orkney Mainland, Glasgow, Inverness (www.visitshetland.com). A970 north through Mainland for 60 miles to the Sandy Lochs. Left here (OS ref. 326771) on west branch of A970 ('Hillswick') through Urafirth. In another mile, right on B9078 through Braewick; in another 2 miles, right (217780) past Loch of Framgord to the lighthouse at Calder's Geo (206788). Park here and walk north or south along the cliffs of Esha Ness.

Shetlanders themselves call Esha Ness the 'back of beyond', and it is certainly a very long way from anywhere that could be called a town or centre of modern life. To get there you have to drive north through the ragged island of Mainland, generally through the weathers of all four seasons one after another, before turning west and roller-coasting over the lochan-riddled moors that blanket the bleak peninsula of Esha Ness. Shetlanders keen on fishing for 'da troots' in the lochs come here, and the occasional birdwatcher, but few other outsiders are seen.

Once you reach the cliffs and strike out on foot you are in a wide, windy world of black rock and thrashing water. Out at sea rise islets and rock stacks, some pierced with great sea-worn arches. A long day's walk north, splashing across burns and through sodden peat hags, will bring you out on the steep brae of Heylor, looking across the shadowed fjord of Ronas Voe to the screes of the Brough, rising 500 feet tall. It was here that the great fiddle teacher and collector of Shetland's traditional tunes, Tom Anderson, received the inspiration to compose one of the most beautiful slow airs to come out of the islands:

There's a story behind every tune, you know, and you cannot play this music properly without having the story in your mind. I composed 'Da Slockit Light' in 1969, at midnight one night up at Esha Ness. I was standing on the side of the voe looking at the lights in the houses going out one by one. A 'slockit' light in Shetland dialect is one that has just been put out. My wife had just died, and I was thinking of her, and of how few houses there were around Esha Ness compared with when I was born there. The tune came to me as I stood on the hillside. I went back to the car and sat in there, writing down the tune in sol-fa on the back of a cigarette packet by the car's interior light.

427. ISLE OF YELL, SHETLAND

Maps: OS Explorer 470; Landranger 1, 2

Travel: A970 through Shetland Mainland to Hillside; A968 north to Booth of Toft; ferry to Ulsta on southern tip of Isle of Yell. A968 north through the island (www.visitshetland.com/area_guides/yell/yell).

Yell is probably the least-known island of its size in Britain. It measures 18 miles long and about 5 broad, but very few non-Shetlanders have heard of it – partly because it is so far north, partly because it forms a stepping stone between Shetland Mainland and the most northerly island in Britain, Unst (see pp. 466–7). I first came here to track down a village dance and a fiery fiddler. I never found the dance or the fiddler, but you wouldn't necessarily expect to in a place as loose and unorganised as Yell. In any case I was sidetracked by the sheer, unalloyed wildness of the island. There seemed at first glance little to tempt me from the main road: open, treeless moorland of damp dark peat and moor grass rolls away, patched with sombre lochs and sodden by burns. But once out in the middle of the moors, floundering on Hesta Mires and the Hill of Arisdale, I discovered with a shock of pure delight that I had the landscape entirely to myself.

Take the less-travelled east coast road through Yell, sidetracking to walk out to Burra Ness, with its basking seals and whales in Basta Voe, or walk north up the craggy cliffs of Lee of Vollister above Whale Firth. At the head of the firth stands the gaunt ruin of Windhouse, tremendously haunted, particularly by a trow, or troll, slain by a traveller who was sleeping here all alone one Christmas Eve. Walk on, skirting the deep inlets in 200-foot cliffs where waves hit at the rock stacks and pour through the sea-cut arches. On North Neaps look out to dark sea stacks – Whilkie Stack, Eagle Stack and Gloup Holm.

On the harbour at Gloup stands a memorial erected in 1981 on the centenary of the Gloup fishing disaster. I pitched up to it soaked, exhausted and high as a kite. It records the names of the fifty-eight men who died on 21 July 1881, when a squall came down out of nowhere on a fleet of ten 'sixareen', or six-oared fishing boats. Six of the boats were from the village, and dozens of children were orphaned and wives widowed. In a full northerly gale, when the whitened sea rolls down Gloup Voe and smashes on the rocks of Gloup Ness outside, it is easy to see how the tragedy came about.

428. FETLAR, SHETLAND

Maps: OS Explorer 470; Landranger 2

Travel: Ferry from Gutcher on Yell or Belmont on Unst (www.fetlar.com).

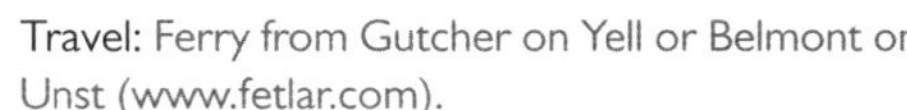

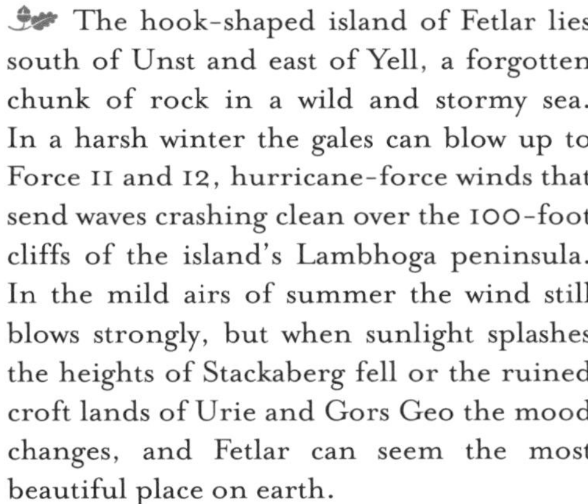

The hook-shaped island of Fetlar lies south of Unst and east of Yell, a forgotten chunk of rock in a wild and stormy sea. In a harsh winter the gales can blow up to Force 11 and 12, hurricane-force winds that send waves crashing clean over the 100-foot cliffs of the island's Lambhoga peninsula. In the mild airs of summer the wind still blows strongly, but when sunlight splashes the heights of Stackaberg fell or the ruined croft lands of Urie and Gors Geo the mood changes, and Fetlar can seem the most beautiful place on earth.

This corner of the Shetland archipelago has suffered, like all the islands, from the curse of depopulation. In 1836 there were 859 inhabitants; by 1891 fewer than half that number still lived on the island. The missing islanders had been cleared from the land by the ruling Nicolson family to make way for sheep. In one year alone, 1839–40, all thirteen crofts in the Gruting district of east Fetlar were emptied. Nowadays about eighty people share the flowery slopes, the sparkling hill burns and lonely valleys with the sheep, the fulmars and the otters. They brave the winters, the poor pickings and the isolation, living for the long days and short nights of summer when the light never leaves the sky and life seems to course at double strength through everyone's veins.

Fetlar, out on its own in the eastern seas of Shetland, is a favoured staging post and refuge for seabirds and waders – whimbrels, delicate cousins of the curlew; fulmars on the impossibly narrow ledges of the cliffs; rare red-necked phalaropes that breed on the marshy grounds. From the 1960s to the early 1990s the best-known birds of all were Fetlar's snowy owls. Snowy owls belong to the tundra of northern Scandinavia. They are extremely seldom seen as far south as the comparatively temperate island of Britain. Yet it was in Fetlar that a pair made an unheralded appearance in 1967, surviving the winter on a diet of rabbits, mice and whimbrels, and staying on to breed the following year.

The blow-ins raised a brood for the next eight years; then the genetic imperative faded and died. The numbers of their offspring steadily declined over twenty years, and after that the 3-foot-high birds with the pale grey plumage and the wrestler's shoulders were seen no more.

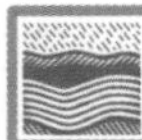

429. HERMANESS, ISLE OF UNST, SHETLAND

Maps: OS Explorer 470; Landranger 1

Travel: A970 through Shetland Mainland to Hillside; A968 north to Booth of Toft; ferry to Ulsta in Isle of Yell: A968 north through Yell to Gutcher, ferry to Belmont in Isle of Unst; A968 north to Haroldswick, left on B9086 past Burrafirth to Stackhoull. Continue for 1 mile to parking place (OS ref. 612149). Follow track for 2 miles north over Hermaness Hill to top of cliffs of Boelie above Looss Wick (606182). See www.unst.org.

The Isle of Unst is the most northerly of the Shetland Isles. It contains the most northerly settlement, the most northerly post office, the most northerly brewery. Even the geography runs north in long parallel ridges, leading inexorably up the island and up the map.

The most northerly 2 miles of Britain are walked along a rising track, leading over the 650-foot top of Hermaness Hill and down a long green slope where, if it is spring or early summer, you are certain to be attacked and torpedo-bombed by a bonxie or great skua. The bonxies, quite reasonably, regard this moorland as their exclusive property, and would dismiss out of hand the concept of a rambler's right to roam, if they had heard of it. Once past these fierce guardians of Hermaness, you will blink and gasp, both at the force of the wind coming unimpeded from the Arctic, and at the view that reveals itself beyond the cliffs. Among shrieking seabirds you stand and look out over a flotilla of bare rock blades, steeply canted in the sea like the hulls of ships about to go under – Vesta Skerry, Rumblings, Tipta Skerry, and Muckle Flugga, its lighthouse planted in a seemingly impossible position on the apex of its sharp spine. A little way north rises the small round button of Out Stack, prosaically named but romantically situated, the northernmost piece of land in the British Isles. From here 1,000 miles of empty sea stretches to the edge of the Arctic.

Looking down from Hermaness it is hard to imagine how Jane Franklin, Victorian skirt billowing, ever managed to scramble from a boat on to Out Stack in 1849, let alone stand and pray there. It was partly an act of devotion – she stood in tears with her hands stretched northwards and murmured, 'Send love on the wings of a prayer' – and partly a publicity stunt to raise awareness and money for yet another expedition in search of her husband. Sir John Franklin had set sail with

134 men four years earlier to seek out the famed and fabled North-West Passage across the roof of the world to India and China. Two months after departing in the steam-heated ships *Erebus* and *Terror*, loaded with candles, wolfskin blankets, lemon juice, 8,000 gallons of liquor and 8,000 tins of meat, soup and vegetables, they vanished off the face of the earth. Lady Franklin cried, prayed, worked like a Trojan and funded four separate rescue missions, all fruitless. Utterly determined to discover the fate of the expedition and at the same time reinforce the perception of her husband as a hero, she became the symbol of an intractable mystery.

Gradually, over the years, bits and pieces of the expedition reappeared – boats, belongings, notes and a few bodies. Tales of murder and of cannibalism began to circulate. At last, scientific research on bodies of expedition members preserved in the permafrost revealed the likely cause of the disaster, a mixture of exhaustion, scurvy, other diseases, and an abnormally high lead content in the bones. The tinned food had been sealed with lead solder, which had leached into the contents. Probably the men had been suffering from lead poisoning and the poor judgement and mental confusion associated with it. Some of the bones had knife cuts in them, suggesting that the desperate men had indeed resorted to eating their dead comrades as they wandered the snowfields of the Arctic after abandoning their frozen-in ships.

Here is the place to ponder their fate, leaning against the wind on Hermaness, staring north over a whitened sea.

13

IRELAND

Ireland's reputation as a treasury of wild places has a lot to do with the image of the Emerald Isle, green and inviolate, separated by the sea from a larger, more powerful and brutally industrialized neighbour. And Ireland has produced a remarkable number of artists, writers and musicians whose work celebrates the wild side of the island's people and its landscapes, particularly of the ruggedly romantic west.

THE WEST OF Ireland is wild, strikingly so. County Donegal has swathes of empty moorlands, Connemara is a patchwork of mountain clusters and open bogland. Down in the south-west you can walk all day and see no one. The emptiness is easily explained; over the past two centuries emigration and famine stripped this land of most of its people. As for the islands off the west coast, a few retain thriving communities, but they are outnumbered by the thinly populated or abandoned ones whose fields and early Christian sites are being repossessed by nature. There is a melancholy to these places of the west, alongside a magnetic beauty and grandeur.

But the west does not have a monopoly on wilderness. The magnificent bogs of the Midlands – glorious heather, wild flowers and iridescent pools – are as wild as can be in their natural state. When stripped for peat extraction they wear an aspect of naked desolation that haunts and mesmerizes. There are mountain ranges inland where very few outsiders venture: the Slieve Blooms or the Blackstairs, the Comeragh or empty Ox ranges. Up until recently such places were considered poor land and therefore poor-value country that was essentially a waste of space. Pressure from inside and influence from outside Ireland are changing that attitude. Conserving wild places has traditionally been a minority concern in the Irish Republic, but it's now gathering pace as a broader education and more contact with overseas visitors opens Irish eyes to the vulnerability of their natural treasures.

While the Republic basks in the fame of its landscape, north of the Border the wild places go virtually unknown. Thirty years of the Troubles put paid to the tourist industry here, and the glories of the North still wait to be properly appreciated. All the better for those who think that wild places and crowds of visitors are mutually exclusive. Some notable conservation efforts in Northern Ireland are bearing fruit, especially in Belfast, where the reserves of Lagan Meadows and Bog Meadows keep patches of wildness in the city. More typical, though, is the back country, which, as in the south, has traditionally been seen as low grade and low status, the kind of place no one sane would want to hang around. A good example is the all-but-unvisited Sperrin Hills in central Tyrone – a county that also contains, in the vicinity of Beaghmore, a most extraordinary prehistoric landscape of stone circles, standing stones and tombs, half emerged from bogland.

Remnants of pre-Christian cultures with their pagan hint of wildness lie thickly on the ground all across Ireland, from County Fermanagh's enigmatic, wide-eyed Janus Man to the giant tomb of Newgrange, where modern-day suppliants crouch at winter solstice in hopes of revelation. Round any corner in rural Ireland, those with tuned antennae will recognize the untamed, unregulated places where Christian belief is still active in meeting older faiths – holy wells, cure-stones, rock chairs that mend your backache, standing stones carved with Christian symbols.

Then, of course, there is the wildness of the music and the talk. You'll meet that in pubs at midnight, in a back-lane conversation over a gate, round a kitchen table, or wherever else people gather to laugh and sing, following a tradition that is still kept up throughout rural Ireland. Whether it is done to keep the wild out of the human circle, or to invite it to enter, is another question.

LINKS VIA THE WAYMARKED WAYS

- **Northern Ireland** (www.walkni.com)
- Causeway Coast Way: Rathlin Island, Port na Spaniagh, Giant's Causeway, Dunluce Castle
- Lecale Way: Mountains of Mourne, Strangford Lough
- Central Sperrins Way: Sperrin Hills
- Ring of Gullion Way: Slieve Gullion
- Antrim Hills Way and Moyle Way: Antrim Glens
- **Republic of Ireland** (www.walkireland.ie)
- South Leinster Way (www.southleinsterway.com): Blackstairs Mountains
- Cavan Way (www.cavantourism.com): Shannon Pot
- Donegal Way: Mount Errigal, Tory Island
- Western Way: Ox Mountains, Nephin Beg, Croagh Patrick, Maumturks, 12 Bens, Iar-Connacht
- Sli Chonamara (Connemara Way): Maumturks, 12 Bens, Iar-Connacht, Gorumna and the causeway islands
- Kerry Way (www.kerryway.net): Old Kenmare Road
- Dingle Way (www.dingleway.net): Great Blasket Island, Mount Brandon
- Slieve Bloom Way: Slieve Blooms
- East Munster Way: Comeragh Mountains
- East Munster Way/Tipperary Heritage Trail (www.tipperaryway.com): Knockmealdown Mountains

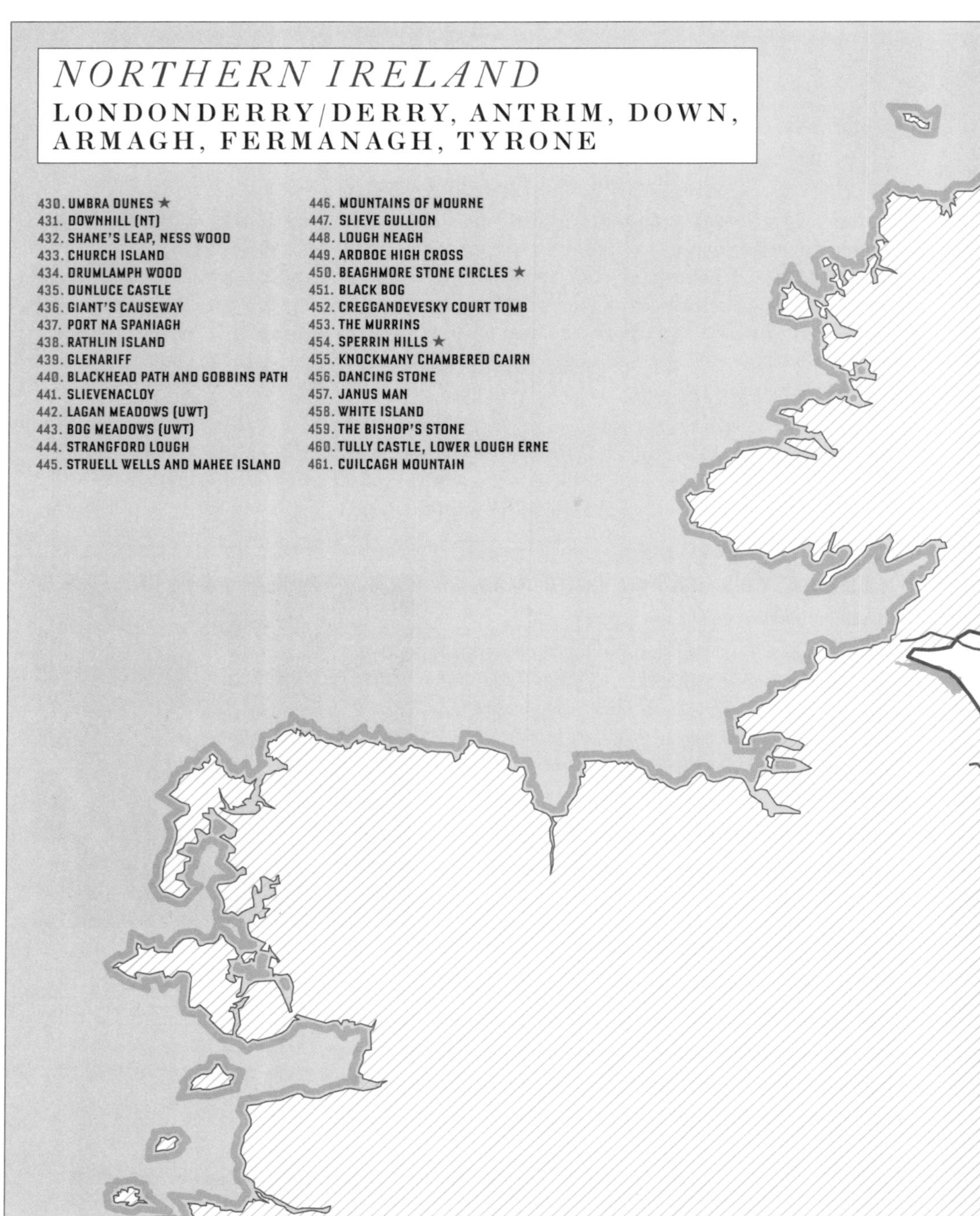
NORTHERN IRELAND
LONDONDERRY/DERRY, ANTRIM, DOWN, ARMAGH, FERMANAGH, TYRONE
430. UMBRA DUNES ★
431. DOWNHILL (NT)
432. SHANE'S LEAP, NESS WOOD
433. CHURCH ISLAND
434. DRUMLAMPH WOOD
435. DUNLUCE CASTLE
436. GIANT'S CAUSEWAY
437. PORT NA SPANIAGH
438. RATHLIN ISLAND
439. GLENARIFF
440. BLACKHEAD PATH AND GOBBINS PATH
441. SLIEVENACLOY
442. LAGAN MEADOWS (UWT)
443. BOG MEADOWS (UWT)
444. STRANGFORD LOUGH
445. STRUELL WELLS AND MAHEE ISLAND
446. MOUNTAINS OF MOURNE
447. SLIEVE GULLION
448. LOUGH NEAGH
449. ARDBOE HIGH CROSS
450. BEAGHMORE STONE CIRCLES ★
451. BLACK BOG
452. CREGGANDEVESKY COURT TOMB
453. THE MURRINS
454. SPERRIN HILLS ★
455. KNOCKMANY CHAMBERED CAIRN
456. DANCING STONE
457. JANUS MAN
458. WHITE ISLAND
459. THE BISHOP'S STONE
460. TULLY CASTLE, LOWER LOUGH ERNE
461. CUILCAGH MOUNTAIN

Londonderry
Coleraine
Portrush
Bushmills
ANTRIM
LONDONDERRY
DERRY
Ballymena
Larne
Strabane
Maghera
TYRONE
Carrickfergus
Newtownabbey
Bangor
Lough Neagh
Cookstown
Omagh
Belfast
Newtownards
Coalisland
Lisburn
Dungannon
Portadown
Craigavon
Lower Lough Erne
Ballynahinch
Enniskillen
Armagh
Downpatrick
DOWN
FERMANAGH
Dundrum
ARMAGH
Upper Lough Erne
Newcastle
Newry
Crossmaglen
Scale 5 m 10 km

430. UMBRA DUNES, CO. DERRY

Map: OS of Northern Ireland Discoverer 4

Travel: A2 Coleraine towards Limavady; through Castlerock and Downhill; in 1 ¼ miles, park just beyond level crossing cottage (OS ref. 724356). Go through gate next to cottage; track through trees leads to Umbra Dunes.

NB: This track is for members of Ulster Wildlife Trust (tel: 01396 830282; www.ulsterwildlifetrust.org). You can also reach the dunes along the strand.

Umbra Dunes is most definitely a spring and summer place. The track through the trees at Umbra seems an ordinary woodland path at first; then you emerge into a dazzling wildflower meadow, and the richness and – to contemporary eyes – strangeness of the scene hits you like a blow. Early purple orchids push up their big milky flower spikes, not in the rare ones and twos you are grateful to spot at most preserved wildflower sites, but in their thousands. Yellow rattle, that infallible indicator of traditionally managed grassland, carpets the grass. Deep purple-blue vetches grow in tangles, along with the frothy, bright yellow flower clusters of lady's bedstraw, a plant with a beautiful sweet smell and an honourable place in Irish herbalists' lore. Lady's bedstraw was chosen by Our Lady as the bedding on which to give birth to her son in the Bethlehem stable, and some of that virtue still clings to a plant which can keep evil spirits away, cure bladder and bone joint problems, curdle milk for cheese-making and soothe the sore feet of wayfarers.

Follow the track past the meadow and you come out among Umbra Dunes, where the wildflower glories continue. Pyramidal orchids send out their spicy vanilla scent from flower clusters in nail-polish pink, and guelder roses bloom on their spiky trails. Lifting your eyes from these floral treasures may be an effort, but it is worth it for the view across the colourful backs of the dunes to the purple cliffs that march eastward behind the sandhills, the pepper-pot shape of Mussenden Temple (see below) perched precariously at the brink.

431. DOWNHILL (NT), CO. DERRY

Map: OS of Northern Ireland Discoverer 4

Travel: A2 from Coleraine towards Limavady; in Liffock pass B119 Castlerock turning on right; entrance to Downhill is ½ mile on your right (OS ref. 757357).

Frederick Hervey, 4th Earl of Bristol and Protestant Bishop of Londonderry, was a splendidly red-blooded and eccentric cleric.

Back in the eighteenth century a man – and particularly an aristocratic Englishman with plenty of money and a robust sense of his own position in life – could do pretty much as he damn well pleased. Hervey indulged a great penchant for foreign travel, having himself conveyed about Rome in a palanquin. He put up at a hotel overlooking the route taken by religious processions on their way to St Peter's Square, and delighted in dropping spaghetti on to their Catholic heads as they passed solemnly below his balcony. Or perhaps it was soup from a tureen in Siena – stories about Hervey grew fat with the telling. King George III called him a 'wicked prelate', and he was certainly fond of many self-indulgent pursuits – travel, practical joking, eating, art-collecting and sex. He could be magisterially rude, 'very blasphemous, and greatly addicted to gallantry'. Yet Frederick Hervey was no intolerant monster (except towards the French, whom he hated) – he was remarkably liberal-minded by the standards of his day, and advocated a relaxation of the Penal Laws, imposed at the beginning of the eighteenth century to crush Irish Catholics with fines and fierce prohibitions on voting and Catholic education.

A force of nature, Hervey was Bishop of Londonderry for thirty-five years, and during that tenure he poured money out on the Downhill Estate that he built between 1774 and 1778 on the cliffs near Castlerock. The Palace of Downhill was designed to house his huge art collection; there was also a handsome walled garden, wide grounds and a number of follies. All now lie in ruins.

You approach the decayed estate through an ornate stone gateway, either the Lion Gate or the Bishop's Gate, and stroll past the roofless, gaunt and crumbling ruins of the bishop's palace. The classical columns of a great abandoned mausoleum rise away to the east. The path leads to the cliff and the rotunda known as the Mussenden Temple, which Hervey sited here on the edge of the drop. The bishop allowed the local Catholic priest to celebrate Mass in the temple, proof of his generosity of spirit. The building housed his library and, locals said, one of his mistresses, too.

432. SHANE'S LEAP, NESS WOOD, CO. DERRY

Map: OS of Northern Ireland Discoverer 7

Travel: A6 from Derry towards Claudy; in 8½ miles, left (brown 'Ness Wood Country Park' sign) to car park (OS ref. 528118). Follow the 3-mile trail through Ness Wood.

Ness Wood takes its name from the Gaelic *an eas*, 'a waterfall', and this place is made thunderous and thrilling after heavy rainfall when the Burntollet River comes down swollen with water from the north Derry mountains and crashes over its falls in the depths of the wood.

A good path leads through thick woodland of oak, birch and hazel, with the sound of the river coming up from below, a rhythmical noise as the water swirls round pockets in its bed of schist. The path descends from a ledge high above the Burntollet to a fork – the right-hand path climbs, the left-hand one carries on down to the floor of the wood, where you turn back to cross the river on a footbridge before climbing to another junction. A left turn here takes you back to rejoin the river. Stained brown with peat

Ness Wood Country Park

from the moors, it tumbles like molten glass through a narrow channel in the rocks under ferns, rhododendrons and trailing lianas of ivy before leaping out and down a double fall, 30 feet into a rock basin in a haze of mist and rainbow spray. Above the fall stands Shane's Leap, a pair of pale rock ledges facing each other like the piers of a vanished arch. Here Shane 'Crossagh' O'Mullan once pulled up, according to legend, with a file of soldiers hot on his heels.

Though 'Crossagh' means 'pocked-marked', Shane is said to have been a handsome devil, a raparee, or cutpurse, very much in favour with the ladies. He would rob the rich, and loved to tease the agents of law and order; on one occasion he forced a company of soldiers, and their general, too, to slink into Derry in their underpants after he had relieved them of their uniforms. Like Robin Hood before him, Crossagh gave generously to the poor and to wenches who caught his fancy, and the threat of the gibbet did not deter him.

When he arrived at the Burntollet fall he sprang off the rocks and leaped down into the basin, breaking his leg on landing. Still too spry for the squaddies chasing him, somehow he managed to hobble away and escape. Crossagh lived to steal and kiss for many another day, until in 1722, on a sad morning for Derry ladies, the hangman finally coiled a hempen rope around the neck of the gallant and reckless raparee.

433. CHURCH ISLAND, LOUGH BEG, CO. DERRY

Maps OS of Northern Ireland Discoverer 14

Travel: From Magherafelt, A31 to Castledawson; A54 towards Bellaghy. In 1 mile turn right on Ballydermot Road (OS ref. 943945). Cross B182 and continue for 1/3 mile to entrance to Lough Beg National Nature Reserve on right (965948).

NB: This entrance is on a dangerous bend; do not park here, but continue along road to park a little way further on and return to entrance on foot. In winter the way to Church Island (975946) is generally impassable owing to flooding.

Church Island looks impossibly romantic on a winter's day, with its tall spire and skeletal trees reflected in a shimmer of water. The island lies right on the brink of the western shore of Lough Beg. In winter, when the lough is swollen with rain, the grassland nature reserve, of which Church

Island is the centrepiece, becomes so sodden that even a tall man with waders would find it impossible to reach the isle on foot. You have to remain a few hundred yards off, watching geese and wading birds stalking the wet ground, and speculating on the nature of the church that lies so isolated among the trees.

In summer the ground dries out and becomes negotiable, though always damp. Lapwings mew overhead and snipe zigzag away as you walk out along the well-worn track through the grass. If you come on the first Sunday in September you will have company in the form of dozens of pilgrims making the annual trek to Church Island, perhaps led there by traditional musicians. The feast day of the island, 7 September, is that of Saint Taoide, or Thaddeus, a friend of St Patrick who inspired the great man to help him found a monastery there in the fifth century AD.

Although there is still a church on Church Island it is not attached to the spire. It was the eccentric and free-spending Bishop of Londonderry and 4th Earl of Bristol, Frederick Hervey of Downhill Estate (see pp. 472–3), who had the spire built as a pleasing folly in the eighteenth century. The twelfth-century church near by lies as a ruin, the beautiful and solemn little graveyard a riot of flowers. Down by the lough lies a bullaun, a quern-stone, whose hollow centre catches rainwater that has healing properties. No wonder – for it was the patron saint of Ireland, St Patrick himself, who made the hollow in the bullaun with one of his knees when he knelt there to pray.

Church Island

434. DRUMLAMPH WOOD, MAGHERA, CO. DERRY

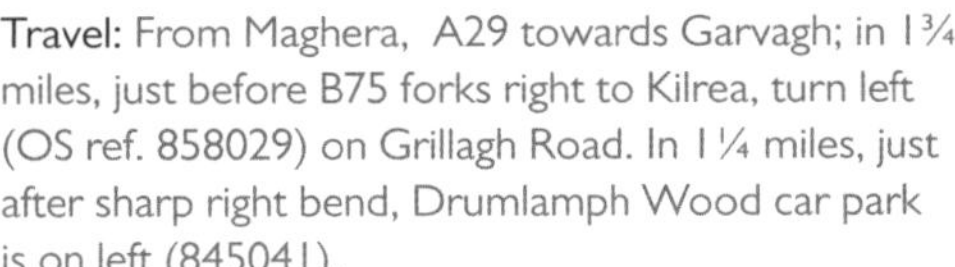

Map: OS of Northern Ireland Discoverer 8

Travel: From Maghera, A29 towards Garvagh; in 1¾ miles, just before B75 forks right to Kilrea, turn left (OS ref. 858029) on Grillagh Road. In 1¼ miles, just after sharp right bend, Drumlamph Wood car park is on left (845041).

Is it Drumlamph or Drumnaph? The signposts don't seem quite certain of the correct Anglicization of the Gaelic *droim chneamh*, 'ridge of wild garlic'. Or is that *dromin nDamh*, 'ox ridge'? Experts also disagree. Whatever the etymology, this is one of Northern Ireland's very few pieces of ancient woodland, having survived the intense exploitation of native forests over the centuries for charcoal-making, shipbuilding and domestic industrial construction. Drumlamph Wood, too, was cut for weapons and tool handles, hacked into to clear ground for agriculture, and harvested to provide timber for building the walls and ship quays of Derry city in the seventeenth century. 'In fact,' says the explanation board at the entrance, 'it's a miracle that any of the woodland has survived.'

Drumlamph Wood

A Red and a Yellow trail take you around the site, which is being intensively replanted in selected patches with native tree species: beech, oak and ash. Children will love the ingenuity with which a dead tree by the path has been carved into the shapes of animals and birds, including a fox, badger, heron, otter, salmon and owl. There is a damp meadow rich in marsh orchids, where sedge warblers send out their sharp clicks and whirrs of alarm, and the entrance to the wood is over ground soggy and flaky with half-rotted fallen boughs smothered in wet mosses. There are no forest giants in Drumlamph Wood. This is more of a thicket, a dense old tangle of low, mossy trees in the grip of ivy, floored with bracken and moss. Rushy streams gurgle across the clearings, and the silence of the wood is pierced from time to time by a rich burble of blackcap or whitethroat song.

435. DUNLUCE CASTLE, CO. ANTRIM

Map: OS of Northern Ireland Discoverer 4

Travel: A2 from Bushmills towards Portrush; car park in 2 miles; walk to Dunluce Castle (OS ref. 904414).

Even if you know nothing of Dunluce Castle's history, first sight of the fourteenth-century stronghold suggests its story should be a sombre one, with its blank windows, weather-blurred battlements and upthrust stubs of masonry, not to mention its precarious position right on the brink of the cliffs. In sunlight the walls glow honey-brown; under cloud the whole broken building darkens to resemble an outcrop of the cliffs that slope 100 feet into the sea. These cliffs contain crevices and hollows, a chasm that makes an island of the castle promontory, and a long cave where the

MacQuillan and later MacDonnell owners of Dunluce concealed their warships.

Two incidents stand out in Dunluce's history of clan sieges and struggles with the English for occupation of the fortress. In 1584, when Tudor repression of the Irish was gaining force all over the island, the English had taken Dunluce from its owner, Sorley Boy MacDonnell. The means by which he won it back were extraordinarily daring; he had his men hauled up the cliffs in baskets, thus achieving a staggering surprise and overwhelming the garrison before they could really take in the fact that they were being invaded from a completely impossible direction – the thin air above the sea.

The second incident, which was responsible for the gradual abandonment and ruin of the castle, took place half a century after Sorley Boy's feat. Between the castle proper and the cliff edge a range of kitchens had been built. It had always been an awkward, storm-lashed spot, and perhaps the builders had skimped on their workmanship, for during a fierce gale in 1639 most of the kitchen quarter split away from the castle and crashed into the sea. Several of the castle servants were killed. The MacDonnell family decided thereafter to live 'on land', leaving Dunluce to its ghosts – especially the pale lady who haunts the north-east tower. Unlucky in love, she walks alone, nursing the broken heart from which she died.

436. GIANT'S CAUSEWAY, CO. ANTRIM

Map: OS of Northern Ireland Discoverer 4

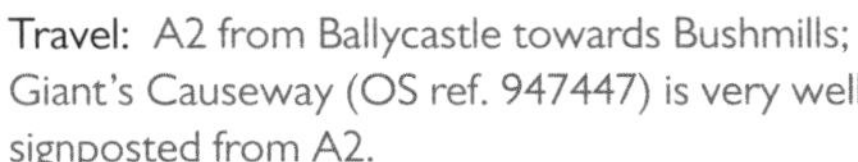

Travel: A2 from Ballycastle towards Bushmills; Giant's Causeway (OS ref. 947447) is very well signposted from A2.

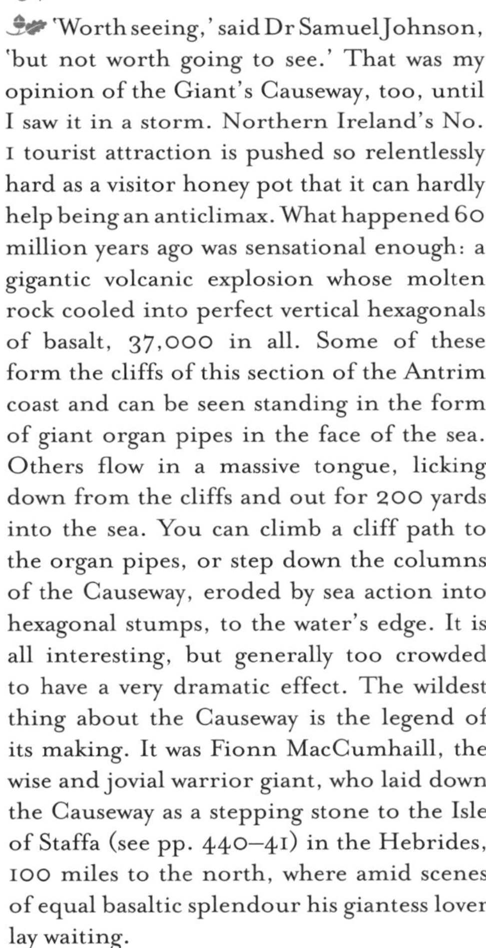

'Worth seeing,' said Dr Samuel Johnson, 'but not worth going to see.' That was my opinion of the Giant's Causeway, too, until I saw it in a storm. Northern Ireland's No. 1 tourist attraction is pushed so relentlessly hard as a visitor honey pot that it can hardly help being an anticlimax. What happened 60 million years ago was sensational enough: a gigantic volcanic explosion whose molten rock cooled into perfect vertical hexagonals of basalt, 37,000 in all. Some of these form the cliffs of this section of the Antrim coast and can be seen standing in the form of giant organ pipes in the face of the sea. Others flow in a massive tongue, licking down from the cliffs and out for 200 yards into the sea. You can climb a cliff path to the organ pipes, or step down the columns of the Causeway, eroded by sea action into hexagonal stumps, to the water's edge. It is all interesting, but generally too crowded to have a very dramatic effect. The wildest thing about the Causeway is the legend of its making. It was Fionn MacCumhaill, the wise and jovial warrior giant, who laid down the Causeway as a stepping stone to the Isle of Staffa (see pp. 440–41) in the Hebrides, 100 miles to the north, where amid scenes of equal basaltic splendour his giantess lover lay waiting.

The stormy day that I ventured to the Giant's Causeway changed my outlook completely. It was an angry white north-easterly of Force 8 or 9 on a rising tide, and the waves came rolling in across the bay to smash with thunder into the flanks of the Causeway. They burst with a boom so deep it could have been a giant's roar, and the rocks themselves shuddered. A cold, dense exhalation of spray hung off the cliffs as thickly as a fog, and the sight of the Causeway buried in white foam, then appearing to heave itself free like a coarse-skinned sea beast, was mesmerizing. I had intended to walk out among the rollers, but a glance told me that it would be suicide. So I climbed the cliffs and sat in a niche with salt in my mouth and eyes, the only soul there, to watch the Causeway fight the sea.

Port Na Spaniagh

437. PORT NA SPANIAGH, CO. ANTRIM

Map: OS of Northern Ireland Discoverer 5

Travel: A2 Antrim Coast Road to Giant's Causeway Visitor Centre (signposted near Bushmills, between Ballycastle and Portrush). A fenced clifftop path starts behind the Visitor Centre and runs east for a mile to reach Port na Spaniagh (headland beyond Giant's Causeway). Viewpoint at OS ref. 955452, wreck site 953456.

The Antrim coast is a formidable rampart, and nowhere more so than in its northernmost sector around the UNESCO World Heritage Site of the Giant's Causeway (see above). Just east of the famous promontory the cliffs push seaward to from the prow of Lacada Point, a fortress-like headland pricked with dark red rock spires, from which another columnar promontory snakes into the sea. Port na Spaniagh (Spaniard's Cove), a narrow bay with a pebbly strand, lies immediately east. A clifftop footpath looks down on the cove, a path spattered in summer with common spotted orchids, wild thyme, bell heather and the white starlike flowers of stonecrop.

The cove derives its name from a tragic incident that occurred in 1588. Around midnight on 26 October, drifting rudderless at the mercy of one of that autumn's ferocious gales, the Spanish galleass *Girona* went down after striking a rock off Lacada Point. *Girona* had been sheltering in the County Donegal port of Killibegs, and had set out earlier that day, hoping to sail clockwise around Ireland and back to Spain. But breaking her rudder at the height of the storm did for her. Of 1,300 souls on board, five only were saved, plucked from the disaster by rescuers from Dunluce Castle (see pp. 476–7) under the orders of local lord and master Sorley Boy MacDonnell.

Once safely recovering on shore, these bedraggled wretches must have considered themselves lucky. Half of the 131 ships of the Spanish Armada that set out from Lisbon on 30 May 1588 never returned home. The great invasion fleet that should have hit mainland

Britain and crushed all opposition was itself knocked for six by the worst autumn storms in living memory. Savaged by Sir Francis Drake's ships in the English Channel in July, in full retreat anticlockwise round the British Isles by August, the clumsy Armada vessels were storm-battered and wave-driven in their dozens on to the wild coasts of western Scotland and Ireland. Eight thousand sailors and soldiers died in the wrecks, many more at the hands of locals when they struggled ashore. Some, on the other hand, were kindly treated by sympathetic Roman Catholics, or those with decent impulses towards fellow humans in trouble.

Girona lay undisturbed for almost 400 years until 1967, when a team led by Belgian diver Robert Stenuit found her. The rich treasure they unearthed from the seabed around the wreck – a fabulous hoard of gold and silver, along with hundreds of intimate personal artifacts such as shoes, buckles, knives and drinking horns – lies on display in the Ulster Museum, Belfast.

438. RATHLIN ISLAND, CO. ANTRIM

Map: OS of Northern Ireland Discoverer 5

Travel: A2 to Ballycastle; ferry to Rathlin Island (www.antrim.net/rathlin)

Swooping through Sloch na Marra, the Valley of the Sea, you may wonder if the little Rathlin Island ferryboat will manage to rise and breast the next green slope of the waves. Sloch na Marra is well named. The liveliest tide-rip off the Atlantic coast of Northern Ireland, it twists and roars in angry furrows between the ferryport of Ballycastle and the L-shaped island of Rathlin, some 5 miles offshore. All things come to an end,

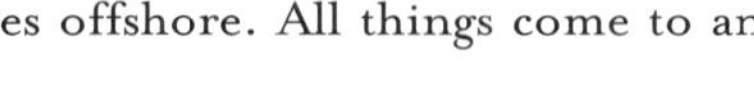

however, and in a few minutes you come bumping out of the foothills of Sloch na Marra into calmer water as Rathlin Island begins to shape itself out of the spray. The island resembles a bent arm, its upper half running from tall western cliffs towards a crooked elbow at the north-east corner. Its forearm, sloping south to Rue Point, shelters the few white houses of the harbour village.

The island's cliffs seem to grin a rugged welcome, a cheerful exposure of white calcareous teeth. Travelling round the coasts of Britain I became so accustomed to seeing chalk as the white icing on the geographical cake that the curious topsy-turviness of Rathlin Island's construction came as a shock. Here it is the lower storey of the island that is pale chalky limestone, the upper layer dark basalt, spread like chocolate by the tremendous volcanic convulsions that formed the Giant's Causeway (see pp. 477–8) and the spectacular cliffs of the Antrim coast.

Rathlin's cliffs are burrowed with caves where grey seals breed. In one of them, the islanders will tell you, the fugitive Scottish King Robert the Bruce sat on a day of despair after his defeat at Perth by the English in 1306 and learned a lesson in perseverance from a patient spider. The cliffs are seamed with ledges where seabirds nest, mate and rear their chicks by the hundred thousand each year. In the cold, clear water around the island flourish sea cucumbers, sponges and soft corals. Rathlin is a sea-surrounded paradise. It's quite extraordinary that the island is not swamped by tourists.

After landing on the little jetty, strike out west along a narrow walled road between

neat hay fields. Blood-red lanterns of fuchsia tremble in the hedges, and thick carpets of heath spotted orchids bend this way and that to the gentle push of the wind. You pass a marshy lake where tufted ducks sail. Irish hares bound away across the grass. These signs of healthy natural balance are sustained by the small-scale, old-fashioned agriculture of Rathlin, the tiny human population of seventy-odd, and the physical isolation of the place.

From the crest of the island you can see the long peninsular silhouette of the Mull of Oa, 15 miles across the sea in the Isle of Islay (see p. 436). For all its lonely situation, Rathlin Island was always a ripe strategic plum for invaders. In 1642 Sir Duncan Campbell landed here from Scotland to deal out slaughter and despair among the islanders. One of Rathlin's hills is still known as Crocknascriedlin, the Hill of Screaming. It was from there that the island women watched Campbell's soldiers butcher their men before they, too, were rounded up and thrown to their deaths on the rocks at Sloak-na-Calliagh, the Pit of the Hags. So the very place names of Rathlin remember its story.

In the seabird breeding season the western end of Rathlin could well be called the Cliffs of Screaming. A quarter of a million birds squabble and swoop around Kebble Cliffs – kittiwakes on black-tipped wings, guillemots and razorbills thronging the sea stacks, puffins at their burrow doors in the grass ledges of the cliffs. The stink and the noise, the everlasting circling and the dizzying height above the creaming waves will make your head spin.

439. GLENARIFF, CO. ANTRIM

Map: OS of Northern Ireland Discoverer 9

Travel: A2 coast road to Glenariff; inland on A43 for 4 miles to Glenariff Forest Park; car park on left (OS ref. 212203).

The Antrim cliffs are the most breathtaking piece of coastal scenery in the whole of Ireland. They are strikingly coloured – white limestone, dusky red sandstone, pale grey puddingstone – but it's basalt that is the rock star hereabouts. The basalt reaches the sea in a series of dramatic, sharp-nosed headlands and cliffs, overspill from a gigantic volcanic explosion some 60 million years ago. The deep clefts eroded by rivers between the basalt ridges form the Glens of Antrim, a succession of nine beautiful, wild river valleys, with pretty little whitewashed villages such as Carnlough, Glenariff, Cushendall and Cushendun at the river mouths. These villages were isolated fishing settlements with no land communication until the coast road was built to link them up in the 1830s. The road was planned as a means for local men to feed themselves and their families by earning money as labourers – for Antrim, like every other part of rural Ireland back then, lay in the grip of desperate poverty.

Glenariff Forest Park has four walks laid out through the best part of the glen, and the most dramatic is the Waterfall Trail. As with so many popular wild places, to appreciate it to the full it is best to come early or late in the day, after heavy rain if possible. At such times there is a magic in the woods as you walk on a pine-needle carpet down by the rain-swollen rivers, Glenariff and Inver, following one and then the other as they rush and plunge over falls and through pools. Wrens trill and chatter, red squirrels bounce among the pine branches. Wooden stairways take you down almost to water level, running along the rock faces where mosses and ferns bulge from dripping clefts. In spring the gorges are filled with bluebells and wood anemones, and are pungent with the reek of wild garlic.

The trail becomes spectacular, a series of curves and tight concertina bends that cling to the rock as they carry you down to the foot of a superb double waterfall in the depths of the cleft. Then the track rises at the confluence of Glenariff and Inver to follow the latter in a canopy of trees. Look up to see the purple-grey basalt rim of the glen high overhead, before climbing steeply to pass unexpectedly through an immaculately kept area of Victorian gardens – rhododendrons, bamboos, flowering cherries. A final section of trail leads to a stunning viewpoint, a high prospect down the length of Glenariff to the sea, sparkling in its cleft 5 miles off and nearly 1,000 feet below.

440. BLACKHEAD PATH AND GOBBINS PATH, ISLAND MAGEE, CO. ANTRIM

Map: OS of Northern Ireland Discoverer 9, 15

Travel: A2 Belfast towards Larne; in Whitehead, turn right ('Whitehead, Island Magee') to the seafront. Park here (OS ref. 478921) and follow Blackhead Path under cliffs.

NB: Do not attempt the Gobbins Path; it is derelict and dangerous.

The Gobbins Path was one of the most dramatic examples of late-Victorian engineering know-how brought to bear for the benefit of the seaside tourist trade. A memorial stone at the start of the Blackhead Path – the more southerly section of the route that begins on Whitehead seafront – commemorates railway engineer and architect Berkeley Deane Wise (1853–1909). He was the designer of a daring series of walkways which united the ingenuity of pier construction and the versatility of cast-iron to enable holidaymakers to walk and climb for miles along the otherwise impassable cliffs and offshore rock stacks of the Antrim coast. Wise's system of railed catwalks, ladders and iron cages allowed the bustled and boatered tourists to admire, from seal's- and bird's-eye level, views into caves and down sheer cliff faces that they could not otherwise have enjoyed.

Notices beside the Blackhead Path reinforce its present-day hazards: unexpected waves caused by passing ferries, cliff slips, falling rocks, slippery sections. It is a badly maintained route, brightened in places by clumps of sea pinks and white sea campion, along a lonely shore which bulges into the dark cliff faces of Blackhead. The path climbs by stairways and steps, crossing bridges of concrete and nosing through clefts in the rock. Rusty sections of rail offer a dubious handhold here and there, though, and soon enough you turn the corner of the cliffs and reach a firmer shore.

This more southerly Blackhead section of the path is subject to closure from time to time, as the state of the overhanging cliffs dictates. It is in any case no more than a taster for the far more dramatic section of path which crosses the face of the Gobbins cliffs, a little further north. This stretch of path starts at the foot of a narrow track down from the coast road, and is really only negotiable by those with sticky fly-feet. It commences by passing through a rough archway, labelled THE GOBBINS in coarsely cut capitals, and from here onward is marked by ancient salt-rusted stanchions, stretches of neatly embanked pathway cut apart by cliff falls, and slippery, weather-eroded staircases leading to perilous ledges – once guarded by rails, but now edged with 100-foot drops to the rocks below. The long bridges, caged-in with iron hoops, that spanned the gaps between cliffs and rock stacks have long ago fallen into the sea or been retrieved for scrap, and the whole path is far too dangerous to be attempted on foot. But from a boat hired from Larne Harbour you can follow the course of this wonderful and extravagant cast-iron road above the sea, marvelling at the energy and 'can-do' attitude of that practical genius the Victorian engineer, so supremely confident in his mastery of nature.

441. SLIEVENACLOY, CO. ANTRIM

Maps: OS of Northern Ireland Discoverer 15, 14

Travel: A26/B101 towards Lisburn. Left along Flowbog Road. In 1½ miles, go through gate on left (OS ref. 250709 – 'Ulster Wildlife Trust'), up track and park by Trust's buildings. Leaflet from dispenser shows footpaths through reserve.

The landscape just west of Belfast has nothing whatsoever to do with a city. It is all about small-scale farming in decline – winding lanes, overgrown hedges, brimming ditches, rushy fields overgrown and run wild with meadowsweet and yellow flags. Cattle graze chin-deep in damp, thistly bogland. Some deep drainage, a dose of Roundup and a brisk tidying session with a hedge-ripper would soon bring this forgotten pocket of countryside up to date, but that hasn't happened so far.

Long, lush grasslands rise up the hill slope of Slievenacloy. Nothing violent has been done to this land; it has been farmed through generations as it is nowadays, under the care of Ulster Wildlife Trust – slowly, much of it by hand, giving flowers time to set seed and birds to lay, hatch and fledge their broods. The long grasses in summer are thick with southern marsh orchids, bright pink starbursts of ragged robin and tall blue

Slievenacloy

spikes of self-heal. Hares lollop off as you climb the track and wander the footpaths. These large and beautiful animals have been on the decline since the arrival of modern farming practices, which see the hay fields cut before they can grow long and the hedges and headlands slashed back to the ground. Hares need the shelter of long grass, and they find it at Slievenacloy.

There are three chief types of habitat here, each complementing and blending with the others: wet heath of sphagnum moss interspersed with patches of heather and purple moor grass; rushy pasture where the delicate pink and blue blobs of milkmaids grow in spring; and the wonderful grassland full of orchids, scabious, ragged robin and straggly purple vetches. Standing with your feet in the flowers and your ears tuned to ecstatic lark song, it is hard to credit that Northern Ireland's roaring capital city lies just over the hill.

442. LAGAN MEADOWS (UWT), BELFAST

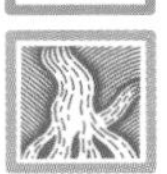

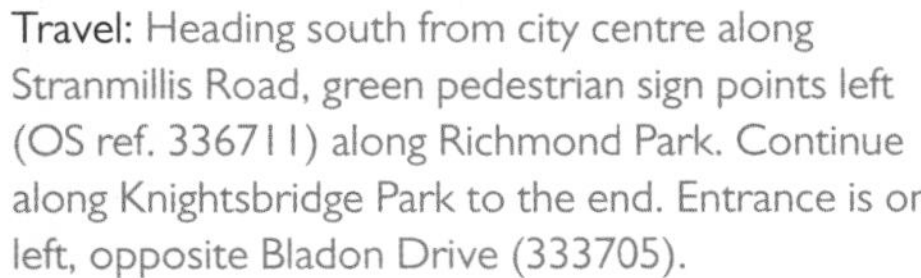

Map: OS of Northern Ireland Discoverer 15

Travel: Heading south from city centre along Stranmillis Road, green pedestrian sign points left (OS ref. 336711) along Richmond Park. Continue along Knightsbridge Park to the end. Entrance is on left, opposite Bladon Drive (333705).

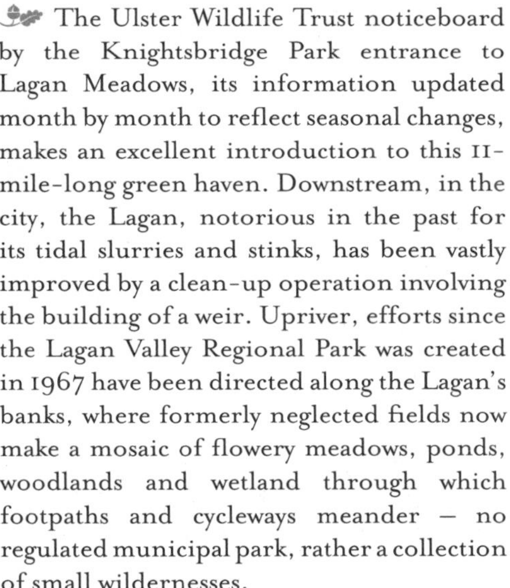

The Ulster Wildlife Trust noticeboard by the Knightsbridge Park entrance to Lagan Meadows, its information updated month by month to reflect seasonal changes, makes an excellent introduction to this 11-mile-long green haven. Downstream, in the city, the Lagan, notorious in the past for its tidal slurries and stinks, has been vastly improved by a clean-up operation involving the building of a weir. Upriver, efforts since the Lagan Valley Regional Park was created in 1967 have been directed along the Lagan's banks, where formerly neglected fields now make a mosaic of flowery meadows, ponds, woodlands and wetland through which footpaths and cycleways meander – no regulated municipal park, rather a collection of small wildernesses.

Dark brown ringlet butterflies flit across meadows of damp grassland full of feathery pink ragged robin, common spotted orchid, buttercups and meadow thistles. From those grassy fields you dip downhill through larch woodland and groves of oak to paths running through lush meadows beside the River Lagan. Lester's Dam forms the centrepiece, a reservoir built at the turn of the nineteenth century to store water for the rapidly expanding and industrializing Belfast. These days it's a sedgy pond fringed with reeds and bulrushes. Young willows are shooting up all round; electric-blue damselflies quiver at a

Lagan Meadows

mid-air standstill over the lily pads before dematerializing in a haze of wing beats to reappear 10 feet off. Reed buntings nest in the reed-beds, and you can hear the songs of two warbler species that love thick cover and wetland surroundings – the 'winding fishing reel' of the grasshopper warbler, and the sedge warbler's monotonous little bursts of chirrups and trills.

443. BOG MEADOWS (UWT), BELFAST

Map: OS of Northern Ireland Discoverer 15

Travel: Leaving city centre along Falls Road, turn left just before Milltown Cemetery down Milltown Row (OS ref. 311727 – brown 'Bog Meadows Nature Reserve' sign). Park at bottom by noticeboard.

Bog Meadows is a very fine example of a wild place in the heart of a city. These 50 acres of marsh, meadow, woodland and water are the carefully shaped and maintained remnant of what was once a wide stretch of wetland, often inundated by floodwater from the River Lagan. Industrial development (especially of the city's linen mills), drainage for agriculture and the building of housing and roads have all eaten away at its margins over the past two centuries, and today it is only the vigilance and hard graft of local volunteers, working alongside the Ulster Wildlife Trust, that preserves Bog Meadows for wildlife, school groups and the many individuals who come here to escape the city.

Hard surfaced paths take you through wet areas of sedges, horsetails, marsh orchids and meadowsweet, through patches of willow

Bog Meadows

scrub where finches chirp and acres of heath where you can hear the 'two-stones-clicking' call of stonechats, down past old flooded clay-pits that are now ponds rich in frogs, dragonflies and waterbirds such as coot, moorhen and tufted duck. Busby-headed reedmace and the shiny yellow flowers of marsh marigold grow on the edges of ponds and watercourses.

444. STRANGFORD LOUGH, CO. DOWN

Map: OS of Northern Ireland Discoverer 21

Travel: A2 (via Bangor and east coast of Ards peninsula) and A20 (via Newtownards and east side of Strangford Lough) meet at Portaferry in south of peninsula. Half-hourly car ferry crosses to Strangford. A25 crosses 'St Patrick's Country' to Downpatrick; A22 returns to Belfast up west side of lough.

Strangford Lough lies sheltered by the Ards Peninsula, which bends southwards from a shoulder of coast just east of Belfast. A seaward outpost of County Down, 23 miles long and some 4 or 5 miles wide, the Ards has a core of gentle green farming county flanked by two contrasting shorelines. Great beaches of sand interspersed with rocky coves face out east into the Irish Sea, while low-tide mudflats – locally called 'slobs', and home to an enormous population of wildfowl – lie on the west along Strangford Lough.

This long sea lough is ideal for wintering birds because it is all sheltered mudflats and sandbanks rich in food. Godwit and redshank, pintail and wigeon spend the cold months here. Shelduck, back from their yearly moulting trip to the German Bight, hoover the mud for invertebrates with quick sideways scoops of their beaks. Lapwing crouch head to wind among the stones, perfectly motionless, superbly camouflaged in their grey-and-white plumage. Huge masses of golden plover congregate on the sandbanks, their backs glittering golden-green in the pale winter sunlight as the wind ruffles their feathers.

Up to 20,000 light-bellied brent geese start off from the Canadian High Arctic each autumn, impelled by instinct or memory and steered by a marvellous and mysterious binnacle in their brains to accomplish a journey of several thousand miles and take up their hereditary winter quarters on this one particular sea lough on the east coast of Northern Ireland. It is a remarkable sight as squadrons of them come in to land. Black webbed feet lowered and held forward, wings shivering to keep them at hovering speed, they plop down one by one. Half a minute with heads held nervously high while they inspect the surroundings for potential dangers; then the blunt beaks are lowered to the green carpet of *Zostera marina*. Gathered to feed in flocks several hundred strong, gabbling like barking hounds, the brent geese make a memorable sight against the green hills of County Down and the grey-and-brown tidal flats of Strangford Lough.

445. STRUELL WELLS AND MAHEE ISLAND, CO. DOWN

Map: OS of Northern Ireland Discoverer 21

Travel: Struell Wells (OS ref. 512442) is signed to left off B1 Ardglass road, 1 mile east of Downpatrick. From Downpatrick, A22 towards Comber; on entering Lisbane, take second right and follow minor road through Ballydrain, over causeways on to Mahee Island. Park near Nendrum monastic site (524637).

St Patrick's Country lies round about the foot of Strangford Lough (see above). Hard facts about Ireland's great patron saint, whose first landing in the country was here in AD 432, are not easy to come by, but you can trace him through his haunts, real or imagined, around the southern and western shores of Strangford Lough. One such is the ancient spa of Struell Wells, in a quiet green valley near Downpatrick. Among the venerable stone buildings set above a stone-cold underground stream are a drinking well, a well for curing eye diseases, and men's and women's bath-houses. Down at the bottom of dark steps in the men's bath-house, your feet in a tank of numbingly cold water, respect for St Patrick increases sharply. Legend says the holy man spent an entire night immersed here, stark naked and singing psalms.

Up along the western shore of Strangford Lough a string of round little drumlin islands rises from the gleaming slobs, or mudflats. Here at the far end of a long chain of causeways is the diminutive green dome of Mahee Island, encircled by three ancient stone walls. A broken round tower and a ruined church, perhaps 1,000 years old, stand side by side at the summit. Foundations of huts and the rugged stone grave slabs of long-forgotten monks lie in the turf. This lonely site is where St Mochaoi, a contemporary and colleague of St Patrick, established the monastery of Nendrum, one of the earliest Christian foundations in the world.

446. MOUNTAINS OF MOURNE, CO. DOWN

Map: OS of Northern Ireland Discoverer 29; 1:25,000 'Mourne Country Outdoor Pursuits' map

Travel: From Belfast, A7 to Downpatrick; A25/ A2 to Newcastle; B180 Hilltown road. In 4½ miles, left (OS ref. 319323 – 'Meelmore Lodge' sign) for 1¼ miles to Meelmore Lodge car park (305307). NB: Mourne Rambler bus runs hourly, 10 a.m.–5 p.m., September–June, Newcastle to Meelmore Lodge car park.

From here 'Mountain Walk' sign on wall points left; follow walled lane and field walls for ¾ mile to bear right (313303) up stony Trassey Track for a mile. Where track zigzags up to right (319290), aim ahead on clear path, then through boulders, up to cross Mourne Wall in Hare's Gap (323287). Left along Brandy Pad path, under Slieve Commedagh for 1⅓ miles to cairn on col between Commedagh and Slieve Beg (342279). Continue to east end of the Castles cliffs (on your left); left here (348279) uphill off Brandy Pad to cross Mourne Wall at The Saddle between Slieve Commedagh and Slieve Donard (350279).

Follow path north-east down Glen River Valley. In 1⅓ miles, pass ice house (364295) to reach dirt road by concrete bridge (366297). Left for 50 yards, then right, down stony track through trees on left of Glen River, to humpbacked second bridge (370299). Turn right to cross it, then left ('Glen River Track' sign); descend on right of river to Donard Bridge (372302). Bear left to cross bridge: descend beside river into Donard Park (373304); continue down to car park in Newcastle (374306).

NB: A walk of 6½ miles, with some tricky stretches underfoot, especially descending from the Saddle into Newcastle. Wear hillwalking boots and take wet-weather gear.

If the beautiful Mountains of Mourne were magically transplanted from the County Down coast across the Irish Sea,

they would be as oversubscribed by ramblers as the Lake District fells. But, in common with most of the rest of Northern Ireland, the high places of the Mountains of Mourne are *terra incognita* to almost everyone. Millions have heard of them, through Percy French's touching but tacky Victorian song. Tens of thousands come to view them each year. But only a handful of hillwalkers actually get to know them. Those who do find themselves intoxicated by the empty skylines of the Mournes.

The old quarry road of the Trassey Track climbs gently towards Hare's Gap, a high saddle between rounded Slievenaglogh and the jagged granite tors on Slieve Bearnagh. Up there you can stop beside the Mourne Wall to gaze back down the Trassey Valley to the wide farmlands beyond. The Mourne Wall is an astonishing structure, a shoulder-high ribbon of stone that circles for 22 miles, running up and over twelve of the highest peaks as it does so. It was built as a boundary marker early in the twentieth century by the company that created the two reservoirs of Silent Valley and Ben Crom in the heart of the mountains; and it stands as a monument to hundreds of local men who dressed its stones and raised it to earn their bread in hard times.

It wasn't only granite quarrymen and the builders of the Mourne Wall who travelled these mountain paths. Back in the eighteenth century, when brandy and tobacco made good profits for anyone bold enough to dodge the Excisemen, the Mournes provided a quick and secure through-route for contraband goods from the Down coast into the heart of Ireland. The path from Hare's Gap eastward under the peaks of Slieve Corragh and Slieve Commedagh is known as the Brandy Pad, an old smugglers' track from which you get superb views down over the darkly gleaming Ben Crom reservoir and the tall mountain slopes that hem it in.

All around the Brandy Pad the peaks of Mourne rise in round green heads, the distant line of the Mourne Wall swooping up and down their napes. You meet the wall again at The Saddle, another high col under the shoulder of Slieve Donard, and go skidding and stumbling down a rubbly track beside the Glen River, with a wonderful prospect ahead over Newcastle and the great sandbank-streaked arc of Dundrum Bay.

447. SLIEVE GULLION, CO. ARMAGH

Map: OS of Northern Ireland Discoverer 29

Travel: A1 from Newry towards Dundalk; in 1 mile, right on B113 towards Forkhill. Half a mile beyond Meigh, right for ½ mile to Slieve Gullion Forest Park's Courtyard Centre car park (OS ref. 042197). Follow waymarked Ring of Gullion Way.

South of Armagh city, down into the back country of South Armagh, the landscape rises from green grazing valleys towards the high backs of a range of craggy hills. The remnants of a volcanic crater 50 million years old, they form a ring 10 miles from side to side. The Ring of Gullion is a magnificent sight, best appreciated from the summit cairn of Slieve Gullion, the hub of the circle, which rises nearly 2,000 feet. Legends are thick about this fine whaleback mountain.

The waymarked Ring of Gullion Way is your guide from the Slieve Gullion Courtyard Centre, climbing steeply up through the forest and then following a green track

Slieve Gullion

up the mountainside, with views opening northwards for 20 miles towards the city of Armagh. Near the top of Slieve Gullion you pass the cold dark pool of Cailleach Beara's Lough. Be sure not to touch the water ... It was here that the hero Fionn MacCumhaill met the sorceress Miluchra in the shape of a beautiful woman. Fionn dived into the lough to retrieve her golden ring, but when he emerged he found that the lovely girl had transformed herself into the Cailleach Beara, an ugly old hag, and he himself had become a bent and feeble old man.

Climb on up to the Stone Age chambered tomb hidden in the huge cairn of stones at the peak of Slieve Gullion, the house of wicked Miluchra. You can creep inside – if you dare – to admire the corbelled roof, the large shallow stone basins where cremation remains were laid, and the burial chamber at the far end. From here the faithful Fianna, the warrior band of Fionn, dragged the Cailleach Beara and made her restore their leader to his rightful stature and age. Or did things come to pass as another legend tells? In this version Fionn's dog, Bran, runs the length of Ireland to Killarney to fetch his master's grandson, Oscar, who snares a fairy man and makes him give Fionn a restorative drink of youth.

Yet other tales tell of how the enchanted youth Setanta, son of the god Lugh the Long-handed, earned a new name on the slopes of Slieve Gullion. When he was seven years old, Setanta dealt with a savage dog that attacked him on the mountain by choking it with his *sliotar*, or hurling ball, and then beating it to death with his hurley stick. The brute turned out to be the favourite guard dog of Culan the Smith, whose forge and castle stood on top of Slieve Gullion, the Mountain of Culan. The blacksmith was incandescent with rage at the loss of his dog, and agreed to spare Setanta's life only on condition that the child would guard his property until he had had a chance to train up another dog. So Setanta took up the dead hound's duties and adopted the name of Cuchulainn, the Hound of Culan. Cuchulainn grew up to be the greatest warrior that Ireland ever knew, Defender of Ulster against the wild hordes of invaders from Connacht.

The view from the cairn is stupendous, 100 miles of Ireland's mountains, coasts and sea spread out at your feet. South Armagh is full of this sort of thing – dramatic mountain views, steep green farmland with hidden lakes, and old tales rich and strange.

448. LOUGH NEAGH, CO. ARMAGH

Maps: OS of Northern Ireland Discoverer 19, 20

Travel: M1 to Junction 10; right on B76 for ¼ mile, then right ('Oxford Island' signs) to park at Oxford Island Discovery Centre (OS ref. 047616).

Lough Neagh is by far the biggest lake in the British Isles; 18 miles long and 11 miles wide, it's a vast sprawling inland sea. The shoreline of the lough stretches nearly 100 miles when its many promontories and bays are taken into account, and it gives a water frontage to five of the six counties of Northern Ireland – only Fermanagh misses out, and that westerly county with its liquid heart of Lough Erne is half water anyway.

It is hard to get a physical overview of Lough Neagh from its flat shores. But the boardwalks and paths of the Oxford Island Discovery Centre offer a series of intimate glimpses into the activities of its wildlife – migratory birds in spring and autumn, wetland flower species, the pike, perch and pollan that edge through the reeds, clouds of flies and midges in summer attracting flights of swallows, nesting sedge warblers spinning out their wheezy little songs. A spectacle worth coming to Oxford Island simply to witness is the remarkable courtship display of the great crested grebes, a show that begins each New Year and continues well into spring.

At night Lough Neagh becomes the hunting ground of boat fishermen who cast nets in the deeper water for eels, one of the lough's great delicacies. It is a hard, wet job, and more often than not a poorly rewarded one, but Lough Neagh's eel fishers form family dynasties, and the skill and stubbornness needed to persist in such tough labour on long dark nights out on the inland sea seems part of their DNA. Once you have eaten a Lough Neagh eel, fried in its own green oil, at midnight on a boat anchored under the stars, and have washed it down with a cup of tea you could stand a spoon in, then you can truly claim to have savoured this place.

449. ARDBOE HIGH CROSS, CO. TYRONE

Map: OS of Northern Ireland Discoverer 14

Travel: B73 from Cookstown east for 10 miles through Coagh and on to the shore of Lough Neagh. Just before reaching the lough, turn right at Moortown on minor road (signposted) for 1½ miles to Ardboe High Cross (OS ref. 966757).

The early Celtic Church in Ireland produced many extremely beautiful, superbly carved stone crosses, up to 20 feet tall, to mark the lands belonging to the monasteries. The High Crosses disseminated biblical stories and sermons in stone to all who passed by. Dozens still stand, some with their carved panels blurred by weathering beyond understanding, others still remarkably sharp in detail. What the High Crosses of Ireland tell us about the rich internal life, the fears and dreams of the people for whose pleasure and instruction they were created, still captivates our imagination, though their moral messages seem far adrift from today's secular anchoring points.

The High Cross at Ardboe stands 18 feet high on the shores of Lough Neagh as it has done for 1,100 or 1,200 years. It may be the only High Cross in Ireland still complete and intact in the place it was originally erected; most of the others are composites of more than one cross, or have had major portions destroyed. The carved panels are weathered but still easily decipherable. Adam and Eve, Abraham sacrificing Isaac, Daniel in the lions' den and Shadrach, Meshach and Abednego in the fiery furnace face the lough and the rising sun. The Three Wise Men, the miracles of the wine into water and the loaves and fishes, and Christ entering Jerusalem on a donkey look towards the sunset. These westerly sculptures are the better preserved.

The tall sandstone cross is rich in legend. Corpses would be carried three times around it before burial to ensure a smooth passage across Jordan; local people on their way to emigrant ships and the New World would chip out a small piece to take with them as a talisman. Behind the cross, in the old graveyard (which is haunted by the little figure of a monk), an ancient beech tree droops dead, its bark crammed with thousands of coins. Copper poisoning did for the tree, but believers say it was the burden of illnesses transferred by those who pushed in the coins, hoping for a miraculous cure from their afflictions.

As for how Ardboe High Cross still stands, tall and strong, after so many centuries—well, you can put that down to the intervention of St Colman of Dromore, who lies buried near the wishing tree. It was he who sent the masons a cow from the depths of Lough Neagh as they were erecting the cross. The miraculous animal gave so much milk that the masons could not drink it all and they mixed the surplus with their mortar. So the Ardboe Cross still stands.

450. BEAGHMORE STONE CIRCLES, CO. TYRONE

Map: OS of Northern Ireland Discoverer 13

Travel: A505 from Cookstown towards Omagh; pass turn-off on right for Wellbrook Beetling Mill, and in 1 ¼ miles turn right at Drumshanbo Glebe for 1 mile to T-junction. Left for ¼ mile, first right for 4½ miles to find Beaghmore Stone Circles on left (OS ref. 684843 – park on road and walk down track to site).

A shallow bog landscape lies between sweeping ranges of hills. There is a seethe and twitter of lark song high overhead, and the occasional harsh belch of a crow, but this is an empty, silent place. Lying low in this desolate bogland, positioned here in the mid Bronze Age, perhaps 4,000 years ago, are seven circles of stone, ten rows and a dozen or so round cairns. The circles stand in three pairs, their stones varying from solid man-size chunks to modest boulders, all creviced with weathering and blotchy with lichens. The seventh circle is entirely different; its centre is almost solid with rocks, about 800 of them – dragons' teeth, according to local lore. Two of the stone rows point towards the rising sun at the summer solstice, and others seem to be aligned with the movements of moon, stars and sun, but there is no proof of anything other than the presence of these patterns in stone.

When these rows and circles were laid out, the landscape was partially wooded. Men had already encroached far into the wildwood of alder, birch, oak and hazel; and once all the trees had been cleared and the climate began to turn wetter, from the first millennium BC onwards, the peat increased and the bog advanced to smother the old stones. They lay under the turf for 3,000 years, until turf-cutters began to stumble upon the mysterious shapes in the 1930s as they stripped the peat for their domestic fires.

What you see today is the Beaghmore Stone Circles as they have been uncovered so far. Under the undulating bog there could lie many more. It is a tantalizing thought – peeling back the turf across the entire wide valley to reveal what could well be the greatest monument of its kind ever brought to light. For the present, though, whatever other treasures Beaghmore holds lie hidden.

451. BLACK BOG, CO. TYRONE

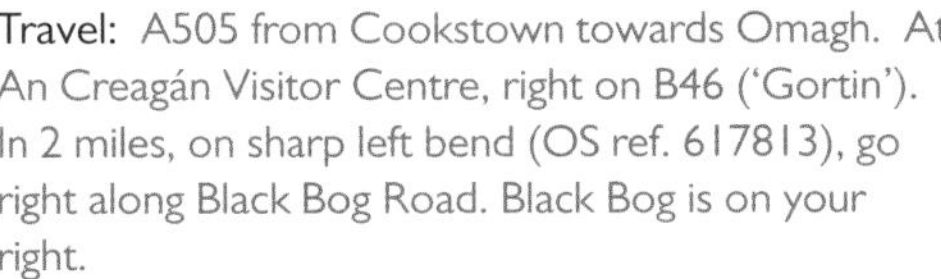

Map: OS of Northern Ireland Discoverer 13

Travel: A505 from Cookstown towards Omagh. At An Creagán Visitor Centre, right on B46 ('Gortin'). In 2 miles, on sharp left bend (OS ref. 617813), go right along Black Bog Road. Black Bog is on your right.

The great bogs of central County Tyrone are mostly blanket bogs, shallow marshes composed of dead grasses, fed by rainwater trickling in off the surrounding hills. Typical of such bogland is that found around the Beaghmore Stone Circles (see above). It is a man-made habitat caused by the felling of forests, subsequent leaching out of soil minerals and formation of an acid, sterile landscape on which peat has formed. Most of this kind of bog lies at high altitudes in the west of Ireland, and most of the other kind of bog, raised bog, is in the Midlands. But in the centre of County Tyrone lies one of the finest raised bogs in the country, Black Bog, a splendid dome in a flat sea of blanket bog and farmland.

It was the formation of hollows in the glacial rubble of Tyrone (see p. 493) that enabled the Black Bog to form. Under the bog lies a hollow, which filled with water to become a lake as the ice retreated. Into the lake fell reeds, millennium after millennium, eventually filling the hollow and absorbing all the lake water. Sphagnum moss formed above the unrotted vegetation, continuing to rise into the high dome. At first sight, in fact, this bog looks flat, but soon you begin to be aware of its wave-like formation and the long raised ridges within it as it rises southward into a dark upturned bowl of sphagnum and heather.

The surface of the Black Bog is crusted with the pale branched fronds of reindeer lichen, and strewn in spring with tiny pink dots of crowberry flowers. Later in the year the hard green crowberry fruit turns pink and then purple, darkening eventually to a lustrous black. Don't bother eating the berries raw, though: they are a taste-free disappointment unless artfully cooked. Better to admire them through the changing seasons, drops of colour in the bog's sombre coat.

452. CREGGANDEVESKY COURT TOMB, CO. TYRONE

Map: OS of Northern Ireland Discoverer 13

Travel: A502 from Omagh towards Cookstown; pas B46 Omagh/Sixmilecross crossroads, and in 300 yards turn right along Loughmallon Road ('Creggandevesky' brown sign). In 2 miles go over crossroads (OS ref. 646758); in another ¾ mile, Creggandevesky is signposted on right through gate. Park on road here (651749).

Out in the grazing country of County Tyrone, Creggandevesky Court Tomb lies in solitary splendour on its bank, overlooking the shallow water of Lough Mallon. The setting is magnificent: wide prospects across a landscape of glacial mounds and ridges now covered in grass, out to the silhouettes of the Sperrin Hills rising on the northern skyline.

The court tomb, repository of the remains of many people, was built some 5,500 years ago, a structure of Stone Age pomp and ceremony. The grass mound that covered it is long gone, and the internal structure lies revealed – three little chambers, joined by low interconnecting doorways with massive jambs and lintels of stone, encased in an enormous heap of small stones some 60 feet long. The cremated remains of twenty-one people were excavated from the tomb, but whether the large courtyard that faces Lough Mallon saw obsequies for the dead within

Creggandevesky Court Tomb

its pincer-shaped walls, or ceremonies to reassert the potency of life, is open to conjecture. In spring the grassy courtyard floor is a mass of orchids, self-heal and dandelions, a wonderful place for sitting and dreaming.

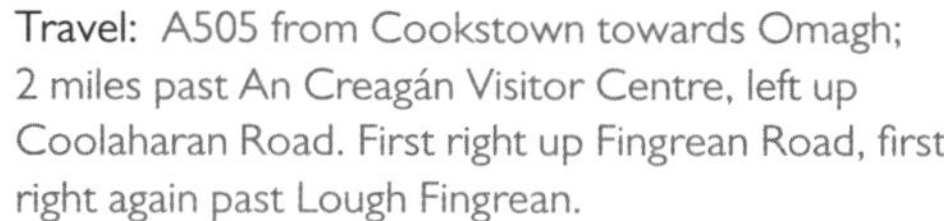

453. THE MURRINS, NEAR OMAGH, CO. TYRONE

Map: OS of Northern Ireland Discoverer 13

Travel: A505 from Cookstown towards Omagh; 2 miles past An Creagán Visitor Centre, left up Coolaharan Road. First right up Fingrean Road, first right again past Lough Fingrean.

NB: Most of the Murrins is a nature reserve with no unarranged access (contact warden on tel: 02838 851102 for access), but on north shore of Lough Fingrean (OS ref. 571780) you can scramble to the top of the bank and view the kettle-holes.

The kettle-holes of the Murrins are hard to find. You drive up the bumpy country road round Lough Fingrean, looking out for little hollows filled with water. These are the kettle-holes, formed in dramatic circumstances at the end of the last Ice Age and now hidden away among the heathery ridges and boggy valleys of the back-country Murrins district. Then you realize that Lough Fingrean itself is a lake without any real inlets or outlets, and that this whole landscape, if you subtract its skin of grass, heather and trees, is formed of the outpourings of a huge melting glacier that was retreating north-eastwards across this plain some 10,000 years ago. You get out of the car and hop up the bank, and there across the next field is a rushy pool among willows, a static bowl of rainwater and ground seepage which has lain like this for the best part of ten millennia.

The Murrins

The framework of this land of hollows and humps was laid down as meltwater gushed out of a glacier, flowing south-west and mounding up a sandy, gravelly rubble of debris into long ridges fanning out like the sandbanks of a river delta. You can pick out these ridges, and also the mounds which piled up when the meltwater was temporarily held up by the ice. Great chunks of ice were trapped in the rubble, and when these in their turn melted they left behind hollows – some as much as half a mile across, others only a few yards wide. Whatever water collected in these hollows, from rain or from seeping water that soaked the soil, stayed there, slowly evaporating, slowly being replenished. Here in the Murrins the watery hollows still lie between the grassy, heathery ridges of gravel, remnants of that extraordinary time when this was a naked landscape of rock, rubble, melting ice and charging rivers.

454. SPERRIN HILLS, CO. TYRONE

Maps: OS of Northern Ireland Discoverer 13, 7

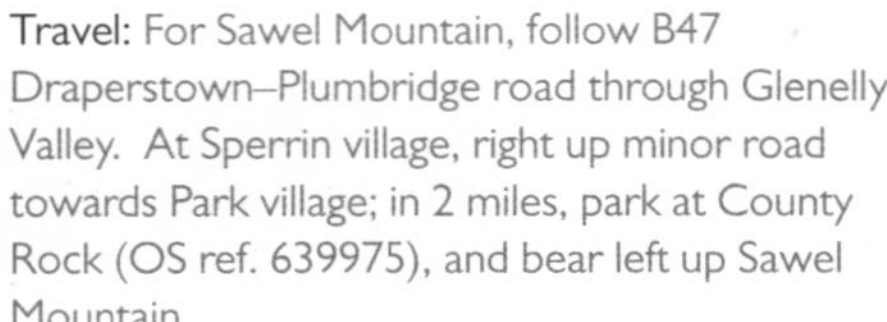

Travel: For Sawel Mountain, follow B47 Draperstown–Plumbridge road through Glenelly Valley. At Sperrin village, right up minor road towards Park village; in 2 miles, park at County Rock (OS ref. 639975), and bear left up Sawel Mountain.

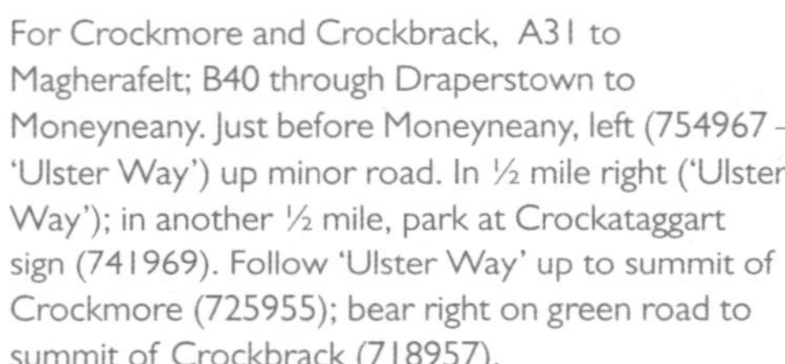

For Crockmore and Crockbrack, A31 to Magherafelt; B40 through Draperstown to Moneyneany. Just before Moneyneany, left (754967 – 'Ulster Way') up minor road. In ½ mile right ('Ulster Way'); in another ½ mile, park at Crockataggart sign (741969). Follow 'Ulster Way' up to summit of Crockmore (725955); bear right on green road to summit of Crockbrack (718957).

NB: Sawel Mountain is a stiff climb of 1,200 feet (2½ miles there and back); the Crockmore and Crockbrack walk is gentler but longer (4 miles there and back).

The Sperrins are not particularly lofty hills – Sawel, the tallest peak in the range, is only 2,226 feet high. But they form a 20-mile barrier of wild country that swells in a steep wall above the green and beautiful Glenelly Valley. A couple of narrow mountain roads cross the range, but for the most part the deep valleys are roadless; pathless, too, since the shepherds' tracks and drove roads are beginning to sink back into the bog and grass again.

The highlands of Sperrin look bare compared with the lush greenness of the Glenelly Valley. Life on the small farmsteads up the slope was always hard, and most of the houses on the mountainside are uninhabited these days. Up among these bleak uplands the mountain road from Sperrin village levels out below the County Rock, a grey lump that shows the meeting place of Counties Tyrone and Derry. From here you aim straight up the steep flank of Sawel, squelching aloft among old peat banks and bright green moss pools until you reach the top. Here you can sit on the rocks, gazing over 20 miles of the two counties – rough mountain slopes folding into fertile valleys, with more ridges and mountain crests beyond.

For an easier climb into equally desolate country, take the splashy lane from Crockataggart, a few miles east of Sawel, to reach the saddle and summit of 1,568-foot Crockmore. A wet green road brings you easily west for half a mile to the top of Crockbrack where, at 1,726 feet, there is a mind-blowing prospect of country, perhaps 100 miles in all, the olive-and-grey shoulders of the Sperrins dominating the middle distance.

From Crockbrack you can continue your clockwise walk, taking in the tops of Oughtmore, Spelhoagh and Craigagh on a demanding but delightful 8-mile circuit. Or you can simply stand and stare.

Sperrin Hills

455. KNOCKMANY CHAMBERED CAIRN, AUGHER, CO. TYRONE

Map: OS of Northern Ireland Discoverer 18

Travel: A4 from Dungannon towards Enniskillen. In Augher, A28 Aughacloy road turns off on left; opposite here, right for 2 miles to crossroads on B83 Seskinore–Clogher road. Bear right here for 1 ¼ miles, then right (signposted) to Knockmany Forest Park car park (OS ref. 544563). Steep path climbs through forest to Knockmany Chambered Cairn at summit (547559).

NB: Cairn gate is kept locked. Key is held at Peatlands Country Park, just off M1 Junction 13, 30 miles east of Knockmany (tel: 02838 851102; www.ehsni.gov.uk/peatlands).

The Knockmany valley is a secret sort of place, overhung with the dark conifers of Knockmany Forest in a cleft of the south Tyrone hills. The knoll of Knockmany rises steeply from the valley, a hilltop that must have commanded an amazing view to all points of the compass before the forest was planted on the hill slopes. As it is, the prospect is striking, especially along the Clogher valley to the south and east. It is the perfect place to honour the life and death of a great man or woman; and so the builders of Knockmany Chambered Cairn must have thought when they constructed the passage grave on the hilltop in the late Stone Age.

It is worth getting hold of the key to the gate of the ugly, out-of-place bomb shelter that was put up over the grave in 1959 to protect the stones from any more damage by weather or vandals. Once inside, the full force of the carvings in the pink sandstone is apparent. There are great swirls like the tails of comets, starry bursts in wheel shapes, scrolly carvings that look like eyes, waves that resemble the painted sea patterns on Minoan pottery. These sinuous forms, the sunburst or starburst shapes and the big concentric waves, are all very reminiscent of those on the tombs at Loughcrew (see pp. 510–11) and Newgrange (see pp. 509–10). Ancient men would have been dedicated watchers of the skies for weather warnings, and probably other signs and wonders, too. One theory is that these carvings were made to propitiate or honour star gods at times of celestial phenomena – shooting stars, comets, sunspots, meteors – which, some evidence seems to suggest, may have been lively around the time these tombs were built. It looks a possibility, but no one can really say.

The power and presence of the monument, though, is palpable. I once witnessed a sunrise dance around the grave by the Armagh Rhymers, a mumming group whose faces were covered with sinister wicker hoods. The clear dawn light glinted on the willow strakes of the sightless hoods, a spectacle that might have been plucked from some spine-tingling ritual of the deep pagan past.

456. DANCING STONE, LETTERBAILEY, CO. FERMANAGH

Map: OS of Northern Ireland Discoverer 18

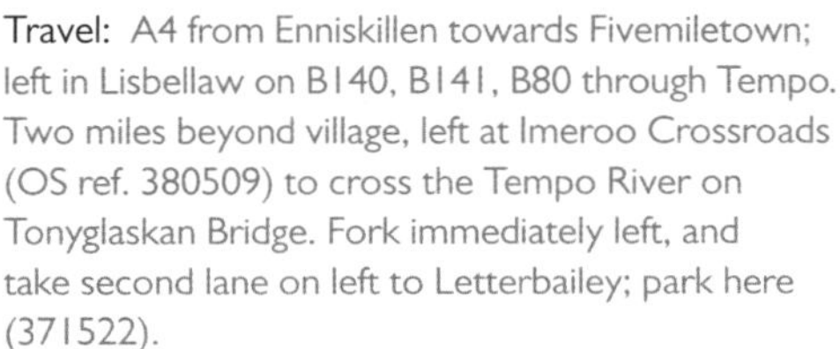

Travel: A4 from Enniskillen towards Fivemiletown; left in Lisbellaw on B140, B141, B80 through Tempo. Two miles beyond village, left at Imeroo Crossroads (OS ref. 380509) to cross the Tempo River on Tonyglaskan Bridge. Fork immediately left, and take second lane on left to Letterbailey; park here (371522).

Brougher Mountain in the east of County Fermanagh has more than its share of stone circles, standing stones and chambered graves. There is a fine stone circle, the Round Pound, at Far Town, up beyond the mountain hamlet of Letterbailey, but it is a hard job to find it because of the bracken that cloaks where it lies. It is far from easy to find Far Town, for that matter. The old settlement is hardly more than a tumble of mossy stones these days, long abandoned for marginally easier land further down the mountain. Ruined houses lean into their doorposts and window frames below the Round Pound – perhaps itself built of the component pieces of a far older stone circle. Near by lies a boulder with a cross deeply incised, a Mass Stone around which the faithful would congregate, in fear of the English soldiers, to hear Mass at the eighteenth-century nadir of the Penal Laws. In those times, to attend Mass was to court fines, imprisonment and beating, not to mention a nasty death for the celebrant (see pp. 537–8 and 539–40).

The scrub here is full of gorse and whippy hazel stems, a painful barrier to negotiate. There in the heart of the neglected thicket lies the Dancing Stone. On a Sunday locals would come from miles around in their good clothes to chatter, court and dance. They stepped out on the old flat stone for the pleasure of hearing the hollow below ring and echo with the click of their heels and toes. You could fit three couples on to the Dancing Stone, if they were good and careful, and the thought of them stamping a measure here on the hillside while their neighbours whistled and whooped is enough to make a stone head smile, as they say hereabouts.

457. JANUS MAN, BOA ISLAND, CO. FERMANAGH

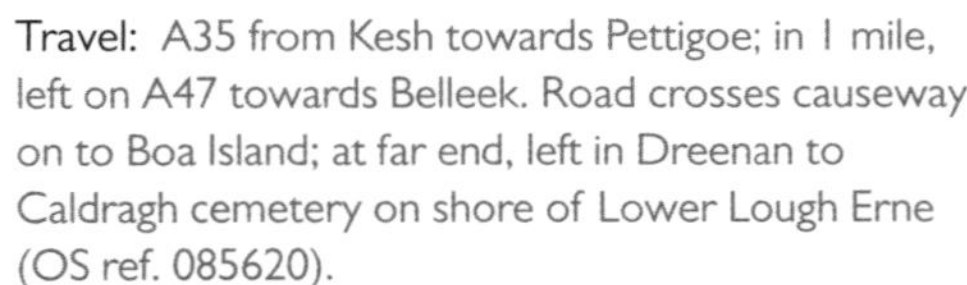

Map: OS of Northern Ireland Discoverer 17

Travel: A35 from Kesh towards Pettigoe; in 1 mile, left on A47 towards Belleek. Road crosses causeway on to Boa Island; at far end, left in Dreenan to Caldragh cemetery on shore of Lower Lough Erne (OS ref. 085620).

Of all the strange stone carvings in which County Fermanagh is so rich, the Janus Man is the most celebrated. That is partly because he stands in an easily accessible place, among the mossy stones of the cemetery on Boa Island. You can drive on to Boa Island via causeways at either end, and Caldragh cemetery is conveniently located near the west end, only 200 yards from the road. But there is nothing easy or everyday about the Janus Man.

Standing chest-high to a modern man, at first sight the Janus Man seems to be a gentleman of the Tudor era carved out of a block of stone – a classic sixteenth-century face with a pointed beard. But there is something very odd about his huge, bulging eyes and the representation of some item that crosses his chest – it might be cross-belts, or a pair of spindly arms which cradle what could be a blurred and eroded phallus. Carved on the other side is the same kind of figure, but the bottom of the face has more of a pointed chin, less of a beard, and the statue has no phallic member. The oversize eyes and protruding tongues are mesmerizing. Between the back-to-back crowns of the twin heads is a deliberately hollowed hole, perhaps original, perhaps dug out to collect rainwater for ritual or miraculous purposes.

The two-faced Janus Man has a cousin, a smaller figure that stands near by. This is the Lusty Man, so named because he was brought to the cemetery from Lusty More Island just offshore – where the Janus Man was probably originally sited, too. This figure's features have been far more badly eroded by wind and weather, but it seems to possess only one properly formed eye. Again the tongue pokes out and the stare is hypnotic. The left hand is bent in front of the body, as if grasping something – again, perhaps a phallus now eroded beyond deciphering. Demonic winks and manic stares: there are certainly messages in the eyes of the Boa Island figures, but fifteen or sixteen centuries have passed since they were fashioned, and what the sculptor had in mind remains unfathomable.

458. WHITE ISLAND, CO. FERMANAGH

Map: OS of Northern Ireland Discoverer 17

Travel: From Enniskillen, A32 towards Irvinestown. In 2½ miles, left on B82 towards Lisnarrick and Kesh. 1 mile past Lisnarrick, left into grounds of Castle Archdale. Park near Drumhoney Holiday Park jetty (www.drumhoneyholidaypark.com/whiteislandferry). Hourly boats to White Island. Church with figures: OS ref. 175600.

While the purpose of the Janus Man (see above) seems completely inscrutable, you can make some sort of guess at that of the Seven Figures of White Island. But that is not to say that, taken collectively, they do not generate a comparable frisson of strangeness.

The Seven Figures stand in the back wall of the ruin of the island's lovely twelfth-century monastic church. Devotional occupation of White Island was long established by the time the church was built; the Vikings were recorded as having destroyed a monastery there in a raid on Lough Erne in AD 837. So the figures, carved on smoothed slabs of white quartzite, probably originally designed to form part of the abbey's furnishings, could date back to the ninth century or before. The style is formal, stiff and archaic, lending them a curiously pagan air.

A sheela-na-gig in a short-sleeved tunic sits cross-legged on the left end of the row, grinning with plump lips and holding open her vulva with both hands. Next to her is a secretively smiling man, supporting a book on his lap. Then comes a cowled monk holding a bishop's crook and bell, probably a figure of St Patrick; and next to him a stout person with a Celtic monastic tonsure, his left hand pointing to his mouth – maybe King David as a young man, indicating his beautiful singing voice. Next are two smaller figures with extravagantly curly fringes. One grips two battling beasts as if banging their heads together; the other wields a sword and a round target shield, and has an elaborate Celtic brooch to pin his cloak – Christ the Warrior, side by side with Christ the Mediator? Last is a roughly outlined head and body, a ghost fading back into the wall. So ends the strange and enigmatic rank of figures, all but the final feature beyond the ghost-stone – a small, sulky face looking out on the beautiful view with an expression of the utmost disgust.

459. THE BISHOP'S STONE, KILLADEAS, CO. FERMANAGH

Map: OS of Northern Ireland Discoverer 17

Travel: From Enniskillen, A32 towards Irvinestown. In 2½ miles, left on B82 towards Kesh. In 4 miles, Killadeas Church stands on left of road (OS ref. 206540).

Killadeas churchyard doesn't seem to have made up its mind whether it is exclusively Christian or open to pagan influences. There are various odd-looking stones among the grave-slab memorials, including a stone set up on end that is indented with several very large and ancient cup marks, like those carried by a bullaun – a stone with holes for pre-Christian offerings.

But the most remarkable monument, the one that sets the ambivalent mood, is the Bishop's Stone, standing by itself under an old yew on the south side of the church near the boundary wall. It might once have formed part of the arch of a window, being cut vertically on one side and convex on the other.

On the north face of the stone is the bishop, a very weathered figure, striding eastwards towards the rising sun, his great bell and crook in hand. His expression is stern, his beard juts aggressively, and his staring eye is turned sideways to keep you under scrutiny. This is the figure of the Church in full authority, ever watchful, ever advancing. Round on the south and more sheltered side of the stone is the counterpart or alter ego of the solemn, self-controlled prelate – a grotesque pagan head with round eyes sunk in debauched bogs, a snub blob of a nose, puffy cheeks and a blubber mouth open in a wicked kind of leer. Interlaced

carving forms its body. If the point of the double stone was to convey the complex nature of man, his double standards and the weight of darkness he drags around on his back, it succeeded admirably.

460. TULLY CASTLE, LOWER LOUGH ERNE, CO. FERMANAGH

Map: OS of Northern Ireland Discoverer 17

Travel: A46 from Enniskillen towards Belleek; in 10 miles, Tully Castle is signed to the right. Park at the castle (OS ref. 126567).

Tully Castle stands tall and gaunt, a sinister-looking ruin on the south shore of Lower Lough Erne. The fortified tower house was built in the very early seventeenth century by Sir John Hume, one of the fortunate immigrant Scots who were granted land when England began the 'plantation' of the north of Ireland with Protestant incomers. Of course all the lands of Ulster already belonged to Catholic landowners. They had had it abruptly confiscated and given to the incoming strangers as a penalty for the continuous uprisings of the Catholic Irish population during the previous century against their Protestant overlords, the mainland British. The Catholics of Ulster were dispossessed, and they were doubly dangerous because of it. The brother of the hereditary possessor of the Tully Castle lands was only too ready to join in a general rebellion in 1641 to try to wreak revenge for his family's lost holdings.

Roderick Maguire arrived outside Tully Castle on Christmas Eve 1641 at the head of 800 men. Sir George Hume, who had inherited Tully from his father, Sir John, two years earlier, was away from the castle, but had left his wife, Mary, in charge. With her were sixteen serving men, and sixty-four women and children. Lady Hume negotiated with Roderick Maguire, and received assurances of a safe passage for them all to Enniskillen. But no sooner were the gates opened in surrender than the Maguires seized the women and children, stripped them and locked them in the cellars of Tully. The male servants they stripped, tied up and threw outside.

On Christmas morning Lady Hume (she had been spared the indignity of being stripped) and a few other gentlefolk were separated from the others and shut in a nearby barn. They were allowed to live, but everyone left in the castle was then attacked and murdered in the cellars or in the bawn, the defensive yard attached to the castle tower. After the massacre the building was set on fire and reduced to a ruin.

These days the old ruin attracts visitors with its picturesque tower, its stance near the lake and the seventeenth-century herb garden that has been established in the bawn. The terrible events of 1641 that took place in and around the building seem entirely forgotten.

461. CUILCAGH MOUNTAIN, CO. FERMANAGH

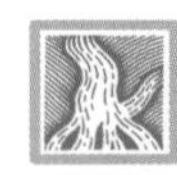

Map: OS of Northern Ireland Discoverer 26

Travel: A4 from Enniskillen to Belcoo; cross border from Northern Ireland into Republic of Ireland on N16 Manorhamilton road, and in 400 yards turn left along minor road towards Florence Court. In 500 yards recross into Northern Ireland (OS ref. 086377). Continue for 5 miles, crossing Cladagh Bridge, to turn right up mountain road (150344 – 'Marble Arch Caves' brown sign). Follow this road uphill for 2 miles, to park car where a track runs off on the left, at the top of a rise on a right-hand bend (126337 – marked 'Cuilcagh Mountain Park'). Follow this track towards Cuilcagh Mountain.

The whole of the limestone region south of Lower Lough Erne is riddled with caves and cracks; if you could cut a slice half a mile deep out of the ground, you would find it as full of holes as a wedge of Emmental. At Marble Arch Caves you can gasp at stalactites, stalagmites, calcite sheets and other natural marvels. But if you want to strike out on your own, away from the crowds, and enjoy the miniature gardens that grow in the water-raddled rock, head for the track across Cuilcagh Mountain to the south of the show-caves.

Cuilcagh Mountain

Very few walkers venture here. The water has insinuated its way into every crack, crevice and weakness in the limestone, dissolving the rock, disappearing down swallet holes, carving cracks and channels that slip away into black nether regions near your feet as you wander the stony hillsides towards the prow of Cuilcagh riding on the southern skyline. Thickets of ash and hawthorn cling to the mouths of small caverns and sprout from ledges a few feet below the upper crust of the limestone.

Past the pool of Pollasumera – a favourite with wagtails – a secret swallet lies hidden in a grove of mossy hazels, a tumble of rocks thick with ferns and mosses piled in the entrance to the cleft. A thick hawthorn root jacketed in moss grows out of the depths of the swallet, where dark green leaves of ferns disappear down into the crack in the earth. A faint trickle and crash of water comes up from far below, and a stone-cold breath of moisture exudes, as if a giant were stirring down there.

Above: Benbulben and below left, Dartry Mountains (pp. 515–17). Centre: Clara Bog (pp. 532–3). Right: Inny River Bog (pp. 514–15)

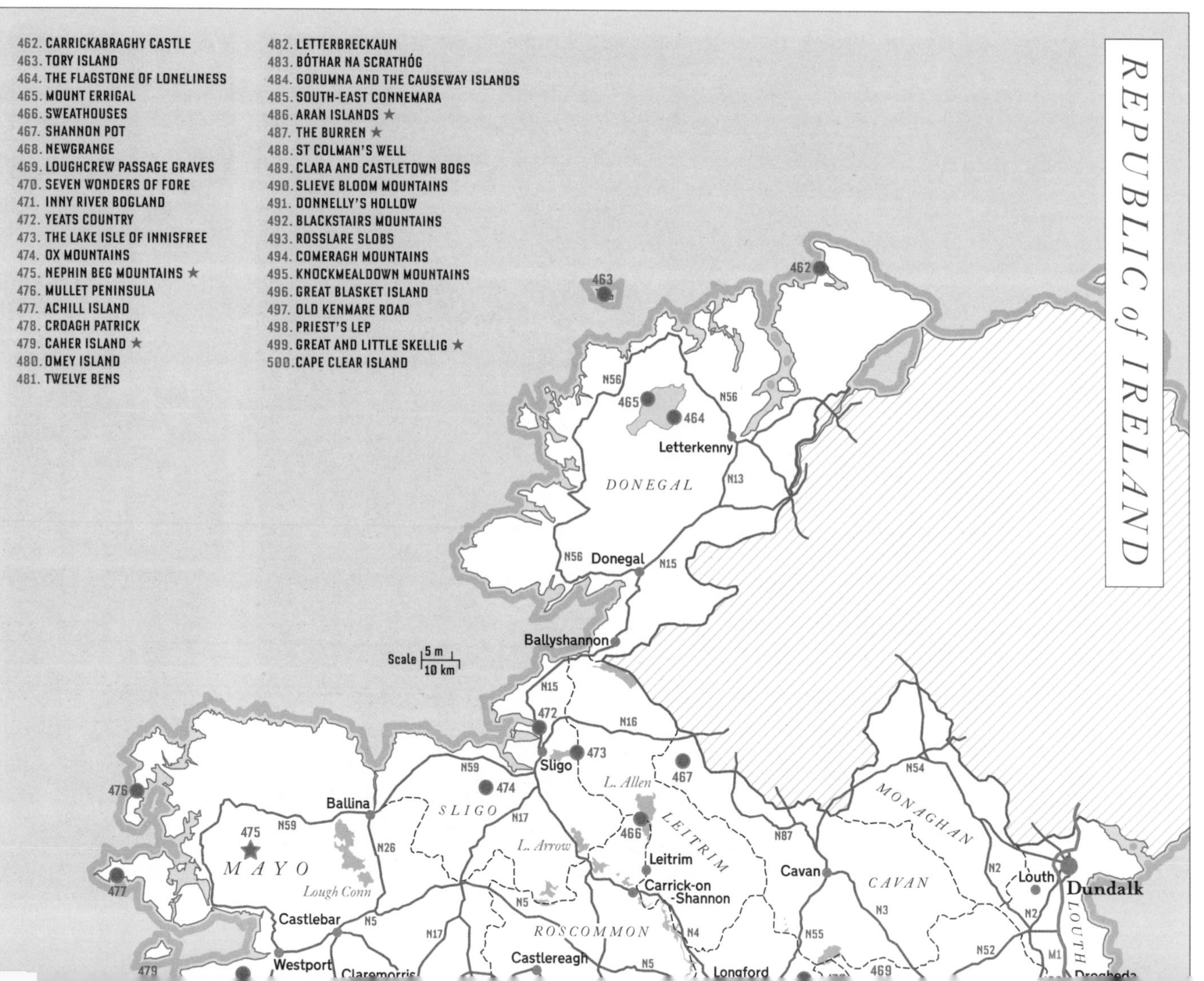
REPUBLIC of IRELAND
462. CARRICKABRAGHY CASTLE
463. TORY ISLAND
464. THE FLAGSTONE OF LONELINESS
465. MOUNT ERRIGAL
466. SWEATHOUSES
467. SHANNON POT
468. NEWGRANGE
469. LOUGHCREW PASSAGE GRAVES
470. SEVEN WONDERS OF FORE
471. INNY RIVER BOGLAND
472. YEATS COUNTRY
473. THE LAKE ISLE OF INNISFREE
474. OX MOUNTAINS
475. NEPHIN BEG MOUNTAINS ★
476. MULLET PENINSULA
477. ACHILL ISLAND
478. CROAGH PATRICK
479. CAHER ISLAND ★
480. OMEY ISLAND
481. TWELVE BENS
482. LETTERBRECKAUN
483. BÓTHAR NA SCRATHÓG
484. GORUMNA AND THE CAUSEWAY ISLANDS
485. SOUTH-EAST CONNEMARA
486. ARAN ISLANDS ★
487. THE BURREN ★
488. ST COLMAN'S WELL
489. CLARA AND CASTLETOWN BOGS
490. SLIEVE BLOOM MOUNTAINS
491. DONNELLY'S HOLLOW
492. BLACKSTAIRS MOUNTAINS
493. ROSSLARE SLOBS
494. COMERAGH MOUNTAINS
495. KNOCKMEALDOWN MOUNTAINS
496. GREAT BLASKET ISLAND
497. OLD KENMARE ROAD
498. PRIEST'S LEP
499. GREAT AND LITTLE SKELLIG ★
500. CAPE CLEAR ISLAND
Scale 5 m 10 km
DONEGAL
Letterkenny
Donegal
Ballyshannon
Sligo
Ballina
Castlebar
Westport
Leitrim
Carrick-on-Shannon
Cavan
Louth
Dundalk
Castlereagh
Longford
MAYO
SLIGO
LEITRIM
ROSCOMMON
MONAGHAN
CAVAN
LOUTH
Lough Conn
L. Allen
L. Arrow
N56
N13
N15
N16
N59
N17
N26
N5
N4
N87
N55
N3
N54
N2
N52
M1
462
463
464
465
466
467
469
472
473
474
475
476
477
479

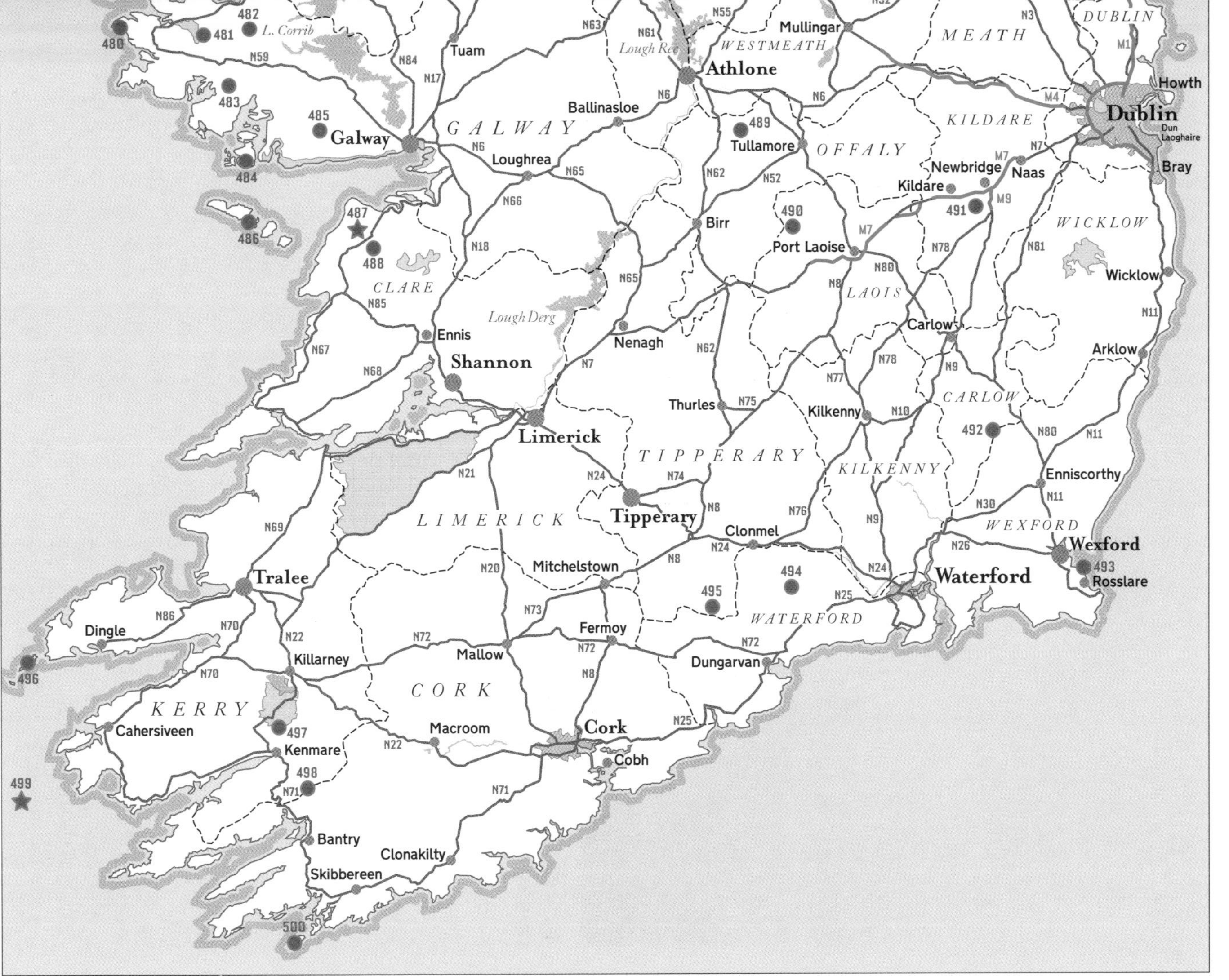

480
481
482
L. Corrib
N59
483
485
Galway
484
486
487
488
Tuam
N84
N17
N63
N61
Lough Ree
N55
Mullingar
WESTMEATH
Athlone
MEATH
N3
DUBLIN
M1
Howth
Dublin
Dun Laoghaire
Bray
M4
N6
Ballinasloe
N6
GALWAY
N6
Loughrea
N65
N66
N18
489
Tullamore
OFFALY
KILDARE
N7
M7
Newbridge
Naas
Kildare
M9
491
N62
N52
Birr
490
Port Laoise
M7
N78
N81
WICKLOW
Wicklow
CLARE
N85
Lough Derg
N65
N80
N8
LAOIS
Ennis
N67
Shannon
N68
Nenagh
N7
N62
Carlow
N11
Arklow
N78
N9
N77
Thurles
N75
Kilkenny
N10
CARLOW
492
N80
N11
Limerick
TIPPERARY
KILKENNY
N21
N24
N74
Enniscorthy
N11
Tipperary
N8
N76
N9
N30
WEXFORD
N69
LIMERICK
Clonmel
N24
N26
Wexford
493
Rosslare
N20
Mitchelstown
N8
494
N24
Waterford
Tralee
495
N25
N73
WATERFORD
N86
N70
Dingle
N22
N72
Fermoy
N72
Mallow
N72
Dungarvan
496
Killarney
N70
CORK
N8
KERRY
Cahersiveen
497
Macroom
Cork
N25
Kenmare
N22
Cobh
499
498
N71
N71
Bantry
Clonakilty
Skibbereen
500

462. CARRICKABRAGHY CASTLE, INISHOWEN, CO. DONEGAL

Map: OS of Ireland Discovery 3

Travel: R238 from Buncrana towards Carndonagh; 1¼ miles beyond Ballyliffin, left on minor road (brown 'Doagh Island' sign) to Carrickabraghy Castle at end of road (OS ref. 398523). To walk to Carrickabraghy: turn left in Ballyliffin for 1 mile to car park on shore (387495) and walk up Pollan Strand for 2¼ miles to castle.

Carrickabraghy Castle stands forgotten at the end of its long road, a monument to Ireland's wild history and a time when every local lordling worth his salt built himself such a stronghold. These days the castle ruin looms above a tiny settlement of houses and a farm, but when Phelemy Brasleigh O'Doherty built it in the sixteenth century it stood by itself at the outer edge of Doagh Island. When complete it boasted seven round towers at the corners of a great bawn, or defensive courtyard, that enclosed a stout, square keep pierced with musket loops. It needed to be strong; O'Doherty sided with the English against his countrymen during the bloody rebellions and oppressions of the Nine Years War around the turn of the seventeenth century, and the castle was besieged more than once. On Pollan Strand, a glorious beach just below the castle, a desperate battle took place in 1600 between the pro-English forces of Niall Garve O'Donnell and the Irish supporters of Red Hugh O'Donnell, chief of the O'Donnell clan. Red Hugh was beaten. The castle fell into disuse after Irish resistance to the British had been snuffed out, and half a century later stood unoccupied, as it has ever since.

Strictly speaking, Doagh is no longer an island. But the place still has an island feel.

Carrickabraghy is a weather-beaten, desolate place, where in rough weather the tide runs in to spurt viciously up in spray from a blowhole near the ruin. Here you stand, looking out at the dark rock hump of Glashedy Island, the craggy silhouette of Reachtain Mhór mountain to the west beyond Pollan Bay, and in the north the long hump of Malin Head among white-capped seas.

463. TORY ISLAND, CO. DONEGAL

Map: OS of Ireland Discovery 1

Travel: Ferry from Bunbeg or Magheroarty (www.toryislandferry.com).

Patsy Dan Rogers greets you off the Tory Island ferry with a handshake or a kiss, depending on your sex and how the day is going. Patsy Dan is a musician, a painter and a very genial man; he is also the King of Tory, elected by his 150 fellow islanders to be monarch of their 2 square miles of storm-battered, cliff-encircled rock. Tory Island needs a protagonist such as Patsy Dan; it is one of the most isolated and frequently cut-off islands of the Irish coast, and life is tough out there. Winter gales can sever communication with the mainland for weeks at a time, and the crossing is usually a rough affair. Any positive promotion the island can get helps to secure its future as a going concern.

Once you have recovered your land legs you will see an all but level and treeless plain of salt-sprayed grass. The land tips to a flattish south shore and rises to harsh cliffs nearly 200 feet tall on the more exposed and rugged north coast. The fields are small, crouched inside stone walls. Birdwatching is excellent on the northern cliffs and down by the loughs (or lochs, as they spell them here) in the west of the island; but sooner or later everyone gravitates to the pubs in the island's single village, out of the wind and into the crack.

Astonishingly, to uninformed visitors, Tory Island is the base for a flourishing art scene – the Tory Island School of naive painting, of which its king is a keen exponent. It started in 1968, when local man James Dixon vowed he could paint a better Tory Island landscape than the one he'd watched being created by English artist Derek Hill. The Englishman gave the untried fisherman brushes and paints, and what resulted was a vigorous 2-D style with immense appeal. Things snowballed from there among the island's fishermen and farmers, in the same sort of way as had happened forty years earlier with the nascent writers of the Blasket Islands of County Kerry (see p. 538). These days an original landscape of the Tory Island School will set you back a good sum.

On a stormy day you might want to enjoy the blast at the promontory fort of Dún Balair, the Fort of Balor. The ferocious Balor of the Evil Eye, god of darkness, was chief of the Fomorians, an ancient race of Tory Island pirates much given to raiding the mainland under the protection of their most potent weapon, the all-slaying Evil Eye of their leader. But when the Fomorians were brought to battle by their implacable foe, the god named Lugh the Long-Handed, they received their come-uppance. Lugh slung a stone which knocked Balor's eye clean through his skull into the back of his head, from which position it glared his followers to death in no time.

464. THE FLAGSTONE OF LONELINESS, GARTAN LOUGH, CO. DONEGAL

Maps OS of Ireland Discovery 6

Travel: From Letterkenny, R250 past Newmills; in 1½ miles, right on R251 for 3 miles. Where R254 Doocharry road bears left, keep ahead on R261 through Church Hill. In 1 mile cross Gartan Bridge and turn left ('Gartan'). Follow brown 'Colmkille's Birthplace' signs to parking place at Lacknacoo (OS ref. 055180). Follow short path to find St Columba's Cross and the Flagstone of Loneliness on the left (054178).

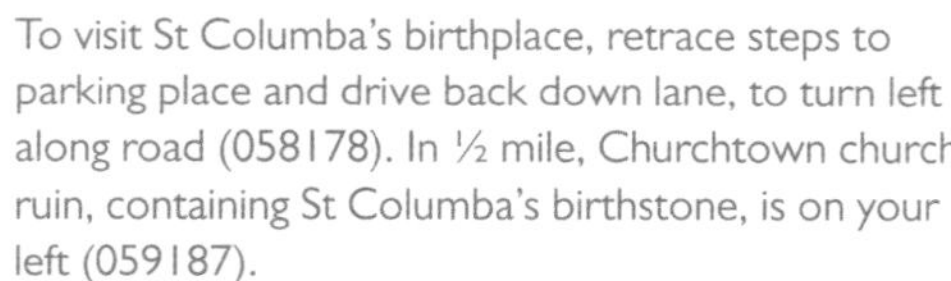
To visit St Columba's birthplace, retrace steps to parking place and drive back down lane, to turn left along road (058178). In ½ mile, Churchtown church ruin, containing St Columba's birthstone, is on your left (059187).

As with so many wild places in Ireland, things are not quite as they appear around St Columba's birthplace. In spite of the large cross that stands beside the Flagstone of Loneliness and proclaims this spot to be the birthplace in AD 521 of the saint called Columba, or perhaps Colmcille, or Colmkille, or Columbkille (versions vary widely), Ireland's greatest native missionary was in fact born – as verifiably as is possible, since it happened 1,500 years ago – half a mile away, on the spot where the ruined old church of Churchtown now stands. There is a stone slab in the old church on which the saint is said to have been born, but many still believe that the birth slab was the one that lies by the cross at Lacknacoo, or Leac na Cumha – the Flagstone of Loneliness.

Some stories say that Columba cured a man dying of homesickness by laying him on the Flagstone of Loneliness. Others assert that it was the saint himself who lay here in agony of mind the night before he was to leave Ireland for ever in self-imposed exile, having provoked the Battle of Cul Dreimne under Benbulben in Sligo (see p. 439). What is certain is that the ancient cup-and-ring-marked stone was a magnet for Irish emigrants in the nineteenth and twentieth centuries. To sleep on the Flagstone of Loneliness insured you against the curse of homesickness, and if you could board the 'coffin ship' to the New World with a pocketful of clay scraped from the old church at Churchtown, you could be additionally sure you would not drown, burn to death, or die unexpectedly and unshriven.

Each of the Stone Age cup marks in the 7-foot-long stone is filled with copper coins, tokens left by the faithful. Rainwater has dissolved the copper and spread it far and wide, so that when the heavens open the Flagstone of Loneliness weeps rusty red tears.

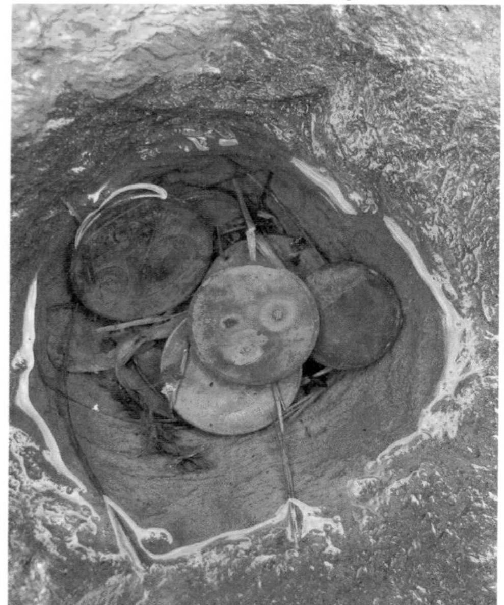
Flagstone of Loneliness

465. MOUNT ERRIGAL, CO. DONEGAL

Map: OS of Ireland Discovery 1

Travel: N56 from Gweedore towards Gortahork; in 2 miles, right on R251 towards Letterkenny. At 2 miles beyond Dunlewy, look for lay-by and 'walking man' sign near Carlaghmohane Bridge (OS ref. 953205). Poles point the way along the obvious track up Mount Errigal. You can in fact climb easily from almost anywhere along the road a mile or so east of Dunlewy, turning left along the ascent path when you reach it.

NB: This is a steep and slippery ascent in parts. Unless experienced at hill navigation, don't try it in heavy rain, low cloud or mist. The summit ridge track is narrow – possibility of vertigo here. Wear hillwalking clothes and boots. Allow 2½–3 hours there and back, depending on fitness.

Mount Errigal stands alone and magnificent, a cone of quartzite 2,466 feet high. It seems to be under snow when viewed from afar in bright sunlight; it is only when you are close to that you see the dazzling whiteness of the quartzite. The mountain appears forbidding from below, especially looking up at the great corries, or hanging valleys, torn by glaciers in its flank. But in fact in good conditions it is an easy climb, though a tiring one, from the road that curls around its south side.

Start from the road over squelchy bog and heather, a sodden trudge to where the slope begins to rise. Here you hit the stony track, worn by countless feet, that bears north-west up the long nape of the mountain. It is a rough, scree-like path, winding among outcrops, steadily gaining height through boulder fields of quartzite where the light reflects off the rock in brilliant star-like twinkles. Near the top the track bends and zigzags among slabs, then straightens out to reach the summit.

Here the mountain plays a good-humoured trick on you: the summit you have had your eyes and mind fixed on as you climbed is not the only one Errigal possesses. A couple of hundred yards ahead another peak rises on the far side of a very narrow ridge, the path only a couple of feet wide in places, a nasty drop plummeting away to the east. Once you are across the ridge and up on this supplementary summit, you can relax and enjoy an astonishing view over lakes and mountains to the Donegal coast, a prospect of 50 miles of country. If the sky is completely clear you might glimpse the Antrim heights and the mountains of Connemara down in Galway, or even the high peaks of Scottish mountains beyond the sea – a panorama of perhaps 150 miles. And no wonder, for Errigal is the highest thing in County Donegal, and so, for the moment, are you.

466. SWEATHOUSES, ARIGNA, CO. LEITRIM

Map: OS of Ireland Discovery 26

Travel: R280 from Drumshanbo towards Drumkeeran. In 2½ miles pass R285 ('Keadew') where it turns left; in another 300 yards, bear left to Arigna. Turn left over Derreenavoggy Bridge (OS ref. 930142) and keep straight ahead uphill past Arigna Fuels. Straight ahead up narrow lane (929140), over crossroads (927146) and on uphill for ½ mile to pass lane on right. In 150 yards look over hedge on right to see pair of sweathouses in a bank (923128). In another 250 yards, park carefully (narrow lane) near 'Miner's Way' fingerpost that stands on the left and points across the road (920127). Follow its direction up steps, over stile and up steep sunken lane for 200 yards. At top bear right (yellow arrow) at another sweathouse (920130).

Lough Allen seems to be the national centre for sweathouses. There are more of these primitive little stone huts around the shores of the big wedge-shaped lake than anywhere else in Ireland. Some have tried to link the sweathouses to the prevalence of iron and coal mining in the region, but no one can really explain their superabundance here.

The sweathouses you see beside the lanes at Crosshill above Arigna are much like the others of their kind, except that the first one you come to is in fact a double or semi-detached sweathouse. Only 3 or 4 feet high, with a crouching doorway and closely fitting drystone walls, sweathouses were roofed with sods of turf when fully operational back in the eighteenth and nineteenth centuries – and perhaps long before that, too. Turf keeps in the heat, and the purpose of the sweathouses is implied in their name – to sweat out fevers, chills, rheumatic pains and cramps.

What seems like crude folk medicine in fact worked on the excellent principle of the sauna. A turf fire was lit in the sweathouse, and the miniature doorway blocked up with bundles of wood or more turf to allow the interior to become baking hot. When it was singing like a kettle, the door would be unblocked, the fire raked out and the sufferer inserted into the roasting-hot chamber. The door was re-blocked and the patient left to cook. When judged sufficiently 'done', the doorway would be opened, the thoroughly sweated-out figure dragged outside and dumped into a freezing cold stream. It was kill or cure in the robust medicine of the countryside in former days – and, surprisingly, a lot more sufferers seem to have been cured than cooked to death.

467. SHANNON POT, CO. CAVAN

Map: OS of Ireland Discovery 26

Travel: N16 from Blacklion towards Manorhamilton; in ¼ mile, left ('Glangevlin') on R206. In 5 miles, brown 'Shannon Pot' sign points left (OS ref. 048322) to car park. Follow path from here to Shannon Pot (053317).

Sinnann, daughter of Lodan, came to the pool below Cuilcagh Mountain to find the Salmon of Wisdom. Anyone who could catch and eat that notable, one-eyed fish would gain all the wisdom of the world. But the salmon saw her coming, and grew so angry he caused the pool to bubble and boil, to overflow and to pour down through Ireland. Or did the maiden eat the salmon and then melt into that mighty river? Either way, Ireland's longest river, the 230-mile Shannon, has its origin in the modest pool that bubbles away to itself in a ring of hazel trees – the very trees, so the story says, whose nuts fed the Salmon of Wisdom.

The Shannon Pot is no roaring hole or jagged cliff torrent, as you might expect of the source of Ireland's talismanic river. An overcast day in summer after heavy rain, early or late when no one else is about, is a good time to visit. Then the Shannon, fed by springs below the mountain, pushes strongly out of the earth, agitating its pool and setting off through the fields as a rushing waterway already too wide to jump across. It leaves its birthplace with the force of a full-blown river going somewhere in a hurry, down through half of Ireland, through Lough Allen, Lough Ree and Lough Derg, draining 6,000 square miles – one-fifth of the country – as it gathers tributaries in their hundreds before entering its long estuary and surging out into the Atlantic. Think of that tremendous journey as you stand and stare at the dimpling water of the Shannon Pot. If a single cold, appraising eye stares back at you from the glass-grey depths, you could reach for your fishing rod – but beware of what you fish for.

468. NEWGRANGE, CO. MEATH

Map: OS of Ireland Discovery 43

Travel: N1 to Drogheda, then follow Brú na Bóinne signs. Newgrange Passage Grave (OS ref. 007727) is part of Brú na Bóinne World Heritage Site.

NB: Visits to witness winter solstice sunrise inside Newgrange Passage Grave are arranged by lottery. All details: www.knowth.com/newgrange.

The late Stone Age tribesmen who lived in the River Boyne valley were hardy, determined and well organized. They were also rich, spiritually and culturally. So much becomes clear the moment you set eyes on Newgrange Passage Grave, the fantastic monument to life in death that they built beyond the river. The tomb stands 40 feet high and nearly 300 feet across, a giant heart-shaped mound dominating its ridge above the river. Something like 200,000 tons of stone went into its construction, from the great slabs of grey-blue sandstone that formed the outside kerb, interior passage and central burial chamber, down to the millions of fist-sized pebbles used to shape the overarching mound. Those who hauled the huge sandstone blocks for miles by rope and log rollers, those who trudged up and down with the filler rubble, may well have spent their entire lives at the task. Newgrange wasn't built in a day: it probably took two or three generations of continual labour to carry out the construction of this extraordinary tomb.

In the lands all round the big tomb, and all over Europe in the fourth millennium BC, Neolithic people were building great passage graves and raising mounds over them. But the tomb-builders of the Boyne outdid all others. Around 30 tombs lie in this one small area, the greatest apart from Newgrange being the tombs of Knowth and Dowth just along the ridge. Brú na Bóinne, the Palace of the Boyne, is unquestionably the finest Neolithic cemetery in Europe. When you consider that the builders had only stone, wood and animal bone with which to make tools, the mighty scale of the Boyne achievements comes more into focus. And these tombs were not mere stone garbage pits in which to throw human remains. The great stone slabs, inside and outside, were carved with elaborate patterns of curlicues and spirals, tessellated triangles and interlocking panels of diamonds; and with circles surrounded by rays, the emblem of the sun.

What notions of life after death and godhead the Boyne tomb-builders entertained one can only guess at. But the sun was clearly central to their religious beliefs. The passage they built into the burial chamber inside Newgrange is exactly aligned with the point on the eastern horizon over which the sun first shows itself at the midwinter solstice. But it is not down the passageway that the sun shines into the tomb. It is the stone-bound slit known as the 'roof box' that catches the rays of the just-risen sun and condenses them into a single beam. A thin intense finger of light pierces straight to the back wall of the innermost burial recess at the

heart of the mound. The chamber floods with a warm, life-affirming glow for a few minutes; then the finger slowly withdraws down the passageway and leaves the tomb to darkness for another year. This drama of light is enacted only for the five or six days that span 21 December.

Newgrange has stood for perhaps 5,000 years, unregarded for most of that time. Today, excavated and presented for public enjoyment, it is Ireland's best-known ancient tomb. There are dozens more (for example Knockmany – see p. 495; and Loughcrew – see below) open for exploration.

469. LOUGHCREW PASSAGE GRAVES, NEAR OLDCASTLE, CO. MEATH

Map: OS of Ireland Discovery 42

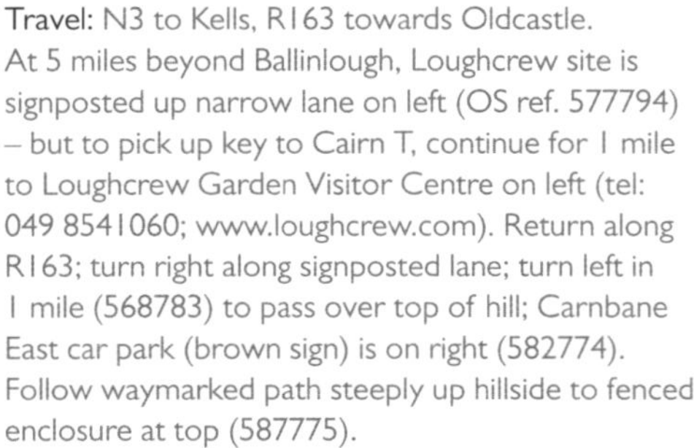

Travel: N3 to Kells, R163 towards Oldcastle. At 5 miles beyond Ballinlough, Loughcrew site is signposted up narrow lane on left (OS ref. 577794) – but to pick up key to Cairn T, continue for 1 mile to Loughcrew Garden Visitor Centre on left (tel: 049 8541060; www.loughcrew.com). Return along R163; turn right along signposted lane; turn left in 1 mile (568783) to pass over top of hill; Carnbane East car park (brown sign) is on right (582774). Follow waymarked path steeply up hillside to fenced enclosure at top (587775).

The Loughcrew Hills of west Meath hold an extraordinary necropolis, spread across the two peaks of Slieve na Calliagh, the Hill of the Witch. No wonder our superstitious forebears felt that these hills must be haunted; on the opposing peaks of Carnbane East and West, 900 feet high, lie thirty-two stone tombs, mostly chambered cairns, built on these heights some 5,000 years ago. The low entrances and humped appearances of the tombs resemble strange

Loughcrew Passage Graves

houses clamped into the earth, and the fact that their doorways lead into blackness in the heart of the hilltops – blackness where human remains and mysterious treasure lay – made them doubly sinister.

Cairn H on Carnbane West shows Iron Age decorations by incision, but it is Cairn T on the summit of Carnbane East that you can unlock with a clang. A dark mouth opens in the stony hillock. The flanking stones of the passageway are carved with rings, sunbursts, whorls and waves. Duck under the waist-high stone lintel and crawl along a passage lined and roofed with massive slabs of stone, green with lichen, then negotiate a kerbstone and enter the central chamber of the tomb. Three compartments, one either side and one at the end, burrow back into the walls under a corbelled roof, open at the top to rain or sun. The back stones of the grave carry carvings beautifully preserved in the cool and dark for five millennia: deeply scored sunburst shapes like flowers, centipede-like motifs, and more waves and whorls, the whole design in shadowy movement in the half-light inside the hill.

470. SEVEN WONDERS OF FORE, CO. WESTMEATH

Map: OS of Ireland Discovery 41

Travel: R394 from Mullingar to Castlepollard; R195 towards Oldcastle, in 2 miles, right (signposted) to Fore. Park on road just before village, beside the Tree That Won't Burn (OS ref. 509706).

The wildness of the Seven Wonders of Fore has more to do with the outer shores of the human spirit and imagination than it does with landscape. County Westmeath is mild dairying country, the Fore Valley a pleasant green retreat – albeit with a scattering of curious objects.

The Seven Wonders of Fore add up to a landscape of peculiar significance in the Christian imagination. Beside the road stands a dead-looking stump, the Tree That Won't Burn. So many copper coins have been pushed edge-on into its bark that what was once a flourishing tree is now a withered wreck. So much of its anatomy now consists of metal that it probably does live up to its legendary property. It still carries streamers of 'clooties' (strips of cloth knotted into its structure to reinforce prayers), as does the sapling that is growing to replace it.

Near by lies the Water That Won't Boil, a muddy puddle. Anyone boiling a kettleful will have bad luck for insulting holy water, for this long-polluted spring is the Holy Well of St Fechin, the pioneering missionary

who founded a monastery at Fore in AD 630. There stands the monastery in the distance, a fine group of late medieval Benedictine buildings, very tightly composed, known as the Monastery in the Quaking Scraw – Fore's third Wonder. Only a miracle could allow such a citadel of God to be built in such a rushy, sloppy bog – that, or a good solid foundation of rock just under the morass. As you visit the monastery you will pass a tumble of mossy stones under a clootie-hung tree on the left of the path. This should by rights be the Eighth Wonder of Fore, since it is St Fechin's Bath – the broken remnants of a holy well where Fechin would spend all night at prayer, kneeling in the freezing water.

Where the path to the monastery joins the road lie two more Wonders – the Mill without a Race, which the saint ordered to be built in spite of the fact that there was no water to turn the wheel, and the Water That Flows Uphill, which he caused to appear as a supply for the mill by striking his staff into the Hill of Lough Lene not far away. Seen against the lie of the field through which it runs, the water does indeed appear to defy gravity and flow uphill.

Across the road stand the two remaining Wonders of Fore. Up the bank in a twelfth-century church you will find the Stone Raised by St Fechin's Prayers. The huge slab is inscribed with a Greek cross inside a circle – a very ancient Eastern Christian symbol – and it was lifted and set as the lintel to the church doorway by the praying power of the saint alone. Further up the slope stands the church-like building where the hermit Patrick Begley, the Anchorite in a Stone, lived incarcerated in a cell four centuries ago. His cell now forms part of the structure of the building, a mausoleum built for the Greville Nugent family that wholly eclipses the humble dwelling of the hermit. Yet it is he, and modest St Fechin of the sore knees and fervent prayers, who are still revered and remembered.

471. INNY RIVER BOGLAND, CO. LONGFORD

Map: OS of Ireland Discovery 41

Travel: R194 from Longford to Granard. Cross N55 in town, and bear left on R396 towards Coole. At 2 miles beyond Abbeylara, park by roadside where it's safe and walk out on to the bog.

County Longford suffers from an image problem. There just isn't that much in the small north Midlands county to make it stand out from its neighbours. Cavan has its lakes and waterways, Leitrim a swathe of mountains and moors that shade into glamorous Galway and Sligo, while Westmeath has great lakes, including the giant Lough Ree, with the mighty Shannon flowing through it.

And Longford? Woods and fields, meadows and streams, a hill here, a valley there. Yet this lack of sparkle lends Longford an understated charm for connoisseurs of Ireland's out-of-the-way places; and the boglands that accompany the Inny River along the Westmeath border are wonderful places to go if you want some peace and quiet.

Walk three minutes out along one of the Inny's bog roads and you will find yourself in a starkly contrasted world. On one hand stand the ominous dark cliffs left by peat-

Inny River bogland

cutting machines harvesting the 'bog gold' on a commercial scale; on the other, and right alongside, uncut bog rolling away to a skyline black with conifer plantations. On the uncut bog the scrub willows and silver birch are riotous with birdsong – wrens, blackbirds, willow warblers, finches, thrushes. There is a soporific hum and buzz of insects. The puddled bog road passes through sulphurous splashes of gorse, coarse pale tussocks of grass and dark brushy banks of heather where hobbies and sparrowhawks skim after dragonflies.

At any one of the machine-cut cliffs of peat you can stop to inspect the inner structure of the bog, and marvel anew at what the underlying acid rock has preserved unrotted – delicate hairs of plant roots, fragile black willow leaves that fall to pieces as you touch them, and swirling hanks of pale material like miniature horse tails that reveal themselves to be fragments of the limbs of 5,000-year-old pine trees that have not seen the light of day since they were felled, until you pull them out from their puddingy dark bed.

472. YEATS COUNTRY, CO. SLIGO

Map: OS of Ireland Discovery 16

Travel: N15 from Ballyshannon, N16 from Manorhamilton, N4 from Boyle, N59 from Ballina and N17 from Galway all converge on Sligo. The 100-mile Yeats Country Drive, signposted with a brown-and-white 'quill-and-inkstand' sign, takes in all the major W. B. and Jack Yeats sites.

In Sligo town, Sligo County Library on Bridge Street has W. B. and Jack Yeats memorabilia (letters, sketches, rough drafts of poems, etc.). The Model Arts and Niland Gallery on the Mall (www.modelart.ie) houses a magnificent collection of Jack Yeats's paintings and drawings. The Yeats Memorial Building on Hyde Bridge contains a photographic exhibition on W. B. Yeats, and is the HQ of the Yeats Society.

Nearest railway station: Sligo

The Yeats brothers, William and Jack, celebrated poet and painter, still cast a long shadow in Sligo, the backwoods county they roamed as boys and later raised from nineteenth-century obscurity to twentieth-century renown. It was William who,

Ruined cottage, Dartry Mountains

through his poetry, spun the legends he learned in childhood of Sligo places: of the hill of Knocknarea, where rapacious Queen Maeve lies buried, and the boat-shaped mountain of Benbulben, on whose slopes the hero Fionn MacCumhaill took a deadly revenge on Diarmuid who had cuckolded him. Benbulben was William Yeats's favourite mountain, a soaring green ship of a hill that looks down on Drumcliffe Church and the churchyard where the poet lies buried under a plain grey Sligo stone slab cut with his self-penned epitaph:

Cast a cold Eye
On Life, on Death.
Horseman, pass by!

Jack, meanwhile, put ghosts and mysteries into Sligo fair days and donkey races with his paintbrush, readying himself for the great expressionist landscapes of the county that would define his art.

From the crown of the great cairn called Queen Maeve's Tomb on Knocknarea, the Hill of the Kings, an extraordinary sculptural landscape unfolds, looking as if it had been mounded up and moulded with a sharp knife. You command a view 50 miles wide, a great stretch of north-west Ireland from the 2,000-foot cliffs of Slieve League in Donegal all the way to Achill Island and the rugged profile of the Nephin Beg mountains, way down into County Mayo. Streaks of drying sand and whorls of water mark the outgoing tide as it sluices past Rosses Point into Sligo Bay. To the north Benbulben climbs out of the coastal plain:

Saddle and ride, I heard a man say,
Out of Ben Bulben and Knocknarea,

What says the clock in the Great Clock
Tower?
All those tragic characters ride
But turn from Rosses' crawling tide,
The meet's upon the mountain-side.
A slow low note and an iron bell.

Three ragged inlets make up the coastline around Sligo. These are exciting shores, where the tide pushes past peninsulas and islands into bays threaded by complicated shipping channels. At Rosses Point surfers swoop in, riding the big Atlantic rollers with the relaxed grace of champion horsemen. This is the place to walk sandy beach and dunes, boots crunching on seaweed and shells, savouring the sea coasts and mountains that haunted all Jack Yeats's paintings, from early studies like *Sailor Home from the Sea* to the wildly impressionistic mystical late paintings such as *The Sea and the Lighthouse*. 'Every painting which I have made,' said the artist, 'has somewhere in it a thought of Sligo.' Most poignant and beautiful of all is *Leaving the Far Point*, with the figures of the painter and his wife and uncle, transparent as ghosts, walking the wet sands of Rosses Point on a wild day long ago.

473. THE LAKE ISLE OF INNISFREE, LOUGH GILL, CO. SLIGO

Maps: OS of Ireland Discovery 16, 25

Travel: R286 from Sligo towards Manorhamilton along north shore of Lough Gill; in 6 miles, park at Parke's Castle on right (OS ref. 782351). Join Rose of Innisfree cruises here (www.roseofinnisfree.com).

William Yeats loved the legends of Sligo. As a boy on holiday from Dublin, staying with his Pollexfen grandparents in Sligo and roaming the countryside near by, the budding poet and his artist brother Jack (see above), heard the story of the city that lies drowned beneath the waters of Lough Gill. They learned of the two friends, Omra and Romra, who ruled over the ancient city of Sligo, which lay in former days under Cairns Hill. All was peace and happiness until Omra chanced to see Romra's beautiful daughter, Gile (Bright One), bathing in a river and fell in love with her. The friends had a furious quarrel, and Romra slew his daughter's would-be lover. Romra was so badly wounded in the fight that he, too, died. In some versions of the tale the combatants are brothers, and Romra slays Omra for entertaining an incestuous passion. Young Gile was so horrified at the disaster sparked by her beauty that she killed herself; whereupon her nursemaid wept so bitterly that her tears filled the hollow under the hill and drowned the city of Sligo. Thus was formed the lake named after Gile. Omra and Romra were buried side by side under twin mounds on Cairns Hill, and these are still to be seen overlooking Lough Gill.

Like the Yeats brothers you can go boating on Lough Gill and listen for the bells of old Sligo tolling under the lake. Towards the south shore lies the Lake Isle of Innisfree, a smother of wood anemones and bluebells among old oaks, where lichen hangs in long streamers. You would be hard pressed to find a small cabin of clay and wattles in a bee-loud glade on the islet today, but that was the fantasy that came to William Yeats in the winter of 1888 as he sat depressed and day-dreaming in a London room, with Ireland in political turmoil and his poetical career not yet off the ground. A Romantic fantasy of a wild place (in a well-ordered kind of way), Yeats's 'The Lake Isle of Innisfree' yearns for rows of beans, beehives and evenings full of the linnet's wings.

The big cruiser *Rose of Innisfree* takes parties from Parke's Castle past Innisfree, but you will scarcely agree with Yeats that 'peace come dropping slow' this way. Better to see if you can persuade someone to lend or hire you a boat. Standing among the mossy stones by the shore and gazing across Lough Gill, you can murmur to yourself:

I will arise and go now, for always night and day
I hear lake water lapping with low sounds by the shore;
While I stand on the roadway, or on the pavements gray,
I hear it in the deep heart's core.

474. OX MOUNTAINS, CO. SLIGO

Maps: OS of Ireland Discovery 24, 25

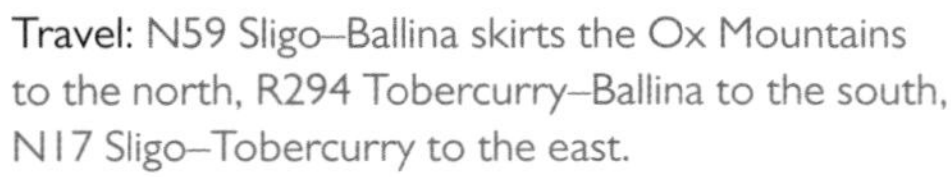

Travel: N59 Sligo–Ballina skirts the Ox Mountains to the north, R294 Tobercurry–Ballina to the south, N17 Sligo–Tobercurry to the east.

The Ox Mountains are some of the least-walked uplands in Ireland. Rising where they do, in an unfrequented rural corner of County Sligo, they are left unexplored. Yet these are beautiful mountains, if you like rugged scenery, wild weather and tough walking.

They have sea to the north and farmlands all round; they stand detached, a massive upland whose green back is scabbed with outcrops of some of the oldest rock in Ireland, volcanic matter that solidified some 600 million years ago. There is sandstone here, too, and plenty of copper and iron. The outcrops are folded together and pushed sideways or on end, so looking out from between two buttresses of rock there will be vertical zigzags on the one side and horizontally squashed rock sandwiches on the other. Over this rough material, where white quartzite lies baked between the folds, bog and heather are spread so thickly that walking the mountains becomes a knee-deep stumble and squelch. Boots plunge down cracks into soft, gulping bog, and tuffets of heather slide underfoot. The reward for the struggle is a complete solitude, with only wheatears and pipits for company.

To get a taste for these wild lands, head for the north-east corner of the range, above Coolaney. The winding hill road into the mountains brings you past the big open-faced bluff called the Hungry Rock. Many died along this road, some in the shadow of the Hungry Rock, during the Great Famine of 1845–9, as they wandered from one workhouse to another in hopes of food. Throw a stone at the rock, and you will avert a similar fate, so says local tradition, and the litter of stones around the rock bears witness to the enduring power of the tradition, and also of the appalling history that bred it.

475. NEPHIN BEG MOUNTAINS, CO. MAYO

Maps: OS of Ireland Discovery 23, 31

Travel: N59 from Ballina to Bangor Erris. Bangor Trail starts from the football pitch on the south side of the Owenmore River (OS ref. 866226) and winds through the Nephin Beg mountains for 27 miles to the road at Srahmore Lodge (974045). The trail crosses the Tarsaghaunmore River (867161), passes Tawnyanruddia Mountain and runs through the Scardaun Valley (919104). You continue by the Bawnduff River and to the edge of Letterkeen Wood to Srahmore Lodge. If continuing on foot, choose either the high or low road to take you

Nephin Beg mountains

south to the foot of Lough Feeagh at the Yellow River bridge (980978), and a final 4 miles into Newport (984937).

NB: This is a very long and demanding walk – about 23 miles from Bangor Erris to the road at Srahmore Lodge, and another 7 into Newport. The track is waymarked, but is boggy, wet and lonely, passing through very wild country. Unless well experienced, do not attempt this walk solo. Wear full hillwalking gear and take food and water.

You will never, ever forget the Bangor Trail if you decide to tackle it. It is the loneliest hill track through the widest extent of blanket bog and the remotest mountain range in Ireland. The trail runs for 30 rugged miles through the heart of the Nephin Beg mountains of north-west Mayo. The quartzite peaks are often veiled in mist; rain hammers in frequently from the Atlantic a few miles to the west. There is no one to talk to or see, no house or road to encounter. You enter the mountains immediately you leave Bangor Erris, and by the time you cross the Tarsaghaunmore River 5 miles down the track you are right out in the wilderness.

The old road has deteriorated since cattle drovers and hardy travellers tramped it across the Nephin Beg. For centuries it was the only route through the remote boglands of Erris. Parts have sunk back into the bog; parts are under grass, stones and heather. It is map-and-compass country, where an unwary walker can go astray far from help. As such, the Bangor Trail is a precious route indeed.

In the depths of the Nephin Beg, halfway along the trail, lies the Scardaun Valley, completely silent and deserted. On the valley floor you can make out the lines of lazybeds, or potato ridges, and the print of the old tracks and field boundaries of the village whose houses crumble beside the track. This roadless valley lies at the hub of a spectacular circle of mountain peaks, and through them you wind in the shadow of Nephin Beg and Glennamong, to trudge the lonely miles down to the road at Srahmore.

With aching legs you face the last quarter, swinging up along the old road high above Lough Feeagh, then limping down the lane into Newport with blistered feet and a head full of marvels. You'll never taste a sweeter thing than that first mouthful of Guinness.

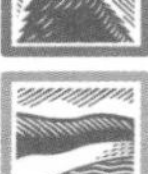

476. MULLET PENINSULA, CO. MAYO

Map: OS of Ireland Discovery 22

Travel: N59 from Westport or Ballina to Bangor Erris; R313 to Belmullet, and on to end of Mullet Peninsula.

Inside the armpit of the Mullet Peninsula, all the way down to the clutch of Blacksod Point, lie tidal mudflats and marshes, the bird-haunted slobs that make the Mullet such a magnet for birdwatchers. On the outer edge is a succession of magnificent sandy beaches, tawny strands pounded by rough seas and heaped with long banks of seaweed. The main body of the peninsula lies low and humped, boggy fields to the east, high flowery machair to the west, lakes all over. Termoncarragh Lake, out towards the north-west corner of Mullet, is reedy and shallow, a place unapproached by any road. This is one of the best places in Ireland to spot rare breeding red-necked phalarope, tiny wading birds with narrow black bills and pillarbox-red necks.

Straight lanes lead through fields and dunes to the hidden strands of the west coast. An all but vanished promontory fort guards the dull silver strand of Belderra, its upper beach studded with coloured pebbles. The peerless white bay of Portmore looks out to the green hummocks of the Duvillaun Islands. Just behind the beach lies St Dervla's holy well with a penitential arch to creep under, a cup for drinking cold, sweet water from the well, and offerings placed by the source – a conch shell, pebbles, flowers, a marriage ring. The strand that lines the most westerly stretch of the Mullet is more than 2 miles long, and is a place to stroll among the browsing cattle and look out on the Inishkea Islands, low in the sea 3 miles offshore. North again off the strand beyond Cross Lough lies Inishglora, where the Children of Lir served out the last three centuries of their 900-year exile from their home. They had been turned into swans and banished by their jealous stepmother, Aoife. When a holy man visited the island, the spell was broken and the Children of Lir were able to resume their human form. But alas! They were 900 years old, and fated to die immediately. The saint baptized them, attended them as they died, and buried them on Inishglora as they had requested, standing upright with their arms round each other, together in death as in life.

477. ACHILL ISLAND, CO. MAYO

Maps: OS of Ireland Discovery 30; Achill Island Map and Guide, available on Achill

Travel: From Galway, N84, R330 to Westport; N59 to Newport and Mulrany; R319 to Achill Sound and Achill Island. From Knock, N5 to Castlebar; R311 to Newport; then as above.

Achill is Ireland's largest offshore island, a great chunk of windswept mountain and moor some 14 miles wide and 12 miles from north to south. It is shaped like a sea monster bunched for a spring, its sharp-nosed head thrust out defiantly deep into the Atlantic Ocean. Around 2,500 people live on this tough and fantastically beautiful island.

The channel between the mainland and Achill is so narrow that a modest bridge spans it. Yet looking across the sound at the Achill houses and the slender tower of Carrickildavnet Castle, rising from the water's edge, the island remains apart, entirely separate from the mainland in character as well as geography. A stunning coastal route known as the Atlantic Drive skirts the south and west shores of Achill by way of Carrickildavnet. In Tudor times the grim tower was a stronghold of Granuaile the pirate queen, otherwise known as Grace O'Malley. Granuaile once refused a conciliatory offer by Queen Elizabeth I to make her a countess, chiding the monarch: 'Is it not presumptuous of Your Majesty to say you would confer this honour on me? I am already a Queen in my own right, in my own place.' It was rumoured that no one could steal any ship of Granuaile's fleet by night, for all their hawsers were fastened to a silken thread which passed through her bedroom window and was tied round her big toe as she slept.

Each twist in the narrow, winding Atlantic Drive opens up a rocky bay, an empty cream-coloured strand or a vista of cliffs and mountains. Motley islands rise offshore: the humped sea-beast of Clare; the long sleeping dog of Inishbofin; Inishturk's craggy spine. At Keel village you reach a 2-mile curve of sand called the Great Beach and can look back to the mighty cliffs of Minaun that turn gold and black in evening sun and shadow. Out at the seaward end of Achill you can walk the westernmost clifftops to Moyteoge Head with its sensational view, down to the perfect yellow horseshoe of Keem Strand, out to the islands and beyond to the Atlantic.

In the shadow of the humpbacked mountain of Slievemore lie the houses of Toir Reabhach, a deserted village facing a wonderful vista of sea and islands. It was a combination of famine and poverty that drove the villagers away from their mountain settlement. The strength and simplicity of dozens of dwellings, the domestic intimacy of their stone storage cupboards and hearths, the rushy fields corrugated with ancient potato ridges and the rutted village road paved with white quartzite, all summon in the mind's eye the ghosts of that vanished community.

478. CROAGH PATRICK, CO. MAYO

Maps: OS of Ireland Discovery 30, 31

Travel: Ascent of Croagh Patrick: R335 from Westport towards Louisburgh; in 6 miles park at Campbell's pub in Murrisk (OS ref. 920823) and turn up the signposted track, climbing 1,650 feet to saddle under Lugnademon (920805); bear right for very steep ascent of 860 feet to summit of Croagh Patrick at 2,510 feet (906802).

NB: This is a very steep climb, the second and steeper part on slippery rubble. Allow 4–5 hours there and back.

Tóchar Phádraig, the Pilgrim Route: N84 from Castlebar towards Ballinrobe; through Ballyhean, and in 2 miles turn left (signed) to park at Ballintober Abbey (154793). Follow route westward for 23 miles to top of Croagh Patrick, by way of Lufferton (140796), Bellaburke Church (097810), Aghagower (034804), Lankhill (004792), Boheh (976785) and Boleybrian (948792).

NB: This is a 23-mile walk with a very steep climb at the end.

Croagh Patrick is Ireland's Holy Mountain, the symbol of all that is ancient and lofty in the island's beloved and fervent Christianity. St Patrick himself climbed the peak in AD 441, casting out demons, exhorting backsliders, hurling his great Cloigin Dubh, the Black Bell, over the precipice of Lugnanarrib, sweeping snakes, toads and other horrible beasts and spirits to their doom. Before the dramatic events of 441, Croagh Patrick had been known as Cruachan Aigil, Eagle Peak, and was the worship place of Celtic gods. The canny Patrick took it over, leaving his One God victorious upon the mountaintop.

Croagh Patrick is a mighty mountain, not so much in size (it is well short of 3,000 feet), but in grace of shape: a perfect cone rising from a high saddle, overlooking the waters of Clew Bay. Its pale form has a stirring effect as it rises above all other peaks into the sky. It is an uplifting mountain – so think the 60,000 or more pilgrims who make the strenuous climb to the chapel on the peak each Garland Sunday, the last Sunday in July.

To catch the mountain at its most impressive, follow Tóchar Phádraig, St Patrick's Path, from Ballintober Abbey 23 miles east of the mountain. This wonderful old pilgrimage way passes holy wells, standing stones, cup-and-ring-marked monoliths, ancient churches, towers and castles, fairy rings and spirit woods to reach the foot of the Reek, as Croagh Patrick is known to locals. Arriving this way your head and heart will be full of signs and miracles even before you gird your loins for the final crunching ascent to the saddle, the last hands-on-knees scramble to the summit. Here you can slump against the chapel wall, getting your breath back and immersing yourself in a truly celestial view.

479. CAHER ISLAND, CO. MAYO

Maps: OS of Ireland Discovery 30, 37

Travel: N4, N5 to Westport; R335 to Louisburgh; minor road west to Roonah Quay (OS ref. 745808); ferry to Clare Island (www.clareisland.info). Onward travel to Caher Island: enquire at Bay View Hotel, Clare Island (tel: 098 26307).

NB: Caher Island is accessible only at certain states of weather and tide. There is an annual pilgrimage to Caher from Roonah Quay on 15 August, weather permitting.

Clare Island measures only 4 miles by 3, and its rich history is written plainly across its face. The hillsides are corrugated with old cultivation ridges, ribbed like corduroy when the sun throws shadows into their furrows. In these raised beds, laboriously fertilized with seaweed and dung, the islanders grew their potatoes and oats until well into this century. Some continue to do so; today there are still well-manured potato strips and tiny fields where oats are scythed by hand, neatly stooked and tied with a wisp of oat straw. Here it is not Greenwich Mean Time that sets the rhythm of the days, but the seasons and the back-and-forth journeys of the ferry.

You can sweat up a switchback cliff path to the summit of Knockmore. Up there at 1,470 feet all the best of Ireland's north-west coast seems spread out: the cone of Croagh Patrick in the east (see above); the Nephin Beg mountains to the north (see pp. 512–13); and the Twelve Bens of Connemara down in the south (see pp. 510–11). This is a view for the angels, and due south, 6 miles off in the sea, is the tiny green slip of Caher Island, lonely and alluring.

There is no quay on the uninhabited

Caher. Landing is by rubber boat on the slippery, rocky beach. You can't get in, even on a calm day, if there is the slightest swell. And flat calms at the mouth of Clew Bay are rarer than horns on a donkey. But if by luck you chance on the right combination of wind and tide, and can negotiate a crossing, what you find on Caher is enough to strike you dumb: wafer-thin crosses carved with faces; delicately decorated standing stones; a bevelled stone hanging lamp perhaps 1,500 years old; a cramped chamber into which penitents would pack themselves to purge their souls with bodily agony; an ancient altar of stacked slabs; and the simple beauty of a tiny, ancient church in ruins.

These stones are not dead, but alive. White quartz pebbles, feathers and fresh flowers lie as offerings, though you have seen no other boat. Someone has placed a silver coin in the lamp. The altar has been washed clean, and bunches of votive flowers laid carefully side by side there.

How have the monuments of Caher survived, inviolate and perfect? The sea itself guards them, local people say, and will rise up against anyone foolish enough to take anything away.

480. OMEY ISLAND, CO. GALWAY

Map: OS of Ireland Discovery 37

Travel: N59 from Galway to Clifden. Continue beyond Clifden on N59 ('Letterfrack'). In 2 miles (OS ref. 647531) left on minor road to Claddaghduff. Park beside church (582569).

Follow lane beside church to its end on shore (578564). Cross sands to Omey Island (573559 – NB: see below) and explore at leisure. Sites are unmarked; but you will find middens in the cliffs not far from the crossing place (568564), the ancient graveyard beyond in the cliffs (564563), the old church (Teampull Fechin) just inland (563561), and the holy well (Tobair Fechin) on the north shore of the west side inlet (562555).

NB: Omey Island is cut off from the mainland at each high tide. Information on tide times from Connemara Walking Centre, Clifden (tel: 095 21379; walkwest@eircom.net), or enquire at Sweeney's pub in Claddaghduff (tel: 095 44345). The crossing is accessible for 3 hours each side of low water. Wear boots; bring rainproof and windproof clothing (no shelter on island), and drink/snack.

Omey Island lies beyond tidal sands at the westernmost point of Connemara. That short half-mile of causeway puts a world between island and mainland. Back in the 1830s, before the Great Famine, there were nearly ten times as many people in Connemara as live here now. Those who did not emigrate existed in extreme poverty, and social rituals were a vital glue holding communities together, in death as in life. Omey Island is one of the few places in Ireland where people are brought from the mainland to be buried. The place has a special reputation as sacred ground going back long before the time of Christ. People seem to have been burying their dead here for ever.

The island wind is genuine west of Ireland wind – a force you can lean against, real solid stuff full of salt and sand grains. Once you have been buffeted and blown across the causeway, the whole island lies open for exploration. In summer the sand-bedded turf is a mass of wild flowers. Layers of cockle and limpet shells in the low cliffs show where the islanders of 800 years ago threw their dinner scrapings. How the Omey islanders, exposed to every gale, endured the west coast winters on an almost exclusive diet of shellfish is hard to imagine. They built their houses low, sunk into the body of the island, out of the worst of the weather.

At the top of the island you can hunker down on a sheet of smoothed granite and stare out west to a scatter of offshore islands, including lonely High Island, where a beautiful little oratory, founded by St Fechin some 1,300 years ago, lies by a seldom-visited lake. It was Fechin who established a monastery on Omey Island. His name lives on in the ruined church of Teampull Fechin, crouched in a hollow in the sand and entirely hidden from view, and in Tobair Fechin, St Fechin's Well, which lies on the west coast. Under a simple wooden crucifix a niche in the wall of Tobair Fechin holds offerings – a toy car, a fishing float, a woven circlet of blue wire, a golf ball, an obituary folded inside a plastic envelope – forms of plea or thanksgiving. The spring itself is a clear pool inside a crack in the ground. A round white quartz stone glimmers through the ice-cold, brackish water – a cure-stone for skin troubles, to be applied and then replaced in the holy well for some other sufferer to use in their turn.

Twelve Bens

481. TWELVE BENS, CONNEMARA, CO. GALWAY

Maps: OS of Ireland Discovery 37, 44

Travel: From Galway – N59 Oughterard, Maam Cross and Recess; right on R344 through Inagh Valley; left on N59 past Kylemore Lough to Kylemore Abbey car park (747582). Turn left on foot along N59 for 1/3 mile (take care!); right off road through gateway (752381 – 'Connemara National Park'). Follow track between rhododendron bushes, past limekiln and quarry (754379), then steeply up, climbing south-east towards cone of Benbaun, up grass shoulder to summit cairn (765568). Head south to summit cairn of Benbrack (764558). Turn right (west), following rocky ridge past little lake (764558) and on north-west, down for ½ mile to fence on saddle between Benbrack and Knockbrack. Cross fence (wires are removable – please replace them as you found them!); bear right over rocks; then north down, on grass, into valley, keeping Mweelin River away on right. Cross stile in fence at bottom (753574); continue on left of fence, aiming for Kylemore Abbey. Ford river where it runs under fence and continue on left of fence, which soon bends right to a pair of stone gateposts (754577). Turn left on stony track to reach limekiln; return to N59; left (take care!) to Kylemore Abbey car park.

NB: A 5-mile walk. Ascent of Benbaun is steep; Benbrack is rocky; descending into the Mweelin valley can be slippery. Wear hillwalking gear and boots.

Hillwalking in Connemara is a treat, especially among the Twelve Bens or Twelve Pins, the magnificent cluster of rugged mini-mountains at the hub of the region.

These hills are Connemara's pride and joy. As you walk their slopes and hollows you will see tombs, holy wells, hut circles and lazybed strips shaping themselves as if by magic out of the grass and heather.

The walk up Benbaun, the White Mountain, rises from the south shore of Kylemore Lough, a pathless ascent that passes a tiny Neolithic court tomb, a jumble of old grave-slabs smothered in yellow iris, and the covered holy well of St Maol. Far below, the big pale grey bulk of Kylemore Abbey lies in full view across the lake. Climb up the ever-steepening grass shoulder of Benbaun over wet ground full of sundews and the pink heads of lousewort, a stiff hands-on-knees pull up over peat hags towards the summit cairn of Benbaun. You could stop here to admire the landscape of Connemara, but beyond Benbaun rises a second summit with an even more dramatic view. The grey rocky hummock of Benbrack, the Speckled Peak, is a different kettle of fish from the grassy slopes of Benbaun – a wilderness of rock, in smooth plates and in broken rubble. From the summit you gaze south to the heights of Bencullagh, Muckanaght and another hill named Benbaun, east to the bulky uplift of the Maumturks (see below), quartzite sisters to the Twelve Bens. Seen from this high point the Connemara mountains look formidable, a cluster of ramparts to wall out the world beyond.

When you have looked your fill, turn and make west along the ridge. The descent off the ridge is a slippery one, and you will have grass and turf stains on your backside by the time you get back to the road. But you have the most fantastic panorama in prospect all the way – mountains and lowlands, sun gleams and cloud shafts, and out beyond the edge of Ireland a shoal of green islands swimming for America.

482. LETTERBRECKAUN, MAUMTURK MOUNTAINS, CO. GALWAY

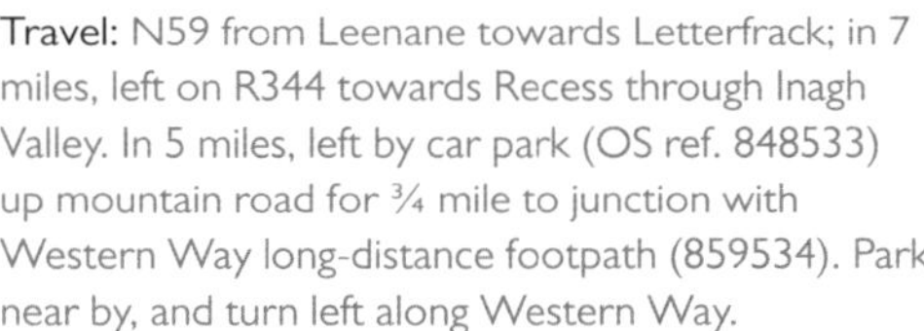

Map: OS of Ireland Discovery 37

Travel: N59 from Leenane towards Letterfrack; in 7 miles, left on R344 towards Recess through Inagh Valley. In 5 miles, left by car park (OS ref. 848533) up mountain road for ¾ mile to junction with Western Way long-distance footpath (859534). Park near by, and turn left along Western Way.

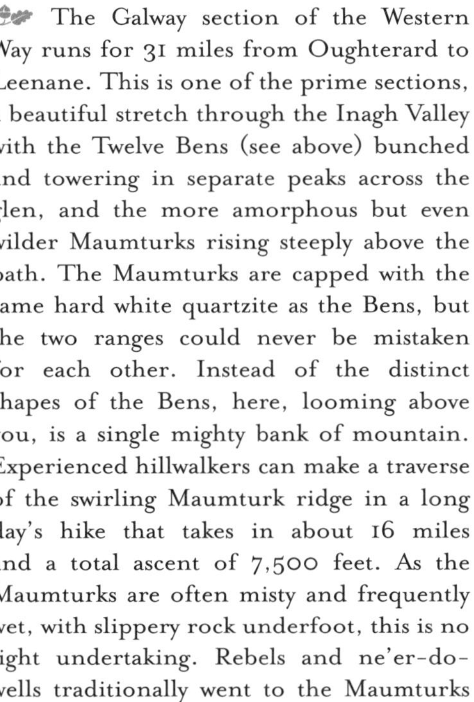

The Galway section of the Western Way runs for 31 miles from Oughterard to Leenane. This is one of the prime sections, a beautiful stretch through the Inagh Valley with the Twelve Bens (see above) bunched and towering in separate peaks across the glen, and the more amorphous but even wilder Maumturks rising steeply above the path. The Maumturks are capped with the same hard white quartzite as the Bens, but the two ranges could never be mistaken for each other. Instead of the distinct shapes of the Bens, here, looming above you, is a single mighty bank of mountain. Experienced hillwalkers can make a traverse of the swirling Maumturk ridge in a long day's hike that takes in about 16 miles and a total ascent of 7,500 feet. As the Maumturks are often misty and frequently wet, with slippery rock underfoot, this is no light undertaking. Rebels and ne'er-do-wells traditionally went to the Maumturks for refuge – with good reason: they are the wildest, loneliest and least accessible piece of country in Connemara.

Walking the puddled Western Way in the skirts of the Maumturks, you can pick out ways to scramble up to higher ground for sensational views of the Twelve Bens reflected in Lough Inagh. If you are sticking to low-level exploration, look out for the long corrugations of lazybed ridges where people grew their potatoes before hunger and desperation drove them away. Here are the broken husks of their houses, the humps of their field walls – and, craftily concealed in the side of a cattle pen, the remnants of a small liquor still, a stone fireplace and a grassy hollow where the mash tun stood. In lonely, exposed places such as this it was the home-distilled whiskey called poitín or poteen – or the Cratur, or Mountain Dew, or the Pure Drop, or simply Itself – that kept heart in people and gave them a reason to sing:

Ye maidens pathetic with lovers athletic,
For liquid cosmetic you can't beat the Drop;
With a glow on your cheek, it'd make your heart leap,
'Twould whiten a stallion or cure an ould cob.
From the mouth you would drool, be reduced to a fool,
You'd kick up your heels and you'd peel to the buff,
And 'tis you'd be athletic while he'd be pathetic –
If only you'd take a few drops of the Stuff.

So stick to the Cratur, the best thing in nature
For sinking your sorrows and raising your joys,
For there's nothing like whiskey for making maids frisky –
It soon separates all the men from the boys!

483. BÓTHAR NA SCRATHÓG, CO. GALWAY

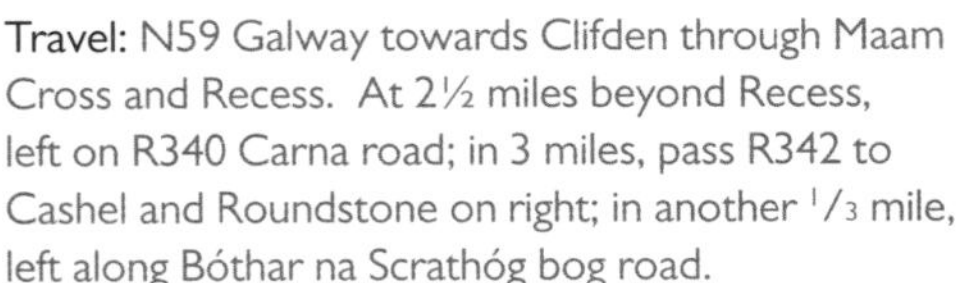
Map: OS of Ireland Discovery 44

Travel: N59 Galway towards Clifden through Maam Cross and Recess. At 2½ miles beyond Recess, left on R340 Carna road; in 3 miles, pass R342 to Cashel and Roundstone on right; in another 1/3 mile, left along Bóthar na Scrathóg bog road.

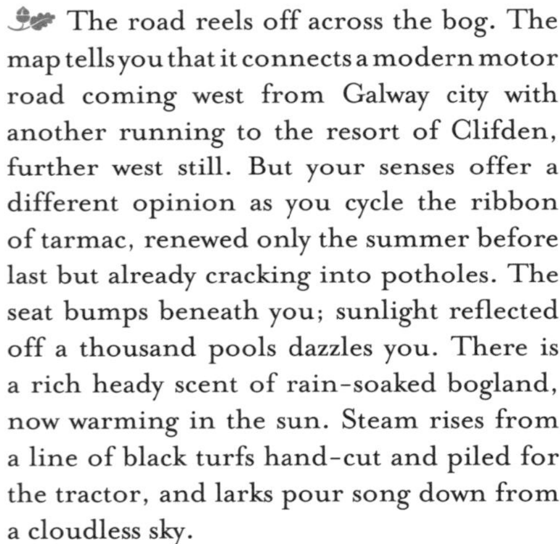
The road reels off across the bog. The map tells you that it connects a modern motor road coming west from Galway city with another running to the resort of Clifden, further west still. But your senses offer a different opinion as you cycle the ribbon of tarmac, renewed only the summer before last but already cracking into potholes. The seat bumps beneath you; sunlight reflected off a thousand pools dazzles you. There is a rich heady scent of rain-soaked bogland, now warming in the sun. Steam rises from a line of black turfs hand-cut and piled for the tractor, and larks pour song down from a cloudless sky.

You pull up and dismount, letting the bike fall where it will, and find a perch on a tussock of heather by the road. On your Folding Landscape map of Connemara, bought in Galway on your way through to the west, the bog road is a scribble of black through an empty white landscape. 'Bóthar na Scrathóg' runs its name in map-maker Tim Robinson's neat script. 'The road of the top-sods', says Robinson's translation from the Gaelic. This must be one of those roads built by destitute local people to earn a few pence for food during the hard times at the turn of the twentieth century.

When playwright John Millington Synge and artist Jack Yeats – brother of poet

Bóthar Na Scrathóg

William (see pp. 513–14) – came to this granite-laden, thin-skinned wasteland in 1905 to report on conditions for the *Manchester Guardian*, the two Irishmen were genuinely shocked by the poverty they found. The reports they filed, published by the newspaper twice a week between 10 June and 8 July 1905, lifted the lid for the outside world on what were known as the 'Congested Districts', and documented the desperation of a hungry, hopeless people who were eking out an existence in wretched conditions that had hardly changed since the terrible days of 1845–9 and the Great Famine.

Men and women had to pay their rent with the shilling-a-day they earned through rough manual labour on new roads such as Bóthar na Scrathóg, and it was a section of road like this that inspired one of Jack Yeats's most powerful illustrations. He depicted downcast men humping stones and levelling the surface while women, bent under back-loads of turf, passed like a line of pack animals. A stout ganger, self-importantly grasping his lapels, was 'swaggering among them and directing their work', Synge noted.

> *Some of the people were cutting out sods from grassy patches near the road, others were carrying down bags of earth in a slow, inert procession ... As we drove quickly by, we could see that every man and woman was working with a sort of hang-dog dejection that would make any casual passer mistake them for a band of convicts.*

You lie back on the sun-warmed grass and the clink of a slean, or turf spade, near by tells you that someone is cutting the bog; in your mind's eye you see a ragged line of men and women, slaves to the ganger and their own poverty, building this empty road to nowhere.

484. GORUMNA AND THE CAUSEWAY ISLANDS, CO. GALWAY

Map: OS of Ireland Discovery 44; Folding Landscape series, 'Connemara' (widely available locally)

Travel: From Galway city, R336 via Spiddal to Casla; R343 towards Carraroe for ½ mile; just beyond petrol station, right on R374 through the islands.

A string of rocky islands, linked by causeways and bridges, curves down into Galway Bay. Annaghvaan, Lettermore, Gorumna, Lettermullan and Furnace; they lie low and lumpy, more granite than grass. Their shores are some of the most beautiful in Ireland – rocky little inlets bright with orange seaweed and silky blue water, a couple of carefully restored Connemara hookers, or wooden sailing freight-boats, a fleet of slim black fishing canoes gently rocking at their moorings by a stumpy stone jetty. To the north rise the sharp outlines of the Connemara mountains; to the south across Galway Bay lie the sleeping-beast shapes of the Aran Islands (see below).

There's little tourist trade in the causeway islands. Visitors tearing by on their way into western Connemara seldom spare the poorly marked road to the isles a second glance. Yet for strollers and chatters, painters and photographers, lovers of huge skies full of weather, there's nothing nearer heaven in the west of Ireland. For the Irish-speaking locals, however, life has always been hard. Houses are built low, out of the path of the wind and rain that rampages in from Galway Bay. Narrow boreen lanes, tufted with grass, run among tiny fields marked off from each other by walls of granite so loosely piled that chinks of sky or sea gleam between the stones. Some people live on minuscule islets

Gorumna

that lie off the causeway islands, such as Inse Ghainimh, or Sand Island, across its own rocky causeway from Lettermore, where the Joyce brothers farm and fish from the single house.

On the shores of Loch Tan on Gorumna, St Anne's holy well – a triangular hollow of springing water in a rock – is cradled by a stone wall into which believers push holy pictures and statues, rosaries, pill bottles and pairs of spectacles in thanks for a cure. The causeway islanders make use of other home-distilled specifics against the chills and the ills, too. Down at the foot of the island the road curves on across the causeways, threading an ever-narrower way through Lettermullan and Furnace islands, petering out at last in a green boreen and a shore of sand and seaweed. If a curl of blue smoke is seen rising across the channel beyond the humped back of Dinish, outermost islet of the archipelago – don't trouble to wade out and see what is causing it. Something pale and potent will be brewing out there.

485. SOUTH-EAST CONNEMARA, CO. GALWAY

Map: OS of Ireland Discovery 45

Travel: The bogland country of south-east Connemara is bounded by a triangle of roads – N59 from Galway to Maam Cross, and R336 Maam Cross–Ballynahawn–Galway.

Everybody rushes through south-east Connemara, and nobody stops. Everyone's eyes are fixed on the romantic and beautiful west. The bare bogland streaks by the car window, and no one pays it any mind. Yet the cranky old road that runs slap through the middle offers fifteen of the loneliest miles of road you will drive in all Ireland. This is the largest expanse of bog in County Galway, patched with a thousand lakes and lakelets.

It is always wet underfoot in this vast wasteland, but a sticky trudge along a boreen or a rutted old bog road is worth every step. Out in the middle of the turf banks and the undulating bog, out by Muckanaghkillew or Lough Fiddaunnavreaghlee, you are many miles from anywhere. Big dark slabs of conifer forest have been imposed upon much of south-east Connemara; ugly and threatening in other settings, here they seem appropriate to the darkness of this misty, rainy country. Yet as with all the boglands of Ireland, once the sun is out and the lakelets have taken on that iridescent, metallic sheen, everything changes. You can climb to the domed top of Lackadunna, the one proper hill in these 80 square miles of forgotten country, and looking out from its 1,135-foot summit you can be monarch of the back of beyond.

486. ARAN ISLANDS, CO. GALWAY

Maps: OS of Ireland Discovery 51; Folding Landscape series, 'The Aran Islands' (widely available locally)

Travel: Ferries run to all three islands from Rossaveal (R336, R372 from Galway) and from Doolin (N18, N67 from Galway to Lisdoonvarna; R478, R459 to Doolin). Ferries also run to Inishmore from Galway City docks. Aer Arann flies from Inverin airport near Galway city. All travel details: www.visitaranislands.com; also www.world66.com/europe/ireland/aranislands.

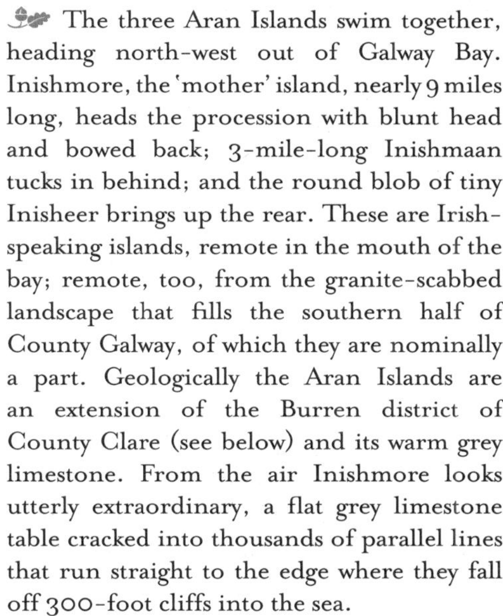

The three Aran Islands swim together, heading north-west out of Galway Bay. Inishmore, the 'mother' island, nearly 9 miles long, heads the procession with blunt head and bowed back; 3-mile-long Inishmaan tucks in behind; and the round blob of tiny Inisheer brings up the rear. These are Irish-speaking islands, remote in the mouth of the bay; remote, too, from the granite-scabbed landscape that fills the southern half of County Galway, of which they are nominally a part. Geologically the Aran Islands are an extension of the Burren district of County Clare (see below) and its warm grey limestone. From the air Inishmore looks utterly extraordinary, a flat grey limestone table cracked into thousands of parallel lines that run straight to the edge where they fall off 300-foot cliffs into the sea.

Getting out to the Aran Islands is easy enough by boat or tiny Aer Arann plane; getting to know them would take a lifetime. The Aran islanders are far from unwelcoming, but they are private people, not too forthcoming until they know you. Then you can expect to learn something, as did the playwright John Millington Synge when he came to stay on Inishmaan several

Aran Islands

times at the turn of the twentieth century. Synge's great book about his experiences, *The Aran Islands*, published in 1906, draws an intimate and detailed portrait of Inishmaan and the 'primitive' people with whom he yarned and played his fiddle over the fire. 'Their grey poteen,' noted Synge, 'which brings a shock of joy to the blood, seems predestined to keep sanity in men who live, forgotten, in these worlds of mist.'

Inishmore has two stunning 2,000-year-old cliff forts, Dún Aengus and Dún Dúchathair; Inisheer has a tremendously jolly music pub, and the complete rusted wreck of a freighter stranded on one of its pebble beaches. But for a taste of old-style Aran it is Inishmaan you want to head for. The middle island of Aran is occasionally cut off by mist and wild seas, always windy, often bleak and forbidding, and endlessly absorbing. Walk out past the thatched house where Synge drank poteen and ceilidhed, out down the winding threads of boreen lanes where the stone walls fit together like the most intricate lacework. On the south shore on a stormy day the blowholes hiss and spout, rollers thunder in to shake the rocks, and flakes of stone fly like bullets across a carpet of wild flowers.

487. THE BURREN, CO. CLARE

Maps: OS of Ireland Discovery 51, 52; Folding Landscape series, 'The Burren' (widely available locally)

Travel: From Limerick and Shannon, follow N18 to Ennis, then R476/R480 into the Burren. Ballyvaughan in the north and Lisdoonvarna in the south-west are connected by the R477 coast road, and by N67 which crosses the interior of the Burren.

The Burren is without question the most magical place in County Clare. The region comprises 500 square miles of rounded grey hills and rocky coast on the southern shores of Galway Bay, a wilderness of naked grey limestone as warm as human skin and as cracked as crocodile hide. Botanists come to North Clare from all corners of the world to roam the wobbly clints, or limestone pavement blocks, of the Burren in search of jaw-dropping floral rarities flourishing

The Burren

in the shadowy grykes – deep cracks in the limestone pavement. The grykes come vividly to life in spring, sprouting the richest and strangest community of wild flowers in Ireland, purple, white, pink, deep yellow and startling blue. Any visitor with a flower book can wander in a daze across this unique landscape of domed and terraced hills, where lakes known as turloughs fill and empty with the rainfall, where the ground is carpeted with flowering plants: creamy blooms of mountain avens; clumps of blue-lipped eyebright; bee, fly and frog orchids; dark pink drifts of bloody cranesbill.

The Burren is an old seabed hoisted high, then scraped by glaciers. Its scrub is still grazed tight each winter by cattle, just as it was thousands of years ago; so there is little to shade out the plants when they start to grow each spring. Plants that would not normally be found within 1,000 miles of each other grow contentedly in neighbouring hollows in the pavements and on the grassy hill slopes: acid-loving heather and lime-loving milkwort; northern species like mountain avens, whose seeds were first dropped by melting glaciers, and southerners like hoary rockrose. Mountain saxifrages grow down at sea level; woodland ivies and violets thrive in this treeless place. All is topsy-turvy here, a rich confusion.

These glorious wild flowers are not the be-all and end-all of the region. For a place whose interior can show only a handful of dwellings, where water hides secretively underground and bare rock forbids habitation, the Burren is remarkably well endowed with historical relics. Ruined churches, ring forts, ancient grave-slabs, stone huts and carved stone crosses lie tucked away unvisited among hazel groves, or stand open to inspection at the roadside.

The most compelling of the many Burren hills is Mullaghmore, out in the east of the region, a bizarre double hump of twisted flowing limestone. The moment that Ireland's Office of Public Works announced their intention to build an Interpretive Centre with EU money out here in the wilderness – a Visitor Centre, car park, restaurant, lavatories, a new road, walkways over the limestone pavement – locals took up passionate positions on both sides. Jobs and tourist money for a depopulated and hard-up area? Or peace and quiet for wildlife, untamed beauty for lone explorers? The OPW started to build, then stopped, then restarted, then stopped again. The issue still seems to hang in the balance.

There are no paths, no waymarks on Mullaghmore. It takes a good hour to crunch and stumble your way up the mountain, scaling the warm limestone cliffs like a spider, jumping from clint to clint among the cranesbills, orchids and ferns. Up on top the wind and the view over 20 miles of Clare countryside make you gasp. Look down on rain-swollen green turloughs, scrubby crevices and tilted limestone pavements, on a swirl of stone that spirals inwards to a vanishing point, as strange and otherworldly as can be.

488. ST COLMAN'S WELL, TOOMAGHERA, CO. CLARE

Maps: OS of Ireland Discovery 51; Folding Landscape series, The Burren (available locally)

Travel: N67 from Lisdoonvarna towards Ballyvaughan; in 2¾ miles turn right on side road to Cahermakerrila and park as soon and as neatly as you can. Return to N67 and turn right along it (please take care!). In 300 yards look for gateway/stile in wall on right, opposite a house. Follow faint path south across two fields for 250 yards to St Colman's Well (OS ref. 173002).

Christian belief mixed with older faith is a living fact in Ireland. All over the island thousands of holy wells are still actively visited, such as the one that lies in the rushy fields near Toomaghera. The little shed-like structure on the back slope of the hill is easy to miss. Inside a neat stone hood steps lead down to a spring of brown water, welling up in a muddy hollow among a lush growth of ferns. Niches hold images of Christ and the Virgin Mary. Old iron horse shoes, bits of rag and rough crucifixes, statues of saints, coins and holy medals have been pushed in among the stones. Fresh flowers are often placed in the niches there.

You move from the Christian to the pagan in the few short steps that take you from the well to a low arch of bevelled stone, perhaps once the window arch of a chapel, that stands in a sea of mud dented with impressions of knees. Push your head through the arch, as so many have evidently done before, and you will be cured of headaches.

The holy well is dedicated to St Colman, son of Duagh, a hermit of the seventh century who founded a monastery a few miles to the east at Kilmacduagh. Legend says that God let Colman know where to establish his cell by causing the holy man's girdle to slip down to the ground – proof positive that the Lord has a sense of humour.

489. CLARA AND CASTLETOWN BOGS, CO. OFFALY

Map: OS of Ireland Discovery 48

Travel: Clara Bog: In Clara, R436 towards Ferbane; just as you leave Clara, bear left on minor road ('Rathan' and brown 'Clara Bog' sign). In 1⅓ miles, park in car park on left (OS ref. 250304), and take track out on to Clara Bog.

Castletown Bog: R436 from Ferbane towards Clara. At ¾ mile beyond Lemanaghan, left (179277) up bog road on to Castletown Bog.

One-third of County Offaly is bog. This strange and wild landscape – until very recently undervalued at best, exploited and destroyed at worst – is lodged in the hearts and minds of Offaly people as central to their daily lives. They see it every day in sombre swathes between their lush green grazing fields. They walk, run and bicycle on it or alongside it; they curse it when it seeps across their roads or through the soles of their shoes. Some cut slices of it by hand for their living-room fires. A few are still harvesting it commercially for fireplace briquettes and horticulture in the employment of Bord na Móna, the Irish Peat

Clara Bog

Board. But that is all slowly coming to an end. The bog is seen increasingly these days for what it really is: a wonderful habitat for flowers, birds, butterflies, frogs and lichens; a vault that locks up carbon that would contribute to global warming if released; and a beautiful, if moody, landscape in its own right. The raised bogs of Offaly, as with those of the Irish Midlands in general, are made up of thick tuffets of sphagnum moss which developed over shallow lakes formed at the end of the last Ice Age 10,000 years ago. They are packed with plants such as bog rosemary and bog myrtle, cranberry with its pink flowers and big wine-coloured berries, and insect-eaters with sticky leaves such as sundews and butterworts. Birds of prey hawk over them, small birds such as whitethroats, sedge warblers and dunnocks sing from the scrub bushes. As for aesthetic qualities – there is something captivating about the fruity smell of a bog after rain, or the rush of sunlight and cloud across its broad back.

Two contrasting bogs lie conveniently near each other in north-west Offaly. Clara Bog is much-studied and well recorded – so much so that 1,000 acres of it are now a National Nature Reserve and have been declared a UNESCO World Heritage Site. Just to the west lies Castletown Bog and its neighbouring bogland, but this landscape has been partly devastated by commercial cutting. Ten-foot cliffs of sheer-cut dark peat stand exposed, speckled white and silver with fragments of ancient trees. Mountains of powdery milled turf loom in swathes of cut bog, as bleak as a Flanders battlefield. Plastic coverings of immense size gleam on ridges of piled peat. At the end of the bog road lies a farmhouse among tall trees, surely the loneliest farm in the most other-worldly – and nowadays redundant – landscape in all the Midland boglands.

490. SLIEVE BLOOM MOUNTAINS, CO. LAOIS

Maps OS of Ireland Discovery 54

Travel: N7 from Kildare through Monasterevin and Jamestown. At 2 miles beyond Ballybrittas, right on R422 through Emo and Mountmellick to Rosenallis.

For Glenbarrow car park: in Rosenallis, pass Cogan's pub on right, and at next right bend keep ahead uphill. In 1 mile, first right (OS ref. 391083); in 1¼ miles, left at crossroads (373090 – brown 'Glenbarrow car park' sign) to Glenbarrow car park (368081).

For Ridge of Capard car park: from Rosenallis follow 'Mountrath', then 'Ridge of Capard' signs to Ridge of Capard car park (363065).

The Slieve Bloom Mountains rise in a gentle blue-green dome where County Laois meets County Tipperary, an unexpected swelling in the flat heart of the Irish Midlands. Slieve Bloom roads are narrow and stony; the paths over the heather-covered hills and through the steep glens are scarcely trodden these days, and for anyone happy to walk in wild country and get wet and muddy, this is a little piece of heaven known only to the fortunate few.

The waymarked Slieve Bloom Way loops round the crests and across the loneliest valleys of the hills, making a fine grandstand route for exploration. There are other paths, notably the track that leaves Glenbarrow car park to run through the forest to Clamphole Falls, a rushing set of rapids on the River Barrow. But it is the Slieve Bloom Way that will take you to the very best of the mountains. You will find squelching black peat and thick bell heather underfoot, curlew and ravens above.

Slieve Bloom mountains

A less-demanding introduction to the path is to walk the Ridge of Capard from its car park to the Stoney Man Cairn, which commands huge views over hayfields, woods and dozens of miles of country mapped out 1,000 feet below. Or you can strike off for yourself, to the 1,100-foot summit of Baunreahcong Mountain, perhaps, or down into the upper glen of the River Barrow, where fallow deer pick their way between the silver birches. Do not fool with the source of this river – legend says it will rise and flood the world if you do. In times past, a priest 'virgin in mind and body' would say Mass here and sprinkle the Barrow with milk to placate the angry spirit. But you can make your peace with the river by taking a draught of its cold, sweet and peaty source.

491. DONNELLY'S HOLLOW, THE CURRAGH, CO. KILDARE

Map: OS of Ireland Discovery 55

Travel: M7 from Naas towards Kildare; take N9 turn, and in 5 miles turn left to Kilcullen. Left here on R413 towards Newbridge. In 3 miles, beyond 'Athgarvan' sign, brown fingerpost points left to Donnelly's Hollow.

Come all ye true born Irishmen
And listen to my song,
And hold your wrist and clench your fist,
For that won't take ye long,
While I a song unfold to ye
Sung with joyous Irish air,
About the Cooper–Dan Donnelly fight
On the Curragh of Kildare.

Into the turf of the Curragh of Kildare, a grassy plain more famous for horse training and racing than for bare-knuckle fighting, a deep green hollow lies sunk. Here, on 13 December 1815, one of the most celebrated boxing matches in the history of the sport took place between Dan Donnelly of Dublin and Englishman George Cooper from Staffordshire.

Donnelly was born in Dublin in 1788 and grew up hard and tough, a quiet man whom it was bad to cross. By the time he was twenty, Donnelly was cock of the walk. In 1814, he met the noted bare-knuckle fighter Tom Hall in this natural amphitheatre of the Curragh, known then as Belcher's Hollow, and easily won a purse of 100 sovereigns by beating Hall in fifteen rounds in front of a crowd of 20,000. Many more than that – some estimated the crowd at 31,000 – turned up on 13 December the following year to see their hero matched for a purse of sixty sovereigns against 'the famous English pugilist George Cooper'.

Belcher's Hollow was ideally placed for an illegal event in front of a big crowd. It lies near the main road, but is concealed by a raised shoulder of ground. Spectators lined the rim and stood on tiptoe dozens deep to see the two men squaring up below. Donnelly was a battling bull of a fighter, George Cooper more of a scientific boxer. The first three rounds were all Donnelly; he floored Cooper three times. The next three rounds were more even, as the Staffordshire man recovered his poise and danced Donnelly around. But then the Dublin bruiser suddenly charged, knocking his opponent about the ring for four brutal rounds before, in the eleventh, he unleashed two tremendous blows, the second of which broke Cooper's jaw and laid him out senseless on the ground.

Donnelly was cheered from the ring, and entered Dublin in glory a few days later, carried shoulder-high through tumultuous crowds while his mother marched before him, striking her breast and calling out: 'There's the breast that sucked him! There's the breast that sucked him!' The scene of the fighter's triumph was immediately dubbed 'Donnelly's Hollow'.

Give three loud cheers for our own Dan
And the way he fought today,
And another cheer for the Englishman
Who could not have his way.
So here's to Dan, our noblest son;
No other need him dare,
For today he made the English run
On the Curragh of Kildare.

Unfortunately Ireland's 'noblest son' was a sucker for the good life and the booze. He drank solidly for a year or two, sobered up enough to go to England in July 1818 and beat the English champion Tom Oliver on his home turf (Donnelly was 'knighted' by the Prince Regent in a pub for his prowess), then sank back into a drinking lifestyle that put an end to him within eighteen months – aged thirty-two and penniless.

The story doesn't end there. Donnelly was buried beside other Irish battle heroes in Bully's Acre cemetery in Dublin, from where his body was dug up by grave-robbers and offered for sale to a surgeon for dissection. The surgeon recognized Donnelly and refused to take his body, but did amputate the right arm and embalm it as a souvenir. The arm travelled from pillar to post over the following century, eventually coming to rest on display at the Hideout pub in Kilcullen, just down the road from Donnelly's Hollow, where it lay on display – a brown, dried-up appendage, the sinews standing out, the index finger pointing forward in ghoulish warning.

An obelisk stands in Donnelly's Hollow today, its inscription recording the events of the Donnelly–Cooper fight and of Dan Donnelly's short, wild life. A set of footprints leads up the side of the amphitheatre, faithfully cut in the place of those made by Donnelly as he walked up to acknowledge the crowd while George Cooper lay unconscious behind him. As for the mummified arm: in early 2008 it was on display in the Irish Arts Center, Manhattan, New York, part of a celebration of that cliché that happened in its original owner's case to be absolutely true – the 'Fighting Irishman'.

492. BLACKSTAIRS MOUNTAINS, CO. CARLOW/WEXFORD BORDERS

Map: OS of Ireland Discovery 68

Travel: N80 from Enniscorthy towards Carlow; leaving Bunclody, left on minor road (OS ref. 908569; brown 'Mount Leinster' sign). In 5 miles, left (835567; 'Nine Stones and TV Transmitter' brown sign) to parking place at top of road (817546).

As you drive north from Waterford or Rosslare towards Dublin, a long range of mountains floats like a pale blue cloud on the left-hand horizon. The mountains stand 10 miles off but seem much further. They are dream hills often seen, often the subject of a vague intention – 'I really must go and look at those hills one day – I wonder which they are?' – but never visited. Anyone who steals a half-day and makes that westward turn into the Blackstairs Mountains will be glad they acted on their impulse. These are beautiful

Blackstairs Mountains

mountains, laden with tales and stories, the resort of rebel Irishmen in the 1798 Rising against the British, which brought blood and terror to Counties Carlow and Wexford. The Blackstairs straddle the border between the two, and bold heroes and bad hats have sought refuge there down the ages.

Mount Leinster, at 2,610 feet, is the highest peak in the range, its sloping summit marked by a tall television mast. You can drive to the Nine Stones, a Neolithic alignment of nine standing stones at the foot of the mountain, and walk up easily to the peak, but the presence of the aerial and attendant paraphernalia milks the height of its wild element. Better to set off on the other side of the car park and climb the gentle hump of Slievebaun, from whose brow of shining quartzite slabs you look out over the flat country of County Carlow to the silhouettes of the Wicklow Mountains, 30 miles off on the north-east skyline. From here there is a really impressive view of Mount Leinster filling the eastern sky. You can also brood over the tale of the Nine Stones – nine foolish shepherds, turned to stone because they refused St Kevin of Glendalough a bite to eat as he was wandering these hills.

Walking in the south of the Blackstairs is equally fine. From the Scullоge Gap across the waist of the range you climb over the long back of Blackstairs Mountain and down the southern slope, passing the jumble of granite rocks called Caher Roe's Den. Legend says this was the hideout of Red Caher O'Dempsey, a wild eighteenth-century robber from County Laois who hid himself and the proceeds of his horse-thieving up here. Red Caher was hung by the neck a long time ago, but his treasure still lies hidden somewhere on this hillside.

493. ROSSLARE SLOBS, CO. WEXFORD

Map: OS of Ireland Discovery 77

Travel: N25 from Wexford towards Rosslare Harbour; 1 mile past Killinick, left on R740 into Rosslare village. Turn left at T-junction; follow 'Golf Club, Golf Links' signs towards Rosslare Point. Park where the Point runs north from the mainland.

Nearest railway station: Rosslare (2 miles)

The word 'slobs' is an excellently descriptive one. How better to sum up the slippery, sloppery glutinousness of the coastal environment that the English call 'tidal wetlands'? Slobs are an integral part of the habitat mosaic around the shores of south-east Ireland, and Wexford Harbour has some of the finest. The Wexford Wildfowl Reserve on the harbour's North Slob is very well known among birdwatchers as a superb place to see seabirds and wildfowl, especially in winter. But access to the slobs themselves is very limited here.

Round on the south side of the harbour

the slobs at Rosslare are open to all. You will see bait diggers out on the mud, spading for lugworms that they'll use in sea fishing. Out beyond them, Rosslare Point runs 2 miles northwards, a narrow spit that shelters an enormous saucer of slobs under its western flank. Wide mudflats lie gleaming at low tide, and a stony ridge brings you out into their midst. Countless millions of worm-casts make pimples in the mud, ancient fishing vessels rot on the flats and old clinker-built boats lie greening over in the reed-beds along the shore. Sea purslane knits together patches of saltmarsh draped with bladderwrack.

Bring your binoculars to this flat no man's land in winter. You'll see black-headed gulls, screeching in their winter plumage of snowy heads with a dark dot. Pale-bellied brent geese, Greenland white-fronted geese, knot and dunlin feed on the muds or stalk the grassy shore. Curlew and oystercatcher send their spine-tingling, melancholy calls along the tideline, and up in the misty air golden plover pipe back hauntingly, the spirit of these lonely, windy shores.

494. COMERAGH MOUNTAINS, CO. WATERFORD

Map: OS of Ireland Discovery 75

Travel: R761 from Clonmel towards Youghal and Dungarvan; in Ballymacarbry, left opposite Melody's Nire View bar. Brown 'Comeragh Drive' signs direct you from here on a fine route through the mountains. To explore Knockanaffin countryside, bear left in 3 miles over Birchell's Bridge (242141); in another mile fork right (244149; 'Cul de Sac' sign) and continue along this narrow country lane under Knockanaffin.

Cradled in the western flank of the Comeragh Mountains lies the damp valley of the River Nire, where floodlands seethe with water in spring and snipe go darting away as you walk the low fields. The Comeraghs are always in view here, especially the long ridge that rises to the pale stony peak of Knockanaffin, the Mountain of the Mass. Fugitive priests and parties of worshippers knew they were safe enough up in these hollows back in the days of the Penal Laws.

You can climb to the summit of Knockanaffin. From here, at 2,477 feet, among boulders and ledges of rock, the low-lying farmlands of west Waterford and south Tipperary seem spread out as if painted on a green cloth. Coumduala Lough lies below, a dark eye in the hill. South from here the range trends upwards into the high plateau of the Comeraghs. Heathery slopes rise to the 2,600-foot peak of the range around Knockaunapeebra, a clunking Anglicization of Cnocan an Piobaire, the Hill of the Piper, a name to make you hum a tune.

Back in the real world a narrow road burrows from the west into the Nire Valley. By following it you will discover what it means to be a back-country farmer in rural Ireland these days. Abandoned farms lie in rushy, forlorn fields. Rusty barns slide imperceptibly into streams that were once well-drained cart tracks. Yellow gorse is taking over the meadows. Scraggy sheep roam the lower slopes of the mountains unclipped, trailing long tendrils of clotted wool. At the end of a stone-strewn lane a farmyard crouches under tattered larches, with a FOR SALE sign jammed into the stones of the wall. The house is locked tight, the yard empty except for a dog raving at the end of its rope. A rocky boreen leads on, to dip across the river and rise towards the mountain, and nothing stirs either along it or anywhere else in sight.

495. KNOCKMEALDOWN MOUNTAINS, CO. TIPPERARY/WATERFORD BORDERS

Map: OS of Ireland Discovery 74

Travel: R669 from Cappoquin towards Clogheen; in 2 miles, right at Knockaun East (OS ref. 110005) towards Newcastle by way of Lyre Bridge and Keane's Bridge (129068). In 2½ miles, road to Ballynamult turns off on right (145100) at Clashganny West. At 200 yards before this junction, park and head left down rough dirt road.

After some 400 yards, as bungalow comes in sight in dip ahead, bear left (138096 approx.) towards prominent face of Mass Rock, at confluence of two streams ½ mile away. Meeting a field bank, bear right; follow it down to stream; cross on stepping stones (136094); follow right bank upstream to Mass Rock (135090).

From here follow right fork of stream. Aim for rounded top of Knockardbounce (125088). From summit, aim for Knockmeal (rounded hill ahead), bearing half left to hold your height and meet track (122082 approx.) under Knocknasculloge. Bear right along it until nearly at road, then left onto road near S-bend sign (112083).

If continuing, turn left up track at S-bend sign to ascend Knockmeal.

NB: Hillwalking clothes and boots recommended.

The Knockmealdown Mountains are a beautiful lumpy line of fells. This is all wonderful walking country where you can wander secret valleys all day and seldom set eyes on another walker. A good place to start is at Clashganny West, at the eastern end of the range. From here you can make a preliminary sortie up the smallish peaks of Knockardbounce and Knocknasculloge.

Under Knockardbounce lies a Mass Rock.

Knockmealdown Mountains

The tall rock face leans out of the hillside at a place where two streams meet. Irish Catholics during the eighteenth century lived under threat of dire penalties if they were seen to practise their religion; so local people would make their way in secret to illicit sites of worship, using the streams as guidelines, walking up the watercourses so as to leave no footprints. Nowadays open-air Masses are said for pleasure and inspiration around the historic old rock.

From here you climb a long slope of knee-high heather and thick tuffets of sphagnum moss to the summit of Knockardbounce, where you can stop to pick blueberries and take a look around before descending to the road on the county border. If you have the day in front of you, climb up to the peak of Knockmeal and take your pick. Either forge north along the ridge to Crohan West and the great cairn that lies in its shadow, or strike west along the border for an exhilarating high-level march along the main ridge of the Knockmealdowns by way of Knocknagauv and the summit of Knockmealdown itself at 2,600 feet. Or you can simply return the way you came, the sharp tang of blueberries on your tongue and the silence of the hillsides broken only by the trickle of streams and the occasional blare of a cross old ewe among the heather.

496. GREAT BLASKET ISLAND, KERRY

Maps OS of Ireland Discovery 70

Travel: N86 from Tralee to Dingle; R559 to Dunquin. Boats to Great Blasket from Dunquin: www.dodingle.com/pages/blasket_island_trips

It is certainly worth visiting the Blasket Centre at Dunquin, a stylish modern interpretive centre, to learn the story of the Blasket Islands. But you will never get the proper picture of what life was like on the little archipelago unless you read three classic books produced in a moment of extraordinary literary flowering by three members of the 120-strong community on Great Blasket Island.

The island and its neighbouring rocks would have remained cloaked in obscurity had it not been for Tomás O'Crohan, Peig Sayers and Maurice O'Sullivan. This trio discovered that the knack of vivid story-telling, as natural as breathing to an isolated and in many ways primitive community, could be transmitted to a wider audience by means of writing. No one from Great Blasket Island had attempted to record what life was like there until O'Crohan was given pen and paper by a visiting student of Gaelic. The diary he kept, thick with idiosyncratic turns of phrase and salty pen portraits, was published in 1928 as *Island Cross-Talk*, and the following year he produced *The Islandman*, another pungent account. In 1933 young Maurice O'Sullivan wrote an exuberant and poetical autobiography, *Twenty Years A-Growing*. Peig Sayers, wife of a Blasket Island native, completed the threesome with her witty, chatty books *Peig* (1936) and *An Old Woman's Reflections* (1939).

Written in Irish but soon translated into English and many other languages, these books opened a door to a previously little-known world. Here, colourfully displayed, was a way of life long abandoned by the mainland – donkey transport, climbing cliffs for birds' eggs, cutting furze for bedding, wrestling cattle into narrow fishing canoes, endless talk to drive away loneliness. Life on Great Blasket was hard and narrow, the sound between island and mainland notorious for its dangers. Crops sometimes failed in the salt-sprayed fields. Eventually the relentless harshness of life on the Blaskets and the curse of depopulation – all the girls had gone ashore to brighter lights and better prospects – drove the remaining islanders on to the mainland in 1953.

A fast boat whips you over the sound these days. You can wander through the ruins of the village and up over the hill. Peig Sayers's house is now a hostel, the perfect place to base yourself for a few days of absolute peace and quiet, exploring the coves where the islanders trapped seals, the rocks they fished from, the pathways where they quarrelled and flirted, and the tumbledown shells of the houses where they sat smoking over the turf fires, spinning stories that never would be caught and set down in print.

497. OLD KENMARE ROAD, CO. KERRY

Maps OS of Ireland Discovery 78

Travel: N71 from Killarney towards Kenmare; in 1½ miles, pass entrance to Muckross Estate on your right; in another 2 miles, park at foot of path to Torc Waterfall (OS ref. 965848). Climb path past waterfall and on ('Kerry Way' waymarks) by way of Esknamucky Glen and Windy Gap, descending to Gowlane (917752) and road into Kenmare.

NB: This 11-mile path passes through remote mountains. Parts are boggy and slippery. Wear hillwalking clothes and boots.

Nearest railway station: Killarney (4 miles)

It is remarkable that the mountains around Killarney have not been robbed of their wildness, considering how many millions of visitors pour into Ireland's Lake District each year to savour the views and explore the foothills and lake shores. The fact is, though, that the further you venture from the valley roads, the less likely you are to have the world and his camera in your face.

The old road that leaves the south shore of Muckross Lake and climbs over the gap in the mountain to Kenmare is the best escape route into the hills. At first you climb on a well-surfaced forest track to reach the beautiful cascade of Torc Waterfall in its mossy channel; then you climb on, leaving almost everyone behind, up through the trees and out into the green groove of Esknamucky Glen. The old drovers' track passes through an oak wood floored with great tussocks of grass, smothered in velvet-smooth moss; a damp grove of liverwort and ferns. Further up you pass the ruins of old houses, then jump the stones over an ice-black river and come to the abandoned settlement under Windy Gap.

Poking around the angles of walls crouching among tattered pines and oaks, it is hard to know how our forefathers managed to survive winter here. The view is sublime, looking over the flooded village street and the rush-grown fields to Peakeen Mountain and Knockanaguish, raising their heads against the sky. You can't eat scenery, say those few farmers who still eke a living in such high and wild places, and that is why the mountains of the west stand empty, for all their hard and dramatic beauty.

498. PRIEST'S LEP, KERRY/CORK BORDER

Map: OS of Ireland Discovery 85

Travel: N71 from Glengarriff towards Bantry; in 3½ miles, left (OS ref. 964546) on minor road ('Kealanine'); in 2½ miles, just before Coomhola Bridge, left (993555) up lane ('Priest's Lep' sign) for 3½ miles to park at the pass at top of lane (985611).

A narrow, gravelly road winds up the side of Coomhola Mountain, with wide, empty valleys dropping away on all sides. This landscape of the Cork and Kerry border is rough country of long high ridges and hill grazing, where the rock pokes through the grass and there does not seem to be cover for a rabbit – let alone for a hunted man, his horse and the dozens of followers who made their way here to receive consolation at his hands.

The pass at the summit of the road is marked by a plain iron cross, rusted and pitted by weather. The view is stunning, out over miles of rugged mountainside running down to Whiddy Island and others scattered in Bantry Bay. This spot is the Priest's Lep,

from which a fugitive priest once made a miraculous jump. So says tradition, and so say the local people even today. It is hard to pinpoint exactly when the tale took hold – it has been noted since late Tudor times – but the story is that the holy man was celebrating Mass out of doors at a clandestine meeting of the faithful at Killabunane near Kenmare, when English soldiers with dogs appeared. Priest and people took to their heels, hotly pursued by the Crown forces. But as the hounds gained on the refugees, the rocks under their paws melted and formed a barrier. You can still see the place by the roadside not far from the town, the Carraig na Gadharaigh, or Dogs' Rock.

The hunted man and his supporters ran up the road to the pass at Cummeenshrule, where the people helped their pastor scramble on to a horse. Out it leaped above the soldiers and hounds, flying through the air until it landed near Bantry. Marks of the hooves, and of the hands and knees of the priest as he tumbled off on landing, are seen there, too. Each time road-menders tar them over, they come to the surface once more.

499. GREAT AND LITTLE SKELLIG, CO. KERRY

Map: OS of Ireland Discovery 83

Travel: N70 'Ring of Kerry' road; between Waterville and Cahersiveen, turn off on R565 towards Valencia Island. Portmagee Pier is just beside the bridge (OS ref. 371730).

Boat trip: contact Des Lavelle (tel: 066 947 6124; www.skellig-boat-trips.com).

NB: Boats run April–September, weather permitting. This can be a rough trip of more than an hour. Boats are small. No facilities on Skellig Michael; bring water, food, weatherproof clothes and walking shoes. There are 544 steps to climb to the monastery.

Great Skellig – Skellig Michael, as it is more often called – is a very wild place in an often wild and windy sea. Landing is by no means guaranteed. But just sailing to the island, 9 miles off the tip of the Iveragh Peninsula, is an unforgettable experience. Skellig Michael slants fiercely out of the sea, its broken crown rearing above cliffs covered in seabirds – gannets, gulls, kittiwakes, fulmars, puffins. If you are able to scramble ashore and begin the long, leg-aching climb up the 544 steps to the summit of Skellig Michael, it is an emotional moment. Here on this storm-whittled rock a community of monks supported itself for over 500 years on whatever fish the brothers could catch and the seabird eggs they harvested, drinking

Skellig Michael

rainwater they caught and stored in home-made cisterns, watching and praying in one of the remotest monastic communities in Europe.

St Fionan's Monastery was founded on the island in AD 588. It was looted by Danes in AD 823; the attackers made off with one of the monks as part of their booty. But the brotherhood rebuilt the monastery and stayed on for another 300 years, until they finally quit their lonely outpost in the sea and moved ashore.

Here on the edge of the cliffs, at the top of a long and crooked stairway, 750 feet above the sea, stand the huts that the monks built stone by stone, beautifully constructed clochans, or beehive-shaped dwellings, their exterior shape round but squared into cell shape inside, entered by a low doorway. The stark grey huts huddle together as if for warmth and strength. Near by are the two churches the monks built, one open to the sky with narrow west window and walls still intact. There is a bleak refectory for communal meals – how chill and threadbare those must have been in a west of Ireland winter! And standing tall, their arms smoothed into shapeless lumps by 1,500 years of weather, are the stone crosses the monks erected to remind themselves what they were doing this for, and to recall their continuing existence to the mind of God.

The austerity, the battling with loneliness, with winter depressions and petty hatreds, the struggle to collect food and water, are almost beyond imagining. But there must have been days of sunny exhilaration, moments of bliss, too. So you hope, anyway, as you stand in the tiny graveyard at the lip of the cliffs and gaze towards the landward world.

500. CAPE CLEAR ISLAND, ROARINGWATER BAY, CO. CORK

Map: OS of Ireland Discovery 88

Travel: N71 from Cork to Skibbereen, R595 to Baltimore; ferry to Cape Clear Island (www.capeclearisland.com).

The most southerly bight in the coast of south-west County Cork goes by the marvellous, elemental name of Roaringwater Bay. What more evocative name could there be with which to end a journey through the wild places of Britain and Ireland? This great deep sea inlet is strewn with 127 islands, islets and blobs of rock on which the south-west wind smashes the sea. Of these the most southerly, and the largest, is Cape Clear Island, lying far out at the mouth of the bay. About 120 people live out here, most of them Irish speakers, all of them defiant of the many storms, the isolation, the problems of supply and the ever-present risk of being cut off from the mainland.

There are no planes to Cape Clear, only the thick-bodied island ferry, *Niamh Ciarán II*. From her pitching deck, as she weaves between the rocks and small islands, Cape Clear Island grows steadily larger, a bulky, hilly island of green walled fields rising to brown heathery ridges, dotted with the white and grey cubes of houses. Once ashore and walking down the quay, the ordinary march of hours is suspended in favour of a slower island time, as thick and irresistible as syrup.

Cape Clear Island's bird observatory is one of the best-known in Ireland, and no wonder. The island lies under the migration pathway of millions of birds, and in spring and autumn it becomes a stopover for huge numbers, hungry and exhausted. The harbour shops sells copies of Cape Clear's Heritage Trail booklet, which also contains a birdwatching trail, and with this in hand you can keep an eye out for avian rarities as you walk the roads between hedges heavy with the blood-red hanging lanterns of fuchsia. The trail leads up the steep little hills and into the hidden valleys of the island, to the Marriage Stones and St Ciarán's Well, the Ogham Stone with its indecipherable inscription, and the birthplace of the 8-foot giant Concubhar who once dredged up a 500-pound anchor that six men couldn't shift. History and legend run together here.

The best, the only fitting place to end the walk and this whole long journey through wild places is on the grassy slope above the southernmost cliffs in Ireland as the sun sinks in the west, looking out to the black spires of the Fastnet Rock, its tall lighthouse, some fantasy of an ocean castle, rising from a patch of sea sunlit to dazzling silver. On a long walk in 1991 from tip to toe of Ireland, I carried for luck a tiny doll's shoe that I'd picked up by chance on Malin Head at the start of the adventure. Here on this Cape Clear hillside I buried it at the end of my walk, on a blustery evening of rain. I can't remember exactly where now, but in any case it is good to feel that here the luck still lies, embedded at the end of the road in a wild place such as this.